GALLIPOLI SOUP

Gallipoli Soup

A War Story of Statecraft and Sacrifice

TIM KNIGHT

First published in 2025 by New Holland Publishers
Sydney

newhollandpublishers.com

Images from New Holland Image Library, Shutterstock, Adobe, Map on page 190 from Australian War Memorial RCDIG1009984

Cover images from Australian War Memorial Front cover: P08678.002, A02781 Background: C03369 Back: A02599, A05301, H11559

A record of this book is held at the National Library of Australia.

ISBN 9781760797775

Managing Director: Fiona Schultz
General Manager/Publisher: Olga Dementiev
Designer: Andrew Davies
Production Director: Arlene Gippert
Printed in China

Keep up with New Holland Publishers:

NewHollandPublishers
@newhollandpublishers

Firstly, for my dear wife Melis, thank you for your loving support. You have challenged and inspired me.

For my children, Corey, Lara, Bryce, Joel and Elissa. I am so proud of each one of you. Always remain willing to ask 'why?'

And for Nathan, you touched so many lives. Sixteen and a half years seems too short, but that was your allotted time. Your battle is over and you are in a better place now. We miss you.

AUTHOR'S NOTE

In the interests of full disclosure to the reader, this is a dramatised account of events that took place during World War I. As such it includes fictional characters, as well as historical characters and events. Purist historians may frown on this style of writing as it blurs the lines between fact and fiction.

However, like many other Australians who have made the pilgrimage to the shores of Anzac Cove and the battlefield cemeteries of the Gallipoli peninsula, I have wondered what it was like for the young men who fought and died there, and why did it happen anyway? I have tried to understand the politics and warfare strategies, as well as imagine the sensations and emotions of those involved. Imagination can provide a powerful connection to the experiences of those who have been before, especially if it is coupled with a fair representation of historical facts as available.

I have, as far as possible, framed the story around actual historical events and dates. Characters who are politicians, senior military or naval commanders and war correspondents are real historical people. Representations of their thoughts and emotions are based on a combination of historical accounts and my imagination to fill the gaps. Characters who are common folk, swept up in the war as soldiers or family and friends of soldiers, are fictional. Their experiences and feelings as described are, in many cases, based on accounts of those who experienced the war.

In places, I have included dialogue and thoughts directly from autobiographical accounts. This is intentional, to preserve the voice of those who lived through these events.

To give credit to the authors whose work has been referred to, and to give the reader the opportunity to understand which parts of what they are reading are based on historical accounts, I have prepared end notes outlining the historical details and references for each chapter. Unfortunately, these end notes are too extensive to have been included in the published work, but they can be freely accessed online at: www.gallipolisoup.com.

Enjoy reading,
Tim Knight

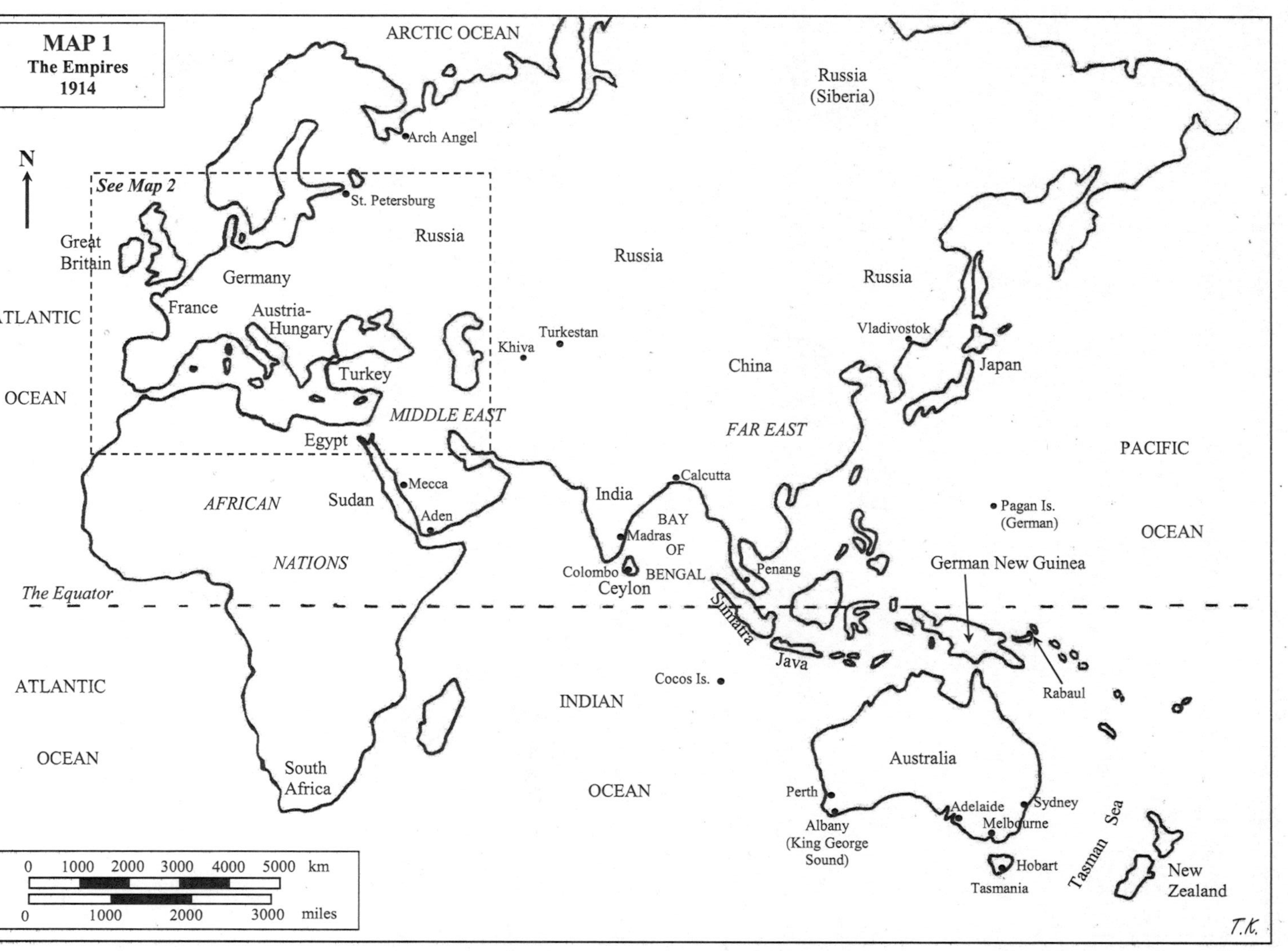
MAP 1
The Empires
1914
N
See Map 2
ARCTIC OCEAN
Arch Angel
St. Petersburg
Russia
Russia
Russia
Russia (Siberia)
Great Britain
Germany
France
Austria-Hungary
Turkey
MIDDLE EAST
Khiva
Turkestan
China
FAR EAST
Vladivostok
Japan
PACIFIC
OCEAN
Pagan Is. (German)
German New Guinea
Rabaul
ATLANTIC
OCEAN
Egypt
Mecca
Sudan
Aden
AFRICAN
NATIONS
India
Calcutta
BAY
Madras
OF
BENGAL
Colombo
Ceylon
Penang
The Equator
Sumatra
Java
Cocos Is.
INDIAN
OCEAN
ATLANTIC
OCEAN
South Africa
Australia
Perth
Albany (King George Sound)
Adelaide
Melbourne
Sydney
Hobart
Tasmania
Tasman Sea
New Zealand
0 1000 2000 3000 4000 5000 km
0 1000 2000 3000 miles
T.K.

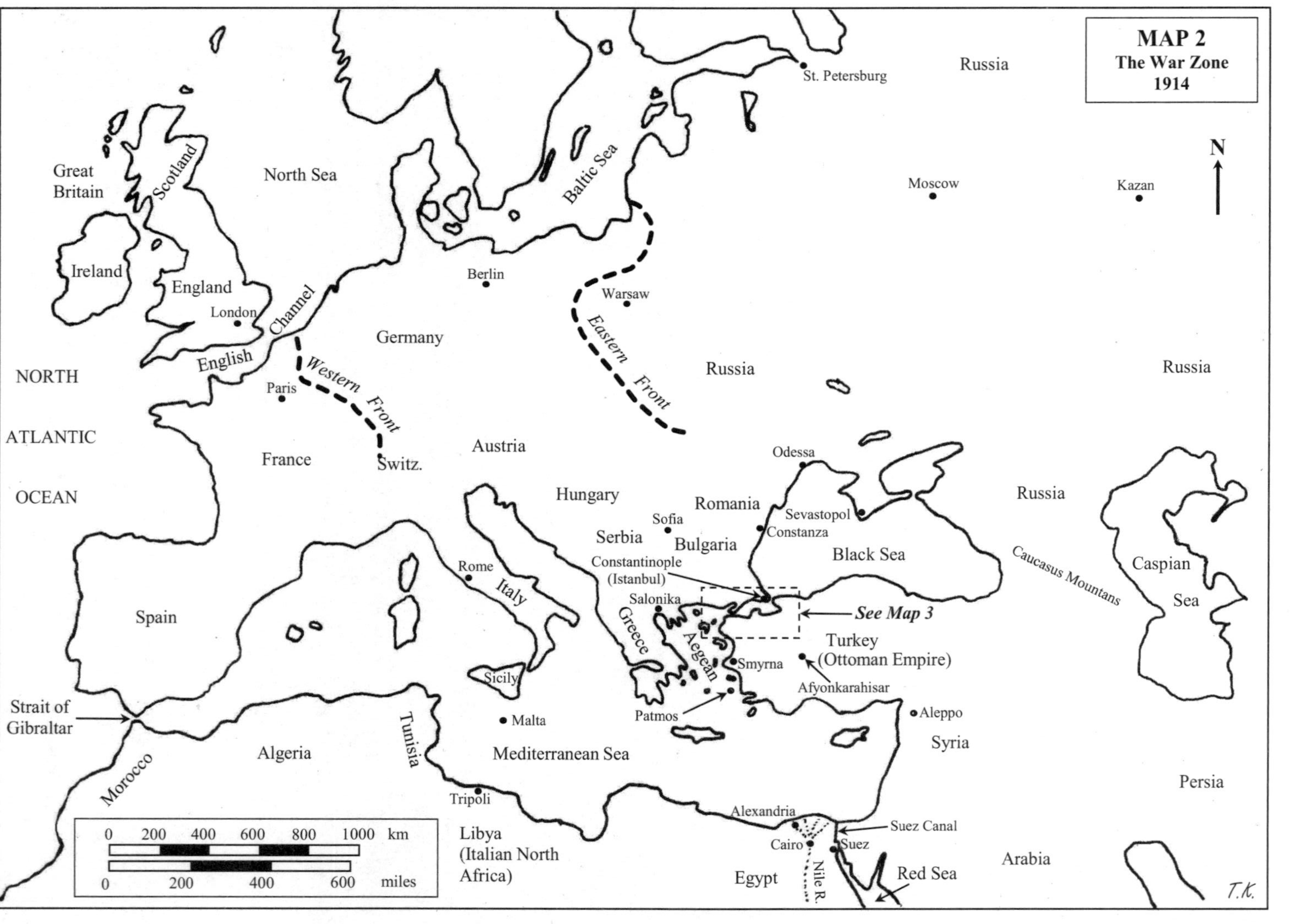

MAP 2
The War Zone
1914
N
St. Petersburg
Russia
Great
Britain
Scotland
North Sea
Baltic Sea
Moscow
Kazan
Ireland
England
London
Channel
English
Berlin
Warsaw
Germany
Eastern Front
Western Front
Paris
NORTH
ATLANTIC
OCEAN
France
Switz.
Austria
Russia
Russia
Odessa
Hungary
Romania
Sofia
Serbia
Bulgaria
Sevastopol
Constanza
Black Sea
Russia
Caucasus Mountans
Caspian
Sea
Constantinople
(Istanbul)
Salonika
Rome
Italy
Greece
Aegean
See Map 3
Turkey
(Ottoman Empire)
Smyrna
Afyonkarahisar
Spain
Sicily
Strait of
Gibraltar
Malta
Patmos
Aleppo
Syria
Tunisia
Algeria
Mediterranean Sea
Morocco
Tripoli
Persia
Alexandria
Suez Canal
Cairo
Suez
Libya
(Italian North
Africa)
Egypt
Nile R.
Red Sea
Arabia
0 200 400 600 800 1000 km
0 200 400 600 miles
T.K.

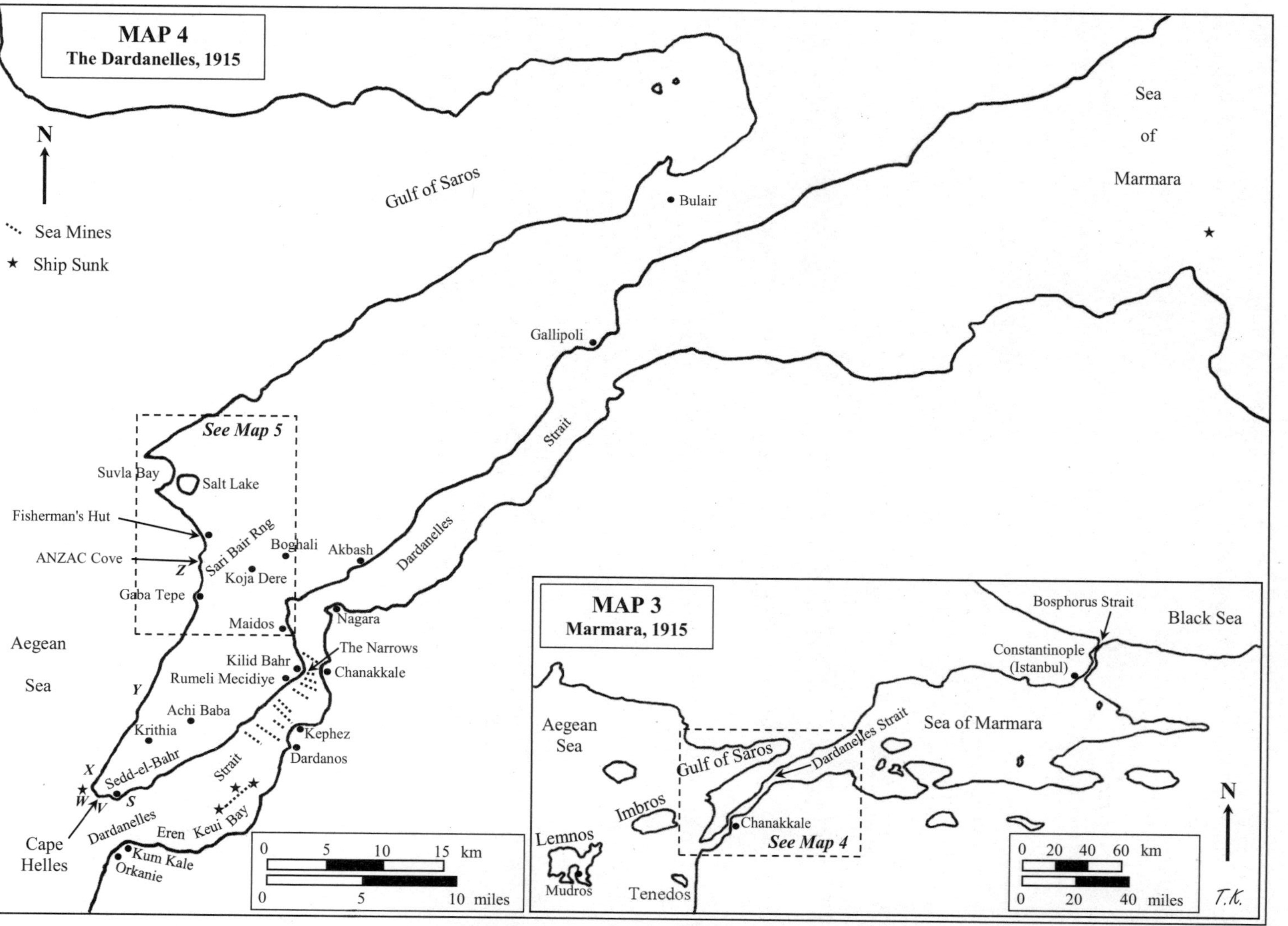
MAP 4
The Dardanelles, 1915
N
Sea Mines
Ship Sunk
Gulf of Saros
Bulair
Sea
of
Marmara
Gallipoli
Strait
Dardanelles
See Map 5
Suvla Bay
Salt Lake
Fisherman's Hut
ANZAC Cove
Sari Bair Rng
Boghali
Akbash
Koja Dere
Z
Gaba Tepe
Maidos
Nagara
Aegean
Sea
Kilid Bahr
The Narrows
Rumeli Mecidiye
Chanakkale
Y
Achi Baba
Krithia
Kephez
Dardanos
X
Sedd-el-Bahr
Strait
W
V
S
Cape
Helles
Dardanelles
Eren Keui Bay
Kum Kale
Orkanie
0 5 10 15 km
0 5 10 miles
MAP 3
Marmara, 1915
Bosphorus Strait
Black Sea
Constantinople
(Istanbul)
Aegean
Sea
Sea of Marmara
Dardanelles Strait
Gulf of Saros
Imbros
Chanakkale
See Map 4
Lemnos
Mudros
Tenedos
0 20 40 60 km
0 20 40 miles
T.K.

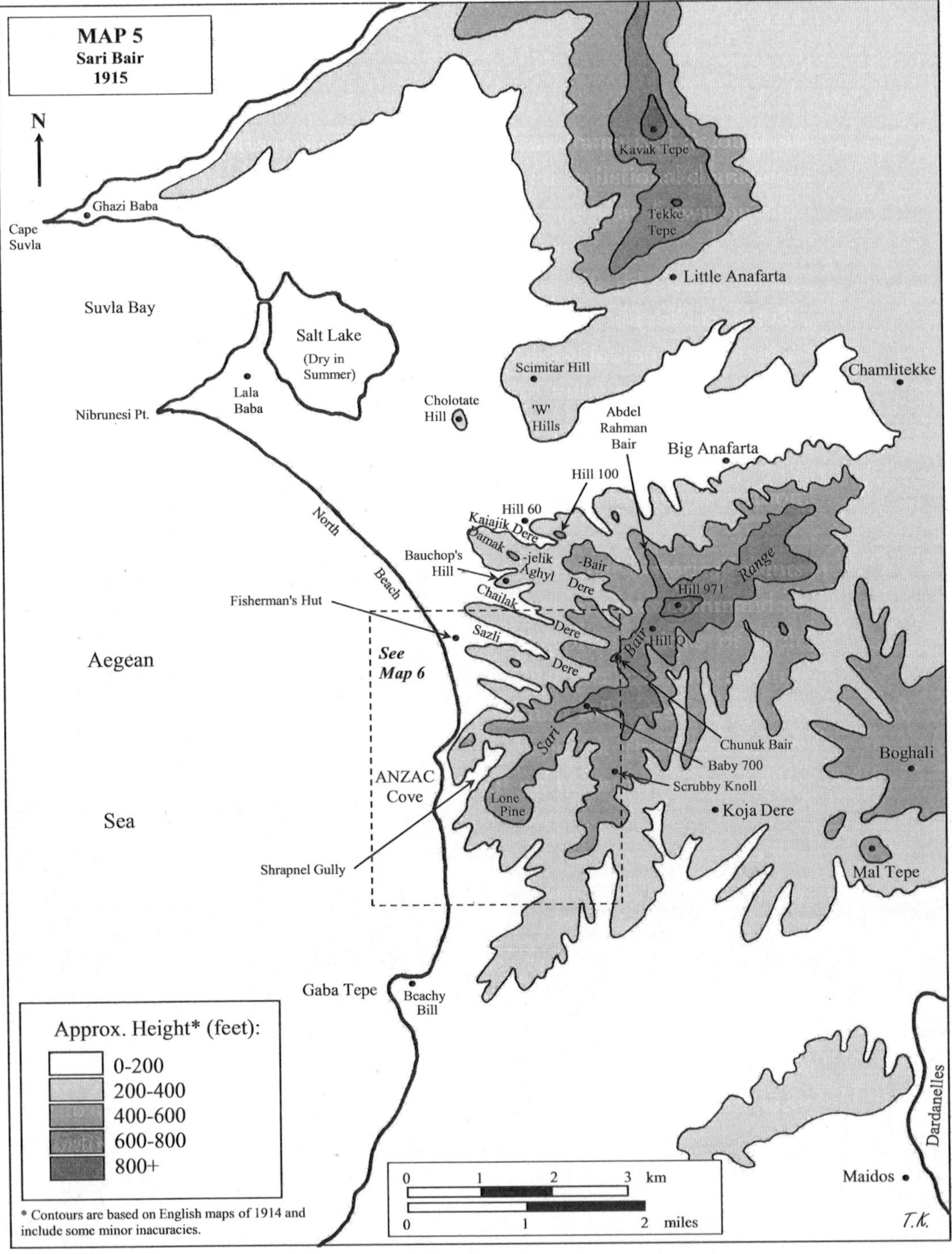
MAP 5
Sari Bair
1915
N
Ghazi Baba
Cape Suvla
Suvla Bay
Salt Lake
(Dry in Summer)
Lala Baba
Nibrunesi Pt.
Cholotate Hill
Scimitar Hill
'W' Hills
Kavak Tepe
Tekke Tepe
Little Anafarta
Chamlitekke
Abdel Rahman Bair
Big Anafarta
Hill 100
Hill 60
Kaiajik Dere
Damak -jelik -Bair
Aghyl Dere
Bauchop's Hill
Chailak Dere
Sazli Dere
Fisherman's Hut
North Beach
Aegean
Sea
See Map 6
Hill 971
Range
Hill Q
Bair
Sari
Chunuk Bair
Baby 700
Scrubby Knoll
ANZAC Cove
Lone Pine
Koja Dere
Boghali
Mal Tepe
Shrapnel Gully
Gaba Tepe
Beachy Bill
Approx. Height* (feet):
0-200
200-400
400-600
600-800
800+
* Contours are based on English maps of 1914 and include some minor inacuracies.
0 1 2 3 km
0 1 2 miles
Dardanelles
Maidos
T.K.

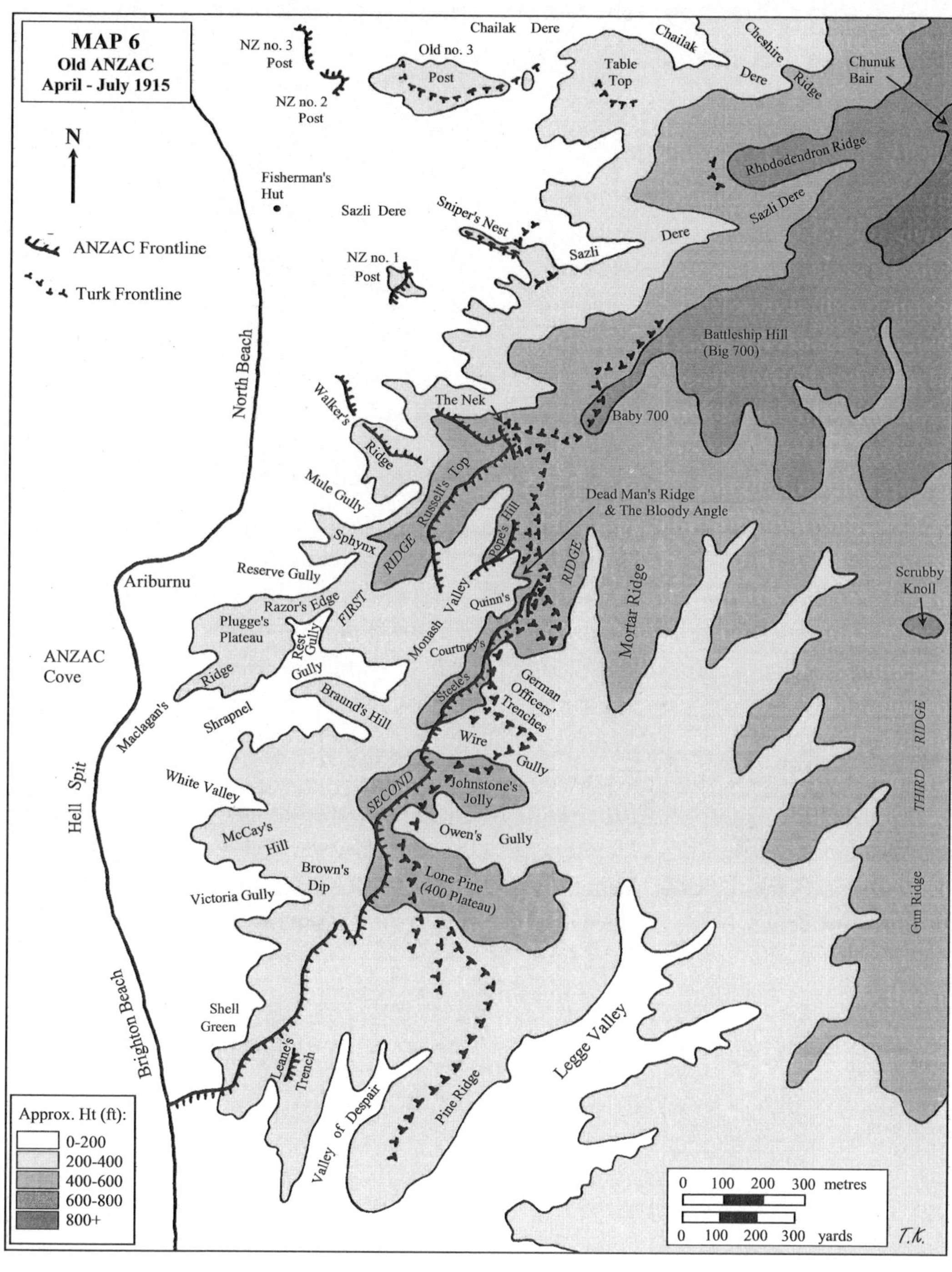
MAP 6
Old ANZAC
April - July 1915
N
ANZAC Frontline
Turk Frontline
NZ no. 3 Post
NZ no. 2 Post
Old no. 3 Post
Chailak Dere
Chailak
Cheshire Ridge
Dere
Table Top
Chunuk Bair
Rhododendron Ridge
Fisherman's Hut
Sazli Dere
Sniper's Nest
Sazli Dere
Dere
Sazli
NZ no. 1 Post
North Beach
Battleship Hill (Big 700)
Walker's Ridge
The Nek
Baby 700
Mule Gully
Russell's Top
Dead Man's Ridge & The Bloody Angle
Sphynx
RIDGE
Pope's Hill
RIDGE
Reserve Gully
Ariburnu
Razor's Edge
FIRST
Monash Valley
Quinn's
Mortar Ridge
Scrubby Knoll
Plugge's Plateau
Rest Gully
ANZAC Cove
Ridge
Gully
Courtney's
Braund's Hill
Steele's
German Officers' Trenches
Maclagan's
Shrapnel
Wire Gully
Hell Spit
White Valley
SECOND
Johnstone's Jolly
THIRD RIDGE
McCay's Hill
Owen's Gully
Brown's Dip
Lone Pine (400 Plateau)
Victoria Gully
Gun Ridge
Brighton Beach
Shell Green
Leane's Trench
Legge Valley
Valley of Despair
Pine Ridge
Approx. Ht (ft):
0-200
200-400
400-600
600-800
800+
0 100 200 300 metres
0 100 200 300 yards
T.K.

GALLIPOLI PLACE NAME TRANSLATION FOR MAPS

English Translation of Turkish Name	Turkish Name	Anzac / English Name
Besim Hill	Besimtepe	Hill Q
Bloody Ridge	Kanlisirt	Lone Pine
Bomb Ridge	Bomba sirt	Quinn's Post
Falcon Ridge	Şahin Sirta	Rhododendron Ridge
Flat Hill	Düztepe	Battleship Hill
High Ridge	Yükseksırt	Russell's Top
Hill of Great Pasture	Koca Çimen Tepe	Hill 971
Hill of Valour	Cesarettepe	The Nek
Junction Hill	Merkez Tepe	German Officers Ridge
Kemal's Place	Kemalyeri	Scrubby Knoll
Little Bee Point	Ariburnu	Anzac Cove (north headland)
Red Ridge	Kırmızısırt	Johnson's Jolly
Reedy Creek	Sazlidere	Sazli Beit Dere
Salt Lake	Tuz Gölü	Suvla
Sheepfold Valley	Ağildere	Argyl Dere
Shrine of Pines	Çamlıtekke	n/a
Sword Slope	Kiliçbayır / Hill 180	Baby 700
Treacherous Hill	Haintepe	Plugges Plateau
Valley of Black Nomads	Karayörük Deresi	Legge Valley
Valley of Fear	Kuruku Dere	Shrapnel-Monash Valley

CAST

The tale is told from the points of view of the following characters:

Ali Private Ali Aslan, 2nd Battalion, 27th Regiment, 9th Division, Ottoman 5th Army. (fictional)

Charles Major Charles Villiers-Stuart, Intelligence Officer, Australian and New Zealand Army Corps (A. & N. Z. A. C.) (historical)

Clarence Charles 'Clarence' Palmer, British Vice Consul in the Dardanelles. Later a Lieutenant in the Royal Navy. (historical)

Dacre Lieutenant Henry 'Dacre' Stoker, Royal Navy, on loan to the Royal Australian Navy, Commander of Australian E class submarine *AE2*. (historical)

Ellis Ellis Ashmead-Bartlett, war correspondent for the London press. (historical)

Hamid Private Hamid Kaya, 1st Battalion, 57th Regiment, 19th Division, Ottoman 5th Army. Father of Ishmail. (fictional)

Hans Baron Hans von Wangenheim, German Ambassador to the Ottoman Empire. (historical)

Harry Colonel Henry 'Harry' Chauvel, Australian Representative, Dominions Section, British Imperial General Staff. Later Commander of 1st Light Horse Brigade. (historical)

Ishmail Private Ishmail Kaya, 1st Battalion, 57th Regiment, 19th Division, Ottoman 5th Army. Son of Hamid. (fictional)

Jayjay Jonathan 'Jayjay' Jones, citizen of Sydney. Later Private, 1st Battalion, 1st Infantry Brigade, 1st Division, Australian Imperial Force (Later A. & N. Z. A. C). Brother of Ronald. (fictional)

John Colonel John Monash, Commander of the Australian 4th Infantry Brigade, Australian and New Zealand Division, Australian Imperial Force (Later A. & N. Z. A. C). (historical)

Karl Captain Karl von Muller, Commander of warship *Emden*, German Navy. (historical)

Larry Lawrence 'Larry' Gillespie, citizen of Sydney. Later Private, 1st Battalion, 1st Infantry Brigade, 1st Division, Australian Imperial Force (Later A. & N. Z. A. C). (fictional)

Mustafa Lieutenant-Colonel Mustafa Kemal, Ottoman Military Attache in Bulgaria. Later Commander of the 19th Division of the Ottoman 5th Army. (historical)

Roger Commodore Roger Keyes, Chief of Staff to the Royal Navy Mediterranean Fleet Commander, Admiral de Robeck. (historical)

Ronald Ronald Jones, citizen of Sydney. Later Private, 1st Battalion, 1st Infantry Brigade, 1st Division, Australian Imperial Force (later A. & N. Z. A. C). Brother of Jayjay. (fictional)

Winston The Honourable Winston Churchill, elected Member of the British Parliament and First Lord of the Admiralty. (historical)

CONTENTS

"Those who cannot remember the past are condemned to repeat it."
– George Santayana, 1906[1]

"Daddy, I don't understand why the Australians came to fight in Turkey. It's so stupid!"
– Lara Knight, age 8 years[2]

---

1 *The Life of Reason, Volume 1 – Introduction and Reason in Common Sense*, 1906, p. 284.

2 To the author during a family holiday in Turkey, whilst on a tour of Gallipoli battlefields and cemeteries. The day this book was conceived.

PART I

For the Empire

CHAPTER 1

Jayjay

Saturday, 8 August 1914

"I wonder what it's like to kill a man."

Jayjay stabbed his spoon into the bowl of porridge without looking. His eyes were fixed on the *Sydney Morning Herald.*

His mother Mary dropped the pot she had been scrubbing into the sink.

"How is your breakfast Jonathan?" Her voice cut the morning like a razor.

He was wide awake now.

"It says here," he said in his calmest morning croak. "That His Majesty's Government gratefully accepts the offer of Australia's ministers to send a force of 20,000 men to England."

His mother shook her head, but said nothing.

"Then it says," Jayjay continued, "that we propose to send the force at the earliest possible moment."

I hope she keeps her views about the war locked up inside this house, otherwise Charlotte might give me a white feather. I'd rather die.

He turned back a page to page 13 and scanned the war related articles. One caught his eye and he read in silence as he ate:

THE DOMINIONS KINGS MESSAGE

"EMPIRE WILL STAND UNITED"

LONDON, Aug. 6.

His Majesty the King has forwarded the following message to the Governments of Canada, Australia, New Zealand and South Africa:–

"I desire to express to the people of the Dominions with what appreciation and pride I have received the messages from their respective governments. These spontaneous assurances of their fullest support recall the generous self-sacrificing help given in the past to the mother country. I shall be strengthened in the discharge of the great responsibilities which rest upon me by the confident belief that in this time of trial my Empire will stand united, calm, and resolute, trusting in God."

He stood and took his empty bowl to the sink.

"What's up Jayjay, did you suck on a lemon for brekkie?" His father stood in the doorway and rubbed one eye.

"I was just reading about the Australian troops who are going to help England in the war against Germany, but I don't think Mum's real keen on the idea."

His father opened his mouth as if about to speak, but said nothing.

Mary looked up from the sink and stared at them both.

"This is not our war!" she said.

"England has declared war on Germany Mum," Jayjay said. "So we are at war."

"Nonsense!"

"We're a part of the British Empire."

"We're a federation of fools if we can't make our own decisions."

"I'm thinking of signing up."

"Hold your horses young man!" The pitch of her voice rang higher. "England only declared war a few days ago. A little more thought would be wise before rushing off to a war half way around the world and throwing your life away for no damned good reason!"

Mum never uses that kind of language. Jayjay hesitated before replying.

"I'm not going to rush into anything. Mum. I promise. I just want to consider it."

"You're not old enough."

"I don't know what the age limit is, but I'll look into that too. I'm a lot bigger than most other nineteen year-olds. I don't see how I could be left out for being too young."

Mary took a step towards him and looked up to his face. Her eyes, a foot lower than his, opened slightly. "Jonathan, I could not bear to see you go off to war and not know if you would return."

"I just want to do my bit Mum."

Without knowing what else to say, Jayjay turned to his father Stanley who sighed and sat at the table.

"Mary, England is at war!" Stanley's voice was slow and firm. "If she wins, she'll remember whether Australia stood by her. If she loses, we'll be spoils for the victor regardless."

She stared at her husband.

"No," she whispered. "Stanley, please."

"Without the Royal Navy to defend our shores," he continued. "Australia is ripe for invasion. We have more than ten thousand miles of coastline and less than five million people to defend it. It is simple mathematics. Jayjay's right. England is at war and so Australia is at war, like it or not. Our boys are old enough to make their own decisions and taking up arms to defend our homeland is not a bad decision to make."

Mary slumped into a chair at the kitchen table and dropped her face into in her hands.

Jayjay looked at his mother, then to the door, then his father. Stanley's jaw was set, as if ready to defend his position, but he said nothing and gave Jayjay a slight nod.

Jayjay slipped out and followed the short corridor to his bedroom to get dressed. His thoughts swirled in a blur of confusion. It had all seemed so simple before breakfast.

Once dressed, Jayjay grabbed his jacket and walked out the front door without saying goodbye. He pulled on the jacket and a waft of eucalyptus scent filled his nostrils. *There's another good reason to sign up. No need to wake at dawn and haul lumber all week for a pittance. I was looking forward to this weekend, but now I'm not so sure.*

Outside, on the path at the front door step of his home, a small circle of yellow-orange sand formed a mound at the junction of two paving bricks. Tiny black ants marched in a line, from a hole in the middle of the mound, with purpose. A jasmine vine clung to a trellis by the window, laden with buds in anticipation of the coming spring.

Jayjay stepped over the ants and walked down the street towards Larry's home. Few people were about this early on a Saturday morning.

Before he had walked a block, Larry rounded the corner ahead and strode towards him. Jayjay grinned and tried to forget the unplanned start to the day.

"Wanna walk down to Wentworth Park to watch the footy?" Larry suggested as the gap between them closed. "I've got two shillings to put on the Tigers to win."

"Sure."

The game wasn't due to start for a few hours, but Larry seemed just as excited as Jayjay had been before breakfast. *We would both rather be out walking the streets than stuck at home in our parent's houses.*

The Sydney winter morning air was crisp and the sky was blue. Jayjay's breath was visible for an instant when it left his mouth, then faded into nothing, but he walked on without feeling the cold.

"I'm signing up for sure," Larry said. "Can't wait to get a crack at the Hun. Teach them a lesson about being bullies."

Jayjay put his hands in his pockets and looked down at the ground. "My mum doesn't want me to go. Dad seems more okay with the idea though."

"What'd you tell your mum for? Women don't understand about war."

"I felt I ought to."

"We've got to start making some big decisions for ourselves Jay. And what could be bigger than this? We can show the world that us Colonials can stand up with the best of them. We'll do Australia proud."

They sauntered on with the lazy gait of those who have all day to get to wherever they are going, but Jayjay could not release the tension that gripped his gut.

On reaching the waterfront at Rozelle, they followed the streets between the narrow terrace cottages and the wharves as they wound around Rozelle Bay.

At the head of Blackwattle Bay, they found a place to sit near the shore. Across the water, twin chimney stacks of the new White Bay electricity generating station stood tall, but the view was far from Jayjay's mind as he sat with Larry, discussing the war and their possible involvement.

Time came for the pair to move towards Wentworth Park Rugby League Field for kick-off. They left the bay behind them and passed beneath the brick arches for the raised railway line that had been under construction for years.

The two Balmain Tigers supporters found a space on a timber bench near the half-way line and watched a hard-fought match, surrounded by vocal supporters of both teams. The full-time score of five-all was a result that might have been called fair by an impartial observer, but there were none present, so the result was unsatisfactory to all concerned and the referee was informed of his shortcomings from all quarters.

A decision in Jayjay's mind was no clearer than the rugby league result.

* * *

The next day, Jayjay walked home from the morning service at St Thomas Church of England with his parents and Ron and Emilia. Sunday family lunch was now a regular event, since Ron had married Emilia in January and moved out with her to a small rented house nearby.

For lunch, Mary Jones served up roast leg of lamb with potatoes, pumpkin and beans. Jayjay piled his plate with meat and vegetables, and drowned the lot in gravy. On the table in front of him, near his right hand, four small dents marked the place where he had hammered his fork into the wood years earlier, during a heated dinner-time discussion about throwing fruit at school. He traced a finger across the row of dents and swallowed the last of his patience with the first mouthful.

"So Ron," he said. "What do you think about signing up?"

His mother, shaking salt on her meal, hesitated for a moment, and then continued. She did not look up.

Ron, chewing, looked at their mother who kept her eyes aimed downward. He swallowed and cleared his throat.

"I think it's our duty," Ron said. "It's as simple as that. We'd be shirking it to stay home now that England is at war."

Good answer Ron!

"What do you think Dad?" Jayjay asked.

Stan glanced at his wife. Now she looked up and glared at him. He reached for his glass of water and took a sip before answering.

"Like Ron said, England is at war, so the question comes to whether Australia should join her in support. We're vulnerable here at the end of the Empire. There aren't many of us looking after this big island, and we have plenty at stake. The Germans or the Chinese could easily invade Australia from the north. The Germans have already colonized New Guinea and everyone knows you can't trust a Chinaman. The German navy is growing strong, and the German army is marching across France towards England as we eat our lunch. Now if we are invaded, I have no doubt that England would be here to help us out. They'd have to. What do you think would happen to Australia if they didn't? I'll tell you what: we'd become servants of the Germans or Chinese, we wouldn't be a part of the British Empire any longer. Now, if Australia is bound to support the English war effort against Germany, it becomes a question of whether you are willing to stay at home while others go off to fight for our freedom. Here is where you boys will have to make up your own mind. You know that your mother and I have different views in this, but no one can tell you what to do. You have to decide within yourselves what you believe is the right thing to do."

A heavy silence blanketed the table.

The sound of Jayjay chewing on a mouthful of lamb gristle squelched in his ears. *The others must be able to hear me.*

He forced himself to swallow to kill the noise.

"When did England ever help us?" Mary's voice dripped with disdain. "Think of all the droughts, floods and fires we've had over the years in Australia. What help did England ever send, other than more convicts?"

"What about you Emilia?" Stanley asked. "You are part of the family now. What do you think about Ron going off to war?"

"Well," Emilia hesitated, then looked at Ron. "I think Ron has to make his own decision. They are saying that the war will likely only last six months, and our boys might even be home by Christmas. I'd worry ever so much if he went, but I know Ron will be careful whatever he does. I don't think he'll take any unnecessary risks."

"It seems that you have all been blinded by loyalty to Mother England." Mary shook her head slowly. "You think England would come running to our aid if we were invaded? Only if it suited Mother England and she was worried about the cost to herself."

"But Mum," Jayjay said. "This is our chance to defend the innocent, isn't that the right thing for us to do? We don't know what England would do if we were invaded, that's true, and there is no way we can know so that doesn't really help us. I know you are worried about the danger. But think of the sermon that Reverend Davies preached this morning. Jesus had the courage to face death for us, and we praise him for it. We worship God at the Church of England. The whole Australian colony would not exist if it wasn't for England. We owe it to England to help. Our Government's offer to England has already been accepted, so we can't very well back out now. What would that say about Australians?"

"It would say that Australians have the good sense to use their God-given brains," Mary said.

"If anyone should stay at home, it should be Ron. At least he's married and has a good job here. I haven't been able to do much right since I left school. I didn't get an apprenticeship. I'm just working as a labourer. I'm bigger and stronger than most down at the sawmill, but business is pretty quiet lately and there's no great prospects there. I'm nearly twenty years old now. What else can I do? I don't want to keep labouring for the rest of my life. Maybe joining up and becoming a soldier is the change that I need. Besides, Larry's going."

I shouldn't have mentioned Larry. As soon as the words passed through his lips he tried to suck the sentence back, but it wouldn't come.

"I see, so if Larry decided to go to Sydney Heads and jump off a cliff you would go right on after him, would you?"

"No Mum, it's just that Larry and most of the other guys my age are going to go, so it would be pretty hard for me to face them when they come home if I stayed here."

"If they come home." Mary said "What do –"

"Well, I expect at least some of them will return." Stanley interjected "And Jayjay has to be able to face those that do. Even if none of them return, he has to be able to face himself in the mirror. No man wants to be named a coward."

From that moment, Jayjay knew what was right and what he would do.

"No way am I going to let my little brother go off to war while I stay here." Ron said, as if reading Jayjay's thoughts. "It has nothing to do with whether I am married, or whether I have a job. I have already discussed it with Emilia, and while she would obviously rather keep me around here, she understands my decision to enlist."

Emilia stared down at her plate and said nothing.

A tear rolled down Mary's nose. It clung to the tip for a moment, then let go and fell onto her plate of untouched food.

Guilt oozed through Jayjay's body like poison.

Why do females have to get all emotional and make a simple thing complex?

He wanted to fight for the freedom of those he loved. He wanted to defend the innocent against the aggressor. He cared that his sister-in-law Emilia was upset, although that was something he could push to the back of his mind without any great effort.

But to make his mother sad.

So sad.

That must be some big kind of sin.

CHAPTER 2

Hans

Tuesday, 11 August 1914

Baron Hans von Wangenheim, German Ambassador to the Ottoman Empire, paced across an ancient Turkish carpet to a window in his summer embassy.

He drew a long breath through a large black German cigar and his gaze drifted across the Bosphorus Strait. A thin strip of water that separated Europe and Asia, and cut through the heart of the ancient city of Constantinople, or Istanbul as the Turks liked to call it. A strip of water that provided much benefit to the Russians, with whom the Fatherland was now at war. *A strip of water that will soon yield check-mate to my diplomatic mastery.*

On the opposite shore, one kilometre away, the antenna structure of his newly-constructed wireless station stood proud against the horizon.

Still no official confirmation of the news, but a small launch pulled away from the wireless station and steamed towards him.

Warm anticipation swelled in his chest and he smiled to himself. *The fruits of three years of my good work are about to be revealed for all to see.*

A knock at the door disturbed his moment.

"Sir, the American Ambassador, Mr Henry Morgenthau is here to see you."

Hans nodded for the visitor to be shown in. "Good morning, Mr Morgenthau. To what do I owe the pleasure?"

Hans paced across the room, turned and hurried back to the window. The approaching launch bobbed halfway across the Bosphorus.

"Good morning, Baron von Wangenheim," Morgenthau waited at the door.

"We are witnessing a great victory for German diplomacy Henry."

"May I come in?"

"Yes, of course. Please sit down." Hans tore himself from the window.

"Something is seriously distracting you Hans," said the American. "I will go, and come again some other time."

"No, no!" Hans almost shouted. "I want you to stay right where you are. This will be a great day for Germany! If you will only remain for a few minutes, you will hear a great piece of news – something that has the utmost bearing upon Turkey's relation to the war."

Hans strode out onto the portico and leaned over the balustrade. The launch was close now. Without further explanation he left the American Ambassador alone and rushed down to the embassy dock.

He seized an envelope from one of the sailors and tore it open.

It is exactly as I had hoped. No, exactly as I planned it to be.

He hurried back inside where Morgenthau waited, looking bemused and a little impatient.

"We've got them!" Hans waved the wireless message as if it was the winning ticket at a horse race.

"Got what?"

"The *Goeben* and the *Breslau* have passed through the Dardenelles."

"How does that help you Hans? By international treaty, Turkey cannot allow German warships to stay in Turkish waters for more than twenty-four hours, and still remain neutral in the war. Is Turkey really ready to declare war on England, France and Russia?"

Hans hesitated and paused. He walked over to Morgenthau, shook his finger and spoke on his best diplomatic voice. "Of course, you understand that we have sold these ships to Turkey! And our Admiral Souchon will enter the Sultan's service!"

"So Turkey is to remain neutral?"

"Of course! We have no wish to drag Turkey into a war that does not concern her. That would not be in her best interests or ours. If she were to join us as an ally, we would be obliged to share the spoils when we win. As soon as we have finished speaking, I will send a message to Admiral Souchon and order him to raise the Turkish flag. There is no longer any *Goeben* and *Breslau*, they are now *Sultan Selim* and *Medilli*, two warships of the Turkish Navy. International prohibitions do not apply!"

Morgenthau walked slowly to the window and stared across the Bosphorus. "It seems to me Hans, that perhaps, it is more than a coincidence that these two German cruisers should have been lurking in the Mediterranean at the moment when war broke out?"

Hans nodded and allowed himself to reveal a hint of a smile. *A little gloating couldn't hurt.*

"The British Navy guards Gibraltar and Suez," Morgenthau continued. "And there is no other way to exit the Mediterranean Sea, but via the Dardanelles Strait. There are not so many places in the Mediterranean where a German warship could take coal these days. And yet, both ships are capable of high speeds. If I am not mistaken, at least one of them has made the voyage to Constantinople previously?"

"Our cruisers took coal at Sicily, where the Italians were careful not to let them stop for more than twenty-four hours. Our ships left the British fleet in their wake and came east at full steam. The British must have had more important business to attend to as they gave up the chase. Your memory is correct, *Goeben* has twice visited Constantinople in recent years. Her officers know their way up the Dardanelles and they found no enemy warships there to challenge them."

Morgenthau continued gazing across the water, scratched at his goatee beard and said nothing.

"I treated the Young Turks with the respect they are entitled to as heads of Government," Hans continued. "And reminded them that Germany is their only friend in the region. The Turkish Minister for War, Enver, understands the value of German assistance in re-organising his army. All other major European powers have carved off slices of the Ottoman Empire and annexed them for themselves. And Winston Churchill unlawfully seized the two dreadnoughts England was building for Turkey, just as they came out of production in the British shipyards. That upset the Turks no end and made my job easier. Did you know that Turkish seamen were already in England ready to man these ships on their maiden voyage?"

"England had the legal and moral right to requisition those warships."

"So they say. The English and French have demonstrated their arrogance and they will pay a high price for it. They have treated the Young Turks with contempt, as if the Turkish government lacks legitimacy."

"The young General Enver did storm the Turkish parliament with a mob, murder the previous Minister for War and take control by way of a forceful coup."

"Nazim's death was an unfortunate accident."

"The Sultan has been placed under house arrest and his son-in-law hanged as an example. The new regime has shown no less of a despotic tendency than the previous one."

"Once a man has had a taste of power, his lust for it grows all the more insatiable. I gave Major-General Enver what he needed to secure his position and he knows who his friends are."

"Did you want this war Hans?"

"I told Enver that the warships must enter the Turkish navy and pass through the Dardanelles, and he crumpled like paper. Only fools believe in coincidences Henry."

* * *

A few days later, Hans walked along the road that followed the shoreline of the Bosphorus Strait. Admiral Souchon had promised a show that Hans didn't want to miss.

Hans found a place where he could see the Russian embassy. He lit a large black German cigar and made no attempt to conceal his presence. A tall man with broad shoulders, he was unlikely to be mistaken for a Turk.

At the scheduled time, a German battle cruiser steamed along the Bosphorus from the north. The *Goeben,* recently re-Christened as *Sultan Selim,* eased to a stop and dropped anchor in front of the Russian embassy.

Out front of the embassy, the Russian Ambassador emerged and stood alone, facing off against the warship's 11-inch guns. His arms straight by his side, as if standing to attention, ready to be blasted into oblivion.

On the top deck of the warship there stood a line of sailors in dress uniform, all wearing Turkish fezzes. The men removed the Fezzes in unison, and replaced them with German caps. At that moment the ship's band began to play "Deutschland über Alles" and the sailors sang along loudly.

After the German National Anthem, the band played "Watch the Rhine."

The Russian ambassador turned his gaze towards Hans, and Hans threw him a casual wave. The Russian stared back for a long moment, then returned his glare to the warship, as if he was the last defender of Russian pride.

After serenading the Russian ambassador for over an hour, the sailors removed their caps and again put on their Turkish fezzes. The warship weighed anchor and started south to her station. Strains of German war songs gradually died away as she disappeared downstream.

Hans lit another cigar and strolled back in the direction of the German Embassy.

Turkey is mine. I have one noose around the Ottoman neck and another around the Russian neck. Now I can watch the ropes tighten slowly. The Kaiser trusted me and I have delivered. The cost of two warships is nothing in the great game. I will be Chancellor of Germany once this war is over. Weeks, maybe months at the outside. The prize is within my grasp.

CHAPTER 3

Jayjay

Wednesday, 19 August 1914

Jayjay had hardly slept.

At the first hint of dawn he rolled out of bed. He dressed into his Sunday best clothes and hat, all laid out ready from the night before, then walked quietly to the kitchen and poured a glass of water.

He swallowed a mouthful, then set the glass down next to the sink and visited the outhouse. The winter's morning air chilled his skin, but not enough to bother him. Nonetheless, when he was done, he hurried back inside.

A window over the kitchen sink framed the grey outline of the backyard he had grown up in. He sipped at his water and stared out into the beginning of a new day.

A thin slither of moon hung above the back fence. The yard he had played in, for hours at a time, now seemed very small.

He placed the empty glass in the sink, gently, so as not to make noise.

A drink of water and a splash on the face. A duck's breakfast will do me today.

"So you're going then?" His mother's voice came from behind him.

I had hoped to get out the door and avoid this conversation.

"It's the right thing for me to do Mum." Jayjay turned to face her.

Her eyes met his in the dim light.

She exhaled slowly.

"Jonathan, I know things have not gone as you had hoped of late, but that can always change. It's the tough times that make us stronger. It's not too late to change your mind, but I can see you will not. You are a grown man now and have to make your own choices. Would that I could have it otherwise."

Jayjay forced a smile. "There's nothing for me here now."

"Just come back to me safely Jonathan, your father and I are here for you. And bring that brother of yours back with you. I'm sure Emilia will appreciate it."

"Don't worry about us Mum. We'll be fine."

Jayjay stooped, gave his mum a hug and walked down the hallway to the front door without looking back. *She'll be teary, but I don't know what else to say. Staying home is not an option for me anymore.*

A ten minute walk had him at Ron's house. The front door was ajar and Jayjay went straight in without knocking. Ron came out of the kitchen with a slice of bread in his hand and gave Jayjay a smile and a grunt, which might have been "G'day" if his mouth wasn't full. Ron's wife Emilia appeared looking surprisingly awake for this hour and gave Ron a parting embrace that lasted longer than was necessary.

Let's go Ron, away from the last female obstacle between us and Victoria Barracks.

Emilia released her husband and smiled, looking as if she was holding back tears. Ron gave her another kiss on the cheek and turned toward the door, then strode past Jayjay without meeting his eyes.

The brothers walked in silence for a minute, then Ron looked up.

"Sorry to hear things didn't work out at the saw mill."

"Yeah," Jayjay nodded. "So much for the rule of 'last in, first out'. Jimmy is the owner's brother-in-law, and the older guys have families, so bad luck for me. It's not fair, but who cares. It doesn't matter now, at least not for the next few months."

On the way to the Balmain line tram stop, the brothers came to Larry's home.

Larry sat waiting on the front door step. A broad grin spread across his face and he jumped up and joined them.

"Let's get going then, I don't wanna miss out! The paper says fellows are streaming in from all over. Soon they're gonna realise they have enough and won't want any more men. Let's not shorten the odds on that happening."

Larry's twin sister Grace stared at them from inside the window and Jayjay waved her a good morning.

At least Grace isn't out here making a fuss.

She caught his gaze and her eye's narrowed. She pulled a face and poked her tongue out at him.

"Don't feel special," Larry chuckled. "Gracey is like that with everyone. You should see how she reacts to people she really doesn't like!"

The three walked on and caught a tram to Sydney Railway Terminus, then they started on the one mile walk to Paddington.

The walk helped to settle Jayjay's nerves and take his mind off the possibility that the army might reject his application to enlist. A few minutes later, he rounded a corner and an imposing sandstone archway came into view, marking the entrance to Victoria Barracks. Any calming benefit from the walk dissipated at that moment.

A small crowd of men gathered on Oxford Street, and loitered about the entrance.

"This way gentlemen, if you please," said a uniformed army officer with a fat moustache and friendly smile as they approached. He waved them through the stone arch.

Jayjay found himself standing straighter already. *I would make a good soldier. I'm bigger and stronger than most, so with the right equipment and training I should be able to do what's required. Hopefully they'll give me a fair go.*

He let the others go to be interviewed by the enlisting officer ahead of himself. After Jayjay sat down, a devastated-looking young chap emerged from a medical.

"What d'ya mean flat feet?" he roared.

"My feet are as good as anyone else's here. Let me have a running race, or a long march, just let me show you. I bet I could outrun that big guy over there!" He pointed at Jayjay.

Heat rose in Jayjay's neck and face.

My skin is turning red. I wish I could stop it from doing that. I must ignore that fellow. I shouldn't have let the others go in first. I hate running races and I hate it when people tell me I must be a fast runner with such long legs. The shorter boys could always pump their legs in a smooth motion and win the race. I could never achieve that smooth motion. It would be just my luck if that officer declared I would have to race the flat-footer and only the winner will be able to enlist.

Jayjay stared at his shoes. The protests against rejection faded into the distance.

"Jonathan Jones!" The enlisting officer called.

Jayjay walked across the room, heart racing, and sat at the table across from the officer.

"What's your age son?"

"Nineteen – nearly twenty years old, Sir."

"Before I write that in ink, you should know that anyone under twenty-one years of age needs written permission from a parent to sign up. If a strapping lad like yourself was to tell me that he was older, say twenty-two, I'd be none the wiser."

The enlistment officer's quill dipped slowly into the inkwell, then hovered above it.

Jayjay reached inside his jacket and pulled out a letter, signed by his father, stating that he had been granted permission to sign up.

"No need for that Sir." Jayjay grinned and handed over the letter.

"Right you are then. It's just that some of the lads have come a long way and didn't quite get around to asking their parents what they thought of the idea."

After a series of questions about who he was and where he lived, the enlisting officer asked if Jayjay had ever fired a rifle.

Jayjay nodded. "At my Uncle David's farm at Miranda. I used to shoot rabbits and crows when I went to stay with him in the holidays, 'cause they're pests. I guess Germans would be a bit easier to hit, being so much bigger and all."

The officer looked up at him with one eyebrow raised in a way that reminded him of his mother's disapproving look.

"I don't suppose the rabbits or crows were shooting back at the time?" The officer replied, his tone dry as dust. A patronising grin formed beneath his moustache.

"Well son, how about you step behind that curtain over there for a medical examination?"

Jayjay hurried to the curtain. The examination took all of two minutes which seemed awfully brief, considering its importance, but he didn't complain when he was sent back with an 'all clear' to the enlistment officer.

"Congratulations," the enlistment officer smiled. He held out a form in one hand and a quill in the other. "You have been accepted to join the Strength if you would like to take the oath. It is important to understand that the oath is binding and should not be taken lightly."

Deep inside Jayjay, pride welled up like a spring. He grabbed the form and quill. *I'm joining 'The Strength!'* It sounded like an elite club that would bring power and success just for being a part of it.

The officer had already written the name 'Jonathan Jones' and the date, as well as the other details confirming the location of enlistment and his own signature as Attesting Officer.

The oath was printed on the form to be read and signed...

OATH TO BE TAKEN BY PERSON BEING ENLISTED.

I, Jonathan Jones *swear that I will well and truly serve our Sovereign Lord the King in the Australian Imperial Force from* 19.8.1914 *until the end of the War, and a further period of four months thereafter unless sooner lawfully discharged, dismissed, or removed therefrom; and that I will resist His Majesty's enemies and cause His Majesty's peace to be kept and maintained; and that I will in all matters appertaining to my service, faithfully discharge my duty according to law.*

SO HELP ME, GOD.

____

Signature of Person Enlisted.

Jayjay said the words of the oath aloud, reading as quickly as he could while the quill quivered in his hand. Semi-human Germans on a violent rampage, depicted on war posters hanging around the room, bore witness to the declaration of his oath.

"Just sign and you are done," added the enlistment officer.

Jayjay dipped the quill into the ink pot and scribbled his name.

He walked away from his interview and a lightheaded sense of euphoria buzzed in his head. Ron and Larry were waiting for him, grinning like school boys. He shook hands with each of them and they all congratulated each other.

"He told me we can march to the 1st Brigade camp at Randwick this afternoon," Ron said. "Or we can return in the morning."

"Easy choice," Jayjay said. "Why go home now? It'd just make Mum cry again."

"You bet," Larry said. "We're here now. Imagine if we came back tomorrow and they decided they didn't need us anymore."

"Yeah," Ron's voice carried less conviction. "I suppose so."

They waited at the barracks until the afternoon, then marched with the other recruits to Randwick Racecourse. Here they were told that due to a shortage of tents, they would be sleeping in the grandstands. After a meal of boiled potatoes and bully beef they were each issued two blankets.

Those men who had signed up on earlier days had positioned themselves under the small amount of roof cover at the back of the grandstand, leaving only the exposed areas for the newer recruits. That night, Jayjay lay on wooden bench wrapped in his two blankets and smiled at the black sky. Clouds shrouded the moon and stars that he knew were smiling down at him.

Today couldn't have gone any better. We could've missed out, but all three of us were accepted. I have no job and Charlotte won't give me the time of day, but none of that matters now. I'm a soldier in the king's army, sworn to a duty, part of the Strength. This is the beginning of a new phase of my life.

At that moment, rain started to fall.

CHAPTER 4

Clarence

Thursday, 20 August 1914

The Kilid Bahr docks always smelt the same in the morning – fish, putrefying refuse and fresh baked bread. The site of an ancient stone fortress, Kilid Bahr was more of a defensive emplacement surrounded by a village than a real township.

Clarence Edward Stanhope Palmer strolled from the ferry wharf with a confident air, as if he had all the time in the world and no particular place to be. It was hard work looking like he wasn't trying to look inconspicuous.

A street vendor selling hot corn provided the perfect excuse for Clarence to sit on an old barrel near the water's edge while he nibbled at the kernels and stared across the water to Chanakkale. Three Ottoman soldiers stood within earshot, engaged in their own discussion and taking no notice of his presence. Clarence was obviously European. His fair complexion and linen suit left little chance of him being mistaken for a local, and he used that to his advantage. Few Europeans bothered to learn the Turkish language and the locals knew it.

One of the soldiers was grumbling, in Turkish, how unreasonable their sergeant had been in beating a young soldier, Ali, with a leather strap for failing to keep up with the platoon on a training run. The lad on the receiving end was only fifteen years old, and didn't have a father or older brother here to look out for him. Not very useful information. *Hopefully they will move to a more interesting topic of discussion before the corn cob runs out of kernels.*

Here at the Narrows, the opposite shore of the Dardanelles Strait was less than a mile away. Behind him the western bank rose steeply to the Kilid Bahr plateau. The terrain was well suited to defence.

Back in his consular office, across the Straits in Chanakkale, his safe contained a map he had marked up in red pencil with several gun emplacements located along the escarpment that followed the western shore.

The water flowed to the south, always to the south from the Black Sea through the Bosphorus Strait into the Marmara Sea. Then from the Marmara Sea into the Aegean Sea through the Dardanelles Strait – the Chanakkale Strait as the Turks called to it – or Hellespont as it was known in ancient times. The peaceful harbour town was cursed by being located at one of the most valuable strategic crossroads on earth. This junction between Europe and Asia had been the scene of conflict since before the ancient armies of Xerxes the Persian or Alexander the Great passed through here. Way back into Greek mythology, recorded by Homer in The Iliad – Troy, the ancient city of the fierce battle between Trojan King Agamemnon and Greek hero Archilles – lay around 10 miles away at the mouth of the Dardanelles near Kum Kale. *The history of this place is delicious.*

Apparently the three Ottoman soldiers were homesick farmers, conscripts who would rather be tending crops. They were part of the 27th Regiment, and about to move up north to the Gulf of Saros. *That's strange. The 25th and 26th Regiments that make up the rest of the 9th Division are stationed to the south near the mouth of the Straits. It is not like the Turks to split a Division like that. I must look into that further.*

He stood and lobbed the finished cob into the water, then walked back towards the wharf where a ferry was pulling in. It was time to head back across the Straits to Chanakkale.

On the way to the ferry wharf, a pair of German officers sat deep in conversation at a table in the morning sun, out front of a waterfront café.

Damned Germans! So relaxed and arrogant, sitting in the local coffee shops while their comrades are stomping through France, murdering innocents on a rampage towards England. Dressed in full uniform, the Germans didn't bother to be discreet about their presence.

Being a diplomat, Clarence was always unarmed, but he could obtain a hand gun easily enough. The option of doing so and taking down three or four Germans had crossed his mind more than once. Being single and a patriot, trading his life for three or four of the enemy seemed worthwhile. But that was against the rules of international diplomacy, and rules were important. It was the Germans and Turks who were not playing by the rules. Ottoman neutrality was a farce. 'Buying' two German warships, and allowing them safe passage to the Marmara Sea. The ships were still manned by Germans and it was doubtful whether any payment had been made. The Ottomans were virtually broke. And the Germans were running the Ottoman army, at least in these parts. Germans who couldn't even communicate with the Turks without an interpreter, giving orders and bringing artillery – *so many big guns.*

Clarence had devised a more effective way to do his bit for the British war effort than killing a few enemy officers who could be replaced before they were missed. *Diplomatic immunity applies in a neutral country, so while the Ottomans claim neutrality, I can remain and use my position to gather information with impunity – the Turks don't even know I'm doing it, much less the Germans.*

No doubt, circumstances would change at some point, but as things stood, he would do what he could. He had worked hard to achieve his role of British Vice Consul in the Dardanelles, and Clarence was determined to make hay while the sun shone, by using diplomacy and gathering valuable information at the same time.

A few days ago, the *Lily Rickmeers* had grabbed Clarence's attention. The steamship appeared in a bay to the north of Chanakkale, flying the German naval flag and equipped with wire strung above the deck that could only be a long wave wireless antenna. Several German officers came on deck to smoke and chat. *What a target! The time has come to act. Maybe a British submarine could find a way under the sea mines and sink the steamship along with the German officers. That would be fine!*

That day, Clarence penned a letter to the captain of HMS *Indefatigable*, one of the British warships patrolling outside the Dardanelles. His letter included details of land-based gun emplacements and the location of three rows of sea mines across The Narrows, as well as details of the *Lily Rickmeers* with her German officers and wireless antenna.

Clarence passed the letter in secret to a merchant sea captain for delivery. There was some risk that the letter might fall into the wrong hands, but the old salt was a fellow patriot and hated the Germans well enough.

The risk paid off, although the letter ended up on a different British warship. A reply message came from the captain of HMS *Indomitable*, acknowledging the value of his information and confirming the importance of any further details of German activity. The British ship's captain promised to send codes which could be used on the public telegraph to the nearby island of Tenedos for specific situations. However, the captain also raised concerns about the risk of using civilians to transport intelligence, and had arranged for one of his officers to meet him in secret. The meeting was to take place later this morning, so Clarence had taken a final chance to glean what information he could in preparation for the meeting. *I didn't really learn anything important today though.*

The ferry carrying Clarence docked at Chanakkale, a bigger town than Kilid Bahr. The morning smell here was similar, only stronger.

He disembarked, bought a local newspaper and sauntered in the direction of the coffee house where he planned to rendezvous with the British naval officer.

The meeting place was only a hundred yards away and the designated meeting time was not for another half hour. *Best that this meeting has the appearance of an unplanned chat between strangers. It might look suspicious if two British men arrived at the same time.*

Clarence arrived at the coffee house and assessed the situation on entering. *Only two other customers inside – that's good.* This meeting place had been his suggestion, close to the docks, but typically quiet in the mornings. The grumpy old woman who ran the place spoke no English and showed little interest in her customers. Also, being on a street corner, it shouldn't be too hard to find based on the simple directions he had provided.

He sat away from the other customers and ordered a coffee in Turkish. *Coffee here always smells so good.* He opened the newspaper, but did not read it. Until now the whole game of espionage had been fun, almost a hobby for spare time, but as if from nowhere, fear stabbed his stomach like a shish kebab skewer. The summer's day was warming up, but he didn't normally sweat like this. *What if the Germans intercepted the meeting plans? What would they do to me?*

He looked up without raising his head and surveyed the room as he reached slowly for the tiny cup. The coffee was thick and strong as ever, an acquired taste.

An old local sat by the window looking half asleep. *I've seen him here before, so he's not out of the ordinary. He looks harmless enough.*

The other fellow sitting near the door looked more European. Could he be a German? A scruffy looking merchant seaman by the look of him. *Hasn't shaved for a week, something isn't quite right. His clothes look awfully clean. Maybe I should be carrying a gun.*

The seaman looked up and met Clarence's gaze for an instant before looking to the old fellow by the door. He cleared his throat and rose from his seat. On the way to Clarence, the seaman reached his right hand into his pocket. Clarence looked to the doorway again, but it was too late. The seaman was already on his feet and could easily block his path if Clarence made a run for it. *Better try to stay calm. Act as if nothing is wrong. I'm only here for a coffee. My mouth is so dry.*

The seaman strolled over and sat at Clarence's table, opposite him, hand still in his pocket. "Vice Consul Palmer, I presume?" He said softly.

Clarence felt faint with relief. That was a Londoner's accent without a doubt. "At your service."

The seaman smiled and removed his hand from his pocket. It contained a folded piece of paper.

CHAPTER 5

Ronald

Sunday, 23 August 1914

Ron shovelled home another mouthful of roast lamb and vegetables, careful not to drip gravy onto his shirt.

"Haven't they been feeding you boys?" His mother frowned.

"There's plenty to eat at Kenso'," Jayjay replied with his mouth full. "It's just not as good as this."

"He's understating the difference Mum," Ron said. "Army food is basic and tastes the same every day. Your cooking is fantastic!"

His wife's eyes narrowed and Ron regretted his enthusiasm immediately.

"I really miss your cooking too Em." He lied.

Emilia sighed.

Ron pretended not to notice and tried to savour his mother's home cooking. He had been looking forward to it for days, but found himself unable to enjoy the taste.

Em might show a bit more cheer when I come to visit. She doesn't smile anymore. I wish I could do something to comfort her. It's a shame I can't go home with her tonight, but I'm not sure it would make any difference.

"Well," his mother said. "It is lovely that you boys were able to get away from your training and visit. We do appreciate you coming home to see us."

"So, apart from the food, what's it like to train as a soldier?" his father asked.

"We're up at first light every morning for reveille, and get to work before breakfast," Ron grinned. "There's a lot of marching and exercise. We haven't done much with weapons yet, but we were issued with our rifles a few days ago, and yesterday we moved camp from Randwick Racecourse, across the road to Kensington Pony Track. Now we have tents to sleep in."

"Where did you sleep before?" his mother asked.

"On the benches in the grandstand," Ron suppressed a shiver. "They weren't too bad. There's a bit of shelter and they gave us blankets. The force is still building. Boys from the bush come in each day, some carrying Matilda on their back. I think when the battalions are full it will be clearer what we have to do and when we'll go."

"We just got our new khaki uniforms," Jayjay blurted. "And they look great. We weren't allowed to wear them home today, but we will wear them when we march through Sydney, so if you come out to see us, you'll see them then. Look for the First Battalion in the First Brigade and that will be us. It's easy to remember, because we're the First."

After they had finished eating, their father stood. "I have some things for you both."

He left the room briefly, then returned with a small bundle wrapped in cloth.

"Firstly, Jayjay, your mother and I gave Ron a wristwatch for his twenty-first birthday. We want to give you one also before you leave. A couple of years early, but no matter."

He withdrew the timepiece from his bundle, and handed it to Jayjay. "We bought you one with a leather cover for the face to protect it. The army runs to a schedule, so it might be helpful for you to know the time, from time to time."

Jayjay leaned forward.

"Thanks Dad, and Mum. I'll wind it each night. If I can keep it ticking, I'm sure it'll be handy."

"The main thing is to look after yourself. It is yours to serve you, not the other way around. Now, for each of you, I have one of these." Their father revealed two sheathed knives from under the cloth. He handed one to Ron and one Jayjay.

"Fair dinkum!" Jayjay pulled the blade from its leather sheath and cut a figure-eight in the air. Light from the window glinted on the polished metal.

Put it down Jayjay. It'll upset Em and Mum'll hit the roof.

But their mother said nothing, her face showed no surprise. *She knew about the knives in advance. She approves.*

Emilia, on the other hand, covered her mouth and gazed with wide eyes at the knife in Ron's hand. She had barely touched her lunch and looked pale.

Ron placed his knife on the table, on the side furthest away from his wife and rested a comforting hand on her shoulder.

"Please excuse me for a moment." Emilia rose and stared at the floor, then walked slowly out the back door and turned towards the outhouse.

"I'll see to some dessert." Their mother's glance lingered in the direction of the back door and her daughter-in-law, then she left the table in the opposite direction.

Mum must be worried about her too. Maybe she could help me make sense of Em's emotions. I'll ask if I get the chance.

Jayjay continued to examine the naked blade and started shaving hairs from the back of his hand.

"I know modern warfare is all about rifles, machine guns and artillery," their father said, "so you can kill the enemy from a distance. But the enemy knows this and they have all these weapons too. There may be a time when you have to face an enemy up close, and these may help you to defend yourself."

Jayjay's head bobbed up and down.

I ought to go and check on Em, but this moment seems important to Dad. Ron stayed seated and nodded.

"Now, these are not official army issue," their father continued. "So I suggest you keep them with your personal things and don't go waving them around until you are in a combat situation, or at least well established in a team you trust. The army can be quite particular about standardising on equipment. I've seen the bayonets they will provide to attach to the barrel of your rifles. They have a seventeen-inch blade which I'm sure is good for spearing someone at arm's length, but on its own it is more of a sword than a knife. I found an interesting shop in Sydney where I bought these. I must admit I have walked past it many times, but never been inside. When I told the owner that they were for my sons who are off to the war, he gave me a discount and a few tips about their use."

Their father reached for Ron's knife.

"This is a small bowie knife. A fighting knife."

He withdrew the blade from the sheath and balanced the knife with the flat of the blade resting across his index finger.

"The knife is balanced between the handle and the blade, to allow you to manoeuvre it easily."

He lifted the knife off his finger with the other hand and held the knife by its handle.

"The bone handle is tough and waterproof. I've had each engraved in case there is any argument about ownership."

Lettering of 'R. Jones' lay neatly scribed across the base of the handle.

Maybe to avoid an argument between us, about which belongs to who? No, more likely in case someone else tries to pilfer it.

"The six-inch blade is long enough to do deadly damage, but small and light so you can carry it easily and use quickly if needed. The leather sheath holds the knife with the blade facing to the rear when it is on your right hip as you are both right-handed. You can grab hold of the handle and remove the knife from its sheath with one hand, and it will have the point facing downwards and the sharp edge of the blade facing back towards your wrist."

Their father returned the knife to its sheath and handed it back to Ron.

"Wow Dad!" Jayjay exclaimed. "I didn't know you knew about fighting knives."

"Well I didn't until a few days ago, but like I said, the good fellow in the shop gave me a lesson."

"I wouldn't have thought you would want to know about that kind of thing,"

Ron said. "Let alone buy them and bring them to the family lunch table."

"War is a terrible thing Ron, but sometimes necessary. This is a significant moment in history. Much of the civilized world is at war. The world is changing and will likely never be the same again. This is the reality, regardless of what we want to believe about how remote we are here in Sydney. If the Germans conquer Europe, there will be little to stop them from expanding their rule throughout the rest of the world. You boys are going to fight in a war to defend the freedom of our nation and that is a noble thing, but I cannot sit at home and pretend you're off to a game of rugby league. I hope neither of you ever have to use these knives to harm a fellow man, but if you do then I'll be glad I gave them to you. May God give you both courage."

"I'm not afraid Dad," Jayjay said.

"And I'm glad of it Jayjay. But only when you taste fear can you know what courage truly is."

"How about you put those away now before Emilia comes back and we'll have some dessert," their mother said, standing in the doorway, holding a cake.

"Ah, yes," their father looked up. "We wouldn't want to cause Emilia any more distress."

He took both of the sheathed knives, re-wrapped them in the cloth and placed the bundle on the floor under the table.

"Good idea," Ron nodded and looked towards the back door. "She hasn't been herself lately. She's still getting used to the idea that I'll be away a while and she's been a bit teary."

"One more thing." Their father reached into his pocket and pulled out two gold sovereigns. "I know this isn't much, but I want to give each of you a bit of emergency money. Keep it on you in case you need it. They're small and light, but gold coins should be recognised anywhere you're going."

"Wow, thanks!" Jayjay pocketed his coin without hesitation.

"Dad," Ron said. "You don't have to… just look out for Em while I'm away, with her dad gone and her mum crook… but thanks."

His mother started serving up cake. "You know you don't have to ask Ronald, of course we will."

Jayjay was into his second helping when Emilia returned from the back yard.

"I'm so sorry," Emilia said as she sat. "I've been a little ill. No cake for me thanks."

Ron stopped eating and returned his hand to her shoulder.

"I know it's hard with me going away, but it won't be forever. I promise I'll come back as soon as I can, after I've done my bit."

Emilia smiled weakly and nodded without speaking.

CHAPTER 6

Hans

Wednesday, 26 August 1914

Baron Hans von Wangenheim, German Ambassador to the Ottoman Empire, sat on his stone bench and exhaled smoke from a large black German cigar.

Behind the stone bench stood a guard hut, and behind the hut there resided the buildings and gardens of the German summer embassy in Istanbul. A road to the north out of the Turkish capital lay between Hans and the Bosphorus Strait, whose waters he could hear lapping gently against the shore.

From this location Hans could smile and blow smoke at ambassadors from England, France and Russia when they walked by. They would avoid his gaze and cross to the opposite side of the road to pass. From his bench Hans could also watch his wireless station on the opposite shore and see any boat that might start in his direction, bringing more good news across the currents of the Bosphorus Strait.

The American Ambassador to the Ottoman Empire, Henry Morgenthau approached up the road on foot. *Henry will not cross to the other side to avoid me.*

"Good afternoon to you Mr Morgenthau." Hans blew smoke towards the water, away from the American.

"Good afternoon, Baron von Wangenheim. Sitting out on your perch again, the war must be continuing to progress in Germany's favour?"

"More news came this morning, we are working our way through Belgium and France. I expect we shall be in Paris within the week."

Morgenthau shook his head and shot Hans a disapproving look which Hans was careful to ignore. "You do understand that the French will re-organise themselves and fight back against your invasion Hans."

"They might try, but they have nothing like our Prussian military pedigree. France is capitulating as we speak. I expect we will offer her terms of peace shortly. She will have to completely demobilise of course, and pay us an indemnity. Five billion American dollars would be enough if she is willing to settle now, but if she persists on continuing the war, it will be more like twenty billion."

"Do you really think the English will watch and do nothing while you crush their allies and take up residence across The Channel? Your forces would be within spitting distance."

"England has a contemptible little army. She shall not trouble us. A shadow of her former self, spread too thinly across the globe. Once we hold France hostage, England will be persuaded to cooperate out of mercy for her ally. We will build a mighty German Empire, a merchant empire. We have no interest in controlling new territories in which the population does not speak German. We have had enough of that trouble in Alsace-Lorraine and Poland. But we will demand harbours and coaling stations everywhere and then German ships will control world trade. This is the way to rule in the modern world!"

"The English have called on their dominions to help build their forces."

"The idea is preposterous! It takes years of militarism to produce anything like the German army. We have been building it up for two hundred years. It takes thirty years of constant training to produce such generals as we have."

"What of the Russians?"

"Russia's alliance with France and England is more of a nuisance than a serious threat to us."

"I have heard that the Russians are putting up a fierce resistance on your eastern front."

"Russia is so big, so much farmland to produce so much grain. Great for trade. And yet she has only four places where her ships can access the rest of the world."

"One less now that your navy controls the Baltic Sea. Russian Ships can't sail far from Saint Petersburg."

"A funny thing about Saint Petersburg, Russia is about to rename the city as Petrograd so that it sounds less German!"

"So I have heard." Henry muttered.

"And Archangel on the Arctic and Vladivostok on the Pacific are both frozen for several months of the year. That makes the strip of water here in front of us quite important as the only remaining route for Russia's ships."

"The passage from the Black Sea to the Mediterranean via the Bosphorus and Dardenelles Straits."

"Did you now that nine tenths of all Russian trade passes through this way, including ammunition from her allies, ammunition that Russia cannot produce herself?"

"International law would prevent Turkey from closing the Bosphorus or the Dardanelles while she remains neutral in the war. You yourself said that Turkey should stay neutral."

"Of course, it would not be in Turkey's interests to join a war that does not concern her. She is still licking her wounds from the Balkans conflict."

"And yet you are preparing the Turks for war."

"Germany is Turkey's friend. We have helped restore pride to the Ottoman Army, and now we are helping to restore Turkish warships that were deliberately left to decay by the English Admiral Limpus and the British Navy's ineffective mission of assistance to the Ottoman Navy."

"You can save your propaganda speech Hans. There are no Young Turk coup leaders within earshot and I am not so easily misled. I can see what is happening here. The Russians are massing an army at the Caucasus and the English are doing the same in Egypt. British warships have prowled about the mouth of the Dardanelles ever since you snuck the two German battle cruisers through."

"And so, England and Russia have already sent significant military resources away from our main battlefields while Turkey remains neutral. What advantage would it bring to us if Turkey joined the war?"

"And if your opinion about German advantage were to change?"

"Not all wars are fought on the battlefield Henry. German officers control the defences at the Dardanelles. In fact, we control the Ottoman Army and Navy. At my word, the Straits can be closed within thirty minutes. How much of a threat do you think Russia will be then? A man cannot live long without oxygen and I have my foot on Russia's throat. Our defences of the Dardanelles are impregnable, but I expect we will not close the Straits unless England attacks them first. England will be responsible for the destruction of her ally. That deed will not go unnoticed and Russia will not forget it. The alliance between England and Russia will be broken for a long time."

"Why are you telling me all this Hans?"

"America is a neutral country. I trust that honour will prevent you from revealing the details of a confidential discussion to our enemies. We will have this war won in two months, three at the most, and then the facts will be plain for all to see."

"Your confidence may be misplaced. These are uncertain times. The world is descending into chaos."

"So it may seem, but everything is as we have planned. After the assassination in Sarajevo, I went to Germany and met with the Kaiser in Potsdam. We had to decide if that would be the trigger for war that we had been waiting for. German military and industry leaders were there and everyone was ready. Only our bankers needed two weeks to sell foreign securities and make loans. Soon we will be in a position to lob bombs across The Channel into England from the French coast. Our Krupp guns will destroy England's ships and cut off food supply to France. Your American ships should beware, they would be wise to steer clear of English harbours. These waters will become very dangerous."

Morgenthau held Hans' gaze and his eyes narrowed. Hans resisted a strong urge to blow smoke into the American ambassador's eyes.

"Good day to you Baron von Wangenheim," Morgenthau checked his pocket watch, his hand shaking slightly. "I must be on my way."

Hans reflected to himself whether he had revealed too much information to the American. *No. Keiser Wilhelm trusts my judgement. The world will know it all soon enough. The war will be over, the Fatherland will be victorious and I will be the German Chancellor. If I can reduce the chance of American ships aiding our enemies in the meanwhile, then so much the better.*

He searched deeper inside himself and knew his own motives pure. *Many men will fight and die with honour in this war. They are courageous, but not heroes. To die with honour is a great thing for a man, not a sacrifice, but a privilege. A luxury I cannot afford. I must rise above, like the great Otto von Bismarck, and be willing to sacrifice everything for the Fatherland – not only life, but honour.*

CHAPTER 7

Jayjay

Wednesday, 9 September 1914

Jayjay pulled the central pole down from his bell tent.

"Don't these people realise that there's a war on and we have important training to do?"

"And what's worse," muttered Larry, "Is that we can't stay here and have a nice day at Kenso' watching the races."

"At least the punters should be able to see the ponies trotting all the way around the track now. We wouldn't want to cause them an inconvenience!"

"I heard we're doing musketry training. Maybe we'll get to shoot these rifles instead of just carrying them about and stabbing hay bales –." Larry's voice faded as he gazed up into the early morning sky. "What the blazes is that?"

"It's an aeroplane," Ron said. "I read about them, but didn't believe it. Amazing it can stay in the air like that. There's a man inside flying that machine."

Jayjay shook his head. "We must look like ants from up there."

The whine of the aeroplane engine was barely audible, but word spread quick and men across the racecourse stopped working on tents and stared into the sky until the flying craft was nothing more than a dot over the horizon.

After dropping their tents, so as not to obscure the race-goers' view, the men of the 1st Battalion formed up at Kensington Pony Track and marched over scrub-covered dunes towards the coast. They arrived at Long Bay Rifle Range mid-morning and separated into platoons. Each man was issued with a charger clip of five rounds of live ammunition.

Waves rumbled against the rocks at the base of the nearby cliffs and seagulls squawked. A light onshore breeze cooled Jayjay's sweat-stained uniform as he stood in the sunshine.

A gruff old sergeant that Jayjay didn't know stood on a mound of earth that raised him a couple of feet above his audience. He addressed Jayjay's platoon with a cockney accent.

"Men, I am told you have had some familiarisation training with your new weapons, and learned how to set the sites. This is not a toy you understand. It is a Short Magazine Lee-Enfield rifle, known affectionately as the S.M.L.E. It is a

0.303-inch calibre SHORT barrel rifle with a ten round MAGAZINE. You have each been issued with a five round charger clip of live ammunition. Two of these charger clips will fit neatly into the rifle magazine here. Do not, I repeat do not, insert the ammunition into the weapon until you are told to. That means you soldier. If anyone is shot here today it will look very bad for me."

The sergeant glared at a private who had been fiddling with his magazine, and now looked as if he wanted to dissolve into the sand beneath his boots. Appearing satisfied with the effect, the sergeant continued to address the men.

"The rifle's bolt mechanism is well proven over several decades of warfare. It was designed by James LEE, and has been reliably produced for many years in the Royal Small Arms Factory in ENFIELD. That's Enfield in London, not out in the Western Suburbs of Sydney where they scraped you sorry lot together. Now, your rifles have not, however, come all the way from Enfield. They have been made in Lithgow, but not to worry, the production in this country has been overseen by English experts and is seen to be to a good English standard. So there you have it, the Short Magazine Lee-Enfield rifle. It is your best friend, take it to bed with you and look after it. Learn how to strip it down, clean it and reassemble it with your eyes closed. In combat you may have to do this in complete darkness. The next morning it might be the difference between life and death.

"Today we will start with some basic grouping training. The targets you can see have a three-inch ring set at 25 yards. You will each fire five rounds at the target and hopefully produce a group of five holes somewhere in the general vicinity of the ring. Now, have any of you boys fired a rifle before?"

At that moment, Jayjay wished he had never fired a rifle, but raised his hand, not wishing to be caught out at not owning up to the truth.

"Only one of a whole platoon 'ey?, or is it just that only one of you has the balls to admit to it. Righto lad, step forward. What's your name son?"

"Private Jones, Sir" Jayjay replied, trying to sound more confident than he felt.

"Well Private Jones, let's see if you have been paying attention, insert the ammunition and pretend that the target is the heart of a Hun and let him have it."

Jayjay took the ammunition and was pleased to find the charger clip slid smoothly into the magazine. He turned to face the target and tried to remember what his uncle had taught him about how to hold the rifle. He stood side-on to the target and looked at it over his left shoulder. He lifted the butt stock to his right shoulder, and looked down the barrel at the three-inch ring that seemed awfully small at a distance of 25 yards. After lining it up at best he could he started to squeeze the trigger.

"Hold it right there Private Jones," burst the Sergeant.

Jayjay flinched, but managed to ease the pressure on his trigger finger before it released the firing pin. He held as still as he could and the Sergeant's cane tapped his left elbow.

"Elbow directly below the rifle, body well balanced, feet shoulder width apart. Bed the butt firmly into the hollow of the shoulder as this will help your aim and help your body to absorb the recoil. Maintain a firm grip with both hands and keep the eye well back from the cocking piece, this makes sighting the target more accurate. Keep the sights upright, you cannot aim a rifle accurately if the sights are leaning to one side."

Jayjay's head spun. He couldn't remember the first instructions, but focused on keeping the sights upright.

"Now take aim, and squeeze the trigger gently," said the sergeant.

Jayjay peered down the barrel at the target.

I must have most things right, or close enough to right. My feet feel like they are about a shoulder width apart, but I can't check now. Maybe the instructions are more for the benefit of the onlookers.

He pulled the trigger. The rifle let out a crack and recoiled into his shoulder. The force was stronger than that of the 0.22 calibre rifle he had used at Uncle David's farm at Miranda, but he was ready for it and his shoulder absorbed the energy with little movement.

A small dot marked the hit, just outside the three-inch ring, slightly to the right and low.

"Okay Private Jones, he is wounded but not dead, continue firing."

Jayjay pulled back the bolt and pushed it forward to load the next round into the firing chamber. He took aim again and fired. He emptied his magazine and was relieved to see that all five rounds had hit the target. Four were in a cluster just outside the ring, and one was a wide shot near the edge of the target.

"Thank you Private Jones. You may return to the line."

Jayjay took his place between Larry and Ron, filled with a sense of relief that he had not embarrassed himself, or been humiliated by the old sergeant.

"The paper Hun is dead," the sergeant continued. "Unfortunately for Private Jones, so is he. The Germans have rifles of their own and a tendency to return fire. There will be times when it is right to shoot from a standing position. When you are entrenched this will often be the case, but in an attacking situation, you may be required to go over the top of the parapet at the front of your trench and raid open terrain. Standing up in the open to shoot at the enemy may seem courageous, but if you get yourself shot dead then you are no good to king or country or the girl of your wet dreams."

"Private Jones, step forward. I don't want you to think that I am picking on you son, it's just that the rest of these boys don't know which end of the rifle to hold and they might end up shooting someone and that would be very embarrassing for me, especially if I am the one who gets shot."

The sergeant tossed Jayjay another charger clip holding five rounds and continued.

"It's your lucky day soldier! Imagine that you are alive again, and so is the paper Hun. But this time he is looking back at you, down the barrel of his Mauser rifle. You have less than one second to react before you're a dead man."

Jayjay threw himself at the base of the mound of earth that the sergeant was standing on. He rolled onto his back and slid the next clip of five rounds into the magazine, careful to keep his head below the mound and the rifle pointing away from the other privates who seemed to be enjoying the lesson much more than Jayjay.

Heart hammering, he rolled onto his front and inched his way towards the top of the mound where the sergeant took a step sideways. Jayjay took aim again but his hands were shaking, and when he squeezed off the shot, it missed the target board completely. The sergeant continued in a raised voice.

"Private Jones, at least you are still alive, but so is the German. You have found cover and so has he. Your hands are shaking from nerves. If you think this is a difficult situation, wait until you are facing a real enemy shooting real bullets at you. Now, get back behind that mound and take three deep breaths to calm yourself. You have some time as the enemy has also ducked for cover. When you feel ready, get back up there and take another shot."

Jayjay slid back down the mound and rolled onto his back again. He could feel many eyes watching him, but looked only at the sergeant as he took a deep breath. He imagined the target to be an armed German soldier and it became the sole focus of his thoughts. He took a second deep breath and forced himself to relax. Rolling onto his front, he wormed his way back up so he could just see the ring target, took a third deep breath and exhaled slowly. His SMLE rifle rested on the earth. The metal ring was the enemy. A calm settled over him as he steadied his aim. There was no sound, there was only the metal ring. He squeezed the trigger.

A cheer erupted from his platoon. His mind was so focused that it took a moment to register that they were cheering his success, having hit the target inside the metal ring. The paper Hun was dead by his hand.

"Enough!" roared the sergeant.

"That will be all Private Jones, rejoin the line."

Jayjay stood tall, dusted himself off and swallowed a grin as he returned to his position between Ron and Larry. "Yes, Sir."

Today the rest of you are going to learn that firing a rifle accurately is not as easy as it looks. We will start shooting from a standing position, but if you remember nothing else from today, remember that your first priority in most situations is to find cover to avoid getting shot yourself. If you remember this you will be a better soldier and you will live longer. Sometimes this is not possible if there is no cover and you are taking part in a charge over open ground. But even in that situation there can be cover from enemy fire. An attack charge would, if possible, be timed to coincide with an artillery barrage to provide a curtain of cover for the charge to advance, but that is a lesson for another day.

"Now, one Section at a time will approach the mound and everyone will have a five-round turn at grouping practice. One at a time lad! No one is getting shot here today."

Jayjay stood back and savoured the moment. Rays from the early spring sun warmed his skin.

The others lined and took turns to fire at the target, some looking nervous, some excited and many a mixture of both.

I always thought I was a reasonable shot, but it's surprising how poor much of the platoon's aim is. I wonder if the others are any better? With practice they'll improve, but we may not have much more time before we go to the front. Presumably we'll have several weeks of travel. I wonder if shooting practice is possible on a ship?

On three separate occasions that afternoon, privates from his platoon, men who Jayjay didn't even know, came up to him to shake his hand or slap his back in congratulations for nice shooting. These were small gestures, but significant to Jayjay who was physically strong, but had never been good at athletics or ball sports.

After a day of musketry training at Long Bay Rifle Range, he marched with the First Infantry Battalion back to Kensington Racecourse. There he re-erected his bell tent with his tent-mates and retired to the mess area.

"Let me guess," Larry said. "Boiled potatoes and bully beef, my favourite!"

Sitting with the others, Jayjay felt something that he hadn't felt for a long time – a true sense of belonging.

* * *

A few days later, on Monday 14th of September, the First Infantry Battalion formed up for the first time with the full New South Wales contingent of the Australian Imperial Force: The First Brigade, made up of the First, Second, Third and Fourth Battalions.

Now I really am part of the strength. Four thousand fighting men from our state alone. Lucky we joined up when we did! If we'd waited until now, with the battalions full, we would've had to wait at Liverpool with the other reserves. Those poor chaps might miss the action all together.

He marched out with the rest, fully loaded up with kit, across the open ground between camp and coast, terrain familiar from recent training exercises. Today's destination of Maroubra lay closer than Long Bay rifle range, a march of around three miles.

At Maroubra, the four battalions of the First Brigade formed up into their companies and platoons. All men stood to attention and the Brigadier, Colonel McLaurin, strode past and inspected his troops.

When the inspection was complete the men of the First Battalion Machine Gun Section set up a pair of Maxim machine guns in front of Jayjay.

Hopefully we get to see of these machine guns in action today. They've been on display at Kenso' often enough, but never fired. They look like a bit of work to set up.

As part of G Company, Jayjay stood near the end of the First Battalion formation, close to the Second Battalion. *I wonder how their training compares with ours.*

Recognition of a familiar face in the Second Battalion caught Jayjay off guard and without warning anger surged within him. Just a few yards away, in a private's uniform just like his own, stood Alfred McKenzie.

I thought I'd never have to see that bastard again.

Alfred looked up. He hesitated for an instant then broke into a grin. His smiles had disarmed school teachers, and made girls swoon. A few inches shorter than Jayjay, he stood around six foot tall. Not only was he athletic and good at all forms of sport, but he was smart. Teachers had often turned a blind eye to the misdemeanours of their favourite student who could do nothing wrong.

I'm not sure if this brigade will be big enough for the two of us. The last thing I want is a constant reminder of what might have been.

One of the Maxim machine guns was loaded with ammunition and the men from the Machine Gun Section set up a target like the targets from Long Bay Rifle Range, at a distance of around 100 yards. From the lectures, Jayjay knew of the weapon's theoretical capability. Firing the same size rounds as their SMLE 0.303 calibre rifles, the machine gun was capable of firing 600 rounds per minute, the equivalent fire power of thirty rifles or two full infantry sections. The water-cooling system, as well as the weight of the gun and ammunition, meant that three or four men were required to move and operate the gun at full efficiency.

The Brigadier strolled past and then after a few words from the First Battalion Commanding officer, Lieutenant-Colonel Dobbin, the machine gun opened fire. The bullets were launched at such a rate that it was difficult to distinguish the sound each individual round firing. The sound was more of a loud and continuous rattle.

The machine gun shook and spat flames for a several seconds. Jayjay's gaze moved from the gun to the target and back to the gun. The firing stopped and Jayjay looked up to see the remains of the target fall to the ground in pieces.

A murmur went through the First and Second Battalions. They had been instructed that this was an important inspection by the Brigadier, and that there was not to be any cheering or unruly behaviour.

Damn that Alfred! I was looking forward to seeing a machine gun in action and it did everything it was supposed to do. Now all I can think of is him, and Charlotte, and what they might have been getting up to together. Damn them both!

CHAPTER 8

Karl

Tuesday, 22 September 1914

Captain Karl von Müller gazed at the lights of Madras Harbour in the distance. *The place is lit up as if this was peace time. A good sign. The town's lack of vigilance will reduce my risk tonight.*

Earlier in the evening, he had approached Madras slowly, under cover of darkness, not knowing whether there might be hostile warships about, but his lookouts had seen none.

Now that the way appeared clear, the *Emden* surged at full steam towards her target.

He shouted the order: "Ready for action!"

A mix of exhilaration and fear tingled up his spine.

* * *

A month earlier, Karl's ship, the *Emden,* had parted company with the rest of the German Pacific naval fleet at Pagan island, part of the German colony of New Guinea. Since this time, his sole support was from a supply ship *Markomannia,* affectionately known by his crew as the 'milking cow'. The *Markomannia* was well provisioned with coal, water and other supplies to support his operations. However, his milking cow was grazing in safe pasture tonight, well away from this hornets' nest he was about to whack with a stick.

Karl allowed himself a smile of pride. He was part of the Kaiser's navy, a major force on the world's oceans, now rivalling even the British naval might. German colonies were expanding and bringing much wealth to the Fatherland. Control of the seas would continue to strengthen the German Empire. If this war against the triple entente of France, Britain and Russia could be won, there would be no one else left to stand in the way. Maybe the Americans, but they seemed intent on keeping their noses out of European affairs and hadn't shown a tendency towards colonial expansion.

During the past two weeks he had been hunting in the Bay of Bengal along the shipping route between Calcutta and Madras. He had successfully captured, raided and scuttled six enemy merchant vessels.

Karl took no pleasure in the suffering or death of fellow men. He did what was necessary to disrupt the enemies' cause, and destroyed their resources with careful intent. However, where possible he tried to spare the innocent.

I will continue to play my part in this war with honour. Regardless of the final outcome, I will not be remembered as a pirate. I am a ship's captain in the German navy, and that means something more than being a marauding bandit.

Each time he captured an enemy merchant vessel, he rounded up the crew with their personal belongings and took them onto the *Markomannia* before sinking the captured ship. He enjoyed watching the faces of the crew as they watched their ship go down and contemplated the salvation they had been granted.

Eventually the *Markomannia* became so crowded with prisoners that something had to be done with them. One of the captured merchant vessels, the *Kabinga*, was spared from being scuttled. The prisoners were transferred to this ship and she was sent on her way to Calcutta. Even to the end, the crew cheered in thanks for being spared along with the ship, rather than being sent to the bottom with her.

He knew he increased his risks of being found by doing this, but he would not murder innocent civilians in cold blood if it could be avoided. He wondered what his orders would be if the German navy commanders knew of his circumstances and were able to communicate with him. He knew the likely answer, but didn't want to acknowledge the truth. He was pleased for the need to maintain radio silence, it gave him more autonomy that a navy ship's captain would ordinarily enjoy, and the freedom to grant mercy.

As soon as the *Kabinga* was out of sight he had changed course and left the shipping route behind. No other vessels had been seen by his lookouts since, and he was confident that the enemy did not know his whereabouts.

That was about to change tonight. He smiled to himself as he watched the flicker and glow of Madras Harbour. He was about to announce his presence loud and clear. The night was young. If all went well, God willing, he would be long gone before dawn.

He checked again that the gunners were at the ready. Their orders were simple and clear.

At around 4,000 yards from shore, he ordered the search lights on. The *Emden* continued surging full steam ahead, towards the harbour town.

Within moments, Karl could make out the faint outline of large oil tanks, located near the waterfront.

Boom!

Boom!

Boom!

The first salvo from *Emden's* guns launched explosive shells at the target. All guns blazed and thundered in rapid succession. One tank burst into flames and lit up the rest of the target like day.

"Kill the searchlights!" Karl yelled, not sure if his voice could be heard until the lights blinked off.

Another tank blew, and another. Soon the whole tank farm was on fire. Flames licked the night sky, casting an eerie orange glow over the surrounding suburbs. The light from the fire was so intense that Karl could see his men's faces glowing orange, even at this distance. He could see that they were enjoying the moment too. *That's good, as long as they remained focused and professional.*

His ship would now be quite visible from shore in the intense light of the fire, even though it was still quite some distance away.

"Cease fire," he yelled.

"Retreat!"

The men were well briefed in the mission plan, and the ship was soon adding to the distance between her and the fire. A battery of guns on the shore opened fire on the *Emden*. Karl could not believe it had taken them so long to come to the town's defence. The shells from the shore battery fell wide and did little to worry Karl as the *Emden* steamed off into the night. He was well out of range before they could improve their accuracy to a point of becoming dangerous.

It was a successful mission. One hundred and twenty-five rounds had been consumed, but to great effect. Hopefully the fire could be contained to the oil tanks, with minimal loss of life. He would likely never know. This was a dangerous business and sooner or later the enemy would catch up with him. He may not have to opportunity to ask for detailed outcomes of his handiwork.

"So now we shall see if the hornets come," Karl said quietly to himself as his ship steamed southwards.

The air buzzed with encoded enemy radio communication signals he could not interpret. He was no longer a hunting wolf, but lonely prey. Any day he might come across another man-of-war on a mission to destroy the *Emden*. In the meanwhile, he would continue to do what he could for the Empire.

CHAPTER 9

Winston

Monday, 28 September 1914

Winston Churchill sat alone, deep in a leather lounge chair in his smoke-filled library in Admiralty House, London.

An empty whisky glass hung from one hand and the stub of a Cuban Havana cigar smouldered between the fingers of the other. A grandfather clock against the wall chimed a quarter to midnight.

His head ached, but not because of the whisky or cigar. *My chance to achieve wartime greatness is slipping through my fingers. Everything I have worked for is falling apart.*

He took a final draw on the Cuban and crushed it into the ash tray, then dragged himself to his feet and opened a window. Cool air flowed in but did little to clear his head. A cloud of smoke streamed out and dissipated into the night.

I'll be forty years old in a few weeks. I've climbed higher than most men can hope to in a lifetime, but at this rate my reputation will plummet to oblivion before my birthday. I cannot let that happen. There is so much more I can achieve. This war is my chance to chisel my name in history.

Number ten Downing Street was only a few hundred yards away, and yet for all the support the British Prime Minister Henry Asquith had given him, Winston had never felt so isolated.

One who serves as a minister in a democratically elected government must expect to take some criticism, but lately negative press against me has been more intense than any Member of Parliament should have to contend with. It doesn't matter that I am a civilian and a politician. As first Lord of the Admiralty, I am held accountable for naval performance and so far my bet on the Royal Navy has not paid off.

He returned to his chair, collapsed into it and sighed.

I have to do something to secure my position.

He cut the tip from a fresh Havana cigar, lit it and inhaled the taste that had given him solace ever since he had acquired it in Cuba, reporting as a war correspondent on the Spanish suppression of local guerrilla rebels.

How can I use this latest disaster to my advantage?

* * *

Taking the position of First Lord of the Admiralty in 1911 had been a wonderful change from being the Home Secretary. Winston had immediately immersed himself in naval strategies, technology and life on the sea. Week after week he had spent away on the *Enchantress,* the Admiralty yacht that came with his new role, a 4,000-ton luxury vessel with a crew of 196. On *Enchantress* he would visit ships and naval facilities around Britain and throughout the Mediterranean. It became clear that the British Navy made Britain a great power, and that the fortunes of the race and Empire would crumble if naval supremacy was lost. The German navy was advancing and becoming a threat that could not be ignored.

He cast aside the view he had espoused as Home Secretary, that the naval budget should be cut to support social policy. Instead, he started arguing for massive increases to naval funding. Since having successfully crossed the floor from the conservative side of politics to join the Liberal party ten years earlier, he was not afraid to change his political position when it suited him.

The budgetary increases that he had successfully argued for were based on building more oil-fired super-dreadnought class battleships with fifteen-inch guns. The previous generation of warships was coal-fired and had thirteen and a half-inch guns. The new oil-fired ships were faster on the water and could refuel much more quickly, and so would be better able to compete with the German fleet, some of which was also oil-fired.

The increase in calibre of the ships' guns also represented a significant technological development. The additional explosive power of the larger shells increased the recoil force experienced by the ship by half as much again. The ships' ability to handle this increase while in service was yet to be proven. The *Queen Elizabeth* was the first of this new class of super-dreadnought battleship to be built. She had been launched, but was still undergoing testing and yet to enter active service.

It had taken all of Winston's negotiating skills to have the additional funding approved. Plenty in the Liberal government openly held a view that the level of naval funding was excessive. Support from the Prime Minister Henry Asquith and the Chancellor of the Exchequer, Lloyd George were the only reason that he had been able to succeed.

The oil needs of his navy were substantial and growing. The strategic value of future oil reserves was obvious to Winston, even if not to the rest of the Liberal party.

To reduce reliance on foreign oil ventures, Winston had successfully argued for the injection of British capital into the Anglo-Persian Oil Company in 1913, establishing a controlling interest for the British Government. In addition to the established oil resources in Persia, the Anglo-Persian Oil Company also held a 50% share in the Turkish Petroleum Company which was undertaking exploration to establish the oil reserves in Mesopotamia. This investment had grown in value to several times the initial outlay, and had helped in Winston's negotiations to expand the navy's financial allowance, a large portion of which was to build the oil-fired fleet.

Having built a significant British oil interest in Persia and Mesopotamia, he saw the potential value in securing these resources further for the Empire. The inevitable collapse of the Ottoman Empire, including its Mesopotamian territory might create an opportunity in this region that could later expand into Persia. It was ripe for the picking. Now, with most of the region at war, and Turkey seeming to side with the enemy, the chance of annexing this territory for the British Empire was real. The stakes of the game would increase with another nation siding with Germany, but the increased risk brought with it increased potential for reward of securing the oil reserves.

Our geologists have snuck into Mesopotamia, pretending to be archaeologists. Our armies will soon secure Basra, then Bagdad and Mosul. Oil will be the new gold, essential for the Empire.

Winston had worked so hard to build up the navy, and when war broke out he had looked forward to demonstrating its prowess. But the navy's strength of reputation worked against him. Success was expected. When the navy had delivered six army divisions to France during the first two weeks after war was declared, it had just been doing its job as expected, and was not credited with any great attention or sensational newspaper headlines.

The failures were different. Everyone noticed these, especially the English press. First there was the early embarrassment when the navy lost the only two German warships in the Mediterranean, the *Goeben* and *Breslau*. After stopping to take on coal at the Sicilian port city of Messina, the German ships were expected to head north-west. However, they steamed off in the opposite direction and evaded the British chasers, entered the Dardanelles Strait and were adopted into the Ottoman Navy.

Then, last week, embarrassment was followed by tragedy when three British armoured cruisers were sunk off the Dutch coast in German U-boat submarine attacks. Nearly 1,400 men were lost in the attacks which all occurred on a single day. The press learned that admiralty instructions were to blame for the ships being in a dangerous location, and suddenly Winston's reputation had been publicly torn apart. Of course, it didn't matter that he had not seen or approved the instructions personally. The press had to allocate blame for a tragedy of this magnitude somewhere, and so far it had been laid directly at his feet.

In the latest disaster, yesterday, his naval squadron off the Dardanelles had intercepted a Turkish torpedo boat. When they found that there were German soldiers on board, they rightly ordered the vessel back to Turkey. The Turkish military, which was known to be heavily infiltrated by the Germans, had retaliated by laying strings of mines and closing the Dardanelles Strait to all shipping.

Russian ships would be queuing up in the Black Sea by the day and building pressure to open the shipping channel. Russia relied heavily on this passage and would be desperate to have it reopened. This might not have been a direct act of war, but it was close enough to show that Turkish loyalties now lay with the Germans.

Maybe the opportunity for my navy to shine resides at the Dardanelles. Everyone wants to keep Russia loyal to the cause. Maybe I can bring about a glorious wartime victory yet.

Winston jumped to his feet, sucked hard on the Cuban and started to pace about his library. Renewed energy surged through his body.

Russia has long had her eyes on Constantinople. The Holy City and warm-water shipping access gives her a strong incentive. Greece remains neutral, but has been feuding with Turkey for centuries and shown an interest in the Gallipoli peninsula. She might be willing to land an army force there as part of a combined operation. The Mesopotamian oil fields would be left for England and everyone would have a slice of the Ottoman pie.

Winston's pacing quickened and he barely noticed the Cuban threaten to burn his fingers.

A sea-based campaign at the Dardanelles could knock the Ottoman Empire out of the war, keep Russia committed, expand British petroleum interests and give me a glorious naval triumph.

Winston allowed himself a smile at his strategic genius, refilled his whisky glass, lit up a new Cuban and returned to his lounge chair. The idea was becoming a plan that continued to crystallise in his mind.

CHAPTER 10

Ronald

Tuesday, 6 October 1914

Ron awoke to the cry of the reveille bugle and groaned.

His younger brother Jayjay stood grinning down at him, fully dressed. *How does that boy do it? I need more sleep.*

Larry snored.

The bugle refused to die.

At least it's light by six o'clock now, and not quite so bloody cold.

Ron rolled off his hip-hole, folded his blankets and reminded himself that he would feel better in a few minutes.

Jayjay gave Larry a shove and the snoring was replaced by more groans of protest.

"Time for physical jerks lads!" Jayjay's voice was much too cheerful for the hour. "There's time for a duck's breakfast if you giddy up."

Ron dressed, visited the latrine and splashed some water on his face. It would be a long two hours before breakfast. *By then I might be hungry.*

* * *

After morning exercises, Ron sat at a trestle table in the open air, with the rest of G Company, and ate a breakfast of bread and jam with coffee. Two extra slices of buttered bread lay on his plate. More than he wanted, but he had taken extra and would offer it to Jayjay when no one else was looking.

Sergeant Baker addressed the men.

"Today we will be taking part in a parade march with the Second, Third and Fourth Battalions, as a full brigade into Sydney. It's no secret that we expect to be away to the war soon. All of Sydney knows it. There's been a public notice that we'll be marching today, so expect a big crowd along the way. They want to see their troops and we're going to give them a good show. This is how the people of Sydney will remember us. Your family and friends. We're going to show them that we're an orderly lot. You are to be formed up in the parade ground with rifles and bayonets, ready to march at nine am. Every man will be clean shaven and your uniforms will be in order. I will be inspecting this platoon personally before we depart. Anyone who does not look like they will do the First Battalion proud will be left behind to peel potatoes and dig a new latrine pit. Any questions? No? Good. As you were."

After breakfast Ron hurried back to the eight-man bell tent to get ready. Men busied themselves with the details of their uniforms and a buzz of excitement hung in the air. He wound the puttees around each leg, from the boot up to his knee. The bandage-like aspect of his uniform always struck him as strange, but it had become part of his morning routine and he had learned that in the army you often had to do things that didn't make sense.

At five minutes to nine, most of G Company was ready at the parade ground in the middle of Kensington Pony Track. The other companies A to H that made up the First Infantry Battalion were also largely present. The men were yet to form up, standing in small groups chatting.

"Do you think we'll see Mum and Dad?" Jayjay asked.

"I dunno, but I reckon they'll see us. Dad knows we are in the First Battalion, and he reads the newspaper every day. Mum wouldn't miss it for the world, it might be the last time she sees us. You know, before we leave, I mean."

"What about Emilia?" Jayjay hesitated, as if not sure whether he should have asked.

"She'll be there." Ron tried to sound like he believed his words. "I'm sure, I hope I can see her. She's had a rough trot since I signed up. It's hard for her to get used to me being away, after we got married and set up the house together. It's not money she's worried about. She's moved back to live with her mum rather than being on her own, so there's no rent to pay, and those of us who are married have to send two fifths of our pay directly to our wives. That's two shillings per day and it will be plenty for her to get by. I think she's just worried that something bad might happen to me. You know how women are."

"No, I bloody well don't." Jayjay said. "I mean, I could tell Mum was pretty worried. You know, that stuff she said about this not being our war, and that we shouldn't go. I would have been embarrassed if she said that in public. At least Dad knew we were doing the right thing. I just don't understand how women's brains work. You're married, maybe you can explain it to me Big Brother?"

He always calls me that when he thinks he's outwitted me.

Ron faced up to his younger brother who stood eight inches taller than he. "They're so emotional. They don't think logically like us. We know the Germans are doing all those terrible atrocities in Belgium and France, and we know they have to be stopped. If we sit back and leave it for others to do it, well that just wouldn't be right. And then, there's what Dad was saying about the German navy up at New Guinea, and the Chinese further north. If we want to stay part of the British Empire and enjoy the peace that comes from the protection of her navy, we have to do our bit when we're called on. We have to pull our own weight. It's simple logic, but women have trouble with it."

Jayjay nodded with an approving look.

"Em's just worried, like Mum." Ron continued. "I'm sure she'll be out today with Mum and Dad, and when they see us as part of this whole Brigade, they'll know we're part of a force to be reckoned –."

"Fall in!" Sergeant Baker cried.

A flurry of movement followed. Ron hurried with Jayjay into formation.

Ten minutes later, the First Infantry Battalion was marching north in parade formation along the Botany tramway tracks on Bunnerong Road past Randwick Racecourse.

They passed between the Zoological Gardens on the left and the Sydney Cricket Ground on the right, and the number of supporters lining the street grew. Those that had come cheered as the column of men marched past.

"On ya boys, ya doin' us proud!" called one old cove from his balcony on Oxford Street as Ron marched past his terrace house, the fellow saluted the troops with a half full glass of beer.

Thousands had gathered in Hyde Park.

The brigade marched between the park and the imposing structure of Saint Mary's Cathedral, and the clapping and cheers of the crowd increased to a continuous din. While holding formation and trying to keep his head facing forward, Ron scanned the crowd on both sides of the road, panning with his full range of eye movement. Onlookers were perched in trees and lined up several layers deep along the road making it difficult to see much beyond the first row. He expected his parents to be on the other side of Sydney, near Saint Andrew's Cathedral or Sydney Town Hall. This was for practical reasons, rather than religious allegiance to the Church of England over the Roman Catholic Church. It was closer to where they lived, coming from west of the city, and also it was a landmark they had previously used as a family meeting place on trips to the city when he was growing up.

The column of men marched along Macquarie Street where they were ordered to halt and form up in front of a temporary stage. The Governor-General took a salute from the brigade, and then the men marched on.

Having travelled the length of the city, almost to Circular Quay, they turned left along Bridge Street, then left again onto George Street to start the return march south.

Sweat dripped down Ron's back and the rifle jolted his right shoulder with each step, his right forearm stiffening from holding a steady position supporting the rifle butt. The roar of the crowd could not take his mind from an imagined vision of his wife's face, eyes filled with sadness.

He glanced across at Jayjay who wore a broad grin as he marched. At least his brother could enjoy soaking in the glory of the moment. Some of the young ladies in the crowd were very attractive and cheering with abandon. *Of course Jayjay is smiling.*

They marched up George Street away from Circular Quay and the street veered slightly to the left. As it did so, the Queen Victoria Market Building appeared in the distance. The Market Building loomed closer and he recognised his wife Emilia in front of it with his parents and Larry's family.

Emilia waved and smiled as he hoped she would. Larry's twin sister Grace pulled a face and poked out her tongue, then burst out laughing.

Ron glanced sideways at Jayjay to check he had seen their parents and a beaming face looking in their direction confirmed he had. Larry looked as if he was trying not to laugh.

Ron gave his head a slow single nod of acknowledgement towards his wife. He figured the brim of his slouch hat would help to make the gesture easily recognisable from where she was standing with his parents, now less than twenty yards away. He maintained his best smile until he had passed them by.

The marching column came towards the end of the Queen Victoria Market Building and Sydney Town Hall emerged from behind its dominant form. Then Saint Andrews Cathedral showed itself and the column turned left onto Park Street back towards Hyde Park. The men skirted around Hyde Park, past a large stone obelisk, and back to Oxford Street. The crowd that lined the streets thinned out as the brigade left the city.

Emilia's face would not leave Ron's mind. She had been smiling today, but the face in his mind remained cheerless.

I made a commitment to her before family, friends and God. Now she needs me and I am abandoning her.

CHAPTER 11

Hans

Thursday, 8 October 1914

Hans strode up the stairs towards the new seat of authority of the Ottoman Empire. He didn't bother to use the handrail.

True power rested no longer with the Sultan or the Young Turk military coup leaders, but with the senior German Navy and Army officers who controlled the Turkish armed forces.

The stairs he climbed led to the deck of a ship. The German merchant ship, *General*, moored in the Golden Horn, near the Galata bridge in the heart of Istanbul.

"Good evening, Baron von Wangenheim," a familiar voice called from the darkness as Hans reached the top."

"Good evening, Admiral Souchon." Hans replied to the man who had guided the two German warships *Goeben* and *Breslau* through the Dardanelles Strait two months earlier.

The Admiral stepped into the glow of an electric light. A short man dressed in an immaculate uniform, he carried the confidence and upright posture that short men often rely on to compensate for their lack of stature.

"Welcome aboard Ambassador," Souchon said. "I had hoped you might join us tonight."

Hans squared his shoulders and lit a large black German cigar. "I cannot stop long. Are you hosting another party this evening Admiral?"

"The wine and beer are good for morale Ambassador. Can I offer you a drink?"

"No, I need to keep my thinking clear."

"Of course. The men don't have much else to keep them occupied at present. We have to give them something to do, so why not let them have a bit of fun while they can? We cannot have them running riot in town, especially since you have worked so hard to maintain good relations with the Turks. It seems that you have won their hearts."

"You don't know the half of it. Are you aware that I recently bought the Turkish newspaper 'Ikdam'?"

"How much did our Kaiser pay for this newspaper?"

"Less than what you might think and it was worth every pfennig. My editors remind local readers every day that England is an unscrupulous liar and Russia is a thief who wants to take away their homes. Germany is Turkey's only true friend. The English say 'God save the king' and now the Turkish man on the street has been taught to say 'Gott strafe England!'"

"I am glad you're not producing propaganda for our enemies Ambassador!"

"I remind my readers that General Enver is a Turkish patriot and a hero. We must keep him in power. The young Minister for War favours a Turkish alliance with Germany and has a mindless tendency towards aggression. He thinks he can restore the Ottoman Empire to its former glory. Have you noticed he now wears his moustache turned up at the corners like Keiser Wilhelm?"

Admiral Souchon gave a blank look, then nodded.

"Our Kaiser," Hans continued, "will be known as 'Hadji Wilhelm', great protector of Islam. My newspaper will say that he has converted to Mohammedanism, and that Muslims in India and Egypt are about to throw off their English tyrants. A call to arms will go out to the Muslim world to rise up against their oppressors. I recommend you read it."

"I cannot speak or read Turkish, few of us can. We rely on local translators and they are in scarce supply."

"I will send you some of the press articles. Have one of your men translate them for you. You must understand what is motivating the Turkish men if you are to command them effectively. Many of them are devout and they are driven by Muhammadan loyalty. I have been flattering the Young Turks and I have them convinced that our enemies fear the return of the great Ottoman Empire, that our enemies will act to suppress any chance of this happening."

"Is that true?"

"Of course it's not true! You miss the point, Admiral. It doesn't matter whether it's true. It only matters whether the Young Turks believe it to be true. The hound doesn't need to bite every sheep in the flock to herd them into the pen. He uses his bark to drive them on with fear. Turkey herself is not the really important matter. Her army is a small one, and we do not expect it to do very much. For the most part it will act on the defensive. But if we can use Turkey to stir up the Mohammedans of the world against England and Russia, we can defeat them. Even if we cannot incite the Mohammedans of the British Empire to revolt, we will promote the idea, and the mere threat of such an uprising may be enough to induce England to abandon Belgium and France to their fate."

Admiral Souchon stared at Hans for a moment, then a smile spread slowly across his face.

"When can we unleash the Turks in the Black Sea? Our ships have been taunting the Russians, but we have been unable to provoke a response. Our officers are spoiling for a fight."

"Unfortunately, it must be sooner than I would like. Our land campaign has lost momentum in France and it has failed to deliver us the quick victory we had planned."

"I heard that the Russian front is not faring well either."

"Russia is putting up some resistance. But now that we have closed the Dardanelles, she will suffer and break. You should have heard the squeals coming from the Turkish Cabinet conference when they learned of the actions of our German General Weber who they themselves had placed in charge of the Dardanelles fortifications. General Weber ordered the strings of mines to be dropped, he extinguished the guiding lights and erected signs that read 'No Thoroughfare'. With that the Dardanelles were closed to all ships. Only Enver was stupid enough to revel in the moment, the rest knew they had been pulled into our war with no way out."

"Didn't the Young Turks resist German intervention in Turkish affairs?"

"They couldn't take a piss without someone to hold their pecker. They can do nothing more than moan. Regardless, a Turkish torpedo boat ventured out of the Dardanelles and was stopped by a British navy ship. When the English officers realised that the torpedo boat was manned by German officers, they refused to let it pass and sent it back under threat. That was enough for our General Weber to declare that England had committed an act of war."

"So, we blamed England."

"Of course. Just like I blamed England for deliberately letting the Turkish navy ships decay under their naval mission here, and then reassured the Turks that Germany has fixed their ships."

"Did they believe that?"

"That is the art of diplomacy. We had been trying to provoke the English ships for days, but there was no need to trouble the Turks with that detail."

"We will continue to harass the Russians," Admiral Souchon said, "with our ships in the Black Sea."

"Fire on them if you must. The Kaiser's orders are clear, we must now engage Turkey as an active ally in the war. The war has gone badly for us this past month. Victory is no longer certain, and is now only possible after a protracted struggle. Our enemies must be forced to commit maximum men and warships to this region. We have driven a wedge between Russia and her western allies and now we must regain the initiative."

"My men are playing their part for the Fatherland. The isolation of Russia is ensured. What a sight that was! For days after the blockade of the Dardanelles, the Bosphorus looked like a harbour that had been stricken by the plague. Hundreds of ships lay at anchor, so dense we had trouble picking a way through with a small motor boat. Then one by one, they gave up waiting and turned back for some Black Sea port. We will draw Russian soldiers away from the German front, and maintain our stranglehold on this shipping route."

"See that you do." Hans drew a long breath through his cigar and exhaled into the night. "Russia cannot continue to fight without a supply of bullets and shells from the west. We must not release our grip on the Dardanelles. Do whatever is required. Is this clear?"

"Yes Ambassador."

CHAPTER 12

Ronald

Saturday, 17 October 1914

"All leave is cancelled!" Sergeant Baker yelled over the sound of rain pounding on the outside of the mess tent. "Pack your kit bags and await further orders. Everyone is to remain in camp. No exceptions. Break this rule and you risk being left behind. Any questions? No? Good. As you were."

"We've heard that before!" cried a voice with Irish accent. "Starting another rumour Sergeant?"

The sergeant hesitated, then added. "Try to get some sleep tonight lads. It looks like we're really going this time. Be ready to break camp tomorrow morning. Dismissed."

Ron filed out of the mess tent into the night with Jayjay, Larry and the others from his platoon and ran as fast as he dared across the mud. Lanterns hanging from poles gave a hint of light, but were spaced far apart and he had to rely on memory to avoid the deeper puddles on the way to his eight-man bell tent in the dark.

"Get some sleep despite being soaked to the bone." Larry grumbled.

"At least our tent hasn't flooded," Ron replied. "We've got a good dry possie here compared to some. Slightly higher ground, and the drainage trenches we dug did the trick."

"I'm just glad we're finally getting away," Jayjay said. "We've been stuck here forever!"

"Me too," Ron said. "Emilia's cheered a little of late. I've said my good-byes and I want to leave on a positive note."

"That's if it's fair dinkum we're going," said Larry. "We've been ready to do a get go for weeks. This send-off will probably be cancelled just like last time. We'll be marching back to Long Bay to shoot more seagulls before we get on any ship. You see if we aren't."

A lance corporal from another company poked his head in the tent flap, water dripping from his face.

"I will be collecting your kit bags in ten minutes." The lance corporal said. "Make sure they are packed and ready. We will be taking them onto the transport ship tonight."

A bolt of reality shot through Ron's body. *This time we are going!*

"At least the matches are dry." Ron lit the lantern hanging from the central tent pole.

Each man rummaged through his kit bag and repacked the small volume allowed for personal items. Ron re-rolled a few items of clothing, amongst which he stashed the bowie knife his father had given him.

The lance corporal returned as promised with two privates and the kit bags disappeared into the dark.

That night Ron couldn't sleep. From the noise of activity outside the tent he was not the only one. Nevertheless, everyone was up early the next morning. By 6:30 am the bell tent that had been his home for two months, along with Jayjay, Larry and five others, was empty. Ron was surprised to feel a pang of sadness at leaving the tent behind and wondered what his accommodation would be like at the other end of the ocean voyage. The routine and comradery of Kensington Racecourse camp had become a way of life that he enjoyed. Often the work was hard, but expectations of him and his role were clear and simple.

A hurried breakfast was followed by Battalion Parade. Soon after 9:00 am they were marching towards Sydney and Circular Quay. It was a route they had taken a number of times on parade marches, but today was different, not just because of the wet weather. This was the last time the First Infantry Battalion would march from camp into Sydney, and come what may, they would not be returning to Kensington.

How will Em cope without me around? She'll worry, no doubt, but hopefully not too much.

I ought to enjoy the excitement of this occasion. We are off to play our part in global affairs, and let the world know that Australia is a part of the British Empire to be taken seriously. A brigade of four battalions and four thousand men. The pride of New South Wales. Today, Australia is growing up as a nation. Australia is going to war.

Orders were clear that the departure was to be kept secret, but the attempt to keep the citizens of Sydney ignorant had failed. Supporters had turned out in great numbers and lined the streets along the parade route. They cheered as usual, their spirits seemingly unaffected by the heavy rain.

The infantry procession held formation to a man, having been warned that breach of discipline would be severely dealt with. However, the crowd of well-wishers was full of mothers, wives and girlfriends who seemed determined not to miss the opportunity for a final farewell with a loved one. A handful of policemen attempted to hold back the crowd at Circular Quay, but were overrun by a mob of women.

Ron might have laughed at the spectacle, but the emotion on the women's faces was real and raw. *How might I react if Emilia behaves like that, or Mum?*

He marched on towards Fort Macquarie at Bennelong Point and picked out Emilia and his parents amongst the sodden crowd. They waved frantically and followed along. Ron sent them a smile and several nods, then lost them in the crowd.

He couldn't decide whether he was relieved that his wife and mother had behaved in a dignified manner, or disappointed that they didn't show the passion of the surging mob.

From Fort Macquarie, the troop transport ship *Afric* could be seen at anchor in Farm Cove. The vessel's identification number was painted as a large 'A19', in black lettering on a white square, on the side of the hull at the bow, and again at the stern. Ferry boats waited ready to take the battalion from Fort Macquarie to the *Afric.*

"Halt!" Sergeant Baker ordered.

Ron stood with the others like a statue.

It would be nice to find Em, and give her a goodbye hug and kiss. And to hug Mum, and shake Dad's hand.

But orders are orders. If we dispersed, it would take hours to get everyone back together again, and some might not come back.

It's cleaner like this. I'm going away for God only knows how long, and Em may become emotional and need consoling. At least I can remember a happy departure. I can think of home and imagine her waiting patiently for me to return so life can get back to normal.

Next thing he knew, they were herded aboard a ferry boat and it cast off. Men lined every inch of balustrade for final farewell waves and cheers. Ron took a position near the stern, and defended it with Jayjay and Larry against the press from behind.

He searched back over the crowd as the Ferry inched away from the dock, but he could not locate Emilia in the sea of yelling faces and waving arms.

CHAPTER 13

Jayjay

Sunday, 18 October 1914

From his vantage point on the ferry, on the way to the transport ship *Afric*, Jayjay tried to find his parents again. Instead, he recognised Charlotte in the crowd and heat rose in his neck despite the rain.

She had already seen him and waved frantically, blowing several kisses in his direction. *Blazes! Why is she doing that?*

He wanted to snub her. Hate her. Pretend he didn't care that she had ignored him for the past year. But he couldn't stop himself from smiling and waving back, happy to see her looking pleased to see him.

"Good luck Jayjay" she mouthed, "God bless you!" At least that is what it seemed like, then she blew another kiss in his direction.

The ferry slid further away from the dock and Charlotte was swallowed by the crowd. He gauged the distance between the ferry and shore to be fifty yards, then stopped to question himself why such a detail mattered at that moment.

Beside him Ron gazed across the crowd as if in a daze.

"Well, well," Larry wore an amused smirk. "Someone got a special send-off. I'm pretty sure that Charlotte wasn't aiming those kisses at me!"

"She hasn't said so much as three words to me for months," Jayjay frowned. "And then she turns up here with that display when I'm leaving."

"Still, you seemed to enjoy it" Larry said. "Maybe it's because you were leaving that she wanted to see you."

Jayjay was only half listening to Larry, and focused on the shoreline. The crowd was still waving and cheering, but the faces shrank with increasing distance and he could not find Charlotte.

"I didn't know you were such an expert in female logic Larry, now you're starting to talk like a sheila yourself."

At least that wiped the smile of his face.

"No," Larry said. "Think about it. You were her friend for years and then she got caught up with Alfred and hardly saw you at all."

"Great, thanks for pointing out the bloody obvious!"

"She knows that the two fellas she cares about are going away and she knows she's been neglecting you so she feels guilty, and confused about why she feels guilty."

"You think she cares about me?"

"You're wasting your time dwelling on her. You could do better."

Jayjay held his focus on the crowds lining the shore as the ferry boat nestled in beside the *Afric*. Thousands of noisy well-wishers lined Farm Cove, around the edge of the Botanical Gardens to Mrs Macquaries Point, but Jayjay could think of only one.

Orders came to transfer onto the larger vessel. The vessel that would take him away from her and to the other side of the world. Jayjay lowered his gaze to the water below, dark, almost black under the heavy clouds. The oily smooth surface peppered by rain drops.

He contemplated the possibility of slipping away onto one of the many smaller craft that were starting to swarm around the *Afric*, and taking a quick trip to shore and see Charlotte again.

No. On my honour, I would not neglect my duty. I am a soldier in the king's army.

He shook his head slightly and pulled his shoulders back.

Larry gave him a nod and they turned to depart the ferry.

By noon the whole First Battalion was on board the transport ship *Afric*, 1,013 men strong. Jayjay lunched with the rest of G company below decks, then returned to the top deck to enjoy the send-off. He saw no more familiar faces in the crowd, but soaked in the excitement of the moment as well as the incessant rain.

At 5:00 pm it was time to depart. With its coal boiler fired up, the *Afric* weighed anchor and steamed off towards the heads of Port Jackson. Once in open water, she turned south into the choppy waters of the Tasman Sea.

Jayjay watched the sandstone cliffs of South Head blend with the horizon. Now there was no option of turning back. This might have settled his thinking, but turmoil inside returned and was made worse by the rocking motion of the ship.

* * *

Later that evening Jayjay leant against the balustrade. He had left his lunch behind long ago, but felt no better for it. They had been assured that it would just take a few days to get their sea legs and Jayjay hoped this would prove to be true. It would take the best part of two months to reach England, and if he felt like this the whole way he couldn't eat or drink and would not be able to survive the voyage.

"Still feeding the fishes?" Larry appeared from behind. Jayjay was focused on watching the horizon and oblivious to anything else that was happening around him. Ron leant at the rail beside him, also in a poor state.

"No mate, I'm all emptied out, but I still feel crook as Rookwood. This is not how I imagined sailing off to glory!"

Jayjay wanted to make light of the situation, but he could hardly move. He knew they would have to string their hammocks and try to sleep in a few hours, but he dreaded the thought of leaving the railing. He had never slept in a hammock before, and was looking forward to trying it, but he worried he might have to stay on deck all night.

"I'll hang up your hammocks," Larry said, as if reading his thoughts. "And there's big vomit bowls nearby in case you need them. No one wants you spewing all over the place below decks. A good sleep might help you to feel better."

The rest of the evening blurred by. Dusk faded into darkness. Eventually Jayjay's platoon sergeant, Sergeant Baker came around and informed those still clinging to the rail that it was time to get some sleep. Jayjay and Ron followed him down to where Larry, true to his word, had strung hammocks for the two of them. Jayjay managed to get himself into the hammock without spinning over and dropping to the tables or floor below as several others had done. He closed his eyes and willed himself to sleep, trying not to think about the urge to vomit, but sleep did not come quickly that night.

Next day the seas and weather remained rough, but Jayjay managed to keep some water down. The day dragged on in a haze, with Jayjay's sole goal to reach the night and escape seasickness in sleep.

The following morning, call for reveille found Jayjay in a state of deep sleep. It was unusual for him to have trouble waking in the morning, but this day he did. He dragged himself to the upper deck and found the sun was shining and the sea was calm. The uneasy feeling in his belly was gone, replaced with hunger.

This was the first day that the Company was brought together on deck for physical jerks. He built up a sweat with the others, but felt light-headed and weak.

Only a handful of men were still seasick. Improved morale across the Company was noticeable.

After physical jerks, Platoon sergeant Baker addressed the men.

"It's good to see you men back on your feet and doing some exercise after a couple of days of holiday. Now that you are finding your sea legs, we will be re-establishing your daily training routine. Apart from a few obvious differences, you will find that life on board the ship is not greatly different from what you were used to at Kensington. Firstly, this is His Majesty's Australian Transport ship number 19, the steamship *Afric*. This ship, along with the other transport vessels in the convoy, has been requisitioned, at significant expense, by the Australian Government for a one-way voyage to England."

At the mention of England, some started to cheer. *Maybe they didn't notice the trip being described as 'one way'. I don't like the sound of that.*

Sergeant Baker raised his right hand and waited for silence.

"The SS *Afric* will be your home for around two months. After the war, when we've taught Germany some manners, other arrangements will be made for those of you wishing to return home. For your information, the *Afric* is a passenger and cargo vessel built in 1899. She transported British troops to South Africa during the Boer War, so treat her with some respect. As a passenger and cargo vessel, she is designed to carry 320 third class passengers only. However, for the purposes of this voyage, we have invented a new class of travel. We call it 'infantry class'. With the installation of some additional temporary galleys and latrines, as well as a few hammock hooks, the SS *Afric* can now comfortably carry 1,400 of us. Granted, comfortably may be too strong a word, but this is wartime transport and not a luxury cruise. I think you will find the quarters and meal provisions adequate. If not, you can always swim home."

The Sergeant looked about, as if hoping for a reaction, but no one moved or spoke. He cleared his throat and continued.

"Righto, there are a few things that you should know to avoid embarrassing yourself on this ship. The front end is called the 'bow' and the back end is called the 'stern'. The right-hand side is called the 'starboard' and the left-hand side is called the 'port'. The large chimney in the middle of the ship is called the 'funnel', and the room up high where Captain Marshall commands the ship is called the 'bridge'. Any questions? No. Good. Dismissed for breakfast.

Jayjay took his hunger as a good sign and hurried below decks where he shovelled down double portions of porridge, toast and eggs. *I wonder how much of this I might lose overboard if the seas pick up?*

The *Afric* continued to travel south, the coast visible on the starboard side. Seas remained calm, but the commanders gave no indication of where their next stop might be.

Days passed, routine was re-established and seasickness didn't trouble Jayjay again.

Battalion officers attempted to keep the men from becoming idle with early starts, physical training, rifle exercises, lectures and enforced bedtime.

Some officers slept in cabins, but the privates had no space to call their own. At night the men strung hammocks on hooks, in tight rows above tables in the open halls. Each morning, they dropped the hammocks and rolled them for storage, so the space could be used for dining.

Melbourne and Tasmania were ruled out as ports of call, as was Adelaide, when they diverged from the shoreline and entered the Great Australian Bight.

One week after leaving Sydney, soon after daybreak on a Sunday, the *Afric* dropped anchor at King George Sound off Albany in Western Australia. A handful of other transport ships lay at anchor nearby. Morning physical jerks were followed by breakfast and church parade where Jayjay joined the other Protestant men to be addressed by the Battalion chaplain. The Roman Catholics and non-conformists had separate parades. More ships arrived that day and on the following days.

* * *

New Zealand transport ships arrived all painted grey. Six days after *Afric* arrived at King George Sound over thirty ships lay in the Sound.

That afternoon during lecture time, Sergeant Baker informed them that the ships were all ready and would be leaving the next morning.

"We will be travelling in convoy, and escorted by four warships. HMAS *Sydney* and *Melbourne* from the Australian Navy, the *Ibuki* from Japan and the convoy will be led by HMS *Minotaur* of the Royal British Navy."

A cheer erupted, and Jayjay yelled along with the others. *A ship from the mightiest navy in the world! That will be something to behold.*

"Righto, righto," Sergeant Baker yelled. "Before we all get too excited, it is important for you men to understand a few things. Firstly, this many troops in a single convoy makes us a very attractive target for the enemy. There are around 30,000 of us including our friends from New Zealand, and I'm sure the German Kaiser would like nothing more than to see every last one of us sink to the bottom. Everything has been done to keep the details of the voyage a secret, but a convoy of this size is difficult to hide. The Germans know we are coming, so there is every chance they will figure out where we are.

"There are three German warships currently unaccounted for in southern oceans and there is a very real chance that our convoy will encounter one or more of these warships. These enemy ships are the *Scharnhorst*, the *Gneisenau* and the *Emden*. The reason that our departure has been delayed over the past month is the Australian Government's concern for your safety and its insistence on providing a naval escort for every transport vessel. The threat is real. We will be taking precautions to minimise the chance of one or more of these Hun warships locating us, and we will be conducting drills to prepare for the possible event that our transport ship is fired upon. Take these precautions and drills seriously men as they might just save your life or the life of a fellow soldier."

Sergeant Baker paused and eyeballed a few of the men as if daring anyone to interrupt. Apparently satisfied that he had placed sufficient emphasis on the importance of his last point, he continued.

"Firstly, the precautions. There will be no lights at night that might be visible from outside the ship. Porthole covers are to be in place if lights are on in your quarters in the hold. There are to be no visible lights on deck, and that includes lighting or smoking a cigarette. If you wish to smoke, you do so inside. We will not be transmitting any wireless signals which might alert the enemy to our presence. All communication with the other ships will be by visual Morse code signals or semaphore flags only."

"Secondly, the evacuation drills. Our SS *Afric* is a merchant vessel. Her hull is made from plate steel thick enough to stay afloat with a load of precious cargo or a battalion of infantrymen. However, this is not an armoured warship and is not built to withstand explosive shells fired from a warship's guns. A few well-placed rounds at the waterline and this ship will sink like a stone. We are at the mercy of our escorts for defence and if an enemy ship manages to get in amongst our convoy, our escorts may not be able to fire in case they hit us or another transport ship. In this case, if you want to survive, you will follow the procedure to your allotted life boat, get your life belt on and remain calm. You will keep quiet and speak only when required to marking the roll at your life boat. Initially we will conduct these drills in the daytime so you can become familiar with the process. Later, we will also conduct drills at night because an enemy warship has a much greater chance of finding its way past our escorts under cover of darkness. Any questions? No. Good. Dismissed."

Sergeant Baker turned and left.

Larry frowned. As soon as the sergeant was out of earshot he grumbled, "Well Sergeant Fishface sure knows how to take the fun out of everything. We are about to leave Australia's shores and he wants us to think we'll have to abandon ship in the middle of the bloody Ocean."

"Sergeant Fishface?" Jayjay replied.

"It's a type of fish, called Sergeant Baker. He does have a bit of a fishy way about him."

"There'll be around forty ships," Jayjay said, but doubted his logic as it left his lips. "Even if our ship is sunk, we'd be picked up by one of the other ships. We have four powerful escorts, from the British, Australian and Japanese navies. The enemy ship would be sunk itself before it did too much damage. I'm looking forward to being underway again and I'm not going to let that wet blanket ruin the occasion!"

The last evening at anchor lacked the usual banter. The anticipation of leaving Australia's shore felt to Jayjay like leaving Sydney Harbour all over again, but this time on a grander scale. It was two weeks ago that they had marched out of Kensington camp, boarded the *Afric* and received a rousing send off from the people of Sydney. Now, together with military might of Australia and New Zealand, they were to depart again in the morning.

* * *

The warship escorts waited outside King George Sound as the convoy of transport ships formed up. It took most of the morning of Sunday 1st November for the thirty-six transport ships to organise themselves into moving columns with a uniform speed. Jayjay had learned to recognise each of the warships during the stop at King George Sound.

The HMS *Minotaur* of the Royal British Navy led the convoy as the vanguard. The Australian transports formed up in three columns. The Australian Navy ships took the flanks, with HMAS *Sydney* on the port side, and HMAS *Melbourne* on the starboard.

The *Afric* was one of the last Australian ships to weigh anchor, being a part of the starboard column which formed up after the central and port side columns. *Afric* joined as fourth transport ship from the front of its column of transport ships.

The Albany residents had come out in force and covered the cliff tops and the slopes of a large hill overlooking King George Sound. They cheered and waved as the ships departed. *The town must be deserted.*

Jayjay stood with Ron, Larry and numerous others leaning against the balustrade at the stern and watched the convoy continue to build behind them.

After the remaining Australian ships joined the line, the grey New Zealand transports formed into two columns at the rear. The ships joining the tail became smaller and smaller until they were lost at the horizon.

By the end of the day most of the ships' captains managed to match their speed with the rest of the convoy, after some overshot their position and had to veer to one side to avoid catching up to the ship in front. Distances were difficult to judge across the water, but Jayjay gauged that there was around half a mile from each ship to the next one in front, and about a mile between each of the three columns of Australian ships. Looking back to the starboard, away from the setting sun, he watched the Australian coast slide past in the fading light.

The following day they passed Fremantle and the final two transport vessels completed the convoy with their Japanese warship escort the *Ibuki*. The *Melbourne* slowed and positioned herself astern to form a rear guard, and the *Ibuki* took her place on the starboard flank. The *Ibuki* appeared to be two or three ships behind the *Afric* in her position out on the flank, but was clearly visible as she steamed into position, sending up thicker, blacker smoke than any of the Australian vessels.

"They must have filthy coal in Japan," Larry said. "That cloud of smoke would be visible from forty miles away."

That afternoon the convoy diverged from the coastline and the setting sun cast a warm glow on the rocky cliffs. Men stood vigil along the starboard balustrade as the West Australian shore faded into the distance. Jayjay stood with them, and watched in silence, until darkness closed around the fleet.

* * *

The next morning, before breakfast, Jayjay hurried back to the balustrade. He squinted at the horizon below the climbing sun, hoping to catch a final glimpse of Australian shores, but there was only water.

The *Ibuki* continued to leave a huge trail of black smoke.

Jayjay wondered about the German warships, the *Scharnhorst*, *Gneisenau* and *Emden* and what damage they might do if they managed to get amongst the convoy. He looked down into the water as it foamed past.

He shivered although he was not cold.

CHAPTER 14

Clarence

Tuesday, 3 November 1914

Finally, it was starting to get light outside. He rolled over to check the time and damp sheets clung to his body – five o'clock.

Thank God another night is coming to an end. Not that there's anything to jump out of bed for. I am a caged animal here. There's nothing more I can do. My war is over before it has even begun, unless I can find a way past the guard and onto a British warship.

Under house arrest, Clarence had tested and found the limits of his diplomatic immunity.

In three months of holding the role of British Vice Consul in Chanakkale, Clarence Palmer had defined his function as more than that of a mere diplomat. Without anyone to guide or support him he had taken the initiative to record details of Turkish and German defensive preparations around the Dardanelles Strait and provide regular updates to the British warships that patrolled close by the opening of the Dardanelles at the Aegean Sea. Artillery emplacements, lines of sea mines, troop camps, a German officers' command ship, even details about Ottoman preparations in Constantinople – all recorded and passed on by whatever means he could find.

It had been a thrill, taking a picnic lunch up the hill behind Kilid Bahr and finding a nice vantage point overlooking the water. A place to take in the view and record locations of individual guns and lines of sea mines around The Narrows. *Such freedom I enjoyed.*

Most British ships in the Marmara Sea and around Constantinople had been blocked from exiting via the Dardanelles, but a handful had found their way through to Chanakkale and beyond. Clarence had made a point to board these in his diplomatic capacity and glean what information he could about defences at Constantinople and Ottoman naval operations. All these details were included in his reports and they were appreciated. The British Naval ships' captains had affirmed the value of his information on more than one occasion. That had been all the encouragement he needed to keep taking the risks.

The local Turkish officials had known. They must have known, at least towards the end in October, but they maintained the ridiculous façade of neutrality that tied their hands when it came to treatment of foreign diplomats.

Finally, the Young Turk coup leaders who commanded the flailing Ottoman Empire had shown their hand. *Quite a clumsy way to enter the war, but those in power must have made the decision based on what information they had. There must be a few things going on between the Turks and Germans that a minor British official stationed hundreds of miles away from Constantinople cannot not know about.*

Nevertheless, Clarence had been amazed to hear that the Ottoman navy, newly reinforced with two recently acquired German cruisers, had launched an attack on the Russian ports Odessa and Sevastopol in the Black Sea, without provocation or a declaration of war. The act was surprisingly belligerent after the Turks had been careful to maintain neutrality for the first three months of the war.

Word of the Ottoman naval attacks five days earlier had travelled fast, and spelt the immediate end of diplomatic freedom for Clarence. He had been forced to remain in his house under armed guard and cut off from the outside world since the moment the news arrived. He had not yet been advised of a formal declaration of war by either the Ottomans or the British, but it hardly mattered now. There was no doubt that the empires were at war. The Russians and French were British Allies in the war with Germany, Austria-Hungary and now the Ottoman Turks. *There are only two sides in this conflict – us and them. At least I haven't been imprisoned yet. I wonder how long I will be able to stay here? Maybe I will be sent home?*

* * *

The reverberation of a distant explosion shook Clarence from sleep. The clock showed quarter to six and light streamed in the window. *I must have dozed off.*

Every now and then an unfortunate soul would accidentally detonate a sea mine in The Narrows, resulting in a loud 'kaboom' and a giant water spray. This was different though, further away, but substantial. Maybe artillery practice? Another blast and another followed. A salvo of some sort. *Who is attacking what?* The thundering vibrations continued in regular succession.

Clarence jumped out of bed and hurried out of his room still wearing his pyjamas.

The young Ottoman soldier stood unflinching by the front door, like a monument to a bygone era.

Clarence walked to him and addressed him in Turkish. "Come, my friend, let us have a look from the front of the house. I will not run off. If I do you have my permission to shoot me."

Only his jaw moved. "We will stay inside. Those are my orders. I have no wish to shoot you Vice Consul Palmer Bey."

The tone that the guard added the formal title of 'Bey', the Turkish equivalent of 'Sir', made it clear that he had little interest in discussing the matter further.

The distant blasts continued for a few minutes, then there was a single almighty thunder. It was as if the initial series of blasts had only been an introduction to the main show. I wonder what that was. Some people must have been killed in that one.

The guard remained unmoved.

The explosions continued for another five minutes, but nothing like that single huge blast again.

Then Silence.

Somewhere a few miles away, the first stage of a battle was concluded. *It must be out at the mouth of the Dardanelles. That's where all our navy fire power is. Would the sound carry that far? I suppose it might. That final blast might have been an ammunition magazine. Was it one of our ships, or a land-based store? If it was a ship, she must be sunk from such a blow. Time will tell. I can't go and find out. Hopefully someone will come and let me know what happened soon. No, I must do something more. Maybe I could lean on my diplomatic credentials one more time.*

Clarence approached the guard again and spoke slowly. "My good man, it is imperative that I see the governor at once. I will dress and you will make the arrangements. Lives are at stake here. The lives of your people."

* * *

An hour later, Clarence stood in front of the civilian governor of Chanakkale.

Information was limited, but he had been able to determine that a combined British and French naval attack had been launched against the defensive fortresses at the mouth of the Dardanelles – Sedd-el-Bahr on the northern shore and Kum Kale on the southern shore. These defences were surrounded by small townships, so civilian casualties were certain, it was only a question of how many. The Germans claimed to have done some damage to the warships and sent them on their way. Maybe that was true, but the big explosion was at Sedd-el-Bahr, on the northern shore, likely an ammunition magazine.

The governor wore a grave face. He waved his hand at an empty chair opposite his ornate timber desk.

"Please sit," he said in Turkish. "You wished to see me."

"Governor Bey," Clarence replied, also in Turkish. "Many thanks for seeing me at such short notice. Good sir, I implore you, again, to think of the young wives that will be widowed and children that will be orphaned if you follow the Germans into this war. I have lived here among your people and this peaceful community. If you align yourselves with Germany, it is your people who will suffer. Ottoman blood will stain the earth red. Your Empire should seek peace and consolidate its position. The Kaiser cares only for German expansion, pushing into Russia and France, colonising southeast Asia. Why sacrifice yourself on the altar of his ambition?"

Decisions made about Ottoman involvement in the war were made in Istanbul, not Chanakkale, and Clarence knew it. In all likelihood the key decisions had already been made and could not be reversed by now. However, it was Clarence's job to represent the British interest and he genuinely cared for the local people. This was not their war. Why should Germans be allowed to walk around like they owned the place when it was Turkish towns and homes that would be destroyed and Turkish lives lost if war was allowed to come here.

The governor leaned forward in his chair and pointed a long finger at Clarence before he spoke.

"Vice Consul Palmer Bey, of course I do not want war here. Everything you say is true. Unfortunately our countries are at war. Maybe it has been inevitable for some months. You have known this – collecting information and sending it out to these warships – the warships that have this very morning launched an attack on my people, killing innocent civilians – women and children! You have played your part in supporting these floating machines of death. How do you feel about that Palmer Bey? You are the enemy here, not the Germans. What am I going to do with you? Maybe I could have you publicly hanged as a spy, as small gesture to appease the people. You will soon become a prisoner of war. Maybe you will have the honour of being the very first one to be executed. What do you think about that, Palmer Bey?"

This is not how the conversation was supposed to go. No, this is no good at all. "I am a Vice Consul, a diplomat here to facilitate communication between our Empires. I am not a combatant. There are protocols sir, diplomatic protocols. When war becomes official, you are free to expel me from your territory, but while you allow me to stay here you know that I have immunity."

"Tell me Palmer Bey, when does war become official? How many of dead bodies should we drag from the rubble before we consider ourselves to be at war? Does it matter if they are soldiers or civilians? Either way you have killed plenty of both."

"I have not killed anybody." The words rang hollow in Clarence's ears, even as he spoke them. "I want to prevent further conflict. This morning's episode is likely in retaliation to attacks launched by the Ottoman navy on our Russian allies. Can you tell me that there were no innocent women and children killed by the salvo's fired into Russian harbour towns from the Black Sea?"

The governor's shoulder's slumped and he shook his head. He turned to the window and gazed out over the Dardanelles. "This waterway, The Chanakkale

Strait, it keeps our town alive and it will be the death of us. Ever the centre of conflict – men have fought and died here for as long as history has been recorded. I had hoped that this day would not come in my lifetime. Neither you or I can prevent this now. Many men will die here. My people and your people. Your ships of destruction will come and try to get through here and kill us to take control of this precious stretch of water. We will stop them my friend. We will sink them. Maybe you can get one more message out to your friends – tell them that the Turks are men of courage and will defend our nation to the last man. Tell them to prepare to face the one true God."

The governor turned to face Clarence. "I think you should return to your residence now. Your guard will escort you. If you are lucky, maybe you will survive this war. Many will not have the luxury of being taken prisoner Palmer Bey."

Clarence stood and extended his hand in a hopeful final gesture. The governor shook his hand, but sad eyes belied his smile.

If there was a chance to escape on the way back to his residence, it went unnoticed and untaken. Clarence was focussed on replaying the conversation with the Governor in his mind. *How can I help these people and my people? Germany is the real enemy. What will they do to me?*

CHAPTER 15

Mustafa

Thursday, 5 November 1914

Lieutenant Colonel Mustafa Kemal, military attaché to the Ottoman Embassy in the Bulgarian capital of Sofia, poured raki into his glass. He added water and watched the two clear liquids swirl into a cloudy white mixture.

A knock at the door of his embassy office disturbed his brooding.

"Kemal Bey," Mustafa's aide-de-camp peered around the door, then entered. "Sorry to disturb you at such a late hour, but a telegram has come for you."

"Of course it has."

"The English –"

"Let me guess, the English have joined their Russian allies and declared war on the Ottoman Empire."

"Have you heard the news already Sir?"

"I heard that the English navy blasted our forts at the mouth of the Chanakkale Strait. It was only a matter of time, since we let those two German warships enter our waters and proceed to shoot up Odessa and Sevastopol. That might be considered aggressive, don't you think Hadji, sinking Russian ships and blowing up Russian oil tanks? I'm only surprised it has taken two days for the English to make the announcement."

"But Germans commanded those warships, not Turks."

"We let the warships fly our flag and we have let ourselves be pulled into the war."

"The Germans are our allies now. They will help us."

Damned Germans! Mustafa resisted the urge to throw his full glass against the wall. Instead he drained it while contemplating how far he could trust his aide-de-camp. Then Mustafa stood, stepped out from behind his desk and threw the empty glass into the fireplace, sending shards sprinkling into the embers.

Mustafa clicked his tongue and tipped his head back in the Turkish gesture for 'no'. "Do you think the Germans seek an Ottoman alliance for our benefit? Is there any benefit to us in such belligerence in the Black Sea? Is there any benefit to us in allowing the Germans to mine our Straits? The Germans control the senior ranks of our army and navy. We borrowed money from them that we cannot afford to repay. We accepted the warships they gave us, without asking what is required of us in return. We allowed the Germans into our bed and we shouldn't be surprised that they screw us whenever it pleases them."

"But the German Mission has helped to rebuild our armies."

"It is unnatural for a nation's military forces to be led by another nation! The Russians have had their eyes on Istanbul and the Straits for centuries and the Germans are fighting a war on two fronts. Both will soon realise that their interests are better served by making peace with each other. What will our German allies do then? Do you think they will remember us while they are still at war with the French and English on another front? I think not. No one cares to defend the Ottoman Empire but Turks, and Turks should command Ottoman forces!"

"The Germans are experts in military tactics and training." Hadji's voice wavered. "Surely there is much we can learn from them?"

"The cost is too high."

"Enver Pasha talks of expanding the empire again, with military expeditions into northern Africa, the Caucasus mountains in Russia, Egypt, Afghanistan and even India. We will need German help for this."

Enver! Mustafa drew a deep breath. *I need another glass to smash.* "In the last two years alone, our military has been humiliated in Libya and here in the Balkans. It is barely in a state to defend Istanbul and the remaining Turkish heartland. The Empire is crumbling."

Hadji's eyes narrowed.

"Hadji, you are a Turk and patriot."

"Yes Sir."

"You would give your life for the Fatherland."

"Of course."

"I am a patriot."

"No one would question that, Kemal Bey."

"Enver would have us believe he is a patriot, but he does not deserve the title of Pasha. He is not a true leader or general."

"Do you doubt the loyalty of our Minister for War? The papers call him the champion of youth against middle-age, and of daring against caution."

"Enver's nationalistic views are simple and popular, but –" Mustafa shook his head. "Last year he forced the retirement of one thousand experienced officers, including thirty generals. How many years of valuable military experience were wasted with that one act of stupidity? And then he went to his friend Baron Hans von Wangenheim and asked for German help to rebuild our military.

"Enver would cheerfully sacrifice thousands of men to achieve his personal ambitions. He has sold our nation's soul to maintain his grip on power. To be a true patriot, a man must be willing to sacrifice everything. Enver is too self-obsessed for this."

"You must be careful what you say Kemal Bey."

Mustafa nodded. "We must all be careful. Enver holds his position because he held a gun and led a mob into our parliament. The former Minister of War, Nazim Pasha, was killed that night. The former Grand Vizier Kamil Pasha resigned his post with a gun at his head."

Hadji stared back at Mustafa wide-eyed.

"Do you know why I am here Hadji, in Bulgaria?"

"I assumed you must have chosen to serve here Sir."

"We were disgraced here. The world watched and laughed as the sick old man of Europe was humiliated."

"The battle of the Balkan Revolt?"

"There was hardly even a battle to speak of. Our forces capitulated and ran like cowards. Vast territory, part of the Ottoman Empire for centuries, was lost in a moment. Our government was weak and unpopular, but Enver saw his opportunity in that disaster. Now he can take some pleasure that my name is associated with the shame that allowed him to seize power."

"You know Enver Pasha?"

"I argued with him about allowing the Germans to command our armies. The moment I spoke against him I was sent away, so now I live here in exile."

"And yet you know much of the workings in Istanbul."

"Others in our Capital think as I do. Communication is dangerous, but I maintain contact as I can. Our armies have been mobilised and it is rumoured that Enver will soon announce a Jihad against the Russians and their allies –."

"A Holy War!"

"We have taken sides in a war between Christian states. There is nothing holy about it. Enver was never overly religious in high school, or at military college, and he has not been since, but this will not be his first Jihad. He uses the devotion of others to help him achieve his political objectives. He can offer our men paradise for their martyrdom. Not one dead soldier has ever complained that the promise went unfulfilled."

Hadji looked at the floor and twisted one foot to left, then to right.

"A man may sit in the seat of power, but that doesn't mean he always speaks the truth. Never forget how he came to that position."

"Kemal Bey, the way you speak." Hadji looked about as if someone might hear, although everyone else had left the embassy hours earlier. "It borders on treason."

"You have already shown me that I can trust you, Hadji. Think about the things I have told you, but keep them to yourself. Our goals are not built on the ambitions of one man. Whatever happens, we must always think of what is best for the Empire and for the Turkish people."

"Yes, Kemal Bey," Hadji hesitated. "Will that be all?"

At a nod the aide-de-camp shuffled out.

Mustafa took a fresh glass and poured himself another raki with water, then slumped in his chair feeling much older than his thirty-four years.

Can anything be done to save the Ottoman Empire?

The days of an Islamic State are over. Having one man as the political ruler and religious leader worked for centuries, but it doesn't make sense in a modern society. Developments in the west have proven that.

We have failed to modernise with the rest Europe and paid the ultimate price. Now we must consolidate our Asian territory, or face total destruction. The English war correspondent Ellis Ashmead-Bartlett got that right in his book about the Turks in Thrace.

We must let go of the old ways and focus on building a nation state to preserve our culture and language, while at the same time enjoying the benefits of technology and civilisation that can be learned from the Christian Europeans.

I must do something. I cannot give up hope for a modern Turkish nation. But I cannot influence politics, not with Enver in power. There is nothing I can do here in Bulgaria.

Mustafa gulped the raki and searched the aniseed flavour for answers to impossible questions.

The English Navy has made its intentions clear. Something must be done to defend the Chanakkale Strait and the Gallipoli peninsula. I know the terrain on the peninsula as well as any man. I could go back there.

Maybe things will be different after this war – if I survive it.

I will seek a frontline appointment, and show the Germans that a Turkish officer is as capable as any. I will defend what is left of Turkish military pride.

CHAPTER 16

Larry

Friday, 6 November 1914

Six images lay in two neat rows, drawn on the floor in chalk: a crown, an anchor, a heart, a diamond, a spade and a club.

After this bet, I'll walk away.

This time for sure.

All or nothing.

He stepped into the middle of the circle, reached into his pocket and pulled out a handful of silver shillings. The circle of onlookers cheered like a crowd of ancients watching a blood sport.

The anchor drew him in. *No, I have already bet my life on this boat, and German warships are still lurking about the ocean.* At the last moment, he pulled his hand back and dumped all the coins on the chalk crown. The circle cheered again.

"For His Majesty!" Larry cried. "King George of England!"

"The King of England," said Seamus O'Shea, "can go shag a sheep on the shamrock green, but I'll take your money."

O'Shea passed the Crown and Anchor dice to Larry.

Larry shook the three dice in his hand for longer than necessary.

The circle crowded closer.

Anticipation surged through him like pure energy.

He rolled the dice and they danced across the floor.

Crown!

Crown!

Crown!

For a moment he was numb. He opened his mouth, but no sound came, then a guffaw took hold of him and the circle erupted in cheers.

His laughter was drowned by the noise. Only when the din died down could Larry speak.

"Well me laddies, I do believe that's a triple crown.

Larry crouched and counted out the coins he had bet. Twenty-two shillings. He laid them out in neat rows.

"One pound, two shillings on the floor," Larry called. "Aye, the luck of the

Irish! Time to pay up – Two pounds, four shillings if you please!"

O'Shea stared at the dice on the floor, still lying where they had stopped. O'Hara starred at the rows of shillings and O'Reilly looked as if he might throw a punch.

It's a good thing we have plenty of witnesses. They'll likely pay up rather than skive off.

"How about one more round?" said Seamus O'Shea. "Your luck is good today!"

"Maybe another day O'Shea," Larry replied. "I think I'll quit while I'm ahead for once."

O'Shea looked about at the circle of onlookers, as if considering his options, then nodded at the other two Irishmen. O'Hara counted out twenty-four silver shillings and handed them over. O'Reilly fished about in his pocket and glared at Larry through narrow slits. He pulled out a gold sovereign and dropped it in Larry's outstretched hand.

Larry closed his fingers around the still-warm coins and pocketed his winnings. He scooped up his shillings from the floor and the circle began to disperse, but Larry's heart pounded, as if he had just sprinted a lap around the top deck.

"What are you lot up to?" Sergeant Baker boomed from the doorway.

Larry stepped back and did his best to blend into the crowd, careful to keep the coins from jingling in his pocket.

"Just getting ready for bed Sergeant." Jayjay said.

"Have you lot been gambling down here again?"

He cannot see the chalk figures with everyone standing about, but if he makes us move away there'll be no denying it.

The men stood in silence.

Baker stared them down.

Larry fought an urge to finger the coins.

"I thought as much," Baker said quietly, then raised his voice.

"I will be back here in five minutes. Your hammocks will be strung up with you all inside them. Make sure I don't catch you breaking the rules again. If I do, I'll confiscate your money and I'll have you all on washing up duty for a week. Any questions? No! Good!"

Baker turned and disappeared out the doorway.

"Thanks Jay." Larry said.

"I don't understand why you keep playing that game," Ron said.

"I know you don't." Larry replied.

"You lose more than you win, and even when you win, there's nothing to spend the money on out here in the middle of the ocean."

"It's not about spending it."

"I heard last week a bloke got caught with a few quid he couldn't explain, so his sergeant assumed it was gambling proceeds and confiscated the lot."

"That bloke was careless. Let's get these hammocks up. I need to get some sleep."

Larry walked off towards the pile of rolled up hammocks. He scuffed his feet over the chalk figures on the way.

Sergeant Baker took longer than five minutes to return, but when he came the men were in their hammocks as ordered.

"You can open the port holes now." Baker turned off the lights. "Damn stinks down here."

Larry lit a cigarette, as did several others about the room. He stared into the darkness not wanting sleep to come, but tiredness overtook him in minutes.

* * *

The world spun.

It was very dark.

Is this another nightmare?

No. In a nightmare I never think to question if it's a nightmare until I wake up. We must be sinking. Shit, I'm going to drown.

Larry's hammock lurched left and right in an unnatural motion. He struggled to get out, fell, bounced off the table under his hammock and thudded onto the floor.

Someone yelled. *That's Jayjay's voice.*

Someone else yelled.

Other noises, a scuffle of feet.

He scrambled to his hands and knees.

The floor was steady.

Most of the boys must be still asleep. It's too quiet.

He lit a match.

By the weak light, he could make out a length of rope looped around the foot end of his hammock and several other hammocks in the row, including Ron's and Jayjay's.

"Nice prank," Larry called, hoping his voice didn't quaver. "Whoever that was. Now piss off and let us sleep!"

He climbed into his hammock and lay back feeling as if he might vomit.

"You alright Mate?" Jayjay croaked.

"Yeah."

This time sleep took a long time in coming.

* * *

Next morning, after physical jerks and breakfast, Larry stood on the top deck, assembled with the other men of G Company. Musketry training took the usual form of a marksmanship competition. Today G Company was to shoot off against F Company.

The men from both companies took their turns firing at the target at the starboard balustrade. Bullets that missed the target flew out to sea, away from the other ships in the convoy.

Jayjay hit the middle ring of the target with every round.

Good on you Jay, I'm glad to have you on my team.

O'Reilly, from F Company stepped up and hit the middle ring himself, then returned to stand with the other two Irishmen who had run the game of Crown and Anchor. He shot Larry a look that said he hadn't forgotten.

"Uh-Oh," Larry said in his best Irish accent. "It's the Irish Uh-Oh's. You feeling okay O'Reilly? You look a bit under the weather this mornin'."

"Aye laddy," O'Hara smirked. "The seas were mighty rough last night."

O'Hara lurched about in a mock stumble and nearly crashed into Larry.

"You Irish can't shoot to save your lives," Larry said. "I bet you a shilling that Jayjay's next shot is closer to the centre of the ring than any of the three of yours. That's if you can afford it."

"O'Hara!" Sergeant Baker yelled. "Get back into formation. You can shoot next. See if you can hit the target this time, otherwise I will deduct three points from F Company."

"Yes, Sergeant."

* * *

Later that evening, Larry scoped the room.

Everything was in place.

Ron gave a nod from the door.

Larry left his hammock and walked over to where O'Shea was setting up his hammock, next to O'Hara and O'Reilly.

"I reckon," Larry folded his arms, "you Irish Uh-Ohs know something about what happened to our hammocks last night."

"I dunno what ya' talkin' about." O'Shea replied.

The three Irishmen faced Larry and stepped towards him. O'Reilly balled his hands into fists.

"The rope. You know. You tied it around our hammocks at gave it a tug in the middle of the night. Sent me flying to the floor."

"Maybe you were just tugging at yourselves in the middle of the night?"

The three Irishmen laughed. At the same moment, Jayjay walked behind them, dropped a raw egg into each of their hammocks and kept walking towards his own hammock without slowing.

"Righto," Sergeant Baker yelled from the doorway. "An early start tomorrow, time for sleep. Come on man, get a move on! Anyone would think you like the foul stench you make down here. Into your hammocks so we can switch these lights of and let in some fresh air."

"I believe you O'Shea," Larry kept his arms folded. "Thousands wouldn't, but I believe you."

Larry turned and retired to his own hammock, slung next to Ron and Jayjay's. Sergeant Baker switched off the lights and ordered the port holes opened.

"What the bloody hell –". The cry from the dark carried an Irish accent.

"Quiet man," Sergeant Baker roared. "Or I'll have you on disciplinary charges, it's time for sleep."

The sergeant stood at the door for several long minutes and no one said another word.

Larry smiled to himself in the dark.

* * *

The next morning, evidence of a successful operation was clear on the three Irishmen's pyjamas. Larry, Jayjay and Ron laughed along with the small crowd that had gathered.

O'Reilly pointed at Larry.

"You did this!" he exploded.

"I dunno what ya' talkin' about." Larry raised both hands palm-up. "Anyway, I couldn't have done it, I came to talk to you when you were standing by your hammocks, and you were with me the whole time until Sergeant Fishface came to tuck us in and kiss us good night. It must have been someone from your own platoon who did it while we were having a nice chat."

O'Shea glared.

"You Irish Uh-Oh's have got it all wrong. When your mum told you about fertilising an egg to make a baby, that ain't what she meant."

"Hey boys," cried a voice from someone behind. "That's called a nocturnal egg-mission!"

Sounds of amusement rippled through the room. *Hopefully wide enough to ensure uncertainty as to the source of the prank.*

Later that morning, at breakfast, after the usual physical jerks exercise drills, the Company Commanding Officer, Captain Swannell, came to address the mess.

"Now you're in trouble Larry," Jayjay muttered under his breath. "He's here to have a go about the eggs you pilfered from the galley."

"No mate, it was the perfect crime. No witnesses, no evidence, no nothing.

Anyway, he'd send Sergeant Fishface if that was all it was about, he must have something more important on his mind."

"Men," said Captain Swannell. "Yesterday we received news that is of grave importance to this convoy and your safety. Listen carefully. At the start of our voyage, you were informed of the threat of three German warships whose location was unknown. These warships are the *Scharnhorst, Gneisenau* and *Emden.*

"I can now confirm that the *Scharnhorst* and *Gneisenau* are known to be off the Pacific coast of South America, too far away from our convoy to be a direct threat to us."

Captain Swannell wore a grim face stood like a statue. A murmur of approval spread through the mess, but an uneasy feeling took hold of Larry.

"We know where the *Scharnhorst* and *Gneisenau* are because they were engaged in a deadly battle with the British Navy. His Majesty's Ships *Goodhope* and *Monmouth* went down with all hands."

Gasps of breath were followed by a heavy silence, then Swannell continued.

"The *Emden* appears to be operating alone and remains a threat in our vicinity. Her last known location is at Sumatra where she caused havoc at the port of Penang nearly two weeks ago."

Two ships went down with all hands – from the most powerful navy in the world. How can that be? Not a single survivor. All drowned. There must be a mistake. Maybe they were caught by surprise?

"HMS *Minotaur* left our convoy this morning," Swannell continued. "Being called away on other business. HMAS *Melbourne* has taken her place at the head of our convoy. We will continue our practice drills in case of an attack by the *Emden*. I trust you men will take these drills seriously. As you were."

With that the Company Commanding Officer turned and left the men to their breakfast.

Larry picked up his toast, stared at it and returned it slowly to his plate.

"I'll eat that," Jayjay said. "If you don't want it."

"The bloody *Emden*'s still out there," Ron said. "And we've lost the *Minotaur*. If the *Melbourne*'s moved to the front, then there's no protection at the back."

"I know," Larry replied. "Went down with all hands. Damn! Why didn't they fire back and sink the German ships? It doesn't make sense."

"Where the hell is Sumatra?" Jayjay asked with his mouth full of toast.

Larry shrugged and stopped himself from voicing the thoughts that followed inside his head.

That could happen to us, we can't fire back. We could all die before we see dry land again.

What does 'havoc' look like in the middle of the ocean when warships are involved? Does it hurt to drown?

Morning parade and drill on the top-deck followed breakfast. Larry went through the motions with little enthusiasm and stole glances towards the horizon in all directions.

* * *

The next morning the usual daily routine continued. After breakfast, Larry lined up on deck awaiting his turn for rifle drill. The surface of the water drifted past glassy smooth and the sun shone hot enough to have him working up a sweat.

Far out to sea, on the port side past the other two columns of transport ships, Larry caught a sight that filled him with dread.

"Hoy," Larry cried. "Where's *Sydney* going?"

Not waiting for answer, he ran with his rifle to the balustrade for an unobstructed view. Larry's platoon followed close behind.

"I don't recall ordering you to charge off!" cried Sergeant Baker, but his protests seemed more forced than serious. Baker got himself a front position at the rail and gazed out to sea with the rest of his men.

HMAS *Sydney* diminished into the horizon quicker than Larry thought possible. A smudge of smoke the only sign of her presence. *Why are you going away? We need you here to protect us.*

"Look at *Ibuki* move," Jayjay said. "She's pumping out even more smoke than usual!"

Larry turned. On the opposite side to *Sydney*, the Japanese battlecruiser *Ibuki* surged up the starboard flank, rapidly gaining on the *Afric* and leaving a trail of thick black smoke. *Ibuki* caught up and moved past, pushing a huge bow wave in front. She left a great cavity in the ocean behind her, with a standing wave following after. The Japanese flag of the rising sun fluttered at her stern. The deck was cleared with only a handful of men visible scurrying about their business. *Ibuki* left *Afric* in her wake and a second larger rising sun unfurled high up atop *Ibuki's* mainmast, in front of the three funnels that continued to belch out smoke.

"*Ibuki* is flying her battle flag!" Ron said.

Larry stared at the flag, then at the water. *So much water. I don't like the stakes of this game.* "We must be the biggest pack of lunatics in the world."

CHAPTER 17

Karl

Monday, 9 November 1914

Karl gazed across Port Refuge, a natural harbour in waters sheltered by the reefs of the Cocos Islands, from the deck of the *Emden*. She lay at anchor, near the northern entrance to a circular atoll, six miles across. Waiting for his landing party to return, Captain Karl von Müller wore a wry grin as he reflected on the irony of the name of the place. *This atoll could become a death trap if we are caught here. The sooner we are away the better.*

His landing party had left the *Emden* soon after 6:00 am, led by First Officer Hellmuth von Mücke in a steam launch towing two boats. They had been gone for around three hours. If all went to plan, they should be returning within the hour.

This mission was to destroy English communications assets on Direction Island at the northern edge of the atoll, just a few thousand yards east of where he waited at anchor. The wireless transmission tower and submarine cable connection point on this island were known to be important elements in the communications between England and her eastern colonies.

He knew he was taking a risk attacking a facility like this, coming out of hiding again and announcing his location to the enemy. But if today's operations were successful, the risks would be worth it.

The wireless operator on the *Emden* had confirmed that English staff manning the communications equipment on the island managed to send a distress radio signal away before the landing party reached the shore. Attempts to block this transmission had been unsuccessful, as an enemy warship acknowledged the distress call and was approaching to assist. Fortunately, his wireless operator was able to determine from the signal strength of the transmission that the enemy ship was around 250 miles away. That should provide enough time to complete the mission, steam off in one direction for 50 miles until out of sight of the island's residents, and then change direction to evade the hunters once again. It was a method he had successfully used numerous times in recent months.

The risks were increased by his decision to send a landing party, rather than pound the installation remotely with the *Emden's* four-inch guns. However, this allowed a more targeted approach, and gave his men a chance to destroy the submarine cables if they could be located. Hopefully it would also eliminate the loss of innocent lives.

He hoped the resident Englishmen did not resist. There was little they could do to stop fifty men armed with rifles and four maxim machine guns, other than throw their lives away. However, in case of armed resistance, he had ordered First Officer von Mücke, to return to the *Emden* immediately and the job would be done with the ship's guns. He could not afford to delay here.

Karl noticed the hint of smoke on the horizon. That would be his latest milking cow, the *Buresk*. She was due to arrive at 9:00 am and was a little late. He contemplated rescheduling the rendezvous with her in light of the fact that an enemy warship was known to be on its way here.

The smudge of black smoke held his gaze and he realised that something was not right. The *Buresk* never produced that much smoke. A pit formed in his stomach. He forced himself not to run as he moved to the mast and climbed up part way to have a better look. There was too much smoke for that to be the *Buresk. The enemy warship should not be here yet.*

As he stared at the horizon, the signalman in the crow's nest called out.

"Enemy man-of-war with four funnels in sight."

Now it was time to run. Karl hurried to the bridge.

"Sound the siren, we need those men back here urgently," he ordered.

Immediately a loud siren blared from the *Emden*. He filled the silence that followed with the next order.

"Prepare for action, clear the decks, fire all boilers."

Men were running in all directions. A hostile warship was approaching and they knew it was time to perform.

Four funnels could mean one of a number of English warships, probably the cruiser *Newcastle*. She was known to be in these waters. It would be a fair fight if he could get the *Emden* into open water before she came within firing range.

Karl's adjutant climbed to the crow's nest above the Bridge, and called out that the warship was the Australian cruiser *Sydney*.

With the flurry of activity around him, Karl took a deep breath and a moment to consider battle tactics.

"So it is to be *Sydney* then. Come *Sydney* and let us dance. This will be the last waltz for one of us."

Karl looked back towards Direction Island. He could see tiny figures scurrying onto the beach. He needed them to man his guns for a sea battle, but if he waited for them to return, he might be trapped in the bay and destroyed. He looked up at the *Sydney*. She was closing the distance between them too quickly. He needed to get to open water to have any chance. He looked back to the landing party.

Their steam launch could only move slowly when towing the two heavily laden boats. The beach was too far away.

I am sorry to leave you behind boys, but you may have a better chance of surviving the day this way. I cannot wait any longer.

He gave the order to weigh anchor.

Karl recalled that the *Sydney* had six-inch guns. Now he was outgunned and undermanned. This was going to be a tough fight. However, the Sydney and her crew were untested in battle, in fact, the Australian navy had never actually done anything that he could remember. Most of the crew are probably still in training. He would have to bluff a little, and hit her hard early before those bigger guns could do too much damage.

He ordered the *Emden* full steam ahead, due north away from the atoll and into deeper water. The enemy approached from the northeast. The distance closed fast. The *Sydney* had some speed up.

"Fire when in range" he ordered.

The limit of the *Emden's* range was around 10,000 yards. At this range his gunners fired the first shot. The *Sydney* had not yet fired. The first salvo fell short, the second overshot. The third hit its mark and burst into flames on the deck, drawing first blood. The *Sydney* had still not fired, maybe this would not be such a tough fight after all.

The *Sydney* turned hard to her starboard, taking a course northward, running parallel to the *Emden*. She opened fire broadside. Initial range finding shots sent huge fountains of water into the air all around the *Emden*.

A deafening blast rattled the bridge as a shell thundered into it, knocking Karl to the floor. Karl immediately picked himself up to inspect the damage. Several of his crew were wounded. The compass and range finder were destroyed.

Somehow he had not been injured, but if he stayed here he might not be able to command the ship in battle for long.

He climbed down into the conning tower below the bridge. Armoured with four-inch steel plate, this small room below the bridge was designed to protect the warship's commander in battle. Visibility was not as good from here, although slots had been cut in the armour to provide some view.

He looked at the *Sydney*, now surging ahead of the *Emden*. His shells did not seem to be having much impact on her. She continued to unleash salvo after salvo in his direction. And they were accurate.

Another shell punched through the bow of the *Emden*, exploded on its way through and left the hull ringing like a bell. The noise was loud from within the conning tower, it must be deafening for the gunners on deck.

The *Emden's* decks shone red with blood and bent steel lay everywhere. Several gun crews had been killed or wounded.

The rate of shellfire from his ship had slowed and was proving to be ineffective against the *Sydney's* armour at this range. He was losing the battle and had to do something. He had to get closer to do more damage before he was destroyed.

He ordered a change course a few points towards the starboard to converge with the *Sydney.* However, as the order was still being carried out, another shell exploded into the deck between two guns in front of the conning tower, killing the gun crews and damaging the guns.

The conning tower was full of black and yellow smoke. Electrical supply was gone. Ammunition winches were destroyed, leaving a number of his guns impotent. An occasional shell was still being fired from the *Emden* now, but it was not enough to have any impact.

The gunnery officer approached Karl.

"Request permission to fire unmanned gun myself sir?"

Karl nodded. There was no one else left to take over the guns that remained operable. The gunnery officer called up more ammunition and sent a few shells away before becoming another victim of the onslaught. His lifeless body lay across the gun in a final embrace.

Enemy shells continued to rain on the *Emden.* A massive explosion tore through the stern when an ammunition store was hit. Karl heard cries from the wounded through a speaking tube. The sound was pitiful. The best he could wish for these men was a rapid death.

He looked towards the stern. The ship's three funnels were all destroyed, laying about the deck like lazy sailors. Flames towered over the wreckage. The whole rear end of the *Emden* was aflame.

The *Sydney* was closing for the kill, now only around 4,000 yards away. She launched a torpedo which sped past, missing its mark.

Another shell hit the *Emden* at the stern and jammed the rudder. Karl knew the battle was over. His guns were silenced and now he could hardly steer the ship to evade incoming shellfire.

The *Emden* had twin steam engines, each driving its own screw. There was some scope to steer by backing off one engine with the other at maximum power.

Karl admired the Engineer and other men in the engine room. They were hot and frantic, shovelling coal to keep the ship moving. Deep inside the ship, they would have no hope of escape if the *Emden* was sunk. *They must know that the Emden is losing the battle, but every man remains at his task.*

He had always imagined that he would be sunk in the end. It was only a matter of time given the destruction he had caused around the Indian Ocean. It seemed a fitting end for himself. He did not mind going down with his ship.

However, it seemed unfair on the men, his men. *They are like sons to me. They have fought so valiantly, willing to fight to the death. This is no longer a fight.* He had no hope of inflicting any further damage to the *Sydney.* The battle was lost and he was only forestalling the inevitable. It was not the German way to surrender, and yet it was not right to sacrifice human life for the principle.

"The dance is over," he said softly.

North Keeling Island lay ahead and within sight. The small uninhabited atoll gave him the opportunity he needed. He sent commands to the engine room to balance the power to continue directly at the island.

The *Emden* could not reach its former top speed as the funnels had been destroyed and the boilers lacked their usual draft. Nonetheless, she hit the reef hard and lurched to a halt with a terrible grinding sound.

At least the *Sydney* had stopped firing those infernal shells.

Karl surveyed the carnage. Steel sheets of deck were curled up like autumn leaves. Glass portholes had melted in the heat. The funnels and other mangled steel made the deck unrecognisable. One of the *Emden's* four-inch guns had a scar gouged into its barrel, in the way a slab of butter might be gouged with a hot spoon. Burned and mutilated bodies lay about, some screaming, some moaning and some silent.

The men looked to him for direction. Even amidst this horror, surrounded by dead and wounded comrades, they waited for him to tell them what to do next.

"Fires out in all boilers. Flood the engine and ammunition rooms, then all hands report on deck," he ordered.

The men leapt to action, likely glad to have something to take their mind off the situation. In the midst of activity, Karl had a moment to think about what to do next. The *Sydney* was steaming away towards the horizon. He wondered if she would return or send help for his men.

A wounded man lying nearby begged in a hoarse voice that was barely audible.

"Water, water, please."

It was the least he could do, but a quick check confirmed that the ship's water tanks had been destroyed along with everything else. There would be no water for anyone. If the *Sydney* was coming back to rescue the helpless crew and wounded, it had better be soon.

Men returned a few at a time, reporting that they had completed his orders.

"Three cheers for the captain!" called one, and the others joined in the chorus.

Karl was touched at their loyalty, despite everything they had been through. He addressed the men.

"Without such a crew I could have done nothing. It has been my great fortune to have under my command some of the keenest and finest of fighting men."

"Now we must prepare in hope that our enemy will return for us on a mission of mercy. Firstly, we must destroy all papers and equipment. We must also tend to the wounded as best we can. Our water tanks are destroyed so we have no water to give them. If any man would care to swim to the island in search of water or coconuts to ease the suffering of these brave men he may do so. Otherwise, we wait."

Some men moved to the remains of balustrade at the edge of the deck and looked down into the waves crashing over the reef. The beach was a good 200 yards away. A few were determined to make the attempt. Maybe they would die trying, maybe they would be the lucky ones.

A terrible smell hung in the air, announcing that the dead were starting to decay in the tropical heat. Noisy sea birds circled above, looking for their next meal. Karl wondered to himself whether it would have been kinder to his men to fight to the death, and end the suffering sooner.

CHAPTER 18

Jayjay

Monday, 9 November 1914

Sweat soaked Jayjay's uniform.

Will this rifle drill never end?

He stole another glance across the deck towards the horizon on the port side, past the *Melbourne* and *Ibuki,* the direction in which *Sydney* had steamed off earlier that morning. *Will it be a friendly ship returning from that direction, or the other kind.*

On *Sydney*'s departure, the two remaining warship escorts had stayed with the convoy. *Ibuki* had overtaken the convoy and crossed in front of it to the other side. There it had taken up a joint position with *Melbourne* at the forward port flank.

Now, in the heat approaching midday, he reflected on the vulnerability of being on an unarmed ship in the middle of the ocean. He didn't even have live ammunition for the rifle he had been training with all morning.

As Jayjay struggled to focus on the rifle drill, a flurry of activity on the bridge caught his eye. Junior officers ran in all directions. Captain Swannell, G Company Commander, walked slowly towards his men training on deck. Other heads turned and drilling paused. No one said a word.

"Men," Captain Swannell's expression gave nothing away. "We have received a message from General Bridges regarding the HMAS *Sydney.* She has engaged in combat with the enemy ship the *Emden.* The following part of the message is repeated directly from a message sent by Captain Glassop of the *Sydney* himself: 'The *Emden* is beached and done for.'"

Relief washed over Jayjay and a roar erupted around him. Men cheered, laughed, whistled and yelled.

"That's our *Sydney*!" cried Larry, slapping Jayjay on the back. "We got 'em, take that you Hun bastards!"

The commissioned and non-commissioned officers to a man all joined in. Any need to maintain order and discipline was set aside for the moment.

After many minutes of celebration, the ruckus died down and Sergeant Baker tried to rekindle the drill routines, but it was no use and he called for an early luncheon.

Over a meal of cold meat, salad and bread there was only one topic of conversation.

With his mouth full of food, Jayjay asked Ron and Larry "What do you think will happen to the *Emden* and her crew?"

Ron replied "The ship'll be left there to rust I reckon, she must be all shot up if she's 'done for', and after all, she's 'beached'."

Larry added "The crew will be taken as prisoners for sure. They can't have been wounded too badly, otherwise they wouldn't have been able to get the ship onto the beach. They were probably running away from the fight, bloody cowards. Our boys on the *Sydney* wouldn't have scarpered like that, they would have stayed and fought to the death. That's the difference between us and them. That's why we'll win the war."

Conversation continued to revel in the *Sydney*'s glory. In the absence of further facts, speculation evolved into undisputed truth about details of the mighty victory.

Following lunch, Sergeant Baker attempted to return the men's attention to rifle drills, but no one seemed willing or able to hear his instructions. Captain Swannell came to the sergeant's rescue when he came to address the men.

"I have an announcement that I am sure will be of great interest to you all. In the honour of the Australian Navy's first great victory on the high seas –."

He paused until the cheers died down.

"The commander of the Australian Imperial Force, General Bridges has declared that the rest of today will be a holiday from drill and other duties."

Again, he had to wait for the noise to subside, but he seemed in no rush. Eventually he raised his hand to indicate there was more.

"And furthermore, in his generosity, the General has offered to stand a drink for every man, at no cost to yourselves, in addition to the single glass of beer that you are each able to purchase this afternoon if you so desire."

This time the cheers were louder than before. Captain Swannell smiled beneath his moustache, turned and left, not bothering to restore order before he walked off.

Jayjay had never been a drinker in Sydney. His parents were teetotallers and when he was young they warned him of the dangers of demon drink. As he grew up, he saw his friends spending their spare money on alcohol, doing stupid things and making themselves sick. This never seemed like a good idea to him.

However, drinking was a part of the culture in the Infantry. Whilst on board the *Afric*, each man was allowed to purchase a single pint of beer each day, at a cost of four pence. This amount, being just a third of a shilling, made a small dent in the five shillings of daily pay that the privates received while on active duty. There was not much else on board the ship they could spend that money on, especially given the ban on gambling. Even those married who were obliged to send two shillings directly to their wives at home still had a surplus of available funds.

Without much else to look forward to each day, four o'clock 'beer parade' had become a highlight of the routine. Jayjay joined in with Ron, Larry and the others in his section. At first he didn't much like the bitter taste or the smell of hops. However, he joined in as he enjoyed the company and the time of relaxation towards the end of the day. With his large frame, the alcohol in one glass of beer was not enough to have any great effect on him.

Soon, he had acquired a taste for the drink. He started to enjoy the taste and aroma as much as the downtime with his mates. As Jayjay drained his bonus second glass, he reflected that this was a clever way to build good will of so many. It was just a shame that he could not have a third to extend the occasion.

He wondered out aloud to Ron and Larry. "If we came under attack, what would you rather… to be blown up by a shell, fall into the ocean to drown, lose a limb and be sent home or be taken prisoner?"

Larry was so quick to answer that Jayjay wondered whether he had thought about this type of question before.

"Well, drowning would be slower than being blown up, so I reckon that would be worse, and I heard that the Germans torture their prisoners to make them reveal secrets, and sometimes cut their balls off just for fun, so I definitely would not want to be taken prisoner."

"But we don't know any secrets," Ron laughed.

Larry continued "Well the Germans don't know that do they, and they might enjoy trying to find out if we do or not. They're cruel sods. Anyway, as I was saying, if I lost a limb and got sent home, I'd miss out on the rest of the action and then the rest of you lot would come home as heroes and I'd just be a cripple who didn't make any contribution. I think I rather just be blown up nice and quick."

Ron was more cautious. "I'm not so sure about wanting to be blown up, it might not be that quick and painless. I would like to get home to Emilia, even if I lost a limb. I'm sure she would like to look after me and I guess the government would give us some money as I couldn't work as a builder anymore."

"I'm sure Emilia would love to look after you, especially in the bedroom, but you can spare us the details. What about you Jayjay, you came up with this evil question, what would you rather?"

Jayjay hesitated. Like Larry, he had always thought he would rather be killed quickly than be maimed and sent home a cripple. But Larry's innuendo fuelled his imagination and the idea of being looked after by Charlotte made him smile.

"I dunno," said Jayjay.

"I dunno!" Larry roared in mock outrage "You can't put a question like that, then listen to our answers and then just say 'I dunno' for yourself."

"You're right," conceded Jayjay, hurrying to conceal his true thoughts. He gave them an answer he thought they would be happy with.

"I think I'm with Larry on this one, I'd like to go quickly and not suffer for too long. I'd want to be blown up too."

He laughed along with the rest of them, but deep inside an urge to live belied his words.

The *Afric* steamed onwards across the Indian Ocean. That night Jayjay slept easier knowing the immediate threat of the *Emden* was gone. In the following days he noticed a sense of relief in those around him. With all major German naval threats to the convoy now accounted for, the men's focus returned to the ship's daily routine, and how to avoid it.

The tight convoy formation of the fleet relaxed a little. The New Zealand transport ships and a few of the faster Australian transport ships surged ahead of the rest of the convoy with HMAS *Melbourne*. The *Afric* remained with the other slower transports and the *Ibuki*.

* * *

Four days after the news of the *Emden's* destruction came the 'crossing of the line'. To Jayjay's surprise, the antics were led by the ship's captain, Captain Marshall and G company commander, Captain Swannell. Both of whom dressed up as King Neptune, and led the dunking ceremonies in the make-shift pool of sea water set up on the deck. Officers and non-commissioned officers were the first ones to be tried for fictitious crimes.

Sergeant Baker was charged with extreme harshness in bedtime enforcement, and proved to be a good sport about being shoved unceremoniously into the water.

Following the officers, men who had not previously crossed the equator were found guilty of any number of charges, and the punishment was always the same, a good dunking in the salt water pool. Some of the English born troops were quick to point out that they had already crossed the equator on their original journey to Australia, but crossing the line as a civilian provided no immunity. Jayjay, Ron and Larry were hauled before King Neptune and found guilty of stealing eggs from the galley. *Not quite the perfect crime.* However, there were no further repercussions, other than a swim on a hot day.

The Irishmen, Seamus O' Shea, Poddy O'Hara and Mick O'Reilly, organisers of the Crown and Anchor game that had led to the egg prank, cheered more heartily than anyone. Jayjay ensured that the Irishmen were charged with interfering with hammocks for their dunking and there were laughs from all concerned.

* * *

Two days after crossing the equator, the *Afric* dropped anchor off Colombo, a bustling harbour town on the western coast of British Ceylon. The faster ships that had left the convoy behind earlier waited at anchor.

Hundreds of small boats rushed around the larger ships, and on land tiny people hurried about their business.

"Sorry lads, but the orders are to stay on board. We only expect to be here for a couple of days before we push on to England. The last thing we want is to have to chase you lot down in pubs and houses of ill repute across the city. We're doing you all a favour. Just think of all the trouble that you won't be getting yourselves into by staying right here."

Sergeant Baker's opening at afternoon parade was met with groans. A long two weeks had passed since they had left Australia's shores at Albany.

There was almost no shade on deck, and the sun's rays punished all who were exposed. In the confined spaces below decks, the heat was concentrated and the air stagnant. Jayjay and most of the others in his platoon took to sleeping on the deck in an attempt to find a little cool breeze. The deck was hard, but at least the air was breathable.

Now they faced another couple of days in the heat, without any new scenery, or chance to seek any liquid refreshments beyond water and the daily allowance of one glass of beer.

Exercise drills at Colombo were conducted early in the morning to avoid the worst of the heat. Some officers from the *Sydney* came to dine on the *Afric*, so some details of the battle were obtained first hand. At least this was what Sergeant Baker claimed when he addressed the men before breakfast, although Jayjay figured that the news was at least third hand by the time it reached the privates.

"Here's what happened chaps," Baker's eyes opened wide. "I heard it straight from the horse's mouth, I did. The *Sydney* chased the *Emden* down with her bigger guns and blew up everything on the deck to the point where it was unrecognisable. The *Emden's* crew had managed to beach her on a small uninhabited island after her guns were all disabled and they flew the white flag of surrender. The *Sydney* went to check on the Cocos Island radio tower and the men there, and then went back the next day to pick up the German captain and crew and took them as prisoners. They looked after 'em real well, fixed up their wounds and all. A mighty fine gesture it was too, if it were the other way around, I dare say the Germans, being Germans, would have left our boys there stranded to die of thirst, if their wounds didn't kill 'em first."

Maybe there was some truth to the version of events they were given, as they had been warned that HMAS *Sydney* would be passing through the convoy with German wounded on board, and asked not to cheer out of respect for them.

However, Jayjay never saw her pass.

Now at Colombo, the *Sydney* lay at anchor some distance away from the *Afric* and was difficult to see.

"Look," Larry yelled. "They're moving some wounded men under guard onto the *Omrah*. They must be German prisoners that the *Sydney* picked up from the *Emden*."

Jayjay hurried with the others to the balustrade to have a look. Australian Transport *Omrah* carried the designation 'A5' and lay anchored near the *Afric*.

Men in tattered uniforms were being guided up a ramp from a smaller boat onto the *Omrah*. Some shuffled hunched over, some nursed wounds and some limped. Many wore bandages the colour of dried blood.

I'm not sure what I thought they'd look like, but I didn't think they'd look so meek. They're nothing like the Germans in the war posters back home, with spiked helmets and murder in their eyes.

CHAPTER 19

Harry

Friday, 20 November 1914

Harry shivered in the drizzle and shook his head.

Another visit to the army camp at Salisbury Plain, south west of London, had left him with more disappointment and growing anger. He turned and walked to the motor car that was waiting to take him back to London.

When he had arrived in England three months earlier the weather was pleasant enough, but it had deteriorated to a point where daily activities of the men at Salisbury Plain were more about survival than military training. He had seen the enthusiasm of the Canadian forces seep away with the summer warmth. The men were living in tents surrounded by deep mud. Sickness was rife and there were only a few hours each day when the men could do anything that remotely resembled combat training.

He had been promised that huts would be built for the men by winter, but this was now clearly impossible. The tradesmen and materials were simply not available. It was too late for much to be done for the Canadians, but he was more concerned about what he could do for his fellow Australians who were en route and only a couple of weeks away.

Colonel Harry Chauvel had been sent from his role in helping to establish the Royal Military College at Duntroon in Canberra for a posting in England. He travelled with his wife Sibyl and young family, to take up his new role as the Australian Representative in the Dominions Section of the Imperial General Staff in London. When he arrived in August, war had been declared and the place was in chaos.

When the Australian offer to send troops had been accepted, he made it a priority to investigate the logistics of Australian troop deployment in the hope of ensuring the men were looked after to the best extent possible. He knew from his experience serving in the Boer War that an army's success or failure was often due more to logistical organisation than the skill or courage of the individual soldiers. He imagined his young sons growing up to be soldiers like himself and believed the military administration had a duty to its men to provide them with the best support and training possible.

With the outbreak of war, he spent much of his time at the War Office where the bureaucracy was infuriating. It was clear that it was pointless to bring thousands of Australian troops to England for training at the start of winter. The war front was in a frozen stalemate and there would be no chance of a major offensive until spring.

Some weeks earlier he had proposed to the War Office that the Australian troops avoid the harsh English winter by stopping to train in Egypt instead. This seemed like such an obvious thing to do that he could not believe the resistance he faced as he argued more and more aggressively for this course of action. The Turks had joined the war and now threatened the Suez Canal which provided critical shipping access to India and the Far East. Additional troops may be required there and the Australians would be sailing right on past.

He had to do something to stop the stupidity.

Maybe the Australian High Commissioner would be willing and able to help. Harry did not like going outside the established chain of command, but time was running out and he could not think of any other course of action that might change the situation.

On returning to London, Harry made an appointment to meet with Sir George Reid, the Australian High Commissioner to London.

* * *

"I'm sorry to bother you sir, but the situation is desperate," Harry began, hoping he appeared more confident than he felt. "The War Office is just not taking us seriously. It isn't right to send our boys out to Salisbury Plain for the winter, especially when there is a much better solution."

Harry outlined his proposal in detail to Sir George, including an account of the woeful conditions at Salisbury Plain and the opportunity for the Australians to train in Egypt and be available help defend the Suez Canal if required.

"After winter, they will be healthy, fit and well trained. If not required to defend the Canal, they could be deployed directly to the front from there. There are just too many advantages in taking this course of action not to do it." Harry concluded.

He remained standing with his arms straight by his side as he waited for Sir George to respond. The portly High Commissioner took his time to consider what he had been presented with, and looked Harry up and down before speaking.

"You are quite right, dear boy, in suggesting our troops stop over at Egypt. You say you have put this idea to the War Office."

"Yes sir, numerous times, but the bureaucracy there is impossible. They simply will not listen to me." Harry replied, pleased that had not been sent away for being impetuous.

Sir George called for his assistant and calmly requested that he put a telephone call through to Lord Kitchener.

Harry felt a sudden need to sit down, but he had not been offered a seat so he did his best to stand still. It went against every protocol that he could think of to presume to make a direct telephone call to the Minister of State for War.

"Please do sit down dear boy, I shall raise this matter with Lord Kitchener myself. We want him to take us Australians seriously don't you think?"

Sir George winked at Harry as he took the telephone and waited for a voice at the other end of the telephone line. Harry just nodded, not sure if he should answer or if the question was purely rhetorical. He didn't want to risk interrupting when Lord Kitchener might speak.

Harry sat in the seat offered to him, but now felt that he should be standing with the impending presence of Lord Kitchener, even if he was communicating by telephone and not here to see whether anyone was sitting or standing.

"Ah Herbert, dear boy, George Reid here. Ordinarily I would not call you directly like this but there is a matter of grave importance that I must discuss with you right away."

Sir George neatly summarised the proposal to stop the Australian troops at Egypt, not mentioning the detail that it was Harry's idea, or that previous requests to War Office had fallen on deaf ears. He also mentioned the urgency as the Australian convoy would be entering the Suez Canal within days.

"Yes, of course I can come tomorrow to discuss this further. Thank you ever so much. I shall look forward to our meeting."

Sir George hung the telephone mouth piece back on its receiver and gave a satisfied smile in Harry's direction.

"Well, I don't imagine that you expected that did you?" he chuckled.

"No sir." Harry allowed himself the slightest of smiles.

He was impressed by the former Premier of New South Wales, and Prime Minister of Australia. Sometimes he gave the impression that he was more interested in showing off his quick wit than dealing with serious matters, but he had shown an ability to digest this issue and act decisively beyond Harry's greatest hopes.

Sir George looked Harry up and down again as if contemplating another decision before continuing.

"There is one more thing, assuming all goes well tomorrow with Lord Kitchener. I will want to be sure that we are doing the right thing by our boys, sending them to train in Egypt for the winter. I can't imagine it will be worse than Salisbury Plain, but nothing is perfect and some will complain no matter where we send them. I will need someone there to make sure everything is in order and report back to me on the wonderful success of this decision. Who knows, if it's that good, I might even come to Egypt to visit the troops myself. I think you had better pack your things together son, if we get our way, you're going on a trip to Egypt."

"Yes sir."

CHAPTER 20

Ronald

Saturday, 28 November 1914

Ron gazed at the sharks gliding through the water.

Australian troop transport ship A19 *Afric* had steamed away from Aden two days earlier, and yet the sharks would not be left behind, darting to and fro, surging forward and drifting back.

Creatures of death, made by God to hunt and kill, like soldiers of the Imperial Force. *Could I be a killer? Will I be killed? I promised Em I'd come home after I'd done my bit. What if I don't come home? Would she think I'm a hero, or hate me, or both? I wonder how she's coping without me. I must write –.*

A hand on Ron's shoulder dragged him back to the present. Jayjay looked over the balustrade and followed Ron's gaze. "Come on Ron, let's get some lunch. Damn, it's hot! But I'm glad I'm not in there swimming with those sharks."

"Yeah."

Ron followed his younger brother below decks. He wasn't hungry, but forced himself to eat some bread, cold meat and salad, then sipped at his water.

After the meal the company Commanding Officer, Captain Swannell, addressed the men.

"Here we go," Jayjay said. "Someone's been pinching eggs again."

"Shut it and listen," Ron said quietly. "Last time you made that joke we got bad news."

"Men," Captain Swannell spoke with a clear voice, but not loud. "This morning we received orders from the Commander of the Australian Imperial Force, General Bridges himself. Following is the message we received: 'Unforeseen circumstances decide that the force shall train in Egypt and go to the front from there. The Australians and New Zealanders are to form a corps under General Birdwood. The locality of the camp is near Cairo.'"

A murmur of grumbles filled the room, Captain Swannell looked up and paused until silence returned.

"We are still going to war, so there is no need for disappointment. In fact, we may even be called upon sooner, to defend the Suez Canal, now that Turkey has entered the war."

"We signed up to go to England, not the flamin' desert," came an anonymous shout in a cockney accent.

"May I remind you that you signed up to faithfully discharge your duty and resist His Majesty's enemies, wherever they may be. Those of you who are familiar with the English winter might be pleased for a stopover in a warmer place. We will be proceeding through the Suez Canal and making for Alexandria where we will disembark, then travel overland to Cairo. That will be all."

Captain Swannell strode out and a buzz of conversation filled the void he left behind.

"Some of the English-born see this adventure as nothing more than free passage back home," Larry said. "Stopping at Egypt on the way to the front is not so bad. Bloody whingeing Poms."

"Maybe they want to see their family?" Ron said.

"I wonder if we'll see the pyramids," Jayjay said. "Are they anywhere near Cairo?"

"I dunno."

* * *

Four days later the *Afric* weighed anchor and steamed towards the canal. The ships of the convoy had been moving at their own pace northwards through the Red Sea and now clogged the bottleneck where the man-made canal began. The First Battalion had waited at Suez for their turn to enter the canal for around 24 hours.

Ron stood with Jayjay and Larry among the throng lining the starboard balustrade. The ship charged the shore, the canal not visible from where he stood. It felt strange after sailing on the open sea for so long. He half expected the ship to come to a grinding halt, but she eased into the canal without incident.

Men on guard duty stood solemn with live ammunition in their weapons.

"Finally something interesting might happen," Jayjay said.

They had all been warned that a Turkish attack on the Canal was possible and guards were to return fire if fired upon.

"This is amazing," said Ron. "Such a thin strip of water can carry such big ships. It's not even wide enough for two ships to pass, but it goes on for 100 miles. Imagine building something like this."

Jayjay nodded slowly. "You always loved building things."

"We don't have anything like this at home."

"Yeah," Larry said. "They cut Africa off from the civilised world. It's lucky it didn't drift away and sink."

"No seriously," Ron said. "Look how long and straight it is and think about how deep the water must be for us to not be scraping along the bottom. This is some real clever construction work. I'd bet it must need constant dredging."

"I don't know," Larry replied "I built something like this once in the sandpit when I was a kid. This is just bigger."

"It's a big sand pit all right," Jayjay gazed towards the horizon. "It goes on forever. Look, there're some tents coming up."

A collection of semicircular sandbag walls formed a defensive boundary between the tents and the desert to the east. The sandbag structures faced towards the desert, each with an opening at the rear. The rows of sandbags lay offset from one another, like brickwork. *The curved structure supports itself, and is less prone to topple than a straight wall. That's a clever method. Solid enough for a temporary fortification and good for stopping bullets from many directions.* In places steel plates were built into the sandbag walls, with loopholes cut to shoot through. The distance closed and men appeared, popping up from trenches and emerging from tents. They waved and cheered.

"Where are you from?" one called from the shore.

"Australia," Larry yelled back. "Who are you?"

"India," cried one.

"England," cried another. "Welcome Australians. You will be here with us soon. Come defend the canal with us."

"No way! We're going to France, just stopping at Egypt for a bit on the way."

The eastern bank was lined with defensive emplacements, every 500 yards or so.

"It feels like we are getting close to the war," Jayjay said.

Yes it does, and closer to enemy bullets.

Cheers bounced between ship and shore, punctuated by regular 'Coo-ees' from the *Afric*.

That evening, Ron loitered on the top deck with Jayjay and Larry. Most of the others had hung their hammocks below and turned in. Sounds of the ship were much louder at night. The muffled fffsh-fffsh – fffsh-fffsh of steam pistons maintained a beat and water protested at being pushed aside.

Camps and defence posts along the sandy shore slid by, visible almost as clear as day under the glow of a full moon.

The ship's search lights probed across the sand, playing hide and seek with an invisible enemy. There was human movement at some of the camps, but they were friendlies.

"How about that," said Larry. "The first real contact we have with the war and it's the most peaceful night we've had since leaving Sydney. And not only that, we're sailing across the desert in a ship!"

Jayjay gazed upwards. "The sky is so clear."

"It feels almost like we're on solid ground," Ron said. "It is so calm on the canal."

Larry shook his head and leaned into the balustrade. "I can't wait to get off this damned ship. Do you know it's been 33 days since we walked on dry land… that march in Western Australia?"

"Won't be long now," Ron said, despite feeling the same way. "A few more days and you'll be marching across soft sand cursing and complaining how much you miss the easy life on the seas."

"I wonder if we'll come back here," Larry said, "to defend the canal with these blokes. There doesn't seem to be much happening. It'd be a bugger if we got stuck here until the end of the war and didn't see any action. Imagine that, going home to everyone who knew that the real war was fought in France while we chased shadows in the desert. This is a flaming sideshow."

"They wouldn't do that to us." Jayjay turned to face Larry. "We came to fight the Germans, to defend England, not to sit out here just in case someone attacks a puddle in the desert."

The others don't seem to be feeling the funk like me. I can't say anything about it, I'm older than them and shouldn't be afraid. Maybe they don't think they have much to lose. Why can't I stop thinking about death?

* * *

The *Afric* emerged from the end of the Suez Canal and anchored at Port Said for two days, then ventured out into the Mediterranean Sea. She made the overnight voyage to Alexandria and anchored at the mouth of a branch of the Nile.

Hundreds of little boats swarmed about, with natives hawking their wares from simple craft that they seemed to live on. A mix of sweet and foul smells drifted across the water.

Several captured German merchant ships huddled along the wharves, tied up like obedient prisoners.

The *Afric* lay offshore for two nights, as if to torment those wishing to reach land, then at 8:00 am on Tuesday, 8th of December 1914, she weighed anchor and eased alongside a wharf at Alexandria. The morning dragged on with anticipation. At lunchtime the company commander Captain Swannell addressed his men.

"Our company will disembark tomorrow morning after breakfast. You are all reminded that you are to stay with your Section and not wander off. Remember that you are in a foreign country with native language and customs that are different to what we are used to in a civilized white society. Men breaking formation or leaving their Section without orders will be severely dealt with. Make sure you have your kit ready first thing in the morning, and remember that you will have to carry it."

"Great, another night on the boat," grumbled Larry.

"It's a ship," Ron said.

"Ship, boat, who cares. It's another afternoon stuck here in this sardine tin and another night in a bloody hammock."

Ron grinned. They could only look on as five other companies of the First Infantry Battalion disembarked early that afternoon.

"See you boys at camp," one called waving to the sea of onlookers who remained on board. "We'll try to save some space for you. Feel that ground, it's so *firm.*"

"*Ahhh*, the air smells so fresh out here," called another. "I didn't realise it stank so bad on that ship until I got off it."

* * *

The next morning they were up early. Ron re-checked is kit. His bowie knife was where it should be, wrapped in some clothes at the bottom. His wallet was accessible, some shaving gear, a great coat, a few other clothes and a waterproof sheet.

He pulled the photo of his wife from his breast pocket, as he did each morning. *Maybe I'll have something interesting to write to you about once we have made camp in Egypt. I miss you Em.*

After morning jerks, Ron forced himself to eat a solid breakfast, taking a second helping, but it didn't compete with what Jayjay consumed. *That boy has the appetite of a horse.*

At 9:00 am Ron marched down the gang way with the rest of his company. His boots touched solid earth for the first time since marching at Albany, forty days earlier. *Noah must have felt the same sense of relief when he stepped off the ark.*

Ron hoped for a chance to explore the ancient harbour city, but they were herded like cattle onto a crowded train carriage. The train pulled out and followed a bank of the Nile.

"It must be in flood," Ron said. "Look at all that water."

"Yeah, funny," Jayjay replied. "So close to the desert, all that good farming land."

"They look like gum trees. What are they doing here?"

Sure enough, ranks of eucalypts stood at ease along the railway line.

"Geez, they're a long way from home. At least this is still part of the Empire. They seem happy enough, I wonder how they came to be here."

"Who knows?" Ron said. "This is a strange place. Look at those houses. They're made from mud bricks, like the Israelites had to make when they were slaves in Egypt thousands of years ago, and they keep chickens on the roof."

"Look there," Larry pointed. "That native's going into his house with his family… and a camel!"

The train ride from Alexandria continued all day and rolled on into the night.

Next to Ron, Jayjay slept in his seat.

"The poor little fella's tired," Larry said.

The poor little fella is six foot, four inches tall, built like an ox and doesn't have a care in the world. Lucky sod.

CHAPTER 21

Jayjay

Wednesday, 9 December 1914

"Wake up Jay, we're getting off."

An orange glow penetrated the darkness.

Where am I? Moving, slowing down – stopped, legs jammed in place. Ron is shoving me. We're on a train.

"Are we at Cairo?" Jayjay groaned. "What time is it?"

"Nearly midnight and yes."

That sleep made me feel worse. I should've stayed awake.

"Good, let's get out of here." Jayjay tried to stand but there was no space to move.

Train doors flew open and men spilled out onto the platform. Jayjay stretched his legs and joined the human flow into the cool night air.

On a gravel road beside the platform, a small crew manned a table piled with bread rolls and a large pot. The crew's spokesman called out once and that was enough to start the migration of the crowd towards his table.

Jayjay shuffled along with the mob. He filed passed the table, received a roll with cheese and a mug of hot cocoa, and wolfed them down. *I should've chewed slower. I wonder if I might snaffle another roll?*

"Form up and move out!" Sergeant Baker's voice cut into the night.

They marched away from the station, without any second helpings, and crunched across a surface that felt to be a mixture of gravel and sand. *Strange that it's so cold, I thought the desert was supposed to be hot, or at least warm.*

The marching column approached a line of electric trams and an order of "Halt" was passed down the line. Officers of the First Battalion scurried about.

"There go the Irish Uh-Ohs." Larry whispered.

The three Irish gamblers skulked off into the shadows while no officers were paying attention. *They're off to take some French leave no doubt.*

Several minutes passed, then Sergeant Baker returned and herded the platoon onto one of the trams and the tram started moving. The triangular outlines of two pyramids loomed in the haze beneath the light of a half-moon and seemed to follow along with the tram. *They must be big.*

The tram rolled on for a couple of miles, and stopped in front of a large stone building.

"All out and form up," Sergeant Baker called. "We will march into Mena Camp where all twelve Australian battalions are to be based. We will sleep there tonight. Look alive man!"

Hopefully it's not far. I'm running out of steam. At least a camp is already established.

They marched across soft sand for half a mile. A handful of bell tents lined the edge of camp, but there were no tents in the area designated for the First Battalion. Men from the first companies to leave the *Afric* lay scattered under the stars.

"Where are the tents for the rest of us?" someone asked the question that Jayjay was thinking.

No answer. Men started to drop their kit on the sand and lie down.

Jayjay checked his watch – 1:30 am.

"I guess this is it boys," Larry said. "At least this sand's soft, no need to dig a hip hole, and it's nice and flat, not like a hammock. I can sleep on my side tonight."

In the sky above, the moon and stars shone bright. *No sign of rain. It'd be too much effort to pitch a tent now anyway.*

He pulled the waterproof sheet from his kit bag. "We may as well lie on this, and keep the sand out of our clothes."

Jayjay, Ron and Larry unpacked their overcoats, wrapped themselves against the cold and lay on the waterproof sheet. Jayjay pulled the collar up around his neck, too tired to feel uncomfortable.

He was walking to the sawmill, cold, winter. Grey dawn marked the beginning of the night's end. His breath was visible under the new electric streetlamps. Something was wrong, no trousers. He didn't have time to go home and dress, it wouldn't do to be late for work, not with people being laid off. He was at work, no trousers. The foreman smiled in sympathy 'Sorry mate, I'd like to keep you on, but you can't work here without trousers.'

Jayjay's workmates were all properly dressed, they stared at him. He covered himself in embarrassment. He turned to run, but his legs wouldn't move. *Why won't my legs move? They're so cold. So cold –.*

His legs kicked out and jolted him awake. *So cold.*

"Well, I guess you can't sleep either" Ron said quietly.

"This is ridiculous," Larry whispered "it's so frigid cold out here."

The moon had moved some distance across the sky since they lay down. *I must have slept for a few hours.* Jayjay uncovered his watch to expose the luminous hands.

"Four o'clock. It'll start to get light soon. Let's just move together and try to keep warm."

The sound of Larry breaking wind was amplified by the quietness of the night. "I thought that might help us to keep warm."

"Righto bugle bum, it's not reveille yet."

The wait until dawn felt like an eternity. At the first hint of light the groans and swearing began, and men rose to find an empty patch of sand to piss on.

"It'll be a while yet before everyone gets organised," Larry Said "Let's go over and explore those pyramids before Sergeant Fishface comes to spoil the fun."

Others were already wandering off towards the pyramids, a few hundred yards away. *We don't have any orders to stay here. Not exactly, and we did miss out on exploring Alexandria, after having watched it from the ship for three days.* "Yeah, let's go, might warm us up a bit."

The pyramids looked closer than they were and grew out of all proportion as the distance closed. Young natives appeared as if from the sand, or the pyramid itself. Jayjay pulled his overcoat around himself. "The little beggars must be freezing out here."

"Mister, Sir, Mister, see pyramid, climb pyramid, come, come," one said.

"Sure, let's go" Jayjay scrambled up the face of the pyramid after him, his legs still stiff from the cold. The boy was surprisingly quick, surging ahead, then pausing to wait.

The desert floor dropped away below, but the top didn't seem to get any closer. *At least I'm warming up.*

After several minutes of climbing they reached the peak. Jayjay was blowing hard and starting to sweat. A few other Australians were carving their names into the stone with pocket knives. Jayjay stopped with Ron and Larry a few stone blocks short of the top and found one to sit on. To the right, miniature soldiers in Mena Camp busied themselves like ants. To the left the Nile River ran silver.

"That's not a bad view before breakfast." Jayjay said.

Ron shook his head "I never thought I'd climb a pyramid and see the sun rise over the Nile. It's amazing."

"Two shillings mister." Jayjay turned to see the native boy holding out his hand towards Jayjay with a broad grin.

"What?"

"Two shillings."

"What for?"

"I show you pyramid, two shillings cost."

Jayjay hesitated.

"Nice try mate, no shillings. I didn't need you to show me the pyramid. It's here for all to see, plain as day."

"Two shillings or I get police, big trouble if you no pay. You agreed."

Heat rose in Jayjay's neck. It didn't help that Ron, Larry and several strangers were barely suppressing open laughter. He reached for his wallet at pulled out two shillings. "This is robbery! You never said it'd cost anything. Two shillings is steeper than this pyramid, now clear off before I think better of it."

The boy took the coins, and turned to Ron. "Two shillings."

"Well aren't you a brazen little thing. You're not doing your people any favours you know." Ron reached into his pocket and pulled out two coins for the boy.

The boy looked to Larry as if seizing up his chances of a third payout. Larry saved him the trouble. "Piss off before I throw you off."

"I get police."

"Not if you're dead you won't." Larry moved as it to stand up and the kid took off like a rat in the ship's galley.

"The little sod," Ron said with a smile. "They told us we were coming here for training, I guess that's the first lesson."

The native boy flew down the giant steps. *He must have been up and down hundreds of times.*

"We better get back to camp," Larry said. "Before we're labelled as deserters."

"Or worse," Jayjay said, "We might miss breakfast."

"But first, I want to leave my name here at the top of the pyramid." Larry pulled out a pocket knife and started work.

"Where' you boys from?" It was one of the others at the peak who had watched the exchange with the native. He had finished carving his name and looked down from a couple of blocks above.

"Sydney," Jayjay replied. "First Infantry Battalion, how 'bout you?"

"Ballarat, Eighth Battalion. You got to watch them bloody natives. They'll take everything you got if you don't watch out. The kids are just as bad as the rest of 'em. They're as cunning as shithouse rats." He climbed down to the same level as Jayjay and held out a hand. "I'm Reginald, call me Reg."

"Jonathan, call me Jayjay." They shook hands. "It was pretty cold last night, was it your first night here?"

"Nah, it was our second night, but the first was just as cold. There's not enough tents for everyone. Even if there were, it's blankets we need."

Jayjay shook his head. "This war doesn't seem to be very well organised. I hope they get things together before we go to the front."

"You mean if we ever go to the front."

"Of course we're going to the front, they didn't bring us all this way just so we could climb a pyramid and enjoy the view. Didn't you get the same message as us – 'we're to train in Egypt and proceed to the front from there.'"

"I reckon that's a bit of a furphy."

"A what?"

"A furphy. A false rumour. At Broadmeadows Camp near Melbourne, we had these carts that come to empty the latrines and they all had the name "Furphy" written across the back."

"So?"

"So," Larry interjected, "Your new friend is trying to tell you that you're full of shit."

"Well," Reg said. "More so the commanding officers who gave us the message, but pretty much that's the idea. I heard we might be sent out to guard the canal from the Turks. Both can't be true. One must be a furphy."

Ron handed the pocket knife to Jayjay and he scratched 'JJ – 1914' in the stone, next to a worn but neatly carved 'Phillipe 1801'.

"Done. Let's get back before we miss breakfast."

They scrambled down, and at the base of the great pyramid, natives swarmed like flies around a fresh dump from a large dog.

"Coffee mister? Coffee?"

"No. How much?"

"Four piastres."

"No. What's a piastre? No."

"Ancient coin, five shillings, true ancient."

"No."

"No."

"No!"

The natives pursued them to the edge of Mena Camp, but then turned back towards the pyramids. *I thought they'd never leave us alone.*

At the First Battalion camping area they blended back in with their Platoon without challenge. No one seemed to know or care that they had wandered off.

"Blankets!" Sergeant Baker called. "Four per man. Come and collect your blanket issue. Then we'll have some breakfast."

"Better late than never I suppose." Larry said.

Thank you God.

* * *

Three days later, the reveille bugle sounded 'wake-up' at 6:00 am after another clear night. The sun's rays warmed Jayjay's face. *My head only just hit the pillow. Not much of a pillow – boots wrapped in a shirt. Still, I must have slept well enough. Another day of training at the Valley of Despair.*

He shook drops of dew off his waterproof sheet, rolled his blankets and brushed the sand off his clothes.

After breakfast he pulled on a pack full of kit, fell in with his platoon and marched with the First Battalion across four miles of soft sand, his boots sinking to the ankles with each step. The marching column stopped at the battalion training area. The sun burned from above and his legs burned from within. He threw his pack to the ground and dropped to the sand for a ten-minute spell before the battalion was split into companies for drill.

The temperature climbed with the sun in the sky. He stood in one line facing off against another, advanced in feigned attack, then retired. Sweat poured into his clothes, but evaporated before it could drip to the sand. He marched, skirmished, bayoneted and drilled some more.

A moment of respite came when the Company was called to be addressed by its Commanding Officer, Captain Swannell. Jayjay squatted in the sun with the others and sucked in the dry air while half listening to instruction before doing it all again.

Lunch, at last, an hour to rest. Some shade would be nice. A dry bread roll and a tin of sardines to share between two. At least there's water to drink, even if it is rationed like everything else.

Afternoon drill blurred like the desert horizon. Three hours taken one step at a time, he could not think any further ahead or reflect back. He completed the final exercise for the afternoon and his body threatened to collapse.

"Collect your packs," Sergeant Baker cried. "Fall in with the other companies. Prepare to return to First Battalion Parade Ground."

Once formed up, they started on the four-mile trek back to Mena camp. Most of the way back was filled with skirmish training. One line of men would run ahead and take a position, then another line charged in attack. *A simple march across the soft sand wouldn't be so bad after all.*

The battalion trudged the final few hundred yards into Mena camp and the waiting band struck up with the French anthem 'Marseillaise' to bring them home. Despite fatigue, Jayjay walked taller and picked up the pace with those around him. Somehow the music dragged out his last reserves of strength.

It only took a moment of rest for Jayjay to know that he was famished. He ate his fill of the sand-soaked stew – bully beef and over-boiled potatoes, cooked over a trench in the open. Afterwards he had a wash, changed into clean, dry clothes, washed the day's clothes and had a brief lie down before night operations. The food in his stomach called on him to sleep, but he talked to the others to keep himself awake.

During night operations the air was cool, the moon was out and he didn't have to carry a heavy pack. Everyone, including the officers had just had a meal and there seemed to be an understanding that they could take it a little slower when skirmishing at night. When the training session was complete, the men walked back to camp in silence.

Jayjay wrapped his boots in a shirt, crawled under his blankets and covered himself with his waterproof sheet at 11:00pm. He rested his head on the boots – he was at Sunday School, learning the Ten Commandments. It was one of his earliest memories. 'Thou shalt not kill' was number six. Of the ten, this was the one that he always thought would be easy to keep. His teacher, Mrs Davies smiled and nodded.

Now he gripped his Lee-Enfield rifle and thrust the bayonet into a defenceless sandbag. He pulled his weapon back, life-sand drained out onto the ground and the bag slumped. Mrs Davies looked down upon him with the same disapproving gaze she wore when he misbehaved during song time. Suddenly she had a bugle at her lips and she was blowing reveille with a gusto that was most out of character *– no it can't be bloody morning already.*

CHAPTER 22

Dacre

Tuesday, 15 December 1914

An Irishman walked into a bar.

He admitted to himself that the Australia Hotel was a reasonable piece of architecture, maybe worthy of the claim to be the finest hotel in the new nation. On the corner of Castlereagh Street and Martin Place, the hotel stood in the heart of Sydney. *I doubt that there's much to compete with it in this primitive country down under. I cannot understand why these Australians are so patriotic, and the obsession of Sydney folk with 'Their Harbour' is ludicrous, as if they are entitled to praise for God's handiwork.*

Dacre hoped to keep his distance from the crowds of khaki-clad gentry refreshing themselves after an arduous day's training. He threaded his way through the Australian soldiers and found himself a seat alone at the end of the lounge bar.

"A whiskey, if I may." Dacre addressed the haughty-eyed mistress who presided over the bar. "No, not that one. Irish whiskey please, with ice. Thank you, ever so much my dear."

He took a strengthening draft and swirled the ice in his glass slowly, until it disappeared.

It is strange to experience weather so hot, this close to Christmas.

"Now, you're a likely looking chap! Why don't ya' volunteer?"

Dacre looked up, disappointed that the fellow was looking straight at him. Dacre stared back without answering. The fellow wore the uniform of a private in the Australian infantry looked to have volunteered within the last few days, as he showed no signs of military discipline.

"Why don't ya' volunteer?" The Australian repeated in a strong accent, running each word into the next.

"Why should I?" Dacre replied.

"The King and Empire are calling Mate! They need us to go and help fight the Germans. So why don't ya' volunteer?"

"Oh well," Dacre hesitated, seeking an excuse. "I think I am not tall enough."

"Not a bit of it. We have many chaps just as small as you."

Dacre swallowed a smile, as the fellow himself stood shorter than Dacre.

"But I don't think I'd like to be a soldier, it must be awfully uncomfortable in the trenches. Besides, it must be so dangerous."

The Australian, after being momentarily lost for words, addressed the bar-mistress. "Have you ever heard anything like it?"

"But," Dacre said. "Surely it's true. You must know – you're a soldier."

"Bah," spat the bar-mistress from behind her ample bosom. "Bah! Some of you things that calls yourself men makes me sick!"

"After all," Dacre said. "There must be many men who ought to go to the trenches before me."

"Why?" demanded the Australian soldier. "Why should there be? Every man is wanted, you just as much as anyone."

"No, I'm afraid I can't agree with you. What about my job – what is going to happen to that?"

"People can't think about their jobs." The Australian's cheeks glowed pink and his rant had grown into a yell which attracted more interest than Dacre would have liked. "Suppose everyone put their own private business before the country's affairs – what then?"

"Well," Dacre said quietly. "Look here, I'll tell you how it really is. I wouldn't mind becoming a soldier a bit, but I'm afraid of the bosses in my business. I don't think they'd be pleased if I ran away."

"That's all right," said the Australian. "We can easily fix that up for you. Employers aren't allowed to stand in the way like that. You tell me who your employers are, and I'll see about having them spoken to."

Dacre placed his empty glass slowly on the counter. "I'll make a bargain with you. If you will get me out of my present job, I will promise to volunteer."

"What's your job?" The Australian made ready to write it down.

"Well," Dacre said in the utmost English drawl he could produce. "I happen to be the captain of the only submarine that is at the present moment in the southern hemisphere."

"Lor!" said the bar-mistress.

The Australian private looked speechless and Dacre continued. "There were two of us, you know, but in the recent operations up north the other submarine was lost with all hands – you probably saw all about it in the papers."

Dacre continued to chat and enjoyed watching the face of the Australian as he digested the situation.

"Will you let me have the honour of shaking your hand?" Asked the Australian private when his powers of speech returned.

At that, Dacre felt a pang of guilt for his prank and insisted on buying the Australian another drink. *After all, the fellow probably had undergone a very arduous day's training.*

At the same time, Dacre was disappointed that the haughty-eye of the bar-mistress remained cold towards him. In his younger days, as a midshipman, philandering his way about the Mediterranean with the Royal Navy, Dacre rarely failed to raise a twinkle in a female eye when he set his mind to the task with a warm smile and tales of derring-do.

* * *

A week later, Lieutenant-Commander Henry Hugh Gordon Dacre Stoker captained the Australian E-Class Submarine *AE2* out through Sydney Heads, under tow by the transport ship A35 *Berrima.* Since childhood, he had been known as Dacre, a name he shared with his wealthy godfather.

Seven months had passed since he and his crew guided the *AE2* into Sydney Harbour for the first time, with twin-sister submarine *AE1,* concluding an eighty-three-day delivery voyage from Portsmouth, England.

Much water had passed under her bows since that cold Sydney morning of May 1914. Dawn on Empire Day it was, 24 May, the day Australians celebrate the fact that they remain part of the mighty British Empire with singing in the streets of 'Rule Britannia' and 'Land of Hope and Glory'.

Two months after the submarines docked at Garden Island Naval Base in Sydney Harbour for the first time, Britain declared war on Germany.

Before the first convoy the Australian Expeditionary Force left Australian shores from King George Sound, the two submarines *AE1* and *AE2* participated in the young Australian Navy's first wartime operations in re-claiming German New Guinea territories for the British Empire. The German Pacific Squadron under Admiral Graf von Spee was reported to be operating in the German South Pacific Colonies, with two cruisers suspected to be harbouring at Rabaul on the island of New Britain.

Rabaul Harbour was found to be clear of enemy ships, and the colony was reclaimed for the British Empire. On arrival, a destroyer and submarine *AE2* patrolled the narrow St George's Strait between New Britain and New Ireland, scouting for enemy ships, but none were seen. Next day, submarine *AE1* and destroyer *Parramatta* patrolled the strait. At the end of the day, Parramatta returned alone having been separated from the submarine.

A garrison force was landed and Australian flags hoisted in place of German flags, but hopes that he *AE1* would return to Rabaul faded the following day. Much to Dacre's dismay, the *AE1* disappeared without explanation and was never seen again despite several days of searching. She was presumed lost with all hands. Each submarine was crewed by thirty-two men, a mixture of Australian trainees and experienced British submariners, all volunteers who earned every shilling of their danger-pay. The submarine crews were well-known to each other and Dacre lost many friends that day, including one close and long-time friend, the submarine's First Officer Lieutenant Leopold Scarlett who he had served with at Gibraltar.

After returning via Fiji with only the ghosts of the *AE1*, Dacre and the crew of the *AE2* faced the prospect of being stranded on the wrong side of the world and unable to join the war effort. Not satisfied with trawling about in Sydney Harbour, Dacre caught a train to Melbourne, and approached the Australian Minister for Defence, Senator Pearce, with the suggestion that *AE2* should be offered to serve with the British Admiralty.

The offer was made and the Admiralty accepted "with many thanks".

The first submarine to sail from England to the 180th degree of longitude, and so travel half way around the world, the *AE2* pushed through the waves in anticipation of retracing her maiden voyage from England.

Now the weather was warm again and Dacre sailed the *AE2* beyond Sydney Heads, towards her next adventure.

CHAPTER 23

John

Friday, 1 January 1915

"Send the signal."

Colonel John Monash glanced at the wall-clock on the bridge of His Majesty's Transport A38 *Ulysses*. The hands read five minutes to eleven o'clock as he knew they would, having checked it immediately before giving the order.

"Yes Sir."

"Yes Sir."

A signalman tapped away at shuttered electric lamp, sending the Morse Code sequence to the column of ships on the port side. Another signalman flashed the same message to the starboard column. The signal would be repeated down the columns, reaching every one of the sixteen other transport ships in less than one minute.

With the German cruiser *Emden* destroyed, the Indian Ocean was clear of known enemy ships, but John would be taking no risks with radio communication when it could be avoided.

"Lieutenant-Colonel Courtney," John said calmly. "Have our men stand to attention."

"Yes Sir." Richard Courtney hurried out and John heard his order being relayed down the decks, and amplified by the voices of sergeants along the way.

John strolled to a location where he could see to the stern of *Ulysses*. The 13th and 14 Battalions covered the top deck. Two thousand men stood to attention, facing the port side.

Following *Ulysses*, in the centre column, sailed another four Australian transport ships, the first of these a mile back. John could see the ship clear enough, but not the men on her deck about to receive an order to stand to attention. Other ships in the centre column sat like miniature painted ships beside the first.

To the starboard side, a mile of dark blue water lay between *Ulysses* and the head of the right column. John counted the five Australian transport ships in a line, each leaving a dark trail of smoke in the windless sky.

Ahead of the command ship *Ulysses*, Australian transport ship *Berrima* lead the fleet across the Indian Ocean. *Berrima* boasted small deck-mounted guns retrofitted at Cockatoo Dockyards in Sydney, and towed behind her the sole remaining Australian E-Class submarine, the *AE2*. The submarine and *Berrima's* deck-guns were the only defences available to the convoy in the event of attack, other than small arms in the thousands.

Hopefully our intelligence is good and no enemy ships will trouble us. Our guns are small calibre with short range and the submarine will have to sneak up close to an enemy ship to aim a torpedo. If the enemy has big guns, they will smash us from a distance. The little submarine is of limited use on the open ocean, I doubt she will have much influence over our fate. One enemy man-of-war would be enough to send us all down to a watery grave.

To the port side, another mile of blue separated *Ulysses* from the head of the left column made up of three Australian transports followed by three New Zealand transports.

John checked the bridge clock again. It read one minute to eleven o'clock. Thirteen thousand men had been standing to attention for about three minutes.

"Send the next signal," John ordered. "All ships to stop all engines."

"Yes Sir."

"Yes Sir."

Signalmen tapped away at the shuttered lamps.

"Captain, stop our engines," John said.

"Yes Colonel."

The captain called instructions into voice tubes and vibrations from *Ulysses'* triple expansion steam engines faded to nothing.

Momentum carried *Ulysses* forward in silence across the calm water, deceleration imperceptible.

Men on deck stood to attention in silence, facing towards a burial service they could not see, for a soldier they did not know. The young fellow had died of Typhoid three hours earlier. The first death at sea, barely twenty-four hours after leaving Australian shores. It would not be the last. Death was an inevitable reality when travelling in such large numbers in close quarters, but John saw the opportunity to remind the men of the serious nature of the expedition and respect for order.

A ship's bell tolled from Australian Transport A30 *Borda*, in the left column. She was nearly three miles away, but the sound carried true over the water. *Likely everyone in the convoy could hear it. That bell marks the death of one soldier and the end of chaos on my watch. A new year's resolution.*

During the three-day stop at King George Sound, off Albany before leaving Australia, it had seemed that everything that could go wrong did go wrong. The final sorting of stores and personnel was a muddle of confusion, communication between ships was near impossible and the tug masters went on strike after refusing to guide ships to their buoys after dark. Two hundred cases of food poisoning on *Ulysses* completed the perfect shemozzle.

Finally, at eight o'clock in the morning of 31 December, the convoy slithered from King George Sound in a snake of floating humanity over twenty miles long, with the tail out of sight from the head. To improve visual communication the fleet reformed into three columns and now occupied a patch of ocean two miles wide by six miles long, all within sight of each other.

John had calculated the cost to the Australian Government of running the fleet, including ship hire, coal, food and other miscellaneous items, to be around eight pounds per minute. In addition, there was the men's pay.

The men have to be paid regardless of what they are doing. Discipline and patience will serve them well when they need it most. We just invested eighty pounds and it was money well spent.

As a Jew and first generation Australian with German heritage, John had experienced plenty of opposition in Australia to his appointment as commander of the 4th Brigade. A successful engineer and businessman, John had always held more than a passing fascination with military command. Before war was declared he was not regular army, but as a citizen soldier he attained the rank of full colonel in the Australian militia. The prospect of leading men into battle tantalized his inner urges like a voluptuous woman with a come-get-me smile.

As the most senior brigadier, John enjoyed command of the second Australian convoy. Now he would have his chance to show his critics his capability, and where his true loyalty lay.

In the distance, a volley of rifle fire announced the end of the burial service for the young soldier from Brisbane. His lifeless body was now sinking to the bottom of the Indian Ocean. The minute hand on the bridge clock ticked to five minutes past eleven.

"Send the signal to all ships: 'proceed at full speed ahead, men to stand down.'"

"Yes Sir."

"Yes Sir."

"Captain," John said. "Proceed at full speed."

"Yes Colonel Monash."

"Lieutenant Courtney," John said. "Have our men stand down and resume normal activities."

"Yes Sir."

Steam throttle valves were opened and the pistons of the steam engine surged to life. Familiar vibrations pulsed through the hull and within minutes *Ulysses* was steaming ahead. The whole fleet resumed the formation march across the ocean.

Order, good planning and targeted use of technology were the key elements of success in modern warfare. To John, war posed an engineering challenge, like the construction of a bridge. When he built the Anderson Street bridge over the Yarra River in Melbourne, John took a risk building the first major structure in Australia to use concrete reinforced with iron bars. The new technology was developed and patented by Joseph Monier, a French gardener who had developed the method to strengthen clay pots for his plants. John read about the method in a German journal and was immediately attracted to the benefits of the idea. His engineering brain understood how the iron took the tensile strain and the concrete took compressive strain, allowing the necessary strength to be achieved in a much lighter structure than required if using stone or unreinforced concrete. Many conservative engineers had criticised his method and a crowd came to see if the three-span bridge would fail under the test of a fifteen-ton steamroller. John walked next to the roller with confidence, but was relieved when the test was completed and no cracks appeared in his bridge.

Always fascinated by the theory and practice of war, John had read all the military literature he could lay his hands on. From the ancient text 'The Art of War' written by Chinese military strategist Sun Tsu in the fifth century B.C. to 'Port Arthur – The Siege and Capitulation', one of John's favourite accounts of modern warfare. In this book, British war correspondent Ellis Ashmead-Bartlett gave a detailed eye-witness account of the tactical errors and lessons about the use of twentieth century war technology and the failures of obsolete formations in attack. Frontal assaults against well defended positions resulted in mass carnage and a lack of medical attention to the wounded resulted in painful death for many who might have been saved.

New tactics were required to use men in conjunction with modern war technology like howitzers, machine guns, bolt action magazine rifles, barbed wire, arc lamp searchlights, hand grenades and wireless radio signalling.

As Ellis Ashmead-Bartlett concluded – we have probably witnessed those old-fashioned methods for the last time. No other nation will repeat the Japanese experiment of 1904, having learned the effect of artillery and machine guns on large numbers of charging men.

John surveyed the formation of ships as they steamed across the ocean towards the enemy, responsive to his orders as to course, formation and speed. *We must help the Empire crush a peril which may mean the end of Australia as a free country.*

Oh, to be entrusted by one's country with so magnificent a responsibility. This is something to have lived for.

CHAPTER 24

Winston

Saturday, 2 January1915

Winston sat waiting and sucked on a Cuban cigar. The black dog of depression rarely left his side of late and smoking was one of the few pleasures remaining in his life.

The English newspapers called for his head with renewed vigour each day. The loss in November of Rear-Admiral Cradock's squadron to the German cruisers *Scharnhorst* and *Gneisenau,* off the Pacific coast of South America, was the latest disaster. The death of 1,600 British seamen could not be swept under the carpet. Yet again the blame came back to him as First Lord of the Admiralty. *I am a civilian and an elected politician, so of course the newspapers feel free to give me a good caning each morning. Damn the German navy and its impertinence.*

Retribution against the *Scharnhorst* and *Gneisenau* had come, but Winston received none of the credit for the savage naval counter attack that was ordered by the First Sea Lord, John "Jacky" Fisher. Having been dragged out of retirement at seventy-three years of age and reinstated as Britain's most senior naval officer, he had taken the initiative and sent two battlecruisers *Invincible* and *Inflexible* to the South Atlantic where they destroyed and sunk the two German cruisers off the Falkland Islands in December. The press praised Fisher for his great naval victory. Over two thousand German sailors lost their lives that day, but what upset Winston was the unfairness that he was being held accountable for all of the British naval losses, but not being given credit for any of its achievements. *Somehow I need to attach my name to a memorable naval victory.*

Winston's right heel hovered above the floor. His knee bounced up and down. *There must be an important development for Kitchener to call a meeting with just the two of us at short notice.* The Cabinet War Council met regularly and provided the official forum for war strategy discussions and decisions, but smaller side discussions were often where the real decisions were made.

"Lord Kitchener is ready to see you now sir," announced an aide to the Secretary of State for War.

Winston rose and was ushered into Lord Kitchener's office.

"Ah, Mister Churchill, please have a seat," offered Lord Kitchener.

"Thank you sir." Winston sat and drew a deep breath through his cigar.

"Russia has requested our help, and I think this will be of interest to you. This morning, the Foreign Office has passed on a request to me from Grand Duke Nicholas. The commander of the Russian army is asking me to mount a naval or military demonstration to draw Ottoman forces away from the Caucasus Mountains where they are harrying his troops."

Winston's heart began to race. *This is the moment that I've been waiting for.*

"I see." He paused to encourage Kitchener to reveal further information and forced the muscles in his face to relax. *I mustn't seem too eager.*

"We have no troops to spare. The western front is our main concern. It is deadlocked and we cannot afford to starve it of resources. If we cannot hold the western front, all is lost."

"Yes, of course" Winston replied.

"And yet, we need Russia to remain committed to the war. She is keeping Germany occupied on the Eastern front, and if she makes peace we are doomed. Hundreds of thousands of battle-hardened Germans would come streaming across to the Western Front and we would be done for. There could be up to half a million of them for heaven's sake."

Kitchener shook his head and paused.

Winston nodded and forced himself to remain silent.

"Our agreement with Russia and France is not even a formal alliance," Kitchener continued. "All we have is an understanding that none of us will conclude a separate peace with Germany. Somehow we have to make the Grand Duke believe that it remains in Russia's best interests to hold to the agreement. If he decides it's time to walk away there is nothing we can do to do stop him."

This was a conundrum they had kicked around at War Council meetings on numerous occasions. The Russian alliance was a delicate thing to be handled with care. The worst-case scenario was that the Russians abandon the agreement and make peace with Germany. However, a close second would be that Germany was crushed and Russia was left holding the balance of power in Europe. A weakening of both empires suited Britain's interests best.

Kitchener thrust his top lip forward and his moustache bristled like a waking beast.

"Sir Edward Grey has promised the Russians Constantinople and the Dardanelles to keep them loyal to the cause. But this might not be enough, in fact it could backfire if Grand Duke Nicholas wants the city and southern shipping access too much. He may be willing to give some ground and walk away from the Eastern front if he can make peace with the Germans and focus on annexing Ottoman territory. The Ottomans are weakened and vulnerable right now and the Grand Duke knows it. We have to keep him focused on the Eastern Front and not let him be distracted to the south. He has asked for our help and we have to make him believe we will do everything we can to deliver him Constantinople and the Dardanelles on a silver platter."

Kitchener paused and shook his head before continuing.

"I don't know what those Young Turks were thinking, throwing their lot in with the Germans and tormenting Russia so. First, they sent their navy to shoot up the Russian ports on the Black Sea, and now they have opened up a war front in the Caucasus Mountains. In the middle of winter of all times, mind you. Damned foolishness. They are a third-rate oriental power from a bygone era, clinging to the memory of grandeur. I think they need to be taught a lesson in modern warfare."

Kitchener leaned forward and pointed a finger at Winston in a pose reminiscent of the war recruitment posters depicting Kitchener announcing 'Your country needs you'.

"You have been arguing for a naval attack on the Dardanelles for some time. Two months ago, your warships gave the Turks a tickle and they didn't put up much resistance, but now it might be time for a more serious expedition. I need to know what you can do without an army on the ground."

Winston drew on his cigar and considered his response. *Everyone defers to Kitchener when it's time to make a strategic decision in the war, but this is the moment for which future generations will remember me.*

"I agree," Winston spoke slowly. "You must reply immediately to the Grand Duke, and let him know that we will provide his demonstration. His request is vague and we do not need to provide him with operational details. Meanwhile, I will make some enquiries with the Admiralty and Mediterranean Fleet as to what we can do and when."

"I will send the reply, but you do understand that this will have to be a naval operation only. Military troop support will not be available."

"Of course." Winston stood to leave.

On returning to Admiralty House, Winston poured himself a whiskey, lit up a fresh Cuban and settled into the leather lounge chair where he did his best thinking.

Jacky Fisher is the problem. Not only did he steal my glory for sinking the German ships in the South Atlantic, he doesn't like my plan to take the Dardanelles with ships alone. The old salt is too conservative and can't see the big picture. He lacks the aggressive instincts that should be ingrained in a wartime officer. The risks of inaction outweigh the risks of action here. It's a nuisance that he commands the Navy. If only I could simply bypass him.

Winston jumped up, strode to his desk and reached for a pen and ink. He composed two messages while the idea was fresh.

The first was a telegram to Vice-Admiral Sackville Carden, Commander of the British Mediterranean Fleet. The second message was to Admiral Sir Henry Jackson at the Admiralty in London, the Chief Planning Officer for the Mediterranean. The essence of each message was the same, requesting the recipient to provide urgent advice on the feasibility of a naval assault on the Dardanelles, by ships alone. He stressed that the importance of the results would justify severe loss.

No need to trouble Fisher with this. He has already made his views clear, insisting that troop support would be required to silence the land guns. I cannot afford a protracted argument. It's not strictly in accordance with protocol for me to write directly to his Admirals, but time is of the essence and I need urgent responses. I'm a Cabinet Member of the British Parliament and part of the War Council. We have a mandate to make decisions for and on behalf of the people of England. It is right and proper, in a democracy at war, that the elected government should make strategic decisions based on first-hand information.

* * *

Two days later, Winston received replies to his two telegrams.

Vice-Admiral Carden replied:

`I do not think that the Dardanelles can be rushed, but they might be forced by extended operations with a large number of ships.`

Admiral Jackson provided a five-page memorandum opposing the whole idea, stating that naval penetration to the Sea of Marmara would not be practical until the Gallipoli peninsula was held by allied troops, or every enemy gun on both sides of the Dardanelles was destroyed.

Not what I was hoping for. Maybe he's been talking to Fisher? Why is the Admiralty always so cautious? At least Carden didn't reject the idea outright.

The next day, Winston framed a reply telegram to Vice-Admiral Carden at the Mediterranean fleet. Again, he bypassed the official chain of communication and did not consult with First Sea Lord Fisher or Admiral Jackson before sending the following message to Carden.

"Your view is agreed by high authorities here. Please telegraph in detail what you think could be done by extended operations, what force would be needed, and how you consider it should be used."

* * *

A week later on Wednesday 13th January 1915, the Cabinet War Council was due to meet, giving Winston his first opportunity to put forward the proposition to force the Dardanelles by ships alone.

Winston's first priority was to silence the conservative naval views about the need for troop support to force the Dardanelles. Fisher was the main concern here. He had shown some interest in the naval mission as a simple "demonstration" from a distance. He had even volunteered the new *Queen Elizabeth* super-dreadnought class battleship to join in to test out her fifteen-inch guns, pounding the ancient stone forts from safely out of range. The guns had not yet been fired in anger and had to be tested somewhere. However, when Winston suggested that the ships blast their way through the Dardanelles on a conquest to take Constantinople, Fisher was adamant that significant military support would be required in the form of troops on the ground.

"The enemy's land-based guns have to be silenced and the sea mines have to be cleared!" Fisher had said.

"The flat trajectory of the warship guns is not suitable for such a mission against land-based targets!" Fisher had said.

Unfortunately, Fisher is too old and too negative. Of course there are risks, this is war.

Others in the Admiralty shared Fisher's views, but they would not be present at the Cabinet War Council. Winston would not mention the five-page memo from Admiral Jackson which outlined his reasons why significant military support would be required. Fisher was required to sit in on the Cabinet War Council to represent the Royal Navy. However, he was officially there only as a technical expert and not an elected Cabinet member, so Winston made it clear to him that he was not to speak out unless he was directly asked a question. *It should be straight forward to ensure he isn't questioned. So far Fisher has been willing to bite his tongue, but this meeting will test his loyalties.*

* * *

At the meeting of the Cabinet War Council, Winston focused the full force of his negotiating charm on the key the decision makers: Prime Minister Herbert Asquith, Secretary of State for War, Lord Herbert Kitchener, and Foreign Secretary, Sir Edward Grey.

Winston put forward the proposal for a naval assault on the Dardanelles and emphasised that troop support was neither needed nor wanted.

Lord Kitchener stated his position that troops could absolutely not be spared from the western front, but gave his full support to the proposed naval operation.

"This will provide the demonstration that we promised to the Grand Duke, and if satisfactory progress is not made, or unexpected difficulties are encountered, then the attack can be broken off."

The other War Councillors, on seeing Kitchener's support, fell into line to endorse the idea in principle.

"We are still planning the operational details to determine the size of the naval force required," Winston Concluded.

Discussion moved on to other matters, and Winston smiled inwardly. The cloud of his depression started to lift for the first time in weeks. His proposal was effectively approved. He did not look at Fisher, not wanting to draw attention to the fact that the most senior naval officer would be fuming. *At least the old salt kept his mouth shut.*

* * *

Two days later, Winston sent a telegram to the Commander of the Mediterranean fleet, Vice-Admiral Carden, headed "Secret and Personal from the First Lord of the Admiralty." Again, he bypassed the most senior naval officer, First Sea Lord Jacky Fisher, and advised:

"Your scheme was laid by the First Sea Lord and myself before the Cabinet War Council yesterday and was approved in principle. We see no difficulty in providing the forces you require. We propose to entrust this operation to you. The sooner we can begin the better."

* * *

The next meeting of the Cabinet War Council was held two weeks later on Thursday 28th January. Winston sought formal sanction of his proposal.

He mentioned the new *Queen Elizabeth* with her fifteen-inch guns, the most powerful naval guns in the world. He drew an analogy to the German seventeen-inch siege howitzers and the destruction they had caused against old stone fortifications in Belgium. He did not mention the differences identified by the naval experts, that howitzers have a high trajectory and are more suitable for close range land-based targets than the low trajectory limitations of warship guns. Nor did he mention the operational detail of sea mines which were known to have been laid in several lines across the Dardanelles, or the lack of dedicated minesweeping vessels that had been raised as a concern by Vice-Admiral Carden.

First Sea Lord Jacky Fisher again remained silent during the meeting, having been reminded by Winston beforehand that he was not a part of the Cabinet and he was only to speak if directly asked for technical advice.

Lord Kitchener again supported the idea of a naval demonstration without the need to commit troops, on the condition that if it did not succeed it would be abandoned.

The Cabinet War Council formally approved a ships alone naval assault on the Dardanelles with Constantinople as the ultimate objective.

CHAPTER 25

Ali

Thursday, 4 February 1915

Ali's short legs ached with every step, but he fought to maintain the tempo. *It wouldn't be so bad without this pack and rifle.*

He was strong enough to carry the weight, but the older men seemed to have reserves of stamina that he lacked.

Sleeping under the stars again tonight. I wish I could lie down right here.

He allowed himself a brief glance upwards.

Stars of God's universe sparkled across the sky. The rising moon was between full and half, providing ample light for the battalion to march up the trail into the hills of the Sari Bair range on the Gallipoli Peninsula. The air was clear and cool. *At least it won't rain on us.*

Lanky moon-shadows strode in front.

Ali's shadow was lagging. He made an effort to accelerate, but his foot slipped on some loose gravel and he lost balance. He crumpled to the ground and his heart sank with him.

His fingers maintained a tight grip on the German-made Mauser rifle despite the gravel grinding into his knuckles. *I must protect the rifle.* The beating from Sergeant Kadir for leaving his rifle lying in the dirt during morning prayers last month burned in his memory.

"Let me guess…Donkey Runt!" the sergeant's voice roared from close by. "Is that Donkey Runt?"

A sea of legs from the 2nd Battalion of the 27th Regiment stomped onwards around Ali as he pushed himself onto his knees in an effort to return to his feet –.

Something slammed into his thigh and he tumbled face first into the ground. Men continued to march past. A dull pain swelled where the Sergeant's boot had hit him.

"God, be merciful!" Ali scrambled to his feet again. He hurried back into the line of marching men, his bleeding fingers still tight around the stock of his Mauser.

"God's mercy won't help you if you fall over when the enemy is attacking. You have to stand on your own feet Donkey Runt. The enemy will show you no mercy. Watch your footing boy."

"Yes, Kadir Efendi."

The pain in his hands and thigh brought with it a renewed state of alertness. For a moment he forgot the fatigue that plagued him.

I've aged a lifetime since joining this army six months ago. Sixteen years old tomorrow. To celebrate with a bruised leg and grazed knuckles!

He could have avoided conscription when the Army was mobilising. Especially being small for his age, hopefully still growing. But he refused to stay at home and miss the action. His family was poor and unless he broke away and became a war hero, there was nothing ahead but a life of hard work and poverty, just like his father had endured.

Also, he figured that Zeynep might show some interest in a war hero.

Her generous curves were difficult to make out beneath loose fitting clothes, but they tantalized him. Her smile was so warm, and she always seemed to have one for Ali, even though she was three years older and from a wealthy family – way out of his reach. When she smiled, her gaze seemed to linger, as if she knew the power it had over him. Ali could never hold her gaze, as much as he wanted to, he always looked away first.

When I return as a war hero I will stare back with confidence, and she will blush –.

Ali nearly walked into the back of the man in front.

Time to bivouac for the night.

Thank you God. I need a rest.

The battalion broke into four companies, and companies each broke into three platoons. Ali's platoon, like the others, was made up of nine squads with nine rifles in each squad.

Suleyman's hand on his shoulder was warm and welcome. "Come Ali, our squad will camp over behind those bushes. They may provide some shelter from the wind. If we sleep facing towards Mecca we can pray and sleep at the same time!"

Ali didn't bother trying to suppress a grin. Suleyman's irreverent humour seemed harmless enough most of the time. Final evening prayers were often brief, or completely overlooked when night operations were on. Even the officers seemed too exhausted to care.

The squad crammed into a slight hollow behind a clump of waist high bushes. *There does seem to be less air movement here.* Ali pulled a great coat from his pack and curled up under it. He enjoyed a minute or two imagining a blushing Zeynep welcoming him home as a hero. *I would like to explore those curves.*

Fatigue overcame his fantasy, and he drifted into an exhausted sleep.

* * *

"Donkey Runt! Donkey Runt! Where is that little shit?"

Ali opened his eyes and disappointment washed over him. *Dawn already! My leg hurts, and my hands.*

He poked his head out from under the great coat and there was Suleyman looking back at him with a finger raised to his lips. Suleyman motioned for Ali to pull the coat back over his head.

Ali did so and hoped that the act of defiance wouldn't earn him another beating.

Sure enough, Sergeant Kadir gave up within a minute and went off chasing after some other poor soul to torment with whatever chore he was trying to allocate.

Ali uncovered his head and grinned in relief.

Suleyman looked concerned. "You have hurt your face."

Ali raised a hand to his face. His right cheek was swollen and his eye couldn't open fully. He felt the graze and winced.

"It was my own stupid fault. I should have been more careful."

Suleyman moved closer with his canteen and splashed some precious water on Ali's cheek. It was icy cold, but felt good.

Ali nodded thanks. He had a sip of water from his own canteen. The few mouthfuls of water left would have to keep him going until breakfast, a two-hour march away at Koja Dere camp. *Once we start walking I won't feel so hungry.*

I carry this cursed rifle everywhere, but I am never allowed to fire it. How am I going to become a war hero if there is no enemy to fight? The only enemy I have here is the bastard Sergeant Kadir, and I can't do anything about him.

Curse the pain!

* * *

Breakfast at Koja Dere was the usual hard stale bread and dried beans, washed down with half a canteen of water. Today as a special extra, the kitchen also issued each man in the company with a hardboiled egg.

"Ali," Suleyman placed his hand on Ali's shoulder. "Today is your birthday. You have this."

Suleyman handed his egg to Ali.

Ali accepted the gift and smiled. *I ought to be more reluctant to accept this, but I don't want to give it back.*

"You remembered! Thank you Suleyman! How did you even know when it was?"

Suleyman shrugged his shoulders. "You are in my squad."

Ali savoured the taste of each mouthful and a sleepy contentment replaced the void in his belly. *I cannot think of a better gift.*

After breakfast, the company was called to stand to. Being Friday, the day of congregation, the battalion Imam came to address the company before morning prayers.

Clothed in clean robes, leather shoes and neat turban, the Imam strode forward with the step of conviction. A flowing beard, streaked with grey, wafted in the cool breeze.

"My brothers…" The Imam raised his palms to the heavens until a hush settled over the men.

"The time for action has come. We shall have to fight with all our strength, with all our soul, with teeth and nails, with all the sinews of our bodies and of our spirits. If we do it, the deliverance of the Muslim kingdoms is assured. Then, if God so wills, we shall march unashamed by the side of our friends who send their greetings to the Crescent. God is our aid and the Prophet is our support.

"The time for courage and honour is near. A threat is approaching our great Empire, God's nation. The unbelievers have been plotting against us and nipping at us like jackals, cowardly trying to weaken the strong beast. The English Imperialists and their allies are determined to destroy us and destroy Islam, but God is with us and we will not know defeat. Our great Caliph, the mighty Sultan Mehmed the Fifth, has issued a fatwa declaring jihad, a holy struggle to defend our very existence. As in the legendary days of old, when Muhammad and his armies had to fight to defend the Muslim way, so it will be again."

The Imam held up a roll of paper, then read from it.

"Oh, people of the faith and oh, beloved Muslims, consider, even though for a brief moment, the present condition of the Islamic world. For if you consider this for but a little, you will weep long. You will behold a bewildering state of affairs which will cause the tear to fall and the fire of grief to blaze. You see the great country of India, which contains hundreds of millions of Muslims, fallen, because of religious divisions and weaknesses, into the grasp of the enemies of God, the infidel English. You see forty million Muslims in Java shackled by the chains of captivity and of affliction under the rule of the Dutch, although these infidels are much fewer in number than the faithful and do not enjoy a much higher civilisation. You see Egypt, Morocco, Tunis, Algeria, and the Sudan suffering the extremes of pain and groaning in the grasp of the enemies of God and His apostle. You see the vast country of Siberia and Turkestan, and Khiva and Bokhara, and the Caucasus and the Crimea, and the Kazan and Ezferhan and Kosahastan, whose Muslim peoples believe in the unity of God, ground under the feet of their oppressors, who are the enemies already of our religion. You behold Persia being prepared for partition and you see the city of the Caliphate, which for ages has unceasingly fought breast to breast with the enemies of our religion, now become the target for oppression and violence. Thus, wherever you look you see that the enemies of the true religion, particularly the English, the Russian, and the French, have oppressed Islam and invaded its rights in every possible way. We cannot enumerate the insults we have received at the hands of these nations who desire totally to destroy Islam and drive all Muslims off the face of the earth. This tyranny has passed all endurable limits. The cup of our oppression is full to over-flowing. In brief, the Muslims work and the infidels eat. The Muslims are hungry and suffer and the infidels gorge themselves and live in luxury. The world of Islam sinks down and goes backward, and the Christian world goes forward and is more and more exalted. The Muslims are enslaved and the infidels are the great rulers. This is all because the Muslims have abandoned the plan set forth in the Koran and ignored the Holy War which it commands. But the time has now come for the Holy War, and by this the land of Islam shall be forever freed from the power of the infidels who oppress it. This Holy War has now become a sacred duty. Know ye that the blood of infidels in the Islamic lands may be shed with impunity – except for that of our German brothers to whom the Muslim power has promised security and who are allied with it. The killing of infidels who rule over Islam has become a sacred duty, whether you do it secretly or openly, as the Koran has decreed: 'Take them and kill them whenever you find them. Behold we have delivered them unto your hands and given you supreme power over them.' He who kills even one unbeliever of those who rule over us, whether he does it secretly or openly, shall be rewarded by God. And let every Muslim, in whatever part of the world he may be, swear a solemn oath to kill at least three or four of the infidels who rule over him, for they are the enemies of God and of the faith. Let every Muslim know that his reward for doing so shall be doubled by the God who created heaven and earth. A Muslim who does this shall be saved from the terrors of the Day of Judgment, of the resurrection of the dead. Who is the man who can refuse such a recompense for such a small deed? Yet the time has come that we should rise up as the rising of one man, in one hand a sword, in the other a gun, in his pocket balls of fire and death-dealing missiles, and in his heart the light of the faith, and that we should lift up our voices, saying – India for the Indian Muslims, Java for the Javanese Muslims, Algeria for the Algerian Muslims, Morocco for the Moroccan Muslims, Tunis for the Tunisan Muslims, Egypt for the Egyptian Muslims, Iran for the Iranian Muslims, Turan for the Turanian Muslims, Bokhara for the Bokharan Muslims, Caucasus for the Caucasian Muslims, and the Ottoman Empire for the Ottoman Turks and Arabs."

Ali struggled to focus on the message as the Imam droned on. The mention of other nations took his mind back to the Gulf of Saros where he had spent countless weeks since conscription last summer. He was naïve then, thinking each night that the Greek naval assault might come before morning, supported by the Bulgarian army charging from the north. He had been ready, sleeping with a knife on his belt and rifle close by. But the attack never came. Other Ottoman regiments came to garrison the Gulf of Saros and his 27th regiment moved back to base near Maidos. *It feels good to be back closer to home, like I'm defending my family.* His village outside Chanakkale was almost visible from the surrounding hills.

The tone of the Imam's voice lifted and Ali dragged his focus back to the message.

"Brothers, the enemy has his sights on Istanbul. He wants to desecrate our great mosques and steal the jewel of our nation like a common thief. But he cannot reach Istanbul by land, he can only come by sea, by the Strait of Chanakkale. To pass through the Strait, he must breach our defences and to do so he must capture this land on which we are standing. We must hold this land for God's sake. Some of us will become martyrs and receive God's glory in paradise. Some of us will live to be known as heroes of our people. All of us will fight without fear because we are defending God's nation against the infidel invasion and we know He will reward us for our sacrifice. There is no greater honour than to die as a martyr while defending God's way and God's people. Those who are slain in the cause of God, He will not bring their deeds to nothing. He will vouchsafe them guidance and ennoble their estate; He will admit them into the Paradise He has made known to them. We must fight on and never give up and ensure that God's great nation can remain for our children and the generations to follow.

"They are coming my brothers," the Imam's tone was urgent now. "And we must stop them at any cost. We must fight bravely for God and our nation. Paradise awaits all martyrs."

The Imam faced the men towards Mecca and led them through morning prayers, then raised his palms again to the morning sky. "May God bless us and our efforts, as He wills."

I will do what is required of me. Live or die. As God wills.

The men started to turn and talk quietly amongst themselves until the next orders came. Suleyman lowered his head towards Ali's. "If the Imam thinks it is so great to be martyred – why doesn't he dress like us and pick up a rifle. Then he can get shot at too? The enemy won't be mistaking him for a soldier in that outfit."

"Hush Suleyman! He is a man of God and should not be mocked. He must preach the word to us who cannot read it for ourselves."

"I could read it for myself if I chose to."

"You can read? You never told me! After all this time we've been in training together."

"You never asked me," Suleyman said. "Maybe I'll teach you when this business is over. A clever lad like you would pick it up quickly."

It had never occurred to Ali that he might learn to read. Only Imams and boys from rich families knew that luxury. *Zeynep would be impressed if I could read. Maybe I could just casually start reading something when she is near… 'Oh yes, of course I can read Zeynep –.'*

"Donkey Runt! Suleyman the Magnificent! Attila the Hun!" Sergeant Kadir yelled, having appeared behind them. "You three and the rest of your squad – get over to the Artillery battalion to help with pulling the howitzer to today's training area – Immediately!"

Joint training with the artillerymen and their big guns again.

A brief sit down would have been nice after standing through the Imam's service, but Ali didn't mind. Hauling guns with the bullocks was heavy work, but using the large weapons made it worthwhile. So much power, and targeted with such accuracy.

Occasionally they were allowed to fire off a round. The stumpy howitzer barrel could be aimed up at almost any angle. The art of selecting the barrel angle and setting the fuse timing fascinated Ali. He had seen them identify a target on the next hill, then fire a shell that exploded directly above the target. The explosion signified the moment when he and the other infantry men were to rush from their cover and charge towards the target. Their regiment commander, Lieutenant Colonel Sefik, had addressed them a number of times to emphasise the importance of coordination between artillery and infantry – a powerful combination.

Maybe today I will see a live round fired from one of the howitzers. I hope so.

CHAPTER 26

Jayjay

Tuesday, 16 February 1915

Soft sand wrapped around his boots with each step towards Mena camp, but Jayjay barely noticed. His body was hard and strong after two months of training in the desert. *If only they'd let me loose on the enemy, instead of having me repeat constant exercises and drills.*

Four days earlier, his First Battalion had joined with the Second, Third and Fourth Battalions in a joint training exercise as the full First Brigade. The brigade marched to Beni Yusef, a patch of dessert eight miles out of camp. For four days and nights, they entrenched, defended, attacked and drilled under eyes of battalion commanders and the Brigadier Colonel MacLaurin.

On the final night of the exercise, Jayjay crossed paths with Alfred McKenzie. Alfred stood with the Second Battalion, under the faint light from a thin slice of moon, but his voice gave him away. The voice that Jayjay would recognise anywhere unleashed a burst of fury within him and the butt of Jayjay's Lee-Enfield connected firmly with Alfred's nose.

"Sorry old mate. Lucky I used the back end of the rifle or your face'd be really messed up."

Alfred, wide-eyed, forced a grin. Blood stained his teeth black in the moonlight. *Alfred was feeling the funk that night. There's no special treatment here for handsome smooth talkers with rich parents.*

* * *

Later that day, back at Mena camp, Jayjay stood to attention with his fellow members of the First Battalion, along with the other battalions of the First Brigade.

The Brigadier, Colonel MacLaurin, concluded his address to his command of four thousand men, his voice amplified though a megaphone.

"Officers, NCOs and men of the First Brigade, you are fit for war!"

Jayjay's cheer was drowned in an eruption of noise. *Ghosts of pharaohs lurking under the pyramids might have wondered what that roar was about. No doubt the Gyppo natives in the nearby village heard us too.*

"To mark your hard work and fine performance," The Brigadier added, "I am granting each man of the First Brigade three days holiday!"

Another cheer and the men were dismissed.

"I expect we'll be leaving for the front soon," Ron said. "That much was implied in our Brigade Commander's speech."

"Let's go into Cairo tonight," Larry said.

"You bet," Jayjay nodded. "I am fit for war!"

"Not tonight for me," Ron said. "I'm knackered. I'm going to write to Em and get some sleep. Tomorrow though."

"Sure old man, we'll still be celebrating tomorrow." Jayjay turned back to Larry and placed a hand on his shoulder. "We better have a wash and change first though. If I smell half as bad as you, I must really stink."

* * *

An hour later Jayjay and Larry crammed into an electric tram carriage, bound for Cairo. It seemed that the whole brigade wanted to get out of Mena camp all at once. Legs of those who had climbed on the roof dangled in front of the windows. The tram groaned under the load and crawled into Cairo.

Larry leaned towards Jayjay. "Let's start with something to eat. I'm starving, and if I start drinking beer on an empty stomach I might collapse."

"Sure, we've got three days and wouldn't want to peak too early. How 'bout the Gyppo place on the corner, near the Wozzer. Last time the stew was well cooked and bread was fresh enough."

"That'll do me fine."

New South Welshmen of the First Brigade poured out of the tram before it stopped and most headed in the direction of the Wozzer district.

A short walk delivered Jayjay and Larry to the street food store they were aiming for. The native was there as usual, with his hot pot of stew. Jayjay looked in and inhaled.

"What do you think? It looks like it has real meat in it today."

Larry grinned. "Rat or cat?"

"No rat. No cat. Goat stew, fresh today." The seller looked indignant. "Hot bread also. Four shillings."

"Come on old friend, you remember us. We ate here last week. Two shillings for him and two shillings for me. Four shillings for two meals. We're Australians."

"Five shillings for two meals. Very fresh. Bread hot."

"That's good enough for me," Jayjay said. "I'm starving."

They handed over the coins and sat on a nearby bench to eat. Jayjay wolfed his down and went back for seconds.

Larry stopped with a second bread roll. "That feels better, now let's get a drink."

"The Wozzer?"

"The Wozzer!"

They strode towards the street Haret el Wasser. This street, and surrounding area, was full of bars, brothels and soldiers on leave from camps near the town. Australian infantrymen from Mena, New Zealanders and more Australians from Zeitoun, and lighthorse troopers from Maadi. Jayjay had come here a few times for a night out drinking, but always avoided the brothels.

'Thou shalt not commit adultery' was the seventh commandment. He had memorized this one as part of the ten commandments well before he understood what it meant. His father had sat down with him and explained it to him plainly when he asked – 'save yourself for your wife Jayjay, and do not take another woman to your bed.' – It wasn't so long ago.

"This place has good cold beer," Larry said.

"Looks fine to me."

Inside was busy but not over-crowded. It was a bar they had visited once before. The floor was stone and the benches were hard. A few oil lamps and a fire cast an uneven orange glow across the smoke-filled room.

"There!" Larry exclaimed. "If it isn't the egg layers from G Company."

The accent was loud and familiar. Jayjay and Larry faced off against the Irishmen, the victims of the eggs-in-hammock prank on the *Afric*.

Adrenalin pumped in Jayjay's veins. He took a step back to size up the situation. *There are three of them and two of us, but I reckon I count for one and a half. These guys are not so big. Chances are the other chaps will come off second best if it comes to a brawl.*

"Whoa, settle there big fella." O'Shea raised his glass towards Jayjay. "Come and sit with us lads, let me buy you a drink. We're all part of D Company now since the merge of our old F and G Companies."

"Uh-oh, it's the Uh-Oh's – O'Shea, O'Hara and O'Reilly." Larry extended his hand and delivered a disarming smile. *Maybe this won't end in violence after all. Nice work Larry.*

"Seamus, Poddy and Mick," O'Shea said, and was first to shake hands.

"Seamus O'Shea," Larry said, sitting. "Well, your parents certainly lacked imagination."

Each of the five took a turn to buy a round of beer. Heroics of the Brigade exercise to Beni Yusef become grander and grander with each round.

Before he knew it, Jayjay was drinking Irish whiskey and recounted how he recognized Alfred and smashed his nose.

"Wow, that laddie must have done something to really upset you back home – this Irish whiskey's better than peat wreaking scotch piss, but it's no Jameson. Liquid manna from heaven that is, triple distilled in our home town Dublin lad.

One taste o' that and you'll never look back – It didn't involve a girl perchance?"

Sobriety returned with a flush. *Why did I say anything about him? I don't want to talk about Charlotte. How to change the subject?*

"Oh yeah," Larry said.

"The thing is," Jayjay said. "The way the second Battalion dug those trenches, they made it easy for us. They weren't deep enough and had too many men packed close together."

"What's her name?" Seamus asked.

Jayjay stared at his glass. "It was a good lesson for them – might save their life when it comes to entrenching against a real enemy."

"Charlotte," Larry said.

Jayjay glared at Larry. *That is a break of trust. There is an unspoken agreement that Charlotte is not an acceptable topic of conversation. Maybe it's like the unspoken understanding I had with Charlotte in the first place. Maybe I need to be clearer.* "I don't want to talk about it."

"Come on lad, I know just the thing to help you forget about her. There's a place not too far from here we've been wanting to visit, to see some nice French girls."

So many of the others had come back to Mena after a night out in Cairo and carried on like the French dancing girls were goddesses. *I don't want to forget about Charlotte, I just don't want to talk about her.* "Sure, let's go. Do they do the cancan? Everyone who's seen it says you've got to see a cancan at least once."

"Maybe they do laddie. Maybe they do."

Jayjay stood to leave as if the decision was made, without making further eye contact with Larry.

To reach their destination, the gang of five had to walk through the Wozzer district. On the way they passed two Australians standing over a native fruit hawker.

"Common mate, just give me my money back and you won't have any trouble. This apple is rotten. You can't sell rubbish like this."

"Apple good," the hawker said. "Apple good!"

The other Australian leaned on the seller's fruit cart so it tipped over, sending apples, oranges and lemons rolling across the street. "I really think you should refund my friend's money."

The seller started yelling something in a foreign language, no doubt expressing his displeasure. He dropped to the ground and started picking up the fruit, gathering them in a fold of his loose-fitting robe. The disgruntled customer started kicking oranges across the street and his accomplice flicked open a pocket knife, then sliced though the cloth of the robe, sending fruit tumbling to the ground again.

More incomprehensible abuse followed from the native.

The fellow with the knife folded his arms, still holding the naked blade. "So, are you going to give my friend his money back, or are we going to have to come back and discuss this again tomorrow?"

The verbal tirade didn't slow as the native pulled some coins from a hidden pocket and handed them over. The Australians turned and went on their way, backs to waving arms and flying spit.

Jayjay chuckled as they walked on. "There's always entertainment here. How about this sign: 'Don't go elsewhere to be cheated Australians. Come here!', or that one: 'French and English spoken; Australian understood'. I mean really, what is wrong with these people?"

"Well," Seamus said. "They do have a point about the way you Australians abuse the King's English."

"Speak for yourself bloody Irishman," Larry said. "What do you care for the King of England anyway? You said he could go shag a sheep, and you don't take kindly to saluting his officers."

"No, that's true enough, they can go to blazes. The English officers walk around here all superior like. If they want me to salute, they can kiss my leprechaun arse. Here we are boys, this is the place."

A sign out front read *French Girls* and featured a crude hand drawing of three dancing girls, each with one leg raised high in the air. A red lantern hung over the door. Jayjay filed in with the others. *Something's not right. It's too quiet, the room's too small. This isn't a French showgirl performance. This is a brothel.*

"No Gyppo filth in here then?" Seamus, in the lead, asked a human form that Jayjay could barely see in the gloom. "Only clean French girls hey?"

"Oui, Oui, yes, yes, messieurs, good clean French girls. All registered and examined. All have a healthy ticket," replied a female voice. "Please come."

A door at the rear of the room opened and the madam led the way though. A fire burned in the hearth. The air was warm and heavy with smoke. Lanterns and candles lined the walls. A tantalizing glow rested on the women, wearing barely enough to cover the essentials. Maybe that was real French underwear, who could tell? The women were seated or reclined. They look so relaxed and comfortable. *I don't feel comfortable.*

"Well, Big Jay," Seamus said. "Take your pick, my shout."

Jayjay's mouth was dry. He opened it but no words came. For a long moment no one moved or said anything, then one of the girls rose and walked slowly towards him. Maybe someone gave her a signal, it was too dark to know. She raised a hand and rested it on his chest. "Hello monsieur Big Jay, I am mademoiselle Josephine – I will look after you – unless you don't like me?"

Josephine licked her lips and pouted. Her eyes were captivating. She reached up to his neck and pulled him down to kiss her. Her lips were like honey, her eyes pure sin.

"Oh, I have been waiting for someone like you," Josephine said with a brazen face and a voice smoother than oil. "So big and strong, and handsome too. Come with me Jay, my bed is covered in fine Egyptian linen. Let us drink deep of love."

A waft of sweet, intoxicating perfume dissolved the last shards of his resistance. He followed her from the room like a bull ox led by his nose ring.

* * *

Did that just happen?

He felt suddenly conscious of every part of his body.

A blanket of silence fell over him and the woman. All he could hear was the sound of his own heavy breathing and a pounding heartbeat inside his ears.

"I think you had better put your clothes back on, monsieur Big Jay." Josephine smiled up at him in the dim lamplight, but not with the same warmth as earlier. "You cannot sleep here. This is not a hotel."

He propped himself up so as not to rest his full weight on her body, fearing she might want to shove him off. *Has her accent changed?*

He stood and the room spun. *I think I might need to vomit. She is watching me. I have never stood naked in front of a woman, other than mum when I was a boy. I suppose it doesn't matter, after what we just did together. We have a connection now.* Jayjay dressed and as he buttoned his shirt he wondered if he should say something, or just leave. She didn't bother to cover herself. *Actually, her features aren't so perfect. That nose could be Egyptian.*

"Goodbye monsieur Jay, do come again."

"Goodbye mademoiselle Josephine. Umm, thank you." Jayjay turned and left, returning along the corridor to the room where he had met Josephine, only minutes before.

A couple of girls remained, still reclining in the same positions as when he left. Larry looked up from where he was standing by the fire, arms folded.

Jayjay searched for words. "Did you…"

Larry shook his head.

"Let's get out of here," Jayjay said.

"Don't you think we should wait for the others?"

"We can wait outside. I feel sick." Jayjay made for the door without waiting to see if Larry would follow. *What have I done? What if I catch a disease? The madam said they had healthy tickets, but never showed us. We were warned about this, but what did the doctor say to do now? I can't remember. I could be locked up and sent on a ship back home like all the others marched out a couple of weeks ago – under armed guard like criminals. It's not fair, after six months of hard work.*

Outside, without caring who was watching, he picked up a handful of dry sand. Being a roadside, it was more a mixture of sand and gravel. He stuffed his hand down the front of his trousers and rubbed the contents into himself until it hurt.

"Go easy Jay! I don't think that's going to help."

Jayjay looked up and tried to suppress the panic. *At least for once Larry isn't making a joke.*

"Damn me for a fool, what was I thinking."

"You weren't thinking with your brain, that's for sure."

"I'm a bloody idiot!"

Larry nodded, his eyes saying 'Yes you are a bloody stupid drongo moron idiot'.

"I suggest we get back to camp so you can have a good wash with some soap. Rubbing his majesty raw with grit might make things worse."

"You can't tell Ron."

"I won't say anything."

"Seriously."

"It's not me you've got to worry about, it's the Irish. If you tell them you want this kept a secret they'll shout if from the pyramids. I suggest say nothing and try to relax. Here they come."

"Ah, Big Jay," Seamus called. "I trust you enjoyed yourself with Mademoiselle Josephine. Want to get another drink?"

The Irishmen were smoking and looking mighty pleased with themselves. *Hopefully they're too occupied with their own conquests to notice anything else.*

"No thanks mate. We're going to head back to camp, had enough for tonight. Have you, ah, been in there before? I mean, how do you know the girls are clean?"

"No we haven't, but I reckon we'll be back though. Next time your turn to pay. They seem clean enough to me, but time will tell. Maybe I'll try Josephine tomorrow, would you recommend her?"

* * *

Next morning Jayjay was back under the shower with more soap. His member was red raw and hurt like hell. His bag of marbles wasn't much better. *Hopefully that's just from the sand and gravel.*

That morning Jayjay discovered that all his money was missing from his wallet, including the gold sovereign from his father. *It could only have been at the brothel, I had money before I went in there and I didn't get my wallet out again.*

He fought the urge to vomit.

I've well and truly let myself be robbed. Do I feel sick from guilt for taking a whore, or am I just worried about catching a disease and being sent home in disgrace.

I can't even tell the difference. I wonder what Dad would say if he knew.

Damn me for a fool.

CHAPTER 27

Winston

Friday, 19 February 1915

Winston leant back in the leather lounge chair and blew Cuban cigar smoke towards the ceiling of his library. *Historians of the world will remember the brilliance of my strategy. This is a pivotal moment in the war.*

His Mediterranean fleet lay deployed off the mouth of the Dardanelles Strait, under the command of Vice-Admiral Carden. This morning his ships had launched the first salvos of explosive shells at the entrance to the Strait since the preliminary attack three months earlier. Initially his warships would target the outer forts of Orkanie, Helles, Sedd-el-Bahr and Kum Kale.

He awaited a telegram with details of how the attack was progressing. *It's only a matter of time now before our superior naval firepower blasts its way through.*

The Ottoman army will turn and run today, or tomorrow, just as they did in North Africa and the Balkans. The sick old man of Europe is on his death bed, and the British lion is roaring at his door. I must write that down.

The Admiralty remained an irritation, still voicing concerns about wanting military support for the naval operation. And Vice-Admiral Carden kept bothering Winston with requests for minesweepers. Specialized heavy sweeping vessels would make his work easier, but Carden had a fleet of fishing vessels that were being used to clear a channel though the minefield and he would have to make do with these. The extra time required to equip and send minesweepers was not worth the few extra casualties that would result from using timber fishing boats. Carden claimed that the fishing boats were not powerful enough and struggled against the constant current running south through the Dardanelles. *While Carden still has fishing boats left at his disposal, he hasn't exhausted this option to clear a channel through the mines.*

The real problem is that Kitchener keeps repeating his view that the attack can be called off if it runs into difficulties. Of course there will be difficulties, this is war. That kind of talk was fine early on, it helped to bring everyone along on the journey, but now we are committed. The operation must be a success.

No one dares to oppose Lord Kitchener. If he declares it time to break off the naval attack on the Dardanelles, the whole operation will be doomed.

I need to ensure that Kitchener and the others are as committed to the Dardanelles campaign as I am. They all want to sit on the fence and watch while the attack is underway, ready to turn and run at the first sign of difficulty.

Maybe I should have a chat with Ellis Ashmead-Bartlett. He's trying to report on the war, but Kitchener won't let correspondents anywhere near the front in France. A shame. The press can be a useful weapon if used carefully.

* * *

War related press releases required approval by the War Council, but this was his naval operation and he had taken a liberty. They couldn't very well say anything against him publicly as he had merely communicated the truth to the English people.

He opened the newspaper and found what he sought on page 6. He scanned quickly through the article and skipped the technical details to find the phrases that he had spent hours crafting…

***THE TIMES*, MONDAY, FEBRUARY 22, 1915**

DARDANELLES ATTACKED.

OPERATIONS BY SEA AND AIR.

FORTS VERSUS SHIPS.

By Our Military Correspondent.

The attack on the Dardanelles by the Allied Fleets has at last begun, and, having begun, it must be successfully carried through at all costs…

…The Defences of the Dardanelles are formidable, and nothing is gained by denying the fact…

…The best way to attack the Dardanelles is by means of a conjoint naval and military expedition, and a purely naval attack can only be justified if the necessary and very large military force cannot be spared, or if our information is so good, and the chances have been so carefully weighed, that the success of a naval attack is reasonably probable…

…It is in every respect a serious operation that is in progress, whether the attack is delivered by ships, or troops, or both, and the arrangements made for prosecuting it will be watched with solicitude, since we cannot afford to fail when we touch upon the East. Nothing, however, is impossible to the Allied Navies of England and France, and if they can master these formidable Straits, and appear before the walls of Constantinople they will have accomplished a feat of arms which will live in the history of the world.

A large map of the Dardanelles and Gallipoli Peninsula on the following page of the newspaper completed the story. Winston lit a fresh Cuban and re-read the whole article more slowly. Havana tobacco tasted especially fine this morning.

* * *

The Cabinet War Council met twice during the following week. At the first meeting Prime Minister Lloyd George reacted as Winston had anticipated.

"You had no right to go to the press without consulting with this Council first, and you knew exactly what you were doing. This changes everything. Now if we retreat the whole world will think we have suffered a defeat at the hands of the flagging Ottoman Empire, after the Italians threw them out of Libya and the Balkan states sent them running back to Constantinople."

"With all due respect Prime Minister," Winston spoke calmly. "There simply wasn't time. The opportunity to present good news to the British people and our allies had to be taken while the news was fresh. With the stalemate in France there has not been much positive publicity of late. It is not as if sending a naval fleet of this size to launch an assault on one of the world's most precious waterways could be treated as a covert operation. I don't recall anyone in this Council stating that the operation was to be kept secret."

Lord Kitchener stroked his moustache and lifted his chin slightly. Discussion stopped and all eyes in the room turned towards him.

"Gentlemen," Kitchener said. "There is no doubt that we ought to see the business through now. Let us focus on the way forward. We have already agreed to send a substantial garrison force to the Dardanelles, including good British troops that were destined for the western front, and the Australian and New Zealand forces training in Egypt. When Mister Churchill's naval operation is complete, these forces will occupy the Gallipoli peninsula and defend the Dardanelles against any possible land based counter-attack."

Good, now I can push harder.

"In light of Admiral Jackson's report that I provided at our meeting last week," Winston said. "I suggest additional troops be sent, including a French Division, the 29th Division of our regular troops, a British Territorial Division and a Russian Division."

Kitchener leaned forward in his chair.

"I say what! That is over one hundred thousand men. Mr Churchill, need I remind you that you proposed this adventure as a naval operation alone? What in the blazes is the purpose for which you would require such a large number of troops? Do you now contemplate a land attack as well?"

"No, Lord Kitchener, of course not. It is simply that our Admiralty is reporting that the naval attacks may be held up by sea mines, and some military supporting operations may be required."

The meeting concluded without resolution of the extent of troop support or the nature of its operations.

* * *

The next meeting of the Cabinet War Council took place two days later, on Friday 26th February 1915.

"The additional troops," Winston addressed Lord Kitchener. "Are required to occupy Constantinople and compel a surrender of all the Turkish forces remaining in Europe after the Fleet has obtained command of the Sea of Marmara."

"I am sorry Mister Churchill, the answer is no. There simply are not sufficient troops available for that purpose."

Winston turned to address Maurice Hankey, the secretary and minute taker for the Cabinet War Council.

"Very well, I wish it to be placed on record that if a disaster occurs in Turkey owing to the insufficiency of troops, I must disclaim all responsibility."

* * *

Over the following week, reports came through to Winston that landing parties of marines had reconnoitred the outer forts following naval bombardment. The landing parties found the forts mainly unoccupied, but most of the guns in these forts were still intact. The marines were able to destroy the guns they found with explosive gun cotton.

Turkish resistance increased, until a company of marines was forced from Sedd-el-Bahr suffering the loss of twenty-two men killed. This loss meant the end of marine landing missions to destroy Turkish guns around the Dardanelles Strait.

After the landing missions had been stopped, Winston received a telegram from Vice-Admiral Carden:

> The methodical reduction of the forts is not feasible without expenditure of ammunition out of all proportion to that available.

Carden always dwells on the negative, but at least he has eased off with his requests for heavy minesweeping vessels. Hopefully he will get on with the work of clearing a channel and make do with the fleet fishing boats he has at his disposal.

* * *

On Wednesday 10th March, 1915, the Cabinet War Council met again and the members looked to Winston like children seeking reassurance.

In the previous week he had confirmed that the forts of the Dardanelles Strait were in the process of being destroyed, with the outer forts around the entrance practically demolished.

"The forts of the Dardanelles are doomed," Winston forced himself to project confidence. "The naval operation is well on schedule. The Admiralty still believes that we can affect the passage of the Straits by naval means alone, but are glad to know military support is available if required."

The War Council needs results. I have been telling them the same thing for three weeks. I need to press harder for advancement.

* * *

A few days later, Winston sent a telegram to Vice-Admiral Carden with orders to push on sweeping a channel through the minefield regardless of casualties. To emphasize the importance of the task, he added that "two or three hundred casualties would be a small price to pay for sweeping as far as the narrows."

The next day Carden replied that the task was beyond the capability of the underpowered fishing vessels, even though they were now commanded by Royal Navy officers. Most of the minesweeping fleet was sunk or severely damaged without having had any impact on the minefield.

While the mines remained, advance was impossible.

Cold fingers tightened around Winston's throat.

They cannot give up. I need them to press on, regardless of losses.

He sent a directive to Vice-Admiral Carden:

> We understand that it is your intention to sweep a good clear passage through the minefields to enable the forts at the Narrows eventually to be attacked at close range, and to cover this operation whether against the forts, or the light and moveable armament, by whatever fire is necessary from the Battle Fleet. If this is your intention, we cordially approve it. We wish it to be pressed forward without hurry, but without loss of time.

Carden replied that he agreed, but that many of his minesweepers were sunk or inoperable due to damage already sustained. He needed more powerful armoured minesweepers urgently to allow the minefield to be cleared. He also stated that in the meanwhile he was fitting out some destroyers for this purpose. He even had the nerve to point out that he had requested these more powerful mine sweepers on numerous previous occasions.

Winston screwed up the telegram and threw it at the wall. *Overly cautious and impertinent! He's just like the rest of the Admiralty. The man needs to learn how to obey orders.*

He sent a brief telegram to Carden, telling him to make do with the means he had at hand.

Later that day, Vice-Admiral Sackville Carden, a long serving senior officer of the Royal Navy, broke down and collapsed. He was unable to continue in his role as commander of the Mediterranean fleet and relieved himself of command.

Two days later, on Wednesday 17th March, Carden was replaced by his second in command, Rear-Admiral John de Robeck.

On the first day of de Robeck's new command, Winston sent him a telegram:

> Secret and Personal from the First Lord. Proceed with the naval attack, without delay and without further reference, at the first favourable opportunity.

CHAPTER 28

Ali

Thursday, 18 March 1915

Ali felt the first blast as much as he heard it. Distant vibrations hung in the air like thunder before a storm.

His stomach tensed and fear rose in his throat. Hunger and all regret over missing breakfast evaporated.

Men all around him were silent, as if it might, in some way, prevent alerting the enemy to their location.

Another distant boom filled the sound void and then faded into the air. This one seemed to be closer. Ali looked towards the stone parapet wall at the top of Rumeli Mecidiye fortress, but he could not see over it to the enemy that he knew was there.

Maybe one of the other forts along the Strait had taken a hit. Maybe it was a second round fired in the enemy's opening salvo.

Ali's mouth was dry. *Enemy warships are coming. We must stop them.*

"Suleyman the Magnificent!" Sergeant Kadir yelled. "You and your squad stay here with Corporal Seyit at gun number three. Take your orders from him. Do everything needed to keep this gun working. Donkey Runt, try not to get in the way!"

The Imam next to Sergeant Kadir raised his palms towards the sun, nearly at its midday peak.

"The jackals are coming!" he said. "As God wills. To your stations men. May God give you courage."

Kadir and the Imam paced off towards the next gun at Rumeli Mecidiye Fortress.

"We are already at our station." Suleyman's face was flushed and his tone dark. "Where is your station, Imam?"

"At least we can fire the gun now!" Ali replied.

Corporal Seyit climbed the five metal steps to the firing platform of his 240mm calibre gun – the biggest weapon Ali had ever seen, its barrel longer than two men lying end to end. The rear of the gun was mounted on railway tracks that swept a perfect arc. A second smaller set of metal tracks ran around behind the gun.

Ali's muscles ached from pushing carts of shells along the smaller tracks all morning. Shells that dwarfed the field howitzer shells he had witnessed when training with the mountain artillery battalion near Maidos. Shells wider than Suleyman's head and as long as his arm. Explosive armour-piercing shells with deadly power.

Corporal Seyit turned and faced the squad.

Another boom came, and another.

"You, little man," Corporal Seyit said to Ali. "Come forward and look over the wall. Tell us what you see."

"Yes Seyit Efendi." Ali hurried forward. The top of the parapet wall dipped lower below the gun barrel to allow it full range of movement left-to-right. Ali hauled himself up against the gun mount and peered over.

He tried to take in every detail for an accurate report. A flash burst from one of the closer warships, and a puff of smoke. The boom followed seconds later, and then on the opposite side of the Strait, a puff of earth fountained into the air like water. A cloud of smoke hung over Dardanos Fortress, but did it not appear to be damaged.

Ali turned to face the Corporal. "Seyit Efendi, I counted sixteen ships and saw one fire its gun. The shell hit the opposite bank, near Dardanos."

"How far is the closest ship."

"Still far off," Ali said. "They look tiny, just inside the mouth of the Strait."

"Twelve to fifteen thousand metres." Corporal Seyit raised an index finger in the direction of Ali's squad. "We must keep them back from Dardanos. Lines of sea mines cross the Strait between Dardanos and here at The Narrows. The minefield is a precious treasure we must protect – if the minefield remains intact, the warships cannot pass."

Seyit lowered his finger and took a deep breath. Another boom. "To disarm the mines, their little minesweeping boats must come close without being blown out of the water. To come close, the minesweeping boats need the warship covering fire to distract us. They have tried a number of times and failed. To provide effective cover, the warships need to come closer. Our job is to stop the warships from coming close. Other smaller guns will hunt the minesweepers – wooden fishing boats, too small to chase with this gun. We will use our powerful weapon to hunt bigger prey. We are defending God's empire. If the warships cannot come close, the Chanakkale Strait is impassable and our holy homeland is safe."

Ali gazed over the sea of men towards the hazy blue horizon. The booms ran together now, like a continuous peel of thunder. Intensity rising and falling, but always a rumble hanging in the air.

He struggled to focus on Corporal Seyit's words. *Why aren't we shooting back?*

Just give me some simple instructions. I don't know what to do next.

A loud blast behind him shook the ground and Ali flinched then forced himself to stand firm. Lucky the bastard Sergeant Kadir isn't here to see. He turned to see a brown cloud falling towards the earth, a hundred paces away.

A runner appeared and delivered a message to Corporal Seyit.

Seyit turned to his gunners. "Load."

The winch clanked and an enormous shell crawled up towards the breech at the rear end of the barrel. When it reached the required height, the shell paused and two gunners rammed it home, ready to fire.

Seyit gazed at the horizon and called out some numbers. His gunners responded by winding handles to adjust the direction and angle of the barrel to reflect Seyit's commands. Finally Seyit was satisfied with the aim and called everyone clear.

"Fire!"

Seyit's command was followed immediately by a deafening blast.

The explosion sucked the air from Ali's lungs, and his ear drums felt as if they had burst.

His hands flew to his ears, but it was too late. His ears continued to ring like someone was blowing a whistle, continuous and direct into each ear. He dropped his hands and looked around rapidly, as if to compensate for sudden loss of hearing.

Suleyman's eyes were wide and he burst into a grin.

Ali smiled back and nodded, scared to talk in case he couldn't hear himself.

This is one powerful gun.

Seyit was already barking orders at his gunners to adjust the aim. Another shell rose in the winch towards the breech.

Ali took a step backwards and covered his ears with his hands.

Seyit looked towards the horizon.

"Fire!"

This time Ali was ready when the gun fired, but the blast still shook his bones and he wondered if his ears were bleeding.

Each of the four big guns at Rumeli Mecidiye Fortress took its turn to hold the warships at bay. Ali tried to listen for the direction of other explosions in the battle, but heavy sound bounced all around him and inside his body. Some of the thunder seemed closer. *Hopefully, if God wills, the other forts and howitzer batteries along the Strait are pounding the invaders as well.*

The gunners were part of the machine – they loaded and fired again and again and again.

Ali could not see what was happening on the water. He focused on his immediate surroundings and role, pushing carts of new shells and removing the spent shell casings.

The sun had passed its peak when he noticed a small dot hanging in the air towards the mouth of the Strait. Aeroplanes had flown over a few times in recent months. The commanders always seemed to know which ones belonged to the enemy. Ali had fired with the others twice with his Mauser, but had never seen one hit. The flying men always seemed to manage to stay out of range.

Others tracked his gaze and pointed to the sky.

Attila, a private in Ali's squad, grabbed a rifle and fired three times in the direction of the aircraft, but had no impact on the enemy spy, inching his way up the Strait towards the Narrows. *I wonder if the flying man can report our position back to the warships.*

Ali stood on the cart to steal a glance over the parapet. The ships were closer than they had been when he looked over earlier.

One ship's gun flashed.

It was difficult to track the trajectory of the explosive shells by eye, but Ali saw this one coming. It appeared to lose speed and hang in the air, heading straight for him. He wanted to hide for cover, but his legs wouldn't move. At the last moment it screamed past and crashed into the rampart.

An almighty explosion threw Ali from his perch. He lost all bearings and couldn't tell where he was or what he landed on. Instinct forced his arms over his head.

Fragments of stone and earth rained around him. *Strange it seems quiet now. It hasn't been quiet for hours. Maybe my ears are destroyed. Is it safe to rise? What should I do now?*

He looked up and saw Corporal Seyit standing and staring in the direction of the blast, a look of grim defiance on his face.

"No! No! God be merciful!" Seyit turned towards Ali and Suleyman. "You, little man, big man. Get up. Go help. Go! Go!"

Suleyman picked himself up off the floor.

"Yes Efendi," he said, and lumbered off in the direction of the impact. Ali jumped up and hurried after to the area where some of the ammunition was stored. He had been hauling shells there minutes before.

He froze and surveyed the scene, unable to move.

A fire in the corner made Ali wonder if there might be more explosions here, even without further enemy attack.

Cordite residue in the air burned his nostrils and stung his eyes. Groans of men pushed the ringing from his ears. It sounded strangely human after hours of deafening gunfire.

A smouldering human leg lay on the ground in front of him, without its owner. A dead gunner lay by the firing platform, barely recognizable, although he did still have both of his legs.

Dirt, shells and shards of stone lay scattered over the floor. Amongst it all lay men. Many men. Some dead, but some alive enough to moan.

Ali felt an urge to vomit. He retched, but his stomach was empty.

He wanted to turn and run. If Suleyman was not there, maybe he would have. *What can I do? These men are dead or dying. If I stay here I will end up like them when the next shell hits or when our own shells explode from the fire.*

He looked to the horizon, half expecting to see the next shell flying towards him. Nothing. Another boom in the distance. Could that be a follow up shell into the same target, now the warship had found its range? His eyes dropped to the destruction that confronted him from all directions and danced left to right, as if looking for an escape.

Suleyman shook his head slowly. "Let's get the wounded away from here. The martyrs can wait. Come."

Ali followed, although every part of him wanted to run away from the place.

The first man they found alive was covered with blood.

"Mother." His voice was barely audible. "Mother forgive me."

Suleyman lifted him under the armpits and Ali took the wounded man's feet. By now, others were coming to see to the wounded.

They carried him a short distance and left him behind a stone wall in the care of a medic. When they returned to the impact site, others had arrived and were clearing the wounded.

"Let's get back to the gun," Suleyman said. "We are needed there. These others can deal with this."

Ali stared at the charred leg and nodded slowly, then dragged his eyes away and turned to follow.

Corporal Seyit looked at the two when they returned to his gun placement on the rampart, but Ali couldn't hold his questioning gaze.

When Ali looked up, Seyit had turned away. He asked no questions.

The ships continued to fire, and the guns of Rumeli Mecidiye Fortress fired back. Ali could not get the charred leg out of his mind. What happened to the rest of the man? Did he feel pain? The sick feeling in his stomach would not go away. I'm not sure if I'll ever be able to eat again.

He wanted to sit in the corner and close his eyes. He wanted to be somewhere else. Anywhere else but here. *Maybe I could slip away, find my way back to my family. But how could I look them in the eye. How could I be a hero? How could I return Zeynep's gaze and make her blush. I cannot run.*

Suleyman tapped him on the shoulder. "Come Ali, help me with these shells."

"Curse you, filthy winch," Seyit yelled. "Work, damn you. You lot by the wall, come and help. What are you looking at?"

"One of the English ships, Seyit Efendi," a gunner replied. "It is sinking. Come see for yourself."

Ali and Suleyman left the shells and hurried to the parapet wall with the others. The men were cheering, but Ali could not see.

The barrel of the gun and surrounding metal was too hot to touch, but he managed to haul himself up enough to see the massive underside of a ship's hull exposed.

"It's rolled over!" Attila punched the air. "Did we hit it?"

"The whole thing will be under soon," Suleyman said.

The sinking ship was on the far side of the Strait. Other ships were in the vicinity where the Strait was widest, still well short of Dardanos. *Could they be turning to retreat?*

The ship's hull, pointing to the sky, shrank as they watched. In minutes the last of it slipped beneath the surface like the hand of a drowning man.

The gunners cheered. Ali joined in, glad of a distraction to take his mind from the death of his countrymen that he had witnessed, and the scorched leg.

"A mine," Seyit nodded. "We must have laid more mines further out. Nice! Very nice! Look another is turning, waiting for me to finish him, but my winch is jammed. Gunner Mestan, come and see to this winch.

Mestan dragged himself from the wall and wiped his hands on his legs as he approached the winch. He stared at it for so long, Ali wondered whether he was still assessing the damage, or trying to think how he would explain that he could not fix it.

He made a clicking sound with his tongue and tilted his head back. "I am sorry Seyit Efendi, the winch is broken and will take hours to repair, that's if I can find the parts I need."

Seyit took a deep breath. "I need another round, even just one more. Help me lift one."

"Efendi, these shells weigh as much as three men." Gunner Mestan looked at Ali. "Or four. We cannot lift them without the winch."

"Take one from the cart," Seyit said. "A few of you, just lift it has high as my back."

Suleyman stepped forward and joined Mestan with another gunner. They cursed, but managed to haul the shell up to Seyit's back, in a horizontal position. Seyit reached behind with both arms, held the shell close to his back, one arm around the base of the shell and the other around the its nose. He rocked forward. Suleyman and the others steadied him and stepped back.

Seyit staggered unaided to the metal structure. His hairy barrel chest thrust forwards from a partially buttoned shirt, looking like it might burst with each lungful of air.

He climbed the first step and paused for a breath, then another, and another. He reached the firing platform still leaning forward, and still holding the shell. Two gunners helped him unload the burden and manoeuvre it into the breech.

Ali would not have believed such a feat of strength possible if he had not seen it.

Seyit leaned against steel balustrade and exhaled numbers in a rasping voice. The gunners adjusted the direction and angle of the gun in response. Seyit carried out final sighting checks.

Ali and the others covered their ears, now familiar with the firing sequence.

"Fire!"

Boom.

Ali hurried to the wall with the others.

Suleyman helped him up to see. Ali looked over the wall and saw flames burst forth from the deck of a ship in the second row. The sunken ship had been part of the first row of four. The remaining ships from the first row continued to steam away. The second row of four steamed forwards and continued to assault the land-based defences. They looked to be bigger than the ships in the first row. Now one of these had a hole in its upper deck spewing fire.

"Yes! Yes!" Seyit said. "That is the price you pay for Ottoman blood – English."

Seyit produced a grim smile, but there was sadness in his eyes.

"Here come the little minesweeping boats," Seyit said. "Come. Come boys. Our howitzers will welcome you. I hope you can swim. Nice and slowly, see, they struggle against the current."

Moments after Seyit spoke the words, sprays of water spouted around wooden fishing boats. The boats bobbed, like toys in a bath tub, under attack from a child's tantrum. One of the boats did an 'about face' and accelerated away with the current. The others turned and followed soon after.

One of the large warships in the second row that was now at the front turned away towards the other side of the Strait. Smoke billowed from its deck and funnels. Some flames were visible on its deck.

The turning ship was somewhere near the wreck of the first sunken ship when a fountain of water erupted from beneath its hull and it started to lean to one side.

Gunners and Suleyman's squad cheered as one. Ali's heart pounded and pride welled up from within. *We are fighting them off.*

The men watched the ship lean to one side and an explosion erupted below the waterline of another ship in the area.

"So you have found a minefield English," Seyit said. "One ship sunk and two sinking. There are plenty more mines for you."

The other warships continued to fire as the afternoon wore on. There was little more Ali could do with gun number three out of action.

A private from another platoon brought some water bottles for the men to drink. When the water hit Ali's parched throat, he realized that he had not had anything to drink since first light.

One of the four 240mm guns at Rumeli Mecidiye Fortress continued to fire. It's final projectile for the day was launched when the sun hung low.

Ali peered over the wall again with the others and drained his water bottle. One of the mined ships had limped away earlier, but the other was still lying wounded in the water. Another ship was attempting to tow it away to safety. The rescue ship looked to be the one Seyit's round had hit earlier, with the final shot from gun three.

Another fountain of water appeared, this time from the hull of the rescue ship. It too leaned over and began to sink. Ali squinted and saw tiny men falling into the water from its deck.

An involuntary giggle escaped before he could think to hold it back. Suleyman joined in with a deep guffaw, and soon the others followed and the whole group of men were laughing, pointing and congratulating themselves. Corporal Seyit, still on his firing platform, watched and nodded.

Ali felt the tension of the day wash away. The other warships were turning around.

"See, the jackals retreat," Suleyman said. "With their tails between their legs."

The explosions were fewer now. Several of the ships had turned broadside. *Could they be giving up?*

Seyit turned to the gunner Mestan. "Get that winch fixed before dawn, work all night if you have to. We'll need it tomorrow."

Ali watched with the other men as the ships turned away. One was listing and taking fire from closer shore batteries. It too leaned over and sank while they looked on.

* * *

That night Ali remembered the scorched leg that he had pushed out of his mind for several hours, but now he was hungry enough to eat. A meal of beans, bread and chicken soup was served up to Suleyman's squad and the gunners he had worked with all day.

After they had eaten, he lay on the ground wrapped in his great coat and surrounded by his brothers in arms.

Ali felt wide awake, but the ground felt more comfortable tonight, not so hard and cold. *Today I helped to defend my country.* He replayed the events of the day in his mind several times until exhaustion overtook him.

It was light when he awoke.

I must have slept for hours.

Men stirred around him. Many were still asleep. *No sign of the bastard Sergeant Kadir. Good.*

Ali rose quietly and climbed up to the rampart where he found Corporal Seyit on the firing platform, peering down the Strait.

Ali approached quietly, but the Corporal turned around and nodded to Ali.

"They will come back little man," Seyit croaked. "The winch is fixed and we'll make them pay – again. We still have plenty of shells and more are on their way. We may have to become martyrs like our brothers yesterday, but more men will come too. Let's see how many ships the English are prepared to sacrifice."

But the ships did not return.

CHAPTER 29

Charles

Tuesday, 23 March 1915

In a smoke-filled room, off the southern corridor of the Shepheard's Hotel in Cairo – ANZAC Headquarters – Charles sat in another briefing session with the Australian General Bridges and the other ANZAC commanders.

Maybe it was due to the oppressive Egyptian heat, but these briefing sessions seemed to cover the same ground over again and continued to lacked the clarity he craved. *If and when we are called upon to help take the Dardanelles Strait, how will a landing against a forewarned and well-prepared defensive army end in anything other than a massacre? If we do land, where will drinking-water come from? When will General Birdwood come back to command his Corps?*

At forty years of age, Major Charles Herbert Villiers-Stuart had spent around half his life in active service as a professional soldier with the British Army.

This was likely to be his last campaign and that was not such a bad thing as far as Charles was concerned. He had recently received news that his wife had given birth to their first child, a son. *I always hoped for a son.* His thoughts drifted back to his own childhood in Tipperary County. The lush green fields of southern Ireland seemed a world away from the dusty heat of Cairo.

Charles had come to join this campaign directly from India where he had been serving with the Punjabi Rifles Field Force. *It will be nice to go home to see Joan and meet my new baby boy, but that's for later – I have a job to do here and now. This campaign will be the one where I make a real difference to the outcome.*

The pieces were falling into place since he had been appointed as intelligence officer for Major-General William Birdwood's Army Corps. The General's antipodean forces included the Australian Imperial Force and New Zealand Expeditionary Force – united as the Australian and New Zealand Army Corps, a mouthful that was now regularly abbreviated to A&NZAC or ANZAC around Corps Headquarters.

It was good to be working with General Birdwood again, or at least it had been until he left a month ago to join the naval operations at the Dardanelles Strait, at around the same time as the Australian Third Infantry Brigade left for the Island of Lemnos near the mouth of the Straits.

In India, Birdwood proved himself to be a capable leader. The general was a good solid British army man, no doubt hand-picked by Lord Kitchener himself after serving with him in South Africa and India.

The colonials from Australia and New Zealand lacked battle experience and were naïve at best. But the officers seemed intelligent and were intent on proving themselves as worthy representatives of the Empire.

These imperial soldiers were mostly recent volunteers with no idea of what a modern conflict involved. They had demonstrated a lack of military order since setting up camp in Egypt. However, Charles had to acknowledge their unbridled enthusiasm and top physical condition. In the dessert training exercises they learned quickly and showed great potential. They were a tough lot, camped out of town at the Mena and Zeitoun camps. *They do lack discipline though, they don't quite seem to be at heart regular soldiers.*

It irked him, like fingernails running down a blackboard, the way the Australians mutilated one of his favourite old songs 'It's a long way to Tipperary' with the bawdy variant 'That's the wrong way to tickle Mary'.

Nevertheless, Charles was ready to seize his opportunity with both hands. The colonial forces were clay for him to mould. With the right direction they could be a powerful force. He would provide the benefit of his military experience and harness the energy and resources available to get the best outcome for the Empire.

News of the British and French naval losses at the Dardanelles on the 18th of March had recently come in. It was hard to keep that kind of disaster a secret. As the Corps intelligence officer, he had a responsibility to gather all information to assist with the early stages of planning, even though the full nature of the mission was unknown.

His focus returned sharply to the smoke-filled present as General Bridges looked expectantly towards him, signalling that it was time for him to provide the intelligence update.

Charles spoke to all present at the briefing session, but addressed his report to the Australian general.

"Sir, we have another informant report broadly confirming the enemy numbers as reported from other sources. We believe that there are five Turkish Army divisions on the Gallipoli peninsula and directly across the Dardanelles, with estimated total troop numbers of 43,000 men from Bulair to Kum Kale. Reinforcements could also be brought from Constantinople where they have 101,000 men in eleven divisions; or from Smyrna where they have another division of 10,000 men. There is a clear trend of increasing enemy troop numbers in this region to defend the Dardanelles – they know we're coming Sir and they're getting ready for us. We know that German officers are leading the Turks, so we expect them to be well organised, but we have very little intelligence on the trenching and field gun emplacements at this time. Our Third Brigade is already at Lemnos Island, and others are likely to be required for a military assault on the Gallipoli peninsula after the unsuccessful naval attempt, we have to plan for strong resistance against our landing."

"Thank you Major," General Bridges replied. "We have not received any official word about landing troops on the peninsula at this time. However, I have recently learned that General Hamilton, Commander in Chief of the Mediterranean Expeditionary Force is on his way to Egypt as we speak. As you say Major, it would seem likely that all of the ANZAC might be needed to take the Dardanelles. I know it is difficult to obtain detailed intelligence on enemy defensive preparations from this distance, but do what you can to make this a priority for future briefings."

General Bridges turned to face others at the table. "Regardless, as Major Villiers-Stuart has indicated, assuming we are to land in force, we will be facing large enemy numbers, and with the Germans involved we should expect a tough fight. The landing will be critical. Our troops will be vulnerable in the landing boats, whether it's just one Brigade or the whole of the A&NZ Corps. The boats move slowly and have no armour. Enemy machine guns and shelling could rip them to pieces before they get anywhere near the shore. We need to find a way to protect our men until they can find some decent cover on dry ground. An option has been raised that I would like your thoughts on. It's unconventional, but it might just work. The idea is to land a covering force by stealth, under cover of darkness. They would secure the beach head and provide a safe landing area for the main body of troops."

Now there's an idea.

"What about a daylight landing supported by covering shell fire from the navy?" one of the staff officers offered.

"That would be a more orthodox approach," Bridges said, "and it's probably what the Turks and Germans are expecting. There would be advantages of landing in daylight, to avoid confusion amongst our own troops for one. Rapid advancement is critical. They have to be able to hit the beach running. Unfortunately, the covering shell fire can only be effective if it can be targeted at the enemy trenches and field guns accurately. Now, as we have just heard from Major Villiers-Stuart, we have no bloody idea where they are. Further, the terrain is pretty damn steep and rugged, so it's about as good as it gets for the defending army. If they are organised and mobile, it will be impossible for our naval brothers to take them all out of action for long enough for us to land the full body of our force."

"What if the enemy has search lights. They could still shell and machine gun us at night. If there is a decent bit of moonlight they could kill us without electric lights." Another dissenter added.

"The peninsula's fifty miles long", Bridges said, "and they don't know where we will land. We don't even know that ourselves yet. I don't think they could have electric searchlights covering all potential landing sites. We know they have some lights covering the Straits inside the Dardanelles so it's a risk, but the lights can only illuminate a few hundred yards and would make for a nice target for our guns on the landing boats. It is easier to see the spotlight from a boat than the boat from behind the light. You're right about the moon though. If we are to try for stealth landing at night, then we would have to choose a time when there is little or no moon."

"But when the shooting starts the enemy will know that we are landing. They can still shoot us as we land in the dark."

The Australian general leaned back in his chair and crossed his arms. "That's *if* the enemy starts shooting. We would need to land silently in the dark and get a covering force to secure the beach head with bayonets before anyone starts shooting. If we have men running around, blasting away in the dark, we'll find half of them shot by dawn even if there is no damned enemy for miles. Look, I know it's not perfect. There are risks and it needs a whole lot more thought and planning, but let's just keep the idea on the table as an option for further consideration. The alternative is a daylight landing and expected losses would be high."

Charles tried not to flinch. *That's one way to describe the carnage of hundreds of men being cut down by machine gun and rifle fire.*

"Please think on this gentlemen," General Bridges said. "We will discuss our tactics further tomorrow."

The participants took that as a signal that the meeting was over. With one exception, they gathered their papers and cigarettes and began to shuffle out. Major Charles Villiers-Stuart sat and reflected for a moment on the idea that General Bridges had just presented. *It is unconventional, but creative. Given the well entrenched enemy defences that we will face at the landing, it might just be what we need.*

General Bridges seemed like a capable commander. He was only a colonial, but did at least have some real military experience. As a professional soldier, few things frustrated Charles more than armchair strategists with opinions and egos, but no field experience. As an intelligence officer he knew that listening, thinking and careful planning were the most effective way to achieve battlefield outcomes.

Yes, this idea of landing a covering force by stealth is definitely worth of further consideration. He gathered his belongings and left the empty briefing room.

In the fighting with the Indian Army on the Afghan border, Charles had witnessed the devastating effects of modern machine gun fire and shrapnel bursts from large field guns, and equally learned the value of concealment and terrain. This weighed heavily on his mind. The level of Turkish defences was likely to be high, particularly with the German officers and weapons that they were sure to have.

Unfortunately, Charles was blind to the terrain, as well as enemy trench and field gun emplacements. General Bridges had latched onto this as a problem as soon as Charles had mentioned it during the briefing.

As intelligence officer for an invading force, it was his responsibility to assemble whatever information he could about the enemy that might assist with the invasion planning. With more time there was plenty he could do, but the landing had to be planned in the coming month. The logistical implications of landing thousands of men on a hostile and well-defended shore were terrific. *We don't even know where to find fresh water for the men to drink. Time is of the essence and information is essential.*

Some old maps of the Gallipoli peninsula were available from the Egyptian War Office. The maps gave a reasonable feeling for the terrain, but were not enough to plan for a military landing of this scale without more detailed intelligence of the enemy preparations.

Somehow I need to find better information.

CHAPTER 30

Ellis

Thursday, 25 March 1915

Italians lack any understanding of the need for urgency.

Ellis threw his bags to the floor of his suite in the Grand Hotel in Rome, then threw himself into a deep leather lounge chair beside the window.

Stuck here for four days before I can cross from Sicily to Malta. I might miss the start of the expedition. I wonder if the Italians still hate me for that story I wrote about their army in Tripoli. Nice scoop that was. Earned me a few quid too.

Ellis savoured the memory of the time had exposed the 'Massacre in the Oasis' in 1911. In the early days of the occupation of Tripoli, Italian troops attacked a village and, seized by bloodlust, killed hundreds of Arabs, including unarmed women and children. Ellis witnessed the final stages of the massacre and saw the bodies of the innocents. He had written up a long despatch and sent it via Malta to bypass the Italian censor. The story was reproduced in most of the European and American papers and caused a great stir across Europe. The Italians accused Ellis of lying, breaking censorship rules and even being drunk, and he had to clear out of the country before he was arrested. Now he was back in Italy for the first time since his hasty departure four years earlier.

It's not quite midday yet, but close enough. I may as well visit the bar.

Ellis hauled himself out of the lounge chair and locked the hotel room door behind him on the way out.

Downstairs near the bar, Ellis recognised Turkish Prince Djemil Tossoun from Constantinople. *Now there's a stroke of luck. Maybe I shouldn't be too quick to quit gambling after all.*

Ellis straightened his tie and his posture, then sauntered in the direction of the prince.

"Ellis Ashmead-Bartlett!" The prince smiled. "How the devil are you? What brings you and your nose for trouble to Rome? I thought you would be crawling through French mud towards the sound of the guns, with a typewriter under one arm and a bottle of champagne under the other."

"Your Highness," Ellis didn't hesitate. "I am always on the lookout for a good scoop, but sadly Lord Kitchener won't let us war correspondents close to the front in France. I am on assignment, but I can't say too much. You know how it is."

"Let me guess," Prince Djemil's grin broadened. "On your way to the British naval base in Malta, and then sailing east to a secret destination in the vicinity of the Dardanelles?"

"There's no fooling you, Your Highness. May I ask why are you here?"

"I have been living in Paris," the prince's smile disappeared. "But I was obliged to leave when England and France declared war on Turkey. I am on my way home to Istanbul, or Constantinople as you English insist on calling it. I must say, I would rather that we had aligned our interests with you than the Germans. I don't trust the Germans." The prince looked about and lowered his voice. "And I don't trust Enver or his Committee of Union and Progress."

"I suppose you cannot do much about that now?" Ellis asked.

"Even Sultan Mehmed is Caliph in name only." Prince Djemil shook his head. "His brother, the former Sultan, Abdul Hamid lives under house arrest as an example to any who would consider opposing the Committee. The Committee controls our army and the new warships we received from the Germans. I do not know where they are taking the remnant of our empire and I am not sure that they do either. You have a large fleet of warships of your own, licking their wounds at Mudros Harbour on the island of Imbros, after the attack on the Chanakkale Strait last week. Our men were concerned at first, but you might want to know that the defence held strong and almost no damage was done. We lost two guns and thirty-five men, that is all. The Straits are impregnable. Maybe you would like to come by the Turkish embassy tomorrow to discuss the details with our Military Attaché and First Secretary?"

Ellis allowed himself a smile at the irony of the Prince's frustrations. In 1913, in an attempt to squeeze a few more pounds sterling from his own experiences in the Balkan revolt of 1912, Ellis had published a book "With the Turks in Thrace". In the final chapter of this work he had indulged himself in a brief commentary on the direction the Turks might take the remnant of the Ottoman Empire. Ellis concluded that 'The future of the Turk lies in Asia. Let him return to the land of his fathers and develop those matchless resources which constant wars and preoccupations in Europe have caused him to neglect.'

"Yes, your highness," Ellis said. "I would like that very much."

* * *

The next day, true to his word, Prince Djemil arranged for Ellis to visit the Turkish Embassy in Rome. Ellis was pleased to find that the Military Attaché was an old friend from the Balkan War days, and that he was also quite out of sympathy with the Young Turks, the leaders of the Committee of Union and Progress who now controlled the Turkish Government.

Ellis was able to read the official account of the naval attack. As the document was intended for Embassy staff eyes only, he believed it likely to be accurate. He left the embassy with his view confirmed. *We have underestimated the magnitude of the task, and our naval attack last week never had a chance of succeeding.*

That afternoon Ellis went to the races, but was more interested in observing humans than horses. The crowd included representatives from all the warring nations, as well as locals. Many Italians seemed to feel that their lot would be improved by joining the war, but opinions were divided as to which side they should join.

The next few days dragged on, but seemed less of a waste for the good intelligence gleaned from the Turkish Embassy. None of the rumours he picked up indicated that he would miss the start of the Dardanelles expedition, so he figured that he and his travelling companion Lester Lawrence might as well try to enjoy themselves.

Lester was another war correspondent on his way to Malta and the Dardanelles expedition, but that was about the only similarity he had with Ellis. Ellis represented the London newspapers and Lester Lawrence had been selected from Reuters Agency to write for the Provincial Press.

Lester had an appearance and demeanour that Ellis could only describe as soft. Severely myopic and completely reliant on heavy lens spectacles, it was a wonder how he would see anything to report. Lester lacked the instinct and experience that Ellis knew he himself could count on again to get the scoop.

* * *

The two war correspondents crossed to Malta on April Fools' Day and checked into the Osborne Hotel late morning.

Ellis wasted no time before he slipped away and headed for the Old Port to seek out Admiral Limpus, as he had been instructed to do by Winston Churchill in England.

The admiral welcomed Ellis and seemed glad of the opportunity to vent his frustration.

"With all due respect, Sir," Ellis said. "I am not sure that I fully understand. You are the most senior naval officer in the Mediterranean?"

"Yes," Admiral Limpus replied.

"And you have come here recently after spending some years heading our Naval Mission in Turkey?"

"That's right."

"So you would know the defences of the Dardanelles better than anyone else?"

"I dare say so."

"And yet, now, you are relegated to the charge of the dockyards of Malta."

"It was not considered good etiquette to employ me against my old pupils."

"Etiquette? Really, despite the fact that we are at war? As I understand it, you were sent to train the Turkish navy at their request. If they are to benefit from your instruction, surely we are entitled to take advantage of your experience."

"One might argue that, Mr Ashmead-Bartlett. And yet, here I am."

"May I ask, did Mr Churchill, or anyone from the Admiralty ask you for your opinions in regards to the attack on the Dardanelles?"

"First I heard of it was after three good ships were sunk and God only knows how many men went down with them. If I had been asked for my view beforehand, I would have told them then what I'm telling you now. That attack should never have been made. The forts and defences are far too strong to be breached by a naval attack alone. Now we have given the Turks warning that we intend to strike, and they'll be ready to give us hell if we send troops to land on the peninsula itself."

"Remarkable Sir. Thank you for your candour."

"I take it that you and Mr Lawrence will be wishing to join the fleet to report on this expedition?"

"Yes Sir. That is the general idea."

"I will send you on the next available boat, but there are no warships going that way, you'll have to travel on a collier or a tramp."

"Thank you sir, I will let Mr Lawrence know."

Ellis left in a state of disbelief, still processing the conversation he just had. *It's amazing the British Empire can continue to survive with such inept decisions being made about how to prosecute a war.*

Back in his hotel room, he scribbled some notes in his diary and then pondered his next campaign while he rested before dinner.

Late in the afternoon, Ellis woke from his nap, dressed for dinner and left his room to find Lester Lawrence.

"I reported to Admiral Limpus," Lester spoke from his doorway. "As per our instructions. It seems that you had already been to pay him a visit."

"Yes," Ellis replied. "He's an interesting old salt, very sceptical about the prospects of the expedition."

"Do you really think so?" Lester seemed genuinely surprised.

"We are press correspondents Man, it is acceptable to ask people questions."

"You are dressed for dinner. Were shall we dine?"

"I was thinking of the Malta Club."

"Splendid. Give me a moment."

After what seemed more like several moments, Lester emerged and the two walked together towards the Malta Club. The spring evening air was a pleasant walking temperature, and Ellis felt renewed enthusiasm for the first time in 1915.

The humiliation of bankruptcy three months earlier was something that even Ellis had struggled to shake off. With over £4,000 of unpaid debts, he needed good work in this war to make another new beginning.

At least Winston Churchill sees the advantage of frontline reporting, being himself an old war correspondent of renown. He's reported on nearly as many wars as I. Those group tours of stale battlefields that Kitchener allowed us to join were a poor substitute for reporting on live action. I cannot imagine why Kitchener hates us so. The readers are starting to complain that the truth is being concealed and they are right. History shows that war correspondents have played an important role in all wars in living memory, and no British army has ever had cause to regret their presence at the front.

It might have helped that this is a naval operation and I know Winston personally. Maybe he feels bad that his blasted brother Jack stole my beloved Gwendoline from me.

On arrival at the Malta Club, the pair of war correspondents found a vast gathering of officers from the Army and Navy. Ellis was surprised to run across several old friends from transports en route for the Dardanelles, all longing to get to the front. Most of these had never shown any interest in the Army before the war, but had risen, with remarkable rapidity, to be colonels, majors and captains. *It's not what you know, it's who you know.*

The cocktails and food were up to a good British standard, but Ellis was unable to learn any more details about the Dardenelles expedition that night. *At least it looks like I won't miss the opening scene, whatever that may be. The way Winston was talking, I thought it might be all over in a matter of days.*

Early the next morning, Ellis received a message from Admiral Limpus. Ellis and Lester Lawrence were invited to sail that afternoon on the oil tank steamer *Sunik*, to join the fleet at a secret destination. Ellis accepted the invitation, as did Lester, and the two war correspondents boarded the ship by lunch time and introduced themselves to the captain.

The captain made them feel most welcome and informed them that the brand new oil tank steamer was carrying 6,000 tons of fresh water to the troops about to land in Gallipoli, which she had brought all the way from Liverpool. Scarcity of water was a known difficulty in the islands of the eastern Mediterranean and on the Gallipoli peninsula itself.

At 4:00 pm the *Sunik* steamed out of Malta Harbour.

Ellis stood at the bow with the afternoon sun warming his back as the tanker pushed through the azure water.

At last, I am away towards the next great clash of might. Our unstoppable force approaches an impenetrable barrier. Many men will die gloriously. To sustain this salary of £165 per month, I shall have to write well of great courage and epic deeds done for the Empire.

"There never was a greater tragedy than the First World War. It engulfed an age, and conditioned the times that followed. It contaminated every ideal for which it was waged, it threw up waste and horror worse than all the evils it sought to avert, and it left legacies of staunchness and savagery equal to any which have bewildered men about their purpose on earth."

– Bill Gammage, 1974[3]

"My mate used to say that there are two days you need not try to escape death: the day you are not going to die, for nothing will harm you on that day; the other time is the day you are to die, for nothing will prevent your death that day. When we were called on to 'Hop-over' my mate would say 'Come on! Let's see which day it is.'"

– An Anzac soldier[4]

3 The Broken Years, page xviii (Author's note)

4 WWI Anzac Soldier unnamed, quoted in *The Anzacs*, by Patsy Adam-Smith, page 8.

PART II

INTO THE POT

CHAPTER 31

Ronald

Friday, 2 April 1915

A piano edged through the balcony door, eight floors up, then fell towards the flames that filled the street below.

A fireman ran past Ron, hauling a red hose.

The piano hit the bonfire, sounded every note at once and sent a squall of sparks into the darkening sky.

An Australian soldier ran after the fireman, stepped on the hose, and severed it with a pocket knife.

The sound of a gunshot echoed between the buildings of the Harret el Wasser, but no one seemed to take any notice.

"Gyppo filth!" Jayjay spat. "Serves them right!"

"What?" Ron spun to face his brother. "Our boys are destroying the place. They'll likely be sent home instead of the war front for this kind of behaviour, just like the ones who caught the sex disease."

"Just a bit of good old-fashioned retribution," Seamus O'Shea grinned, his face glowing red in the light of the flames. "For the lads wounded in horizontal combat. And for the bad drink. The Gyppo's pissed in it to give it colour, to be sure."

"We ought to be careful to not get caught up in this chaos," Ron said. "We could be sent home too if we're accused of being involved. It's only days before we go to war, after travelling half way around the world, and all that training. Why take the risk of staying here watching?"

"I think that's why our boys are a bit out of control," Jayjay laughed. "Because they know we're about to leave, and they've got a few scores to settle before we go."

A mattress flew out a window, into the fire, and a bed followed.

Why is Jayjay so cheerful about this destruction? That's not like him.

Ron peered about, half-expecting a squad of military police to storm around the corner at any moment, arrest him along with Jayjay and Larry, and lock them up for affray.

What would Mum and Dad and Em think if I was sent home in disgrace for rioting? Would it matter that I am innocent?

* * *

Two nights later, in the small hours of Easter Sunday morning, Ronald Jones marched out of Mena camp, with the 1st Battalion of the Australian Imperial Force.

Someone ahead started to sing and within seconds the whole platoon joined in. Ron sang along as he marched.

Rally round the banner of your country,
    Take the field with brothers o'er the foam;
On land or sea, wherever you be,
    Keep your eye on Germany.
But England home and beauty have no cause to fear,
    Should Auld acquaintance be forgot,
No! No!   No! No! No!   Australia will be there,
    Australia will be there.

Ron barely noticed the weight of the pack on his back. *Finally we are on our way to the true test. Australia will be there and I will be there. I will fight for what is right and defend the innocent. Ten miles to Cairo. Easy work compared to the usual night drills.*

"The Battle of the Wozzer," Jayjay said. "Has gained legendary status."

"I still can't believe no one was charged," Ron said. "Just orders to pack up and get ready to march. No consequences for the riot, it didn't even rate a mention."

"I heard a couple of officers laughing about it afterwards." Jayjay gazed up towards the crescent moon. "They didn't seem too concerned."

"No one did," Larry said. "Except the Gyppos."

Ron shook his head.

Another marching song started ahead in the column.

They took me out to Pharaoh's land
    To train me for a soldier,
I got fed up with mummy's sand
    While training for a soldier.
I marched through deserts day and night
    'Twas said 'twould fit me for a fight,
My feelings felt it wasn't right,
    And so my feet grew colder.

Good-bye Sydney, Sydney, good-bye
    Sydney, Sydney,

Good-bye Sydney, good-bye,
My heart is aching, aching,
My back is breaking, breaking,
Good-bye Sydney, good-bye.

I wonder how Em is coping back home. We never really said a proper good-bye before I left Sydney, but I will do her proud. She would have liked to see the Pyramids. She would have loved the native children, she's good with children. God I miss her, please keep her safe.

The battalion marched for three hours, then snaked into Cairo in pre-dawn dark. Ron waited out the rest of the night with the noisy throng beside the railway line. Few men slept and at eight o'clock in the morning they boarded the train bound for Alexandria.

Ron dozed on the train that delivered the battalion to the edge of the Mediterranean Sea, then he woke to be herded off the train and onto the *Minnewaska* just before dinner time.

He marched up the gang plank and his mind went back to the day he had stepped off the transport ship A19 *Afric*, at the same dockyard four months ago. The nervous anticipation he experienced on that day returned. This ship would deliver him to the battlefield. Rumour was that it would be a waterway in Turkey called The Dardanelles. Ron had never heard of it before, but it was supposedly defended by Turks and Germans. *God help me to fight like a soldier when my time comes. I'm not sure if I have the violence in me.*

Sergeant Baker called the men to fall in on deck.

"Good news lads," the platoon's sergeant barked. "Tonight you'll be getting your first taste of war. It's called iron rations. Bully beef and hard biscuits."

He paused and men stood silent. It was as if he wanted them to respond, but no one did.

"This ship," the sergeant continued, "is a cattle transport ship, so she's quite well suited to her current purpose. She can cater for up to one hundred first class passengers and a mob of beasts. Do any of you qualify to travel first class? No? Right you are. In a few days we will be joined by the ANZAC general staff, including General Birdwood himself, so you lot will be on your best behaviour. We will all be travelling cattle class. On your last voyage from Sydney you might have become accustomed to certain luxuries, like fresh food and hammocks. This is not the *Afric*. When you are trying to sleep, remember that this is not a holiday voyage. Tomorrow you will be up early to load stores. Any questions? No? Good. Now have something to eat and get some rest. You can sleep up here on deck or below with the horses."

Rain started to fall.

Ron's mind drifted back to the day he signed up in Sydney, and his first night as an enlisted man, trying to sleep, in the rain, on a timber bench at Randwick Racecourse. *The first night since our marriage that Em and I slept apart. I hope she's coping without me. I hate leaving her alone. The decision to sign up seemed so much clearer when I was at home. I never would have thought doing my duty would be so hard.*

* * *

A week after embarking on the *Minnewaska*, and one day after finally steaming away from Alexandria, Ron stood to attention on deck at Church of England Church Parade.

Today's attendance was greater than usual. Maybe because men knew that death for some lay waiting over the horizon, or maybe because they knew they would be addressed by the ANZAC commander, General Birdwood himself.

"Boys," the general said. "As this may be the last occasion on which I shall have the opportunity of speaking with so many of you together there are just two or three things I want to say to you. I wrote the other day to the High Commissioner and to Lord Kitchener and I told him that I had perfect confidence in your ability to fight. I feel absolute confidence in you but there are one or two things that I can say that may be of help to you. We have been given a very big task. You know that away in France the two armies are facing one another and things are almost at a standstill. Well, we have been given a very important mission – to turn the German flank. We are to land at the Dardanelles. There will not only be Turks opposing us, but Germans; they will do everything they can to foil us. They will have done everything with their accustomed thoroughness, barbed wire, aeroplanes, trenches. Your officers will exercise cunning to meet and outwit them. They will give you what you want – straight leading – any amount of it. There are just three things I want you to do for yourselves – and they concern first ammunition, secondly water and thirdly food. You may be landed under opposition and it may be some considerable time before the supplies can be sent up to you. You will have to take 200 rounds of ammunition, full water bottles, and three days rations. That is a very heavy load but it has to be done somehow. Now what I want to ask you is this: first don't waste ammunition. The time will come when you will want it – you will reach a point when the enemy will be in front of you and you will have to pump in as much of it as possible into him. Don't waste it or throw it away whatever you do to start with. Secondly water. I have seen men begin to pull at their water bottles five minutes after leaving camp. If you once begin that you can't stop. It may be evening before we can get the watercarts up to you, so don't waste your water. Thirdly food. You will have to take three days rations. Some men are inclined to just nibble at a biscuit or two and then throw them away. For God's sake don't do that. Remember those three things. As I say, I have complete confidence that you will do all the honour of England and Australia demand of you."

The General dismissed the congregation and Ron wandered to the starboard balustrade with Jayjay and Larry.

"After all this," Larry shook his head, "we still don't get to go to France."

"No, but still fighting the Germans," Ron replied. "General Birdwood said this is a very important mission. I suppose we wouldn't be here if it wasn't."

"Yeah," Jayjay said. "I want to go to France too, but Ron's right, as usual."

Larry looked unconvinced. "What do you think 'landing under opposition' will be like?"

"I don't think it means," Ron said, "that the Turks and Germans will be standing on the shore, waving their arms about and yelling insults."

"Maybe they'll ask us politely to sod off," Jayjay said.

"There are so many islands," Larry shook his head, "and the water is so blue. A swim'd be nice. They reckon there are no sharks here. I might come back for a holiday some time."

"Another one?" asked Jayjay.

"Yeah," Larry said. "A holiday where I don't have to sleep on the damn floor. Everything about this ship is iron. Sleeping on the iron floor, eating iron rations. And you know what the new commander of the Mediterranean Expeditionary Force is called? Sir Iron Hamilton!"

"Not growling again are you Private Gillespie?" Sergeant Baker had appeared from behind as if from nowhere. "I hope you're not getting soft. You know good soldiers have to get used to hard-ships!"

Sergeant Baker chuckled alone.

Ron had heard him make the same joke earlier. *Likely I'll hear it again before the end of today.*

"See that island there?" the sergeant pointed. "Being good Church of England lads, you might be interested to know that that is the Island of Patmos. You know what happened there don't you."

"Saint John the apostle," Ron said, "received the Revelation of Jesus Christ, and wrote it down – the last book of the bible."

"Right you are Jones."

Baker sauntered off.

The largest hill on the island was capped in white, like snow, but it was too warm for snow. Ron squinted and made out the shapes of white buildings. At the peak a grey stone fortress stood proud.

"I wonder why he was there," Ron said. "An island in the middle of nowhere. It's not very big, can't be more than five miles across."

"I always found Revelation confusing," Jayjay said. "All that talk of war and the four horsemen, Armageddon and the apocalypse."

"I never understood that stuff either," Ron said. "But we are going to fight for what's right, so I reckon God will be on our side. That's good enough for me."

Jayjay and Larry nodded and the three stared at the water and islands drifting past.

After lunch no attempt was made to have the men drill, so there was little else to do but stand around on the crowded deck. The *Minnewaska*, fitted out to carry a cargo of cattle and 100 people, was carrying 500 horses and 1,900 men.

Late in the afternoon a speck in the sky caught Ron's eye, hovering above an island way off ahead.

"There's an aeroplane," Ron said. "Like the one we saw at Kenso'."

"No way," Jayjay said. "It must be a bird. Aeroplanes can't fly that high, it must be thousands of feet in the air."

"No, look," Larry replied. "It's too steady to be a bird. It's moving east, back towards the mainland. Maybe it's German, spying on our forces. General Birdwood said the Germans have aeroplanes."

"That's ridiculous!" Jayjay said. "We'd just shoot it out of the sky if it wasn't one of ours. Look how slow it's moving."

"Yeah, I s'pose."

* * *

Next morning, Ron woke at first light and rolled over with a pain in his hip from lying on the hard deck.

A destroyer was guiding the *Minnewaska* into the mouth of an enormous body of calm water. Rolling hills lined either side, about a mile away in both directions.

Ahead lay a fleet of warships and transport ships, maybe fifty or sixty large vessels. A variety of smaller boats moved in between. *This waterway must be three times the size of Sydney Harbour, it's more like Botany Bay. Where are we?*

Jayjay sat with his back to a wall and looked wide awake. He nodded at Ron and gave Larry a shove. "Larry, Mate, wake up and take a look at this."

Larry groaned and took in a moment to absorb the surrounds.

"Blazes! This must be the Dardanelles."

CHAPTER 32

Charles

Tuesday, 13 April 1915

Since leaving the Shepheard's Hotel in Cairo a week earlier, the Corps Intelligence Officer for ANZAC, Major Charles Villiers-Stuart had resided in an officer's berth with Corps Headquarters staff on the ship *Minnewaska*. Comfortable accommodation was something to enjoy while it lasted, but it wouldn't last much longer.

Enemy forces on the Gallipoli peninsula and in the Dardanelles area were now, according to the Egyptian War Office, estimated at 73,000 men.

The *Minnewaska* had anchored in Mudros Harbour off the island of Lemnos yesterday after the voyage from Alexandria. This wet and windy morning he was ready to transfer onto the *Queen* for a two day reconnoitre in the Gulf of Saros, scheduled to conclude with a flight in an aeroplane.

I was always ready to stop a bullet in the heat of battle, but falling out of the sky is not the way I want to depart this life. If God had meant for men to fly He would have given us wings like a bird. Heights make me feel dizzy. I wonder if it's possible to fly as high as the clouds. What happens if we hit one?

There was no arguing with the need. Intelligence brought back from aerial reconnaissance flights by Wing Commander Samson's No.3 Air Squadron was remarkable. This was exactly the information he needed to plan the troop landing. Many lives would depend on it. He wanted to see the enemy preparations with his own eyes.

Charles walked out from under cover to transfer to the *Queen* and cold rain stung his face. He wore a wry smile as he walked past the men from the First Battalion. They climbed over the balustrade again, after God knows how many times to practice for a landing. Heavy rain lashed at their backs and there was plenty of grumbling and swearing.

Just wait lads 'til it rains lead – then you'll have something to complain about. You Australians have no idea what you're in for.

Charles stepped onto the *Queen* and his heart rate quickened. A hard, grey skeleton exposed, with no pretence to cover the machinery of war. Inside, the dimly lit corridors were no softer. He followed the others and stepped through a watertight doorway that would be sealed in the event of hull penetration. *This campaign is more than a plan now.*

* * *

The *Queen* steamed up the Gulf of Saros, well away from the enemy shore and Charles sat in on a briefing session along with other ANZAC, British and French officers in the ward room. A British General Staff officer presented the landing plan as a coordinated assault along the Gallipoli peninsula and Asian coast. At each landing site, a covering force would be sent to claim and defend the beachhead before the landing of the main force. The ANZAC landing site was designated as beach Z, designed to cut off enemy access to Cape Helles at the toe of the peninsula. Cape Helles would be the site where the main landing assault was to take place at a series of beaches designated as S, V, W, X and Y.

Charles focused on the written ANZAC orders, addressed to General Birdwood, the General Officer Commanding. The orders were neatly typed:

SECRET.

INSTRUCTIONS FOR G.O.C. A. & N.Z. ARMY CORPS.

GENERAL HEADQUARTERS

13th April 1915.

1. Information regarding the enemy.
The enemy holds the KILID BAHR plateau in strength, and is believed to have a number of troops concentrated in the neighbourhood of the ANAFARTA villages and MAIDOS. There may be two Divisions (20,000 men) distributed in these areas. Gun emplacements have been located at KABA TEPE and NIBRUNESI POINT, but repeated air reconnaissances have failed, as yet, to disclose any guns.

2. Objective.
A landing force is to be made by the A. & N. Z. Army Corps on the beach between KABA TEPE and FISHERMAN'S HUT. The objective assigned to the Army Corps is the ridge over which the GALLIPOLI-MAIDOS and BOGHALI-KOJADERE roads run, and especially MAL TEPE. Gaining such a position the Army Corps would threaten, and perhaps cut, the line of retreat of the enemy's forces on the KILID BAHR plateau, and must, even by their preliminary operations, prevent the said plateau being reinforced, during the attack of the 29th Division, from MAIDOS, GALLIPOLI or BULAIR.

3. Naval arrangements for landing covering force.

Four transports can be worked simultaneously on the beach selected (Beach "Z"). Three steam pinnaces, or picket boats, with 12 cutters or lifeboats, will be available for each transport of the covering force. These boats will be formed into 3 tows, each with a carrying capacity of 120-130 men. There will therefore be 12 tows available in all, with a total capacity of 1450 to 1500 men.

On the afternoon before the landing is to take place, the troops detailed for the first trip of the tows will be transferred, under naval arrangements to be notified later, from their respective transports to H. M. ships Queen, London and Prince of Wales, which will steam during the night to a position off KABA TEPE. The 12 tows will be brought alongside H. M. ships, under naval arrangements, in time to admit of the landing taking place on Beach "Z" at ________________ a.m.

Transports A1, A2, A3 and A4 carrying the remainder of the covering force will also rendezvous off KABA TEPE during the night, attended by eight torpedo boat destroyers, two of which will be ready to stand by each transport to take off the remaining troops.

The landing of the covering force will be effected in three stages as follows:-

1st stage.	Landing of 1450-1500 men from H.M. Ships in the first trip of the tows.
2nd stage.	Embarkation of the remainder of the covering force with eight torpedo boat destroyers (t. b. d.) which will follow in to shore immediately after the despatch of the first tows.
3rd stage.	Landing of the remainder of covering force from t. b. d. in succeeding trips of the tows. Three tows will be allotted to each pair of t. b. destroyers.

In order to enable t. b. d. to be emptied in three trips of the tows it may be necessary to effect some redistribution of the troops left in the transports before the latter start for the rendezvous off Beach "Z".

4. Naval arrangements for landing the main body
Subsequently, when the covering force is ashore, the transports of the Army Corps will come in and anchor, and the disembarkation will proceed in accordance with instructions given by you. Four transports can be worked simultaneously - three steam pinnaces or picket boats, four lighters, four horseboats and eight cutters or lifeboats being available for each transport.

5. Artillery support by the fleet.
During the disembarkation of the Army Corps, the guns of the fleet will be available to support it by their fire.

6. Topography.
The first essential for the covering force will be to establish itself in Squares 224, 237 and 238 (SARIBAIR on War Office map) in order to protect the landing of the remainder of the Army Corps. From the ridge between squares 237.Z. and 224.F. spurs run northwest and southwest to the sea. This semi-circular system of ridges seems to lend itself to the establishment of a strong covering position. Whether it will be necessary or not to include the crest of the mountain must be left to your discretion.

7. General plan of operation of the Army Corps.
As soon as the first division is landed with an irreducible minimum of animals and vehicles, the disembarkation of the second division will commence.

By the time the second division begins to land, sufficient troops should be available to admit of a further advance. Leaving the covering force to protect the northern flank of the landing place and line of communication, an effort will be made to storm MAL TEPE which is the centre and key to the ridge over which the GALLIPOLI-MAIDOS and BOGHALI-KOJADERE roads run. Should the A. & N. Z. Army Corps succeed in securing this ridge the results should be more vital and valuable than capture of the KILID BAHR plateau itself.

Times and dates have purposely been omitted in these instructions, and will be telegraphed later.

W. P. Braithwaite
Major-General
C.G.S.
Med. Ex. Force

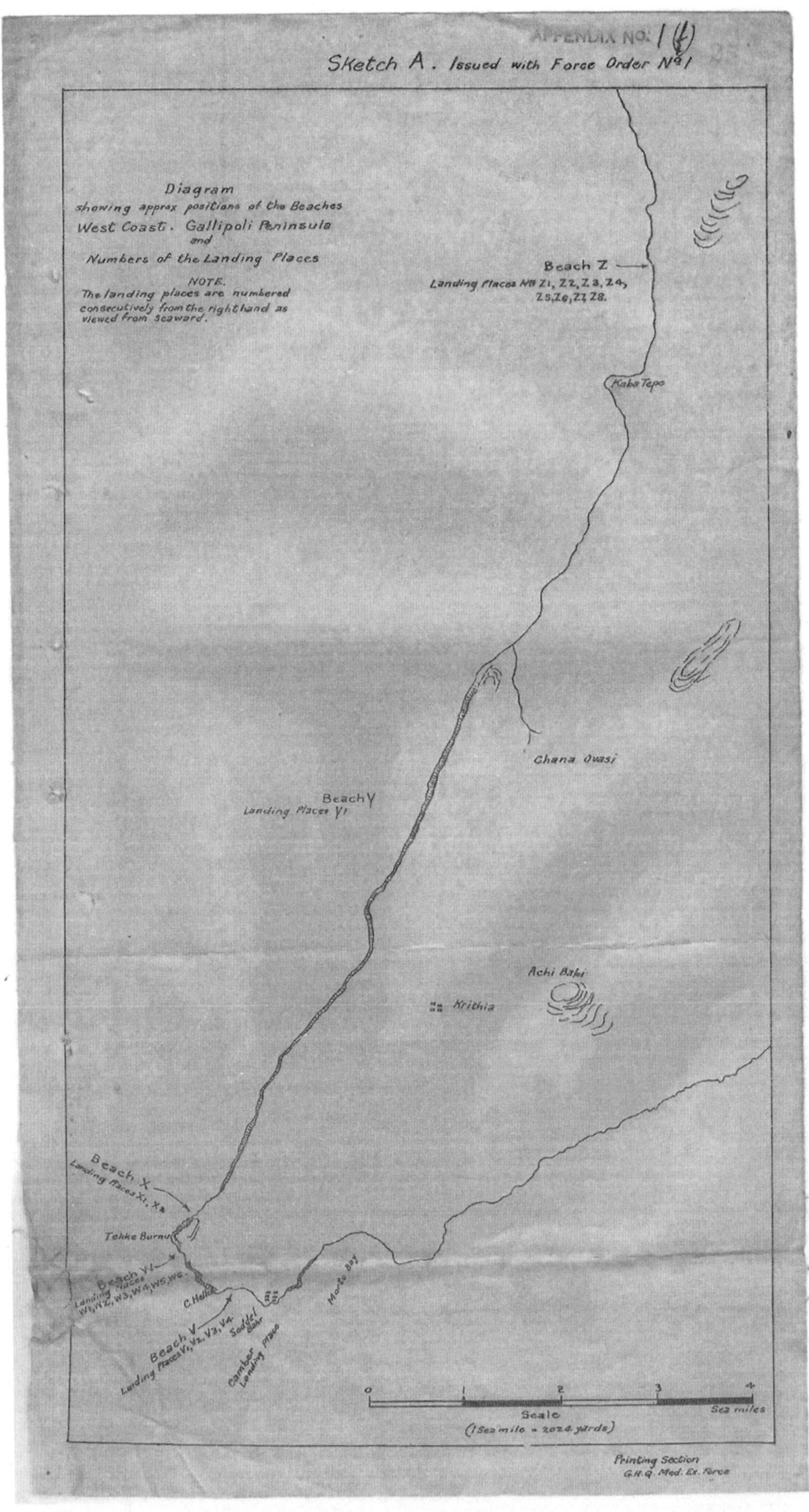
APPENDIX No. 1 (4)
Sketch A. Issued with Force Order No 1
Diagram
showing approx positions of the Beaches
West Coast. Gallipoli Peninsula
and
Numbers of the Landing Places
NOTE.
The landing places are numbered consecutively from the right hand as viewed from seaward.
Beach Z
Landing Places Nos Z1, Z2, Z3, Z4, Z5, Z6, Z7, Z8.
Kaba Tepe
Chana Ovasi
Beach Y
Landing Places Y1
Achi Baba
Krithia
Beach X
Landing Places X1, X2
Tekke Burnu
Beach W
Landing Places W1, W2, W3, W4, W5, W6.
C. Helles
Beach V
Landing Places V1, V2, V3, V4.
Seddel Bahr
Camber Landing Place
Morto Bay
0 1 2 3 4
Scale
Sea miles
(1 Sea mile = 2024 yards)
Printing Section
G.H.Q. Med. Ex. Force

Charles pulled out his note book and recorded the salient details for the A&NZAC landing zone: Beach Z, the whole Corps, from Gaba Tepe to the Fisherman's Hut, about three miles of coastline. The men would land in lifeboats, the first wave of the covering force to be towed in by steam pinnaces, and the rest to be towed by larger torpedo boat destroyers.

Sketch A was attached, a crude, hand drawn map, but he recognized the outline of the Gallipoli peninsula well enough. The headland of Gaba Tepe, spelt 'Kaba Tepe' on the map and orders, stuck out like the nose on a face. The Fisherman's Hut to the north was not shown, but he knew where it was from the aerial reconnaissance reports and maps he had reviewed, a small stone structure by the beach, nestled below the dominating Sari Bair range near the top of the sketch map.

The rest of the day was filled with nervous anticipation. Charles could feel it in himself and see it in others. It was one thing to pore over maps and theorize about how a landing might work, but to see the terrain would give a whole new perspective on the vision for the operation. Conversation amongst the officers during the evening meal was subdued. The lives of over thirty thousand A&NZAC men were in their hands.

* * *

The next morning, part way up the Gallipoli peninsula, the *Queen* turned about and steamed southwards along the coastline. A mile and a half offshore was close enough to have a good look at the terrain through the magnification of field glasses, and far enough away to minimize exposure to enemy gunfire.

Charles stood high on the viewing platform, wearing a blue naval uniform like the other officers, so enemy observers would not see the unusual presence of khaki-clad army folk surveying their shoreline.

Hopefully we will look like a crowd of curious sailors doing some sightseeing. I need to determine how to get our men ashore with minimal losses and the last thing we need is to alert the enemy to our intentions.

The terrain was scrubby with a harsh and uninviting feel. There were very few tall trees, but plenty of steep embankments on eroded spurs and tortured gullies groping upwards to an ill-defined ridge. There was no evidence of any serious attempt to clear the land for crops or grazing, at least not along the visible foreshore.

"There's the fisherman's hut," someone called from nearby.

Charles had already spied the small stone building close to the shore, marking the northern end of the Z beach landing zone. There was no sign of fishing boats or fisherman, or anyone else for that matter. The ridges of hills and gullies behind the fisherman's hut looked steep in places. It was difficult to tell from this distance which parts would be accessible by troops on the ground. Occasional weathered cliffs provided some clear barriers.

Beyond the fisherman's hut, the escarpment took on a clearer ridgeline and converged towards the sea. Maybe half a mile to the south of the stone dwelling, maybe more – distances were difficult to gauge, a narrow outcrop of rock thrust towards them from the top ridge, the scars of its naked face darkened in shadow. Continuing to the south, immediately past the rocky outcrop, a large spur ran towards the *Queen*, and plunged steep into the sea. At the foot of the spur, a sheltered cove lay hidden from all but the seaward approach, bookended by two stumpy toes.

The beach within the cove was narrow and looked to be half a mile long. This cove marked the approximate centre of the three-mile ANZAC landing zone.

Beyond the sheltered cove, a large gully followed behind the spur away from the sea towards the main ridgeline. The main ridge continued to follow the shoreline, but dropped gently behind a long white beach to provide much more open and inviting terrain. Charles knew from his maps that this beach was around a mile and a half long. It had been affectionately named Brighton Beach, no doubt by some homesick officer from southern England.

Brighton Beach ended at a rocky headland, rising up to overlook the open ground to the north. This headland was well known to Charles from his maps – Gaba Tepe.

Gaba Tebe was known from aerial reconnaissance reports to be home to a well-defended artillery battery. Tents and trenches around the gun emplacements indicated that the Turks would not give up the headland easily. I can't see much of it from here though. A bit of barbed wire along the beach was the only sign of an unwelcoming reception.

"That beach looks to be suitable for landing," said one of the nearby Australian First Division officers. "At least as far as one can tell from this distance."

Charles looked to see that he was gazing at the shores of Brighton Beach and shook his head slowly.

That's where the enemy might expect us to land, but there is no cover there. They are well entrenched and ready for us – losses would be disastrous. It helps to see the terrain in reality after staring at maps for so long, but looking from the sea is so limiting. If I didn't know better I would think that the enemy has abandoned the place. It looks so desolate – not good for anything other than defending the waterway behind it.

* * *

Charles waved off the picket boat and shook beads of seawater from his boots. The Jack Tar in control of the small boat threw him a casual salute and turned with his vessel back towards the *Queen*. Charles stood on the beach alone and took a moment to watch the small boat steaming away.

I've been in some difficult squeezes before. Why am I so terrified? Armed with only his notebook, map and a pencil, he turned and walked up the beach. *I've had to confront fear before, but never quite like this.*

The island of Tenedos was a slight detour from the direct route between the toe of the Gallipoli Peninsula to Mudros Harbour. The *Queen* took the detour after the inspection voyage to deliver one Major Charles Villiers-Stuart.

British No. 3 Air Squadron had established an aerodrome on Tenedos, and had provided some exceptional intelligence information on enemy defensive preparations. This would be the place for the start of his first reconnaissance flight in an aeroplane – and hopefully the place for his safe return as well.

The pilot, Flight Lieutenant Herb Collet, was ready for him. "Welcome Major, ever flown in an aeroplane before?"

Charles shook his head. *At least he looks relaxed. That aeroplane looks awfully flimsy. I wonder if they ever break apart in the air.*

"None to worry. It's quite safe really, safer than being on the ground and running at a machine gun eh?" Collet chuckled.

"Just a few details before we take off," Flight Lieutenant Collet continued. "This is a Maurice Farman pusher biplane, driven by a Renault 110 horsepower engine. Normally she's quite reliable, but you might notice she lurches up and down a bit with the air currents around the place."

Charles stared at the flying vehicle. *Makes sense so far – it has two sets of wings and the engine is at the back with a propeller to push it along. It just looks so ungainly.* The only part that looked remotely solid appeared to be an oversized baby's cradle mounted precariously between the top and bottom wings. *The two of us are going to sit in that?*

"Once we get to 300 feet I have to back the engine off a little so she doesn't overheat. Sometimes she coughs a bit, but it's nothing to worry about. Although, sometimes the engine does cut out. Now if that happens, I want you to reach down and check the main petrol tap under your seat. Sometimes the vibrations cause it to close and it needs to be opened back up to get the engine firing again."

Charles dragged his gaze from the aeroplane back to Flight Lieutenant Collet. *He's not laughing. He's serious. I must check the location of the fuel tap before we leave the ground.*

"Wear this leather jacket and flying helmet to keep the cold wind out, and these goggles otherwise your eyes will water so much you won't be able to see a thing, and that would be kind of a shame since you're going to all this trouble to look at the view."

Collet chuckled again.

Charles climbed carefully onto the fragile-looking frame and eased himself down into the back seat of the baby's cradle. The engine was directly behind him, and a large propeller behind that. He reached down and was relieved to find the fuel tap.

Collet climbed up carrying two empty petrol tins and handed one to Charles.

"Now, one last thing," he said. "Life jackets have been hard to come by with all the ships sinking of late, so if we come down in the drink, hang on to this."

"You must be joking," Charles said.

"I wouldn't joke about something serious like this Major. This is for your safely. But don't worry, we haven't had to use the tins yet."

A fellow in a dirty uniform came over and started the Renault engine by doing something behind Charles where he couldn't see. The engine roared to life and the aeroplane started to roll forward. Charles fought the urge to vomit, and checked that, if necessary, he could lean far enough over the side.

The Maurice Farman biplane accelerated along the dirt runway and the ground blurred, then fell away beneath them.

Charles was thankful the engine maintained its constant drone. The air was much smoother than the bumpy runway on the shrinking island of Tenedos behind him. *I can't climb down and walk away now.* He felt a sensation that reminded him of going into battle. An acceptance of his own impending doom settled on him and anxiety melted into exhilaration as the aeroplane gained altitude.

The toe of the peninsula started to take shape above the Dardanelles Strait that opened out into the Aegean Sea.

Tiny toy ships smoked below like discarded cigarettes. One fired a salvo in a ball of flame, followed by a gentle 'crump' when the sound of the ship's gun reached him. A brown dust cloud plumed from the hillside where the explosive shell landed. Maybe that was a devastating blast to mark the end of someone's war, maybe it took out a whole platoon, but it seemed such a trivial puff from the box seat in the sky. The dust cloud drifted away into nothing and Charles looked down to the map flapping in his clutches. *Now let us see what we can see.*

They flew along the coastline, up the western edge of the peninsula. Anti-aircraft explosive shells occasionally burst above, but they seemed to be somewhat speculative. *Thank God they cannot aim those guns better.*

The prominent form of the Gaba Tepe headland loomed ahead. Enemy camps, gun placements and trenches around this area were already marked by hand on his map, but seeing them sent a chill down his spine. The open ground behind Brighton Beach in the southern half of the Z beach landing zone was horribly exposed. A great place for a picnic, but no good for landing an army in the face of a well-prepared enemy.

A glint of light caught his eye, just for a moment. That could only be the reflection from shiny metal. A close look revealed a battery of four field guns on the northern slopes of Gaba Tepe, aimed directly into the exposed flatland behind Brighton Beach.

Charles rechecked the map – these guns were not marked. He scrawled a cross at their location.

The biplane continued towards the sheltered cove that he had observed with interest from the *Queen* earlier that day. It didn't look like much on the map, but the ridge at the southern end looked to break the direct line of fire from the Gaba Tepe guns.

The ridge coming down to the northern end of the cove was marked on his map as Ariburnu, it provided a similar shelter against attack from the north.

There are some trenches on Ariburnu, but they are small and isolated. They could be rushed and overcome. If the men can land here without being decimated in the water, they will have some hope of fighting towards the objectives.

That gully to the south of the cove might provide an accessible route towards the main ridge. So much relies on securing the beachhead early.

The men might have a chance to push overland to the guns at Gaba Tepe and storm them, but attempting to land men in large numbers along that plain, without disabling the guns first, would be a massacre.

I think I can see what we are up against here, this is going to be a tough fight. Hopefully this aeroplane will return me to solid ground alive.

CHAPTER 33

Roger

Wednesday, 14 April 1915

Roger hated the algebra.

"The Germans at Krupps," continued Lieutenant Charles Brodie, "when trying to sell submarines to the Greeks in 1913, gave these figures to demonstrate it could be done, but they wanted to sell their submarines and were likely basing their calculations on optimistic assumptions. They allowed for a current of four knots at the Narrows, and one knot in the wider stretches. They recommended diving to twenty-five metres, that's eighty feet, for the Narrows, and push on for one hour at seven knots. The suggested depth must be due to an undercurrent, but even travelling at a higher speed against the stronger current in the Narrows... It's marginal."

"Stoker thought he could do it," Roger said.

Lieutenant-Commander Dacre Stoker was a fellow optimist. After taking the Australian E-class submarine *AE2* half-way around the world to Sydney, he had captained her most of the way back again to the Mediterranean, and was the first to propose a submarine attempt to penetrate the Dardanelles. Stoker's written proposal was concise and well thought out, concluding that given skilful navigation, the passage is feasible.

However, soon after submitting his proposal, Stoker drove his submarine *AE2* onto the rocks inside Mudros Harbour one night after the French had removed a warning beacon.

Despite the setback, Roger recognised that the potential benefits of success remained enormous. To cripple enemy supplies and communications from behind their lines would seriously hamper their campaign and would allow the Navy to assist the Army attack more than any other way Roger could imagine. The Navy had failed in its overt attempt to make the Dardanelles with battleships on 18 March, but maybe it could succeed with a covert attempt beneath the surface.

As the former Commodore of Submarines, Roger knew the submarine captains personally and had great faith in them as well as the craft. He had sent for three more E-class submarines from England and two of these, *E14* and *E15*, had arrived a few hours earlier that day in Mudros Harbour.

The *E11* and Dacre Stoker's *AE2* had remained in Malta where their crews undertook repairs.

The captains of *E14* and *E15* sat at a table in a cabin of the Super-Dreadnought-Class battleship, the flagship *Queen Elizabeth,* in conference with Commodore Roger Keyes, Chief of Staff to Admiral John de Robeck, the naval Commander-in-Chief of the Mediterranean campaign.

Also at Roger's conference sat his assistant Lieutenant Charles Brodie, who was a former submarine commander, and two other naval officers with local experience of submarine operations, Lieutenants Pownall and Somerville.

"We know the Strait is thirty-five miles long," Brodie pointed at the map on the table. "With a continuous current running into the Mediterranean at three to five knots. We know the Strait is mined and other obstructions may have been introduced. We know powerful electric search lights are located here, here and here. A submarine will likely be seen and come under enemy attack and we know the difficulties of navigating a narrow passage while submerged. The critical unknown of the equation is the current at depth. Then there is also the battery endurance of these new E-class submarines and the surface current. Rumours of the return of the corpse of a redundant member of the Sultan's household, a few days after being dropped in the Bosphorus in a weighted sack, hardly constitute reliable intelligence on a deep undercurrent."

"Do you think an E boat can make it?" Roger blurted when he felt that all known information had been stated at least once. He looked at Somerville as the senior submarine officer.

Somerville straitened up, deliberated a second or two, then answered firmly "No."

Not the answer I wanted.

Roger looked to Pownall.

"No," Pownall said without a hint of doubt in his voice.

Roger looked to his assistant, Lieutenant Charles Brodie.

Brodie looked uncomfortable, like a child asked to choose a favourite parent. He shook his head, "No Sir."

Roger looked to Lieutenant-Commander Boyle, captain of *E14.*

If he agrees, he knows he will be the one who has to do it.

"No Sir," Boyle replied.

One remained. Roger looked to the most junior officer present, Lieutenant-Commander Theodore Brodie, captain of submarine *E15* and twin brother to Roger's assistant Charles Brodie.

Theodore Brodie stared at the map, then at his twin.

Rudyard Kipling's poem 'If' came into Roger's head.

'...If you can trust yourself when all men doubt you,
But make allowance for their doubting too...'

Roger had a copy of this poem above his wash basin in his cabin, and read it every morning. *These men have their doubts, but I have to trust myself.*

The captain of *E15* swallowed and met Roger's gaze. "Yes Sir."

"Well then," Roger jumped to his feet, excitement pulsed through him. "It's got to be tried and you shall do it."

CHAPTER 34

Clarence

Friday, 16 April 1915

A tiny kit bag was all he was allowed to bring. Space on a submarine was limited.

It didn't take long for Clarence Palmer to pack a few personal items. For some reason it seemed important to bring his Certificate of Commission with him on his first mission. *'Lieutenant C. Palmer of the Royal Navy.' I like the sound of that.* The role of Vice Consul at Chanakkale had been exciting, especially with the reconnaissance initiative he had taken, mapping out sea mines and guns, but the role of unofficial spy had become untenable once Turkey joined the war. *Now I'm back here, so soon. Wouldn't the Turks love to get their hands on me.*

The American Consul, Cornelius van Engert had been sent from Constantinople with an escape plan for Clarence soon after the British and French naval attacks on the forts at the mouth of the Dardanelles. *Oh, to see the looks on the Turkish and German officers' faces when they discovered I had escaped from house arrest.*

The fishing boat had rendezvoused with the British Destroyer *Beagle*, which then took him straight to Vice Admiral Carden's flag ship the *Indefatigable* for a debriefing.

I was such a hero. I had made it out with information. Good information about the defensive preparations inside the Dardanelles. The officers wanted to know all about it first hand, even the Vice Admiral himself.

Clarence Palmer had made his way back to England after a couple of weeks on the *Indefatigable*. Once back home he resigned his post at Vice Consul and applied for commission as an intelligence officer with the Royal Navy. Intelligence was where he knew he could contribute the most. Decision makers needed good information, otherwise men would die for no benefit.

When he heard about Lieutenant Brodie's submarine mission to penetrate the Dardanelles, Clarence had asked his commanding officer Commodore Roger Keyes to let him go along, based on his intimate knowledge of the tight waterway and Turkish language skills that might come in handy if something went wrong.

Naval plans to assist the military landing on the Gallipoli peninsula were in place, only the final timing was yet to be determined. Clarence figured his expertise would not be missed for the three week jaunt. This submarine mission would be a rare opportunity to gain field experience. *Submarines are becoming an important part of the war machine and if I have taken part in a live mission I will have credibility for future intelligence work and planning where submarines are involved.*

Clarence had expected to be denied his request, but the Commodore had surprised him by embracing the idea with enthusiasm. *Hopefully we can find a good strategic target. With provisions for a three week patrol mission in the Sea of Marmara, surely we will find a worthy prey for our torpedoes.*

The tiny B-class submarine *B11* had found its way past the enemy defences four months ago, only to waste the opportunity of attacking the German command ship *Lily Rickmeers,* that Clarence had specifically identified. Instead, *B11* torpedoed and sunk an obsolete warship that was of no strategic value. Nevertheless, the crew returned as heroes and Captain Holbrook was awarded a Victoria Cross. *No doubt they took on a dangerous mission with great courage, but for the risks taken they could have achieved a much greater prize.*

Now, on the way to the submarine across the deck of the accommodation ship, Clarence shook his head. It was infuriating to see good, hard-earned intelligence information go to waste. Just two weeks ago, he had been called into a conference with Expedition Commander, General Hamilton himself, who seemed genuinely surprised when told of the extent of Turkish defences building on the peninsula. *It has all been in my reports – didn't anyone read them?*

Clarence clambered down the rope ladder to the British built E-class submarine *E15. I wonder why the warships can have glamorous names, but the submarines only have numbers. That hardly seems fair. I say, she is awfully small.* Voices and other sounds of preparation echoed up through the hatch to greet him.

He pulled himself onto the vertical steel ladder in the conning tower and paused to gaze across Mudros Harbour. There was no moon, but electric lights from a floating city danced across the water. *I have an adventure ahead of me before I climb back out of this little hole.*

He climbed down the ladder and the conning tower closed in around him. *I don't suppose there are many fat submariners.* The control room opened below, but the space was cramped. He didn't know where to go next and stood to the side as others descended the ladder. Having never been on board a submarine he looked about and tried to take in important details, then one of the other officers took him to their shared quarters. There was small cupboard for his kit bag, and a bunk that the two of them would share – one at a time judging by the size of it.

Clarence stowed his gear and returned to the control room as the submarine prepared to undock. Lieutenant-Commander Theodore Brodie ordered that the ship be untied from the adjacent ship and the Submarine eased off under power of her diesel engines.

From the crowded conning tower above, the signalman called out a final message that must have been flashed by blinking lights from another ship.

"From Admiral – no – personal to Lieutenant-Commander Brodie. I wish you God speed in your gallant enterprise."

"Damn all hot air," Brodie spat. "We ought to be off."

A few minutes later, the roar of masses cheering thundered down the conning tower.

Clarence looked up, but could see nothing. As if in answer to his unasked question a voice called down.

"It's only the Australians giving us a send-off. There's a transport liner coming into the harbour, she's packed full of troops from down under."

Once out of the harbour, Lieutenant-Commander Brodie pulled the hatch closed himself with a clang that hung in the air. He ordered the diesel engines shut down and electric power from the Submarines batteries took over. It was time to dive.

The hiss and slosh of ballast tanks filling were new sounds for Clarence. He was surprised that they made him feel uneasy. Good oxygen bubbled away, displaced with seawater like air from a bottle held underwater, able to sink under its own weight once emptied of air. He drew in a deep breath. There was no sensation of descent, and no window for a visual reference. *I suppose we are under the water now. We are still out in the open sea, just off Lemnos, well away from the enemy position. Why do I feel terrified?* At each new sound Clarence imagined an enemy torpedo surging through the water towards him. He looked around, everyone else seemed focused but calm. *It must take a certain temperament to be a submariner. I wonder if I have it.*

Without operational responsibilities, Clarence sat at the chart table in the control room and watched closely as progress towards the mouth of the Dardanelles was plotted in wax pencil. *Thirty feet, at least we aren't very deep.* The periscope could reach the surface at this depth, but when Commander Brodie checked he reported that there was nothing but blackness.

One of the ratings offered Clarence a coffee. It came weak, and full of sugar and milk. *The English certainly know how to ruin good coffee. I know where we could get some nice strong Turkish coffee in tiny cups – a place on a street corner, not far from here.*

Later that evening, Commander Brodie checked the periscope again and reported enemy searchlights at the cliffs of Cape Helles.

"We are at the mouth of the Dardanelles. The current is pushing against us as expected. Dive to fifty feet."

By some clever method that Clarence didn't fully understand, the Commander managed to navigate a route against the current with a stopwatch and compass bearings, and only an occasional check of position with the periscope.

It became clear to Clarence that, as yet, his presence on the mission wasn't adding any real value. His knowledge of the minefield ahead was already transcribed onto the charts. Inside the hull, he was as blind as the rest of them. *I wonder if the crew resent my presence as an invasion of their mission, their moment. They have sailed this submarine from England and all have a good reason to be here.*

Commander Brodie guided the submarine past Erin Keui Bay, ever closer to the first curtain of mines near Kephez Point. The cover of night had lifted, so the periscope was used only when necessary.

Clarence was staring at the chart when the submarine lurched up and his nose crunched into the table in front of him.

What the blazes – ?

He grabbed his face and looked about, vision blurred, his nose slippery with blood.

Men who were standing had been thrown off their feet. Swearing erupted from fore and aft.

Commander Brodie remained calm "We must have hit a thermocline or change in water density. We can't have hit the bottom surely. Hold her steady lads."

Two ratings wrestled with the hydroplane controls in an attempt to hold the submarine level, but it was an impossible task.

The bow breached the surface with an unmistakable splash. Clarence felt like he might vomit. Commander Brodie started yelling orders, but Clarence could only focus on the angle of the floor. Up then down, the submarine was pitching out of control.

Slam!

"What –"

He was thrown to the floor and others flew forwards, stopping only when part of the submarine blocked their trajectory. Exposed piping and other irregular steel shapes were unforgiving. This time the men were slower to rise. Some bleeding heavily.

Brodie was still yelling, "Reverse thrust! Full speed."

The bow was up and the Submarine would not move. They were stuck. *We must have hit a sand bar. How much of our hull is above the water line?*

Brodie flew up the ladder. The hatch creaked open and then came a sound as if the conning tower had been hit with a sledge hammer.

The Commander fell back down the shaft and slammed onto the chart table in front of Clarence with a thud. He groaned weakly and reached towards his belly. He managed to lift his head enough to gaze wide-eyed at a handful of his own intestines. Life drained from his eyes before they could refocus.

Another shell hit the Submarine and detonated in the engine room with a deafening blast. The hull screeched, as if mourning the loss of her captain. *Our vessel is lost. If we stay here much longer we will all be lost with her.* Acid fumes from the destroyed batteries burned into Clarence's lungs.

He joined the flow of men up the ladder, ready to abandon ship. A hole on each side of the conning tower told the story of the first shell that failed to detonate, but nonetheless killed the submarine *E15* and her Commander on the way through. He climbed out on top of the hull with the others. The shelling had stopped. *Thank God.* Men held their hands in the air in the universal signal of surrender.

Clarence recognized the location immediately. "Dardanos," he mumbled.

Maybe they won't recognize me. How many have we lost? That blast in the engine room must have killed a few men.

Some of the wounded needed help up the ladders, but soon they were all swimming for the shore. Turkish soldiers waited on the bank. Some even entered the water to help the struggling submariners.

The prisoners were herded together on the grassy bank on the Asian side of the Dardanelles and soon were marching towards Dardanos Fortress. A Turkish aeroplane flew overhead. *Flying in that machine must be even more cramped than traveling in a submarine, but at least the pilot can see out.* Clarence was relieved to see that there did not appear to be any civilians around. Relieved that they had moved out of harm's way, but even more relieved that they weren't here to recognize him.

From Dardanos, their captors forced the crew to march to Chanakkale, along a road that was painfully familiar to Clarence, and yet so different from the last time he had been there. Streets were devoid of life. So many buildings damaged by explosion or fire.

At Chanakkale each of the men was required to provide name and rank. Maybe I should lie, but chances are they will learn my true identity regardless. No. I am an officer in the Royal Navy. I shall be a prisoner of war like the rest of these men, and answer only in English.

"I am Lieutenant C. Palmer, Royal British Navy."

The officer leading the interrogation hesitated, then smiled and addressed him in Turkish.

"I thought your face looked familiar, welcome back to our country Palmer Bey. I think there might be some men here who would like to talk with you."

Their eyes met for a split second and then Clarence looked at the floor. He said nothing, but he didn't have to. It was too late. *The officer knows I understand.* Clarence refused to meet his gaze, but could feel gleeful eyes burning into him.

He replied in English.

"I am Lieutenant C. Palmer, Royal British Navy."

* * *

Later each of the officers was questioned individually. The interrogator had little further to say to Clarence, but instead paraded him in front of the military commander of Chanakkale, Colonel Djevad Bey. Clarence had met Djevad previously so there was no point in attempting to continue the charade any further.

"So, my old friend, what brings you back to our town. Did you miss our fine cuisine? Have you returned for a nice shish kebab?"

Clarence looked Djevad in the eye and replied in Turkish. "I am Lieutenant C. Palmer, Royal British Navy."

"Maybe you have come back for another reconnaissance mission. You are a spy are you not? Do you know what we do with spies here Palmer Bey?"

"I was a diplomatic representative of His Majesty's Government," Clarence said. "You held me under house arrest against diplomatic protocols. I escaped, returned to London and was commissioned as an officer in the Royal British Navy. My vessel was destroyed in your waters and I was captured with the rest of the crew. I am a prisoner of war."

"Your vessel. Your submarine. A vessel of stealth. How appropriate for a spy like you. Maybe you wanted to look at our guns one last time before you bring your army to our land?"

Djevad Bey might have been watching for a reaction to that last statement. Clarence tried to remain calm and give nothing away.

"Oh yes," Djevad continued. "We know about your army massing at Mudros harbour and we are ready to greet them. Such a welcome they shall receive. I can have you hanged as a spy Palmer Bey. The evidence against you is clear. I recognize your face myself and I could sentence you to death this very day. Tell me why I shouldn't Palmer Bey. Tell me. Tell me where your army will land on our shores and maybe you will live. Our German friends are skilled at extracting information, although I understand it can be rather… unpleasant. Tell me what you know Palmer Bey, and save yourself some… trouble."

Djevad watched Clarence for a moment and then turned to speak to the two German officers who were standing by the door watching. Clarence could not understand the guttural sounds, but their grins left little doubt about the intent of their exchange.

"I am Lieutenant C. Palmer, Royal British Navy."

"As you wish… Lieutenant Palmer. Guards, return this man to the lock-up, for now."

Clarence was returned to the cell where the rest of the submarine survivors were being held, two other officers and seventeen ratings in a small room. The wounded lay about, but there was hardly room for the others to even sit on the hard floor. There was a bucket of water, and another bucket in the corner for the men to relieve themselves. A stench hanging in the stagnant air told Clarence that the second bucket had already been put to use.

They had done what they could for the wounded. Without any dressings or morphine they tore strips of clothing as bandages to control bleeding as best they could. Clarence was silent in his own thoughts. *I wonder if the others were threatened like I was. Probably not, they are genuine prisoners of war, and they don't know the landing plans like I do.* Clarence was not scared to die for his country. At thirty-one years of age and single, he was ready to make the sacrifice, but the threat of torture was a problem. *I might tell them where we intend to land our forces, and still suffer and die. I have to think of another way. Voluntarily giving up secrets to the enemy is treason, and that would not do, but what if it could be done in such a way as to cause the enemy maximum confusion. That wouldn't be treason.*

Clarence looked around the crowded room and then approached the two other British officers.

"These men need some medical help, or at least some morphine. I will call the guard to plead their case in Turkish."

The officers nodded.

"Do what you can," said Lieutenant Price, first officer of *E15*.

"Guard. Guard!" Clarence called out.

A young Turkish soldier wandered towards the cell. *He is just a boy, but he will have to do.* Clarence addressed him in Turkish.

"Guard Bey, please, look at these men." Clarence looked back and waved his hand towards the corner where the wounded lay.

"They need a doctor and some morphine immediately."

The Turkish word for morphine is essentially the same as in English with a different accent and Clarence repeated this slowly and clearly. He then leaned closer to the bars and guard.

"Listen, I need to speak with Djevad Bey. It is very important. Will you go and tell him immediately. Ask him to summon me alone. Do you understand?"

The lad nodded and turned to leave without saying a word.

Clarence clutched his elbows and turned to face the dim room. A couple of the men mumbled thanks, but most were looking down, deep in their own thoughts or pain or both. No one appeared to suspect a betrayal. *Now I wait in this stink-hole. At least I only have minor cuts and bruises – for now. I think I need to use that bucket.*

* * *

One hour later the guard returned and unlocked the cell door. He pointed to Clarence and gestured.

"You come," he said in Turkish.

"Morphine?" Clarence replied.

The guard raised his chin and clicked his tongue. The Turkish gesture for 'no'.

Clarence moved slowly towards the door and looked only at the guard. *If I look the men in the eye I might give myself away.*

Soon he stood in front of the Chanakkale Commander Colonel Djevad.

"I will tell you what I know Commander Djevad Bey."

Djevad waved at a chair in front of a desk that separated them.

Clarence sat on the front edge of the chair.

"I am Lieutenant C. Palmer, Royal British Navy."

Djevad spat on the floor. "You waste my time."

"Wait, let me continue. Please. When I left my post as His Majesty's Vice Consul here in Chanakkale, I returned to London and obtained a commission as an intelligence officer in the Royal Navy. The other officers and men you have captured are only submariners and do not know about the landing plans. I am the only one from the Submarine who can tell you what you wish to know. I came along on this mission because of my knowledge of the minefields and Turkish language skills. The other men should be treated fairly as prisoners of war and not tortured for information. This would be inhumane and would tell you nothing."

Djevad leaned forward in his chair. "That is very noble of you Palmer Bey, now are you going to tell me anything useful?"

"Will you treat me as a prisoner of war like the others, if I tell you what I know? I'm not here to be noble, I don't want to hang."

Djevad leaned back. "If you can tell me something useful Palmer Bey, I will spare your life…as far as I am able."

Clarence looked him in the eye for a long moment. *This man is my enemy. Can I trust him? I hope so, I have no alternative.* Djevad took a cigarette and held out the open packet.

"Would you like to smoke, Palmer Bey?"

Clarence took a cigarette, lit it and continued. "We have one hundred thousand men at Mudros Harbour, preparing to launch an assault on your shores under General Hamilton. Originally the plan was for a combined landing at Cape Helles and Gabe Tepe, but that plan has been abandoned."

"Why abandoned?"

"Our aerial reconnaissance has revealed that the terrain is unsuitable and too well-defended. We believe that you had somehow learned of this plan and we no longer believe that it can be successful."

"So what is the latest plan, Palmer Bey?"

Clarence drew a deep breath. "Bulair – there will be feints at Cape Helles, Gabe Tepe and Kum Kale but the real assault will be further to the north, at the Gulf of Suros, in an attempt to cut off your forces on the Gallipoli Peninsula by taking control of the narrowest point."

"And when will this attack take place?"

"The decision to concentrate our attack at the northern neck of the peninsula is only recent. We would have landed weeks ago, but changing plans have caused a series of delays. I tell you honestly Djevad Bey, I do not know when the landing will take place, but I expect it will be soon."

Clarence could feel his heart racing.

He took a final draw on the last of the cigarette, it was close to burning his fingers. His eyes left Djevad's only for a split second to confirm the location of an ash tray on the desk to press the stub into.

That's all I've got.

CHAPTER 35

John

Friday, 23 April 1915

John folded the letter from Bertha with care and returned it to his breast-pocket. Encouragement and complete confidence from his daughter were the perfect things that Colonel John Monash needed to reinforce his own resolve.

General Godley was in a foul temper again today. God only knows how that English gentleman came to be in command of my division. Back at home, a weekend outing of the Wallaby Bushwalking Club would be equipped with better maps and a clearer objective than the 4th Brigade's role in this expedition. That man's lack of attention to detail will cost Australian lives.

"Coo-ee! Coo-ee!" A cluster of privates hollered loudly in the direction of another ship with the familiar cry of the outback.

"I say, look out chaps." An Australian soldier charged past on one of John's newly acquired brigade donkeys. The fellow held up a limp celery like a sword, his boots almost dragging on the deck as the beast clopped by and brayed a mournful sound.

"Come on lads," the rider cried. "You must salute me! I am a British officer! You colonial boys should know how to respect your betters. I say, know your place and we'll all be tickety-boo!"

A wave of laughter rippled through the onlookers.

No harm in letting them have a bit of fun while they can. I must stay positive in front of the men, and focus on the objective. The objective is everything, even though our role is not yet clear. We must take the Gallipoli Peninsula so the warships can pass the Dardanelles Strait. Many of these young men will die under my command, some within days from now. Naïve boys, they have no understanding of the hard road that lies before them or the cost of going to war in their prime years. They have so much future to sacrifice.

John reflected on the words of his speech to the men, ten days earlier on leaving Alexandria, and wondered what impact, if any, his words might have had…

'Now lads, you are shortly going on active service… I told the general on your behalf you are ready to go anywhere and do anything. You may be faced with privation

and hardship, sometimes hungry, often tired and miserable. That is what soldiering amounts to… I call on you with confidence to do your level best for the sake of your manhood, for the sake of Australia and for the sake of the British Empire.'

So far, his men had done everything asked of them. In Cairo, Generals Godley and Birdwood had declared the 4th Brigade to be the best Brigade in Egypt. On 19 April, John had commanded a practice disembarkation of the whole New Zealand and Australian Division, including his 4th Brigade and the exercise had run like clockwork. At times the clock seemed to run a bit slow as it had taken fourteen hours to unload everyone, but that was due to a lack of small boats and nothing to do with the men's performance.

Training is one thing, battle is another. The true test will be on us soon enough.

John leant against the balustrade of Australian transport ship *Seang Choon* and refused to dwell on loss that might lie ahead. Instead he surveyed the floating city of war, built by naval architects on the water of Mudros Harbour.

Askold nestled amongst the British and French vessels. The Russian cruiser, known as 'Packet of Woodbines' for her five tall thin funnels, had fought in a savage battle against the Japanese in 1904 at Port Arthur in China. Ten years later, she worked alongside Japanese warships scouring the Indian Ocean for the German raider *Emden*. On John's arrival with his 4th Brigade in Mudros Harbour, the commander of *Askold* had stood beside one of her six-inch guns and waved his cap as the Australian *Seang Choon* edged past. John waved back and drank in the history of the moment like a fine wine.

That Russo-Japanese war was a bloody siege – a fine conquest for the Japs in the end, but they paid dearly for their prize. This operation we are about to embark on will put Port Arthur in the shade. Army and Navy working together, multiple landing sites. This is possibly the greatest feat of arms of this nature ever attempted.

One British ship held a captive balloon on a long rope. The balloon, large enough to lift a carriage containing three officers, drifted in the breeze and likely practiced signalling enemy position information to gunners below. Another Royal Navy cruiser had lost a mast and lay with a great hole in her after funnel.

French battleship *Jaureguiberry* looked like she had enjoyed too much fine cuisine with her short fat funnels and bulging hull.

Australian submarine *AE2* had found some submarine friends in the Royal navy and joined their pack.

The famous British battleship *Agamemnon* looked alert with her twelve-inch guns fore and aft, and the mighty *Queen Elizabeth* lazed like a sleeping lion in the sun, ready to roar at a moment's notice. The first of a new generation of oil-fired, Super-Dreadnought-class battleship with fifteen-inch guns, she boasted greater firepower than any other vessel on the oceans of the world.

It is strange to sit in this beautiful place, on calm water, and yet to know we are about to go into a mighty clash of battle.

And it is strange that we should be fighting the Turks instead of Germans. At least a probable outcome will be the freeing of Jerusalem and Palestine from the Turkish yoke. Then my Jewish people might finally know peace.

"Colonel, the men have each been issued with two-hundred rounds and three day's iron rations."

The voice interrupting his thoughts was that of John's Chief of Staff, Lieutenant-Colonel McGlinn.

John turned to face his most important administrative support officer and immediately John's head returned to planning mode. So many logistical details had to be considered and prepared before the landing.

"Good," John replied. "Be sure that each man also brings his entrenching tool, two empty sand bags and as much water as he can carry. We must ensure the men remain with their officers and NCOs. The whole brigade should form up when we land, or at least each battalion, to await orders to advance together. And ammunition, we must stockpile plenty of ammunition and maintain a supply line to the front, otherwise the men cannot do what is required of them."

* * *

An afternoon of planning and preparation left John exhausted, but next morning he woke earlier than usual and his mind buzzed with details to organise for the landing.

Unable to get back to sleep, he dressed and returned to the balustrade of the main deck where he could collect his thoughts in the quiet cool air.

Some ships were moving out, across the black water.

In the dim light of dawn he made out the designation of an Australian ship, and three others, all Australian. The four ships that carried MacLagan's Australian 3rd Brigade were on their way out of Mudros Harbour.

So it begins.

The 3rd Brigade, made up of the 9th, 10th, 11th and 12th Battalions, had been given the honour of landing as the covering force. In just under twenty-four hours these men would be the first to set foot on Turkish soil in a pre-dawn attack.

The 1st and 2nd Brigades would follow, then John's 4th Brigade.

At that moment, as he watched the ships steam out of the safety of Mudros Harbour, reality pierced his soul like a sabre. *There will be death and pain. Will I pass the test? I might be shot. Will it hurt? How will I cope with my own pain, or the pain of others? I must not lose sight of the objective. I might not return home alive, but I must lead the men to the end. I must be willing to sacrifice everything.*

He reached up to his breast pocket and, through the cloth, he felt the collection of most recent letters from his wife Victoria, daughter Bertha and sister Mathilde.

Sailing orders for John's 4th Brigade gave him one more day to plan and organise before they joined the battle. It would be a busy day, but something else suddenly seemed more important.

John hurried back to his cabin began to write a letter that he knew might be his last:

Transport A.31
Seang Choon
April 24/15.

Dearest Wife,
We have received our sailing orders, and inside of a few hours shall be in the thick of the greatest combined naval and military operation in history, with Australia in the pride of place. That we will succeed I do not entertain any doubt, but that I shall come through unscathed and alive is not so certain. As this may be the last opportunity I have of talking to you, I want to say briefly that, in the event of my going out, you are to believe that I do so with only one regret, which is the grief that this will bring to you and Bert and Mat. For myself, I am prepared to take my chance. While, on one hand, to win through safely would mean honour and achievement, on the other hand to fall would mean an honourable end. At best I have only a few years of vigour left, and then would come decay and the chill of old age, and perhaps lingering illness. So, with the full and active life I have had, I need not regret the prospect of a sudden end with dismay. I am greatly comforted to know that you will be well provided for, and will be surrounded by many friends, who, for my sake, will help you to come through all difficulties that may beset you in the future. I am sure you know how deeply I have always loved you, and how in all things I have tried to act in your best interests. I know also that you have loved me dearly, and will honour my memory.

Your Husband,
John Monash

CHAPTER 36

Dacre

Saturday, 24 April 1915

The ladder to board the first-of-its-class, Super-Dreadnought battleship *Queen Elizabeth* climbed eternal. A combination of disappointment and shame weighed upon Dacre and he felt very small as he ascended to the Imperial command centre on the mightiest warship in the world.

A day ago he had looked Admiral de Robeck in the eye and assured him, again, that it was possible for a submarine to penetrate the Dardanelles Strait. Then like each member of his crew, in anticipation of a dangerous mission, he had written letters to his family and left these with others with instructions that they should only be sent on confirmation of his death. Not two hours into the mission, barely inside the mouth of the Straits, the shaft which worked the foremost diving rudders broke and could not be repaired without returning to base. Unable to dive, there was no point in continuing and he had to return to preserve the submarine.

The broken shaft was repaired this morning and a test dive completed with success, but the opportunity of many lifetimes, to achieve the greatest wartime feat in submarine history, had passed. The British Submarine *E15* had been lost and with yesterday's failure of the *AE2*, the challenge must now be seen as too difficult. Other E-class submarine captains had argued against the attempt due to the excessive risk.

Half-way around the world and back again, only to be cheated of a chance at success by a broken rod of iron.

This evening, with the flagship *Queen Elizabeth* back in Mudros Harbour after the day's operations, Admiral de Robeck had sent for Lieutenant-Commander Dacre Stoker, the Irish captain of Australian submarine *AE2*. The Admiral could only have sent for Dacre on hearing of his failure and early return, for if the mission was progressing as planned, Dacre would be far into the Dardanelles and possibly in the Marmara Sea by this time.

Dacre reached the main deck of the *Queen Elizabeth* and forced himself to stand tall as he strode past a fifteen-inch gun, towards the quarterdeck. He braced himself for a dressing down, and worse, the bad news he might have to give his crew, that the army landing was imminent and there was no longer any need for a submarine attempt at the Dardanelles.

Dacre found Admiral de Robeck in the ward room and when given the nod he approached. With a dry mouth, Dacre gave an outline of the short mission, cause of failure and subsequent repairs.

The Admiral listened without interrupting and stared at Dacre without blinking, as if considering an important decision.

"It was very bad luck," the Admiral said. "You did well to get so far. Try again to-morrow. If you succeed in getting through, there is nothing we will not do for you."

"Yes Sir, thank you Sir." Dacre didn't trouble himself to conceal a smile of relief. "We will give it our very best."

"One more thing Stoker," said Commodore Roger Keyes, the Admiral's Chief of Staff. "We will be landing our army from dawn and once the Turks realise this, they might start floating mines down the Straits with the current. Instead of trying to pass Chanak without being seen, you are to attack and sink, if possible, any mine-dropping ships you might find in The Narrows – if you get there. Generally run amok!"

A laugh escaped from Dacre's throat, then he remembered decorum and, at the same instant, realised that Commodore Keyes was serious.

Submarines are not fast or manoeuvrable by comparison with a surface vessel. A submarine commander must rely on his ability to hide beneath the surface to evade enemy attack. The Straits were lined with guns, screened with mines and the water itself pushed back against those that would attempt to pass with treacherous currents. The Dardanelles posed a more difficult objective for a submarine than any other sea passage Dacre could imagine. At the Narrows, the passage spanned less than a mile across. To reveal himself to the enemy there would give away his stealth advantage and draw enemy attack in the tightest of locations.

He wondered idly if a submarine had ever previously been used as cannon fodder, and what were the odds that his submarine might connect with an untethered mine adrift in the current.

Still, nothing is impossible until it has been given a good go and proven to be so. The Admiral of the fleet knows the risks and believes it is important enough to try. The last chap who took a submarine past the mines to the Narrows, Lieutenant-Commander Holbrook, sunk a ship and returned a few hours later in his little B-class B11 and was awarded a Victoria Cross for his trouble. I can only imagine the accolades if I can take my E-class all the way through, let alone running a bit of amok on the way. But, either we shall get through, or we shan't, and we shall know soon enough. Tomorrow is almost here.

* * *

At three o'clock on the morning of 25th April, darkness was absolute, the air hung still and the water lay dead calm.

The Submarine *AE2* crept into the Dardanelles Strait and crawled along the surface with the same plan as the previous night. Broken clouds shut out any hint of light from the stars in the moonless sky, but the intensity of the darkness made the searchlights seem more powerful.

A light beam reached out from the Asian side and swept slowly over the water. Systematically the finger of light traced the southern shore towards the entrance, and then along the distant gloom under the steepness of the northern shore.

The beam touched *AE2*, but continued without pause.

Dacre stood in the conning tower and called instructions to those below through a voice tube, his eyes the only ones on board that could see anything outside the submarine. He edged *AE2* closer to the European shore.

The light beam traced another circuit and Dacre held his breath as it approached, but it passed by again.

Ahead a second search light penetrated the darkness from Kephez Point on the Asian shore, near the ancient fortress of Dardanos. Together they probed, like the fingers of a stranger, groping about in an intimate place where they were not welcome.

I doubt we will be able to travel on the surface to the point we reached last night. One of these search lights must catch us soon.

And yet the beam passed by again and again without grasping hold of *AE2*. The submarine pushed on at a dead slow speed, running on only one of its two eight-cylinder diesel engines.

Crump! The retort of a gun on the European shore shook the night sky. The shell overshot its mark and swished passed Dacre's head, closer than he would have liked. He paused a moment with his mouth next to the voice tube, before calling instructions to those below. He took a deep breath to ready his voice so it might sound deep and calm when he called the first order while engaged in combat.

"Diving stations. Prepare to dive."

The crew knew the plan and each man knew his own role. On their commander's signal, they worked as one make the transition with a full understanding of the urgency. By the time Dacre had sealed the hatch and descended from the conning tower into the main hull, the diesel engine had been shut down, the electric motors were running on batteries and the ballast tanks were filling with sea water. Within a minute of the first shell, the submarine was submerged to twenty feet.

"Maintain depth at twenty feet," Dacre ordered. "Up Periscope."

The darkness was so complete that Dacre could see nothing through the periscope but a faint glimmer of light in the eastern sky.

Daylight will be upon us too soon.

Dacre guided *AE2* slowly, at periscope depth, on a course towards the minefield.

Through the periscope, the growing pre-dawn light showed faint contours of the hills on the northern shore. When he was as close as he dared to the first known string of mines, he lowered the periscope and ordered a dive to seventy feet. *AE2* plunged to a new depth in search of a passage beneath the minefield.

With a map, compass and theoretical speed against the current, a calculated position was all he would know until he ordered the submarine to rise for observation through the periscope, but choosing the wrong moment to approach the surface in the middle of a minefield was something he didn't want to think about. By his reckoning, he would have to rise and steal a look thrice before he passed the minefield and reached The Narrows of Chanak.

SSSCCCRRRR – the mooring wire of a mine scraped along the hull, making the sound of a giant violin in the hands of a beginner. Bow to stern, it worked along the submarine, as if feeling for something to grab hold of. The long, tortured note played on and the crew looked about at where the wire might be, but no one said a word. Dacre imagined the wire catching on a dive rudder or becoming entangled in the screw. His heart pounded in his ears and sweat dripped from his forehead.

The mooring wires were anchored to the bottom, and the buoyancy of the mines held the wires taut. Usual convention was to set the depth of mines underwater where they were difficult to see, but close enough to the surface so that only small vessels with a shallow draught might pass over without making contact. To the best of Dacre's knowledge, setting mines deeper to defend against submarines was not done, but he could not shake the idea that the Turks might have given it a try.

Another mooring wire caught the bow and rasped its way along the submarine – DONNGGGG – this sound made everyone freeze.

DONNGGG – DONNGGG – DONNGGG.

The sound continued, as if some lunatic was crawling along the outside and thumping the hull with a club hammer.

A rating near Dacre reached out slowly and grabbed hold of a control wheel. He had no cause to turn the wheel and did not make to move it, but his knuckles turned white with the grip.

After the longest minute, one last thump at the stern and whatever it was parted company with the *AE2*. Dacre breathed again.

Was that a mine that we dragged down? I cannot think what else it might have been. Why didn't it detonate?

Dacre looked about the submarine. Fore and aft, every man of his crew remained at his post and wore a look of grim determination. He gave them a nod and convinced himself that no words were necessary at this moment.

Towards the bow, the mooring wire of another mine began to scape along the hull.

CHAPTER 37

Charles

Sunday, 25 April 1915, dawn

The ANZAC Intelligence Officer, Major Charles Villiers-Stuart, checked his wristwatch. Luminous hands told him it was five minutes past five, although it was almost light enough for him to read the time without the glow.

The first hint of dawn had started to appear an hour earlier. The sun was not due to rise for another thirty five minutes, but the cover of darkness was almost gone.

He sat in silence next to Major Glasfurd, a staff officer of the Australian First Division.

We'll be like ducks sitting on a pond, waiting to be shot, if it gets much lighter before we get to shore.

It had been agonizing to sit through the narrow window of darkness since moonset at 3:00am.

More time would have been better. Damn the winds, delayed our landing by two nights and each night the moonset was just that little bit later. Hopefully the boys from the earlier boatloads of the covering force have secured the beachhead for us.

The two ANZAC officers sat sardined in a landing boat, surrounded by men from the final wave of the ANZAC covering force, the Australian Third Infantry Brigade.

Men of the first wave of the covering force had set foot on the enemy shore around half an hour earlier. Charles had heard the shooting from a distance, first shots fired at 4:30am by his watch. It was difficult to tell in the darkness how the landing was progressing, but there were sounds and muzzle flashes from fighting at the top of the first ridge, so at least they had reached that far.

The Royal Navy's feint at Bulair should keep the northern Turkish Divisions away for a day, maybe two at best. Time will tell if that is long enough for a landing and general advance to establish a position here at Z Beach.

The destroyer towing their boat cast them off and men lowered the oars to row the final couple of hundred yards to the beach. The sheltered cove ahead was lost in darkness behind the spur ridge that loomed high over the beach.

It looks like we are coming in just north of the sheltered cove. Our lads should have control of that first spur ridge to the plateau above soon, if not already. Otherwise, enemy fire will destroy our hopes of landing here when they can see boatloads slowly chugging in.

Rifle fire and shouts grew louder and the shore emerged from the darkness. A few bodies lay on the beach, presumably dead, but many more alive. Some ran directly away from shore, in disorganised groups too small to be effective. Some men stood in a daze, disoriented by their first exposure to enemy resistance and oblivious to the danger they were in or the need to seek cover. Charles had seen it all before. There are many ways a man reacts to his first battle, none can predict it before the time comes. Some wounded lay near the back of the beach, moving occasionally, interspersed by mounds of packs.

At least the men had the good sense to leave their kit behind and charge up the hill with only rifles and ammunition webbing.

Rowers stopped rowing and raised the oars. Men jumped out into knee-deep water and ran towards the beach. Several tripped or slipped on the uneven bottom and fell over, dowsing themselves and their rifles in seawater.

Charles hurried cautiously, holding the edge of the boat to the bow.

A private in front of him fell, and then struggled in a clumsy crawl towards the shore. At the edge of the beach he grabbed a handful of grit and collapsed with his legs still in the water.

Charles grabbed the fallen man's webbing on the way past and hauled him a few paces up the beach. He rolled the fellow over. Blood seeped from a bullet hole in the soldier's chest. He was quite dead. *There must be at least one enemy sniper hidden with a line of sight.* Charles glanced up at the terrain confronting him. Patches of black covered the bluffs and gullies above and away to the left.

One of the fallen man's mates stood nearby and stared at the body.

"He's gone," Charles yelled. "Stay with your Company and go to make it count for something."

The fellow nodded, but stood still, gazing down, "Shouldn't we bury him, or do something?"

"Later. Not now. We need to secure this beach so more men don't get shot when they land here. We will bury the dead later."

Charles turned and looked for some cover. There was precious little shelter at the back of the beach – a bit of a scrubby rise that might solve his immediate problem but nothing more. He was running towards the cover before he made the conscious decision to do so.

If that fellow can't get on and fight then so be it. I have a more important mission.

He looked for Major Glasfurd and saw that he was already crouched behind the embankment ahead. *Why can't my legs move any faster? Surely I can run faster than this, I must be getting old.*

After a few more seconds that seemed like an eternity, Charles sat next to Major Glasfurd with his back to the embankment.

The next boat ground onto the shingle and its oars raised in unison. Men poured over the sides into knee-deep water, and again, two or three tumbled, dowsing themselves and their weapons. At least these ones returned to their feet.

A tall lad from the near the front of the boat won the race to shore, then stopped and let out a victory cry. He took two more steps up the beach and collapsed, falling face first into the coarse sand and pebbles. Men streamed past him. Two of them paused and started to drag the tall lad up the beach, but his limp body didn't respond to their urging. They left him where he lay and ran on.

Charles turned to Major Glasfurd. *He sees it too. This place is exposed to enemy sniper fire. The growing light will be the death of many men here.*

Clusters of men drifted south to the shelter of the headland and the cove.

"Landing is no good here," Charles yelled. "Let's move around the corner to see if it's any safer there."

Glasfurd looked about for a moment, then nodded and ran along the beach to the south.

Charles followed, trying to hunch below the embankment and move quickly at the same time. It was an awkward compromise, and he felt like he achieved neither. He dodged around groups of men and urged them on, running past without slowing, then he rounded the headland into the cove.

Boats were landing in the cove also, and many men were loitering on the beach. Some officers and sergeants yelled to rally the privates. Groups formed and scrambled up the steep embankment that led up to the first ridge.

A few dead bodies lay about the place but, judging by the numbers standing around, no one had been shot here in the last few minutes.

Mounds of packs cluttered the top of the beach. *This looks to be where most of the men have advanced from.*

Charles looked south along the cove. It was still dark, but he could make out the swollen form of the southern spur which provided some cover from the south.

An explosion flashed in the sky above the cove. A sound like heavy rain on the ocean followed, lasting only a few seconds – Shrapnel. The small metal pellets fell harmlessly into an unoccupied patch of water.

That shell must have come from one of the guns at Gaba Tepe. At least it doesn't have a direct line of sight to the beach in this cove. The breaking dawn gave barely enough light to confirm this visually, but he had memorised maps and aerial photographs, and pictured the topography in his mind.

Charles turned to Major Glasfurd. "I think we better limit landing to the cove. The north beach where we came in is too exposed to the northern ridges we don't hold. Brighton Beach to the south is well defended and come sunrise it's in the direct line of sight for shellfire from Gaba Tepe."

"I agree. This's the only place now that it's getting light. We hold the beach, but the enemy is still resisting on the main ridge to the north and south. Landing outside this cove will cost too many men. They'll have to find their way up and out overland from here."

Another shell burst above the beach to the south and a number of men below fell to the sand. They all rose but one, and hurried up the beach towards the hill behind. The figure lying in the dark moved his arm and then lay still. Charles felt a pang of sadness that another man would not live to see the sunrise after his long journey to the enemy shore, but pushed the thought from his head. The air and land seemed to be erupting all around with deafening explosions. The ringing in Charles's ears never quite had the chance to fade away before the next blast.

He tore a page from his notebook and scribbled a note to General Bridges confirming the coordinates of their landing place:

"Landing effected 237W 224B. Steep slopes inland afford cover. Landing appears possible south of this present place. Will signal when can find MacLagan."

Both men signed the note and Charles dashed out to an empty lifeboat that was being turned around by four young Jack Tars.

"Who is in charge of this boat?" Charles yelled.

"I am," one replied, "and I have orders to return it immediately to bring more men, sir."

"Good. Good." *He can't be more than sixteen years old.* "We have an important message that must be taken back to General Bridges on the *Queen*."

The lad hesitated.

"Listen," Charles held out the torn page. "I am Major Villiers-Stuart, Corps Intelligence. This is Major Glasfurd, First Division staff. The rest of the landing boats have to come into this cove, otherwise losses will be severe. That is the message written on this paper. It must get back to Corps HQ. If you return with a boatful of men and land around that corner, many will die, likely you included. Do you understand?"

The Jack Tar took the note and nodded. "Yes sir. I will deliver your message sir."

He stuffed it in his pocket and turned to the others. "Let's go boys. Time to row. We gotta deliver a message and get some more men."

Charles stood with Major Glasfurd and watched them take the first few strokes towards a gap between two landing boats that surged towards the beach.

Charles turned to survey the beach. Beyond the mounds of packs dumped at the top of the beach, the spur rose at a sharp incline, on and on up into the dark grey sky.

A sergeant called for his section.

An officer yelled for his platoons to form up.

No one responded.

Small groups of men stood in huddles. The growing light exposed their presence when they should be pushing up the hill fighting with the rest.

This will do as a landing zone, and maybe for a section of fifteen men to meet and gather, but there is barely room for much more than that. Platoons of four sections could form up in the gullies immediately above the beach. They are steep, but somewhat sheltered from bursting shrapnel shells coming in from the south. More space will be required for companies of four platoons to rendezvous, and assemble into Battalions.

Glasfurd pointed across the beach to the water. "With these boats coming in now, all four battalions of Colonel Sinclair-MacLagan's Third Brigade must be fully ashore. The full covering force. I expect we should control some fair distance inland by now. Four thousand men landed before daybreak, a well-planned operation Major."

Charles nodded. "Let's find MacLagan so we can discuss the options for rendezvous. This beach is too narrow. They can form up in these gullies, but they'll have to move out of here pretty quick to keep the beach clear. South I'm thinking."

Without answering, Major Glasfurd chased after an officer nearby who turned and pointed up the steep incline behind the beach. Glasfurd saluted, turned back to Charles and pointed up the spur. Before Charles could respond, Glasfurd was scrambling up the hill.

Charles sheathed his notebook in a small satchel and drew his revolver. *I'm coming, one hand to climb and one hand to shoot back if required.*

Both men were breathing hard when they found Colonel Sinclair-MacLagan established at a field headquarters for the Third Brigade near the top of a gully leading to a plateau.

The dawn light had grown enough that the red bands around their caps, and red gorget patches on their collars, introduced them as staff officers.

"Ah yes," the Colonel said. "I was expecting you boys to arrive sometime soon. It's no good trying to go any further up this ridge, it narrows down to a razor's edge beyond the plateau. Too hard for men to cross in any numbers. Possible, but very slow, single file. A good marksman could pick them off one by one – very exposed to enemy fire up there."

"We need to determine suitable places for the main force to rendezvous and form up. We were thinking of the gully south of here." Glasfurd said.

"I think the gully is your best bet," the colonel nodded. "Still copping a lot of shrapnel from the south, but relatively clear of enemy troops on the ground by now. I suggest you have a look for yourselves, but keep your heads down now it's starting to get light. You can head straight over from here, but you'll want to check access from the beach. It's impossible to tell what's going on out there, but I think I need more men to the right. I'll be dropping over into the gully myself shortly to follow the 9th and 10th Battalions and see what I can see for myself."

"Thank you sir," Charles said. "We'll look into this."

He knew the shape of the ridge and gully behind well from weeks of analysing maps and constructing a clay model of the terrain to help other officers appreciate the complex topography during the planning.

Charles and Major Glasfurd saluted the Colonel, and scurried down the ridge towards the southern spit. The slope was gentler this way, but it was more exposed than the direct route by which they ascended. A group of maybe twenty men rushed past them, cutting across their path and dropping into the gully. *Lucky we're all wearing the same Tommy-style caps or they might have shot us.*

The two officers paused to catch their breath behind a mound of earth.

Acrid smoke from gunpowder and cordite hung in the air. Sporadic tapping of rifle fire reverberated from all directions.

A warship's explosive shell flew overhead and burst on impact up on the escarpment, sending a brown dust cloud above the horizon.

Another explosion thundered much closer, maybe thirty or forty yards away. A split second after the explosion, came the sound of heavy rain on the scrub, followed by yells and cries of men.

A small innocent-looking white cloud hung in the air to mark the place where the enemy shrapnel shell had burst, releasing its deadly rain of metal pellets.

Further inland, other similar white clouds traced the path of the gully as it laboured upwards to the main ridge.

"All these shrapnel shells are coming from Gaba Tepe," Glasfurd Said.

Charles was still breathing hard. He nodded and sucked in a lungful. "Maybe there is an area on the far side of the valley, in the lee of the next ridge.

"Yes," Glasfurd replied. "That's the place. The men can make their way to the south end of the cove and over the toe of this ridge, then into the gully and rendezvous over there on the other side. That's about as much shelter as we'll have from this infernal shrapnel."

CHAPTER 38

Ali

Sunday, 25 April 1915, just before sunrise

Ali's heart pounded and his hands shook.

He tried to slow his breathing.

Never had he felt so exhausted. Never had he felt so terrified. Never had he felt so alive.

He squeezed the trigger of his Mauser and watched another invader drop onto the beach below. At this range of a few hundred metres, he was able to hit a human target with at least one of each three rounds he fired.

Platoon commander, Second Lieutenant Ibrahim, had addressed the troops himself this morning, signifying the importance of the occasion. His main concern seemed to be preserving ammunition, he repeated this request several times.

Ali crouched amongst men of his platoon. First Platoon of 8th Company, 2nd Battalion, 27th Regiment. His initial issue of 150 bullets had seemed ample before the attack, but was nearly spent.

The platoon of ninety men held shallow trenches on top of two small hillocks. Ali's squad and several others were perched on the smaller hillock, rising maybe twenty metres behind a stone fisherman's hut. The trenches were old and neglected, bushes grew in the parapet obscuring the view, but also providing some camouflage. The rest of the platoon occupied a larger hill to the south, twice as high. Some invaders had crossed the beach and were starting to climb the larger hill, but had not yet reached the fisherman's hut.

Either side of Ali, men crowded in the trench facing south-west, overlooking bodies of invaders, scattered along the beach towards the headland known as Ariburnu.

The sun was yet to climb over the Sari Bair Range behind them, but there was ample light in the early morning to see the scale of the invasion. Another line of boats was heading for the shore, this one coming straight towards Ali, as if seeking him out. Four boats in single file, each carrying thirty to forty men.

Fear swelled in his throat, as it had five weeks earlier when the fleet of English warships steamed towards him and the Chanakkale Strait. *No breakfast again today. I might not live to eat another meal.*

The warships had not returned, until today. This time they floated offshore, still and in silence. Somehow they seemed more menacing now without guns blazing. Now they were delivering invaders, countless invaders. More kept coming to replace those killed. Soon this position would be overrun and there was no one else. His battalion was all that stood between this stretch of coastline and empty country. One thousand men were not many to defend several kilometres of steep terrain.

Today there was no hiding behind a big gun. No cannon, no howitzers, just men with rifles. *If only we had some artillery. Even just one machine gun would do the job. The boats coming to shore are moving slowly. A machine gun with plenty of ammunition would be enough to kill them all before they reached the shore. Once landed they will be much harder to stop.*

Ali took aim at the front boat. It bobbed along half a kilometre away.

"Hold your fire." Second Lieutenant Ibrahim glanced at the next hill where the remainder of his men faced attackers crawling up the slopes, then he lifted his gaze up towards the Sari Bair clifftops before he returned his focus to the men in front of him.

"Wait until the boats are within two hundred metres. Meanwhile, do what you can to defend our brothers on the next hill, but preserve our ammunition! Be ready to withdraw. Once we have stopped these four boats, we will start a fighting retreat up Sazli Dere towards the ridge. Bring only your rifle, ammunition and water. Everything else must be left here. This ground is lost to the invaders – for now – but we can slow their advance. We must hold the high ground. When the boats are close enough, kill them all."

Ibrahim turned to Sergeant Kadir briefly, then Kadir hurried to the last ammunition box and started distributing rounds to each man. *Strange that Kadir is doing it himself, normally he would yell at someone else to do the menial work.*

Ali turned towards the hill where his comrades fought off the advance of invaders and wondered whether they would withdraw also, or whether they would stay and fight to the death.

Movement on the ridge above caught his eye. He squinted to see. Men were running. A muzzle flashed. Men were fighting at the top of the ridge. They looked like ants from this distance, but the fighting was deadly.

The invaders are already up on the ridge. Ibrahim said we must hold the high ground. Sazli Dere is a dry gully at this time of year, and following it upstream leads directly east. This will take us up towards the main ridge, but higher up and further inland than the place where the fighting is taking place. This is the best way for our platoon to defend against the invaders, but it is a long climb. God give me strength to defend my people and my family and my home.

"The boats are approaching to within two-hundred metres," Second Lieutenant Ibrahim called. "Ready yourselves…fire when ready."

Ali chambered a round and took aim at the front boat. *And preserve ammunition.* Mausers all around him spat bullets. Already he could see men slumped in the front boat and an oar dragged in the water. The invader next to the dead rower stood and moved to take the limp oar, Ali lined him up in his sites. The rifle fire around Ali seemed to pause and he squeezed his trigger. The replacement rower collapsed and tumbled into the water.

He felt a hand on his shoulder and turned to see Ibrahim Bey's grim smile looking back at him.

"Nice shooting brother."

"Thank you Ibrahim Bey." Ali beamed. Those three words would keep him going longer than any breakfast could.

Ali turned and continued the methodical process of reloading his Mauser, taking aim at the closest living invader he could see and shooting. The first boat scraped onto the beach, they were close enough now that he hit more often than he missed.

The white boat rocked, as if waiting for someone to pull it up onto the beach or tie it off, but it was abandoned by all but the dead. Ali wondered whether it might drift off, but there was no wind and no current, so it sat where it was and rolled peacefully on small pink wavelets.

Invaders ran up the narrow beach and some managed to reach the cover of a small embankment at its edge.

The next boat edged close to the beach and men jumped into the water, despite it being too deep to walk. Ali shot at one of these and watched the bobbing head sink below the surface.

Ali shot a man running across the beach. Someone tried to drag this fellow along, and Ali shot him too.

One machine gun and we could hold this hill all day.

The last two boats ground onto the beach, carrying living and dead passengers. Some of the living reached the beach before they fell and stained the sand red. A few invaders crossed the beach, but there couldn't be more than thirty or forty of them from the cluster of four boats. The survivors couldn't be counted now as they hid behind the embankment.

A distant boom shook the air, and in that moment Ali's mind flashed back to the naval bombardment he witnessed five weeks earlier. In that moment he also knew the difference in his circumstances now, being exposed on a hilltop without a big gun to fire back.

A warship's shell screamed overhead and crashed into the valley behind. Ali's bladder let go briefly, but it was not full and he stemmed the flow before anyone could notice.

"Hold fire. Prepare to withdraw." Ibrahim Bey's eyes again drifted to the next hill and the rest of his platoon. Ali's gaze followed that of his commander and what he saw made his gut tighten.

Invaders scrambled upward near the top of the hill, and a line of bayonets pointed to the sky from behind its crest. *That hill is lost. Our brothers there are martyrs, or soon will be.*

Another boom shook the air.

"This is a fighting withdrawal," Ibrahim yelled, "so be ready to stand and return fire as we climb up the gully. All our ammunition is distributed. We have nothing more than what you are carrying, so use it carefully. We will go one squad at a time. You first, you next. Kadir, follow last with Suleyman's squad."

Ibrahim Bey turned and disappeared over the back of the hill with the squad he had nominated to accompany him.

Ali felt a pang of disappointment.

Why did he leave me here to be last with Kadir? He said I shot well. Why didn't he pick me to go with him?

The next squad disappeared over the back of the hill.

Suleyman and Sergeant Kadir fired at the invaders on the next hill.

Only one squad and a sergeant were left on the hill. Ten men against an invading army.

He checked his Mauser's internal magazine. It was full with five rounds and he decided against firing it again before leaving.

Preserve ammunition.

"Let's go Donkey Runt. Keep on your feet. Go! Go!"

Ali's knees felt weak as he stumbled towards the back of the hill.

"Come Ali!" Suleyman was at his side. "We must get off this hill or we'll be blown to bits."

Ali scurried down the back of the small hill and ran with the others past a second small hut. A flat paddock opened out in front of him and a single olive tree stood defiantly, as if guarding the crops for a farmer who might return one day. *Someone must have enjoyed a peaceful existence at this place once.*

Two brown craters gouged the paddock where the naval range-finders had landed.

This must be the only patch of flat land this side of the range.

Ali sprinted across the field with the others, his heart felt as if it might burst through his ribs.

With each step it seemed more likely he would live to reach cover in the gully beyond.

CHAPTER 39

Dacre

Sunday, 25 April 1915, sunrise

The Australian submarine *AE2* rose towards the surface for the third time since entering the minefields of the Dardanelles Strait.

The first two hasty observations had shown Lieutenant-Commander Dacre Stoker that he was progressing faster than he anticipated. Each time he corrected his course and hurried back to safer depths.

At twenty feet he raised the periscope and was surprised to find that he was clear of the known mine-strings and within three-hundred yards of the Narrows. Conscious of his order to attack mine-droppers, Dacre held the periscope up for longer than he would have liked to take stock of the situation above.

The surface of the water lay dead flat like a sheet of glass. *Not good for hiding.*

Before Dacre had seen enough to determine his next course of action, guns from forts on both sides of the Strait opened fire. Projectiles pounded the water above, but only subdued thuds from the blasts penetrated to the submarine. Sounds like hailstones told of burst shrapnel that fell through the water and bounced off the hull.

Around the top of the periscope, explosions lashed the water and made observation difficult, but Dacre made out the form of an old battleship hulk anchored ahead at the narrowest point of Chanak. *Maybe that could be used to drop mines?*

Further up the Strait, a number of destroyers and other small boats bore down on the submarine at great speed.

He lowered the periscope and continued on towards the old battleship.

On raising the periscope again, the hail of fire immediately reopened, but Dacre saw a smaller gunboat cruiser hurry out from behind the battleship.

That gunboat looks like a mine-dropper, and judging by her course she hopes to drop mines across our bow.

Deciding quickly that the gunboat was a better quarry, Dacre continued at periscope depth and when he reached a range of three-hundred yards, fired the bow torpedo-tube at her.

At the moment of firing the torpedo, one of the destroyers was very close and shaping to ram *AE2* on the port side. Dacre ordered a dive to seventy feet as soon as the torpedo was released. At last glance, as the telescope dipped, the destroyer looked to be right on top of the submarine, then amidst the noise of her propeller whizzing overhead a huge percussion shook the walls of the submarine and Dacre knew his torpedo had hit its mark.

On hearing the explosion, the thought of becoming entangled in the sinking ship ahead forced its way to Dacre's immediate concern. The small gunboat would likely sink quickly and Dacre ordered a change of course to the starboard with an intention to pass astern of her.

Changing direction blind in the swirling currents of the Narrows was not in Dacre's ideal plan of attack, but the prospect of being dragged to the bottom by a vessel he sunk himself demanded an alternative. After three minutes he changed back to what he considered the correct course to return to the centre of the Strait.

"Rise to twenty feet depth," Dacre ordered for a periscope observation.

Slam! – At a depth of forty feet the submarine struck bottom hard. Men not holding onto something fell and crashed into unyielding metal. Before Dacre could react, *AE2* slid up the bank to a depth of ten feet.

Dacre groaned.

The depth gauge was located near the bottom of the submarine and when it indicated ten feet, a considerable amount of the conning tower and bridge protruded above the surface of the water.

Through the periscope, Dacre observed that the submarine was grounded on the eastern shore, right under the guns of a fort. As he looked, one of the guns fired, seemingly right into his eye and he jumped back from the eyepiece of the periscope in a reflex response.

Everyone must remain calm. If there is panic we are all dead men. Remember the maiden of Vesuvius.

A silhouette took shape in his mind.

The trim and dainty form of a young female stood defiant, facing the crater at the top of Vesuvius, undeterred by the thunderous eruption or cloud of ash the volcano launched skyward. She casually stepped from side to side, dodging the glowing rocks as they fell. Dacre, the young midshipman, did not know her and never met her again, but when his eye was caught by her figure as he ran away from the exploding crater, he was compelled to stop and stand by her. Pluck personified, she inspired courage.

"Remain cool men and all will go well. Reverse thrust, full astern."

Unfortunately I cannot see the glowing rocks coming, and even if I could see them, I cannot dodge. We need to get underwater.

Electric motors groaned and the submarine hull rocked slightly, but held fast on the shore. Blasts of falling shells close by rocked the hull.

Why haven't the guns blown us apart by now? Maybe we are too close and they cannot aim this low?

"Stop starboard propeller, reverse port propeller full astern." Dacre heard his own voice deep and calm, as if it belonged to someone else.

Slowly, *AE2* began to slide down the bank.

Another shell landed nearby and rocked the hull.

The submarine dragged itself backwards towards deeper water.

"Depth twenty feet Captain," cried a voice from nearby.

"Reverse thrust, both propellers, full astern," Dacre said.

"Depth thirty feet."

Dacre checked his wristwatch. The submarine had been exposed on the Asian shore for the longest five minutes of his life.

"Depth forty feet."

"Depth fifty feet."

"Depth sixty feet."

Dacre checked the gyrocompass. The act of sliding the submarine down the bank and returning to deeper water had left her bow pointing south down the strait, back towards the Narrows and minefield he had just passed through.

"Depth seventy feet."

"Stop reverse thrust," called Dacre. "Forward thrust port propeller, full ahead. Helm hard a-port. Maintain depth at seventy feet."

Seemingly backwards to landlubbers, the instruction 'helm hard a-port' would drive the steering rudder such that the aft of the vessel would tend to the port side and drive the bow in the opposite direction. This combined with thrust from the port propeller only would turn the submarine towards the starboard as quickly as possible.

The propellers of two or three ships buzzed overhead.

"Well done men," Dacre called. "We are making much trouble for the enemy on the surface. We have passed the Narrows and sunk an enemy ship, running amok exactly as ordered. Your calm heads got us out of that pinch."

When Dacre believed the submarine was again on her proper course he ordered her ahead on both propellers.

Bump! – from a depth of seventy feet the submarine slid smoothly up a sandbank to eight feet.

Where on earth are we now?

Dacre raised the periscope and found that *AE2* was beached on the European shore, immediately below another fort.

The current that had swept the submarine off course continued to push against the hull and swung her stern round to port, leaving her high and dry. The bow nosed downwards towards deeper water.

A gun boat and some destroyers lay a little more than a hundred yards off and blazed away with all their broadsides. Dead ahead lay a clear view up the Strait.

If we can get off this bank we are heading on the correct course.

"Forward thrust, full ahead, both propellers!"

The propellers ground into the bottom and groaned in protest.

"Stop thrust!"

The submarine might destroy itself, but we have to get back underwater or we are doomed.

"Full ahead, both propellers!"

The submarine bumped and surged, then slithered ahead down to thirty feet.

Dacre checked his wrist watch again. Four minutes at eight feet seemed longer than the first beaching.

The enemy must have thought they had us stuck, otherwise they could have destroyed us on that bank.

"Dive to seventy feet."

The water buzzed overhead with a host of small vessels giving chase.

It would be miraculous if we haven't sustained serious damage crashing twice under fire. Steering and dive rudders appear to be functional. We still have to navigate our way around Nagara Point and I don't want to beach us again, but enemy vessels are on top of us and I dare not show myself.

I need to get a signal back to the General Headquarters that we have got this far and sunk a ship. Other submarines will be sent once they know we have got through the Narrows, but the Marconi wireless requires that I surface and erect the antenna.

We've consumed one and a half hours of our twelve hours of good air, as well as a good portion of our battery charge. The sun is risen and we haven't a hope of escape until darkness falls at nine o'clock tonight – nearly fifteen hours away.

I wonder if we have any leaks.

CHAPTER 40

Mustafa

Sunday, 25 April 1915, soon after sunrise

The gentle slopes of the Sari Bair range glowed yellow-green. The sun's early rays lit up the hills, but were yet to provide any warmth to Lieutenant-Colonel Mustafa Kemal at his 19th Division headquarters on the plains near Boghali.

Koja Chemen Tepe was the highest point on the Gallipoli peninsula. It looked quiet and peaceful as usual, but this morning it was crying out to be defended from the English invasion force surging towards it.

A fundamental principle of battle – hold the high ground. We should be on our way there already. While we wait, the enemy is charging towards it.

At dawn, Mustafa had received his first report of an enemy landing at Ariburnu. Immediately, he alerted the regimental commanders of his 19th Division and ordered them to prepare to move out. He also sent off cavalry patrols to reconnoitre the roads towards Koja Chemen Tepe, and to the north and south.

The cavalry patrols had not returned.

The 57th Regiment had been on early morning operations and was ready to deploy. This regiment was made up mostly of native Turks and had proven itself to be more reliable than the other two regiments in his division. The 57th would be his first choice for confronting the enemy. The 72nd and 77th Regiments had too many Arab units and raw conscripts. They were unpredictable and lacked discipline. Many seemed to be more concerned about returning home alive than performing their duty.

Major Izzettin approached from the communications hut. *Maybe he carries our orders to commit. Why doesn't he run faster?*

It chafed to command the reserve 19th Division. Regiments from the 9th Divisional were already engaged with the enemy. *Using men and weapons to defend the Fatherland like I should be doing right now.*

Mustafa fought the urge to ride over to meet his Chief of Staff, but tracked him from the edge of his vision as he gazed at the Sari Bair range.

Izzettin drew closer, his face red, nostrils flaring with each breath. "Kemal

Bey, An enemy force has landed at Ariburnu. They are advancing inland and up the Sari Bair Range towards Koja Chemen Tepe. One platoon from the 27th Regiment is defending this area, but they will surely be overrun. Lieutenant-Colonel Sami has ordered the rest of the regiment forward to engage the enemy and push them back into the sea. He has requested that you send a battalion in support."

Mustafa reached down from his saddle and grabbed the paper from Izzettin's hand. He read it quickly, hoping for more detail that would allow him to deploy his troops where they were clearly needed. *Only one battalion. One thousand men. It's not enough. We need the whole division, or at least a full regiment.*

"Is there word of any other enemy landings elsewhere, down at the Straits or up in the Gulf of Saros?"

"No, Kemal Bey."

Mustafa shifted in his saddle. "I have a Division here, ready to deploy. But these are reserves for the whole 5th Army. I cannot commit without orders from Major-General Esat or Field Marshal von Sanders."

"I am sorry, Kemal Bey, Esat Pasha and von Sanders Pasha are at Bulair but we have not been able to make contact with them this morning." His Chief of Staff's eyes darted from side to side, like those of a school boy searching for an escape from a certain thrashing.

Mustafa looked back up to the Sari Bair Range. From the peak at Koja Chemen Tepe, a gentle saddle lead south, down towards the next major peak, Chunuk Bair. From here the ridge split in multiple directions. Two main arms reached south-west and south. These two main arms formed the second and third ridgelines from the sea. The spur running south-west, the second ridge, split again to form the first ridge. *The enemy is advancing on the first ridge now, and maybe onto the second ridge.*

Other lesser spurs ran east and west from Chunuk Bair. It was like the hub of a giant wheel. *Chunuk Bair is the key to the lock. If we lose it to the enemy, they will dominate the lower ground between there and here. But if we can hold Chunuk Bair, we can push them back down the hill into the sea.*

"That will be all," Kemal said, forcing a calmer tone. "For now."

"Yes, Kemal Bey."

Before Major Izzettin had finished his response, Mustafa jammed his spurs into the horse's ribs, and galloped off towards Mal Tepe and his regimental camps.

Masses of tents filled the camps of his 19th Division. Ten thousand men held in reserve, and ready to mobilize. *But where will they be needed?* The enemy had been planning to attack for months. Intelligence reports from Egypt gave plenty of warning of the invasion. Recent aerial reconnaissance over the island of Imbros had confirmed the magnitude of the attacking force, but no one had been able to determine the location of the intended landing place – or places.

Defence in Depth. Mustafa spat on the ground. *A stupid German's idea. One month ago I had the 27th Regiment under my command and artillery well positioned to hit a landing force hard as soon as they set foot on our beaches. The enemy should be made to earn every metre of our precious ground. Now we only have a few companies along the coast and all our strength waiting inland in reserve. Letting the enemy take a foothold easily. Too easily.*

Von Sanders is obsessed with Bulair. The narrow neck of land is vulnerable and the English navy could support an invasion that might strangle supplies to the rest of the peninsula. It could be an effective strategy, but the English wouldn't do it. Bulair is 50 kilometres away from their objective of the Strait and would result in a siege of the whole peninsula. The English would have to cut supplies from the Asiatic side of the Strait and the Marmara Sea. This would be impractical, and even if they could do it, it would take too long. The English are too impatient to try this approach. Their warships are lined up ready to steam through the Strait at the first opportunity.

The English have taken the direct, brute force approach until now, with their failed naval assaults on the forts of the Strait. They will try a landing closer to the Strait in an attempt to neutralize the Strait's defences quickly.

Mustafa stopped at the tent of Major Avni, commander of the 57th Regiment.

Huseyin Avni was returning to his tent as Mustafa dismounted.

"Have the men rested after morning exercises?" Mustafa asked.

"Some, Kemal Bey," Avni said. "Most have eaten and all are ready to engage with the enemy – as soon as we are permitted."

Mustafa looked into Avni's eyes. They looked tired, but determined. "There will be no more rest today. The enemy has landed at Ariburnu. Make your Regiment ready to move out immediately. Each infantryman in all three battalions must have a full allocation of ammunition. Mobilise the mountain howitzer battery and machine gun company, and ready the medical detachment. Form up on the west trail. We will march towards Koja Dere, and then up to Koja Chemen Tepe."

"Yes Kemal Bey." Major Avni hurried off to pass the order down the chain of command.

Kemal re-mounted, searched out his other two regimental commanders and ordered the 72nd and 77th Regiments to call to arms, and then await further orders.

The camp was large and it took longer than he would have liked to initiate readiness of the 19th Division to move out and face the enemy.

He needed more information. Time was being wasted waiting for orders. Committing more than one battalion may be seen as overstepping his authority. Other parts of his reserve division might be needed elsewhere. *If the enemy does land at Bulair and I fail to provide reserve troops when called on, my career will be over. I might be court-martialled and shot.*

Mustafa stopped at the communications hut, dismounted and strode in. "Are there any reports of invasion landings anywhere else?"

The signals officer stood to attention. "Kemal Bey, Ships have been sighted off Bulair, Sedd-el-Bahr and Kum Kale. Ariburnu is the only landing that has been reported to us at this time."

"Connect me to Field Marshal Liman von Sanders. Immediately!"

"Sir, we have been unable to –."

"Or Major-General Esat! Try again! I need to deploy our reserves! The enemy has landed and is advancing up towards the highest ground as we speak. They are virtually unopposed because our army is sitting outside that door, waiting for my orders."

"I will try again, Kemal Bey." The signalman busied himself with the telephone set and repeated the request he had sent numerous times since dawn.

Mustafa paced the small hut like a caged animal. His heart raced as if he had been running. He took a deep breath, and another, and another. *I must act now.*

"I am sorry Kemal Bey." The signalman's voice was tight, he leaned back slightly on his stool. "Esat Pasha is still in the field, attempting to locate Liman von Sanders Pasha. The commanders cannot be contacted at this time."

Mustafa felt a tight pain in his chest, as if it was being compressed. *Why do they hold the decision making authority and make themselves unavailable at the critical moment?* Earlier in the morning, Mustafa had contacted Esat at Bulair by telephone, and requested permission to deploy his reserves. Esat had refused, wanting to consult with Liman von Sanders first. But Liman von Sanders could not be found. *Off somewhere with his German field glasses no doubt, looking for an enemy that isn't there.*

"Send this message to Lieutenant-Colonel Sami at Corps Headquarters: 'I have received your confirmation that the enemy has landed in force at Ariburnu. I will lead the 57th Regiment towards Ariburnu via Koja Chemen Tepe at once, to assist your 27th Regiment throw the enemy back into the sea. The remaining two Regiments of my 19th Division will remain at Boghali as reserves until called upon.'"

"Yes Kemal Bey."

"Read it back to me first."

The signalman was still scribbling the script on a notepad with his pencil. Once he had read the message back, Kemal stood and watched as the message was sent.

"Headquarters has confirmed receipt of your message Kemal Bey."

"Now, take down these orders for the 72nd and 77th Regiment commanders: 'The enemy has landed at Ariburnu. I am leading the 57th Regiment to face them.

You are to remain ready for deployment at short notice. You may be required at Ariburnu or elsewhere, subject to enemy landing force strength and 5th Army defensive requirements.'"

"Yes Kemal Bey."

"And send copies of both orders to Esat Pasha and von Sanders Pasha at the Bulair Head Quarters. They will receive the information eventually."

"Of course, Kemal Bey."

Mustafa turned and strode out to his horse. *Lieutenant-Colonel Sami asked for one battalion of reinforcements, I will bring one regiment. Hopefully it is enough.*

He spurred the horse hard on the way back to the 57th Regiment camp. *Many men will suffer and die today. Why should a horse get off lightly?*

The three infantry battalions of the 57th Regiment stood sprawled around the edge of camp and onto a rough trail leading west. Three thousand men was too great a number of men to leave waiting idle for long.

The regimental commander Major Avni was at the head of the column in conference with his battalion commanders. He stopped talking and all four men looked up expectantly as Mustafa approached.

"The 57th Regiment will march for Koja Chemen Tepe," Mustafa said. "We will hold the high ground and throw the enemy into the sea. We leave immediately."

Mustafa nudged his horse forward, more slowly now. A column of men of this size has much inertia. It would take time for each battalion's runners to spread the word to move out. The artillery battery would move slowly, although bullock teams were already hitched up to each of the four guns.

The little Mehmets will follow me. He wanted to look back and see, but forced himself to face forwards. *Only forwards. If they won't follow me now then we are all doomed anyway.*

He rode on at a canter and pulled out his pocket watch. It was five minutes to eight o'clock.

CHAPTER 41

Jayjay

Sunday, 25 April 1915, two hours after sunrise [8:00am]

A friendly destroyer steamed towards *Minnewaska* from the beach. Three Funnels stood proud of her deck and belched smoke.

Jayjay stood in line and stared over capped heads. His tongue stuck to the roof of his mouth.

Another blast from a warship's gun rent the sky and smothered the chatter of far-off rifles.

A puff of earth rose from a distant hill, silhouetted against the morning sunshine, then the tapping of small arms fire drifted across the water again.

The destroyer surged closer and bloodied human forms on her deck grew visible. Men lay in rows like bent sausages on a barbeque plate. Fear gripped Jayjay's gut like never before and he lost control of his bladder for a moment.

"God help us!" he breathed.

"Sweet Mary!" Seamus O'Shea traced a cross with a finger from his forehead to his belly, then to each shoulder.

"Those boys must've tried to haggle with the natives," Larry said. "Remember no haggling when we land lads!"

Nervous laughter faded quickly and they waited with the other men of the 1st Battalion. Most stood in silence, or murmured an occasional word to a neighbour.

The destroyer eased alongside and the first of the wounded was hoisted up onto the *Minnewaska,* in full view of the rows of waiting men. Jayjay hated the hoist. He hated the destroyer and he hated the *Minnewaska* for bringing him to this place.

The taste of blood filled his mouth. He had bit into his lower lip, but felt no pain.

No haggling? These poor bastards still have all their Turkish cash in their bloody pockets! Months of training and they got shot to bits on the first morning. This is not like the exercises.

On any other day, a hot breakfast of steak and bread would have been a treat to savour, but today it sat in Jayjay's stomach like a stone. The sea was calm and not the reason for his urge to vomit.

The straps of his pack pulled down at his shoulders. Some of the smaller men must have been struggling with the weight, but not one complained. Two hundred rounds of ammunition, two water bottles, three day's iron rations, a great coat and bits hanging off everywhere – an entrenching tool, a bayonet, a bowie knife on his belt and an unloaded rifle slung over his shoulder.

The hoist lifted the last of the wounded out of the way and a voice called that it was D Company's turn to board the destroyer for delivery to the beach.

Men carried their loads, one at a time, down the narrow rope ladders, rifles over shoulders like in practice at Mudros. Jayjay had fallen into Mudros Harbour more than once when the ladder wobbled and spun. A fall today would result in a hard landing on a deck already smeared with Australian blood.

Jayjay's turn came and Ron gave him a nod.

"Hang on tight Mate!" Larry grinned but his eyes showed concern.

Jayjay climbed over the balustrade and onto the ladder. He spun immediately and crashed into the rail in full view of those waiting on deck. Hot embarrassment rose in his neck, but no one said a word or even smirked. He clung tight and took a deep breath while the swinging slowed. *I might take longer than anyone else to get down, but I am going to do it no matter what… one tiny rung at a time… one more… one more… nearly there… I could jump from here… made it.*

"Move back from the ladder soldier," Sergeant Baker barked.

Jayjay paced across the deck, slippery under his boots, and felt as if his knees might buckle at any moment.

He fell into line and his father's words rang to his head, as if intended for this moment. '*Only when you know fear Son, then can you be truly brave.*'

The destroyer funnel close by was riddled with bullet holes, but stood true. *I will be brave Dad.*

The last of D company reached the deck without anyone falling, and the destroyer steamed away from *Minnewaska*. Only a few hundred yards and it was time for the next transfer, into the whale boats that were to be towed as far as possible, then rowed to the beach.

Jayjay climbed down the short distance into the row boat and waited. The boat was under command of a British navy midshipman. *Funny he's the youngest on board, the little middie' can't be more than fifteen years old. I heard that the navy allowed under age Jack Tars to fill these non-combat roles.*

Oars pointed skywards and the destroyer pulled a string of three row boats a short distance towards the beach, then cast the rope away and turned from the shallows. The midshipman called for rowers to drop the oars and start rowing.

The limpid water looked so peaceful in the early morning sun. On another day the narrow beach ahead, with its rugged backdrop, might be a pleasant place to visit.

Jayjay stared into the blue-green water and tried to gauge the depth – zip, splash – a bullet sent up a small spray a few yards away and Jayjay's fingers tightened around the rifle jammed between his knees. Small bubbles disappeared in the swirl of the oars and drifted behind. *We're very exposed. We need to fire back, but orders are to keep rifles unloaded until we land. I wouldn't know what to aim at from here anyway. I'd be just as likely to shoot one of our own blokes as an enemy.*

"We're riding in a boat full of bloody lunatics," Larry whispered. "Only sane bloke here's that middie' who's going to turn her around and get right on back to the ship."

Jayjay grinned and nodded. His throat was tight and felt as if his voice might crack if he tried to talk.

He looked down at his freshly washed uniform. Medical staff had instructed the company to ensure that their clothes were clean for the landing. At first, the order seemed as useless as the expectation to salute British officers on Cairo streets, but the explanation that followed dampened much bravado. Many of them were expected to be wounded. Bullets and shrapnel bring pieces of clothing with them into the body and the extra filth can lead to infection.

The beach ahead stretched half a mile long, curved around a slight headland at each end and lay at the base of a steep hill, rising several hundred feet from the back of the sand. Beyond the hill, and to its left and right, a tangle of gullies and ridges commanded a view over the men arriving in a small boat, as if in contempt.

Men of the Australian Imperial Force walked about on the beach, some with purpose and some without. Above the beach, clusters of tiny figures scurried along the ridge like ants. Some looked to be firing at an unseen enemy, some running, some hiding for cover. *The 3rd Brigade. When we hit the beach, someone will give us orders where to join the fight.*

Left of the beach, a large rocky outcrop jutted towards the sea from the first ridge, a giant nose of sandstone. Steep and yellow, it stood barren of the scrub that covered everything else. Fear summoned the words of a hymn into his mind.

Rock of ages, cleft for me.
Let me hide myself in Thee…

It seemed strange that he couldn't remember the next words of the hymn he had sung in church many times since childhood, as if his brain didn't want to move past the plea for a safe hiding place. Instead the first two lines repeated over and over in his mind.

Rock of ages, cleft for me.
Let me hide myself in Thee…

Sounds of rifle fire grew louder as the boat approached the beach, and came from distinct directions. Some from the left, some straight above and some far off along the lower ridge to the right.

Several yards from the beach the boat ground against the bottom and men poured over the gunnels into the water. Jayjay was amongst the first to splash in waist deep. He held his Lee-Enfield above his head with both hands and worked to keep his footing on the uneven seabed.

Wizzzz – the sound of an angry wasp chirped past at an impossible speed, then a gasp and gurgling cry called out from behind.

Jayjay spun around.

The young midshipman at the tiller clutched at his throat. Blood seeped between his fingers and his eyes met Jayjay's in a questioning gaze, then he collapsed forward. His face thudded into the bench Jayjay had vacated moments before.

That boy was alive and doing his duty seconds ago, now he's dying face down in his own boat. Is he already dead? Who will take the boat back now? Who will tell his parents? What will his mum say? What would my mum say?

Something pulled at Jayjay's middle, near the surface of the water. Everything around him was quiet and slow. Small waves lapped against the boat and it rocked gently like a cradle. The pulling grew stronger. A red puddle spread slowly along the bench, then dripped onto floor of the boat. *The lad looks like he's asleep. Maybe he's asleep.*

The pulling at his middle wouldn't stop.

Jayjay looked down.

Ron was tugging at his belt.

Ron looked to be yelling, but there was no sound.

I need to stay with this boy. His face smashed into my seat and there's no one else here to help him. How will his parents know what happened? They raised him, but they might never know. Maybe I can wake him?

No.

He's not asleep.

He's dead.

Silence smudged into noise. Roaring noise. He allowed himself to be pulled forward and took a step towards the shore. The beach came into focus, men from his platoon ran towards the base of the steep hill, maybe ten or fifteen yards behind the water's edge. He forced his legs to move. He was in a school running race, coming last as usual. *Why can't you run faster with those long legs?* A fellow lay on the beach, arms and legs splayed as if he collapsed midstride and no one had bothered to straighten him up. Jayjay ran past and tried to remember the orders. *Take control of the high ground and work inland to cut off Turkish supply lines. Push on at all costs. Follow your commanding officers. No haggling with the natives.*

The embankment in front reached to the sky and filled his field of vision left and right. The Rock of Ages and the rest of the ridgeline were hidden from view in this sheltered cove. Booming guns pounded a tattoo that shook Jayjay's insides to liquid, it was impossible to tell which came from ship guns and which came from the Turks.

A shell exploded over the water near a drifting boat, still under command of a dead boy. Shrapnel sprayed a patch of water in a local storm that was over in a moment.

The company commander yelled something unintelligible. Others around Jayjay started to move. The company hurried along the beach close to the base of the hill to their left. At the end of the beach the column rounded a headland and a wide gully opened up.

A shell screeched past and burst over a point fifty yards up the gully. A delicate white cloud appeared to mark the detonation and hung in the air. The scrub below bent under the hail of shrapnel and two men dropped in the area of impact. The bushes sprang back, but only one of the men stood, the other rolled over and curled into a ball.

Jayjay followed Larry. *Someone ahead must know where we are going.* A pair of stretcher bearers passed in the opposite direction, carrying a fellow who might have been alive or dead. His limp arm hung off the stretcher and caught on the bushes as if he was trying to grab them on the way past.

Larry turned and pointed into the scrub beside the track. A man lay motionless on his back, clutching at a dark blood stain on his belly. The dead man had a black beard and strange hat that looked as if it was made from wrapped strips of cloth. *A Turk.* He was short and thin and didn't much look like an enemy. Like the Germans from the Emden. *They should look more evil somehow – like in the war posters.*

Explosive smoke filled the gully with haze and burned his nostrils. The screech of another shell built to announce its arrival. Jayjay looked up but could not see it. Others around him dropped to the ground. The shell burst over the beach behind him and he ducked for cover himself.

Sergeant Baker stood and looked to be yelling, but Jayjay couldn't make out the words. Men up front stood, removed their packs and lined them up on the valley floor. They fixed their bayonets and loaded clips of ammunition into the magazines of their rifles.

Baker waved the men forward.

Maybe we should just wait here for a spell. The sound of artillery pounded Jayjay's head like a club and he felt as if his brain might leak out his ears.

Ron knelt and was staring at him.

Creases of concern framed Ron's eyes, but he said nothing.

Jayjay forced a grin and fought heavy gravity to lift himself off the ground, then dropped his pack with the rest.

"Let's go find some Turks Ron." Jayjay stood. "No one to shoot at down here."

"Yeah," Ron clicked his bayonet into place. "We'll come back for the packs later, if no one nicks them."

"Our blokes won't touch them, and the Turks will be too busy running away."

Jayjay jammed two clips of five rounds each into the magazine. Ten bullets loaded and he felt as if he woke from a dream. *This is real now. I may need to shoot a man.*

His heartbeat seemed to accelerate. He shook his head clear and forced his mind back to training exercises. *This is just like in training. Keep calm. Be aware of your surroundings. Know where your enemy is. Maintain your cover soldier and get moving. Breathe.*

He pushed ahead and scrambled up the valley with his company. Smaller groups of men hurried in other directions, but he hadn't seen anyone from the other companies of the 1st Battalion since leaving the beach. *They must have gone to reinforce other parts of the firing line. The left front only needs one company of two hundred and fifty men. That's good, they must be pushing forward without too much resistance.*

Careful to maintain his footing across the uneven scrub, he stole a glance up the valley and then to the left and right. The main ridge looked to consist of a series of hills all jammed together, spurs breaking toward the sea complicated the geometry and made it difficult to figure where a firing line might be. Hillsides rose steeply, but rarely broke into a sheer cliff, unlike the terrain in the Blue Mountains near Sydney. In many places it seemed that a persistent fellow, willing to take hold of scrub with his hands and climb a little, might take, more or less, a direct route up the hill.

Another angry wasp zipped past and exploded into a rock.

Jayjay turned to Ron. "I don't much like these hellish insects!"

"Yeah," Ron grinned past the worry lines. "Shoulda' brought a fly swat."

"I wanna shoot back," Jayjay said. "But haven't seen any Turks 'cept a dead one."

"These bullets gotta' come from somewhere," Larry puffed. "Must be crazy bastard Turk snipers. Watch out for them hiding in the bushes."

Jayjay scrambled upwards and thought he saw leaves move on a bush a few yards away from the line his Company followed. Maybe it was a bullet. Maybe it was nothing.

How can we shoot the Turks if we can't see them. I thought they were going to run away or surrender. We gotta find them.

CHAPTER 42

Ali

Sunday, 25 April 1915, mid-morning

Ali's legs threatened to give up.

The gap between himself and the next man up the hill was growing.

He turned and looked back – *no one.*

I am the last defender.

Platoon Commander, Second Lieutenant Ibrahim had called it a fighting withdrawal, but it felt to Ali as if they were running away from the invaders.

A bayonet appeared from below the rise on which he stood, thirty paces back, forty at most. It marched towards him, stabbing up at the blue horizon.

The invaders are too close.

'God's mercy won't help you if you fall over when the enemy is attacking.' Sergeant Kadir was way up ahead, but the memory of his harsh words rang inside Ali's head, as real as the boom of the enemy warships' guns.

'You have to stand on your own feet Donkey Runt.' Kadir had said on the other side of this very hill two months earlier.

'The enemy will show you no mercy. Watch your footing boy.' The rebuke had followed a vicious kick to the thigh from the sergeant at night training when Ali fell over while marching.

Maybe Kadir was right. I am just a runt. Too young and too small to be a soldier. Now I will die for nothing.

Ali dropped to one knee and pulled the butt of his Mauser up to his shoulder. Too exhausted to keep running up the hill, he sucked in another lungful of sea air and tried to steady the shaking rifle as he exhaled as slowly as he could.

If the unbelievers join battle with you, they shall be put to flight. They shall find none to protect or help them.

A calm came over Ali with the realization he was about to die – A martyr for God and His nation. *Not what I planned. I want to return to Mum and Dad as a hero. And Zeynep, could she have loved me? Or at least respected me? I think so.*

He stared down the steady barrel and a khaki clad figure with a flat circular hat appeared in his rifle sites.

As God wills. Ali squeezed the trigger.

The man crumpled into a heap, still and silent.

Another circular-hatted-head emerged from behind the rise, and then disappeared back down before Ali could chamber another round.

They're trying to kill me, but I killed another one of them instead and they know it.

They're scared like me, but they can choose to wait. They have the luxury of caution.

New strength surged through Ali's body with the realisation that he might live on. He slung his rifle on his shoulder and fresh legs carried him up the hill towards his comrades. Immediate survival was his pure focus. He pulled at scrub on the way, hauling himself up the hill with every muscle. One small bush let go of its grip on the hillside and Ali nearly overbalanced with the uprooted plant still in his hand.

A rifle shot chased him. The distance from behind difficult to tell, but it was close.

Another rifle shot, and this time, at the same moment the bullet sung past his ear and a puff of dust burst from the hill in front of his face. *That was closer. The next one will get me.*

Ali dove sideways behind some scrub before the marksman had a chance to try for the third shot.

He was both terrified and relieved to realise that he almost landed on Sergeant Kadir.

Kadir calmly held his finger up to his lips. "Nice. Very nice Donkey Runt. I thought you were a dead man for sure."

Ali lay flat on the ground and sucked in air. "So did I." It was the most positive thing he had ever heard from Kadir's mouth – about anyone.

Kadir raised his hand and waved it forwards, in a large arc towards the enemy and the sea.

Men emerged from bushes around and took aim to fire at the invaders. Most remained crouched and were concealed from the enemy below. One or two rounds at the most, then they lowered their profile again.

Several of the invaders dropped, exposed and motionless. Victims of the latest onslaught. One rolled around, writhing in pain, but other than that there was no movement.

"Good," Kadir said. "They have stopped again. First Platoon to me. Keep low, do not let the enemy see you."

Men crowded around. Ali was pleased to see Suleyman's huge form and moved to crouch near him.

"Anyone who has ammunition left," Kadir continued, "give it to me. We have held the enemy for as long as we can with what we have. You must get word to the commanders that the enemy has landed here in force and we need reinforcements."

Ali handed over three rounds, keeping one round chambered in his rifle in case he needed it himself.

A new respect for Sergeant Kadir caught Ali by surprise. The man had always been so cruel towards Ali and others. Kadir could have led the retreat himself, and posted others as a rear guard. Yet he ordered the others away, choosing to stay himself.

Suleyman refused to hand over his ammunition. "I will stay. Give me some of those bullets."

Suleyman turned to Ali. "Someone else will have to teach you to read Ali. Go! Warn the commanders."

Suleyman smiled grimly and turned away.

Kadir aimed his Mauser and fired a single shot towards Ariburnu, over the top of a mound of earth that he would surely die defending.

Ali wanted to say something to Suleyman to acknowledge his brave decision, and even to the Sergeant, but he couldn't think of words that seemed worthy of the situation. The rest of the men were already scrambling up the hill.

"May God bless you Suleyman, and Kadir Efendi. You are brave men. You will enter into Paradise today. As God wills." It was the best Ali could do. He turned and ran after the others.

Ali hauled himself up the range towards the local peak at Chunuk Bair and the sounds of rifle fire drifted away behind.

Covering fire from the two rear guard defenders bought only a few minutes of time and too soon the rifle shots grew closer again. Running for his life with a one-shot rifle, Ali did not look back. He kept low as best he could and charged upwards with the rest.

A few paces ahead, Attila stumbled to the ground and lay still. Ali caught up to him seconds later. Blood oozed onto Attila's shirt through a hole the middle of his back. Ali grabbed Attila's shoulder and pulled him over, but Attila's eyes stared blankly back and his body was limp. The rest of his squad sped on ahead and either did not notice Attila's fall, or chose to ignore it. *You were always the aggressive one. I never thought you would have been shot in the back.*

A puff of dust burst from the ground next to Ali's foot. He dropped Attila and sprinted on towards the crest at Chunuk Bair.

Ali was on the verge of collapsing from exhaustion when he caught up with the remaining members of his Platoon. They stood at the crest with other men who also wore the Turkish army uniform.

There was only a small number, not even a full squad, but one man had an officer's uniform. His air of confidence left no doubt that he was in charge.

"Why are you running away?" The officer demanded without introduction. Ali saw by his insignia that he was a lieutenant-colonel and then recognised him as Mustafa Kemal. Ali's 27th Regiment had come under Kemal's command for around one month earlier in the year, between one re-organisation and the next.

"The enemy has landed," Ali forced out the words between deep breaths, "and has overrun our trenches at Ariburnu. We have no ammunition left. They are right behind us and we have orders to inform the commanders."

The lieutenant-colonel looked past Ali down the hill towards the sea, and then quickly turned to back one of his own men. "Go back to the 57th Regiment and bring all battalions forward to defend Chunuk Bair. I need them all here! Immediately!"

"Yes, Kemal Bey!" The man sprinted off.

Lieutenant-colonel Mustafa Kemal turned back to the remnant of Ali's squad. "Well you have given me the message, and now I must give you another order – you do not run from the enemy! If you don't have ammunition you have your bayonets! You must let the enemy see you and lie down. Reinforcements are coming. The enemy must be slowed here so we can hold this high ground until the reinforcements arrive."

Ali held the lieutenant-colonel's gaze. His throat was dry, it seemed that a whole canteen of water would make no difference.

Many thoughts ran through his head all at once.

Ali loved his family and friends, and suddenly longed to return to the simple peaceful existence he had known up until a few months earlier. He had wanted to be a hero, to kill God's enemies. After months of gruelling training, this morning he had had his opportunity. So many came. So many died, and yet they kept coming. Ali had lost count of the men he had shot since dawn. Tens. Many tens had died by his hand. *Why do they keep coming?*

He thought of Zeynep and whether his family and hers could ever support a marriage.

However, the morning's battle had prepared Ali for such an order in a way that months of training never could have. Having seen his squad leader Suleyman and Sergeant Kadir sacrifice themselves for the other men, and his friend Attila killed by the invaders, there seemed now to be no alternative. Ali loved his family and his homeland and he had to defend it with his life. Reinforcements were on the way, but they were not here yet. He was here.

"Yes Kemal Bey."

Ali turned away from Lieutenant-Colonel Kemal without another word and walked back down the hill towards the enemy. Every remaining member of his unit also turned and walked with him.

Enemy soldiers climbed the hill towards him. Less than one hundred paces away now.

Ali made sure that the invaders saw him approaching and watched them go to ground. He lay down himself, taking what cover he could behind thin vegetation.

Peering through the scrub, he watched them creep closer. They were close enough that no great marksmanship would be required to make a kill. Bullets, however, were the problem. The enemy didn't know he only had one bullet left, but somehow he still expected them to charge up the hill at any moment.

Ali waited in position for several minutes, not sure what to do next. *The approaching enemy must have slowed in their advance.*

He listened for any indication of the invaders approaching, but could only hear Lieutenant-Colonel Kemal shouting orders. *At least some of the reinforcements from the 57th Regiment must have arrived.*

Ali had heard others talk of Lieutenant-Colonel Mustafa Kemal. The young officer was reputed to be aggressive, but well respected by his men. Ali craned his head and concentrated on listening to hear the commands in the distance. He could just make out the words:

"I am not ordering you to attack, I am ordering you to die! During the time that will elapse until we die, new forces and commanders can arrive and replace us."

God be merciful. Ali felt a pit deep in his gut. *The bastard has already given us up for dead, and the reinforcements behind us. What hope is there to stop these invaders?*

Ali crawled forwards, down the hill. He was alone and used his small size to remain invisible. *The English must be close.*

Foreign words in a harsh tongue came from too close and he froze, willing his body to blend with the sparse scrub he lay beneath.

What should I do? I only have one bullet. I could shoot one of them and die. Maybe if I wait until they pass I could shoot one of them and live.

Yells and a groan were followed by rifle fire and a gang of enemy soldiers rushed past Ali's position without slowing, maybe ten or fifteen of them. The groaning one stayed behind and Ali allowed himself to breathe again. *The groaner won't be causing us much more trouble. I wouldn't waste the bullet on him, but I don't want him to see me in case he can still manage his rifle.*

Ali listened for a moment to be sure that the wounded enemy was alone, and then continued to crawl downhill. He dared not raise his head to peer after the crowd that had just hurried past, but dragged himself away until he found a small clearing.

He crouched behind a bush and made sure he was well balanced, in a position such that he could jump up and charge quickly when he needed to. He raised the butt of his Mauser to his shoulder and waited.

An eternity of time seemed to pass and Ali's knees started to ache. He stood to stretch his legs.

Movement in the scrub down the hill caught his eye. His focus narrowed on the location. All sound disappeared.

Ali watched the movement down the barrel of his Mauser. *One shot left. Then what? Maybe I could shoot one and then surrender. What chance is there that they might take me alive? Would they torture me? I should be ready to die a martyr. Paradise awaits those who trade their lives fighting for God.* He had not seen the enemy take any prisoners, nor had his platoon taken any invaders as prisoner. It wasn't practical in a running battle. Both sides had taken the easy option of killing unarmed or wounded men so they could keep fighting and push on themselves. *Maybe I can hide and keep still while they pass, then creep back to safety at night. Without ammunition, I cannot do any more than I've done today.*

A face appeared in the moving bush and looked straight at him. The invader's eye's opened wide and his mouth started to move. Before any sound came, Ali squeezed the trigger. He knew immediately that the invader was dead. A small bullet hole was visible between the eyes for a moment before the face fell forward into the dirt. The bullet had deformed on entry, and taken out a large piece of skull at the back of his head on exit, leaving red and grey spatters of brain hanging in the bush behind.

Another invader appeared from behind the brain-festooned bush. *Why do they keep coming? This one is a giant, bigger than Suleyman.* The big man looked to his dead comrade and raised his rifle, looking back at Ali along the barrel.

The two stood motionless, aiming at each other. Ali's legs were frozen. *Why doesn't he shoot?* Ali lowered his rifle, hoping the invader might do the same. He couldn't breathe.

The invader started frantically working the bolt action of his rifle.

The fool doesn't have a round chambered. Otherwise I would already be dead. I could have killed him too, if I just had one more bullet. Ali's legs sprang to life before he could think about the action, and he charged at the invader.

He levelled his bayonet and aimed it somewhere between the invader's chest and gut.

For a moment, Ali thought he would win the race, his legs pumped hard, gravity helping with the downhill sprint. He knew he was moving faster than he had ever run, and yet, at the same time he felt that he was moving slowly, as if pushing through waist-deep water.

Only a few paces separated the two when the invader looked up. His eye narrow behind the rifle and the muzzle flashed.

Ali felt as if he had been punched in the stomach. All strength drained from his legs and the ground rose towards him. *I have to stop this one last opponent.* He stabbed his rifle towards the giant and felt the bayonet bite into his enemy's thigh on the way past.

Ali hit the ground and kept sliding into the bush that was bedecked with brains. His Mauser fell out of reach, but he hardly knew or cared. He rolled onto his side and pulled his knees up towards the fire in his belly.

His vision blurred.

Through the intensity of pain, Ali was vaguely aware that he was being shoved over onto his back. He fought to focus his vision on the invader looking down at him.

The invader worked the bolt to chamber another round. This time slowly and deliberately. *He is about to shoot me.*

It took all of his remaining strength to pull one hand away from his gut and raise an open palm towards the enemy, but it seemed that somehow this simple act might win mercy.

Blood trickled down the back of his shaking fingers. *I cannot harm you now. Let me live. Please!*

The giant stared down, his eyes flickered to his dead comrade and then back to Ali. He said something in a deep voice. Foreign words – slurred and harsh. He raised the tip of his bayonet and rested it on the centre of Ali's chest.

Mum will be sad. I hope Dad will be proud. Will they ever know?

Ali's hand was still in the air when the invader leaned his weight against the buttstock of his rifle and ran Ali through.

CHAPTER 43

Jayjay

Sunday, 25 April 1915, midday

"Damn Turk!"

Jayjay looked down at the dead enemy soldier and tried not to think about the look in those eyes when he had pushed the steel blade into the fellow's tiny chest.

Why didn't you shoot me when you had the chance? Maybe you were thinking about what you did to Poddy? You're only a boy, like the middie who delivered me to the beach – barely old enough to shave. Still, you deserved to die for what you did. Damn near blew Poddy's head clean off.

Jayjay's platoon blurred away up the hill.

Blood from the bayonet wound to his leg stained the gash in his uniform and trickled onto his boot.

He pulled back on his rifle, but it wouldn't come. *I need to keep up with the others. My bayonet must be jammed between the lad's ribs. I should've gone in lower, or turned the blade sideways first. Damn my leg hurts.*

A demon wasp whizzed loud past his ear and he dropped hard to the ground. *I wonder how close a bullet has to be to sound like that. No more than a few inches I reckon.*

His thoughts flashed back to the first day of musketry training at Long Bay Rifle Range in Sydney.

'Standing up in the open to shoot at the enemy may seem courageous, but if you get yourself shot dead then you are no good to king or country or the girl of your wet dreams… It's your lucky day soldier!'

Poddy O'Hara lay face-down, still, as if resting but for the crater in the back of his head. A small fly buzzed onto a broken edge of skull and walked around to investigate. Jayjay shooed it away, careful to keep low.

"I'll come back and make sure you get buried properly old mate. Find a Catholic chaplain to say a few Catholic words and pray to Mary. I never did understand why you don't just pray directly to God like a true Christian."

Jayjay made a sign of a cross like he had seen the Irish and other Roman Catholics do, touching his forehead, belly then each shoulder. He took three deep breaths, then reached up and grabbed the buttstock of his Lee-Enfield which pointed to the sky. He pulled sideways on the rifle and the skewered Turk rolled towards him with the motion. A dead-man's-groan came with the last of the air from the small body's lungs. It sounded more like a dead-boy's-sigh. *Maybe his voice hadn't broken yet.*

Jayjay, still lying on the ground, lifted his left boot to the Turk's chest and pulled back on his rifle. A surprising amount force was required before the blade would budge, then a sucking sound came with the blade as it came free.

He made a quick attempt to wipe the blood from his bayonet onto the dead boy's sleeve, then scrambled to his feet and limped after his platoon who had paused fifty yards ahead.

The men stood at the rolling crest of the ridge and breathed heavily. Sweat darkened their armpits and chests. Jayjay felt an urge to kneel to reduce his profile, but stood with the others and looked around from the high viewpoint.

Ron looked at Jayjay's red bayonet, and his bleeding leg. His eye's held a questioning look, but he said nothing.

Jayjay grinned back and nodded, hoping he looked more confident than he felt. *I just stabbed an unarmed boy to death while he begged for mercy. I should have let him live. It wasn't right, despite what he did to Poddy, but how could I do it? We can't take prisoners with us. I need to focus, or I'll get myself shot.*

He looked about, trying to make sense of the lay of the land and looking for Turks at the same time. Ridgelines and spurs ran in all directions like the broken ribs of a tortured beast.

Take control of the high ground and work inland to cut off Turkish supply lines. Push on at all costs. Follow your commanding officers. No haggling with the natives.

The ridge they had been following continued to rise to the north-east, diverging from the coast which was away to the west and two hundred yards below their position. Inland, there lay a valley, and beyond the valley, any view to a distant horizon was obstructed by another ridge that ran northward towards a junction with the ridge on which he stood. There was no shimmer of water to mark the Dardanelles, only more green scrub and yellow-grey weathered sandstone. *Maybe we'll see some water when we reach the next ridge.*

"Take cover!" Someone yelled. "Bloody Turks!"

A swarm of hot metal wasps zipped by and some chirped into the bushes. A groan close by announced that someone had been hit. *Hopefully not too bad. Hopefully not Ron or Larry. This is an unhealthy business.*

Jayjay stole a glance up the hill and dropped to the ground.

Another swarm attacked the branches and leaves around him. *How is it that they can shoot at us, but we can't see them to fire back or attack? None of our training exercises were like this. They're hiding and shooting at us.*

Pulsating pain in his thigh demanded attention. He pulled out his field dressing, pressed it against the wound, looped the bandage around his leg and tied it off. *That will have to do for now. Hopefully it will stop the bleeding until I can get a doctor to take look.*

A shell approached from inland with the sound of a steam train speeding through a cutting. It burst over the ridge ahead and strafed a strip of ground two hundred yards long and twenty yards wide. The brief hail storm of lead pellets sounded like a flight of parrots and kicked up puffs of dust in places where the scrub was sparse.

As if in response, one of *Queen Elizabeth's* guns flashed and a shell screeched in from over the sea. It slammed into the ridge, higher up than the shrapnel shell, maybe half a mile ahead, and sent a brown spray into the air.

Sergeant Baker stood and looked about. Furrows cut into his forehead. He turned to the remnant of his platoon as if to speak, then a bullet bit into his upper arm.

"Bastard!" He grabbed at the wound with his other hand and opened his mouth, but no words came.

He kneeled slowly and bowed his head like a man in prayer, wounded arm hanging limp at his side.

Men looked on, but no one said a word. After a long moment, Baker looked up, his face lighter in colour and creases cut deeper into his forehead.

"We move to the left," his voice was dry, "to the seaward side of this ridge. The ship's guns might protect us there, and help us to get further up this ridge. Keep low. Move forward."

* * *

The afternoon sun hung low over the warships and none but a small group of New Zealanders had arrived as reinforcements. *Why don't they send us more help? There must be hard fighting elsewhere.*

Jayjay huddled with about twenty others behind a fresh mound of earth next to a naval shell crater, unable to move forwards or back.

"Turk's don't seem to want to turn and run like the brass thought they might," Ron said.

"No way," Larry said. "They're fighting like crazy bastards. The Maori-landers are just as insane. Did you hear 'em yell when they charged forward? 'Eggs is cooked!' – as if they were a pack of Gyppo lunatics, escaping from the asylum kitchens."

The seaward side of the ridge proved to be little better than inland. The platoon had joined forces with some New Zealanders, but Turkish rifle fire prevented the newly-formed group of ANZAC infantry from advancing any further.

Sergeant Baker sat with his back to the mound and his eyes closed. He nursed his wounded arm and breathed heavily.

We need more bullets, and reinforcements, and artillery cover, and a clear goal. Otherwise charging ahead will achieve nothing more than getting us all killed.

Sounds of yelling and rapid rifle fire came from further up the ridge. Jayjay raised his head and peered over the mound. Sprinting directly towards him, was a company-sized stampede of Australian soldiers. Within a minute the front runners streaked past.

"Get to buggery!" one yelled. "The Turks are coming on – there's thousands of them."

He ran on and others followed. Some limped, some nursed wounds. One fellow lagged behind, carrying another who might have been dead by the look of him.

Jayjay looked to Baker for direction and wondered who might decide what to do next if the sergeant was unable to. Baker made as if to stand, then paused, and slumped back against the mound.

"Tell me what you see up the hill," he barked without aiming his gaze at anyone in particular.

Jayjay raised his head again. Countless tiny bayonets pierced the horizon in a long line.

"There's a bloody lot of 'em." Jayjay ducked back down. "Might not be thousands, but at least hundreds. I can see bayonets pointing to the sky, all lined up further up the hill, several hundred yards back. Without more men and a trench we're all good as dead if we stay here, Sergeant."

Ridges in Baker's forehead swelled like waves approaching the shore. He inhaled slow and deep, then released a whisper. "Fall Back."

"Fall Back!" Baker yelled. "We need to regroup in a position we can defend. An enemy attack is coming. Godspeed men. Now move. Run!"

Some leapt to their feet and bounded downhill like rabbits, but many hesitated.

Jayjay stole another glance up the hill where an enemy force of at least a battalion size was massing. Then, as one, the force started to roll downhill in a torrent. Slowly at first, but the speed was difficult to judge from front on. Distant cries of "Allah! Allah!" reached his ears. He turned to Ron and Larry who, being shorter, could not have seen what he saw.

"Let's go!" Jayjay cried. "They're coming fast and there's a bloody horde."

Another group of Australians came running down the ridge, along the seaward side.

Jayjay ran with them, and the others from his platoon, but struggled to keep up the pace. His leg burned. He was in a school boy running race, falling behind no matter how hard he tried. *Come on, you have such long legs. Why can't you run faster?*

Further down the hill someone was winning the race, bounding nimbly over the uneven ground. *Is that Mick? It's Mick O'Reilly the Irish Uh-oh. Short legs, but he's a fast bastard. The boys with short legs always were the fastest.*

Jayjay nearly lost his footing and focused on the clumps of scrub in front of him.

He glanced ahead again. Mick's body went limp mid-stride, like a marionette with the strings cut. Momentum carried the Irishman forward and he tumbled twice before a bush dragged him to a stop.

Jayjay re-focussed on the ground in front of each step. Bushes bounced off his puttees and blurred past.

Hot metal wasps tore through the air, overtaking all humans in the race towards the sea. A man ahead fell with a grunt and howled a pitiful sound as Jayjay left him behind. *What will happen to him? I'm lagging behind myself. What will happen to me?*

One fellow ahead veered to the right and hurled himself into the head of a gully that dropped away from the ridge.

In a split-second decision that seemed much too important to be taken without more consideration, Jayjay darted to the right himself. The ground dropped away below him into a gully of green prickly scrub and steeper patches of bleached yellow earth.

He half ran and half tumbled downwards and held his Lee-Enfield across his body, tight in both hands. *I mustn't stab myself with my own bayonet.*

The gully slope flattened a little and the rifle Jayjay held across his body dragged in the bushes to help slow his fall. He skidded to a stop and dared not move, expecting to be shot by a Turk hiding in waiting. He tensed the muscles in one leg, then the other. Both seemed functional, with no new pain beyond the cut in his right thigh, received from the little Turk who had shot Poddy in the face.

Both arms seemed okay, fingers a bit sore but he could bend and straighten them. He lifted his head slowly and looked around. Battle chaos sounded strangely distant. Up at the head of the gully – no movement. *This gully was a good option, although I am separated from the others. It looks to lead down to the beach. At least there's no one here from home to see me run from the enemy and get myself lost.*

He looked up at the weathered yellow cliffs lining the Turkish stronghold. The place had an ancient feeling about it.

A shrapnel shell burst in the distance.

Rock of Ages cleft for me,
Let me hide myself in Thee.

Before the retreat, when advance was impossible, the joking had died down, and bravado dissipated. *Likely many of the others felt as I did. Thinking this is the end. We have failed and we will be killed.*

Now I am alone. Mum and Dad might never know what happened to me. I wonder if they have even heard of Gallipoli. Does it hurt to be shot, or blasted with shrapnel?

I never really said a proper good-bye to Mum. Dad would have understood, in his quiet way, he knew I was doing the right thing, but Mum hated the idea of us going to war. I never knew what to say to her.

"It's not our war," she had said. *"Let the English sort out their own differences."*

"Come on mate. How about dragging yourself out of the open and get behind these bushes?"

Jayjay's head spun so fast his neck hurt.

A fellow in an Australian uniform crouched amongst a clump of bushes and waved him over.

The fellow had a face that might have been considered handsome, if not for a nose that looked to have been broken and then allowed to heal crooked. *I know that voice and I know that face.*

Jayjay's legs wouldn't move.

The two eyes looking back at him locked on his in a moment of recognition.

The crooked nose below those eyes was the same nose that Jayjay had smashed with his rifle butt in a training exercise against the 2nd Battalion in Egypt.

Alfred McKenzie – Charlotte is his best girl, and she oughta' be mine.

CHAPTER 44

Dacre

Monday, 25 April 1915, early evening

Percival droned across the surface of the Dardanelles Strait, eighty feet above. The few moments immediately after his passing were the bad ones.

The single engine ship had been sweeping back and forth while the Australian E-class submarine *AE2* lay still, hiding on the bottom. If any sweep Percival dragged after him were to catch the submarine, it would be only a short time before the hull would be blown in upon Dacre and his crew.

Dacre checked his wristwatch – a quarter to seven in the evening. It had been a very long day.

* * *

Earlier that morning, having beached *AE2* twice under enemy fire, Lieutenant-Commander Dacre Stoker and his submarine crew had escaped the Narrows with a flotilla of hostile warships in pursuit.

Anticipating more treacherous eddy currents near the surface, and fearful of enemy fire, Dacre rounded Nagara Point blind, at a depth of ninety feet. He travelled as far as he dared without an external reference, then took *AE2* to twenty feet and raised his periscope to the welcome sight of the wider reaches of the upper Dardanelles. This time he had managed to keep the submarine in course despite the currents.

But, when he turned the periscope to look back down the Strait, the host of pursuant vessels hurried and scurried in all directions about Nagara Point, including a gun boat, three destroyers and number of tugs and other small craft.

Even as he looked across the glassy surface, his periscope was seen, a ship's gun fired and the chase resumed.

"Dive to seventy feet," Dacre lowered the periscope. "Well done lads! We are around Nagara Point and shall have a nice straight run ahead. The surface is like glass so we'll hold our course and keep the periscope down for a bit of time."

The submarine glided up the straits at a peaceful depth for three quarters of an hour when Dacre decided to approach the surface again, hoping to have shaken off the hunters.

This time, when he raised the periscope, the enemy vessels were so close that he thought he must have caught an observation net and been dragging a tell-tale buoy along the surface.

He scanned the surface behind and could see no such buoy, but ahead saw an equally disturbing sight. Dead ahead, not a hundred yards away, two tugs trawled for a submarine. Between the two tugs stretched a wire rope right across the path of *AE2*.

"Dive to eighty feet. Helm hard a-port." Dacre called the orders to turn the submarine towards the starboard and contemplated his options.

I am like a wounded elephant trying to flee a pride of lions. I might be able to destroy one or two, but they are too many for me to fight them all. The Dardanelles Strait runs another twenty miles before it opens out into the Marmara Sea. I cannot outrun them and, if I try to, my batteries will discharge before I reach the end, leaving me stranded on the surface. We must hide until dark.

He checked the charts and confirmed that the bottom shoaled gently south-east towards the Asiatic shore.

"Make depth seventy feet," Dacre ordered. "Maintain present course. Slow engines to minimum speed. Prepare to stop on the bottom."

Within minutes *AE2* rested on the seabed as Dacre intended. He looked about the interior of the submarine and his crew returned his gaze like hungry children waiting for dinner.

"Well done again lads!" Dacre called for all to hear. "So far, we have done everything asked of us. We've made the Narrows, sunk an enemy ship and generally run amok along the way. We are going to stop here for a spell."

After about an hour a single engine ship passed overhead, and was immediately followed by a knock at the submarine's side as something hit and jumped over. The sound sent a chill down Dacre's spine. He could only deduce that the ship was sweeping with an anchor, or grappling hook, in an attempt to locate the submarine. If a marker buoy was attached to the *AE2*, an explosive charge would surely follow, leaving little hope of escape.

Shortly after the knock, two other vessels passed over.

They must have deduced that we are hiding around here.

The single engine ship, whose solitary screw made a unique noise, continued to pass at regular intervals. This ship was dubbed 'Percival' by a torpedoman.

We are well out of the passage for ships following their ordinary course up and down the Strait. Percival must be hunting us.

The next few hours passed very slowly and Dacre decided to try to move the submarine away from Percival and his sweep that was contributing to everyone's anxiety.

Being Sunday, he read prayers to the crew before sending them to their diving stations.

The submarine edged forwards.

"Depth eighty feet Captain."

"Captain, we have lost diving control. The ballast tanks must be leaking sir."

"Depth ninety feet."

"Depth one hundred feet."

The depth gauge of an E-class submarine reads a range of zero to one hundred feet as the hull is designed to withstand a maximum pressure of one hundred feet. Instructions to Dacre from the engineers at the shipyard at Barrow-in-Furness were simple: 'Do not, under any circumstances, exceed a depth of one hundred feet.'

"Depth off scale captain."

Dacre checked the depth gauge himself and saw the tip of the needle hard against the end-stop at the one-hundred feet marking. The usually-straight needle was bent from pushing against the end-stop.

"Reverse thrust, both propellers, full astern," Dacre called.

"Depth one hundred feet."

"Depth ninety feet."

"Depth eighty feet."

"Stop motors. Rest her on the mud. We will have to wait until dark to get to the surface and readjust the ballast tanks. Try to get some sleep if you can men, it will be a long wait."

We will lie still and wait, hiding in our coffin throughout the day, then skulk about under cover of night, like my cousin Bram's Count Dracula.

Dacre Stoker lay on his bunk to set the example, although he knew he would not sleep. If some of the men were able sleep, they would consume less of the precious oxygen. All but one had been ordered to rest.

One rating had the job of watch-keeper for the day, his sole duty to watch the depth gauge and report any change. *Not the most interesting job. A job that might leave any man tending to daydream, but an important job. If a swirl of current causes us to drift along the bottom and sink below one hundred feet the hull will collapse and we will never be heard of again, like the poor lads on AE1.*

Throughout the rest of the day, Percival continued to pass at steady intervals of around twenty minutes, and each time the single engine ship approached, Dacre fought to suppress cold fingers of fear that squeezed on his innards.

* * *

Dacre checked his wristwatch. *Percival is due to have passed over again by now. Maybe he has given up for the day.*

Another hour passed and before Dacre allowed himself to hope. He was starting to feel sleepy and wondered if the lack of oxygen might be a cause.

He rose from his bunk and started to rouse the men. Some had managed to sleep. He wanted to get to the surface, but didn't want to emerge before dark.

At a quarter to nine that evening, submarine *AE2* surfaced, having been submerged for over sixteen hours, four hours longer than the recommended limit for a fully manned E-class submarine.

Dacre climbed the conning tower and opened the main hatch.

Warm air surged up past him for a moment, then cool fresh air streamed in and filled his lungs.

Below, inside the submarine, a white mist formed.

Outside, the final stages of twilight were fading, but the moon shone bright. Too bright for Dacre's liking, but there were no enemy ships in sight.

He climbed out on the deck and the crew swarmed after him into the clean night air.

The submarine lay about half a mile from the Asiatic shore, in the sweep of the bay above Nagara Point. The shore looked to be marshy swamp land, devoid of habitation. Dacre figured that any ships travelling the Straits by night would be unlikely to see the submarine against land. The main danger of discovery lay in being found by a patrolling vessel.

Dacre ordered the diesel engines to be started to recharge the submarine batteries and reminded the men not to smoke on the deck for fear of giving away their position.

Some ratings re-entered the hull to smoke, but found that the matches would not burn for long enough to light their cigarettes due to the bad air. Only when they stood at the base of the conning tower, did sufficient fresh air waft down to sustain a flame.

Enemy supply lines here are vulnerable. I need to get a message to Admiral de Robeck. Once he knows of our success he will send more submarines.

Dacre ordered that the antenna mast be erected for signal transmission.

Earlier generations of submarines had relied on homing pigeons when they strayed from their tender ships, but the E-class submarine was a modern weapon of war. At an additional cost to the Australian Government of seventy-five pounds per submarine, just before leaving England, *AE1* and *AE2* were hastily fit out with newly developed Marconi wireless communication sets.

Dacre composed a message in his mind, that *AE2* had made the Narrows, having torpedoed an enemy gunboat on the way, and that the most difficult part of the task was accomplished. He dictated the message to submarine telegrapher William Falconer.

Dacre and crew watched on as Falconer tapped out the longs and shorts of Morse code. During the transmission, the damp aerial wire threw purple and blue sparks against the mast.

On completion of the signal, an answering signal of acknowledgement should have been sent by the telegrapher at General Headquarters, but the signal didn't come.

"Send it again Falconer," Dacre ordered.

The submarine telegrapher tapped out the message and more sparks followed, but again no reply came.

"What does it mean?" Dacre stared at the antenna mast in disbelief.

"There is a problem with our receiving instruments, Sir," the telegrapher replied.

"What about the sending instruments? Are they working? They seemed to be doing something with all those sparks jumping about."

"Can't say Sir," Falconer replied. "All I know is that I sent the signal, but received no reply, so I don't know if they got it."

"We have to stay on the surface for three to four hours to recharge the batteries. Dry off that aerial wire as best you can and wait one hour, then send the signal again. Let me know the moment you receive any response."

"Yes Sir."

"We should have brought a homing pigeon."

"Yes Sir."

"Or a well-trained falcon."

"Yes Sir."

CHAPTER 45

Ellis

Sunday, 25 April 1915, soon after dark [9:30pm]

Ellis climbed down from the Formidable-class battleship *London* to a pinnace that had pulled up alongside for fuel and water. The Jacob's ladder that he clung to swung towards the hull of the warship. *How do the infantry men manage to descend these rope ladders carrying all their kit without falling.*

The English war correspondent had observed the Australian landing from the *London* throughout the day, and was determined to visit the beach to learn what he could this evening before writing his first despatch.

Ellis stepped onto the boat, then the Naval Landing Officer pushed off and a small crew guided the pinnace through the darkness. Ellis was the only passenger.

The chug of a small steam engine and the splash of wavelets bumping against the side of the boat gave a welcome change from the incessant blasts of warship guns that had left Ellis with a headache and ringing ears.

"Like pissing on an ants' nest" was the way the young navy gunner had described it. "Position yourself as close as you dare. Aim, fire, correct your aim, keep firing and watch the ants scurry."

All day, signals had come through to the *London* calling fire from her twelve-inch guns to bombard various positions on the landscape. When daylight faded, the Australians looked to be digging in along the top of the ridgeline, as far as it was visible from the sea. *Those Australians are a race of athletes. Bigger and stronger than our boys. Didn't do them much good though. The defenders still won the day like I thought they might.*

Boats had returned to the *London* during the day, and each brought similar news of heavy casualties, beaches choked with wounded who could not be moved and strong Turkish defences that showed no sign of abating. There seemed to be confusion as to where the unending stream of wounded should be taken once the single hospital ship was full. Some casualties were delivered to the *London*, then taken off again after lying for hours without receiving care. *No doubt many colonials died for the lack of proper medical provision.*

A bullet splashed into the black water not far away, and another. The steam engine slowed. Ellis felt his heart rate accelerate and savoured the anticipation.

This was the kind of thrill he lived for.

The pinnace approached the beach and bumped up against a barge. One of the crew tied off against it. Ellis scrambled over the barge and managed to reach the shore with dry shoes. He hurried up the narrow beach and found that the steep rise behind the beach provided good shelter from stray bullets.

He paused to examine the scene of confusion he had entered under the faint light of a crescent moon. The beach was piled with ammunition and stores, dumped from boats without order. Among the crates lay the dead and wounded, and maybe some who had collapsed from exhaustion. It was impossible to distinguish between the sleeping and the dead. Ghostlike silhouettes of groups of men wandered about in the gloom, apparently going to, or returning from, the firing line. On the hills above, a struggle raged, lit up by bursting shells. The night air hummed with bullets like the droning of countless bees on a summer's day.

Where do I go now? I need to find some reliable information about the position of the Australian troops.

A small group of men stood with the confident look of officers, apart from the others by the hillside, under a tarpaulin. At the centre of the circle, a short man appeared to be giving instructions by the light of two candles.

Ellis walked towards the group and as he drew closer he recognised the short man to be General Birdwood, commander of the Australian forces. Ellis had a memory that rarely failed him. He had never met Birdwood previously, but had seen a photograph once and that was enough.

"Who are you?" One of the officers cried at Ellis. A big man with an Australian accent. "What are you doing there?"

Ellis was wearing his uniform, but realised he was still wearing an old green hat.

"Seize that man, he is a spy!" The big officer shouted Before Ellis could answer.

Soldiers rushed up and grabbed Ellis by each arm.

This is the third time this war I have been arrested as a spy. If I was truly a spy I think I might have taken the trouble to dress like everyone else.

"I am Ellis Ashmead-Bartlett," he said calmly. "The official War Correspondent attached to the Expedition. I have a pass here from Captain Armstrong of HMS *London*, if you will allow me one hand free to retrieve it and show you."

Ellis had no formal connection with the army as yet, but, in anticipation of something like this happening, he had convinced Captain Armstrong to sign a pass permitting him to come ashore.

"How do I know who you are?" the big Australian yelled. The volume of his voice was none diminished for the short distance now between them. "Does anyone here know this man?"

"Yes, I do," came a gruff voice from somewhere out of the darkness.

Soon Ellis found himself free once again, but he had no knowledge of who had vouched for him. *That was lucky. This is definitely not the time to give up gambling.*

The big Australian introduced himself as Colonel Street, Chief-of-Staff to General Birdwood. Street presented Ellis to General Birdwood, who, despite the noise and chaos, appeared to be the embodiment of calmness.

"How did you come ashore?" Birdwood asked.

"In a pinnace, from *London*."

As soon as the words passed his lips, Ellis flinched, hoping his answer would not be taken as a wise crack, but the officers all seemed too flustered to notice the possible double meaning.

"You must keep him here," Colonel Street exclaimed. "We have no other steam launch ashore at this hour."

"Do not send your boat away," The Naval Beach Officer said. "Whatever you do. We have to go around all the transports and get them to send in their boats. It is impossible for the Australians to hold out during the night, they are being too hard pressed."

Under enemy fire, in the confusion of night, trying to evacuate now would be impossible. There will be a massacre on the beach.

"I have no intention of sending the boat away Sir," Ellis said. "Not without being on it myself."

"Godley, write this down:" Birdwood spoke slowly to dictate a message. "Both my Divisional Generals and Brigadiers have represented to me that they fear their men are thoroughly demoralised by shrapnel fire to which they have been subjected all day after exhaustion and gallant work in morning."

Ellis hung on each word of the communication from General Birdwood, scribed under candlelight by General Sir Alexander Godley, commander of the New Zealand and Australian Division. Birdwood continued.

"Numbers have dribbled back from the firing line and cannot be collected in this difficult country. Even the New Zealand Brigade, which has only recently engaged, has lost heavily and is to some extent demoralised. If troops are to be subjected to shell fire again tomorrow morning there is likely to be a fiasco as I have no fresh troops with which to replace those in the firing line. I know my representation is serious, but if we are to re-embark it must be at once."

Birdwood waited until Godley stopped writing, then took the note and quill. He re-read the message by the light of a candle, signed the note and handed it to the Naval Landing Officer who dashed off towards the pinnace.

Ellis hurried after the Naval Landing Officer, driven by the sense that he was witnessing historical events unfold, as well as an urge not to be left behind on the beach where men might shortly be killing each other in large numbers.

On the pinnace, the naval officer shouted "Go to the battleship *Queen,*" as Ellis scrambled on board. *I don't think he was going to wait for me.*

The pinnace chugged away from the beach and steamed for the battleship *Queen*. On reaching the *Queen*, the Naval Landing Officer made climbing a Jacob's ladder look easy and disappeared on board for several minutes, then returned to report that he had handed the letter to Admiral Thursby.

"Where to now?" Ellis asked.

"We've got to go to every transport in turn and order them to ready their boats immediately to bring off the Australians."

"Clearly," Ellis said, "that is impossible in the darkness and confusion. The only chance the Australians have is to hold on till daybreak."

"I know, but I must obey my orders."

The *Queen* weighed anchor and steamed away into the night, towards Cape Helles at the southern tip of the Gallipoli Peninsula. Off Cape Helles floated a new Super-Dreadnought-class battleship, the flagship *Queen Elizabeth,* carrying the Commander-in-Chief, General Sir Ian Hamilton. Also on board a warship floating off Cape Helles, was the British war correspondent Lester Lawrence. Lester had won the coin toss, and so the right to witness the main landing of British troops, leaving Ellis to observe the Australians at the secondary landing at Z Beach. *Curse my luck. Lester is at the main battle front and is closer to the ship with cable access to England. What hope have I got of getting the best despatch out first? What's worse, it looks like the Colonial sideshow here is over.*

The Naval Landing Officer steered for the nearest transport ship, and when close he shouted through a megaphone, "Hold your boats in readiness to send them ashore at a moment's notice."

Illuminated under the steady glow of an electric lamp, a sailor on watch waved in acknowledgement.

The Naval Landing Officer manoeuvred the pinnace about and directed her to the next transport ship. Despite circumnavigating this ship, not a sailor could be found on her decks. He shouted the order several times, but could not rouse any response.

"We can't do any more here," he spat.

For the next two hours, Ellis and the Naval Landing Officer systematically approached the transport ships to deliver orders to ready the boats to evacuate the landed men. Many of the transports gave no acknowledgement, with not a solitary sailor left on watch and no one interested to take the message.

After visiting all the transports, the Naval Landing Officer steered the pinnace back to the beach. By this time, it was clear to Ellis that re-embarking the Colonial army this night would be impossible.

On shore, the situation seemed to have improved. Rifle fire continued, but with less intensity than earlier in the evening, and the Turkish guns were almost silent.

Ellis hurried along behind the Naval Landing Officer who located the Command Staff.

"Seize that man, he is a spy!" It was the familiar yell of Colonel Street.

You must be joking.

"Ashmead-Bartlett here Sir," Ellis said. "War Correspondent, Sir."

"Right you are then," said the colonel whose nerves seemed to have completely deserted him.

"I delivered the orders as best I could Sir," The Naval officer reported to General Birdwood. "But several transports had not set a watchman and did not appear to receive the message. I think it might be particularly difficult to re-embark the men tonight Sir, if you don't mind my saying so Sir."

The staff said little, even Birdwood, and despite the darkness Ellis sensed an air of despondency from the leaders.

They are still awaiting a response from Hamilton and they don't know what to do. At least the troops cannot witness this dithering. The men at the frontline will hold on until morning now.

On the walk back to the pinnace, Ellis recognised the Principal Medical Officer from the *London*. Dark stains of blood covered his shirt, visible in the moonlight.

"How would you like a ride back to our ship?" Ellis asked. "I have a pinnace heading that way now."

"I cannot," the Medical Officer sighed and his voice twanged with exhaustion. "There is much work for me to do here. We are very short of surgeons."

On the pinnace back to the *London*, Ellis and the Naval Officer sat in silence. Ellis began to conjure ideas and phrases he might use in his first despatch. *The Australians rose to the occasion. They did not wait for orders or for the boats to reach the beach…found themselves facing an almost perpendicular cliff…here was a tough proposition to tackle in the darkness, but those colonials were practical above all else…race of athletes proceeded to scale the cliff…when daylight came, the warships endeavoured to support them by heavy fire…Turks relied on snipers until reinforcements came…Australians were counter-attacked…had to fall back after suffering heavy losses…Australians did not yield a foot of the main ridge…General Birdwood and staff devoted their energies to securing the position so as to hold firm until next morning…A serious problem was the getting of the wounded from the shore…the courage displayed by these wounded Australians will never be forgotten… raw colonial troops proved worthy to fight side by side with the heroes of Mons, the Aisne, Ypres and Neuve Chapelle.*

The word-smithing would likely occupy him through till dawn, but the broad outline was clear in his mind. A little poetic license was acceptable.

Though many were shot almost to bits, without hope of recovery, their cheers resounded... They were happy because they knew they had been tried for the first time in the war and had not been found wanting.

CHAPTER 46

Roger

Monday, 26 April 1915, small hours (around 1:00am)

"We need the Army's Commander-in-Chief," Admiral Thursby exclaimed. "You go and wake him up Braithwaite, you're his Chief of Staff."

"Sir Ian," General Braithwaite looked as if he had just been asked to charge at a machine gun. "Sir Ian has been overwhelmed with anxiety over the Turkish counter-attacks on the beaches at Cape Helles, and the failure of troops to get ashore from the *River Clyde*. He has only had one hour of sleep."

"Do you want to make this decision yourself then General, and explain it to Sir Ian in the morning?"

General Braithwaite opened his mouth as if to protest further, but after a moment of hesitation he turned and left the dining saloon of super-dreadnought battleship *Queen Elizabeth*.

Roger watched the exchange with interest. Political struggles between navy and army had no doubt raged since the first time some king had the idea of exercising his consolidated might of arms in the conquest of some enemy across some sea.

"Lieutenant Brodie," Roger said to his assistant. "When Sir Ian arrives, stand sentry outside the door and see that we are not interrupted."

"Yes Sir," Brodie replied.

Commodore Roger Keyes, Chief of Staff to the naval Commander-in-Chief, stood beside his superior Admiral John de Robeck. Next to de Robeck sat Admiral Cecil Thursby.

Thursby, squadron commander in charge of landing the Anzac forces at Z beach, looked to be pleased with himself, having just sent Braithwaite away to retrieve his master. Thursby picked up the note from General Birdwood that he had come to deliver, the note that had been delivered to a sentry on his ship *Queen* by a messenger from shore. The note was not addressed to anyone, or dated, but the contents were such that it required attention at the highest level. Thursby remained adamant that he must deliver the message to Sir Ian himself.

Two ANZAC officers completed the gathering, including Generals Robert Carruthers and Cunliffe Owen who had come with Admiral Thursby from the

ANZAC command ship *Queen*. Carruthers was the ANZAC Quartermaster General and Birdwood's chief administrative officer. He looked to be shell-shocked by the news that his commander had requested evacuation less than twenty-four hours after the landing of the first troops.

Sir Ian shuffled in through the door wrapped in a British Warm overcoat, bent with the stoop of an old man. The coat stopped at his knees, revealing the legs of his pyjamas below.

All eyes of those standing around the dining table were on the Army's Commander-in-Chief and he stopped at the door, as if assessing danger, before coming over to join them at the table.

Lieutenant-Commander Brodie slipped quietly out and closed the door behind him.

Carruthers took the note from Thursby and passed it to Sir Ian.

Sir Ian looked down at the note, and then back at the men standing around the table as if awaiting some explanation as to why his sleep had been interrupted. No one said a word, and Sir Ian returned his eyes to the note in his hand and read it aloud:

"Both my Divisional Generals and Brigadiers have represented to me that they fear their men are thoroughly demoralised by shrapnel fire, to which they have been subjected all day after exhaustion and gallant work in morning. Numbers have dribbled back from the firing line and cannot be collected in this difficult country. Even the New Zealand Brigade, which has only recently engaged, has lost heavily and is to some extent demoralised. If troops are to be subjected to shell fire again tomorrow morning there is likely to be a fiasco, as I have no fresh troops with which to replace those in the firing line. I know my representation is serious, but if we are to re-embark it must be at once. Birdwood."

Sir Ian drew a long breath and looked up.

"This is a difficult business," Sir Ian said. "What are we to do about it?"

No response.

General Braithwaite chewed on his moustache.

"You Australians." Sir Ian addressed the ANZAC staff generals. "These are your chaps. What can you tell me about their tactical position on the shore?"

"We've landed them Sir," replied Cunliffe Owen. "But the units are scattered and we don't know where they all are right now. They are facing some stiff opposition."

Sir Ian shook his head slowly and turned to Admiral Thursby.

"Admiral, what do you think?"

"Many of the boats have been smashed and sunk," Thursby replied. "The transports have been shelled and forced further out to sea. It will take the best part of three days to get that crowd off the beaches."

"And where are the Turks?"

"On top of 'em!"

"Well then, tell me Admiral, what do you think?"

"What do I think? Well, I think myself that they will damn well stick it out if only it is put to them that they must."

"What do you think Carruthers?" Sir Ian asked the ANZAC Quartermaster General.

"It seems impossible to re-embark the force within the necessary time."

Sir Ian pursed his lips and there was a knock at the door.

Lieutenant Brodie stuck his head in the door, "Commodore Keyes, might I have a moment?"

"I think it can wait until we are finished here Lieutenant." Roger fought to contain his anger at the intrusion. *It was a simple instruction – See that we are not interrupted.*

"The Yeoman of Signals has just delivered an important message Sir. I think it would be best if you came to read it now."

Learn to follow orders Brodie.

Roger left the room and closed the door behind him before whispering in harsh tones.

"What is it that cannot wait? I told you we were not to be interrupted."

"Dacre Stoker has done it Sir!" Brodie didn't show a hint of remorse. "He has taken the *AE2* under the minefield and passed the Narrows. And he torpedoed a Turkish gunboat on the way."

"Run amok!" Roger's anger evaporated.

He snatched the message and hurried back into the dining saloon where Sir Ian Hamilton sat, pen in hand, with a sheet of paper on the table before him.

"Sir," Roger said. "I think you will be interested to know that our Captain Stoker has taken the Australian submarine *AE2* under the minefields of the Dardanelles and passed through the Narrows. He has torpedoed a gunship at Chanak."

Sir Ian Hamilton looked up, his pen hovered over the page.

"Tell them this Sir," Roger felt emboldened by the news he bore. "It is an omen. An Australian submarine has done the finest feat in submarine history and is going to torpedo all the ships bringing reinforcements, supplies and ammunition to Gallipoli."

Sir Ian nodded and wrote in silence.

"Admiral Thursby," Sir Ian said when he had finished writing. "This is the reply for you to take to General Birdwood."

Before handing over the page, Sir Ian read the message out aloud:

"Your news is indeed serious. But there is nothing for it but to dig yourselves right in and stick it out. It would take at least two days to re-embark you as Admiral Thursby will explain to you. Meanwhile, the Australian submarine has got up through the Narrows and has torpedoed a gunboat at Chunuk. Hunter-Weston, despite his heavy losses, will be advancing tomorrow, which should divert pressure from you. Make a personal appeal to your men and Godley's to make a supreme effort to hold their ground.
Ian Hamilton
P.S. You have got through the difficult business, now you only have to dig, dig, dig, until you are safe. Ian H."

"Good show Sir!" Admiral de Robeck said.

"Yes, well done Sir," Roger said, then he darted out of the room to the corridor where his aid Lieutenant Charles Brodie waited.

Brodie must feel a tender spot for the E-class submarines and might take some comfort from the impact of this success. Charles Brodie was twin brother to Theodore Brodie, Commander of English submarine *E15,* who had failed an attempt to pass the Dardanelles days earlier. Theodore Brodie had never learned that he was sent a personal message wishing him Godspeed on the gallant enterprise from the First Lord of the Admiralty, Winston Churchill.

Charles Brodie had flown on an aeroplane mission that day and seen his twin's *E15* from the air, beached on the shore. He subsequently participated in a mission to destroy the abandoned *E15* with a torpedo from another submarine and came within one hundred yards of her damaged hull.

As yet no news had been received as yet whether the captain of *E15* was killed or taken prisoner.

"It's done the trick!" Roger nodded to his assistant.

Stoker's message could not have come at a more opportune time. My faith in our submarines was justified. At first light we shall plaster the enemy hillside with high-explosive and shrapnel shell of all calibres.

CHAPTER 47

Mustafa

Sunday, 26 April 1915, daybreak

Another brown cloud erupted from the second ridge, followed by a heavy crump.

Mustafa drained the last drops of water from his aluminium canteen, threw it to the ground and raised his field glasses.

Precious ground won back yesterday, at great cost, was slipping away under a ferocious naval bombardment. Explosive shells designed to penetrate armoured warships were ripping into the hillside and re-defining the landscape.

Dust settled and revealed new additions to the tally of dead Turkish soldiers that littered the ridge. Hundreds of them.

The second battalion of the 57th Regiment is virtually annihilated. There is no defending the seaward slopes against this kind of onslaught.

Mustafa lowered the field glasses, rubbed his eyes and let out a long breath. *I could use some sleep.* He stood behind a camouflaged embankment at the top of a slight rise on the third ridge.

The first ridge was lost. It ran up to the more substantial second ridge from the small cove that the English had chosen as their landing place. Steep ground around the cove sheltered the enemy's beachhead against land-based attack.

The second ridge now formed the main battle front and it was becoming a natural stalemate. Ottoman counter-attacks onto to seaward side of the second ridge were stifled by fire from the landed infantry force, supported by terrific shelling from the warships. Conversely, enemy advancement beyond the eastern side of the second ridgeline was, so far, being repulsed by Turkish infantry battalions that were supported by artillery fire from the third ridge.

We must hold Chunuk Bair – the junction where the second and third ridge come together. Then the enemy can be contained to the seaward side of the second ridge. Once contained, they can be pushed back. We will counter-attack tonight, when their warships cannot see us.

"Kemal Bey, an urgent message from the 27th Regiment, sir!"

Mustafa turned to see a runner covered in sweat and breathing heavily.

The runner struggled to compose himself. "Our 1st Battalion has had to withdraw. The 77th Regiment has retreated in the face of enemy attack. We are trying to hold the enemy back but are badly exposed at the left and need reinforcement."

Mustafa took a moment to absorb what he had just been told. If the left flank collapsed, the enemy could charge across the valley to the third ridge and beyond. *I knew I couldn't rely on the 77th. Arabs cannot fight like Turks.*

In deploying the 72nd and 77th Regiments, Mustafa had overstepped his authority.

Part of his training as an Ottoman officer was a key principle, never to hesitate in a command void. Taking the three battalions of the 57th Regiment, instead of the single requested battalion, could be justified under this principle. But he had now committed the full reserve force of the 5th Army, without consultation with the Army commander Field Marshal Liman von Sanders. *I would have consulted him if he wasn't sitting on his arse at Bulair waiting for an enemy landing that was going on elsewhere. Why is he so obsessed with that place?*

If successful, Mustafa's decision to deploy all three regiments of the 19th Division would be tolerated, but if not it would likely be career ending. *If we fall to this invading force, my career is nothing anyway.*

Mustafa dismissed the runner and turned to his Chief of Staff, Major Izzettin. "Send an order to the 57th Regiment. They must pull back from the seaward slopes exposed to naval shellfire. They are to dig in and consolidate their position on our right flank."

He glanced at the runner scurrying down the hill, and back to Izzettin. "Then we will go and see what's happening on the left flank."

"Again, Kemal Bey?" Izzettin replied. "We spent half the night patrolling the front line in the rain. We were there only hours ago!"

"We'll walk again, riding would make us easy targets."

Mustafa stepped back from his observation point and turned his attention to a junior staff officer while he waited for Izzettin to write out the order and send another runner.

"This observation post needs to be enlarged with some proper support trenches and better camouflage at the front, but don't let men work out the front in the daylight. If this place becomes a target, we are all dead men."

Mustafa waited for the junior officer to nod in acknowledgement of this important detail before continuing. "I will establish field headquarters on the sheltered side of this ridge, see to it that some shelter is constructed here. I will need to sleep eventually."

"Yes Kemal Bey," the junior officer replied, and scurried off.

Mustafa strode down the safe side of the hill, followed by Major Izzettin. He found the gendarme scout who had led them along the full length of the battle line in the rain during the night.

"We need to return to the 77th Regiment at the left flank," Mustafa said. "Can you take us there without bringing us into the line of enemy fire?"

"I will do my best Kemal Bey."

"Lead on."

The scout turned silently and led the two officers around a spur on the eastern side of the third ridge. After around fifteen minutes he stopped and raised a hand. He spoke softly, as if the enemy might hear. "We must cross over the ridge here, and drop into the next gully. There is some risk once your silhouette is above the horizon, but the sun is rising behind us so we will be harder to see here. We must cross over quickly."

The scout disappeared over the rise.

Mustafa glanced at his Chief of Staff. Deep furrows in Izzettin's brow were like a miniature model of the terrain they were navigating, but at least he had the respect to hold his silence.

"See you on the other side." Mustafa realised the double meaning of his words as he scrambled up the hill. He allowed himself a smile and a quick look around from the top of the ridge before he saw the scout deep in the gully below waving furiously. *I guess he will have some explaining to do if he lets me get killed.*

Mustafa scrambled down the hill and Izzettin nearly landed on top of him at the bottom.

They were alongside a creek bed, a trickle of water flowed from last night's rain, although it looked like it was most often dry.

The scout's pistol and eyes were tracing a path down the gully. "We can follow this gully. It is mostly sheltered from the fighting, but the situation is always changing. Please keep your weapon ready Kemal Bey."

* * *

Izzettin's brow was still deeply furrowed when they reached the 77th Regiment command post. They completed the journey without incident, but the situation on the left flank was worse than Mustafa feared.

Casualties were high, many hundreds, that was to be expected, but the desertions made him want to grab someone by the throat and squeeze.

He cursed the Ottoman High Command. Only weeks ago, they had taken his 55th and 56th Regiments away to strengthen the 4th Army in Syria. The 72nd and 77th regiments he received in exchange were not of the same calibre. He had argued against the swap, but the complaints fell on deaf army ears.

The 77th Regiment had been the worst, mainly conscripted from Aleppo, a province in Syria where they didn't have a military tradition. Roughly half the regiment's number was made up of Arabs and the rest were a mixed bag, including nomadic Turks, Kurds, Yazidis and Nusayris. Many were very old or very young with no combat experience. None had any knowledge of the local terrain.

They need time to adjust to military life, but there is no time available. I must accelerate their acceptance of this reality.

Mustafa shook his head slowly and turned to Izzettin. "Bring the rest of our reserves from the 72nd Regiment. They must fill this gap."

"Yes Kemal Bey," replied his Chief of Staff.

"And bring the cavalry to set up a security line behind the 77th Regiment position. They are to catch any further deserters and anyone else who becomes confused about where they should be."

"Yes Kemal Bey."

"It will be everything we can do to consolidate our position and hold it now. We are too vulnerable without reinforcements. The enemy must know it, they are probably planning for a major attack later today. That's what I would do in their place. Our counter-attack will have to wait until tomorrow."

* * *

Later in the day some welcome news arrived from Fifth Army General Headquarters.

An enemy landing at Kum Kale was a feint, and two regiments were being allocated from the Asian side of the strait as reinforcements for Mustafa's Ariburnu area. The regiments were marching towards Chanakkale to be ferried across the strait.

And Field Marshal von Sanders was sending a battalion of reinforcements from Bulair, although he was still holding the best part of two full divisions in the north.

At least he has acknowledged we have a serious enemy force to deal with here, and my decision to commit the full reserve division has been accepted.

An artillery battalion had also arrived, and Mustafa immediately deployed all available field guns along the third ridge on either side of his field headquarters. These guns, added to those already positioned in the area, were now enough to provide some meaningful support to the frontline troops.

It seemed that the enemy had landed in two main thrusts. One at Ariburnu, and one to the south at the toe of the peninsula.

Lieutenant-Colonel Sami and his 9th Division was defending the toe and Mustafa had been nominated as Ariburnu Area Commander. Reinforcement regiments sent to Ariburnu would all come under Mustafa's command.

Now I can coordinate an effective defence and counter attack on this front, but what to do about the troublesome 77th Regiment?

Mustafa called the 77th Regiment commander, Major Saip, and his battalion commanders together to discuss the unsatisfactory performance of the regiment. Like any large group of people, it was made up of individuals with various abilities and attitudes. Some reorganisation was required to make the best of a bad situation. Despite the losses already sustained, a composite battalion was assembled from surviving members who were capable and motivated. It was well under strength, only 400 strong, but at least it formed a fighting unit. A number of others were sent back behind the lines for re-training before they would be ready for active service.

That left Mustafa with around two dozen recalcitrants. The troublemakers. They would not respond to discipline and would surely abandon their weapons to flee at the first opportunity, taking others with them no doubt.

These men are a liability, but maybe I can use them as an example for the others.

With Izzettin and some cavalry officers, Mustafa set up a field court-martial there in the valley. The troublemakers were tried and found guilty of refusing to do their duty and abandoning their posts.

Mustafa ordered that the guilty be tied up in groups in a central open area of the valley, visible to the surrounding regiments, including the remnant of the 77th. He then called forward the cavalry troop who had been acting as a security force behind the 77th line.

Mustafa looked around to check that there would be plenty of witnesses amongst the infantry and then gave the order to the cavalry troopers in a voice that was calm, but clear and loud:

"Execute them."

CHAPTER 48

Jayjay

Monday, 26 April 1915, sunset

Dirt flew.

A metal wasp bored into the earth.

Jayjay's arms and back ached but he dared not pause for rest.

He hacked into virgin ground with the entrenching tool. The iron head and timber handle had seemed cumbersome hanging from his belt on the first day, but now they were too small for the need, like a child's toy in a man's hand.

Alfred McKenzie crouched beside him in the pit, a hole of a size that might make a shallow grave for a short man.

Out front, a mound of excavated dirt swelled with enemy bullets, dragged to a halt inches from their target.

Alfred raised his Lee-Enfield, fired a round and dropped quickly back behind the parapet mound with the smooth movement of an athlete.

Fading light marked the setting of the sun behind the ships for the second time since the landing. Sleep had not been possible for Jayjay since he had set foot on Turkish soil and there was no indication that this night might be any different. Sweat soaked his shirt, body fluid he couldn't replace since his water bottle had emptied itself through a bullet hole some time on the first day. *What I wouldn't give for a sip of water. Hopefully the night will bring some cooler air. Maybe when it's dark they'll be able to get some supplies up to us.*

Others worked in pairs or small groups along a crude line that might form a trench if digging continued for another day. Orders were to entrench and defend the position.

The firing line was taking root several hundred yards back from the most advanced position Jayjay reached on the first day with Ron, Larry, Sergeant Baker and the others from his platoon. *I guess we'll regroup and hold here until reinforcements are available and then launch a new attack to push further forward.*

A bullet ricocheted off Jayjay's entrenching tool on the upswing and he ducked, although he knew his head was already below the parapet.

Rock of ages cleft for me,
Let me hide myself in Thee.

"You're a sharp shot Jon," Alfred said. "You want to let me dig and you take a rest for a spell? Fire off a round at Johnny Turk every once in a while?"

"What do you know about my shooting?" Jayjay paused from digging, but kept his head low.

"You helped your platoon to win shooting competitions on more than one occasion from what I heard."

Jayjay fought to hold back a grin. *I wouldn't have thought that news of my shooting successes might have extended outside the 1st Battalion.*

"Of course, I mainly witnessed your skills with the back end of the rifle."

Jayjay swallowed the grin quick as a schoolboy caught with a picture of a naked woman. "Yeah look. About that. I'm sorry I –"

Alfred chuckled and Jayjay stopped himself before finishing the sentence.

"Thing is," Alfred said. "At the time, I was pretty upset with you, being such a bad sport about Charlotte and all. But it doesn't really matter now does it? Bloody Turks might shoot us both full of holes before morning. There's no sheilas here to help with the fight. War's a man's game. No point in gettin' caught up over a girl when we got man's business to attend to."

It's easy to call someone else a bad sport when you're the winner. I'm surprised you even noticed my feelings about Charlotte.

Part of Jayjay wanted to stay angry with Alfred, having invested months of negative feeling towards him, but at the same time a burden was lifted from him. *I cannot argue with Alfred's logic. War is a man's business and there is a very real chance we might not live to see the sunrise.* He let go of the anger buried deep down and dug with renewed strength.

"Just a little deeper," Jayjay said. "Then we can work across and join with the next bit of trench. I'll keep going for a bit, then we can swap."

Colonel Braund of the 2nd Battalion crawled behind the ditch. The colonel had pulled together all the Australians and New Zealanders he could find and organised them to hold this ridge. It seemed that he had been in contact with headquarters and was receiving up to date orders.

"Keep digging boys," Braund yelled. "We must hold this ridge. I have demanded reinforcements but do not know when they will come. We have to hold on to the last man."

"Yes Sir!" Alfred cried.

Jayjay nodded once and kept digging.

Braund moved on and Alfred laughed. "Old bastard can't hear at the best of times. He's got no chance with all this noise."

Jayjay smiled. "At least he's got us all working together. The first day was chaos."

* * *

Cool moonlight carried enough light to make standing in the shallow trench deadly.

Jayjay's ditch now joined with others on either side. The trench zig-zagged along the ridge, as they had been taught, to prevent an enemy being able to fire any distance along the trench if they penetrated it. The trench was only two foot deep, but wide enough that a messenger could squeeze past without exposing himself to the enemy. A mound of excavated dirt above the trench, along the Turkish side, formed a parapet and increased the effective height of the front wall.

He sat with his back to the trench wall and sucked in night air.

"I reckon," Alfred said, "this bit of trench is good enough for time being. How about one of us takes a bit of a spell and the other keeps watch, for Turks and officers? Then we swap. I didn't sleep last night and barely slept the night before. My eyes are starting to blur. You must be the same."

"Let me guess," Jayjay replied. "You take the first rest?"

"Nah, you're the work horse, you can take the first break. I'll rouse you in an hour."

"I don't need your charity, we'll toss for it." Jayjay pulled out a silver shilling and flicked it into the air. Moonlight flashed off it and for an instant he half expected a metal wasp to fly out of the night and send the coin to oblivion. A bullet zipped past, but the coin landed in his hand.

"You call."

"Tails I rest first," Alfred said. "Heads you do."

Jayjay revealed the coin and King George's head gleamed in the moonlight.

"There you have it," Jayjay said. "You did your share of the digging too, but no one can argue with a coin toss.

"I'm a thoroughbred, not a draft horse. You dug most of this. Enjoy your break soldier."

Show pony more like it. Actually I did do most of the digging and I do need a rest, and some water.

"I'll just have a bit of a spell, I don't plan to sleep. Give me a shove if anything looks like happening, or if an officer comes by."

"Sweet dreams sunshine." Alfred picked up his Lee-Enfield.

In one smooth movement he raised his rifle over the parapet, fired off a round and dropped back down for cover. Return fire followed within seconds as several bullets thudded into the parapet in front.

"Try not to get yourself shot mate," Jayjay muttered and dozed off.

* * *

Alfred leaned over and dropped his full weight on Jayjay, waking him in an instant.

"What the blazes? I said just give me a shove, there's no need to jump on top of me."

Jayjay took a moment to get his bearings. The moon hadn't moved so he couldn't have been asleep for long. He gave Alfred a shove, but instead of reacting or pushing back, Alfred rolled over onto the trench floor. *Blazes, Alfred Stop being a bloody idiot. I need more rest. Something isn't right.*

He shook his head in an attempt to clear the fog of sleep and kicked Alfred hard in the leg.

Alfred lay still and stared at the stars.

Jayjay reached down and grabbed Alfred's sleeve at his shoulder. He opened his mouth to tell Alfred to stop fooling around, but no words came as he lifted Alfred by his shoulder and saw a dark stain on his chest glisten wet in the moonlight.

Jayjay gagged, an empty stomach the only reason he didn't vomit. He looked up, expecting to see a line of Turks standing on the parapet, aiming Mauser barrels at him, but there was no one there.

Nothing else had changed. The moon hung in the sky and covered everything in the same blue glow. Intermittent rifle fire continued.

Men to his left and right dug on, and looked intent to focus on their own circumstances. One fellow raised himself just high enough to fire off a shot and dropped back behind the parapet.

The zig-zag alignment of the trench limited any view further along it.

No one was looking at Jayjay or Alfred.

In all probability, no one had seen what happened.

There was no way to know if anyone had come past while he was sleeping, but it seemed unlikely, otherwise Alfred would have woken him. Anger and grief for Alfred were forced to the back of his mind as fear gripped him. A nauseous feeling returned to his empty belly.

What if they know I was sleeping and it was my fault? I might be court-martialled and sent home in disgrace, or shot as an example! Thoughts blurred through his mind as he imagined worse and worse punishments and humiliations that he might face.

"He's dead Mate, best let 'im go," came a voice from behind him.

Jayjay spun around, half expecting to see a couple of officers there with their pistols levelled at his face, ready to make the arrest. Instead it was someone he didn't know on hands and knees, likely a private from his uniform.

"Sorry cobber, I guess he's a mate of yours."

"Yes he is," was all Jayjay could manage in return. He stared at Alfred's body lying face-up on the floor of the shallow trench and refused to meet the soldier's eyes.

"Our boys are droppin' like flies up and down the line," the private said.

"Here's some more ammo mate. Go easy with it. Word is to hang on, no more reinforcements comin' tonight. We best get your mate out of the trench. Stretcher bearers might come and take him down to the beach cemetery when they come by. Want a hand to move 'im?"

Jayjay paused before answering.

"No, I'll do it. You can keep going. Deliver your message and bullets. Got any water?"

"I wish I did. Maybe in the morning?"

The fellow moved to crawl past. He took care to keep low in the tight space and dragged a boot across Alfred's bent nose on the way.

It seemed somehow disrespectful, and yet, what did it matter? *Alfred is dead. God help me. That might have been me, but for the toss of a coin. No one knows I was asleep at my post. I will never tell a soul. If anyone asks, I was sitting, wide awake, taking a brief rest from the digging.*

Poddy and Mick died on ground we cannot get to now. They won't be recovered for burial for some time yet. So much for the luck of the Irish. Should I take Alfred's identity disk from his neck? No. It must remain with the body. What if I die. How will Mum and Dad find out. They would want to know what happened to me, whether I suffered. Maybe his wallet, to send home to his parents. I don't know what –.

Zip! Another bullet flew past his ear and he dropped to the trench floor. A foul smell emanated from Alfred's trousers, inches from Jayjay's face.

Without further thought he scooped Alfred's limp body in both arms and pushed him out over the back of his section of trench.

"Sorry mate, you'll just have to lie up there for now. Bullets won't hurt you anymore. I'll do the digging and shooting myself tonight."

Rock of ages cleft for me,
Let me hide myself in Thee.

CHAPTER 49

Hamid

Tuesday, 27 April 1915

He couldn't produce enough saliva to spit at the ground he sat on, though never had he experienced a situation more deserving of it.

Under different circumstances, the sunset over water might have triggered praise to God. Today it signalled the end of a wretched day and time for a difficult discussion. Incessant rifle fire echoed around the valley below and made it difficult to think. Another shrapnel shell burst over the valley, level with their height. A gentle swish of metal pellets landing followed, like a bucket of water thrown across good lawn. The tiny smoke cloud hung in the air, in memory of the miniature death storm.

There was no breeze.

"Here. Drink this." Hamid's whisper scraped in his throat. "The last of our water. Soon it will be dark. We might stay here one more day and return to our battalion tomorrow night. How many rounds do we have left?"

Hamid knew the answer, but he also knew Ishmail would resist staying. *That boy is determined to become a martyr before his time.*

Maybe if they worked through the decision together good sense might prevail.

"Twenty-three bullets," Ishmail replied, too loud. "Plus five in each of our rifles."

"By God's mercy," Hamid whispered, quieter than before. "We have lived another day, and stopped forty-one invaders, maybe more. Not bad for an old man and his boy."

"I am no boy." Ishmail's voice had the tone of an angry child.

"No, that's true son."

"I say we make our way back tonight," Ishmail was still talking too loudly. "As soon as it is dark. We are both soldiers in the Sultan's holy army and need to return to our commanders. You do not rule me here."

Hamid judged the risks in an instant.

He delivered an open handed slap to his son's face. The impact of his palm was dulled by a heavy beard, making the situation seem even more absurd. Ishmail was a grown man now, but it was too late to back down.

Ishmail's eyes brimmed with defiance.

Hamid grabbed Ishmail's collar and pulled their faces close. "Listen! Lower your damned voice and listen."

Ishmail stared back, but said nothing.

"While my heart beats you will show me respect! Sergeant Zahid ordered us to take up a concealed position and fire at the invaders to slow their advance. That is what we are doing and that is what we are going to do tomorrow. If we can hit the target with even half of the twenty three rounds, that will slow the invaders, and fill their hearts with fear. They are godless and do not know our hope of paradise in martyrdom."

Ishmail's mouth opened slightly. "I am not afraid to die."

"Good! We will all lie under the cypress pines one day. You heard Kemal Bey," Hamid continued. "He knows we will die, but he knows more time is needed to bring more men to defend our country. Our commanders know the invaders are here, they will bring a whole army to crush them. Each one we stop will make a dozen others hesitate."

Ishmail shook his head slowly. "I feel like a coward. Hiding in the bushes while the invaders desecrate our land with their arrogance. I want to show courage, so I will be welcomed into heaven."

"You could run down the hill, screaming like an animal, and throw your life away. Plenty of our brave brothers have done that already, but it has not stopped the enemy. They keep coming. Think son, use the brain God gave you. If you were the enemy who would you rather face? Defenders who run at you making easy targets? Or hidden assassins who might strike at any moment?"

"But our commanders might think we have deserted."

"Our squad is likely all in paradise already, maybe the whole company. Even our battalion commander Zeki Bey was wounded on the first day, he could be dead too for all we know. Men are dying all around us. We cannot go back and ask for orders whether we should stay here or return –."

Movement in the valley below caught Hamid's eye and he froze immediately. He raised a finger slowly to his lips and motioned towards the movement. He picked up his Mauser, flicked off the safety catch and raised the stock to his shoulder where he sat.

"The enemy gets lazy with the fading light," he whispered, glad for the interruption.

There was barely enough light to make out the form of six or seven men, maybe a hundred paces away. They were hunched over, with rifles aimed at the early stars. A pause, and then the one in front straightened a little to look around. *Perfect, he is the leader.*

Hamid squeezed the trigger and the leader dropped into the scrub. Screams of pain carried across the valley to confirm Hamid's aim was good.

"Another belly-hit." Hamid smiled, but kept his focus on the view below. "The bastard will die slowly and his friends won't leave him to die alone. One or two will carry him back to the beach. The others will not forget. They will wonder – what is it like to feel such pain? Pain that makes a man scream like a girl. They will see phantoms in shadows and hesitate to push forward. This is why we must stay here."

Cries of the wounded invader continued, barely audible over the constant chatter of rifle and machine gun fire that echoed around the valley.

Hamid chambered another round in his Mauser. "One more before this day ends. As God Wills."

Hamid locked his gaze on the black bush where the last invader fell. Clumsy movement from this location heading down the valley towards the beach told him that his earlier prediction was accurate. At least one able-bodied invader was helping his wounded comrade away. He let them go, and waited to see what the rest would do.

"That is why we must stay here," Hamid said. "We are obeying our orders. Even if we return to our battalion and the commanders do not believe us, we will know. When we enter paradise, God will know."

Minutes passed and Hamid's arms ached from holding his Mauser up in readiness. He started thinking about how to re-start the conversation with his son. Vision blurred and he closed his eyes to rest them for a moment.

His eyes protested at opening, but Hamid forced them to focus in the last hint of dusk. There was no moon yet and soon darkness would be complete. *If they are moving this way, we will be overrun before morning.*

He squinted tight and watched through flickering eyelashes. Black shapes sharpened a hint. Yes, there was movement.

Hamid closed his left eye and stared down the barrel for a full minute before he squeezed the trigger. Then he exhaled and lay back on the ground, embracing his Mauser to his chest.

"Did you hit him?" Ishmail asked.

Hamid shook his head. "I can't be sure. There was movement. Maybe. As God wills. We won't count that one."

Hamid loaded two fresh rounds into his Mauser. "Twenty-one left for tomorrow, then we retreat with five rounds and a bayonet each."

Ishmail hesitated. "Yes Father."

Hamid smiled into the darkness.

The only light now came from powerful searchlights on the enemy warships, sweeping across the seaward slopes in search of movement. "Get some rest son, I'll take the first watch. Tomorrow will be a long day."

Ishmail sat up. "What's that sound?"

Hamid closed his eyes in the dark and tuned his ears to the distant hum. He recognised the chant and had to fight to suppress a moan.

"There is no God but God," a thousand men chorused in unison, up the ridge towards the head of the valley, "and Muhammad is his prophet."

The same words that Hamid and Ishmail had cried with the rest of the 1st Battalion of the 57th Regiment two days ago, before a mad charge at the invaders and their ships of death.

"There is no God but God, and Muhammad is his prophet."

"God, God!"

"God, God!"

Machine guns rattled and smothered the cries of men. Hamid looked up and saw muzzle flashes but could not make out the attack. Then a flash out to sea caught the edge of his peripheral vision. *No!*

A scream as if the night air was being ripped apart was immediately followed by a terrific blast up the ridge from their position.

Vibrations from the explosive shell faded. Sounds of earth and human debris landing resembled a brief rain shower.

"Those are our brothers from the 57th Regiment Ishmail."

"We should be with them."

"You know we cannot."

The grunt of acknowledgement was as good as Hamid could hope for from his son. The argument was over, for tonight at least.

Hamid knew he could not sleep while warship searchlights narrowed their focus and the battle raged. It might be for the best. Who knew what the enemy would be up to this night?

Machine gun chatter and rifle fire continued up the hill for around twenty minutes and then died away.

Ishmail snored.

The lad hasn't slept for two nights. Too long for a young man. Hamid gave his son a gentle prod. The snoring stopped, but he did not wake.

Hamid straightened his long legs one at a time. *My knees ache.* He closed his eyes and tried to block out the cries of the wounded and listened for any movement nearby.

Nothing.

Hamid felt relieved that Ishmail had put up little resistance to staying at the sniper post. Returning to the 57th Regiment now would be suicide.

Thank you God for keeping my son alive for another day. I didn't raise him and work so hard to put him through architect school to have him throw it all away.

* * *

"Wake up. Father, wake up."

Hamid released an involuntary groan and then remembered where he was. Pressure pain throbbed in his hip.

The moon was up.

It must be close to morning.

I should not have slept.

Ishmail is awake.

We are alive.

He held his Mauser close and peered through the scrub towards the valley. Sporadic rifle fire continued but he saw no movement. He reached out and slowly parted the thorny branches for a wider view.

"They will come with dawn," Hamid whispered. "If not sooner. Have you been awake for long?"

"I did not sleep."

Hamid considered apologising to Ishmail for slapping him, but thought better of it. *I would do it again. It was for his own good. I have been a good father and have never needed to apologise before.*

"You were right Father," Ishmail said quietly. "It is right to stay another day."

Hamid met his son's eye's.

It was difficult to see his face in the low light, but something about the tone of voice let Hamid know that his son needed reassurance.

Hamid grabbed Ishmail's upper arm and gave a gentle squeeze. He nodded and reached for two sealed tins they had taken from a dead invader on the first day. They had no other rations left.

"Let's see if we can have some breakfast before light comes." Hamid whispered. "What do these infidels eat?"

He opened the larger tin and the smell of a stewed meat filled the small hollow of their hide-away.

"It's not pork is it Father?"

He dipped two fingers into the fatty slop and took a mouthful. Any hint of flavour was smothered by the extreme saltiness. The texture was soft and unsatisfying. *There's no way to know what that is, but it's better than nothing.*

"No, it's goat. Have some."

The smaller tin contained a sweet apricot preserve. Hamid had a small mouthful and gave the rest to Ishmail.

He felt as if the tinned meat would take all day to digest. *As God wills, if I should live out the day.*

Within half an hour darkness started to lift. Hamid and Ishmail were ready for another day of sniping. Both Mausers fully loaded with five rounds. Ishmail held the spare rounds in his pockets.

A basic plan for retreat was agreed, over the ridge behind them and into the next valley to the east. If the enemy looked likely to overrun their position in large numbers, or when they were down to the last ten rounds, they would retreat. If enemy raiding parties hurried past, Hamid and Ishmail would lie in waiting and let them pass, concealing themselves as best they could. If ten rounds of ammunition could be preserved until it was fully dark, they would wait a further two hours and then make their way back towards the Ottoman front line. Hopefully not to be shot by their fellow defenders.

"Father." Ishmail pointed at movement in the valley, through the prickly scrub that concealed their position.

Hamid nodded and watched the location in his Mauser sites. It was close to the same bush where last night's victim took his stomach shot. Sunrise was still some way off, but there was plenty of dawn light to see by.

A head with a round English style cap emerged from behind the bush.

Hamid applied gentle pressure to the trigger.

A pink mist burst from the invader's head and the shape dropped from view.

Hamid exhaled. "Forty-three."

CHAPTER 50

John

Wednesday, 28 April 1915

Colonel John Monash crouched beside the temporary wall as men of the 14th Battalion worked to fortify his headquarters. Men stacked the sandbags with each row offset from the row below, in a brickwork pattern to maximise strength of the temporary structure. John dragged a deep breath through a much needed cigarette. His head spun, but not due to the tobacco.

The first days since the landing had not gone well. Chaos blighted every aspect of the operation and John was too tired to reflect that he couldn't think of a way in which the attack could have gone any worse.

The original objective, to stream across the peninsula and cut off the Turks to the south at Cape Helles, had failed. On the first night, before John had landed himself, the other Australian commanders were ready to give up and requested evacuation. Instead of pushing on with the attack, the new orders were to dig in and defend the toehold the men had gained. The ANZAC attack was becoming the siege of a hillside, not even a mile inland from the landing beach.

How are we going to help the navy pass the Dardanelles Strait now? What is the strategic objective of digging in to create a defensive position? When I built bridges, so much work went into the requirements specification and design details, then the digging of foundations and construction of formwork for the main spans. Pouring concrete into the mould was the easy part. This military operation is like dumping masses of wet concrete onto unmade ground and then trying to decide how to work it into a useful structure with unclear requirements. Now the mix is hardening, devoid of form. Successful projects cannot be engineered in this way.

The New Zealand Brigade held his left flank and the brigades of the Australian 1st Division held the right. John's 4th Brigade held the centre, assigned the task of defending the head of the main valley that ran inland from the southern end of the landing cove. The main valley had become known as Shrapnel Gully, for the explosive shells sent by Turkish artillery that burst into hailstorms of vicious lead peas. In the upper reaches of Shrapnel Gully, John had made his brigade headquarters in a location he judged to be around one hundred yards back from the firing line.

Some had started to refer to these upper reaches as Monash Valley. *That name will never stick. I'm not sure I'd want it to, this place is likely to become infamous.*

After landing the battalions of his 4th Brigade piecemeal, over two days, John came ashore with men of the 14th Battalion, but could not locate the others. Rumours flew that 150 men from his 15th Battalion had been killed while coming ashore, and that his 13th and 16th Battalions had been split apart with their companies being sent to reinforce various parts of the front line. He felt naked, a commander in name only. He couldn't very well lead his men if he couldn't find three of his four battalions.

Units of John's brigade had returned gradually, and then, after floundering for over a full day, he was called to a conference of the ANZAC division and brigade commanders, to divide up the front line. John was promised the return of the rest of his brigade, in return for which, he was ordered to hold the head of Shrapnel Gully where many of his men had already relieved the first landing force of the 3rd Brigade.

The head of the valley was also the most advanced point position, closest to the Turkish front line and most aggressively attacked for the commanding aspect it held over the other ANZAC positions. This high ground was the most vulnerable point on the firing line and the Turks knew it.

Immediately after the conference, commander of the 1st Brigade, Lieutenant-Colonel MacLaurin and his brigade Major Irvine both insisted on viewing the situation for themselves, and in separate incidents, both managed to get themselves shot dead after peering over the defences and refusing to listen to cries of caution from the men on John's section of the firing line.

The waste of their own lives did nothing to inspire the men, but further depleted the leadership ranks and damaged the prospect of re-organising the force. John had only experienced two days of active service, but he was determined to learn fast. He knew he had to learn from others' mistakes. To do otherwise would limit his chance of success and survival.

John's task of re-organising his own men was disrupted by an incident which he could not ignore. After advancing up Shrapnel Valley to reinforce Quinn's Post, the 14th Battalion came under heavy machine gun fire whilst digging in. The spray of bullets cut down two hundred men, including twelve officers, and came from the direction of an area occupied by the 15th Battalion. The intensity of the fusillade led some of the 14th to believe that their sister battalion was responsible for the attack.

John listened to the claims and investigated the matter himself. In the end John was satisfied that the fire came from the entrenched Turks on the ridgeline, but tension between the battalions remained.

A telephone bell tinkled, out of place amongst the continuous bark of small arms fire and the thunder of artillery. The musical sound from ten paces away roused John from his reflections. He was expecting a call on the field telephone from his commander General Godley, and knew it would be the general who was calling. John sucked the last goodness from his cigarette and flicked the butt into the dirt.

"Colonel Monash," the clerk called. "It's for you."

John stood from his crouched position and his knees creaked. *I must lose some weight.* He started towards the phone and, at that moment, the clerk collapsed to the ground.

A nearby stretcher-bearer had witnessed the event and hurried over. John helped him drag the body onto a stretcher, although the clerk was quite dead, shot through the chest.

A staff sergeant picked up the telephone handset from the ground and caught a bullet in his arm for his trouble.

"Best hurry with those sandbags lads," John called and reached for the telephone himself.

Another member of John's staff shoved him away from the handset, at that moment another bullet zipped into the exposed bunker and thudded into a sandbag.

"Sniper's got us in his sites," said the staff officer. "He's seen the telephone and he wants to bag himself a senior officer like yourself. I suggest you stay behind that pile of sandbags, Sir."

"Yes, of course." A calm alertness settled over John. *I must not take unnecessary risks like that.*

The staff officer dragged the telephone across the dirt with a bayonet and handed it to John.

"Colonel Monash here." John spoke loudly into the mouthpiece, to be heard over the incessant percussion.

"Ah, there you are!" General Godley's voice crackled in John's ear. "I was beginning to wonder if we had lost the line."

"No Sir, It's just that two men were shot getting the telephone to me. One of them killed."

"I say, how about that? You might want to be a bit careful up there yourself, but listen, you must entrench and hold the head of that valley."

"Yes, I know that is the idea Sir, but I need all my men back, and more ammunition, and periscopes, and bombs. Captain Quinn's post is the apex of our whole firing line. The Turks are right on top of us there. You can hear them talking only yards away, and they have small bombs, the size of cricket balls, that they lob into us by hand. They know that if they can knock us out of that position they will command the valley and they are throwing everything they've got at us up here. My men here are doing all they can, but you have got to help us otherwise the position is untenable."

Another bullet zipped by and kicked up a small cloud of dust from the floor.

"Try to keep your spirits up old boy. I know it seems worse than what it really is when you get your first taste of the game. We are doing what we can here to get supplies to the whole front. Remember you must hold the head of the valley, no matter the cost in men."

A click terminated the conversation.

Damn that man, he will be of no help to us. I must protect Quinn's Post.

John closed his eyes and pictured the topography of the ridge above. A keen bushwalker and lover of good maps, John enjoyed the ability to produce a three-dimensional image of complex terrain inside his head. Defending Quinn's Post from Quinn's Post alone was impossible. With the number of men the Turks were willing to launch from trenches so close, it would only be a matter of time before the position was overrun by a sheer weight of numbers.

Overlapping machine gun fire from either flank to enfilade no-man's-land would make it impassable for the enemy. The angles must be exactly right, or there will be more accusations that we are shooting our own men, but it's the only way. The 16th Battalion on Lieutenant-Colonel Pope's Hill to the left, and the 14th Battalion at Lieutenant-Colonel Courtney's Post to the right. That might just work.

John waved to summon his Chief-of-Staff and Lieutenant-Colonel McGlinn scurried over with his head ducked low and an awkward motion that seemed too slow for the circumstances. Like John, McGlinn was losing his own personal war on obesity.

"Write a field order," John yelled so McGlinn would hear over the background fire. "Get a machine gun to Pope's Hill and a machine gun to Courtney's Post. They are each to provide flanking fire into the ground in front of Quinn's Post to protect Quinn's from frontal attack, overlapping each other if possible."

McGlinn scribbled notes on the field order book with a pencil and passed it to John to review and sign. Once John had initialled each order, McGlinn hurried away towards a more junior staff officer to have the order issued.

It's time to use our resources in a less haphazard way.

John de-pocketed his own small notebook and started to list agenda items for discussion with his subordinates. Soon he would make time for a meeting of his brigade officers and restore order.

Distribution of ammunition, food and water; sanitation; rosters to cycle men at the firing line; safe access between back lines and firing line; entrenchment plans; encampment areas; casualty counts…

The English tendency to describe war as a sport underestimates its complexity and disrespects the men who suffer and die. Modern warfare is an engineering problem.

CHAPTER 51

Jayjay

Thursday, 29 April 1915

Royal Marines huddled along the trench in single file and two of them took up position in the area of trench that Jayjay considered to be his own.

Days earlier, Jayjay would have been in awe of the British Navy landing force, but this lot looked like a pack of fearful puppies.

"The trench needs more work," Jayjay said to one, "but you should be all right if you keep low. Whatever you do, don't go poking your head up for a look around, especially during the day, unless you want to get it shot off. If you decide to do it anyway, don't be dallying about it, one second at the most, maybe two or three in the moonlight. Mind if I take a sip of your water? I'm out of food and haven't had a drink for a day and a half."

The fellow looked to be ten years older than Jayjay, but he nodded in silence like a schoolboy taking instruction from the headmaster. He handed over a full canteen without hesitation and it was all Jayjay could do not to drink the lot.

"Thanks mate, good luck."

Alfred's personal possessions weighed heavy in Jayjay's pocket, a wallet and fob-watch. *I'm not sure what to do with these, but I need to figure out how to send them home for him.*

Jayjay took one last look over the ditch that had been his home for three days. A ditch where Alfred, the one who enticed Charlotte away from him, had been shot dead while Jayjay dozed. He turned in the direction that the marines had come from and shuffled, hunched almost in half, to a communication sap that had been cut perpendicular to the front line trench. The sap provided some cover and relative safety when he turned his back on the enemy.

The sap floor rose towards ground level sooner than Jayjay would have liked. A sergeant crouched near the shallow end of the sap and barked orders as Jayjay and others shuffled past.

"Keep moving down this way, double time, stay low along the seaward side of the ridge. When it narrows right down into a razor's edge between you and the next hill, drop down into the gully past the razor's edge and then follow the gully to the beach. Roll call for all battalions of the First Brigade tomorrow morning.

Seaward side mind, away from the line of sight of Turk snipers."

Jayjay limped on and kept his tall frame as low as he could.

Away from the sea, undulations in the land provided some protection, such that any Turkish snipers would have to be well behind enemy lines, or a long way off on a flank, but a rifle in skilled hands could be deadly at half a mile or more. He hurried along, as fast as his wounded leg would allow, then slowed as he approached a narrow rocky outcrop to his right. *That can't be the razor's edge, it goes to nowhere. It's the Rock of Ages I saw from below.* A nose of bleached sandstone reached out towards the sea and marked the level of a larger rock platform that might once have been, then dropped in a sheer cliff to the gullies below.

He followed a freshly worn track along the seaward side of the ridge, but lagged behind the more able-bodied men from the 2nd Battalion who ran on. Ahead an isolated plateau stood between the toe of the ridge he followed and the sea. The plateau sloped away towards the sea and was connected to the rest of the ridge by what had to be the 'razor's edge' – the narrow bridge of earth had eroded well below the high ground on either side. Steep sides came together along a jagged crest, like the blade of a serrated knife.

Beyond the razor's edge, the newly worn path dropped into the head of a gully. Men emerged, and others disappeared at the edge, like ants coming and going from the entry to their nest. Jayjay scrambled fifty yards down into the gully, then paused.

Several Australians sat about on the ground and seemed to have no business to attend to. The gully was perfectly sheltered from enemy fire, unless a shrapnel shell managed to burst directly above.

Relief and exhaustion hit him like combination punches. He dropped to the ground, lay on his back with his arm around his rifle and stared at the sky.

Ron or Larry might be dead, maybe both of them. He had known this from the moment he was separated from them, but had pushed the thought from his mind and focussed on immediate survival. *No, it was more than that. My duty as a soldier in the imperial force was to fight the king's enemies. I was trained to seek cover under fire and I did. When re-united with another group of Australians I fought with them and resisted the enemy as best I could. I couldn't just leave my post. Should I have done something different? The advance has stopped and the Turks are digging in. I thought we were going to push over these hills and meet up with the English 29th Division?*

He sat up and looked around, half-expecting to see Ron and Larry watching him, but they were not there. A pair of stretcher bearers walked past, down the gully with the confidence of those who had trod the path a number of times. The fellow lying in the stretcher between them held his belly with two bloody hands, as if trying to stop something important from leaking out.

It was no-one he recognised.

There was no one here he recognised.

God, please let Ron and Larry be alive.

What would I say to Mum, or Mrs Gillespie if they were killed? I need to find out. They might be down at the beach waiting.

Yet, Jayjay's body refused to move. He needed a rest, but felt guilty for it. *I can sleep later. I'll just lie here for a spell.*

Enough ground to lie outstretched without someone shooting at him was a luxury Jayjay had craved for days. He barely noticed the slope or prickles of the scrub, exhaustion overtook him and he drifted into a dreamless sleep.

* * *

The afternoon sun hung over the sea, well past the warships when Jayjay woke. His slumber seemed to last only seconds, but he felt surprisingly refreshed. He checked his wrist watch. *I slept for three hours. Strange no one woke me.*

He remembered Ron and Larry and a sick feeling returned. *I need to find them, or someone who knows what happened to them, before dark. God, please let them be alive.*

His arm still embraced the rifle, but he disentangled himself and examined his wounded leg. The field dressing hung loose leaving the wound exposed. The gash was full of dirt and congealed blood, weeping from one side. *I better have that looked at. Damn thing hurts like a bastard.*

Jayjay hauled himself to his feet and limped downhill using his rifle like an old man's cane.

"Watch yourself leaving Rest Gully mate." A stretcher bearer carried the back end of an empty stretcher, on his way up towards the front line with a partner. "Shrapnel Gully's a pretty unhealthy place, get yourself back to the beach quick as you can."

Jayjay nodded. "Got any water? My bottle's shot."

The stretcher bearer hesitated a moment, then passed over a water bottle with only a few mouthfuls left in it.

Jayjay took a swig and tried not to drink it all, but the bottle he returned held only a few drops.

"Thanks mate."

The gully dropped steeply for around a hundred yards and opened into a larger valley that swung right towards the beach.

A shell burst over the valley ahead near the beach. A small white cloud hung in the air to mark the place of detonation and looked artificial against the blue sky. Men on the ground scurried for cover. *Why are they down here and not at the front line? They must be coming back for roll call or carrying supplies.*

Another shell burst, this one closer. Jayjay didn't need to prop himself on the rifle on the flatter ground, but when he tried to hurry the leg resisted. *Come on leg. You'll be dead along the rest of me if we get caught in a shrapnel storm.*

Fresh blood leaked from his leg wound as Jayjay stumbled onto the beach at the mouth of Shrapnel Valley. He shuffled around the headland to the sheltered cove where he had landed on the first day, then stopped on the beach to take in the sight that confronted him.

Men covered the beach in ripples of khaki. Some moved with purpose, carting boxes from small boats to the back of the beach. Walking wounded trudged towards a hospital tent marked with a red cross. Stretcher bearers carried those unable to carry themselves. Some men stood or sat about, as if waiting for something.

A shell burst over the water and sprayed shrapnel into the water near a small boat that chugged towards the beach like a mouse trying to outrun a cat across an open field.

Behind the narrow beach, a steep hill climbed up to his right. Human activity continued up the slope, as if protesting that the narrow beach would not meet the space requirements of this army. Engineers cut steps and made pathways. All over the face of the hill men cut small benches, or dugout shelters.

How am I going to find the others? I need to find them before dark, but I can hardly move on this leg. There are thousands of men here.

He trudged on across the coarse pebbly sand, leg muscles tugging at the wound with each step. *About half a mile of beach, maybe a bit less. At least it's flat.*

His eyes scanned from face to face, but he saw no one he recognised. *The Australian Imperial Force, able to march in perfect formation up George Street, but sitting around confused in a battle on the other side of the world.*

At the hospital tent he expected someone to come out and call him in, but the medics hurried about their business and didn't even glance in his direction. Walking wounded milled about the place and sat on the beach.

He limped past.

Within a hundred yards of the end of the beach he hadn't yet seen anyone he knew from the 1st Battalion. Unease inside him was growing into panic when he recognised a familiar face.

It wasn't Ron or Larry, but Seamus O'Shea, wearing bandage stained with old blood around one arm. Seamus was talking to others from the 1st Battalion, but they were from a different company and Jayjay didn't know them by name.

Where to start? "Seamus!"

"Big Jay!" Surprise lit up Seamus's eyes. "I thought you were dead! Aye, you wanted to make sure you could play hide the sausage with Josephine again. To be sure, she did have a nice pair of paps and a silky slit!"

"Seamus, listen, do you know where Ron and Larry are? Are they okay?"

"Oh, Matey, the first day we got all mixed up. We were scrambled! Word is we have a roll call for the whole battalion tomorrow morning, they might turn up then. I haven't seen 'em Lad."

Searching eyes asked an unspoken question that Jayjay didn't want to answer.

"Seamus, I'm sorry." Jayjay shook his head. "Poddy's dead. Shot in the face. Right in front of me. I killed the Turk who did it, stabbed him through with my bayonet."

Seamus nodded and looked to the ground. "You seen Mick? I ain't seen 'im since the first day."

Jayjay look down as well and stared at the pebbles in the sand. In his mind, he saw a vision of the fellow collapsing midstride while sprinting downhill. "I thought I saw him, late afternoon on the second day, but I couldn't be sure if it was him."

"Killed?"

"Like I said, it mighta' been someone else."

"Damn! We just wanted a ticket back to England to visit home. I'd murder a man for a bottle of Irish Whiskey right now. I'd drink the whole thing and get blind drunk. Damn!"

Jayjay put a hand on Seamus's shoulder. "I need to try and find Ron and Larry before it gets dark. I'll try and come back to see you later."

Seamus might have nodded, but the movement was so slight that it was difficult to tell.

Jayjay walked on. There was not much beach left before the end of the cove, but Ron and Larry were nowhere to be seen.

Sunset bathed the cove in an orange glow when Jayjay recognised the shoulder patches of a sergeant of the 2nd Battalion.

"Sergeant." Jayjay reached into his pocket and fingered Alfred's watch. "I was with some of the boys from the 2nd Battalion up on that ridge. One fellow I was with – I knew him from Sydney – he was shot – killed – I have some of his things and I want to make sure they are sent back to his parents – maybe send them a letter. Can you help me with that?

"What was his name?"

"Alfred McKenzie."

The sergeant nodded slowly and his eye's told Jayjay that Alfred was known to him. "You can leave Mackenzie's things with me. I'll make sure they are sent to his next of kin. Killed in action up on Walker's Ridge you say?"

"At the front line, during our second night here, so it was a couple of days ago now."

The sergeant kept nodding as if trying to commit the details to memory, but looking like there was a good chance he might forget. "The official letter that will be sent home with McKenzie's things is will be short and to the point. You want to write to the family as well you say? You know his address?"

Jayjay nodded and handed over Alfred's personal items. He wanted to ask more about how the family would be informed, but the sergeant turned away to the next fellow that approached him with another enquiry.

Jayjay stood for a moment, then shuffled on his way. *I don't like the chances of Alfred's things making it home, but I don't know what else I could do with them. And where am I going to start with a letter to his parents? I never was much good at writing at school. I had trouble finding the right words and the teachers always said my writing was too messy. There should be someone else better able to do it than me.*

* * *

After one more trip back along the beach Jayjay paused to rest near the southern end. The leg throbbed and it was difficult to recognise anyone more than a few yards away in the fading light of dusk. Soon it would be dark and there was no sign of Ron or Larry.

He held in his hand three sheets of paper and one pencil, supplies he had managed to extract from a quarter master's clerk on the beach.

Unable to think of anything else he could do, Jayjay found a small patch of unoccupied embankment at the back of the beach and half sat, half lay back against the hillside. He hadn't seen his pack since dropping it on the first day and had no covering against the night. *At least the sky is clear of clouds.*

Glad of the excuse of darkness to avoid starting a letter, he pocketed the paper and pencil, curled up against the cool night air and fell asleep.

* * *

A thin slither of moon peaked over the hill above and Jayjay shivered with cold.

Rifle fire cracked in the distance.

I must have slept for a few hours at least. I wonder how long until morning. Damn, it's cold!

He rolled over and tried to get back to sleep, but the ground was hard and cold and his leg wound ached.

He pulled the pencil and one sheet of paper from his pocket and wrote by the barest hint of moonlight, starting with the McKenzie's address in the top right corner. He didn't know where to start or how to go about writing such a letter, but he wanted them to know that Alfred died fighting bravely and made his best attempt.

It was too dark to re-read it once he had finished. *Probably for the best as it must be terribly messy.* He folded it up and returned it with the pencil to his top pocket.

Please God don't let me have to write any more of those. Now I'll never get back to sleep.

* * *

"Wake up sleepy head!"

Ron and Larry grinned down at him in the colourless light of dawn.

"We've got roll call in a few hours. You better have a shave little brother, you look terrible."

Thank you God, please don't let this be a dream. I'll never let myself fall asleep on duty again, no matter how tired I get.

CHAPTER 52

Dacre

Friday, 30 April 1915

Lieutenant-Commander Dacre Stoker awoke to the sound of a torpedoman taking a morning grunt into a bucket positioned below one of the two fold-down toilet seats in Australian submarine *AE2*. The cloth curtain did little to screen sound or smell.

He reminded himself that this was no dream, he lay seventy feet below the surface of the Sea of Marmara.

Today we have orders, for the first time since making it through the Dardanelles and generally causing trouble for the Turks.

* * *

Four days earlier, once the batteries were charged and fresh night air replaced the stale air inside the hull, *AE2* continued her journey up the Dardanelles Strait. Dacre guided her along the surface under cover of darkness. When dawn started to break he dived to twenty feet and kept lookout through the periscope.

No wireless response was received from General Headquarters, and Dacre had no way of knowing if his telegraph signal declaring *AE2* success had made it through.

At one point along the Strait, Dacre fired a torpedo at an enemy cruiser, but missed. He was furious with himself for the lost opportunity, but knew that two sleepless nights impacted his ability to focus as required in such difficult conditions of bad light and smooth sea.

At about seven o'clock of the next morning, 26 April, *AE2* passed Gallipoli town, with its vast collection of fishing boats, and dived to seventy feet to enter the Sea of Marmara unmolested.

On reaching this point, Dacre realised that he had no idea what to do next. All his efforts had gone into the goal of making the Dardanelles passage. In some ways, the odds of success were so long that the idea of actually achieving the goal seemed more like a distant hope than a real prospect. Now suddenly he had made it through and he had a whole sea in which to roam. His orders were to attempt to make the passage, but he had no orders for action once he reached the Sea of Marmara.

Dacre decided to make sure his presence was felt by the enemy who relied on this shipping channel to move troops and supplies to the Gallipoli Peninsula. With only six torpedoes left and no guns, he had to be selective in his targets, but could allow himself be seen by smaller boats who would spread the word of submarine threat in the Sea. He fired another torpedo that failed to meet its mark, and harassed a number of small fishing vessels, to the great excitement of the fishermen and amusement of the submarine crew.

Nightly attempts at wireless communications proved no more successful than at the first attempt.

Another torpedo attempt was thwarted when the torpedo engine failed to fire, at a range of only two hundred yards to a ship escorted by two destroyers. *A lucky escape for that ship, nothing would have saved her had the torpedo run. I wonder what she was carrying, maybe troops? If she was worth guarding, she was worth sinking. Damn! Four torpedoes left.*

At night, when not chasing Turkish vessels, the *AE2* rested on the seabed to allow the crew to sleep. All but one watch-keeper, his sole duty to watch the depth gauge to see that the submarine did not unexpectedly rise to the surface or slip along the bottom to a greater depth.

One quiet day, with *AE2* positioned within sight of the entrance to Constantinople harbour, Dacre and his crew formed plans to attack it the following day. The appearance of a gunboat distracted Dacre from this planning to give chase and harass it. On deciding that the quarry was too small to waste a torpedo on, Dacre dived and evaded the small gunboat. Once clear, he returned to the surface and steered back towards Constantinople to see out a quiet afternoon.

"There's something ahead there, Sir, looks like a periscope."

"It is a submarine," Dacre said without quite believing it himself. "And she's coming up!"

Not two hundred yards off, there rose slowly and gracefully, first the periscope, then the conning tower, and then the grey, dripping hull of a sister E-class submarine.

"It's *E14* by all the gods!" Dacre exclaimed.

Five days isolated in a submarine under constant threat seemed more like five years and the unplanned meeting of friends in an enemy sea caught Dacre by surprise. Relief washed over him like fresh water and a weight seemed to lift from his shoulders.

The submarines drew close to each other and greetings were exchanged through megaphones.

"What are your plans for tomorrow?" Asked Lieutenant-Commander Edward Boyle, commanding officer of *E14*.

Boyle was senior to Dacre, so with him lay the future direction for *AE2* and *E14* joint operations.

"We propose to continue on to Constantinople," Dacre replied. "To attack the harbour at the mouth of the Bosphorus Strait."

"We are expecting orders from Admiral de Robeck by wireless telegraph tonight. It would be advisable to await his instructions before initiating further action. Let us rendezvous here at ten a.m, on the morrow."

"As you say, Sir," Dacre replied and the two submarines parted company for the night.

* * *

Dacre rolled out of his narrow bunk and inhaled the thick morning air.

Today we have orders. Rendezvous with submarine E14 *at ten o'clock, and see what the Admiral will have us do today.*

"Dive stations, prepare to surface."

Submarine *AE2* rose to the surface with the smooth operation of man and machine working as one. Dacre had come to accept this as normal, but this morning felt a renewed sense of pride in his submarine and crew.

We were the first to force a passage through the Dardanelles, and others followed. Commodore Keyes said there was nothing he would not do for us if we could do it. We have surpassed the efforts of Holbrook and all the others. We will enter submarine folk-lore for this achievement.

The submarine cruised along the surface, batteries fully charged and ready for action. Four torpedoes left.

At one stage Dacre thought he saw *E14* some five miles ahead, but by the time *AE2* reached the rendezvous location, *E14* was nowhere to be seen.

Smoke to the west told of a ship approaching.

Maybe Commander Boyle took E14 *after that prey?*

When the mast and funnels came into view, Dacre saw she was only a small torpedo boat. More smoke told of another ship to the south.

We will dive out of the way of this torpedo boat, and make south to investigate this other ship.

"Dive stations. Prepare to dive."

"Dive to fifty feet. All ahead south."

Water sloshed into the ballast tanks and *AE2* slipped below the surface.

Without warning, the submarine tipped up at the bows. Aimed up for the surface, she started rising rapidly and refused to respond to any attempts to regain control, by dive rudders or shifting ballast water forward.

Only when she broke the surface, did *AE2* stop rising.

Through the periscope Dacre saw the torpedo boat barely one hundred yards off, guns firing hard in his direction.

I don't know what just happened, but we must get under at all costs. Remember the maiden of Vesuvius and remain calm.

"Flood forward ballast tank," Dacre ordered.

After one or two long minutes, the bow tipped down and *AE2* slipped underwater.

"Close forward ballast tank," Dacre called. "Hold ballast water in aft tanks. Dive to fifty feet and level out."

As the instruction to level out passed his lips, Dacre knew something was wrong. Opposite to his intention, the bow continued to dip lower at an ever-increasing inclination.

"Sixty feet Captain."

"Dive rudders are powerless to right her Captain."

"Seventy feet."

"Blow all ballast tanks," Dacre yelled.

"Eighty feet."

"Blow those ballast tanks," Dacre repeated.

"Expelling ballast water as fast as we can Captain."

"Ninety feet."

"Reverse thrust, full astern," Dacre ordered.

"One hundred feet."

"Depth off scale Captain."

What is wrong with this submarine? This could be the end of us.

"She's coming up Sir!"

The needle of the depth gauge jerked away from the end-stop at one hundred feet and raced towards zero.

Without water in the ballast tanks, *AE2* was buoyant and surged backwards towards the surface where she breached like a whale.

"Re-flood ballast tanks," Dacre yelled.

"Up periscope. First officer, tell me what you see."

"The torpedo boat is circling around us Sir. A gunboat is approaching fast from the south."

"Dive!"

This time, as soon as the submarine slipped under the water, Dacre ordered ballast water be expelled, but nothing he could do would prevent her nosing down steeper and steeper, plummeting faster than ever before.

"Sixty feet."

"Eighty feet."

"One hundred feet."

We are going to the bottom, just like AE1.

"Reverse thrust, full astern."

Dacre looked around at his men, all holding onto something to prevent themselves from falling down the slope towards the bow. For an instant time seemed to stop. *They must all know how close they are to death, but they are remaining cool and calm, as I told them to. A fine collection of men, loyal to the last.*

Eggs, bread, food of all sorts, knives, forks and plates came tumbling forward from the petty officers' mess.

In Heaven's name, what depth are we at? Why don't the sides cave in under the pressure and finish it?

Then, once again, the small needle of the depth gauge jumped back from its limit and *AE2* surged backwards to the surface.

BANG! – A cloud of smoke burst from the engine room.

"We are hit and holed Captain!" The cry came from aft. "Two holes above the water line!"

The game was up. The submarine couldn't dive with holes in the hull and she had no guns with which to defend herself on the surface. All Dacre could do now was to try to avoid useless loss of life, if that was still possible. *I owe them that at least.*

"All hands on deck," Dacre ordered. "Overboard if you can swim. We are sinking."

The crew scrambled up the conning tower, but one officer stood by Dacre. First officer Lieutenant Haggard remained to help prepare *AE2* to be scuttled. The two officers had discussed such a situation previously and agreed that under no circumstances should the submarine fall into enemy hands.

Holes above the waterline prevented *AE2* from diving but she was not sinking and could be saved, but saving the vessel at this moment would be handing the submarine to the enemy. Instead she must be sacrificed.

Dacre and his first officer flooded the ballast tanks.

"Hurry Sir," came an anxious cry from above. "She's going down."

At that moment he knew his final responsibility as captain of the submarine was running to plan. Dacre exhaled and tried to smile, but felt as if he was betraying a loyal friend.

"Up you go Haggard. Get out of here."

Dacre cast a final look about the small space that had become his home, now in chaos with food and clothes floating about on the water that rushed in. He spied his private dispatch-case in the wardroom. A thought that the money it contained might be important gripped him, so he ran to pick it up, then darted up the conning tower, reluctant to abandon his submarine until the last.

On climbing out the hatch, water lapped about two feet from the top of the conning tower. Besides this, only a small portion of the stern was exposed and on it the last half dozen of the crew huddled. The remainder of the men were overboard.

Water lapped over the stern and one of the engine-room ratings performed a neat dive into the Sea of Marmara. The image of the smooth motion of the dive burned itself into Dacre's memory. Last to leave, Dacre followed his men into the Sea.

Perhaps a minute passed, and then, slowly and gracefully, like the lady she was, without sound or sigh, without causing an eddy or a ripple on the water, *AE2* just slid away on her last and longest dive.

AE2 had carried him and his crew half way around the world and most of the way back again. She had done everything asked of her, and more than any other submarine in history. A deep sadness filled Dacre as he tread water and watched the dark shadow of the submarine disappear below him.

"Effendi, Give me your hand."

A man reached over the bow of a dinghy that bobbed near him.

Clothes, boots and a dispatch case made swimming difficult and Dacre reached up to take the enemy hand without hesitation.

The Turk dragged him from the water with surprising strength.

"Thank you. Is your captain a German or Turk?" Dacre asked.

"Turk."

Dacre nodded. *Good, I have no desire to surrender to a German. It looks like all the men are saved. Hopefully they will not live to regret surrendering to the enemy.*

The dinghy delivered Dacre and his men onto the torpedo boat.

"Our game is over lads," Dacre said to those close by him. "Best do as they ask."

The men followed his lead and complied like sheep with the gestures of their captors.

Why did my submarine misbehave like that? She must have hit a change in density layers. Maybe a thermocline? More likely boundary between fresh water and salt water. Whatever it was, she bounced right off it.

The torpedo boat carried the submariners back down the Dardanelles Strait to the Narrows. Here, she birthed at a dock on the eastern shore at Chanakkale.

A crowd of Turkish soldiers gathered around with much pointing at the prisoners, but there were no civilians about.

Dacre and his men were marched to a nearby fortress and guided to a dungeon underneath. Dacre and Lieutenant Haggard were pulled away from the crew.

"Chins up lads," Dacre cried out. "We are prisoners of war now. There are rules as to how they must treat us."

Dacre and Haggard were shoved through a door into a small cell.

"Welcome to the officers' quarters," came a voice from the darkness at the back of the cell.

"Who's there?" Dacre asked.

"Lieutenant C. Palmer of the Royal British Navy."

CHAPTER 53

John

Saturday, 1 May 1915

In his dugout headquarters, Colonel John Monash sat on a biscuit box and organised his thoughts with notebook and pencil. A more detailed plan was required, based on first-hand reconnaissance, if this attack was to succeed.

The strategic need to drive the Turks from the high ground was clear. Since the beginning, John had argued that while the Turks held the top of the main ridge, his men would face a constant struggle to hold their ground below.

His concern was that, to mount an operation of that nature against an entrenched enemy, much planning would be required as well as well-timed coordination with artillery covering fire. The proposal, put to him by his commander General Godley, lacked details or any tactical method. Godley remained at his headquarters and had not yet ventured up Monash Valley to inspect the 4th Brigade section of the firing line for himself.

John's pencil scratched against the paper.

Our men of the New Zealand and Australian Division should advance with the Australian 1st Division in a unified Corps assault. The 14th Battalion will advance over Courtney's Post and wheel to the north. The 15th Battalion will advance from Pope's Hill towards Baby 700. Then the 13th Battalion will follow the 15th and head east until they touch the left of the 14th to allow for expanding front.

Baby 700 was the prize. This hill, little more than a patch of sloping ground 700 feet above sea level, lead up the ridge to the next rise of Big 700, now more commonly known as Battleship Hill for the regular pounding it received from naval guns. Baby 700 formed a key junction of the battlefield geometry where the spur that rose from Anzac Cove to Russell's Top connected with the main range via The Nek. For the Anzacs to control Baby 700 would fill a gap in the front line, eliminate much of the sniper threat to the valley and dominate some of the Turkish stronghold.

The New Zealanders will rush The Nek from Russell's Top, under orchestrated cover from navy guns, and the Brigades of the 1st Division will advance on the right, across 400 Plateau, with at least one battalion in reserve to support our advance up the main ridge. The attack will be at dusk to use darkness to our advantage, especially since artillery is so limited.

We will need 200,000 rounds of ammunition by 1:00pm on the day of the attack and we will feed the men two hours before they advance. Engineers will follow the infantry to construct a mule access track for resupply of the troops at the new front line.

When John had completed his proposal, he made the journey to pay a visit to the commander of the New Zealand and Australian Division in General Godley's dugout and discuss the attack face to face.

"General Walker doesn't like it," Godley said when John arrived.

"I know," John replied. "I met with him this morning. We both have concerns about the strength of the men and then nature of the attack. It needs to be a well-planned operation with targeted support from artillery and ship's guns. I have a more detailed tactical plan to discuss with you."

"Your Australian General Bridges will go along with whatever Walker says."

General Walker was a battle-hardened officer of the British regular army. Until recently, Chief of Staff to ANZAC Commander General Birdwood, Walker had taken over command of the 1st Brigade under General Bridges, after MacLaurin's death a few days earlier.

"Perhaps we should discuss this plan with them then Sir?"

"No Monash, that won't be necessary. General Birdwood has accepted the view of Walker and Bridges that the 1st Division men on the right flank should not attack."

"So the attack is called off?" John felt a breath of relief in the hope that the operation might not have to be organised in haste.

"General Birdwood and I have agreed that the attack should proceed without the 1st Division. This will now be an attack by the New Zealand and Australian Division only."

"But we are only two brigades!" John struggled to believe his commander was being serious and the short-felt relief was replaced with a sick feeling in his stomach. "We cannot take Baby 700 without a supporting attack on the right flank. Our men will be butchered from behind as they charge up the hill. We do not have sufficient artillery support to rely on that alone. The New Zealanders will be coming from a different direction. If they, or we, are delayed, the other brigade will be stranded in a very exposed position."

"There will be losses, of course."

"Not just losses, we would be throwing men's lives away for no good reason. This plan is weak and cannot be sustained with such limited numbers. Why would you go into battle unless you have fair chance of victory?"

"Soldiers die in war Monash, that's how it works. General Birdwood and I have agreed to push on regardless, the attack will go ahead."

"When?"

"Not today, you will be informed when a new time is set."

"With all due respect, Sir, it's bloody madness."

Without a salute or waiting for a reply, John turned and stormed out of his commander's dugout.

* * *

The next day, John started to wonder if common sense might have prevailed, but in the early afternoon he received the order. The attack was to proceed at 7:15pm, after a fifteen minute bombardment of the enemy position.

He checked his pocket watch – the hands showed a quarter past two. *Five hours to prepare. The attack is ill-conceived and under-resourced, but if I refuse I would be disobeying a direct order. Walker refused and they respected his views, but he is an English General. Even with more time to prepare I cannot think how I could improve our chances of success, but we must make a fist of it.*

He took several deep breaths to clear his head. There was much to do.

"McGlinn," John called to his Chief of Staff who was never far away. "Our brigade is to attack Baby 700 with the New Zealand Brigade at 7:15pm tonight. We need to spread the word immediately. Men are to be fed at 5:00 and in position by 6:30…"

* * *

At seven o'clock, half an hour after sunset, the first of the ship's guns opened fire.

From John's location at 4th Brigade headquarters, deep in the throat of the winding Monash Valley, he could not see the naval vessels firing, nor the target of Baby 700 hidden behind Pope's Hill. He didn't need visibility to know that the first phase of the attack was playing out as planned, this was the beauty of operating to a plan, even a poor plan. Distant rumbles from the guns faded behind the thunder of high explosive tearing into the hillside to the north.

Guns from at least eight warships pounded the rhythm in a syncopation of destruction. The bombardment rose to a crescendo more intense than any John had experienced. Compression waves resonated in his chest. *How can anyone survive such an onslaught? If these shells are well aimed, maybe our attack can succeed.*

At 7:10pm, John's ear's felt as if they had absorbed a month of sound in minutes. He wondered whether he might have sustained permanent hearing damage and if he would ever enjoy the intricate notes of a symphony orchestra again.

A machine gun rattled on the right flank, and the high pitch of a rifle fusillade joined the score, right on time.

The men would hear it too. They would know it is about time to charge. They had responded with enthusiasm during the afternoon when they learned of the attack.

Before the landing the men had been led to expect that they would soon be marching to Istanbul. In the weeks prior, each man had drawn his pay in English gold or ten shilling notes overprinted in Turkish script with their value in piasters. An atmosphere of frustration had built up with the constant digging of trenches that none expected to occupy for long.

Minutes after the machine guns started the rattle ceased and an intense silence blanketed the valley, but a high pitched ring persisted in John's ears.

A cheer of many drifted down the valley, then deep voices of men singing and a John allowed himself a smile at the familiar tune.

There has been a lot of argument going on they say,
As to whether Dear Old England should have gone into the fray,
But right thinking people all wanted her to fight;
For when there's shady business, Britannia puts it right.
Rally round the banner of your country,
    Take the field with brothers o'er the foam;
On land or sea, wherever you be,
    Keep your eye on Germany.
But England home and beauty have no cause to fear,
    Should Auld acquaintance be forgot,
No! No! No! No! No! Australia will be there,
    Australia will be there.

The Turks had been silenced by the barrage, at least for now. *Take their ground for your own lads.*

Singing continued. "It's a long way to Tipper –"

Machine guns barked.

Rifles spat.

Artillery crumped.

A single candle was all John allowed in his dugout, unless an order had to be written. *No need to tempt fate with enemy snipers about.* He sat on a biscuit box in the darkness and had no way of knowing whether the attack was progressing as planned.

Hours passed slowly that night. Sounds of fighting did not fade into the distance as they should have.

As dawn approached John feared the worst. Neither he, nor any of his staff officers had slept. Confused messages had dribbled in during the night – Turk defences were strong – the New Zealanders had been held up – advance was restricted – men were digging in where they could. None of it sounded like the plan.

At the first hint of grey light, John could bear the waiting no longer and left his dugout with a junior staff officer to reconnoitre the situation for himself.

The climb up to Pope's Hill was hard work, but John wanted to take a good look up and down the ridge. To attempt this from Quinn's Post or Courtney's Post would be an invitation to the sniper's bullet.

He hauled his well-rounded form up the rope ascent to Pope's Hill and reached the top puffing and blowing.

A garrison of the 13th Battalion held the hill and a sergeant greeted John with a grimace.

"I suggest you take a look with this Sir." The sergeant handed a periscope to John and a sinking pit formed in John's gut. He wanted to turn and climb back down without seeing what it was that made the sergeant look that way, but he lifted the periscope and peered through it.

Pope's Hill split the head of Monash Valley into two forks. In truth it was more of a short spur from the main ridge than a hill. Only accessible by a steep climb from the rear, the firing line of Pope's Hill stood like an Australian island in a sea of Turks.

To the right of Pope's Hill, the closest friendly position was Quinn's Post, nearly two hundred yards away. Between Pope's Hill and Quinn's Post, the southern fork of Monash Valley ran up to the main ridge where it was strongly held by the Turks and infested with snipers. This area had become known as The Bloody Angle.

Two hundred yards to the left of Pope's Hill, the northern fork of Monash Valley ran up to the junction of Russell's Top and the main ridge. Near the junction, Russell's Top narrowed to an isthmus, less than thirty yards wide, that favoured defenders over attackers like the draw-bridge to a castle. The isthmus was known as The Nek.

John peered into the mirror and swept the periscope in an arc. Early dawn visibility was poor, but there was no denying the human forms strewn across no-man's land from Quinn's Post to The Nek.

"Some of our boys are digging in up on the ridge between here and the Nek Sir," The sergeant said. "The New Zealanders arrived late at The Nek and couldn't hold the ground they reached so they pulled back into the valley. Our boys have built some new trenches overnight, but when there's good light to see by, the Turks will give 'em hell."

Australian artillery fired from somewhere behind John, in the direction of the beach. Explosive shells tore into the very trenches the sergeant was describing and sent sprays of black earth into the air. His men were being shelled by their own guns.

An urge to vomit swelled from John's belly to his throat.

They are completely isolated up there.

At this rate, there will be nothing left of my brigade within days.

I must order them to withdraw.

I have failed those men.

CHAPTER 54

Jayjay

Wednesday, 5 May 1915

The view from the latrine pole was a peaceful contrast to the frontline trench at Steele's Post. Small waves lapped at the beach below and dissolved into the shingle.

Sounds of war were slightly more distant here. Metal wasps zipped past high overhead. Artillery boomed occasionally.

Warships sat at sea like dogs behind a fence and gave a welcome reminder of British might. One fired off a round that whooshed over and thundered into a hill somewhere behind.

Relief filled the void left by the first dump Jayjay had taken for three days.

"You stink Jay!" Larry sat next to him on the same pole perched over a pit, long enough for four or five men to use at one time.

"Queen Lizzie just let go," Jayjay replied, pleased with the timing, although he knew it was a smaller warship than *Queen Elizabeth* that had just fired her gun.

"Imagine if you stopped a sniper's bullet here," Ron sat on the other side of Jayjay. "You'd fall back into the cesspit and breathe your last with a lungful of that. What a way to go!"

"Look at those galahs splashing about in the water," Larry said. "As if they're on a Sunday picnic."

"I was thinking we might take a quick swim after this myself," Ron said. "Especially since there's no toilet paper."

"They say there's mixed bathing here," Larry said.

"I'd like to see that," Jayjay laughed. "There are no sheilas so how does that work?"

"Men and bullets!"

"I'm done," Jayjay said. "See you boys down at the beach. Sergeant Baker won't miss us for a few extra minutes. At least we didn't foul up the trench like those boys from the bush did yesterday."

"Although," Larry said, "flinging the turds with a shovel, over no-man's-land at the Joe Bourkes, wasn't a bad response to their damn cricket ball bombs. I can't believe the brass sent us to dig in here against a defending army with no bombs to throw. It doesn't take great military strategy genius to figure that bombs might help in a situation like this, and the enemy has loads of them to lob at us."

Jayjay scrambled down the steep track to the beach and stripped off. Naked men splashed and lay about in the water in small groups.

One fellow emerged from the water, clutching at a fresh wound on his arm, surrounded by cheering mates.

"Cripes, I've been torpedoed!" he yelled.

Watery blood seeped through his fingers and ran down his arm.

Jayjay felt a slap on his bare behind.

"Are you going in," Larry asked, "or are you going to stand there and pose nude all day?"

"That guy just got shot in the arm while he was swimming, right here."

"You're a bigger target on the beach than in the water mate. If you moon at the enemy you might get shot in the arse!" Larry ran naked towards the water and threw himself in.

Jayjay hurried in after and wondered if the chance of being shot was greater on the beach or in the water. *How far can a bullet travel underwater before it loses its speed?*

The brisk sea felt pleasant on his skin, until it reached the wound on his thigh. The sting brought a fresh reminder of the bayonet wound that he had received from a small Turk. A Turk who had died by Jayjay's hand. An image appeared in Jayjay's mind of the pleading look on the lad's face when the tip of Jayjay's bayonet penetrated his small body.

Guilt swelled within him, but he shook it off and forced the memory away. He focused on the present. Some crude stitches held his wound together and it seemed to be free of infection. It was good to have a wash – the first since landing ten days earlier. He rubbed himself all over and kept an eye on the pile of clothes on the beach that included his watch and wallet. After a few minutes, he agreed with Ron and Larry on the story for Sergeant Baker as to why they had taken so long, and hurried back towards where they had left their clothes.

"Here's a chance for a lark," Larry said. "A British officer is coming up the beach. Let's give him the salute that these guys crave so much."

The officer approached to within a few yards and the three stood to attention, unclothed, and swung up their right arms to salute in unison.

The officer was a short fellow with orange hair, greying at the temples. He paused and Jayjay realised to his horror that the officer wore a general's insignia. English officers weren't known for their sense of humour, and senior officers could make life difficult.

"Been for a swim have we?" The general looked the naked men up and down. "I am pleased to see the water wasn't too cold!"

The general strode off chuckling to himself. A more junior staff officer trailed behind and gave a sneer.

"I'm getting dressed." Jayjay tried not laugh, but failed. "It's more dangerous down here than up at the front line."

The trio dressed and hurried south along the beach towards the mouth of Shrapnel Gully. Boxes and men crowded the narrow strip of sand. Beyond the sheltered cove more space opened out.

"Watch and listen for shrapnel shells on the way back up lads," Ron said as they scrambled up the gully track towards their front line position at Steele's Post.

"Did you hear Colonel Braund was killed last night?" Larry asked. "Shot by one of his own sentries. Didn't hear their challenge and didn't answer, so the bastard shot him!"

"No way, that's a furphy!" Jayjay didn't want to believe it, but the tale had the ring of truth about it. Braund was partially deaf, Alfred had made fun of his old commander from the 2nd Battalion for this reason.

Ron paused and gasped, then reached for his chest. Jayjay looked up instinctively but there had been no explosions overhead, certainly none close by.

Ron dropped to his knees and Jayjay saw that blood seeped between Ron's fingers, still holding at his chest.

"Sniper!" Larry cried. "Get down and drag him aside!"

Jayjay dropped to the ground in an instant. Ron fell with him.

"Em," Ron said weakly.

"Save your breath," Jayjay hauled Ron behind a bush. "You can tell her yourself.

"I'll go for stretcher bearers," Larry said. "Or that bloke with the donkey. You stay with Ron."

Before Jayjay could think or respond, Larry scurried away through the scrub and was gone.

"Hang on big brother, you're going to be all right."

Ron smiled weakly and Jayjay tried to look confident. Jayjay stole a glance through the bushes up Shrapnel Gully to the green ridgeline above. *The sniper could be anywhere up there.*

Pink frothy blood leaked from the corner of Ron's mouth. *I don't know what that means, but I reckon it's bad. I need to get you to a doctor.*

Jayjay dropped his rifle and scooped his brother up like a child, one arm under Ron's back and the other behind his thighs. He found a hole in Ron's back that shouldn't be there and a sticky liquid that oozed between his fingers.

He ran down Shrapnel Gulley to the beach, and tried to support Ron's body to avoid transferring the jolts from each step. Ron lay limp and clutched at his chest near the pocket. A bullet or two might have zipped past on the way, but

Jayjay didn't notice and later could not recall.

At the beach he turned right and didn't stop running across the crowded sand until he reached the hospital tents in the shelter of the cove.

"I need a doctor! Urgent! My brother's been shot! Please!"

A doctor stood over a man lying on a table and looked up on Jayjay's entrance. The patient appeared to be unconscious and the doctor's hands were red with blood.

"I'll be with you as soon as I can. Please wait to the side. We have a lot of wounded here."

"Please! My brother. He's been shot."

"Everyone here is someone's brother, or mate or son or Dad. You'll have to wait and if you don't settle down you'll have to leave. While I'm talking to you I am not giving these men the care they need. There are not many of us to do this work and we can only do so much."

"Please, there's pink froth coming from his mouth. He might die!"

The doctor paused and said something to a fellow standing nearby, who looked to be a medical orderly and looked directly at Jayjay. "Bring your brother over here."

Jayjay hurried over with Ron cradled in his arms.

The doctor looked at the chest wound, opened Ron's mouth to look inside and then checked the pulse at Ron's throat.

"He will be dead within half an hour, likely sooner. There is nothing I can do. I am sorry. I need to focus on men who I can help."

All feeling left Jayjay's body.

I need to argue harder.

"There must be something you can do. He's still alive now right?"

The doctor moved back to the fellow lying on the table and shook his head. "Your brother has a been shot though a lung and God only knows what else is damaged. His pulse is weak and he is drowning in his own blood. If I was properly equipped and had no other patients I might be able to help him, but even then he might not survive. In these circumstances he has no chance. I am sorry, I must attend to this fellow now. I suggest you say goodbye to your brother. The chaplain can help you if you like."

The doctor didn't meet Jayjay's eyes again.

"Are you Church of England?" The chaplain stood at the entrance to tent, hands clasped on a bible in front of him.

Jayjay's mouth was dry. He was still breathing heavily and could only manage a weak nod.

"Follow me." The chaplain turned and left.

Jayjay didn't know what else to do next and followed the chaplain to a small clearing near the back of the beach, not far from the hospital tent.

He placed Ron on the coarse sand as gently as he could and looked into his eyes. Ron stared back, still clutching at his chest pocket.

Jayjay sat and rested Ron's head in his lap.

"Em," Ron whispered, in a watery rattle that was barely audible.

"I'm sorry Ron," Jayjay said. "I'm going to stay here with you." *I should cry out or yell or do something. I should feel something. Why don't I feel anything?*

"You're a good big brother Ron, you taught me a lot. You're a good Christian. Make peace with God."

The chaplain was standing back, but looked to be listening.

Jayjay ignored him and talked to Ron of home and Mum and Dad and Emilia. He talked of summer holidays and train trips to Cronulla beach. He talked of Ron's childhood friends. He talked about exploring the pyramids of Egypt and the damn training routine day after day. He talked about taking a dump together on the latrine pole while looking out over the beach, and swimming, a few hundred yards away from where he sat.

Ron lay peacefully and stared at the blue sky. His hand never left his chest pocket.

Jayjay stared at his brother's face.

He's not breathing.

He's not blinking.

The chaplain ambled over and knelt beside Ron. He reached for Ron's throat to check for a pulse and shook his head.

"I'm sorry." He looked at Jayjay with sad eyes. "He's gone. Would you like help carrying him to the cemetery?"

Jayjay stared back.

We can't just bury him straight away.

What if he's not really dead?

He might come good.

Shouldn't we wait a bit?

Just to be sure?

He opened his mouth but no words came.

He looked at his watch. *Twenty minutes past ten o'clock.* It seemed important somehow to take note of the time.

Larry came hurrying along the beach. "Sorry Jay, I got back as quick as I could, but you were gone. I've been looking everywhere. Is he – ?"

Jayjay shook his head.

The chaplain closed Ron's eyes, then closed his own eyes and bowed his head for a several seconds.

"Fuck," Larry whispered.

The chaplain stood. "Follow me."

Jayjay lifted Ron from where he lay, cradled him in his arms and carried him along the beach back towards Shrapnel Gully. But this time Ron's arms hung limp from the shoulder.

A cemetery had been laid out near the mouth of the gully and a queue of dead men lay beside waiting to be buried.

"I was going to put one of these fellows in this grave," The chaplain said. "I don't imagine they'll mind waiting a little longer."

It's not very deep.

I thought graves should be deeper.

Maybe we should wait.

"I'll help." Larry grabbed Ron's feet. Jayjay shifted Ron's weight and supported Ron's armpits.

Larry stepped down into the hole and Jayjay had little choice but to follow. They placed him lying face up and climbed out.

The chaplain started to speak, but Jayjay jumped back in the hole. "I have to get his things, to send them home."

Jayjay removed the metal shirt badges, identity discs, a wrist watch and the bowie knife their father had given. He systematically checked each of Ron's pockets and retrieved a wallet from the trousers and a photograph of Emilia from the chest pocket near the place where the bullet entered.

"What's his name?" The chaplain asked.

"Ronald Archibald Jones."

"Your brother?"

"Yes."

"What's your name son?"

"Jay – Jonathan."

"We will mark Ronald's grave with a cross Jonathan. I have some timber here," the chaplain said. "Maybe someone will want to identify the body one day. Maybe take him home."

Jayjay nodded slowly. He returned the photo of Emilia to Ron's chest pocket and climbed out of the grave.

"You can throw in the first handful. The men on grave fatigues will finish the work."

Jayjay handed the bowie knife to Larry, pocketed Ron's other possessions and picked up a handful of dirt from the mound he stood next to. The earth was cool despite the morning sun. His hand closed around it. He squeezed tight and stretched his arm out straight, over Ron. Finger nails bit into the palm of his hand. He squeezed tighter, not wanting to let go. His hand started to shake.

A shell burst far up the valley. A delicate white cloud hung in the air and deadly rain fell below.

Jayjay stood unmoving.

Larry, the chaplain and a few others looked on, but no one said a word.

Jayjay forced his hand to relax.

A few grains fell onto Ron's face and Jayjay moved his hand so the trickle landed on Ron's chest. He half expected Ron to spit out the mouthful of sand and berate him for not being more careful, but Ron lay still.

"The Lord is my shepherd," the chaplain intoned. "I shall not want."

Jayjay's hand was emptied, but he scooped up another fistful and the words that he had memorised with Ron, years earlier in Sunday School, returned to his head.

More dirt fell from his hand and he spoke aloud with the chaplain. He tried not to doubt the words, and even felt a vague sense that the Psalm could have been written for this time and place. But the words that left his mouth were as dry as the dust falling from his hand, devoid of life, belief, or meaning…

"He maketh me to lie down in green pastures. He leadeth me beside the still waters. He restoreth my soul. He leadeth me in the paths of righteousness for his name's sake. Yea, though I walk through the valley of the shadow of death, I will fear no evil, for thou art with me, thy rod and thy staff they comfort me. Thou preparest a table before me in the presence of mine enemies. Thou anointest my head with oil, my cup runneth over. Surely goodness and mercy shall follow me all the days of my life and I will dwell in the house of the Lord for ever."

CHAPTER 55

Ishmail

Friday, 7 May 1915

Ishmail waved the flies away from his bowl of chicken broth.

One remained half submerged, kicking legs and buzzing wings in a vain attempt to escape from the tepid liquid.

He scooped the fly up with his spoon, picked it out with his fingers, crushed it and flicked it to the dirt, careful not to waste any precious soup. He picked up his crust of stale bread and dusted it off. Rock hard bread was just as good as fresh when dipped in soup. At least there was no mould on it today.

Fresh bread was a distant memory, made in the village wood-fire oven by his mother and the other women. Smokey and hot. *Such aroma!* He remembered a different life. *A hard life, but at least there was enough to eat, a warm bed and no one trying to kill me. There were so many smells of life. Here there is only the stench of death.*

His muscles ached and hands stung from digging. Always digging. Front line trenches with firing steps to stand on behind earth mound parapets facing the enemy, communication saps running away to the rear, second line trenches, reserve trenches, all interconnected. Always they had to be bigger and deeper and longer.

Blisters on his hands from the first days never had a chance to heal. Something between scabs and callouses covered his palms. They protested with the making of a fist and cracked if he opened his fingers too far.

"Here, finish this." Ishmail's father Hamid had only nibbled his crust and half his broth remained. He passed the bowl discretely to Ishmail.

"You eat it Father. You need your strength."

"I'm not hungry." Hamid licked at crumbs in his flowing white beard. "Better it's not wasted."

Ishmail shrugged and took the bowl. He finished the meal without meeting his father's eyes, and felt guilty for accepting it so readily.

Platoon sergeant Zahid appeared, flanked by the 1st Battalion Mufti, and addressed the newly-formed squad.

Ishmail and Hamid were the only surviving members from their original squad of nine. The 1st Battalion of the 57th Regiment had been reorganised since the first day. Squads were merged and strengthened with new-comers. Squad commanders became Platoon commanders. Platoon commanders became company commanders. Still the whole Regiment seemed to be way below full strength, despite the reinforcements.

Sergeant Zahid was one of the few survivors from their original platoon. Neither he, nor anyone else had questioned the pair's safe return after the time away from their post, but no one believed the tally of enemy kills they claimed. No one said as much, but it was clear by the looks on their faces.

Returning after three days in hiding had been a harrowing experience. On the final day, by some miracle, enemy soldiers rushed past their position several times, once almost stepping on them. Ishmail and his father waited until after dark as planned, then crept past enemy positions behind their hide-away. They came across a new shallow trench that was unattended, but deep voices in an unintelligible, drawling accent announced the enemy was approaching. Ishmail raised his rifle, but his father pushed it down and signalled to run. Both scrambled over the waist-high wall of the invaders' front line trench, and sprinted, chased along by rifle fire.

"There is no God but God," they cried as they ran towards the Ottoman front line. "And Muhammad is his prophet."

Ishmail noticed his father stumble in the dark and paused to help him.

"Run you fool!" Hamid yelled and scrambled to his feet.

Ishmail kept running and yelling. He reached a friendly frontline trench surprisingly quickly. Surprised faces greeted him in the darkness. He warned them that another Turk was coming. Relief flooded over him when his father tumbled over the parapet and groaned thanks to God.

Now, ten days later, Sergeant Zahid addressed the newly formed squad. The frontline trench was deep enough to stand upright without exposure to the enemy. The trench overlooked the head of the valley the invaders had flooded through on the first day, now known as Valley of Fear.

Ishmail sat and listened with his father, a few hundred metres up the ridge from the place where they reached safety ten days earlier.

"Tonight, there is to be an attack against enemy trenches…" Sergeant Zahid said.

Ishmail's heart raced. *Will I become a martyr tonight?* He wanted to be pleased, but instead terror flooded through his body and he wanted to run back towards the support trenches.

"…by the 2nd and 3rd Battalions of our 57th Regiment," Zahid continued. "The attack against trenches facing their position will begin at nine o'clock. You are to provide covering rifle fire and bombing support."

News of another attack was news that many men would die this night. The reality that his 1st Battalion would not take part in the charge took a few moments to register in Ishmail's brain.

Terror dissolved and he felt he might soon be able to start digesting the food that sat heavy in his belly. His father's reassuring hand rested on his thigh, but another familiar feeling grew in his gut, a gnawing guilt he had known all his life. *The faithful man would gladly take any opportunity to exchange this life for glory in martyrdom. The faithful would have courage.*

"Our attack will be coordinated with a raid by our brothers on the left flank, led by First Lieutenant Safvet of the 125th Regiment. The raid will be at Martyrs' Hill on Bloody Ridge."

Ishmail nodded slowly. *Martyrs' Hill. Named for the memory of true believers who willingly trade their lives for a guarantee of God's forgiveness and entry into paradise. Why am I so relieved to be staying in the trench?*

"The raid at Martyrs' Hill will take place at ten o'clock," Zahid continued. "The enemy here at the top of the Valley of Fear must be fully occupied with our efforts. Hamid, you claim to have a good aim. Let's see you finish off a few more English tonight."

Yells from the direction of the enemy trenches grabbed Ishmail's attention. Something seemed strange about it but he couldn't figure why, yelling was commonplace. Then he realised that the cries were in a familiar tongue. Several heads around him looked up and listened to the call.

"…we look after our prisoners." The voice called from the English trenches in fluent Turkish. "If you surrender we will treat you well. Our quarrel is with the Germans, not with Turks. English and Turks have long been friends. Turks were our friends in Crimea. An old friend cannot be an enemy."

Sergeant Zahid spat on the trench floor. "Do not listen to the lies, they would torture and kill you at the first chance. Be careful what you say. They have spies who can listen to our words."

He looked as if he was wondering about his own recent words, more than worried about what others might say.

"Someone throw a bomb in that direction." Zahid turned and walked off.

The 1st Battalion Mufti stepped forward "My brothers, the English are still here, defiling our soil, defiling God's nation! They offend God by their very presence. Tonight some will be called to the privilege of martyrdom, trading this hard life for entry into paradise. Dark-eyed maidens await the faithful in the garden."

Under different circumstances, Ishmail might have grinned at the thought.

"The enemy is here to steal our land. To take what is ours and our children's. We must defend God's nation and God's people, as did Muhammad in the holy wars long ago. God has ordained it so. We may die, but God will prevail. In the end, His will cannot be challenged. There is no God but God, and Muhammad is his prophet."

"There is no God but God," Ishmail said in unison with the others, "and Muhammad is his prophet."

The Mufti commenced the chant for evening prayers.

* * *

Ishmail looked up at the night sky. There was no moon yet, but the stars were bright.

The 2nd and 3rd Battalions next to Ishmail's 1st Battalion had been throwing bombs for about ten minutes.

Platoon Sergeant Zahid walked along the trench with a purposeful step. "Up and start firing Men," he yelled. "Throw your bombs."

Zahid hurried on, repeating the instructions along the trench.

Ishmail looked down at the two bombs he held, one in each hand. He placed one carefully on the fire step in front and examined the other in the darkness. He wrapped his fingers around it and caressed it with his thumb.

The bomb was a perfect ball-shape, the size of an orange. The cast iron surface cool and slightly rough to touch. Much heavier than it looked like it should be. A thing of beauty. Nicely weighted and capable of killing English invaders in their trenches without the risk of line-of-sight rifle fire.

He looked up and could barely see his father give a nod.

Ishmail struck a match and lit the fuse. He waited a few long seconds to reduce the risk of the bomb returning before detonation, judged the distance and lobbed the bomb with a straight arm over his head as trained.

Seconds later, the explosion was barely distinguishable in the cacophony of battle, but it was there.

Another private looked down from the fire step. "Too long, you cleared the enemy trench by about ten metres."

Ishmail nodded, armed the next bomb and lobbed it with less force.

At the time he judged it should be landing, urgent yells in a foreign tongue told him he had dropped it on target.

A cry of "Bastard –" was silenced by a muffled explosion.

"Yes Ishmail! They called on their god, but he did not answer. Nice throw." Hamid held a Mauser in each hand and passed one to his son.

"These bombs are good," Ishmail said. Why don't the English use them? They have such awesome warships, but don't throw hand bombs from their trenches."

As he was stepping up onto the fire step something thudded into the rear wall of the trench. A glowing ember like a lit cigarette coughed and spat on the trench floor. He stepped back down to investigate and picked up a small food tin. It was like the tin of apricot conserve that he found on the dead enemy soldier, and ate with his father when they were in hiding. The spluttering cigarette was a burning fuse.

The fuse was still quite long. Its flickering light mesmerizing. *I wonder if I should wait for it to burn down further before throwing it back. It might be a prank, it doesn't look like a real weapon.*

Hamid reached down and snatched the tin from Ishmail's hand. He hurled it high into the air and it came down in no-man's-land still hissing and spitting. The explosion was close and loud. Clinks and small impacts nearby told of the shrapnel pieces blown from the tin.

"There is your answer son," Hamid passed Ishmail his Mauser. "They know how effective our bombs are, but don't have any of their own. Now they are making them from what they have. Watch out for these, there might be more. They are like deadly black cats with their tail on fire. We must tell Sergeant Zahid of this new enemy tactic when he comes past."

Ishmail stepped up and peered over the parapet. He looked down the barrel of his Mauser and searched for movement.

Cries of "God! God!" erupted from the flanking trenches to the right. Men from the 2nd and 3rd Battalions of his 57th Regiment leapt from their trenches and surged forwards, bayonets leading the way.

He saw an enemy muzzle flash, aimed his Mauser towards it and fired. Men charged into the night. Some appeared to be reaching enemy trenches. It was difficult to tell in the dark.

That could have been me. One day, soon, I will have to run at the enemy and face death. I will die. All men must die. I will claim my place in paradise, in the garden with dark-eyed maidens.

God, I am terrified.

When my time comes, let me die with honour.

CHAPTER 56

Jayjay

Saturday, 8 May 1915

"Maybe Sergeant Fish-face isn't so bad after all," Larry said. "I take back at least some of those bad things I said about him."

A pair of empty petrol tins hung over Larry's shoulders and clanked as he walked down Shrapnel Valley towards the beach.

"I think I'll go to the beach and pick up a few white pebbles," Jayjay said. "For Ron's grave. Make it look a bit different from all the others."

Jayjay also carried a pair of empty petrol tins over his shoulders, tied together with rope.

Sergeant Baker had handed out mail this morning, the first mail they had received since leaving Egypt. On seeing the letter addressed to Ron, the sergeant gave it to Jayjay and put him and Larry on water fatigue. He said that since things up at Steele's Post were a bit quiet, it would be fine for them to stop by the cemetery briefly on the way back.

The unopened letter lay in Jayjay's pocket and filled him with dread.

What will I write to Emilia, and Mum and Dad. Maybe the letter will have some information that will help me to know what to write to them?

In the three days since Ron's death, Jayjay had sat down several times with paper and pencil to write home. But he couldn't decide who to write to first, or whether it should be a combined letter to Emilia and his parents, or what words to use.

The burial had taken place way too soon. This morning Jayjay woke up and forgot that Ron was gone for several minutes, until noticing he wasn't around and then he remembered with a fresh hit of pain.

"Do you want me to come with you to read the letter?" Larry asked. "I mean, I don't have to read it, but I can come with you to the cemetery."

"Yeah," Jayjay said, "let's read it together. He was your mate too. There might be some good news from home. We could both use some of that."

They ambled down Shrapnel Gully in silence and the cemetery drew closer on their right.

"Let's stop there now and read it together, then fill the water tins and grab a few pebbles."

At the cemetery, two pairs of men were digging two fresh graves in a new line in front of the rows that were already full. A sinking feeling formed in the pit of Jayjay's stomach. *Where is Ron's grave? With all this digging and new graves, how can I be sure I have the right one. It all looks different now.*

"I hope the Chaplain made up the cross with Ron's name on it." Larry said, as if having the same thoughts.

"Yeah, what if we can't figure out which one is his?"

"I'll have a look around."

Most of the graves had a timber cross, some painted white, some raw timber, many bearing stencilled labels from biscuit or jam tin crates. Some had names and dates, some had nothing.

I'm so sorry Ron. I've lost you.

"Here!" Larry yelled.

Jayjay hurried over.

True to his word, the chaplain had erected a small timber cross that looked to be made from the sides of a biscuit box. Neatly written in black paint was the inscription "IN MEMORY OF RONALD JONES, 1 BTN, KILLED IN ACTION 5.5.1915".

This isn't real. You can't really be dead.

Larry placed his two tins on the ground next to each other and sat one buttock on each. Jayjay put his tins down and did the same.

The cemetery was not a peaceful place to rest. Men got about their business digging and carrying materials. A pair of stretcher bearers delivered a new corpse. The sounds of war were never far away. Rifles and machine guns chattered away up at the ridge. Deeper rumbles exploded periodically in the distance.

Jayjay pulled the envelope from his pocket and stared at the ink copperplate addressing it to Ronald Jones. *Emilia has very neat writing.*

"Well Ron, big brother." Jayjay used his bowie knife as a letter opener so as not to tear the envelope. "This letter is for you. I'm sorry you can't read it yourself, but I'm going to read it out for you."

He took a deep breath and opened the page to read.

8 December, 1914.

Beloved Ron,

I trust this letter finds you well. I do worry for you and pray for your safety every day.

I have some wonderful news and I will just come right out and say it, I am pregnant with our first child! I have known for some weeks, but wanted to be sure everything was progressed to a reasonable stage before letting you know. I felt a bit sick early on, but not so bad now. I am four months along and our little one is due to be born in early May.

Your parents are well and your mother has been ever so helpful when I have found it difficult without you, although she does look forward to you and Jonathan returning home.

The newspapers tell us little of where you are, but I imagine you will be training in England or fighting in France by the time this reaches you. I cannot imagine what a battlefield might be like, but I am sure terrible things must happen there. Perhaps I am just worrying too much and letting a woman's imagination run out of control.

More men here are signing up each week, so I dare say another convoy of ships might be heading your way sometime soon.

I wish you a merry Christmas, although I know it will be 1915 by the time this reaches you. Do come home safe and soon.

Remember my love is with you always.

Your dear wife,
Em.
XXX OOO

Jayjay's voice cracked and he had to pause several times to hold his composure and read to the end.

His throat was tight. It was hard to breathe, let alone speak aloud.

This can't be happening.

I don't want to be a soldier in this damned war anymore.

Tears welled in his eyes. He stared at the words, but could not focus. A drop rolled down his nose and fell onto the letter. He wiped it off quickly but the ink smudged.

I want to go home to Mum and Dad, and take Ron home to Emilia, and Larry to his family.

Ron is going to be a dad and he never got to hear the good news. I wonder if he suspected? He must have known it was a possibility. How will Emilia cope without him? How can their child grow up without a father?

He thought of Emilia holding a baby on the other side of the world. It could be being born today, maybe it was born on the day Ron was shot. He tried to imagine her face when she heard the news for the first time. He tried to imagine Ron's reaction when he learned about the baby, and how he might have shared the news with Jayjay and Larry and the others here. How they might have congratulated him. Pain stabbed his gut like cold steel and drove its edge up into his chest.

I might already be an uncle and I might never know if it was a boy or a girl. Our family doesn't even know we're here. They think we're fighting in France. Ron is dead.

Jayjay looked at Larry who gave a weak smile but no words.

Larry's not crying.

God, how can you let this happen?

I want to go home.

Ron is dead!

Jayjay rested his elbows on his knees and held his head in his hands. A tear formed in one eye, then the other. A footprint in the dust in front of him blurred and he sobbed like a child.

CHAPTER 57

Ellis

Sunday, 9 May 1915

Ellis fought an urge to lug his Remington typewriter up the near-vertical steps of the Formidable-class battleship *Implacable* and hurl it from the top deck into the Aegean Sea.

Maybe then I could resign from this role of war correspondent and return home to expose these blunders, instead of writing half-truths and lies about the useless slaughter of thousands of my countrymen.

Any satisfaction that had come from getting out the first despatch to describe the landing was long gone. It was over a week ago that he handed over the despatch, and even now, Ellis could not be sure if it had got through. Five days after the initial assault and still unable to secure a cable service, Ellis had left his censored account of the ANZAC landing in the hands of a navy communications officer on the armoured cruiser *Euryalus*. The officer promised to send the message on a destroyer bound for Alexandria or Malta, where the despatch would be cabled to England. The cable office at the warfront was fully occupied with war communications, and could not be spared for a press article, despite Ellis' best attempts to bend the rules.

At least Lester Lawrence hasn't submitted any writing to be censored yet. Hopefully my despatch made it home. I was quite pleased with that one. It's out of my control now, in the hands of Allah as they say in Constantinople.

* * *

Three days earlier, after being forewarned of an upcoming operation by the Commander-in-Chief, General Sir Ian Hamilton, Ellis had landed at Cape Helles, the main British battle front at the southern tip of the Gallipoli Peninsula, and paid a visit to the local commander, General Aylmer Hunter-Weston.

Hunter-Weston was, as usual, the embodiment of optimism and seemed absolutely certain of success. He was adamant that Krithia would be taken that afternoon, and possibly Achi Baba. If there was no time to take Achi Baba that day, he assured Ellis, then it would surely fall the following day.

Ellis felt most uncomfortable during the conversation with the general and could not see on what his optimism was based, but Ellis resisted his usual tendency to voice his concerns.

Hunter-Weston was preparing to host the Commander-in-Chief and had limited time for Ellis, but guided him to a hill above the beach that commanded a grand view. From this location, an artist could have painted an accurate panorama of the whole battlefield, but word pictures would have to do. Crafting vivid word pictures was what Ellis did best.

Beyond the foreground of green farmland and the distant village of Krithia, the solitary peak of Achi Baba stood like an ancient Chinese idol. A great round head rested on two short, thickset shoulders, and two long arms stretched out on either side to the sea. *The old Chinese idol looks to have been placed there to devour in his fiendish grasp, all the soldiers, guns and material discharged from the attacking ships. I must write that down and use it.*

Somewhere on the plain, between the Chinese idol and the English-French front line, lay an army of Turks, entrenched up to their necks. The enemy was invisible. *Invisible to me, invisible to our troops and invisible to gunners on the warships.*

Forces of the English nations held the left flank from the Aegean Sea to the Krithia Road. Forces of the French nations held the right flank, from the Krithia Road to the Dardanelles. *The army of the last Crusade against the infidel. This campaign is shaping up to be about as successful as the Crusades in its attempt to crush the Muhammadan forces. We have under-estimated them again and history is repeating.*

The objective of Constantinople seemed very far away.

The first salvo came from one of the British warships, Ellis could not be sure which one started the brawl. Other ships joined in for a few minutes, then ceased fire and a wave of British infantry surged towards the unseen enemy.

If the ships' guns had done anything to demoralise the Turks, there was no evidence as the entrenched enemy poured return fire into the advancing troops and prevented them from reaching any place close to the first objective of Krithia village.

Throughout the day, the sequence was repeated. Naval guns fired explosive shells at low trajectory towards enemy trenches, but did little damage the Turkish defence and could not slow enemy fire. Land based artillery added some assistance, but lacked field howitzers which, with their high trajectory, were known to be most effective against an entrenched enemy. After the artillery bombardment, a wave of men was hurled over open ground into a hailstorm of metal and they dropped like insects, sacrificed to the ancient Chinese idol.

Ellis witnessed the same pattern all along the frontline, throughout that day and the next. Shells flew, then an infantry advance melted before a storm of shrapnel and bullets. Time after time, the assault achieved nothing more than to claw back a few hundred yards of no-man's-land and to prove the defensive dominance that could be achieved against charging men by entrenched defenders with modern artillery, rifles and machine guns.

The third and final day of the Battle for Krithia repeated the method on a grander scale.

At 10:15am, a tremendous fire from the ships and batteries was released on the enemy's positions. From the intensity of the sound, it seemed impossible that the enemy could have lived through such an inferno. Lines of reinforcements rushed forward behind the projectiles to reinforce the new firing line in anticipation of a general advance along the whole front. New Zealanders, shipped in from the ANZAC front, reinforced the front line, but could not advance. The French, also, were held in check by Turkish fire. By 1:30pm, another two hundred yards had been gained and progress stalled.

An afternoon lull settled over the battlefield, as if a giant game of chess between General Headquarters and the Chinese idol was locked in stalemate. The afternoon passed very slowly, until around 4:30pm when Ellis noticed men from the Australian 2nd Brigade trickling into the frontline. The Australians had been ferried from ANZAC as general reserve for this attack. Committing the general reserve was the last roll of the dice for the Commander-in-Chief.

At 5:15pm, there suddenly burst forth from every ship afloat and every battery ashore, the most stupendous bombardment Ellis had ever witnessed.

Shells of all sizes searched the ground from the firing line to the shoulders of Achi Baba. Smoke veiled the scene and the earth boiled with fiery eruptions.

After exactly a quarter of an hour, as if controlled by a single will, the guns ceased fire for a few seconds. At this signal, the infantry who had been lying in wait and rose as one to rush towards Krithia.

No sooner were they clear of the trenches than the bombardment was resumed. The ships' guns hit the higher ground and the land batteries maintained a white surf of shrapnel fifty yards in front of the Anglo-French firing line.

Somehow, beneath the display of destruction, the enemy remained ready and waiting. At the same moment that the artillery bombardment resumed, Turkish rifle and machine gun fire opened from concealed trenches and generated a continuous roar of their own, despite the rain of bursting shells that fell on them.

All along the frontline, men faced the unnatural storm. On the extreme left, the depleted English 87th Brigade struggled to advance. To the right of the 87th Brigade, the New Zealanders reached a Turkish trench and bayoneted the occupants.

On the right of the New Zealanders, the Australian 2nd Brigade charged at the same moment, but over much more open ground that provided no cover.

A fury of bullets met the Australians, but lines of infantry advanced without hesitation. No man, except the wounded, attempted to return to the trenches although the fusillade of bullets thinned their ranks.

On the right flank, the French attacked at the same time as the British forces. Lines of light blue French infantry charged, retired under a hail of shrapnel, then renewed the attack.

A light blue regiment, the 8th Chasseurs, stormed a trench and clashed with Turks at the parapet. The French took the trench and held it for a few moments, and then a remnant was driven back by fire from another trench beyond.

Poor devils, the lot of them. They all bleed and die the same when their bodies are peppered with bullets.

After an hour, the general attack stalled and the army was a spent force. Little ground had been gained, darkness began to fall and men at the new front line dug for their lives. Come daylight the Turks would unleash hell's fury to drive them back.

Ellis gazed numb for a long time, then sighed and took in a final view through a haze of smoke that hung over the battlefield. What had recently been green pastures of good farmland was now brown broken earth and littered with three days of dead. *So many dead.* Behind the lines, hundreds of wounded hobbled towards the dressing stations. It was obvious that nothing more could be accomplished by using this approach.

Krithia and Achi Baba remained beyond the Turkish lines and looked further away than ever. Now a defensive effort would be required just to hold the new line against Turkish counter-attacks. The Turkish stronghold at The Narrows of the Dardanelles Strait was well beyond Achi Baba, and Constantinople could be no further out of reach if it was located on the moon. *This is orchestrated mass murder. The campaign has failed. Why are we still here?*

* * *

Back in his small cabin on the pre-dreadnought battleship *Implacable*, Ellis stared at the keys of his Remington in the dim yellow glow of an electric lamp. Q-W-E-R-T-Y. Innocuous enough on their own, but his tired eyes traced the keys that accused him: L-I-A-R, then he relaxed his eyes and lost focus. *I plead Guilty as charged.*

It grated against his inner being to know the truth of the situation and write something different. And it was as if his trusted typewriter knew it too and resented being dragged along as an accomplice.

How can I keep writing this commentary without critique of poor military strategy? If only I could resign and sail home. Then I would have to play no further part in this disaster. But I cannot.

He was duty-bound to stay, as much so as a soldier who would take a deep breath and run at a machine gun. In fact, he owed it to that soldier, and all the others. His employers had incurred much expense to deliver him to the warfront and his descriptions were needed for the benefit of the public at home. He also knew that if he turned his back, the truth of the situation might never be known, other than by those who might benefit from hiding it. This prospect upset him most of all.

I will write what I must for now, and record the truth in my diary for later. One day I will publish the truth, uncensored.

Having decided he must stay on, he stared down the accusing keys and picked up a bundle of typed pages.

This despatch will have to pass the censor, so only half-truths will be allowed. Any criticism must be subtle, and buried deep enough that only those willing to dig can see it.

He began to re-read parts of his work:

...From a hill above the beach a perfect view is obtained of the entire battlefield, and it is from this standpoint that I shall attempt to describe the memorable scenes which have occurred during the past few days...

...I suppose this three days' struggle will go down to history as the battle of Achi Baba, but it might well be called the Battle of the Nations. I doubt whether so many different nationalities have ever before been brought together to one battlefield. Side by side in the Anglo-French Army there fought English, Scottish, and Irish Regiments, Australians and New Zealanders, Sikhs, Punjabis and Gurkhas...

...On the other side of the Krithia road, in the French ranks, were drawn up Frenchmen, Algerians, Zouaves, Goumiers, Senegalese, and the heterogeneous elements which form the Foreign Legion...

...But what of the enemy? What was this great army drawn from so many climes and so many nations facing? That was a mystery we were about to solve. Not a Turk, nor a Hun, nor a gun, or hardly even a trench was visible. Achi Baba and his two long arms might have been deserted for all we knew on this beautiful spring morning...

...Our army was drawn up in the following order on this the first day of the battle...

...our ships opened up a furious bombardment...

...our infantry, advancing in perfect order...

...obliged to retire under a tremendous hail of bullets from machine guns...

...But these great waves of khaki never hesitated...

...this battle, which had now lasted for two days without cessation, was continued with even greater violence...

...On the right of the New Zealanders, the Australians advanced at the same moment...

...The manner in which these Dominion troops went forward will never be forgotten by those who witnessed it. The lines of infantry were enveloped in dust from the patter of countless bullets in the sandy soil, and from the hail of shrapnel poured on them, for now the enemy's artillery concentrated furiously on the whole line.

The lines advanced steadily as if on parade, sometimes doubling, sometimes walking, and you saw them melt away under this dreadful fusillade, only to be renewed again as the reserves and supports moved forward to replace those who had fallen.

In spite of all obstacles, a considerable advance towards Krithia was made, but at length a point was reached from which it was impossible to proceed further. Not a man attempted to return to the trenches. They simply lay down where they were and attempted to reply to their concealed enemy, not one of whom disclosed his position. Only a few hundred yards had been won, it is true, but these Australians and New Zealanders were determined not to budge, and proceeded to entrench themselves where they were...

...On the right, much the same scenes were being enacted on the ground over which the French were advancing...

Ellis turned to the final page. *The ending must have a positive aspect. That is what people will remember and that is what the censor will take most note of.*

He rubbed his eyes and read the final paragraph:

Confused fighting went on all along the line, until at 7.30 p.m. the gradual approach of darkness put an end to this terrible combat. Everywhere the Allies had gained some ground, but the main object of the attack had not yet been achieved. Achi Baba still looks defiantly on the plain beneath, and it is obvious that positions such as those held by a foe as indomitable as the Turks can only be won by extreme patience. Our men have done everything a mortal man can do.

CHAPTER 58

Mustafa

Tuesday, 11 May 1915

The procession waddled up the hillside like a parade of geese. *I would love to see a shrapnel shell burst over the whole gaggle.*

Lieutenant-Colonel Mustafa Kemal stood in his headquarters and watched them approaching on horseback. He was very careful not to sneer.

He had known, for some days now, that Enver was coming. Mustafa's connections in Istanbul had kept him informed of this and other events related to this visit by the Turkish Minister for War.

Nine days ago, the Russian Navy had attacked the northern entrance to the Bosphorus Strait, dangerously close to Istanbul. Enver, wanting to protect the capital, was becoming impatient with the enemy presence threatening the southern waterway at the Chanakkale Strait.

Enver had since dispatched three full divisions of reinforcements to the Gallipoli peninsula, including the well proven 2nd Division from the First Army in Istanbul. Apparently he was looking to break the stalemate, starting with the Ariburnu area. Mustafa's information was that the German Field Marshal von Sanders had been talking up the prospects of a victory here with more reinforcements.

Standard negotiating practice for any military commander – create the upwards perception that victory is within reach, tantalize high command with the prospect and entice them to provide much needed reinforcements.

Enver will be looking for a major assault.

Mustafa knew that his immediate commander would be reluctant, and for good reason. General Esat, former director of studies at the War College in Istanbul, was much more cautious. He would resist wasting men from his III Corps. *He knows that we hold the high ground and are entrenched well enough to hold the enemy back indefinitely with adequate supplies and reinforcements. A major assault could leave the defences weakened and vulnerable.*

The procession was close enough now that Mustafa could see Enver leading the group up the hill. Field Marshal Liman von Sanders was half a horse-length behind. Esat was next. The German pointed up towards Mustafa's headquarters.

Enver looked up the hill and his eyes met Mustafa's.

There was recognition despite the distance.

A wave of hate surged up from Mustafa's gut, demanding release. *No, He must see me as a loyal and effective soldier. He was surely involved in sending me away to Bulgaria last time I disagreed with him and the other coup leaders. Next time he might seek a more permanent way to silence me. He tried to have the central commandant of Salonica assassinated before taking power, and botched it, leaving me to clean up the mess. Now he's in power, he could have me killed with impunity.*

General Enver, as Minister for War, held the official title of 'Deputy Commander-in-Chief', second only to the caliph, the sultan himself.

What a farce!

Sultan Mehmed V is a puppet, appointed by Enver and the coup leaders from the Committee of Union and Progress. The CUP runs the empire now.

The entourage arrived and Enver was the first to dismount.

"Mustafa Kemal, my old friend." Enver's voice was warm, but his eyes had narrowed. "It has been too long. Your heroic exploits in defending our shores are the talk of Istanbul. I believe the enemy is well contained here and clinging to the slopes with the last of their remaining strength. They tell me this hill is called 'Kemal's Place'."

Mustafa nodded his head once slowly, not taking his eyes from Enver's. "Your excellency. Welcome to my humble hill, Enver Pasha."

"Can you see the enemy from here, Lieutenant-Colonel?"

"The front line trenches are on the next ridge, the enemy trenches and ours are very close together. They can be seen from over this rise, so please be careful of your visibility if you approach and look over."

"Indeed." Enver made a show of peering out from the lookout. From this vantage point it was impossible to fully appreciate the complexity of the terrain or the nature of the enemy position, but after a brief inspection he appeared to have seen all he needed to.

"I would like to see this campaign concluded," Enver said. "We have won some famous victories against the English. Their Naval attack on the Strait was repelled and, of course, you have been instrumental in preventing enemy ground-troops from reaching defensive forts of the Strait. And yet the English are still here. This irks me. If we can free up our forces on this front, we can move south and expel the enemy there also."

"What do you think, Mustafa? Can we rid ourselves this nuisance? Can we throw the English back into the sea?"

All eyes from the group were on him now. They would have already discussed strategy in a more private setting. There would have been differences of opinion, surely. This was supposed to be a field inspection, not a strategy planning meeting.

Mustafa took a deep breath and spoke slowly.

"With more reserves – at least one more division and more artillery, we could achieve this. We must not let the enemy take any more ground. If we allow our forces to retreat slightly as some have suggested, the enemy at Bloody Ridge and to the north will have a chance to consolidate their position and advance."

Esat folded his arms. Mustafa allowed himself a brief glance in that direction and saw Esat's eyes glaring back, as if they were about to fire off a few rounds in his direction.

"We should select some key enemy positions," Mustafa said, "and assault these hard, day and night if necessary, until we take them. This will allow us to command their lower ground and reserve areas. We could then cause the enemy great turmoil and desertion."

Enver nodded. "And yet, you have not done this already? The enemy has been here for nearly three weeks."

"There have been attempts, your excellency," Mustafa said. "But reinforcements have been limited, as has artillery ammunition. The enemy forces are well entrenched and defend their territory vigorously."

"Thank you, Lieutenant-Colonel. I know you will continue to do your duty here."

"Of course, your excellency."

Enver turned and strode to his horse. The other members of his entourage moved to depart.

General Esat was the last man to turn away. He walked slower than the others.

* * *

Next morning Mustafa received a message from III Corps headquarters. General Esat ordered him to expel the enemy from Ariburnu according to his views. Esat noted that he was seeking additional reinforcements and artillery as requested to support an attack. His message also clarified that his previous proposal to establish reinforcement points at the rear of each flank did not involve withdrawing the forward line as Mustafa had insinuated to Enver on his field inspection.

The old man is a diplomat as much as a soldier. Better that I upset him than Enver. Enver would cut my balls off without hesitation. The worst Esat would do is give them a gentle squeeze.

* * *

A few days later, Mustafa received a surprise visit from a German. Major Rayman was one of Field Marshal von Sanders' many compatriot staff officers.

Rayman came in secret. At least that was his stated intention.

The Field Marshal of the Ottoman Fifth Army was bypassing the official chain of command by coming to Mustafa directly, rather than through III Corps commander General Esat.

"Can you do it?" The major asked. "If we provide you with a full division of reinforcements and the extra artillery you requested, can you push the enemy into the sea within twenty-four hours?"

Mustafa knew he could not back away from the position he gave Enver in front of the other commanders, but he did feel uncomfortable having this discussion with Esat being excluded.

"The time is right for final decisive action. The enemy is reinforcing his position. All of our Northern Group should participate, but this decision rests with higher command. We are part of III Corps and Esat Pasha gives me my orders."

Major Rayman kept the visit short. *It was a mistake for Liman von Sanders to bypass his general. Such a practice can never remain secret for long and Esat Pasha will not be pleased.*

Mustafa composed a report for Esat, expressing the same views that he had presented to Major Rayman, hoping it would reach his commander before the news that von Sanders had been consulting with Mustafa independently. In the report, he outlined evidence the enemy was reinforcing and recommended that an immediate attack should be planned with the arrival of the fresh 2nd Division.

The division was 10,000 men strong, and had arrived at Akbash from Istanbul over the past two days. The men were marching to Ariburnu by a circuitous route, first looping south. English aircraft patrolled the sky most days, and the intention was to deceive enemy aerial reconnaissance into thinking the reinforcements were headed for the southern front at Cape Helles.

* * *

The next day, General Esat's chief of staff, Lieutenant-Colonel Fahrettin came to Kemal's Place with a message.

"Lieutenant-Colonel Kemal," Fahrettin was being unusually formal. "Esat Pasha wishes to congratulate you on your good service as a Divisional Commander and your impromptu role as Ariburnu Area Commander under these difficult conditions facing the initial phase of enemy invasion. He is presenting you with the Sword of Sovereignty Golden Legion of Merit."

"Thank you Lieutenant-Colonel." Mustafa sensed there was something more to this visit than his being decorated with a medal.

Fahrettin paused stiffly. "And now, with the arrival of the 2nd Division to the Northern Group, Esat Pasha orders you to assist the major attack of the 2nd Division by leading the 19th Division alongside them. Esat Pasha will govern this battle front from your headquarters. Von Sanders Pasha has ordered a major advance along the full front line. Here are the written congratulations and orders signed by Esat Pasha."

Mustafa was numb. "Only a week ago, you suggested we name my headquarters "Kemal's Place" and you obtained Esat Pasha's approval. It is shown on all our maps now. Are you going to throw me out so soon?

Fahrettin turned and disappeared down the safe side of the ridge from Kemal's Place.

'Kemal's Place.' But Esat is stripping me of much of my command, taking control of the major offensive and is even taking my sleeping quarters.

The 2nd Division is too close to delay the attack.

The enemy will likely be alerted by us waiting even one day. They are well enough entrenched as it is. If they are forewarned and well prepared, the attack will be a massacre.

Now a major offensive will be hastily organised under a split command with unclear objectives. A 'major advance along the full front line' is very different to the targeted approach that I proposed. Many will die for no gain. Damn Enver and his ignorant meddling.

I cannot stay here now. I will have to make a new headquarters. We attack in two days. This is not what we need. This is a disaster.

He wondered absently if the name of his hill would soon be changed to 'Esat's Place'.

CHAPTER 59

Charles

Monday, 17 May 1915

This stalemate is so frustrating.

Charles scrambled up the steep slopes towards the frontline trenches. The revolver at his hip his only weapon. Carrying anything more was not practical when he was working on the mapping updates.

A shell burst behind him over Shrapnel Gully, but he barely noticed.

The ANZAC force had failed to take control of the heights in the first few days after the landing. Turkish reinforcements had arrived and both sides dug in. The British Tommies down at Cape Helles hadn't done any better. They had landed but were also entrenched in a deadlock.

The enemy was too strong and well prepared. They hadn't given up as was hoped, and were quite willing to fight to the death. They were well equipped and had plenty of numbers.

In truth, the ANZAC men were clinging to a small and steep patch of hillside with their fingernails.

At least our landing went well enough to plan, despite the wind delaying us by two nights. Bringing the covering force in cloaked in darkness proved much more effective than General Hunter-Weston's approach of landing at Cape Helles in broad daylight – what a disaster that was. Thousands of men lost due to his lack of imagination.

Not that that does us much good now. Without control of the heights above, it will be difficult for us to hold on to what we have, let alone advance on the enemy.

A major enemy offensive is coming.

He was sure of it.

The ANZAC intelligence officer Major Charles Villiers-Stuart didn't have any hard evidence of his own, but the Turks at the front lines had become less active, as if they were waiting for something to happen. They must be up to something.

The constant tapping of rifle fire and bursts from machine guns continued. Charles hardly noticed them anymore, but they seemed somehow less intense. Shells burst over Shrapnel Gully and the beach with irritating regularity, generating a constant stream of dead and wounded.

Surprising the Turks haven't had a big push already. They must have been waiting for fresh troops.

Most concerning was the intelligence from yesterday's aerial reconnaissance. The report from No. 3 Air Squadron at Tenedos indicated a massive increase in the number of early morning cooking fires around the enemy camps near Boghali and Koja Dere.

He paused to think of his own flight in an aeroplane from Tenedos. So terrifying and thrilling, something he would never forget. And that was just the flying part. The ability to overlook enemy lines and see enemy activity changed the planning and tactics of war.

The enemy had aeroplanes too, although they had seemed to be less common than friendly aircraft since the landing.

"Keep ya bloody red head down mate!"

Charles resisted the urge to duck his head down, and instead turned to face the Australian – a private from the 14th Infantry Battalion, according to his coloured patch. A cigarette hung from the corner of his mouth and weighed down that side of his lower lip. He hadn't troubled the razor for a week or more.

Charles was careful to keep his voice steady and low. "You might start with saluting an officer."

"Soochyabloodyself," the private spat on the ground. "Bu' don' stan' near me with thad bloody red target on ya' head, lookin' like a bloody king parrot. Johnnie Turk's aim's not sa good see, he might aim for you and hit me instead."

Charles stared back, but the fellow held his gaze. His mates failed in poorly disguised attempts to contain laughter.

Charles shook his head and turned to continue along the trench. His red cap band and collar badges marked him as a Staff Officer. They made him a target in more ways than one, but if he was to inspire courage in the men, he had to let them see that he was willing to face danger himself. The colonials had shown themselves to be capable fighters with no small amount of courage, but they were so disrespectful. That sort of insubordination wouldn't be tolerated in the British regular army. Neither would such an atrocious mangling of the King's English.

His focus returned to the map in his hand. This area was known as Courtney's Post, manned by Lieutenant-Colonel Courtney's 14th Battalion, of Colonel John Monash's 4th Brigade.

At least that private is in the right area. The fellow might be shot dead today or tomorrow, so threatening him with disciplinary action would be a waste of breath. Why bother trying to stop his having a bit of fun with his mates.

The enemy trenches were close here, as close as anywhere along the front line. Twenty yards away in places, across a deadly no-man's land.

German officers had been observed in some of the opposing trenches. Maybe they had a headquarters somewhere nearby.

Charles moved on without speaking further and marked up details to correct trench lines and contours on his map. Every bit of information and accurate mapping might help to save lives and fight off the inevitable onslaught. *The Turks and Germans won't be happy to endure this stand-off for much longer without trying something different.*

He sat behind a mound of earth looking back down Monash Valley and Shrapnel Gully to the shimmering sea. *It would look so peaceful if it wasn't for the menacing pride of warships. A shame their weaponry is designed for battles on the open seas. Powerful guns limited to firing with flat trajectory, capable of sending explosive armour-piercing shells many miles to detonate on impact, but of limited effectiveness against an enemy entrenched on the other side of a hill.*

A small white cloud of smoke appeared in the blue sky over the valley in front of him. The sound of the enemy's shrapnel shell reached him a second later. *Not so loud from this –.*

A bright flash right in front of him and the terrific thunder was instantaneous. Charles right hand grabbed reflexively at his chest, then the pain hit him.

Damn, that hurts!

Everything faded into blackness. Death took him before he realised he was dying, and before he could drag his thoughts back for one last time to his wife Joan or their newborn son that he would never see.

CHAPTER 60

Hamid

Wednesday, 19 May 1915, small hours (from 00:10)

Machine guns stuttered, then stopped as suddenly as they started.

"Hold your fire!" Sergeant Zahid yelled up and down the trench. "Hold your fire!"

Hamid stood on the fire step, beside his son Ishmail, jammed in the overcrowded trench. He stood tall and stared over the parapet towards the enemy. No movement. The moon had set around half an hour ago. The night was clear, but very dark.

A single muzzle flash spat and the sound of a bullet past his left ear caused him to stoop quickly. A second shot might be more accurate.

Whatever enemy activity triggered the outpouring of rifle and machine gun fire, it was not a coordinated attack of any sort.

Nerves were on edge tonight.

Turkish troop movements had been taking place since darkness fell. Hamid and his company had moved south a few hundred metres, almost as far as Bomb Ridge.

They were close to the area that Hamid and his son Ishmail had escaped to in the early days after the invasion, when they left their sniping post and rushed through enemy lines to a friendly trench.

Enemy trenches were close at Bomb Ridge, within bomb throwing distance. Bomb throwing had become a two way activity since the English started lobbing their black cats – exploding tins packed with shrapnel. Crude, but dangerous things that had killed many and wounded many more. The exchange of bombs at Bomb Ridge was continuous, day and night.

Trenches were full of reinforcements. Fresh troops had been arriving for days. A full division had moved in on the left flank at Bloody Ridge after dark tonight – ready for the great assault, but never having seen the terrain in daylight. Word was that it was the 2nd Division. An Ottoman Army I Corps prime division. Direct from Istanbul, well trained and at full strength with ten thousand men.

Here, between Bomb Ridge and the head of Valley of Fear, companies and platoons seemed to be interspersed. *I don't know how they are going to coordinate such a large attack. At least it will be a surprise. Even if we cannot push the English back into the sea, we should be able to take significant ground from them. Once we command the Valley of Fear, they will have nowhere to hide.*

"Night watch duty only," Sergeant Zahid said on the way past. "The rest of you get some sleep. As best as you can. We attack in three hours. Then we will push down into the Valley of Fear and give the English something to dread!"

Two of their squad held their ground on the firing step. Hamid, Ishmail and the rest stood down.

"I cannot sleep," Ishmail shook his head slowly. "Even if there was space to lie down."

"I know, neither can I Son."

"We might enter paradise tonight."

Hamid nodded. He wished it were otherwise, but knew their chances of surviving this night were low. "As God wills. That is always a prospect here."

The two sat on the fire step, backs leaning against the front wall. Hamid rested his hand on Ishmail's shoulder and spoke softly for his son's hearing only. "I would do what I could that you live and return to complete your studies and have a family of your own."

"No Father," Ishmail's voice was tight. "Do not speak like this. To become a martyr for God is the highest honour."

"It is also possible to live with honour."

"I am not afraid to die."

"Without fear, there is no need for courage."

Ishmail looked up with questioning eyes.

Hamid nodded. "I am afraid, but we will charge at the English together Ishmail. Rest as best you can. Think of home and pray for your mother and sisters."

Ishmail nodded and stared at the stars.

Hamid left his son to reflect and drifted into his own thoughts. This was the moment he knew would come. Charging at an entrenched enemy was a suicide mission. He did not want to deprive his son the opportunity to die with honour and enter paradise as a faithful martyr, but wanted him to know a full life, know a woman and raise his own children. Ishmail was his only son and represented so many of his own unfulfilled dreams. Having toiled the hard ground all his life, he wanted more for his son. Ishmail was going to be an architect. He would earn good money and not have to labour with his hands. He would have his choice of women to take for a wife.

The thought of doing something to deliberately injure his son crept into Hamid's mind with disturbing regularity. It could not appear to be a self-inflicted wound, or something Ishmail was complicit in. If he was suspected of self-harm he might be disgraced and executed.

There might be a way, but the risks were too high.

This assault was a big push. A surprise attack of multiple divisions would be unstoppable. The enemy might be thrown into the sea in a great victory. The distance to force them back was not great. Ishmail might return as a war hero.

The English surely could not resist such an attack. Massive numbers of men, all moved in after dark so the enemy would not know what was coming. A surprise bayonet attack an hour before dawn. The hardest time to defend.

At the very least we will tighten our grip on the high ground, and once we command a better view into the Valley of Fear they cannot endure. We will have to be wary of the warships. Those cursed warships.

Hamid's knees ached. There was no space in the trench, but he managed to straighten one leg at a time, and apologise to those he pushed his feet past in the darkness.

He closed his eyes and travelled back to the village where his wife Fatma and daughters would be waiting and wondering. A village of women, boys and old men. He smelled fresh bread, herbs and garlic. He embraced Fatma's soft warmth.

They will be sad, but I cannot rob my son of his honour. Curse these invaders, stealing our land and our peace. Ishmail will be part of a great attack, maybe a great victory, and remembered as a hero. Part of a mighty force unleashed to crush the enemy. Maybe this night will be remembered by future generations, and commemorated as a feat of valour.

Hamid strolled through childhood moments in a semi-conscious state of exhaustion, somewhere between dreaming sleep and wakeful memory.

Father beat Mother for spilling milk, and turned as if looking for an excuse to deal out the same treatment to Hamid, or one of the other five children. Hamid stared at the stone floor until Father stormed out. Hamid stole away to the nearby creek with his friend Osman. Cool mud oozed between his toes. Hamid and Osman had a pretend sword fight with sticks, then Hamid threw his stick at a bird, like a hunter with a spear. The bird escaped.

"Stand to!"

Already?

Hamid stood up against protesting knees and used his height to steal a glimpse over the parapet.

It took a moment to interpret shapes he could barely make out in the dark-grey pre-dawn light. *No. This cannot be.* He felt as if someone had jammed a fist into his belly, reached up inside him and squeezed his heart until it stopped beating.

Moonlight glinted off enemy bayonets pointing back at him. Continuous rifles marked the line of the enemy trench, as far has he could see to the left. To the right Valley of Fear dropped away into the black, but if the enemy was alerted to the left then they would also be alerted to the right from Treacherous Hill to Hill of Valour.

The enemy knows. They're ready for us. The attack will have to be called off. The attack won't be called off. We will be slaughtered. Ishmail's life will be wasted for nothing. How can I save him?

"Ready yourselves for attack." Sergeant Zahid's voice was strangely calm.

"There is no God but God." The Mufti was at Zahid's shoulder. "And Muhammad is his prophet. Tonight we will smash God's enemies like a clay pot. We will throw them into the sea before dawn. Some of you will live to see this and some of you will enter heaven. There is no greater honour than to trade your life as a martyr for God. Have courage men and know that paradise awaits you."

Ishmail nodded and so did several others.

The trench was packed with men now. Mausers had to be held upright, bayonets pointing at the stars.

The enemy trench came to life with the roar of many rifles all firing at once. The deeper percussion of enemy machine guns counted time and the cries of men completed the tragic symphony.

"God, God!"

"God, God!"

Hamid pushed his way up onto the firing step next to Sergeant Zahid and cautiously peered over the parapet.

The left flank at Junction Hill was charging. Muzzle flashes marked the enemy frontline trench for hundreds of metres, as far down the ridge as he could see. Bodies were mounding up at the parapet. Those charging had to first climb over several of their dead comrades.

Hamid turned and looked up the ridge. At the head of Valley of Fear and on Hill of Valour the same thing was happening. It was further away, but the intensity of enemy fire was the same.

He turned to Sergeant Zahid witnessing the same events next to him. "This is madness. A waste of good men. The attack must be stopped. The English are ready for us."

"Have courage private," Zahid said. "This is a coordinated attack. I cannot not stop it. We will enter paradise this night."

Zahid turned away before Hamid could respond, and yelled to the sky. "God, God! Strike, Strike!"

Men climbed ladders and boosted each other off the firing step, up and over the front wall.

Hamid looked around for Ishmail, for a moment he worried that they might be separated, but he was close by. He reached out and hugged his son.

"As God wills."

"As God wills," Ishmail replied.

"Help me up son, my knees."

Ishmail locked his fingers together to make a step with his hands and bent down so his father could put his foot in. He lifted up and Hamid scrambled over the front wall, keeping low behind the parapet as best he could. Somehow Ishmail appeared next to him and before he could think they were charging at the enemy trench.

Ishmail was short, but a fast runner. Everything seemed to be happening slowly, but Ishmail was surging ahead. Hamid struggled to keep up, but sprinted with all his strength. He lent forwards and stumbled. As he regained his footing he looked down to the tip of his bayonet next to Ishmail's pumping feet.

Out of pure instinct, Hamid thrust his Mauser forward as far as he could reach and angled the bayonet down and across to the right.

At Ishmail's next step, his left calf kicked up into the space occupied by the tip of Hamid's bayonet. Hamid felt the blade bite into his son's flesh.

Ishmail staggered a few steps and fell to the ground as Hamid ran past.

Did I just do that deliberately? Was it an accident? Either way it was for the best. Forgive me God. My son has much good to do yet. Please accept me in his place and keep a place ready for him when his time is right.

"God, God!"

Hamid surged forward.

His knees knew no pain.

The ground was uneven, but he hopped from mound to mound with the nimbleness of a younger man.

He was running fast now.

Time almost stopped.

Sounds surrounded him but could not penetrate his being. Noise was intense and nothing.

His own voice was foreign, outside his head.

He raised his Mauser in one hand like a spear, like an ancient warrior from the times of Muhammad, charging to paradise.

"God! God! There is no God but Go –."

"They bought us anew with their blood, forbearing to blame us,
Those hours which we had not made good when the Judgment o'ercame us.
They believed us and perished for it. Our statecraft, our learning
Delivered them bound to the Pit and alive to the burning
Whither they mirthfully hastened as jostling for honour –
Nor since her birth has our Earth seen such worth loosed upon her.

Nor was their agony brief, or once only imposed on them.
The wounded, the war-spent, the sick received no exemption:
Being cured they returned and endured and achieved our redemption,
Hopeless themselves of relief, till Death, marvelling, closed on them."
– Rudyard Kipling 1917[5]

5 Extract from poem 'The Children', from a *A Diversity of Creatures*, 1917.

PART III

The Burning

CHAPTER 61

Jayjay

Wednesday, 19 May 1915, from ~3:45am

"Die Muhammadan!"

Jayjay squeezed the trigger.

Away to the left the old coot holding his rifle above his head, like a spear, tumbled face first into Dead Man's Ridge.

He must have been as old as Muhammad himself. Probably looked like him too with that long white beard.

"Another one down!" Jayjay yelled at the pre-dawn sky. "A dead Turk's a good Turk. Die you bastards!"

Another wave of dead-men-to-be rose from the enemy trench in front and charged across no-man's-land towards Steele's Post. The 1st Battalion machine gun to his right rattled a familiar rhythm and the Turks started falling. It couldn't cut them all down though and Jayjay worked the Lee-Enfield like it was part of his body.

Nine rounds left in the mag'.

Slide the bolt to chamber a round.

Squeeze the trigger.

Watch one drop.

Eight rounds left.

Slide the bolt.

Squeeze.

Another one dead.

Seven rounds left.

Slide the bolt.

Squeeze.

Got another one…

Jayjay had welcomed news earlier in the night that a Turkish attack was expected and he didn't complain at orders to stand to arms at three o'clock this morning, an hour earlier than usual. The brass must have had good information as extra boxes of ammunition were delivered and placed along the trench in preparation.

Jayjay had cleaned his Lee-Enfield by candlelight and sharpened the bayonet while others slept. His pockets bulged with rifle charger clips, each holding five rounds.

Now the latest mass of attackers dissipated like a wave that could push no further up the beach and collapsed one man at a time. Jayjay paused to jam two new chargers into the magazine.

Ten deaths, neatly packed.

Wisps of smoke wafted from the wooden stock where it touched the barrel of his rifle. He was careful not to touch the hot metal as he reloaded.

"How about stepping back," someone behind him yelled. "Give us a go at them. Come on mate."

"Piss off and I'm not your mate." Jayjay didn't turn around, but stood his ground on the firing step. "My platoon's holding this trench. Keep out of the way, or get ready to pass up a loaded rifle if this one jams!"

Jayjay kept count of the men he killed that night. Each one was for Ron and Jayjay decided that later he would carve a notch in the buttstock of his rifle for each kill, as if to keep score. The Turks kept on coming and most were easier to hit than the target at Long Bay musketry training.

Ron's death had taken several days to hit Jayjay, but after he read the letter from Emilia about the baby, anger stronger than he had ever known burned inside him like a bushfire in a summer squall.

Men from his platoon had started to give him some extra space, but there wasn't much space to give while living together in a trench. No one had said anything to him about it yet, but maybe they would soon. *Maybe they'll put Larry up to it.*

Jayjay's rifle clicked and a Turk lived to take three more steps before succumbing to fire from another source. *Empty again.* Jayjay grabbed two fresh charger clips and reloaded, but by the time he was ready to fire again the attack had paused.

No Turks ran across no-man's-land, but plenty of wounded lay in the dark and announced their presence in the universal language of moans and whimpers. *No doubt a few playing possum as well.*

Jayjay squinted into the darkness and saw a body moving as if to drag itself across the ground. He lined it up and fired. The movement stopped. *He won't be troubling us again, but I won't count that one. Someone else might have already claimed him and he probably would have died by sunrise anyway.*

A strange beat drifted across no-man's-land and reached his ears. It sounded like drums and other musical instruments. *Is that a band playing?*

The music seemed foreign, in so many ways, so out of place that Jayjay lowered his rifle and paused to listen.

"These Joe Bourkes are fucking lunatics!" Larry shook his head and laughed at the pre-dawn sky like a kookaburra whose soul had been touched by the devil.

"Come on, give us a go." The voice from behind was the same as before. "I'll pay you a quid for your pozzy!"

Jayjay didn't turn around.

"Allah, Allah!" This time the Turkish war cry preceded the charge.

They must have given up on the idea of surprising us. It is pretty obvious now that we know they're attacking.

The Turks ran, still yelling "Allah, Allah!"

Jayjay and Larry stood shoulder to shoulder, partly side on, jammed together in amongst their platoon, and raised their rifles as one.

Rows of men approached like waves rolling towards a rocky shore, none slowed by the failure of those who went before them, until this charge too dissipated into nothing.

The Turks paid a high price and gained nothing tonight, at least on our part of the line.

Jayjay had avenged Ron's death many times over, but the release he sought eluded him. He stabbed his bayonet into the parapet, turned and forced a grin at Larry in the grey of early dawn. Larry stared back, eyes wide with blood lust.

Jayjay returned his gaze to no-man's-land, one hundred yards across at this point. Not many Turks had got close to the Australian trench. One or two had reached the goal and tumbled over the parapet, only to be finished off with the bayonet. In the middle, the dead lay thick. Anyone who tried to cross it now would struggle to take more than a few steps without treading on fresh meat.

Bile rose in the back of his throat.

Damn you Ron.

Why?

Damn you.

CHAPTER 62

Ishmail

Wednesday, 19 May 1915, pre-dawn

The words echoed inside Ishmail's head, as if sung by a chorus of ghosts.

My mother raised me and sent me to these foreign lands,
Handed me this banner, farewelled me to God,
'Don't sit idle,' she said, 'Work and serve the Motherland,
Unless you attack the enemy you won't have the blessing of my milk.'

The Ottoman army band had stopped playing the popular anthem some time earlier. Ishmail could not tell how long ago. It felt like hours, but the attack had started at half-past three and it was not yet light, so less than an hour in reality.

It must have been that new 2nd Division from Istanbul. No one who has been here more than one day would be stupid enough to have a full military band playing music during a surprise attack in the dead of night.

Damn my leg hurts!

A dead man lay across his wounded leg. *Poor bastard must have enjoyed his food when he was alive. He carries the weight of an ox.* Ishmail struggled to move his leg again and winced at the pain as dirt ground into the open wound in his left calf.

In truth he could have moved away earlier with genuine effort, but he had not done so.

He replayed the attack and his fall again in his mind, and tried again to make sense of what had happened...

He helped his father up over the frontline trench wall and they charged together. Something caught in his legs. He fell and lost his Mauser in the dark.

Stabbing pain below the knee in the back of his left leg rose from a dull throb to excruciating before he could locate his Mauser. He glanced up at his comrades running on towards the enemy and saw each of their silhouettes fall before a hellfire of bullets. Rifles or machine guns he could not tell, but each of them dropped well short of their objective, as if ordered to dive for cover in a training exercise.

Ishmail knew his father was amongst the fallen.

He collapsed on his back and realised he was lying next to a dead man. A true martyr.

I could get up and charge, but I don't have a weapon. Not even a bayonet. A full platoon of armed men was wiped out in front of me. What could I do with my bare hands? I want to fight for God and become a martyr, but if I throw my life away in waste God might not be pleased. It would be nothing more than suicide to limp at the enemy empty handed. Father would not approve.

As he lay motionless, the next wave attacked.

Another row of men, charging for God at the enemy, in defence of the nation.

Rifle fire intensified and a heavy-set man running directly at Ishmail's location collapsed and fell, his chest landing across Ishmail's knees. The man writhed for a moment and muttered something about his mother, then lay still. Ishmail's own screams contributed to the din of noise.

Pain in his leg made it difficult to think.

With no clear right choice of action he lay there and looked at the stars. Dead bodies provided the only shelter from enemy fire that ebbed and flowed with charging attacks up and down the line.

Running at an entrenched enemy across open ground is ineffective and pure madness. Our commanders must see that now.

Another thought pushed itself into his consciousness.

The cover of darkness will soon fade away.

I cannot lie still all day, in the sun, without water.

One movement and I will be shot.

If I am still here when dawn comes I will be as dead as the rest of them.

Ishmail sat up and gave the overweight dead man a shove with what strength he could muster. He moved a little, but didn't roll fully over, and dropped back on Ishmail's legs with a painful jolt.

He tried again, and lifted the knee of his good leg at the same time. *Why does that leg hurt as well? Everything hurts.* The weight of the dead man shifted and Ishmail wriggled out. His calf dragged across the ground and the open wound felt as if it was being seared with hot embers.

He looked back to towards safety and could make out the hint of an outline of the parapet.

I could grope around for my Mauser first, or just start back for the trench? I can hardly move even without it. Crawling back with a rifle would be awkward and make me more visible to the enemy. It's gone.

He rolled onto his front and dragged himself in the direction of safety. Movement triggered fresh pain and he released an involuntary groan. It was an ugly crawl, his left leg trailing like a corpse.

Twenty paces back to the trench by the look, maybe less, but the ground was covered with obstacles. Bare earth was the exception in a carpet of the dead. *So many dead.*

When he was half way back to safety, the parapet was clearly visible in the early grey.

A bullet zipped past and buried itself into the dead man next to him. Ishmail immediately dropped and lay flat. *Leave me be, I'm wounded. That's the rule. I don't shoot at your wounded.*

He counted to one hundred and then hauled himself forward, slower than before. If the English think I am fit and strong the bastards will put a bullet into me.

What if I make it back alive? What will they say? – 'You failed!' – 'You gave up when you should have attacked the enemy!' – 'You lost your rifle!' – 'You achieved nothing.' – 'You are nothing!' – 'You cannot go to paradise, you will go to hell!'

The parapet loomed. A small mountain of earth delineating the border between death and life.

Dawn was breaking too fast.

I need to get over that mound.

"Help me," he said. "Can you hear?"

Sounds of movement came from the trench and then a thrown rope landed next to him, knotted at uneven intervals with a loop tied at the end. A beautiful bloodied lifeline.

He pulled the loop around his body and tucked it under his armpits.

"Thank you brothers. I'm ready. Pull if you can."

Ishmail started to haul himself forward and the rope pulled tight. It dragged him along, sending his face into the dirt. The ground slid past and his flailing arms could not help him regain his balance. The parapet mound pushed underneath him and lifted him up, then the earth dropped away. He fell into nothing. Someone tried to catch him and collapsed, but cushioned his landing on the trench floor.

He lay where he fell and groaned thanks. Burning legs would not respond. Bullets burrowed into the parapet above. He looked up at the dim stars fading in the dawn sky, still there as always, as if nothing had happened. He turned and focused on the maggots wriggling on the trench floor. The fellow beneath him shoved him off and the maggots grew too close to focus on in the dim grey. *Maybe they are coming for me? They think I am dead. They were almost right.*

Ishmail tried to stand, but his legs collapsed.

Someone held him and cried out, "Medic!"

* * *

"You are very fortunate private. God was smiling on you."

Ishmail forced his eyes to focus.

An army doctor stood over him and looked down, the sun shone behind him.

"I will need to clean the wound on your leg and remove the bullet. Drink this."

Ishmail propped himself on an elbow and took the small cup.

"What bullet?"

A sip of the contents burned his throat and sent him into a coughing fit, unleashing new spasms of pain in both legs.

"What is this poison?"

"Cognac my friend," the Doctor chuckled. "The French wouldn't like to hear you call it poison."

"Alcohol? No, my lips have never touched alcohol. It is forbidden. 'Drinking and gambling, there is gross sin in them both.'"

"Yes, you know your Koran, so you know it continues… 'there is gross sin in them both, and some benefits.' There is also great harm in getting shot and stabbed. Brother, you have been wounded fighting in God's holy war, this is medicine. Not great medicine, but it is what we have. I must clean the dirt out of the wound on your leg. This will cause some pain, and so will stitching it up. You can bite the stick. But then I must remove the bullet from your other leg. It is buried deep in the muscle and you will feel pain. If it stays there, it might cost you your leg, or your life. I have no ether to give you. Drink what you can to dull the pain brother."

I have been shot. A sense of peace filled him from within. *I will not be branded a failure or a coward.*

He took a larger mouthful and tried to swallow it quickly to avoid the taste. Fire followed the cognac down his throat and into his stomach. He worked hard to prevent himself from coughing and exhaled, alcohol fumes burned in his nostrils. He drained the cup and held it out for more of the foul liquid.

The doctor refilled the cup and handed Ishmail a finger-thick piece of stick, as long as the span of his hand. Small tooth-shaped dents covered the smooth surface.

Several minutes later Ishmail's head was spinning and he felt as if he might vomit. He lay on his front with the stick clamped between his teeth. *Never will I be tempted to drink alcohol for pleasure. It did nothing for the pain. When the doctor cleaned gravel out of the wound it still felt like a mongrel dog gnawing at my flesh.*

The next stitch tugged at his calf, and throbbed, new pain building on top of the last.

"That is done brother," The doctor sounded haggard, but in a hurry. "Your leg is stitched back together. Now we must remove that bullet from your thigh. There will be pain."

Ishmail made a fist with each hand and his molars bit deep into the stick.

The doctor moved around to the other side of the table and probed into Ishmail's right thigh.

That doesn't hurt too badly. Maybe the French poison has finally done some good after all.

Then a searing pain shot up Ishmail's leg and filled his body to every extremity. A foreign-sounding cry escaped from his mouth and pieces of stick bounced across the ground.

CHAPTER 63

John

Thursday, 20 May 1915

There was a fine line between bravery and bravado.

General Bridges was the most senior Australian officer and news of his death would demoralise the men.

Death was inevitable in war and no one was exempt from the risk, generals included, but John was furious at the waste that could so easily have been avoided. Bridges had been warned, so many times, to stay behind the sandbag barriers. Lessons learnt by the men of Monash Valley had come at a high cost, but Bridges chose to ignore the men's pleas and wandered into the valley to smoke a cigarette. Within seconds, he caught a sniper's bullet in his leg. The bleeding from his thigh was profuse and, as was so often the case, a severed femoral artery became a mortal wound. The general lasted three days, but when the news came from the hospital ship that the commander of the 1st Australian Division had died, John was not surprised.

So many men have lost their lives in this valley, just getting on with what needed to be done. A valley that now carries my name and I will not be remembered fondly for it. They are the true heroes. All the work of the last three weeks, fortifying the trenches, establishing order, evacuating the wounded, organising the defence… They have never shirked, despite exhaustion and constant enemy fire. That is why we were able to hold our ground when the Turks threw everything at us.

From his headquarters, John looked a short distance across valley to the place where General Bridges was shot. Close to that location, another man had recently lost his life. A man never likely to be remembered like the general, but a common private willing to risk his life each day, not in a reckless display of bravado, but with a humble commitment to getting on with what needed to be done.

John was determined that his men should receive the recognition they deserved and had made some enquiries about the dead private. His findings were unexpected, but nonetheless, John wanted to see credit given where it was deserved and would do what he could to see that this was done. Maybe it would come to nothing, but at least he would try.

He shooed away a giant blue fly from his face and re-read the letter he was about to send:

20 May 1915
H.Q. N.Z. & A. Division,

I desire to bring under special notice, for favour of transmission to the proper authority, the case of Private Simpson, stated to belong to C. Section of the 3rd Field Ambulance. This man has been working in this valley since 26 April, in collecting the wounded, and carrying them to the dressing stations. He had a small donkey which he used to carry all cases unable to walk.

Private Simpson and his little beast earned the admiration of everyone in the upper end of the valley. They worked all day and night throughout the whole period since landing, and the help rendered to the wounded was invaluable. Simpson knew no fear, and moved unconcernedly amid shrapnel and rifle-fire, steadily carrying out his self-imposed task day by day, and he frequently earned the applause of the personnel for his many fearless rescues of wounded men from areas subject to rifle- and shrapnel-fire.

Simpson and his donkey were yesterday killed by a shrapnel shell, and inquiry then elicited that he belonged to none of the A.M.C. units with this brigade, but had become separated from his own unit, and had carried on his perilous work on his own initiative.

John Monash, Col.
C.O. 4th A.J Brigade

* * *

Two days after sending the letter to his commander about Private Simpson and his donkey, John hauled himself up the track to Courtney's Post. His lungs craved oxygen, but the air was thick with the taste of rotting corpses and he fought to minimise each breath.

At the firing line, men greeted him with salutes and expectant faces. John couldn't help noticing that the trench floor crawled with giant maggots, but he made a point not to look twice at what wriggled under his boots.

A sergeant handed him a periscope and John peered into the mirror to view no-man's-land and beyond.

Above the opposing Turkish trench, fifty yards away, flew a white flag emblazoned with a red crescent.

"Docteur!" The cry drifted unchallenged over the army of dead. Firing had ceased at this part of the battle front. "Docteur!"

"Hold fire. Proceed with the flag," John ordered without taking his eyes from the Turkish lines.

John sensed the movement of the flag at the edge of his field of vision, and at that instant, all along the Turkish firing line, men sprang up out of their trench waving white rags and red crescent pennants.

"Hold your fire!"

Two Australian doctors, led by an orderly who carried a Red Cross flag, marched slowly forward, having to step over dead Turks on the way. The Australian delegation met enemy representatives half-way across no-man's-land.

After a minute of discussion and gesticulating, Doctor McGregor turned back to face towards Courtney's Post.

"They want an armistice," called the doctor. "For the burying of their dead."

"Tell their officer to come forward," John called back, and wondered what the heartrates of the men in the middle might be at that moment. One nervous trigger finger and they would all be full of holes.

The handsome young Turkish staff officer, smartly dressed, walked towards John. He stood on the parapet above and showed no fear when he greeted John in fluent French, despite hundreds of hostile eyes that tracked the Turk, ready to unleash retribution at any hint of falsehood.

"I have no power to treat," John replied in French. "This will have to be arranged, if at all, between the Army Corps commanders and with property Articles of Armistice. If your commander wishes to pursue this course, he must send an accredited representative, under a white flag, along the beach from Gaba Tepe, to meet with our representative to discuss the matter."

The Turkish officer nodded once. "Yes Sir, I will pass this on to my commander."

"Now you had better go back," John said. "I will see that you have safe passage, but do not linger. You have ten minutes to return to your trenches, otherwise you shall be fired upon."

"Oui. Merci Monsieur."

* * *

Two days after the informal truce at Courtney's Post, John stood on no-man's-land in front of Pope's Hill. In full view of the Turkish Trenches. He stood with General Godley and together they surveyed the crest of the ridge with their field glasses.

The drone of flies filled the sound void left by a lack of fire from rifles, machine guns and artillery.

In places the Australians and Turks shook hands and seemed to be making friends. *This is no good. We should not be fraternising with the enemy. It will destroy the will to kill and should not be allowed to happen. Men ought to be taught that they are to eradicate the enemy like human vermin. If we cannot dehumanise the enemy we are lost.*

About one hundred yards away, a Turk worked at repairing a loophole at the front of a Turkish trench.

"Can you see what that fellow is up to over there?" John pointed at the Turk.

"Yes," Godley replied. "I believe he looks to be fortifying up the parapet! That's not very sporting of him."

John waved to a Turkish officer nearby and pointed towards the Turk in the act of trench repair.

When the officer understood, he immediately ran over to Turk at the loophole and made a display of dressing him down, then gave him a sound belting with a stick.

The Turkish officer returned and intimated with hand gestures and facial expressions that he was very sorry for the act of the soldier that went against the rules of the armistice. The officer then pointed at John's field glasses and shook his head in disapproval.

John nodded in acknowledgement and removed the field glasses strap from his neck, as did General Godley with his own field glasses. Gaining any advantage by viewing enemy position was also forbidden under the rules of the armistice.

The Turkish officer smiled with a look that showed he was pleased with himself and he moved on up the ridge.

"I think we might stroll towards Quinn's Post, and Courtney's." General Godley said. "Here comes General Birdwood. Let us all take a walk with him and keep an eye on the burial proceeding down that way. They can't very well stop us looking about while we are at it. You have a good eye for terrain Monash, be sure to take a good look at Turkish Quinn's. They seem to give you such a devil of a time from those trenches."

"That they do, Sir. That they do."

CHAPTER 64

Jayjay

Monday, 24 May 1915, early afternoon

Sweat soaked Jayjay's back, but gave little relief from the heat and none from the stench that filled his nostrils. Dead men, in their sixth day of lying in the sun, covered the ground around him. Faces blackened and barely recognisable. Gases inside bloated the bellies like leavened bread dough.

He picked up the boots of a dead Turk and Private Timothy Simmonds, another tall fellow from his platoon, lifted the other end of the body by the wrists. The pair half carried, half dragged the corpse to an abandoned length of trench near the Turkish side of no-man's-land and shoved it into what had become a mass grave. The body tumbled and slumped onto the heap with the others.

After the night of the failed enemy attack, Jayjay had told himself that these masses of Turks died to avenge Ron's death, but it hadn't helped. Now, walking amongst them and burying them, his rage faded into an empty sensation, devoid of happiness.

In recent days, word about the trenches was that the Turks had requested a ceasefire to bury their dead. *A good thing too. They stink to high heaven.*

This morning's orders were that the biggest and strongest men were to be selected to intimidate the Turks, let them know that they were dealing with a formidable enemy.

Climbing up onto no-man's-land in broad daylight felt like a most unnatural act, like leaping from a cliff without being able to see what was below. Sergeant Baker claimed it was an honour to be chosen to represent the Imperial Force. *Honour or not, hauling stinking corpse after stinking corpse in the heat of the day is foul work.*

"I'm going to go up and take a look around Turkish Quinn's and Dead Man's Ridge," Jayjay said.

Simmonds nodded. "I'll go down this way and see if I can sneak a peak at German Officer's Trench."

The rules of the ceasefire forbade spying out enemy positions and collecting rifles or other equipment. Sergeant Baker, who explained the rules, also noted with a wink that it would be difficult to stop someone glancing in the general direction of the enemy trenches and taking a mental note of what they could see.

Jayjay picked up his shovel and wandered up the gentle slope of the ridge past Quinn's Post where the strip of land between trenches narrowed and density of dead bodies increased. His mouth was dry, but the stink of the dead was so strong he could taste them. He wouldn't contemplate putting anything in his mouth and his water bottle remained full.

Curiosity drove him on towards the place where the old Turk had fallen while holding his rifle over his head like a spear. The spur known as Dead Man's Ridge lay in no-man's-land near Pope's Hill and came under fire from all directions.

A body with a long white beard lay in the area where he thought it should be. A Turkish soldier crouched near the body and looked to be examining the bayonet fixed to a rifle that lay nearby.

"Hoy!" Jayjay exclaimed. "No weapons!"

The Turk looked up and held the rifle closer. There was understanding in his eyes, but no defiance, more a look of sadness.

"No weapons Mate." Jayjay pointed to the rifle.

The fellow took another look at the bayonet, it appeared to have dried blood and dirt caked to the tip. He nodded slowly and placed the weapon on the ground alongside the old man.

"Babam." The Turk touched his own chest, intimating at himself and then the old bearded corpse. "Benim Babam."

What the hell are you trying to say?

Jayjay shook his head and showed his palms.

The Turk looked left and right, as if searching for the right words.

"Pere," the Turk said. "Pere, Papa."

"Papa?" Jayjay pointed at the dead Turk, then the living. "Your Papa? Your father?"

"Evet," the Turk nodded and touched his chest again. "Papa."

Jayjay stared down at the old man for a long moment, then stepped forward and scratched the outline of a grave with his shovel beside the body.

He started to dig.

The Turk had a small digging tool and joined in without speaking. He favoured one leg. *That looks awfully like one of our entrenching tools.*

Jayjay hacked into the virgin ground without a pause. He couldn't figure why, but it seemed important to give it his all and dig the hole to a good depth.

Maybe it's to impress the Turk that his enemy has stamina.

Maybe it's to let him know that we can outdo them at anything.

Maybe it's just to help the poor bastard bury his Dad with a bit of dignity. I think I would appreciate that if my Dad was the one lying here dead.

The hole was two foot deep when Jayjay stood and looked the Turk in the eye, much deeper than most of the graves dug for an individual man.

The Turk nodded and some of the sadness was gone from his sweaty face.

Jayjay stepped out of the hole, moved towards the feet of the body and waited for the Turk to take the other end. Together they picked the old man up and lowered him gently into the grave.

The Turk said a few unintelligible words and wiped away a tear. He took out two cigarettes and offered one which Jayjay accepted. *It might mask the smell of rotting flesh.*

Rules didn't allow fraternising with the enemy, but Jayjay had seen plenty of others swapping cigarettes and trinkets. He pulled out his wallet and took out the silver shilling that won him a coin toss on the night Alfred McKenzie was shot. He hadn't been able to bring himself to part with it. *This coin saved my life.*

He handed the coin to the Turk.

The Turk stared at the bearded face of King George and then the other side displaying a kangaroo and emu holding up the Australian coat of arms. *He must hate our king, I reckon. I wonder if he's ever heard of a kangaroo?*

The Turk nodded thanks and rummaged through his pockets but his hands returned empty. He grabbed at a metal button on his uniform and gestured as if to pull it off.

Jayjay nodded, but the Turk's attempts to pull the button off looked like they might tear the tattered uniform apart.

"Wait Mate." Jayjay pointed at the bayonet still fixed to the old man's rifle.

The Turk nodded, crouched down beside the weapon and used the blade to remove the button. Some shards of material came away with the cut.

With the exchange complete, the Turk placed the weapon into the trench beside his father and the two men filled the hole without words.

On completion the Turk nodded thanks again.

"Johnny?" The Turk said in a thick accent.

"Yeah," Jayjay laughed and nodded. "Yeah, I'm Johnny."

"You Abdul?"

The Turk made a clicking noise and jerked his head back. "Ishmail." He touched his chest. "Ishmail." He extended his hand "Johnny".

The Turk's hand felt strangely human to Jayjay. Warm and sweaty and calloused like his own. At that moment, the orders about not fraternising with the enemy, and instructions to intimidate them, flashed into his head. An impulse to squeeze the Turk's hand hard came over him, but he resisted it, as if a higher authority, or respect for human decency, forbade such a mean-spirited act.

The two shook hands, firm and fair. While maintaining the grip, Ishmail reached out with his other hand and closed it about the back of Jayjay's right hand.

Jayjay's eyes met Ishmail's and the Turk nodded slowly. A nod as if to say thank you for our help. As if to say that was a good hand shake. As if to say 'I am sad, but do not blame you for killing my father'.

Ishmail turned and limped off towards his trenches. He didn't look back.

Jayjay watched him go, then wandered back towards Steele's Post where his 1st Battalion was stationed.

On the way, a small cluster of officers from both sides stood near a burial party. Jayjay made a beeline so as to walk past and eavesdrop, but at first he couldn't understand what was being said in the foreign language. A Turkish officer gesticulated at the burial activities as he spoke.

Jayjay moved closer and caught what must have been the translation to English by one Australian officer speaking to another.

"That's politics," the officer pointed at a row of graves.

"That's diplomacy," he pointed at a pile of bodies. "God pity all of us poor soldiers."

Jayjay sucked foul air in through the last of the Turkish cigarette. *Exactly. God pity all of us poor soldiers, Muhammadans and Christians alike.*

He made the appearance of helping with the burials for the remainder of the afternoon, but his heart was not in it. He felt sorry for the other Anzac men. He felt sorry for the Turks, living and dead. Most of all though, he felt sorry for himself.

What the hell are we doing here? Killing and burying each other – for what?

A whistle blew and a shiver ran up his spine. He felt suddenly exposed. It was the same sound that sent men over the top of the parapet to attack. Today it announced that the truce was about to finish and burials were to stop.

He walked directly back to the ladder and climbed down into the trench with his shovel. Only a few of those not chosen to participate in the burial activities sat around, the others must have been given fatigue duties or taken the chance to go for a swim.

Jayjay was glad of the respite to brood. He sat on the firing step and took the brass button from his pocket. Strands of thread clung to a small metal loop on the back. On the front the shape of a crescent moon encircled a single star.

Maybe they look to the moon and stars to remember peaceful times like I do.

The silence was broken by the sounds of rifle fire, away in the distance at first, then closer and from all directions.

A deep sadness settled on him. *What was his name? An Old Testament name – Ishmael. The poor bastard was defending his homeland with his father. At least he knew what he was fighting for.*

A whistle blew, a machine gun rattled and his hand closed around the button.

God pity all of us poor soldiers…
God, how can you let this happen?
God, why have you abandoned us?

CHAPTER 65

Ellis

Tuesday, 25 May 1915

The hull of the pre-dreadnought battleship *Triumph* plunged from an angle of forty-five degrees in the air, then she rolled over slowly.

As she turned, tiny men flew into the sea. Some fell, some jumped and some looked to be flung, as if from a trebuchet. *They're the lucky ones. If they can swim I'd give them an even money chance of being plucked alive from the water by a rescue boat. Those below decks will ride her to the bottom and never see the light of day again.*

She lumbered like a giant whale lazing in the midday sun. Her bottom exposed for all to see, bright red as if she was embarrassed at ending her days of active service in such an undignified fashion.

Jack-tars jostled Ellis for a position at the rail, on the top deck of the *Swiftsure,* sister-ship to the blushing whale. The two vessels had been built for Chilli during the Russo-Japanese war, but taken over by the British government to prevent them from falling into the hands of the Russians. They made a unique pair, at least until this day, with no other battleships like them in the Royal Navy.

Ellis slid back and let the navy men take the front position. He had seen enough and it was they who were losing one of their own.

So the rumours about the arrival of German submarines are true. I'm surprised they took so long to get here, with such a large number of the British fleet concentrated around the Dardanelles. The warships will have to scamper now, likely hide in Mudros harbour behind the anti-submarine nets.

The *Swiftsure*, the fourth warship Ellis had called home since the start of the campaign remained, for now at least, a sturdy floating platform on the sea and Admiral Nicholson's flag ship. On the platform, the crew and officers stood motionless for around twenty minutes, watching until the final dive. The navy men removed their hats and stood to attention when the *Triumph* sank beneath the waves in a cloud of smoke and steam.

"Gentlemen," Admiral Nicholson said. "The *Triumph* has gone."

Yes, we did all see her go under, but I suppose that makes it official.

* * *

Late that afternoon, Ellis surveyed the distant hills of Anzac from his new floating home, the battleship *Majestic*. After the sinking of the *Triumph*, Admiral Nicholson, in a great hurry, had transferred his flag to the *Majestic* and invited Ellis to join him before sending the *Swiftsure* away.

Commissioned twenty years earlier, and once the pride of the British navy, the pre-dreadnought *Majestic* was the oldest battleship in the Dardanelles fleet and now she formed the rear-guard. All the other newer warships had retreated as Ellis had anticipated.

The poor infantry watched it all from those hills. I expect they will feel the loneliness tonight. The Turks must have let out a cheer, no more navy guns to stop them advancing down the seaward slopes.

That night, even the rear-guard *Majestic* harboured in the refuge of Kaphalos Bay off the island of Imbros. Phantom submarines were sighted by those on watch, but none materialised into real danger. Next morning Ellis caught a small motor boat to the nearby *Arcadian*, the floating base of Dardanelles Commander-in-Chief, General Sir Ian Hamilton, and his General Headquarters.

On board the *Arcadian*, Ellis spied Hamilton and headed in his direction, then came to an abrupt halt. Before turning his back on Ellis, Hamilton gave him a look of pure disdain, as if the correspondent was a sticky glob of human turd that refused to be kicked off the sole of the general's best parade boots.

"He read your latest memorandum," Maxwell, the censor stood nearby and had observed the interaction. "He wrote in the margin that it must not be allowed to pass under any circumstances. I won't repeat what he said about you."

Ellis was not surprised. He had given the memorandum to Maxwell five days earlier as a test. The despatch was addressed to 'the Press' and gave a blunt assessment of the Dardanelles campaign as a failure that had become a stalemate, likely to drag on indefinitely. *Maybe I shouldn't have written that Hamilton was living in a fool's paradise.*

No, damn it! If the Emperor is wearing no clothes, I will shout it from the roof-top until I am forced to stop.

Ellis was still stewing in his frustration when he saw the *Majestic* steaming out of Kaphalos harbour towards Cape Helles. *I meant to be on that ship, even if it is the last battleship target out there for the German submarine.*

While he waited for a trawler that might take him to Cape Helles and allow him to re-join the *Majestic*, Ellis allowed himself a sardonic chuckle at staff officers of the *Arcadian* all in a fluster thanks to the naval commander Admiral John de Robeck. Due to concerns about submarines, the Admiral had announced that the Army's General Headquarters would have to relocate from his ship to a land-based camp on Imbros island.

* * *

That evening, back on board the rear-guard battleship *Majestic*, Ellis re-filled his champagne glass to the brim.

There might have been some naval rule that forbade holding a farewell party for a ship, in anticipation of her sinking at the hands of an enemy submarine. However, if there was such a rule, none of the officers present in the wardroom seemed to know or care. *It would be a worse crime to leave all this good champagne and port unopened on the bottom of the sea.*

Ellis was used to being labelled as a pessimist, but was not usually given to premonitions of his own impending doom. In this case, it was simple logic, and he felt certain that the end was near for the *Majestic*. They were on board the only battleship in the vicinity of the Dardanelles that dared to show herself on open water. Tonight, she cowered between the shores of Cape Helles and transport vessels. Once it was the role of the navy to protect commercial ships, but submarines changed the rules and this night the liners provided protection for the warship.

"It is after midnight." The Principle Medical Officer stared at his pocket watch for longer than might have been necessary. "And I feel I have saved as much of the captain's port as I can from the watery grave."

The Medical Officer picked up two life-belts, of the bicycle tyre variety, and handed one to Ellis. "Keep this with you. Inflate it by blowing into it here."

Ellis took the life-belt and said his own good-nights. He swayed along the gangways to his cabin, although the sea was calm. The small cabin lay on the exposed seaward side of the ship, and by his reckoning, several yards below the waterline. At the moment he opened the cabin door, he felt horribly sober and hated the cabin that might become his coffin.

Rather than waiting to find out, Ellis asked a marine to carry his mattress up onto the deck and started to pack a hand bag with his notes, diaries and other valuable documents.

He had one foot out the cabin door when tendrils of guilt caught him and he could move no further. *What impression might it create with the crew if they see me preparing to leave the ship before it has been struck?*

Ellis paused for a moment, then turned and left his bag on the mattress-less bed. He departed the cabin in his pyjamas, with thirty pounds in bank notes and a cigarette case in his pocket, and a life-belt over his shoulder. On deck he found his mattress and soon drifted into a deep, alcohol-assisted sleep.

* * *

Something crashed into his chest. *Am I drowning?* Daylight blinded him for an instant. Men ran past. He lay on a mattress on the deck and remembered deciding to sleep there in the small hours of this morning.

"What's the matter?" Ellis called out, to the situation rather than to anyone in particular.

"There's a torpedo coming," a voice replied from somewhere.

Ellis scrambled to his feet and a dull explosion thudded from below the waterline on the port side. The *Majestic* jerked towards the explosion and remained with a heavy list to one side. Then there came a sound as if the contents of every pantry in the world had fallen at the same moment. Ellis knew at once that the ship had been mortally wounded somewhere in her vitals, and sensed that she would not long stay afloat.

Having been prepared for days for this outcome, the realisation came as no great shock. He proceeded to carry out his plan and stooped down to pick up his life-belt, only to see that it remained limp for lack of air. *Fool, you should have asked a marine to inflate it last night.*

The slope across the deck grew steeper and it seemed the *Majestic* might turn turtle at any moment.

Forget the life-belt part of the plan. Get off the ship before she drags you under.

He hurried aft and was swept down the ladder to the main deck in a torrent of human urgency that bordered on panic, then he reached the quarter-deck which was crowded with men. Some wore life-belts and some did not, but regardless, the general mass moved towards the lower edge where men climbed up the side and jumped into the sea, launching themselves clear of the sinking battleship.

A cloud of black smoke drifted across the deck and by the time Ellis reached the front of the throng, his eyes watered and his lungs burned. He peered down through the semi-darkness and saw that he was clear of the torpedo nets. *Not so effective today, the old torpedo nets. At least they won't drag me down from here.*

He flung one leg over the rail, then the other, and made ready to slide down a stanchion into the water, but a human surge from behind shoved him clear before he could grab hold. He fell and thudded into the net shelf where the nets are stored when not out, then bounced out of control with flailing arms and legs unable grip any of the hard surfaces that he crashed into.

From the frothing chaos below, a patch of dark blue rushed up to meet him.

Cool water wrapped around him like a giant sound-proof blanket. For a moment Ellis stopped moving and tried to determine which way was up. He hoped that half a lungful of air would be enough to drag him to the surface, but he sensed he was not moving up or down, and panic clawed at him from within. He imagined an up-side-down version of the quarter-deck he had just leapt from coming down through the water, dragging him down and trapping him at the sea floor like a rat under a bucket.

His legs kicked and his arms flailed, propelling him towards what he hoped was daylight. Air trickled from his mouth and at the moment he felt he might no longer be able to prevent himself from sucking in two lungsful of seawater, his head broke through the surface and the sound-proof blanket was ripped away from his ears. Sweet oxygen poured into his lungs.

Ellis wiped the water from his eyes, breathing heavily, and realised he still clung to an airless life-belt. The water about him was as crowded as the deck he had just left and it foamed with activity. Some men swam deliberately towards a small boat that bobbed few yards away, already overloaded and threatening to dip under herself. Some men splashed with the pathetic desperation of those who could not master the simple physical motion to keep their head above water and swim a short distance to safety.

He discarded the life-belt and was surprised to see it's limp form float to the surface. Determined to stay afloat himself, he dog-paddled to the boat and clutched at the gunwale.

All his strength was required to hang on. To the left and right others clambered at the boat, but it was impossible to climb on board. He looked around at the *Majestic* which was lying only a few yards away at a steep angle. *If she turns over, our boat will likely be dragged under with her.*

He wondered whether it might be safer to let go and swim away, then his foot discovered a man-grip, a small slit in the keel to provide something to hang onto in the event of the boat turning over. The foot-hold allowed Ellis to rest a moment and consider the options, but before he knew it a sailor hauled him from the water and into the crowded cutter. Ellis lost skin on the way, but was too pleased at being out of the water to care.

More men clung to the gunwale, but there was no more space on the boat. The *Majestic* now had such a list to the port side that it would be impossible to stand on her deck. Many of the crew still hung on to the rails or clung to her side, refusing to part company. All around the sea was full of men, some struggling to stay afloat. Nearby transport vessels were lowering boats.

Without warning, the *Majestic* rolled over to the port side and proceeded to sink like a great stone in a swirl of water and steam. As she turned over, a sailor ran the whole length of her green keel, from aft to bow. Luckily for this fellow, the bow must have rested on a sandbank and he was able to sit astride the ram, which remained the only part of the old battleship above the water's surface, until he was rescued without getting wet. Others who remained on board, or tangled in the torpedo nets, were not so fortunate.

Within minutes a steam pinnace came alongside and took Ellis, along with ninety-three other men, from the cutter that was intended to carry thirty.

The rescued men, looking more like drowned rodents, were dumped on a French transport vessel and the pinnace steamed off in search of more survivors.

* * *

Four days later Ellis sailed into port at Malta, still wearing the blue trousers and white shirt of the French naval uniform that he was given on being rescued. His worldly possessions consisted of thirty pounds in bank notes, a cigarette box loaded with French tobacco and a clean pair of pyjamas.

In the belief that most things can be replaced, Ellis was thankful that he had not gone down with the *Majestic* and come to a watery end, but the loss of his diaries and notes did upset him. They were a key part of his plan to keep a record of the truth. If only he had he taken the bag that contained them onto the deck with the mattress he might still have these documents in his possession, but he had not done so and they were gone.

After his rescue, without consulting the disagreeable staff of the Dardanelles General Headquarters, Ellis had approached Admiral de Robeck for permission to go to Malta to get a fresh outfit and replace various items of his kit. The prospect of writing anything of substance without his beloved Remington typewriter was not something Ellis wished to contemplate. Next day, Ellis boarded the store-ship *Baron Ardrossan* bound for Malta.

On arrival at the British Navy Port at Malta, Ellis went to see Admiral Limpus who had been one of the few fellow pessimists prior to the Gallipoli landings. The admiral was out, but his Staff Captain Congreve gave Ellis the necessary pass for him to go ashore. Ellis checked himself into the Osborne Hotel and went in search of replacement clothes and equipment.

After spending the afternoon combing the wares of Malta, Ellis could see that he would not be able to find many of the things he wanted there, and certainly not a typewriter of the quality that he required.

Back at the Osborne Hotel a message was waiting on his return, from the Governor of Malta, that Ellis was not to send any cables from Malta without his express sanction.

Ellis allowed himself a chuckle at the thought of the Dardanelles General Headquarters staff learning that Admiral de Robeck had granted Ellis leave to Malta without consulting them. *General Hamilton must have blown steam out his ears and bloody Braithwaite probably exploded like an Anzac jam-tin bomb.*

Another fact that Ellis had learned during the afternoon was that a French message boat was leaving for Marseilles on the following day.

Now I'm off the leash, maybe I could make a brief visit to England? I could re-equip myself there and tell a few hard truths to some people in high places. No need to send a cable if I can go there myself.

CHAPTER 66

John

Wednesday, 2 June 1915

"Colonel Monash, Officers, N.C.O.s and men of the 4th Infantry Brigade! I have come here today to tell you all with what great pride and satisfaction I have watched your performances during the past five weeks, and to tell you also that not only your comrades in this division, but also those of the whole Australian Army Corps have looked on with the greatest admiration at your gallant doings from the moment you landed on the Gallipoli Peninsula. You have been for five weeks continuously in the front trenches fighting particularly hard the whole of that time. Never have troops been subjected to such heavy shell and rifle-fire, not to speak of the bombs and hand-grenades, and you have lived and fought in a din and turmoil which would have sorely tried many men indeed. You began your fighting immediately on landing, pitchforked, I might say, into the middle of the battle, with the whole brigade scattered in small fragments along the firing-line, as the various units landed. You were in the firing line continuously for five days with nothing but what you carried on you. It took days of hard work on the part of the brigadier and his staff to collect the battalions together and consolidate the section of defence allotted to this brigade. During this time many acts of heroism, many acts of gallantry, were performed which will remain unknown and go unrewarded, and there were many of your comrades killed and wounded."

John Monash worked his pencil as fast as he could, to keep a record in his notebook of the rare praise from his division commander. The British General Godley barely paused for a breath.

"Again on 2 and 3 May," General Godley continued, "this brigade undertook a sortie in force from its lines, which was very far reaching in its results, operations on your part which shattered the enemy plans for a combined assault most effectually. Again on 9 May this brigade made another highly successful sortie, and only a few days ago during the greater part of 18 and 19 May you bore the brunt of the very severe Turkish attacks by which the enemy hoped to drive this Army Corps into the sea."

The attack of 2 May was a perfect disaster. Many men were lost and no ground gained. That attack should never have gone ahead and I said as much beforehand.

"Yours is a fine record and one of which you yourselves and the whole of Australia have the fullest reason to be proud. You have made and are making the military history of Australia – a military history equal to that of any other brigade or body of troops in the Empire or in the world – and you have performed deeds and achieved successes of which the Commonwealth have the fullest reason to be proud."

Where is our press-man Charles Bean? I wish he was here to listen and record this. Probably off with his beloved 1st Division somewhere.

"Pope's Hill position," General Godley continued, "is named after the gallant commander of your 16th Battalion; Courtney's Post will forever be associated with the 14th Battalion, which has defended it against all attacks for the whole period. To the most difficult post of all, Quinn's Post, is named after Major Quinn, who bravely died at his post in the service of his country, and who, I am sure, would have preferred no more glorious death."

"He might have preferred to have lived on a bit longer." The voice in the crowd triggered a local murmur of laughter. John looked up, but the general did not appear to have heard and continued.

"Among so many whose names are worthy of record and distinction, it has been very hard to single out individuals, but as commander of this division I have had the honour of sending on the names of some twenty officers and men, from that of your brigadier downwards, for special and honourable mention in dispatches for most meritorious service and conspicuous gallantry. It has pleased His Majesty, the King to confer upon this brigade, two Distinguished Service Orders, two Military Crosses, and seven Distinguished Conduct Medals. Those rewards between the landing of this brigade on 25 April and 5 May are surely a grand and enviable record.

"I am sure now that you will soon be wanting to get back to the front line, after you have had a little while to reorganise and refit. I am glad to have had this opportunity of meeting you and sincerely thanking all for the gallant work you have done.

"On behalf of the Imperial Government, because of the great services you have rendered to the glory of the Empire, greater services than you probably yourselves realise, I thank you Colonel Monash, your staff, your commanding officers and all your personnel from the highest to the lowest, for the work you have done during the past five weeks."

John looked up and nodded in recognition of the mention of his name, but to be sure he captured the full speech, he kept writing for a minute after General Godley had finished addressing the men. By the time John pocketed his pencil, Godley had disappeared.

I think I shall send a copy of Godley's speech to Vic and see if she can use it to raise our profile at home.

It's an embarrassment that our general has taken five weeks to make the effort to meet his troops. He only has two brigades. This is half of his command, and our brigade has done the lion's share of the work. Less than half of the originals are left to receive his thanks.

John wondered whether the men might be becoming cynical. They were intelligent enough to see the disconnect between the general's generous words of this morning and his usual absence. A scrappy looking lot they were, most unshaven for weeks, but John could not wish for better fighting men to have under his command. They were loyal to the death, but beyond being impressed by a man for the mere fact that he bore the rank of general in the British Army.

At a nod from John, battalion commanders dismissed their companies and the men began to disperse towards the upper reaches of Reserve Gully.

A few days earlier, the 4th Brigade had handed over the head of Monash Valley to the 1st Light Horse Brigade, commanded by Colonel Harry Chauvel. The troops of the light horse had arrived recently from Egypt without their horses and were deployed as infantry. The 4th Brigade was then able to withdraw from the front line for a few days of rest in Reserve Gully. Wedged between The Sphinx and Plugge's Plateau, Reserve Gully was crowded, but steep cliffs gave shelter from enemy fire in all the important directions. The lower reaches of the valley opened out onto North Beach.

Between piles of boxes stacked at the back of the beach, a lanky bespectacled man with red hair strode from the direction of Anzac Cove and paused to gaze up Reserve Gully, then lowered his head and started to climb up the valley.

Speak of the devil! It's about time he started to show a bit of interest in my 4th Brigade. Our lamp has been hidden under a bushel for too long.

John collected his thoughts for an encounter he had been contemplating for some time and started down the steep track. Etiquette would dictate that the discussion he was about to have should be held in private, but all was fair in war. It wouldn't hurt to let some of his men see that their brigadier cared enough to go into battle for them. They would spread the word amongst their mates.

"Bean," Monash called when the Australian war correspondent was within hearing. "What's all this dribble you have been writing about the 4th Brigade? I thought your job was to report the facts!"

Bean ignored the stab until he looked up and saw that it was John who delivered it, then he looked about like a cornered cat.

That reporter doesn't like the idea of an Australian brigade being led by a Jew with a German bloodline. He doesn't trust me and I don't trust him, but I have to use him.

Bean spent most of his time with troops of the Australian 1st Division and this showed in the reporting. John didn't plan to let the bias go unnoticed.

"I have reported the facts," Bean replied in a calm voice, "as accurately as I am able, in relation to all the Australian soldiers, not just the 4th Brigade."

"You spend all of your time with the Australian 1st Division and your reports are biased towards the achievements of its 1st, 2nd and 3rd Brigades."

"I seem to be here with the 4th Brigade now."

"You have misrepresented our role!" John raised his voice. "Your article about the Turkish attack on Quinn's Post claimed that it was held by the second contingent, 'who with the exception of the first few days of the Landing, had been subject to probably the severest strain of any portion of the force.' On several occasions you have gone out of your way to emphasise that the troops of the 4th Brigade did not take part in the first landing. This is simply incorrect. Three of our four battalions landed on the first day and were flung into the fray with units sent to positions all along the firing line. If you had been here a few minutes earlier you would have heard it from a British General's mouth, maybe then you would believe it. I am not sure quite how else to get you to see the truth of it as you don't often come by our way."

"My role is to report the facts for the Australian people at home, not to promote the exploits of a particular unit or officer. As part of the New Zealand and Australian Division, your brigade landed after the covering force and the rest of the 1st Australian Division."

"The people at home," John thrust his chin forward with an air if righteous indignation, "have been led to believe that the only activity of any significance took place on the day of the landing, thanks to the dramatic exposition by your colleague Ellis Ashmead-Bartlett. That was only one day, and we were a part of that day, but then we stayed here and worked methodically for weeks to fortify our position and hold the line. These men lived in squalor and nearly dropped from exhaustion, but they continued nonetheless. They worked like beasts and suffered heavy losses. We fought off a massive attack by the Turks and our defence was unyielding. Don't you think the Australian people might like to know about that?"

"I have written a piece on the Turkish attack of 19 May, and the armistice."

"You didn't trouble yourself to come and see me or any of my staff for a week after the attack. Tell me, where did you find your facts? Does your piece mention the role of the Australian 4th Infantry Brigade in holding the most advanced Australian position that bore the brunt of the Turkish onslaught?"

"All my work is reviewed by the censor for accuracy before it is sent."

"The censor wasn't here either. I am not sure how he would know whether your reports are accurate. You might consider asking an eyewitness."

"I am here to report the facts Colonel, not embellish them." Bean paused, as if considering a further response, but turned without another word and started down the hill.

John watched him go and maintained his best look of disdain for several seconds, then turned himself and began the climb up Reserve Gully to his headquarters. He did not meet the eyes of any of his men who stood within earshot. He would appear oblivious to them, but at the edge of his field of vision he observed that several of the men had paused to watch the confrontation with Bean. Word of it would spread through the ranks and foster loyalty.

Loyalty is essential in war.

CHAPTER 67

Jayjay

Saturday, 5 June 1915

The waiting is the worst part. The uncertainty of it.

A crescent moon waxed, a few days from new, and gave the barest hint of light. *Just like the thin crescent moon on my Turkish button. A good thing as light would favour the enemy this night.*

Jayjay fingered the smooth metal of the Turkish button, but he dared not remove it from his pocket. *If I drop it now, I'll never see it again.*

"Funny," Larry said with a taste of sarcasm. "Orders to attack an invisible laughing Turk before moonrise. In case the genius at Division H.Q. who came up with this plan didn't notice, the moon is, in fact, already up!"

"Any sign of fire from the machine gun yet?" Jayjay asked.

"None." Larry stepped down from the firing step. "I don't know what those Moari-landers are complaining about. There are no laughing Turks around here tonight."

Several others had made the same observation: the machine gun that was claimed to be harassing the trenches to the north wasn't firing from where it was supposed to be.

Earlier, some New Zealanders had taken control of Turkish Quinn's Trench, opposite Quinn's Post. Orders were that the captured trench should be held at all costs, but there was trouble with enfilading machine fire from the direction of German Officers' Trench.

German Officers' Trench was the Turkish position that lay opposite Steele's Post, so the responsibility for silencing the machine gun fell to the 1st Battalion who manned Steele's Post.

A stealth attack earlier in the night, by a small group armed with high explosive gun cotton, had failed. Orders followed from Division Headquarters that a larger raid of one hundred men should be launched before moonrise.

"Forget the moon," Jayjay said. "If they don't get those engineers back here with their gun cotton soon, the sun will be up. It's nearly three o'clock."

"Stand to arms!" Sergeant Baker called. "New orders lads, we're going over the top in a few minutes. Fix bayonets, listen for the whistle to go. Take the machine gun if you can, otherwise just do as much damage as possible to the trench and overhead cover."

"Where are the engineers?" Larry asked. "And the explosives?"

"We're going without them, they aren't here. We'll do what we can with our rifles."

"But how can we destroy a machine gun without gun cotton?"

No answer.

Sergeant Baker moved further along the trench to repeat the orders and men clicked bayonets into place over the muzzles of their Lee-Enfields.

Jayjay shook his head in the darkness. *This must be the most poorly organised war in the history of war.*

He secured his bayonet. Moonlight danced on the freshly sharpened edge.

Ten bullets in the magazine, ready to kill.

Keep count and save them as long as possible.

No damned explosives to do the real work.

Spare charger clips in the webbing pouches in case they are needed.

Pausing to reload might cost you your life.

Bowie knife on the hip.

Mind your footing while running in the dark.

He stood in line with the others and checked that the Turkish button was still in his pocket. His heart pounded, as if he had already been running. He needed to urinate, but only managed to squeeze out a few drops onto the trench floor.

If only Ron was here.

If only we could go back and not volunteer for this stupid war.

Blazes Ron, why did you have to go and get yourself shot.

I would swap with you if I could. God why won't you let me swap with Ron. I would do it. Please look after Emilia and his little child. If only I could go back and stop him from getting shot. If I could have got him to the doctor quicker. Maybe argued harder that the doctor should help him.

God please let me wake up from this nightmare.

If only I could have saved him.

Then he would be here with us. Maybe he would cop it now instead, chasing after a machine gun that doesn't –.

A shrill whistle blast cut through the night air like a blade.

Men scurried up the ladders and charged forwards.

Jayjay had to wait for three others for his turn at the ladder, then he followed Larry up.

In the early days, it seemed safer to hang back and not go over first, but he had since learned that the opposite was true. The first ones had the element of surprise and could cover some ground before the enemy knew of their approach.

Once alerted by the steps and yells, the enemy was better able to fire at those who followed.

Jayjay stepped off the top of the ladder and sprinted. A few men lay rolling on the ground not far out, their forms barely visible in the dark. He pumped his legs as hard as he could but something caught one of his feet and felt as if it might rip his leg off.

He fell like a tree to the axeman. Both hands clung to the Lee-Enfield and he fought to keep the bayonet away from himself as he fell, instead his face dragged across the stony ground of no-man's-land.

Have I been hit? Is this the end? I thought it might hurt more.

He lay stunned for a moment. Wire pulled against the pain in his ankle.

That's our wire. I have tripped over our own wire.

He kicked out of the wire, scrambled to his feet and charged into the darkness.

The front runners in the race had already reached the finish line. Turkish rifles spat fire along the enemy trench and somewhere in the distance a machine gun rattled a familiar percussion. *God, please let that be one of ours.*

Jayjay sprinted across the fifty yards of no-man's-land and caught up with the raiding party who spread left and right along the enemy front line in search of the mystery machine gun. The enemy parapet was heavily sandbagged, and studded with loopholes. The roof was fortified with logs and bayonets jabbed outwards between the gaps. One spat fire at a raider trying to lift a log and the fellow collapsed onto the trench roof.

Another man cried out, dropped his rifle and clutched at his arm.

Jayjay hunched over, hurried to the nearest loophole and crouched beside it. Likely a Turk sat inches away, waiting to fire out the small opening in the steel plate.

Jayjay checked he had a round chambered and safety catch off. In one smooth movement he swung his rifle around, jammed the bayonet into the loophole to the hilt, and pulled the trigger. Immediately he pulled it back and dropped back down beside the loop hole.

No machine gun here, but maybe I'll hit a rifleman in the trench.

He repeated the action of firing into the loophole and was considering whether he should venture further afield when a bomb dropped out of the loophole and landed near his feet.

A cricket ball bomb. Maximum fuse time four seconds.

An orange glow from the spitting fuse gave enough light for Jayjay to see one inch of fuse left to burn. It was barely enough, but he had no time to think. He reached down, snatched the bomb from where it lay and flung it back through the loophole. Any delay from a fumble would likely have taken his hand off or worse, but not this night.

Instead he heard unintelligible yells of high pitched panic from inside the covered trench, then a muffled blast.

The yelling stopped and a wisp of smoke drifted out the loophole.

A swam of hot metal wasps zipped past. *Machine gun. They know we're here now. We can't stay much longer and live.*

Jayjay dove to the ground and raised is head only enough to look around.

Others kicked at the sandbag parapet, but the structure resisted.

A bomb exploded somewhere close, this one outside the trench.

"Fall back," someone yelled.

"The machine gun's down. Get back!"

Others started running back towards the home trench.

Men ran in all directions.

Maybe I will survive this night after all.

"Fall back!" Jayjay repeated the cry, leapt up and started to run away from the enemy trench.

Metal wasps filled the air. Some sounded too close, but the friendly parapet loomed as a faint outline in the dark and he tumbled over unscathed.

Larry dropped on top of him and laughed.

"Nice Jay! I saw you return the bomb. Blew those Turks to Muhammadan kingdom come!"

Jayjay's heart pounded in his chest and he sucked in the cool night air. He reached into his pocket and felt the Turkish button. *Still there. I wonder if it might have been Ishmael that I blew up tonight. I hope not, that would be a shame.*

"I never thought I'd be so happy to be in this shitty trench." Jayjay released his own laugh and checked his watch. "I feel so alive. That little outing took less than ten minutes, and I reckon I just aged ten years."

"Better that than the alternative," Larry said. "I saw at least two of our boys we left behind for dead. We're mad bastards doing this. Fair dinkum! Certifiable stark raving bloody lunatics."

"I heard someone yell the machine gun was down," Jayjay said. "I don't know how they could tell in the dark, especially without explosives."

"Ah, we'll never know," Larry said. "We were all over the place like a mad woman's breakfast, but why let the truth get in the way of a good story. Tonight the 1st Battalion raided the German Officers' Trench and destroyed a laughing Turk. Young Jonathan Jones should be mentioned in the dispatches for killing ten Joe Bourkes with their own cricket ball bomb. You might be a contender for a DCM."

"I wouldn't mind a 'Don't Come Monday' letter, just like I got from the timber yard. Send me home. Thanks Mr Jones for all your good work, but your services are no longer required here."

"Sorry old chum," Larry said. "No can do, I'm talking about a Distinguished Conduct Medal."

"I don't think so. No one else saw what happened, except you. What good would a medal do me anyway? Come Monday, I'm still here with you lot, complaining about the bloody flies, the bloody heat, the bloody lice, the bloody stink, the bloody food, the bloody digging, and the bloody King's Royal navy that pissed off and left us here to die."

Jayjay looked up into the sky. A crescent moon hung in the same place where it was before the raid.

What did that achieve? Even if a machine gun was destroyed, it can be replaced easily enough. Good men died tonight. Larry's right, this is madness.

I'm still alive. For now.

Ron is still dead.

CHAPTER 68

Ellis

Thursday, 10 June 1915

The English war correspondent Ellis Ashmead-Bartlett covered his mouth with his hand and swallowed a yawn, induced by good food, good wine and boring conversation.

Why do women feel it necessary to discuss changes in the weather or the latest fashions when the country is at war? Maybe coming here was a mistake. Winston hasn't said a word. He looks pale, and years older than when I saw him last, as if he is yesterday's man. He has no one to blame but himself. He ought to snap out of this depressed state. If he had only curbed his impetuosity and listened to his advisors, he would still be First Lord of the Admiralty. A war correspondent who has seen a few wars and written a war novel does not automatically know enough to create history single-handed.

The dining party sat at a long table, hosted by Lady Churchill, Winston's mother, widow to Lord Randolph Churchill, former Chancellor of the Exchequer and late Tory radical. Ellis allowed his mind to lose focus on the tedium and drift over some of the frantic activity of the past four days since he had completed his journey from the Gallipoli battlefront to London. He was pleased that interest at home remained high in the Dardanelles campaign.

As usual in London, factions and partisan intrigue stifled the ability of the Government to make a decision. Many from both sides of politics had approached Ellis for information and were ready to use the Dardanelles situation for their personal advantage. Ellis decided early on to limit his meetings to members of Cabinet and the War Office, in the hope that this might allow him to provide the truth to decision makers without it being misused.

In his meetings so far, he had observed an air of determination to carry the campaign through, but no one seemed to have any idea how to do it. Cabinet would be meeting later that week and would discuss the future of the Dardanelles, but there was no harmony in the government. Many were frustrated with Lord Kitchener, and Winston had become quite out of favour despite having advocated for the expedition at its inception, or perhaps because of this fact. *They will have to do something. Even continuing to dither will be a decision to leave the men in the trenches without a new initiative and this would be a poor outcome.*

The idea of a peaceful week, seeing friends and buying new clothes, had become a lost fantasy. In addition to meeting with war decision-makers, Ellis had re-acquainted himself with the National Press Association and satisfied himself that his employers would continue to pay the bills. His literary agent, Hughes Massie, gave Ellis a cinematograph and ten-thousand feet of film to capture moving pictures of the war. The idea was fascinating, but Ellis had no experience in the use of this type of camera, other than a quick lesson this afternoon. The automatic machine supposedly captured moving pictures when the user switched it on and wound the handle whilst aiming it at the subject. Ellis would have liked to see the output of this process to be convinced that it actually worked. It all seemed a little too easy, but ten thousand feet of film was quite a load to lug back to the war front. *I wonder what the Dardanelles General Headquarters staff might have to say about my recording of moving pictures that cannot be easily censored. Actually, I don't want to think about the first conversation with them when I return.*

"You know Mother," Winston blurted and raised his chin slightly. Conversation around the table ceased at once, as if an important announcement was anticipated. "The Dardanelles Expedition is a brilliant bit of strategy." He paused and shook his head, as if giving a speech in Parliament. A slight rash of red rose from his collar. "If only the ships had pushed on and seen the battle through to the finish. They were so close to the goal and the Turks were low on ammunition, on the brink of capitulation. It would have been a rout, like in the Balkans. The mighty British navy was upon them, but turned back at the critical moment. They just turned away. Gave up when it got a bit hot. Sacrifice must be made in war and more sacrifice was needed to achieve the objective…"

The poor fellow is delusional.

He forgets the facts, or is ignorant of them. The forts unsilenced and saving their ammunition, the main lines of sea-mines intact, three battleships lying at the bottom of the Straits, other ships damaged, no plan to refuel or re-arm the fleet in the Marmara Sea if it found the Narrows closed against its return. He cares nothing for the loss of ships or men, only that the sacrifices made were too small. He probably would have rather left office after the destruction of the entire Dardanelles fleet, if only the affair had been fought to the finish.

"…They could have passed the Narrows. They were right there, but they gave up too soon." Winston leaned back into his chair, drained his wine glass and slammed it down onto the white table cloth, like a judge banging his gavel on declaration of the verdict: 'Guilty'.

He took a deep breath and looked tired, but calmer, as if he had experienced a cathartic moment, or revealed a shameful secret and felt relief that the burden of knowing the truth was now shared by those present.

At this juncture, the ladies took their leave, and looked glad for the opportunity. Once they had left the room, Winston lit a cigar and pointed an accusing finger at Ellis.

"Bartlett, you have come home to run down the expedition! You wish to spread gossip and ridicule so you can make a story of it." Again Winston's neck reddened.

"Not so Winston," Ellis replied. "I am a keen as everybody to see it through, but it must be handled in the right manner. I have seen the defences and the weapons our men face, and the losses we have taken. We need to change our method or we will achieve nothing."

"Very well then." Winston took a deep breath, poured two glasses of whiskey and handed one to Ellis. "You must do everything you can to stiffen the resolve of any ministers you meet and induce them to send the necessary reinforcements. It is imperative for our war effort that we take Constantinople. Imperative man! We must push through the Dardanelles, whatever the cost."

Imperative for your vindication and the restoration of your prestige. That is no concern of mine, I am concerned with the best interests of our country. Fortunately for you, these two causes align in this case.

Ellis held Winston's gaze, a gaze that intimidated so many, and tried to lighten the moment with his most disarming smile. "General attacks across a wide front, against an entrenched enemy are futile. Casualties are extreme for the gain of little ground. Men have been killed in the thousands for a few hundred yards of ground. At this rate we would exhaust the entire population of England and her dominions before we reached Constantinople."

"Tell me your thoughts then, as to what might be done."

"The first and foremost maxim of war," Ellis said, "constantly reiterated by Napoleon, and accepted by every other recognised master of strategy, is to strike at your enemy's most vulnerable point with every available man and gun at your disposal. Concentration alone assures success on the battlefield. Dispersion of strength almost invariably leads to failure."

Winston's eye's opened slightly wider. "I take it you have identified such a chink in the Turkish armour."

"The isthmus at the throat of the peninsula – Bulair. If we strangle the Turkish supply lines and starve their army of food and ammunition, they would capitulate within a week."

"Cabinet is divided as to what to do," Winston pursed his lips. "But it will have to come to a decision this week. I will arrange for you to meet Prime Minister Asquith tomorrow."

A grandfather clock at the far end of the room chimed midnight.

"I will meet with the Prime Minister," Ellis said, feeling suddenly exhausted.

"But I must be off to my hotel now for some sleep. It has been a most busy few days."

"Walk with me first, to Admiralty House. I wish to explore your ideas further, and consult the maps."

Ellis forced himself not to groan.

"Very well."

They bade farewell to Lady Churchill and the other dinner guests who also were making preparations to depart. The press correspondent and politician walked together along the dark streets, almost deserted at this hour.

"I felt sure it might be done with the fleet alone, and I am still convinced that it might have been." Winston spoke in a pathetic tone, and seemed to be talking half to Ellis, half to himself. "As long as we tried it with our old reserve ships it mattered little, because, even if they were lost, we were none the weaker. I told them over and over again, once an army was landed, it would be quite another affair, and that they would be dragged into a great enterprise from which they could not withdraw. As for me, when I resigned from the Admiralty, I had only one desire, namely to go and serve with my regiment in France, but the Prime Minister, and all my colleagues, implored me to remain in the Cabinet, and at a great personal sacrifice I consented to do so."

This man is delusional and obsessed. He was forced to resign from his role as First Lord of the Admiralty after the Dardanelles disaster.

On arrival at Admiralty House, Winston rang the bell at a side entrance. After a brief wait, an attendant opened the door and passively absorbed the abuse Winston heaped upon him for the delay.

The rooms of Admiralty House were in a state of disorder, as if a metaphor for the fallen minister who was staying there, under sufferance until his own townhouse was ready for him to move into. Packed boxes stood in piles in a corner, a book lay here, a letter there. The ornate rooms and official papers seemed to mock him. Deserted halls, so recently full of sycophants, now only echoed the sound of his own voice.

"They never fought it out to the finish." Winston clutched a Brandy bottle and drank in great gulps like a poor wretch strengthening his hand for suicide. "They never gave my schemes a fair trial."

"Actually they did," Ellis replied. "They lost three ships, and two others were badly damaged before ever reaching the minefield.

"That does not matter! They ought to have gone on. What did it matter if more ships were lost with their crews. The ships were old and useless and the crews were mostly old reservists. They were sent out there to die, it was their duty. That is what they were mobilised for."

Their duty to die to give your schemes a fair trial?

Winston is incapable of realising that the world will go on just the same whether he is at the Admiralty or not, as if his fall might mean the fall of England and mark a general calamity to the whole world and modern civilisation.

"Winston, you cannot write history like a serial in Macmillan's Magazine. We are not talking about conflict in some fictitious nation of Laurania here and you are not Savrola. We are constrained by reality man."

Winston flung himself into a chair, slammed the brandy bottle on the table beside him, lit a cigar and proceeded to recount the details of the expedition once more.

"Now," Winston said. "We will try and work out a scheme to show what must be done to ensure success if the Cabinet decide to send large reinforcements."

Winston produced several maps, and the two poured over the known positions in detail. Hours passed and a hint of cheer returned to Winston's face, as if he once again believed that his dreams of victory might come true.

At three o'clock Ellis insisted that he must leave and headed to the door. By this time, Winston looked more like his old self again.

"You have nothing to fear for your reputation in the future," Ellis said. "Because all the errors will be speedily forgotten in the immensity of the achievement, if we get Constantinople."

"We must see the expedition is carried through. I will arrange for you to see the Prime Minister tomorrow, and will be present myself. The paramount interests of England and her Allies depend on our taking Constantinople with a minimum of delay. It is your duty to assist this in every way in your power. You must remain at my disposition, for any time you may be wanted tomorrow."

Ellis nodded consent and stepped into the darkness, looking forward to a few hours of sleep in his suite at the nearby Carlton Hotel. In the next thirty-six hours he planned to meet with Prime Minister Asquith, Lord Kitchener the Minister for War, and Lady Hamilton, the wife of Dardanelles Commander-in-Chief. *I'm not sure which of those meetings unnerves me the most.*

Before he had taken a dozen steps, his musing was interrupted.

"We are all working for a common end," Winston called from the doorway. "If Constantinople is taken there is enough glory for all."

CHAPTER 69

Mustafa

Friday, 11 June 1915

"Maybe it won't be necessary for us to patrol the full front line of our sector again tomorrow."

Sweat dripped from Major Izzettin's face and soaked his uniform. "Little has changed since yesterday. Enemy activity is minimal."

"To command our forces effectively we must remain aware," replied Lieutenant-Colonel Mustafa Kemal. "The situation can change at any time."

Mustafa picked up a canteen of water and his chief of staff did likewise. *He is great at organising the division, but he would sit in the shade writing orders all day if he had his way.*

The sun had only been up for a few of hours, but it was beating down with strength-sapping intensity. Shade in Mustafa's divisional field headquarters provided welcome relief after the walk.

General Esat was still occupying 'Kemal's Place' for III Corps headquarters. Mustafa's field headquarters were now located on the lee side of Flat Hill, sheltered from low trajectory naval shellfire.

"Little has changed, as you say," Kemal said. "How long can this last? They will not tolerate this situation indefinitely. They will want to break out somewhere, but where?"

"They remember the massacre of our great offensive last month." Izzettin shook his head. "One does not easily forget such a thing. They are focusing their strength on targeted raids, like Junction Hill last week. They cannot afford losses like we took. They would destroy themselves. They are mining too, those mounds of earth that appear each morning – maybe they will tunnel right underneath us!"

"They are doing what they can without wasting men," Kemal said. "But their high command will be growing impatient. They are fighting uphill every day, and have not gained any ground since the day they landed here. They must be thinking to try something different."

"I have heard that Limon von Sanders Pasha is expecting an attack around Bulair. He his reinforcing the area with fresh troops, and Kum Kale also."

Mustafa slammed his empty canteen down and the rickety field table threatened to collapse. He looked around to check for other ears and spoke in a voice that was both a whisper and a shout.

"Von Sanders is a fool! The German is still obsessed with the Gulf of Saros! Why would the enemy attack there? It is too far from their objective. I would not. Come with me!"

Mustafa strode out of his shelter without waiting for the inevitable resistance from his chief of staff.

The trench wound its way west, around the gentle crest of Flat Hill, to a lookout. From here he was blind to his left flank at Red Ridge, but he held a commanding view over Hill of Valour to his left and the tangle of ridges and valleys away to Salt Lake in the north – an area that he was now, at least in part, responsible for defending.

Izzettin caught up, red faced.

"Write to Esat Pasha. Again," Mustafa said while his chief of staff was still catching his breath. "These valleys and ridges provide a path for the enemy to outflank us at Chunuk Bair or Koja Chemen Tepe. They are too vulnerable. If the enemy comes behind us onto the higher ground, we may not be able to stop their advance."

"Kemal Bey, he knows your views on this!"

"The split command was a disaster during Enver's great offensive, and it will be so again. Now another German has come, he doesn't know the terrain, and the boundary between his area and mine is somewhere down there around Sazli Dere, the very area the English are likely to attack. How can we respond effectively when the command is not clear?"

"Mainly Australians, and some New Zealanders and Indians sir."

"They're English dogs, they do as their English masters command."

"Kemal Bey, Major Wilhelm Willmer and his Anafarta Group was brought to reinforce our position in the north, and he is very close to von Sanders Pasha. We must be careful what we say."

"Write the message! And show it to me before you send it. I don't want it watered down with your diplomatic language.

* * *

"Izzettin! Send another message to Esat Pasha. I want him to come here and see for himself."

A week had passed since the last message.

General Esat continued to ignore Mustafa's concerns.

Esat's responses provided reassurance that limited reinforcements were being deployed effectively in all areas where an enemy attack was likely, but were non-committal about this sector.

"Carry the message yourself, I hope he is comfortable at 'Kemal's Place'. You can tell me if he is keeping it tidy."

Izzettin delivered the message under protest and the next day Esat came with his chief of staff, Lieutenant-Colonel Fahrettin.

Mustafa led them along the trench he traversed daily to the lookout from Flat Hill.

"I know you are concerned about your sector Kemal Bey," Esat said. "This is right for a good field commander like yourself. What is it you would like to show me?"

Mustafa could sense his own frustration starting to build. *The old man is not going to take this seriously.* He pointed to Sazli Dere, as well as the territory to its north and south. "These ridges and gullies are vulnerable to enemy attack. We need reinforcements and a unified command in this area."

The morning sun left pockets of dark shadow scattered down the crumpled terrain, making it appear impassable in places.

"Only a small detachment of guerrilla soldiers could advance through there," Fahrettin said.

Esat held up his hand, his lips pursed. "Where will the enemy come from?"

Mustafa made a sweeping gesture with his hand, tracing the coastline from Ariburnu, up the long beach to Salty Lake. "From there!"

"Let's assume that they do come from there," Esat replied. "How will they proceed?"

Mustafa pointed at Ariburnu and drew a semi-circle with his finger, sweeping up to Koja Chemen Tepe. "They will find a way up here, to the higher ground."

Esat Pasha laughed and patted Mustafa on the shoulder. "Don't worry yourself, they cannot advance there. Our reinforcements are being deployed where they are most needed. The terrain here is our ally and our best defence."

A heat of rage rose under Mustafa's collar and he looked away from Esat. *It's a waste of time trying to reason with this man.*

"Sir, I hope it will happen as you foretold."

"There is another matter I wanted to discuss with you Kemal Bey. Your old friend, Enver Pasha is coming for another visit."

Kemal dragged his eyes back to meet Esat's gaze. It was like being punched in the gut and then kneed in the face.

"When?"

"One week."

Mustafa took a deep breath. "He still blames me for that disastrous offensive he insisted on last month. No thanks to you or von Sanders Pasha."

"We all played our part. You were awarded the Iron Cross for yours. This is an honourable German decoration. And you have just been promoted to full

Colonel. Your dedication and field command skills are well recognized here."

"Why should an Ottoman officer consider it an honour to be decorated with a Christian cross?" Kemal spat.

"Enver Pasha is concerned that we should be conserving men and not wasting them on attacks that don't have a clear objective."

"I'm sure he is. He has spent so many men he must be running out of them!"

"As I said, Mustafa, your commitment and skill are acknowledged, but you would be well advised to choose your words more carefully."

* * *

Mustafa was still smouldering a week and a half later when word came of an English attack at Krithia from the southern front.

Remote enough from Mustafa's sector for him to ignore, except that Esat sent reserves from Maidos to assist. The cunning Australians executed a feint at Gaba Tepe and lured Esat into diverting the reserves in that direction. The reserves were then cut to pieces by naval shellfire.

I need a successful counter-attack. Enver is on the peninsula and will be happy for any excuse to undermine me.

Mustafa's 19th Division remained responsible for defence of the Ariburnu sector, from Red Ridge to Sazli Dere. The front lines remained relatively quiet, other than a few trench raids by both sides here and there.

If I can take High Ridge, I can command the Valley of Fear and the beach north of Ariburnu. Then they will have to abandon much of their position.

The attack plan was simple. A feint by the 57th Regiment at Junction Hill, and quick withdrawal would be coordinated with the main attack by the 18th Regiment at the Hill of Valour. They would charge across the narrow ridge that connected the enemy position on High Ridge. The 18th Regiment were fresh reinforcements to the 19th Division, recently arrived from Istanbul. The regiment had a fierce reputation, as did their commander until he took a sniper's bullet to the head a few days earlier.

Early in the evening of the night when the attack was due, a freak thunder and wind storm came. Dust and foreign newspapers blew across from no-mans-land, accompanied by a hail of bullets. Neither side could see, so both unleashed a flurry of rifle and machine gun fire, just in case.

Reports of enemy attack proved to be false when the wind died away. Rain might have provided some welcome cover for the attack, but the storm dissipated before there were more than a few drops.

Soon after midnight on the morning of 30 June the attack took place as planned.

The familiar war cry that was also a simple prayer: 'God, God', was loud enough be heard across the valleys.

Mustafa positioned himself close by. A first-hand perspective was important.

It was always difficult to tell how a night attack was progressing. The men disappeared into the black and the sounds of fighting followed – rifle fire mixed with the primal cries of men killing and dying.

An early report came back that two enemy machine guns had been captured along with the first line of English trenches, and that some men had penetrated into the second line.

Mustafa relayed this information to Esat at III Corps headquarters, still located at the hill known as 'Kemal's Place'. Tonight Enver Pasha was staying there also, as part of the Commander-in-Chief's tour of the peninsula.

Soon sounds revealed the truth of the situation.

War cries were replaced with groans of anguish and pleas in a familiar tongue. Enemy flares and fire balls lit up the ridge and Mustafa saw that many men were burning and not far advanced.

The amount of rifle fire drifted down to usual levels, but the groans continued. The advance was halted. *Where are all my little Mehmets?* Wounded returned as usual, some bringing confused tales about having fallen into large pits, but they were too few. A battalion and a half of men had simply disappeared.

The attack was a failure.

Mustafa realized that if the enemy counter-attacked across the Hill of Valour, they would find his trenches empty. He moved his headquarters close up to the front line and rushed reserves in to defend it.

A message arrived from Enver. He questioned the purpose of the attack, and wanted to see the two captured machine guns.

Mustafa looked out across the Hill of Valour and High Ridge.

Flickering flames and flares exposed the disaster against the darkness.

Wounded and dead were countless, but there were no captured enemy machine guns.

CHAPTER 70

Jayjay

Wednesday, 30 June 1915, small hours

Jayjay sat in the dark, on a thunderbox made from an old biscuit crate. Cramps gripped his stomach, then faded, then came again, but he experienced no cathartic relief. His body had already purged itself of all it could.

I better get back to the others. It must be after midnight. Finally a chance to get away from this damned place and I don't want to be left behind.

Before he moved, he paused to listen, but the activity over the hill behind him was over. Echoes of the silenced cries resounded in his ears, as if ghosts of the dead refused to give up.

"Allah. Allah!"

"Allah. Allah!"

The distant yells had been snuffed out by machine guns and rifles.

The charge must have been up around Russell's Top. God, when will this end? More men throwing their lives away. That attack by the Turks was probably about as pointless as our raid on German Officer's Trench.

He pulled up his trousers and crunched across the sand, away from the latrine to the place where the remnant of the 1st Battalion waited, near Watson's Pier on the beach of Anzac Cove. *Can't be more than half the original battalion still here and fighting fit.* Some stood, some sat, their forms difficult to make out in the dark.

Jayjay shuffled slowly across the sand, partly to avoid bumping into anyone and partly to nurse his aching belly.

Larry sat alone and stared towards the waves, inky waves almost indistinguishable, but for the sound, from the black sky beyond. Jayjay sat on the sand next to him.

A thin slither of moon showed itself through a gap in the clouds, but gave little light. The foam of the waves pushing up the beach made dark grey lines against the black. The sea was rougher than usual, choppy from the heavy winds earlier in the night.

"How you holding up soldier?" Larry asked.

"Still got the Gallipoli trots. How do you reckon?"

"I think you need a holiday. You should take a week off."

"Thanks Doc."

Lightning flashed. Natural thunder sounded strange compared to the usual artillery blasts. More distant, but the rumble hung in the air for longer, as if as a reminder that manmade thunder was not as powerful as the forces of God's creation.

The dark form of a minesweeper bobbed in close to Watson's Pier and a murmur rippled through those waiting. Sergeant Baker didn't have to work too hard with the other sergeants and lance corporals to round up the men and get them moving onto the pier.

Jayjay and Larry groped forwards like sheep lining up to be dipped, until a voice declared that the boat was full, then they waited with the rest of the flock for a second minesweeper.

Soon after the raid on German Officers' Trench, the 1st Battalion had been moved to Braund's Hill for a 'rest', but the fatigue work hadn't stopped, especially at night. *Poor old bastard, Colonel Braund was a bit hard of hearing and got himself shot by his own sentry for not answering a challenge. He did a good job of organising us in the early days. That's when Alfred McKenzie died, I haven't thought of him for a while. He only lasted a few days. I wonder if his watch and wallet or my letter ever reached his parents back home. I wonder how Charlotte took the news of his death.*

Their turn came, and Jayjay and Larry boarded the second minesweeper as it was being tied off. *This boat is going to take me away from this cursed place, even if only for a week. A whole week with no one trying to kill me.*

He shuffled to the stern and stood at the balustrade looking back towards the black hillside of Maclagan's Ridge. The boat filled from the rear, as if those boarding could not turn their backs on a connection with the battlefield.

The throttle valve opened, the steam engine pumped and the minesweeper eased slowly away from Anzac Cove.

The boat bobbed like a cork on the sea and Jayjay wondered if the motion might make him feel worse, but seasickness didn't trouble him.

"A week of leave," Larry said. "At least the chances of getting shot at in the next little while are low."

At that moment splash in the water on the port side told of an overshot bullet. Larry laughed and Jayjay joined him. Others were absorbed in their own conversations and didn't notice.

"Maybe that was a flying fish?" Larry suggested.

"You'd have to be the unluckiest man at Gallipoli to cop it now." Jayjay said.

A cloud drifted in front of the moon, leaving only a faint smudge of light against the dark sky. Boat lights were off and smoking was not allowed. Darkness cloaked them so completely that he could not see any white foam behind the minesweeper as it pushed through the waves. His hand closed around the Turkish button within his pocket, the button embossed with the shape of crescent moon and a star. *The new moon is a sign of new beginnings. That must be why they give it a place on their uniform – to remind them what they are fighting for.*

"I got a letter from Gracey," Larry said.

"I know, I was there when the mail bag came. How is your twin sister? Did she sign it off with a portrait of herself poking her tongue out?"

Larry laughed, more than Jayjay felt his question was worth. Not the usual cynical laugh, but a genuine, almost happy laugh.

"She does have a way about her. She's all right you know. Sometimes she's a bit crazy, but she just likes to get a reaction from people."

"That she does."

"She says there's talk of bringing in conscription."

"No way!"

"Nothing official yet, just talk."

"And we were worried that we might miss out on all this."

"Yeah, well, now it seems they're running short on lunatics who are willing to volunteer to come and get shot at."

"Do you reckon they'd force blokes to come?"

"Can't see how that'd work. I mean, what could they threaten them with? 'If you don't go and get yourself killed in the war, then you will be severely punished. You're only making it worse for yourself!'"

"You going to write back to her?"

"Yeah, I'll tell her that conscription's a stupid bloody idea."

"The censors might not let that through."

"I wanna write to her anyway, let her know we're still alive and having a great time here. I'll use a code only she and I know for anything that might get censored."

"I didn't think I'd leave this place alive," Jayjay said.

"We're not leaving it. Not really. Just taking a break for a spell, then we'll come back to keep rolling the dice in the asylum."

Larry's words told Jayjay nothing that he didn't already know, but at the thought of returning to Gallipoli, his heart sank to his boots.

A raindrop landed on Jayjay's arm.

A few more drops followed. Large drops, but not many.

"Imagine what it will be like when it rains heavy," Jayjay said. "It rained on the first day, but the place was clean then. It'll rain here again sometime, maybe tonight – mud, dead Aussies and Maori-landers, dead Tommies, dead Abduls, dead Indians, flies and bloody maggots, turds from all over the world, solid ones from the new boys and runny slop from the rest of us. Dead bloody donkeys. All washed out of shallow graves and mixed up in a giant bog at the bottom of the hill."

Jayjay stared into the night for a long moment before continuing. "Sad thing is, it wouldn't shock me. Once, the thought of it all would have seemed disgusting. Now, if I live to see it, I'll only be disappointed that all that good rainwater has been ruined and I'll still be thirsty 'cause I can't drink it."

"Sounds like a perfect recipe for Gallipoli soup mate, just add nightmares to taste."

"Yeah, well there's no shortage of those either." Jayjay shook his head. "I wish it was just a nightmare. At least then we might wake up. The place is hell, pure and simple. We've been left here to die. No one cares. Back home they probably have no idea what it's like here. They probably know more about what's happening in France. I bet no one else had heard of Gallipoli before we came here either. Nothing counts for anything here anymore. We're hardly getting any reinforcements – they're all going to France and we're not winning there either. You've read the telegrams from Reuters News Bureau at the notice boards."

"Did you get up on the wrong side of the trench this morning? You're growling like a dog. That's normally my job!"

"It's all a recipe for misery, this Godforsaken place. This whole expedition is a complete blunder. We came to take the bloody Dardanelles and we never even saw the waterway. It may not exist for all we know. The whole thing was a giant Furphy – go and fight Germans, defend the innocent. There is no glory here. It was all a lie."

"We joined up too early you know," Larry said.

"We should never have joined up at all. Next big rain, we'll be there with the rest of the poor dead bastards in the giant shit-hole at the bottom of the hill."

"No, think about it. Eventually this war will be over and the ones who are left will get to go home. The girls will hooray and the survivors will be hailed in the papers, only there won't be any of the 1st Battalion left. No one will remember us. We'll be long gone and forgotten. We shoulda' waited to join the 100th Battalion. They'll be the ones who come at the last minute, dodge a few bullets, maybe some'll take a hit, then they can all go home as heroes, march up George Street and tell stories about how they won the war."

"Now I feel worse than before." Jayjay lowered his voice. "Blazes Larry, I don't know how much longer I can keep doing this."

"Come on, chin up mate. They say there's nurses at Imbros. Australian nurses."

"Probably one for every hundred of us. They'll only want to socialise with officers."

"Who knows, you might even find there's a surprise visit from Josephine. And they might have some nice rough gravel on their roads."

Bastard! You must have been saving that one up for a special occasion. Jayjay was grateful for the darkness to mask the red heat of embarrassment rising up his neck. This was the first time Larry had mentioned the Cairo prostitute encounter since leaving Egypt.

I had hoped that Josephine would never be spoken of again.

It's hard to stay grumpy with Larry around.

Jayjay held his silence for as long as he could, then burst out laughing.

CHAPTER 71

Ellis

Friday, 9 July 1915

The small steam engine chugged a rhythmical putt-putt-putt and pushed the pinnace through the water towards the steep slopes of Anzac Cove.

Ahead, the looming hills were denuded of vegetation and pocked with the excavations of an ant-hill. Pockets of activity gave the appearance that the ant-hill had been kicked by a curious boy.

Ellis steeled himself in anticipation of the swarms of flies that plagued the beach and hills of the battlefield, having fattened themselves on Infidel and Christian corpses alike. The pinnace drew up to a new pier, still under construction, where men hauled a rope through a pulley-block to lift an improvised piling rig made from an unexploded enemy shell, under the supervision of the pipe-smoking Lieutenant Watson.

At the pier a continuous hum from the beat of millions of tiny wings droned on behind the swearing of men and distant chatter of small arms fire.

Ellis climbed up to the pier, passed by the working men who took little notice, and walked onto the beach of Anzac Cove past stacks of crates and piles of materials. Without hesitation, he strode along the beach and up a short track towards the particular dugout he was seeking, located about fifty yards from the pier. At a point where the track veered to the right, a series of steep steps, cut into the earth on the left, led up to the dugout. This dugout stood a little larger than those surrounding it, but was otherwise unremarkable. A lean-to roof of sheet-iron raked towards the track, buried under a layer of dirt, giving the appearance that the primitive structure was part of the hillside when viewed from above.

He climbed the steps and stopped outside the entrance to the dugout, the entrance being nothing more than an opening between a sandbag wall and the hillside. Above the opening, at around eye-height for a short man, a small hand-painted sign was nailed to a timber roof-beam. The sign bore three letters: 'G.O.C.'

He stooped and peered into the gloom and waited a moment for his eyes to adjust to the darkness.

"Knock, knock," he called. There was no door to knock on, and even if there was, a knocking sound would have been lost against the background noise. Careful to duck under the roof-beam, he entered.

Ellis was pleased to find General Birdwood in residence, but surprised to find the Anzac Commander, more formally known as General Officer Commanding or G.O.C., lying in his make-shift camp bed in the corner.

The British general was a true leader who held the respect of the Dominion troops and set a personal example in every way. Always active and seen to be active, he bathed with them, lived amongst them, visited the trenches and ate their food.

At first, Ellis thought that General Birdwood might be wounded, but there was no evidence of medical staff, bandages or blood.

"Good morning Sir," Ellis said with caution. "I trust I am not disturbing you."

"Ellis Ashmead-Bartlett, back from London I see, do come in." The general sat up, but lacked his usual colour. "I have had my vaccination shot against cholera. Knocked me around a little is all. We might have a bit of a chat here. I don't think I'll be taking my usual tour of the front line trenches today."

"Certainly Sir."

"I think we have the whip hand of the Turks within our grasp," the general croaked. "One more big push should do it. We must get astride this peninsula at any cost, then we will cut off the Turkish armies to the south and force them to capitulate. First, we must take this Sari Bair Range, right up to Chunuk Bair and Hill 971. Once we control the high ground, we can command the other side of the ridge."

"But the difficulties of this terrain Sir," Ellis hoped to encourage General Birdwood to elaborate on his vision. "The Turks are entrenched right on top of us."

"It cannot be done by a regular attack, but these Australians are an independent lot. I propose that we launch them north, along the shore with instructions to crawl up the hills in any way they can, to reach objectives along the top of the ridge, and there to establish themselves."

Ellis could see that Birdwood had not finished his train of thinking and so Ellis fought the urge to interrupt the general with all of the reasons why his proposal might not work.

"At the same time," General Birdwood continued. "One of the new divisions would land at Suvla Bay and push inland, to occupy the Anafarta Ridge. Turks have some heavy guns and about two thousand infantry there. The combination of these two movements will allow us to cross the peninsula and cut off the Kilid Bahr Plateau. Such operations would, of course, be very hazardous. Little is known about the country. The troops would have to act largely on their own initiative. We will lose control over them in this broken, mountainous country.

But if it can be done, the Dominion soldiers should certainly be the men for the job."

The general paused before continuing. "I would love to unleash five hundred of the Australian Light Horse in their rear, with instructions to raise hell and burn their supplies and depots. It would cause a regular panic among the Turks, but the great difficulty is to get their horses ashore and water them. However, we must see if it can be done."

"Yes, I see Sir. Has your plan been accepted by General Headquarters?"

Birdwood shook his head. "It is still under consideration, but I expect it is almost sure to be adopted. Of course, you must give me your pledge of secrecy."

"Of course… I wonder Sir, what are your thoughts of a landing further north, at Bulair?"

"Well, there has been talk that the Greeks might be induced to join the fray and if they were to land at Bulair as well, that would be excellent. In that case, the success of our operations would be assured, but otherwise we shan't have enough men. The 13th Division of Lord Kitchener's new army has arrived and will be deployed at Cape Helles. We are only expecting one further division for the big push. Will you be visiting the front line today?"

"Well, I had planned to Sir, should the opportunity arise, but I would not want to cause you inconvenience."

"None of it!" Birdwood coughed. "My A.D.C. shall take you. Onslow! Take our friend Mr Ashmead-Bartlett up to the Posts, it should be quiet enough today. No short-cuts across exposed areas." He pointed a finger at Ellis. "You mind yourself up there. It can get unhealthy, mighty quick. Especially at Quinn's, the Turks are only a cricket pitch away and they're always throwing their damned bombs. Good bombs too, not backyard fire crackers like our jam-tins. What I wouldn't give for a good supply of those bombs. Stick with Onslow and keep your bloody head down."

"Yes Sir, thank you General."

Ellis turned and followed the general's aide-de-camp, Captain Brian Onslow, through the slot into daylight and had to squint while his pupils adjusted to the daylight.

Captain Onslow led Ellis to the beach, then south to the end of Anzac Cove and past Hell Spit. Beyond Hell Spit, the mouth of a wide valley opened up. Here the pair turned inland and trudged up a track that followed the lowest part of Shrapnel Gully. The upper reaches were known as Monash Valley, where the trail grew steeper and narrower until the final climb up Pope's Hill, which required the use of rope and what Ellis considered to be a considerable amount of upper-body strength.

Pope's Hill, named for Colonel Pope, commander of the Australian 16th

Infantry Battalion, part of Colonel John Monash's 4th Brigade, was a lonely place. Isolated from frontline trenches on either side by a steep drop, it commanded a perfect view down the Monash Valley. If the Turks took Pope's Hill they could flush the Anzacs out of the valley and they knew it. The place was under a constant barrage of bombs and bullets. Ellis stayed no longer than he had to.

From Pope's Hill's to Quinn's Post was no more than two hundred yards as the crow flies, but Ellis was no crow and to walk a direct line along the ridge would have required the crossing of a spur, owned by Turkish snipers, known as Dead Man's Ridge.

A less dangerous route required Ellis to climb down the rear of Pope's Hill into Monash Valley, and then follow a track up the next gully to the south, towards the main Anzac frontline trench. This gully led Ellis and Captain Onslow to Quinn's Post, named for Major Quinn of the Australian 15th Infantry Battalion, also part of Monash's 4th Brigade.

Men at Quinn's wore the grim faces of men who might be about to face a firing squad. No one spoke unless it was necessary, there was no banter here. Periscopes poked skyward every few yards, peaking over the parapet.

Ellis heard a familiar voice and a chill surged up his spine. Not that the voice belonged to someone he knew, but rather the words and accent were the unmistakable tongue of a Turkish soldier. He remembered General Birdwood's words *...only a cricket pitch away and they're always throwing their damned bombs.*

Only two years earlier, Ellis had travelled with the Turkish Army in Bulgaria and achieved one of the great achievements of his writing career after witnessing the army's capitulation in the Balkan war. He knew the Turks in Constantinople would never allow him to transmit the truth, but he stole passage on a ship to Constanza in Romania and cabled the story to London from there.

The adventure had paid off, not only for the scoop newsprint article, but afterwards Ellis wrote a more detailed account and published this in a book 'With the Turks in Thrace'. The royalties from that book kept debt collectors at bay for a time.

Now, the same Turkish army was within easy ear-shot and would, given half the opportunity, happily kill him and his fellow members of the British Empire.

A Turkish cricket ball bomb careered into the wire netting in front of the trench which creaked in protest, but held firm. The bomb fell to the ground beyond the parapet where it exploded in an ear-splitting crack. In a reflex action, Ellis flinched. Australians about him remained unmoved, other than to continue with the lackadaisical waving away of flies and a few undisguised wry grins at his reaction.

Onslow hurried them along to Courtney's Post, named for Lieutenant-Colonel Courtney, commander of the Australian 14th Infantry Battalion, 4th Brigade.

The final stage of the firing trench visit passed without incident and the pair of visitors re-traced their steps down into Monash Valley and back to Anzac Cove.

"Thank you for the tour, Captain," Ellis shook hands with the aide-de-camp. "Please thank General Birdwood for me, and do wish him my best regards for a quick recovery."

Ellis turned and negotiated his way past the stockpiles on the beach and the men working on the pier, then boarded the pinnace that awaited his return.

A stoker fired up the steam engine, then the pinnace moved out from the pier and pushed through the wavelets as it drew away from Anzac Cove. On the way, Ellis reflected on General Birdwood's new plan of attack and dread ached within him like an old wound.

The steam engine chugged putt-putt-putt.

CHAPTER 72

John

Friday, 16 July 1915

"Arghyl Dere."

"No. Kaiajik Dere."

"I think Kaiajik Dere is that next gully to the left." Despite John's passion for cartography, the tangle of ridges and gullies proved difficult to correlate to the map in his hands.

"Then that ridge between them, that winds right up to the peak of Hill 971, that must be Damakjelik Bair."

"Yes, I think so." Colonel John Monash knew that his voice lacked the confidence he wanted it to have. "When the day comes, the final maps will be explicit and clear. We will have guides, men who have reconnoitred the path, at least most of the way."

"Hopefully these guides will know an easier passage than what we came across yesterday," said Lieutenant-Colonel McGlinn, John's Chief of Staff. "The maze of dry watercourses led us to nothing but sheer cliffs."

John wanted to disagree, but could not, and said nothing. North of the New Zealand trenches at the extreme left flank of the Anzac position, the terrain thwarted each of their attempts to explore inland on a secret reconnaissance mission as soon as he had left the beach with his staff officers.

Now they observed the lie of the land from half a mile offshore, on the deck of a torpedo boat destroyer. Field glasses provided magnification and allowed a clear perspective from a distance. Even so, the twisted ridges of the Sari Bair Range ran into one another like a slump of spaghetti, and the gullies shown on the map hid behind the heights so that their path was obscured from view.

"General Hamilton is taking secrecy very seriously for this operation. General Godley is being even more frugal with the truth than usual. He almost had a guilty look on his face when he told me to sharpen my bushwalking and compass skills, and talked of a left hook."

"Can the men do it? McGlinn asked. "Some of them struggle to drag themselves to the latrine in Reserve Gully."

"The doctors are not confident." John lowered his field glasses. "Four of them have examined most of our men this month and only one doctor believes the men are capable of a half day march, and he was clear that that was on the proviso that they are provided plenty of food, water and rest."

"What of the other three?"

"They said the men are not fit to shovel trenches or do any other meaningful work."

"I know which doctor you will listen to."

"What choice do we have?" John said. "Reinforcements are coming, that will perk the men up. We've had them digging extra terraces for weeks, so there must be a good number of extras on the way."

"We need reinforcements. Last week we lost nearly one hundred men from our brigade to disease alone."

"It would help if some of our wounded and sick actually returned to service. Hundreds of men have left our brigade with minor ailments. Off to Egypt, or Malta, or God only knows where. How many of them have returned?"

"Very few Sir."

"Approximately zero! I have complained to Godley, someone ought to be sent to Egypt to round them up, but he has done nothing."

A puff of smoke appeared near the peak of the Sari Bair Range and several seconds later the gentle thud of a field gun drifted across the water. The range finder shell landed well short.

A young rating emerged from the bridge and approached John, then paused at a respectful distance.

"Beg pardon Sir," said the rating. "The captain asked me to inform you that the Turks have opened fire. We will continue north and evade their shelling as we go, then move further offshore for the return trip."

"Very good," John replied.

The rating turned on his heels and hurried back to the bridge.

"Remarkable," John said, "that one man can handle a vessel of this size, as easily as a motor car. She goes like a greyhound."

As if to confirm his statement, the destroyer accelerated and veered away from the coastline. A spray of water burst from the wake where a shell landed fifty yards behind her stern.

Well-engineered machines like this are the future of modern warfare. Fast and manoeuvrable torpedo boat destroyers that can sink a battleship, and submarines, and armoured land vehicles mounted with weapons, and aeroplanes. This approach of sending men with rifles against well-fortified defences is like throwing buckets of water against a brick wall. Even old Ned Kelly engineered himself better armour than what we equip our soldiers with, and he survived plenty of gun battles before he succumbed to the noose.

John smiled as he recalled his meeting with the bushranger as a twelve-year-old child. Ned Kelly had stopped by John's father's farm in Jerilderie and paid John a shilling to mind his horse and then got about selling other stolen horses. John's father Louis always boasted to have driven a good cash bargain for the horse he acquired that day.

* * *

"Colonel, four new guns have arrived."

Two days after the reconnaissance mission on the water, a familiar voice invaded John's dreamless sleep.

John rubbed grit from his eyes and groaned. "What am I going to do with artillery in Reserve Gully?"

Dawn light crept in through the doorway, around the edges of McGlinn's well-rounded form, and illuminated the dirt floor of his hole in the side of the hill, six feet by seven feet and four feet deep, with outer walls of sandbags and a roof of three waterproof sheets lashed together.

John's body protested against the awakening and his hips ached. *Once I get up and move about a bit the pain will go. One day I will sleep in a bed again.*

A fortnight earlier, John had celebrated his fiftieth birthday. To date John's health had held up better than any of the younger Anzac brigadiers, all of whom had been out of action for a period due to either wounds or sickness. It was only when he woke up that he felt his age, otherwise the hard living conditions had agreed with him. He only drank boiled water and ate small portions. Since leaving Australia's shores he had lost around ten percent of his body weight. Not wanting to make a big show of his birthday, John was pleasantly surprised at the number of officers from all over the Anzac sector who made the effort to come to shake his hand and wish him many happy returns. He received gifts of cigars, French champagne and Greek retsina, and General Godley brought a birthday cake that his wife had made in Cairo where she was carrying out her self-imposed role of transporting the wounded to hospitals in her own motor car.

The guns should be hauled up to Russell's Top, or towards Lone Pine where they can properly target enemy defences and be used to provide cover for men advancing in attack. They are probably here because we don't have the men or beasts to do the hard work of hauling them up the hill. Motorised vehicles should be engineered for such a task, and fitted with armour to protect them from enemy fire.

"There is a crew of English gunners arrived with the guns Sir," McGlinn said. "Their commanding officer is here and would like to know where he should deploy the guns."

And I should like to know where I am to deploy my brigade in the coming advance, but clear direction is somewhat lacking at present.

* * *

A few more days passed in relative quiet on the firing line, but rumours flew about Reserve Gully, telling of the imminent big push and of mass reinforcements. Numbers of casualties due to enemy activity remained low, but losses to disease were crippling.

John was certain that his 4th Brigade would play a key role in the upcoming attack, to make a left flank advance as part of a coordinated operation involving multiple divisions. He looked forward to receiving detailed maps and meeting the New Zealander guides who had scouted the route.

"Colonel, a cablegram has arrived for you. I believe it is from your wife Sir."

John flinched.

Victoria's regular letters maintained a theme of anxiety and sorrow. A cablegram would likely mean more of the same, if not genuine bad news. *Some positive cheer would be nice. I have let go of worrying for myself long ago, I wish she could do the same and be more positive. I have enough difficulties to deal with here, without stresses from home to add to them.*

In a letter he posted to Victoria a day earlier, John had acknowledged her concerns as only natural, but urged her to overcome them.

He tore open the paper slip and read the message dated 10 July 1915:

```
Congratulations on promotion brigadier-general well love.
```

"McGlinn," John called. "Vic has sent me congratulations on being promoted to the rank of general. Do you know anything about that? She sent it eleven days ago."

"No Sir, but maybe congratulations are in order. Is it true?"

"I don't know. This is the first I've heard of it."

We are in the thick of the action here, but so much important information is being withheld from me.

CHAPTER 73

Ishmail

Tuesday, 20 July 1915

Osman stared into the top of Yusuf's empty skull for several long seconds and then vomited onto the trench floor beside his dead friend.

The two were from the same village near Smyrna and had befriended Ishmail since the death of his father in the disastrous May offensive.

Minutes earlier, Osman and Yusuf had been joking about the terrible lunch. Stale bread washed down with stale water – hardly worth postponing Ramadan for.

Now the top of Yusuf's skull and brain were gone, the inside of his head was empty. Part of the spinal cord was visible where blue veins dangled. The roots of his eyeballs were exposed, and from the front his black eyes were half open. His teeth gleamed and his scalp hung in strips.

Tears left clean trails down Osman's cheeks as he cradled the body of his friend.

"No, no, no!"

"No, no, no!"

Ishmail looked down, his own big toe visible through the split in his right boot. He wriggled the toe.

With blurred vision he watched maggots on the trench floor. They wriggled too, as if they were dancing at the prospect of another feast.

Death had become less common of late, but flies still filled the air as thick as ever. Both sides were deeply entrenched and seemed intent on holding their ground. Localised trench raids were ordered from time to time, but not a full-frontal attack since the night in May when Ishmail's father was killed. The night Ishmail escaped with leg wounds, one of which he suspected came from his father's bayonet, by accident, or in a final act of parental protection.

The lack of recent deaths somehow made Yusuf's death more tragic.

"As God wills." Ishmail mouthed the words in silence so Osman would not hear. The words stuck to his tongue like dry ashes. *How can God will this?*

"Come Osman, Yusuf has gone to paradise. The dark eyed maidens are welcoming him now. Let us take him and give him the burial he deserves."

Osman had not yet produced any words, other than "no". He nodded slowly and turned Yusuf's body around to support it under the armpits. Ishmail picked up Yusuf's feet and noticed that the dead man wore two good boots about the same size as his own.

They carried their dead friend away from Red Ridge, down a supply trench, towards a reserve training area in the Valley of Black Nomads.

Men they passed made no effort to conceal their stares. Every man on the front line had seen his share of death. Enough to know that today could be his day, but never enough to stop the morbid fascination with seeing another. Ishmail's right thigh ached from where the bullet had been removed. His left calf didn't feel quite as it should either, although the bayonet wound had healed without infection. As he walked the calf muscle felt tight and uncomfortable, as if everything under the skin had been joined back together in a different way than God made it in the first place.

Yusuf's dirty face looked almost normal from the foot end of his body. Lifeless eyes gazed back towards Ishmail, but not directly at him. The missing top of Yusuf's head pressed against Osman's chest, as if Osman was trying to contain any remnant of brain that might be left in its container.

They found the burial area and dug with tools left there for the purpose.

The sun flogged the diggers like a cruel slave driver.

It occurred to Ishmail to suggest leaving Yusuf to wait until late in the afternoon, or even early next morning when they could return and dig in a cooler part of the day. Then he remembered what the heat and flies had done to his father. When Ishmail located his father's body, it, like all the others, had been lying in the sun for five days. Apart from his long white beard, the old man would have been unrecognisable. The blackened skin boiled with maggots and the body almost fell apart when Ishmail dragged him into a shallow grave with the big Australian.

Ishmail and Osman dug for an hour and produced a shallow grave next to the template of Yusuf's body, exactly the right length and tapered at the head end.

Osman paused and surveyed the hole. Sweat darkened his armpits and dripped from his face. He gave a nod and looked up at Ishmail. Their eyes met for the first time since the incident.

Ishmail nodded in return and moved to pick up Yusuf's feet, still wearing the good boots.

They lowered the corpse into the tomb.

Osman looked around as if to see if the Battalion Mufti might be about, but there was no one. "Thank you, God, for my friend Yusuf. He gave his life for your cause. Please welcome him into the cool gardens of heaven and give him rest."

Ishmail waited for Osman to shovel the first load of dirt back into the hole, then started shovelling himself and hoped Osman wouldn't notice him watching the boots disappear under the dirt. The loosened earth went back in much easier than it came out. Somehow there was only just enough to fill the void, despite space taken up by the body.

"I will avenge you my brother." Osman stared at the disturbed ground when they had finished, then looked around.

"I must find the Mufti and ask him to write to Yusuf's family. His wife will be most upset. His little girl is not yet one year old and she will never know her father."

Yusuf had talked of his wife and daughter enough times that Ishmail knew the dead man would be missed at home.

Ishmail remembered the words of his own father when they talked of the glory of martyrdom – 'it is also possible to live with honour'. *He wanted me to survive.* An urge to live solidified in Ishmail's chest.

Will I ever have a sweetheart of my own, or a child who will call me 'Daddy'? Please God, allow me to live to see that day. Damn this war.

"Thank you Ishmail." Osman said.

Ishmail nodded and turned away. "Come, we must return to our trench."

"Have you heard the rumours of a major enemy attack?" Ishmail asked as they walked.

"There are always rumours."

"Yusuf heard it from Sergeant Zahid. The old goat always seems to know what's going on. He said our commanders know it's coming, they just don't know if it will be here or further north up the Gulf of Saros, maybe as far as Bulair.

"Further north makes sense. The enemy wouldn't be stupid enough to attack here. He saw how easy it was to defend against our pointless charges at their trenches."

"Be careful Osman, you don't know who will hear."

"I am ready to join Yusuf. I don't care who hears what I say."

"I am willing to die as a martyr. It would be an honour, but what good does it do to throw life away?

"The Mufti said God has ordained it this way," Osman said.

"The enemy is not stupid. He killed thousands of us charging at his trenches. No, he will attack somewhere else I think."

"Maybe, but our Ramadan fasting should have started last week, and was postponed, so the commanders must have some reasons to remain vigilant here."

A stone found its way into the split in Ishmail's boot and wedged itself under his foot. He tried to kick it out as he walked, but it would not come.

"I need new boots."

"There are no new boots," Osman replied.

Ishmail stopped and lifted his foot in a more serious attempt to remove the stone.

"Yusuf had good boots," Osman paused and waited. "You should have taken them if they fit you. He can walk barefoot in the garden of paradise."

"Where have you two been?" Sergeant Zahid appeared in the trench in front of them, as if from nowhere.

"We buried our brother Yusuf," Osman's voice had just a hint of defiance. "He was martyred today."

"You should have let the medic's take him, your responsibilities are at the front line."

Osman did not back down. "He was my friend since we were young boys. I could not leave him to be buried by strangers. Anyway, there were no medics to be seen. Beat me if you must, but leave Ishmail. He came because I needed help to move the body. We could not leave Yusuf in the trench with the men, half his head was shot off."

Sergeant looked Osman over as if considering what to do with him. "Get back to your trench, you are both on watch duty all night tonight."

"Yes Efendi," Osman replied.

"Zahid Efendi," Ishmail hesitated. "Might I see the quartermaster about some new boots? These are worn out."

Ishmail lifted is right foot, but knew by Zahid's face that his request was a waste of words.

"We are all worn out!" Zahid spat. "Find some boots on a dead man, and be thankful you are alive."

The sergeant turned and strode off along the trench, barking orders along the way.

"Tomorrow," Osman said. "If we can get away, I will come with you and we will recover Yusuf's boots. He would be happy for you to have them."

Ishmail nodded in thanks. "Let's find a drink and take some rest. We might even sleep for an hour or two before night watch."

* * *

Later that afternoon, Ishmail sat on the knee-high firing step with his back against the front wall of the trench. He reached behind the ammunition pouch on his belt and fingered the foreign coin that lived in the pocket of his tunic.

Sunset approached and he had not slept. *Why? I am so tired and I have to stay up all night.*

He pulled out the silver coin and examined it. A kangaroo and large bird stood tall, as if partially human. The creatures faced each other and held a shield between them, embossed with a cross of stars. Another larger star hung over the shield. An ornate banner unfurled below the creatures, inscribed with hard-edged lettering. More hard-edged lettering formed an arc above the creatures and star, reinforcing the dominance of the image. At the bottom, below the banner, the numbers "1914" showed the Christian date.

The other side of the coin featured a man's head. The ornate crown left no doubt that this was the English king. More hard-edged characters encircled the head. *Who knows what that says? Maybe 'English will conquer the world!'?*

The fellow who swapped the silver coin for a button was a big man. He dug the hard earth with the strength of an ox, but his handshake was gentle, warm.

He was from Australia! I never thought I would meet a person from so far away. The English empire must be mighty to command allegiance from these men from the other side of the world. I wonder what this coin would buy in Australia?

Distant booms from the south confirmed Ishmail's thinking that the enemy was focusing attention elsewhere. The explosions at the southern front increased a week ago and hammered away for two days, then returned to normal levels. There were always explosions somewhere.

South or north, as long as it isn't here.

He thought of his father, when alive. He would often say 'While horses kick out, donkeys allow themselves to be crushed.' He talked of making a better life for his children. An easier life of education and privilege.

Ishmail rested his head back against the trench wall and hoped that sleep might come.

I need the courage to die a martyr and the purpose to live a life of honour. I'm being crushed between two millstones. God when will this horror end? Help me!

CHAPTER 74

Jayjay

Friday, 6 August 1915

Jayjay strode along Artillery Road at the head of his section. The sun was hot and his burden heavy, but he held his head high.

A distant boom shook the air. Another boom followed, then a third and he smiled to himself. *Three tunnel mines. Good. Blown to clear the way and help us surprise Abdul when the afternoon sun is low in his eyes.*

The march from Braund's Hill to Brown's Dip took the long way around, but taking a direct route would mean exposure to the Turks at the front line trenches. Instead, once the 5th Battalion had taken over the trenches of Braund's Hill, Jayjay and the other men of the 1st Battalion filed down Shrapnel Gully towards the beach, then south to Artillery Road, a deep, wide sap used to haul field guns up the ridge and provide safe passage for infantry along the southern sector. Jayjay hadn't fought at the southern sector before, but explored it one time with Larry on an afternoon break.

A biscuit box sign identified a smaller path off to the right as Gun Lane. Gun Lane took them to Brown's Dip where they dropped their load and began the wait.

"It's not right," Simmonds said. "We've been here from the beginning and we're held back in reserve for the big push. Meanwhile all the fresh reinforcements in the other battalions slip straight into the first charge."

The same complaint was rife through 1st Battalion originals. Being held back in reserve while the 2nd, 3rd and 4th Battalions hit Lone Pine was a great disappointment to most, and taken as an insult by some.

Internally, Jayjay shared the frustration, but now he was a lance corporal, a non-commissioned officer in charge of a section of eight men, and he had to hold the official line. He looked to Larry for some help, but Larry only smiled and shrugged.

"Okay Simmo," Jayjay said. "Here's how it is. We're part of the 1st Brigade, the New South Wales Brigade, and this is our chance to show the Empire what we can do. The 3rd Brigade took the landing and got all the headlines in the newspapers. The 2nd Brigade earned their stripes with the British down at Cape

Helles, and now it's our moment. This day will be remembered as the day the boys from New South Wales took Lone Pine. The other battalions of the 1st Brigade will go in first and stir Abdul up a bit, but there'll be plenty of pain to go around. We'll be into it before you know it. Abdul's not going to give up The Pine lying down and experienced reserves will be needed to go where the fighting is hottest. Now unless you want to go back down the hill to dig a latrine pit, I suggest you stop moaning like a bloody sheila."

"Blazes Jones," said Albert, the Aborigine. "You starting to sound like Sergeant bloody Fishface!"

"Shut up Darky!" Jayjay searched for a better come back, but found nothing and laughed with the rest of his section, relieved for a break in the tension.

A fatigue working party brought an issue of rice and tea that was supposedly laced with rum, but the taste of rum was barely perceptible. After the last meal was complete and bayonets were sharpened, three white calico patches were issued to each man, one to be attached to each arm and one to the back. Needle and thread were provided for stitching.

"These will reduce the chance of you getting blown up by our own artillery," Jayjay said, "So try and stitch it right. You can growl about sewing being woman's work but you new lads have to get used to the idea that your mother's not here to look after you and we gotta do everything for ourselves."

"Are we going to carry all this kit when we attack?" asked Raymond Hunter, the latest reinforcement assigned to Jayjay's section. The fellow had arrived at Gallipoli by ship from Egypt less than twenty-four hours earlier and dutifully carried a shovel from Braund's Hill."

"Yes Sunny," Jayjay replied. "When you're running across no-man's-land you can hold the blade of the shovel in front of your chest. It might save your life. Everyone carrying two hundred rounds? A couple of empty sandbags, a day's iron rations and water? We'll leave all packs here. Letters home at the top of your packs. If anyone doesn't make it back, those that do will make sure the letters are posted."

Nods and grunts gave Jayjay as much of a positive response as he could expect and the wait continued.

* * *

The afternoon sun hung over warships that lay waiting, sunbeams danced on the water between ships and shore.

A column of men strode up Gun Lane, loaded up with their own kit and shirts darkened with sweat. Silence fell over the waiting 1st Battalion as men of the 2nd, 3rd and 4th Battalions filed past towards The Pimple and other frontline trench positions facing the Turks' Lone Pine position.

Several of the passers-by nodded in the direction of the 1st Battalion, but the reserves sat like statues until the last man had passed.

Once the four battalions of the 1st Brigade were in place, Anzac artillery pounded the Turkish position at Lone Pine. It seemed as if every land-based gun focused on the one place. At the same time, the British warships that had returned for the occasion unleashed a terrific barrage.

The bombardment rose in intensity for fifteen minutes, to a point where it was impossible to distinguish one blast from the next. A continuous roar shook the air and the ground. *How can anyone survive there?*

Minutes passed and the roar continued, then an explosion sent earth skyward from down Gun Lane, maybe fifty yards away. *If that was one of ours it was way off the mark. Must be Turk shelling.*

Dirt and stones rained on Jayjay and the others where they sat. When the fallout stopped, Jayjay uncovered his head and gazed southwards. *The Turks are firing on us.* A shell from the Turkish gun Beachy Bill sailed through the air and looked to be headed directly at him. His body froze and it was all he could do to yell "Incoming!"

The shell continued directly at him and seemed to stall in the air. Diving to the left or right now would be futile. His eyes locked on the shell as it loomed slowly larger, then screeched over his head and buried itself into the ground with an almighty thud. Around three yards away from where he sat, a new hole marked the point of impact, the size as if it might have been dug by a small wombat. *Blazes! If that one detonated, we'd all be gone. Now what to do? They have our range, but orders are to wait here. Moving away will probably get us killed anyway. It'd be safer to run at a machine gun.*

Another Turkish shell was launched at them from Beachy Bill. It sailed through the air with an identical trajectory to the previous one. *This one can't miss.*

"Incoming!" Larry yelled.

The shell looked to Jayjay to be coming directly at him. *They have us. We're all gone before the charge.*

"Hold your ground!" Jayjay was surprised how calm he sounded. It was as if someone else was speaking with his voice. He watched the projectile sail towards him for a long moment, unable to move. This one hit closer than the last, one yard away from where he sat. The dud bored deep into the ground leaving a second wombat burrow. *What are the chances of that?*

A dark stain on Raymond 'Sunny' Hunter's uniform revealed that the fresh reinforcement had wet himself. Jayjay pretended not to notice and if anyone else realized they didn't say anything about it.

The cloud of artillery dust lifted and the roar faded.

Jayjay's ears felt like they might be bleeding and a high-pitched ringing filled his head. In the distance a whistle sounded three sharp blasts, then yells followed. He checked his wristwatch. Half past five. The first charge was away.

More whistles and more yells announced the following charges of the 2nd, 3rd and 4th Battalions. Some would be going over the top of the frontline trench and some would be using the tunnels to get closer before exposing themselves.

Jayjay's men said nothing, but occasionally looked at him expectantly.

He wanted to say something inspirational, but he could think of no words to fit the occasion, so he just stared back and nodded.

Minutes dragged into an hour.

The battle sounds were difficult to interpret. The fight was on at Lone Pine, but it was impossible to tell how the 1st Brigade boys were fairing.

One company of the 1st Battalion reserves was called forward, and another.

"Won't be long now lads." Jayjay took a sip from his water bottle.

More long minutes passed.

Flies buzzed as if in anticipation, unperturbed by the occasional hand waving them away.

Distant yells and rifle fire from the battle continued.

"D Company," Sergeant Baker called. "Move forward to the firing line."

Jayjay stood and his men followed him up the hill.

"The 1st Brigade holds Lone Pine," Sergeant Baker addressed the company. "Jacko Turk's not happy and is trying to take it back. You are going to make sure we hang onto it. Remember that you are going in as reinforcements. Listen for our own men up front. Let them know who you are and where you are. Don't be shooting them and don't let them shoot you. Their blood will be up and they are liable to shoot at anything that moves if they don't know who it is. Rifles ready, fix bayonets those who haven't. Oh, and rip those white patches off, they'll just make nice targets for the Turks. Our artillery's stopped firing now. On my whistle proceed through this tunnel, then run across no-man's-land and give 'em hell. Any questions? No. Good."

Baker raised the whistle to his lips and blew three long blasts.

Jayjay led his men, some still tearing at the white patches, into B5 tunnel in single file. Not the same thrill as going over the top, but it was some relief to be moving closer to the Turkish front line without coming under fire. His eyes fought to adjust to the darkness as he hunched forwards, careful not to jab the next fellow with the point of his bayonet and hoping that whoever was behind him was taking the same care. *Someone has put some serious work into digging this tunnel.*

Mother earth blocked out battle sounds, the peaceful shuffle of feet in the dirt was all that dampened the ringing in his ears. No one spoke.

A pinhole of light ahead grew into dazzling late afternoon yellow.

After fifty yards the tunnel ended in an opening that looked like a large shell crater. *The mines that blew the opening must have used a lot of explosive.*

The din of battle returned as if it had never stopped. Blinding light obscured men ahead as they scrambled out of the crater. A gang of sappers dug from the crater towards the Turks.

Jayjay stood in the crater, clear of the tunnel opening, until all eight men of his section crowded around.

"We charge together. Ready?"

Nods.

"Go!"

He leapt from the crater clutching his rifle in both hands. Eyes focused on the Turkish parapet ahead, he ran as fast as he could run. His vision narrowed as if he was in a tunnel again, but he felt the presence of his men on either side. They ran as a unit, racing against a common enemy and he did not lag behind. *Maybe they are slowing for me, or maybe I am keeping up because I am running so fast.*

Seconds later, Jayjay's section was across the final thirty yards of no-man's-land and slowed at the enemy parapet. Behind the parapet, pine logs covered the trench forming a heavy roof. *That's where all the pine trees went.* He thought of the old timber mill at home where he once hauled lumber. It seemed a lifetime ago. *Maybe I'll have to lift some of this roofing out of the way to get in.*

Several yards along the trench, a few logs had been pulled aside and lay across the direction of the others.

"There's a gap," Jayjay puffed.

He led his section along parapet of the Turkish trench to the opening where earlier attackers must have penetrated the defence. Below he could see bodies, but no movement. Sounds of fighting were clear, but remained some distance away.

Life-blood surged through his veins.

A bullet sung over his head but he didn't flinch.

Any second might be his last on God's earth, but he felt more alive than ever before. No remnant of stomach cramps remained. Weeks of boredom and sickness had melted away before the heat of battle.

The men of his section encircled him and looked to him for direction.

"We'll go in here."

He climbed down and sat on the log for the briefest of moments, maybe one or two seconds, then lent his weight forwards to lead the way into the enemy trench.

Another log in front provided a platform on which to rest the rifle that he held in both hands, and give resistance to slow his drop into the darkness of the trench below.

As he started to descend, something crashed into his right knee and shock waves of pain shook his leg, as if he had been smacked hard with a cricket bat.

A pitiful scream filled his ears and then he realized the sound came from his own mouth. Pain smothered other senses and he crumpled onto the trench floor, barely aware of the lifeless human bodies that broke his fall.

Directly above, a man-shaped silhouette filled the slot between pine logs.

Jayjay's vision blurred.

"Fuck that hurts!"

He managed to roll to one side just in time to prevent Larry landing on him, but a fresh bolt of pain shot up from his knee.

"I think I stopped one Larry," Jayjay managed to grunt. "Check for the shooter."

Other men from Jayjay's section poured down through the opening in the trench roof and spread in both directions.

Light was dim, but sufficient to show the human slaughterhouse he lay in. Bodies of Turks and New South Welshmen carpeted the floor and lent against the walls in a sculpture of death.

Pain fogged his thinking.

There was yelling.

I think that's all Aussie yelling.

His knee throbbed as if it would explode.

Everything was happening at lightning speed and slowly at the same time.

His eye's struggled to focus.

Am I crying?

Am I dying?

"Jay! Jay!"

Someone was grabbing at him, shaking him.

The voice was familiar.

"Larry!" Jayay cried. "My knee is shot. I can't move. God it hurts!"

"You're okay Jay," Larry said. "This is our trench now. I'll get your field dressing onto your knee and then we can push forward, to help the others – but I'll stay here with you if you want me to – the bleeding's not too bad – you tell me mate."

Jayjay knew the rules. Wounded men had to be left for the stretcher bearers. Advancing soldiers were neglecting their duty and could be charged if they stopped to give more than first aid.

But there was a higher duty. Duty to your mates came first. Jayjay had seen it plenty of times. A man would break any rules and take stupid risks for his mates.

He lifted himself to see his wounded knee, but even that small amount of strain added a new layer of pain. Larry already had Jayjay's field dressing out and pressed against the knee. He worked a length of bandage around Jayjay's leg in what seemed to be an overly rough manner.

Jayjay tried not to groan and grabbed at his leg. Sticky blood was already congealing in the late afternoon heat.

Someone pronounced the trench to be clear. Men stood around Jayjay, as if waiting for direction. Judging by the different heights they stood at, some were standing on one or more dead bodies.

Larry was still crouching close.

Jayjay reached to Larry's shoulder and marked a crude corporal's stripe with his bloody finger.

"Get forward and make sure we hold this trench," Jayjay forced a smile through gritted teeth. "Others need you more than me right now. Remember… You are the First Brigade… And you are fit for war!"

He wanted to sound more convincing but he was drunk with pain.

"Stretcher bearers will be here soon Jay," Larry checked the knee dressing and then brought his face close to Jayjay's and stared into his eyes. Jayjay struggled to focus.

"Listen Jay! Keep strong! The engineers are cutting a sap to join our old front line to this one. We saw them working at the end of the tunnel. They will be here by morning. You gotta hang on for the stretcher bearers. Okay? You can do that Jay – okay?"

"Get going Lance Corporal Larry Gillespie." Jayjay's vision blurred and he knew he grimaced but fought it and forced his eyes to focus on Larry's face. "You take my boys. I'll just wait here for a bit."

"You hang on Jay! You hang on okay!"

Part of Jayjay hoped that Larry would refuse to leave him, but before he knew it Jayjay lay alone with the dead in a mass grave.

Cramped spaces had never caused him concerns before, but now earth walls seemed to be closing in around him. The stench of dead bowels and stifling heat were trapped under the pine log roof. Throbbing pain made him nauseous and he vomited rice with liquid biscuit onto himself and the dead Australian under him.

Poor bastard deserves better. Sorry old mate.

The walls steadied and he felt a little better for emptying his stomach. He propped himself up, back to the wall and looked about the Turkish trench.

Just another bloody hole dug in the ground. Just like ours apart from the log roof.

Who shot me? The bullet hit the front of my knee, so it came from that direction. Must have run off. Bastard.

Rays of sunshine penetrated gaps between roof logs, but came at a low angle and stayed high, as if to deliberately avoid touching the carnage below.

Jayjay cast his gaze along the trench. No side could be declared winner here.

Flies swarmed, spoiled for choice. The drone of their frenzy was interrupted by rifle fire, bombs and yells. Sounds from outside were muffled, but the swearing told him Australian fighters were not far away.

Our attack has stalled. How far have we pushed them back? Can we hold what we have taken? If not, then I'm as dead as these buggers. This trench is a death trap.

Lifeless men from both sides stared, as if lamenting the futility of trading life for life. *Men never shut their eyes to die.*

Some stared at the roof. Some at the wall. Two men stood leaning against the wall and starred at each other, rifles held tight in death and bayonets jammed into each other's gut, as if refusing to accept the reality of their circumstance.

One Turk seemed to be staring directly back at Jayjay.

That's unusual. Normally the dead stare vacantly into nothing. Did that eye blink? I must be going crazy. No, he blinked again. Oh Hell.

Jayjay looked away and pretended not to notice the hidden enemy. He released a deliberate groan to be sure the Turk knew he was wounded. He checked his knee. The dressing had stopped most of the bleeding. *Good.* Men often bled to death from wounds higher up on the leg. The bullet hadn't come out the back of his knee, so must be still in there. He probed to see if he could feel the knee cap, but stabbing agony stopped the investigation before he could determine anything.

He gave himself a few seconds to swallow the pain and looked about to see what weapons were available to him. His bowie knife was still in its sheath at his hip. He wanted to feel the comfort of its bone handle, but he dared not move to touch it.

I need my rifle. All these dead, there must be a rifle.

Nothing within reach. At least nothing without the weight of a body or two jamming it in place.

Notches carved on the butt of his own rifle mocked him from several feet away. At least it lay on top of the bodies, but it was almost half way between him and the blinking eyes.

Bodies around the blinking eyes rose like a wave approaching the beach, then fell away as the Turk stood. *He's a big bastard.* Dried blood from a head wound covered half his bearded face. His belly was covered in blood, but it was impossible to tell if it was his. No signs that his movement was being hampered by wounds. *Damn.*

"Neden Ingiliz?" His voice was low, with a questioning tone.

"Neden Ingiliz?" Louder this time. He moved towards Jayjay, raised one hand waved it around, as if pointing out a problem that Jayjay might not have noticed.

"Neden Ingiliz?" He yelled. "Neden Ingiliz?"

He stopped at Jayjay's rifle and picked it up. He held it out towards Jayjay as if to offer it to him with a mock smile. "Seninki mi?"

Jayjay sat motionless, eyes locked on the Turk's.

His rifle was still out of reach and now in enemy hands.

The Turk released a mirthless laugh, but stopped abruptly to examine the rifle butt. He fingered the notches one by one.

"Seninki mi?"

"Seninki mi?" He yelled.

Jayjay shook his head and managed to croak. "I don't understand mate."

The Turk pointed the rifle at Jayjay's chest.

In that instant Jayjay knew he was about to die. The safety catch was off and a round chambered. All the Turk had to do was pull the trigger. It was impossible to miss at this range, even shooting from the hip. The bullet would enter through a small hole and tear its way out through a large hole at the back. Death would come quickly. Jayjay had seen it often enough.

His bladder let go.

At least the pain will stop when I die.

He stared down the barrel of his own rifle. End-on, past the tip of his own bayonet.

God forgive me for everything.

"Allaha git Ingiliz!" The Turk took a step forward. It was an awkward step on the uneven floor of bodies, but he maintained his balance.

Jayjay remained fixed in place, back against the wall. He gazed back at the Turk through the fingers of his own left hand – outstretched – palm forwards – fingers loosely splayed. His focus shifted for a moment onto the back of his hand. Covered in blood and dirt. The hand of a man about to die.

A fly landed on his thumb, walked a circle, and then buzzed off as if it knew it would be the first to lay maggot eggs into this one's warm meat.

Focus returned to the steel blade that inched towards him.

I looked along that same rifle, from the other end, at the first man I killed. A boy really. The lad held out his small hand in the same silent plea, then I stuck him like an animal, and jammed the bayonet between his ribs.

Why hasn't he fired?

Something wasn't right about the way the Turk held the rifle low at his side. One hand on the butt, the other in front of the magazine. His fingers were not at the trigger.

He means to stick me with my own bayonet.

Jayjay's eyes sharpened and his mind quickened, desperately seeking options. Being shot through the chest for a quick death was one thing, but being bayoneted in the belly and left to die slowly was a different prospect, and one worth fighting against. The belly was the usual bayonet target of choice, as less energy and time were required to push it in and pull it out, as compared with stabbing the chest where the blade had a tendency to jam between ribs.

"Shoot me! Pull the trigger you stupid bastard!"

"Allaha git Ingiliz!" The Turk lowered the bayonet slightly and aimed it at Jayjay's gut, as if reading his fear.

Fingers on Jayjay's outstretched hand stiffened. He let out a deliberate groan and moved the fingers on his left hand slightly to hold the Turks focus. At the same time he inched his right hand to up towards the bowie sheath, making the appearance of shifting his weight defensively.

The Turk lunged forwards, but Jayjay was ready.

A lifetime of events happened in the next second.

Jayjay grabbed the approaching bayonet with his outstretched hand and pulled it across himself down to the right. Damage to his hand was deep, but he was ready for this and kept pulling the Turk towards himself.

At the same time his right hand closed around the bone handle of the bowie knife and slipped it out of the sheath. He struck like a taipan and stabbed the bowie blade into the side of his attacker's neck.

The bayonet plunged harmlessly into the body of another man who had stopped caring earlier that day.

The Turk's eyes opened wide and his mouth opened a little as blood from his severed jugular vein seeped out around the entry of the six-inch blade.

Jayjay pulled the knife towards himself.

The Turk fell forwards.

Jayjay pulled the blade out and it flew by his face, clipping his own ear on the way past.

The Turk landed on top of him, the beard, crusted with dried blood, crashed into Jayjay's nose and scratched against his face.

Jayjay's knee screamed and the fresh wound on his left hand throbbed.

The Turk's body relaxed and it seemed as if he still struggled to fight.

Jayjay called on the last of his strength to push the body off his own. The bone knife handle was slippery with blood, but white knuckles held it in a vice-grip. Elbow bent, he was ready to stab again, but there was no need.

The Turk lay still, looking back. One eye twitched. Blood dribbled from the corner of his mouth. A few more heart beats pushed pulses of blood from the gaping neck wound, each weaker than the last, then the flow changed to a steady trickle.

Lifeless eyes stared back, but looked straight through Jayjay into the distance.

Without conscious thought he returned the bloody knife to its sheath, then he pulled his rifle from under the dead Turk and slid the safety catch on.

He looked about the trench of the damned and wanted to cry out. Not for the horror of his circumstance. Not for what he had just done to a fellow man. Not for the stench of a trench full of dead who had lost bowel control and started to rot in the heat, but from the agony that surged from his knee and pain building from his sliced hand. The best he could manage was a weak moan.

Time lost meaning.

Stomach cramps came and went.

Pain exceeded his threshold of endurance.

He called on God for the mercy of death, but God gave no more response than the soulless bodies lying about him.

Sounds of fighting continued as afternoon light faded.

He cried for his mother.

This must be what hell is like.

Am I already there?

My mouth is so dry. I need water.

Consciousness faded, but pain remained.

Flies buzzed in celebration.

CHAPTER 75

John

Friday, 6 August 1915, evening

The first men of the 4th Brigade marched down Reserve Gully in the dark. They passed the official starting point of No. 5 Supply Depot at precisely the scheduled departure time of 9:35pm.

According to John's schedule, in ten minutes they would reach the end of the gully and turn right at Beach Road. At 10:30pm they would reach the northern tip of Anzac territory at New Zealand No. 3 Outpost. Beyond No. 3 Outpost, the schedule had question marks against the estimated progress times, and a note "Assuming no halts or checks".

General John Monash hated question marks and assumptions, but he had been left with no alternative. His brigade's mission was by far the most arduous of all the operations to take place this night. His men in the left assault column were being asked to cover twice the distance required of the right assault column in the same amount of time. The great unknown was three miles of unreconnoitred ground, all uphill and all controlled by the enemy.

To the north, a destroyer opened fire again. By now, per the schedule, her electric-arc search lamp and guns would be aimed at Table Top, as they had at this time each night for the past six weeks. The Turks had been trained to expect the evening bombardment, but this night the New Zealand Mounted Rifles, having already taken back Old No. 3 Outpost, would continue up the valley of Chailak Dere and, the moment the guns ceased fire, would attack the Turks on Table Top from behind. The bright light would stay on for several minutes to distract the Turks from the front.

The rest of the New Zealanders of the right assault column had been encamped at No. 1 and No. 2 Outposts for two days, so were in good position to start their advance on Chunuk Bair once the covering force of their Mounted Rifles secured the foothills.

John would have preferred to start the march of his own 4th Brigade from No. 1 and No.2 Outposts, to take a mile off the distance of the night's advance, but he had lost that argument. These were New Zealand positions and the New Zealanders were entitled to use them.

"McGlinn," John called to his Chief-of-Staff. "The 13th Battalion is almost away. Have the 14th Battalion stand to."

"Yes Sir." McGlinn hurried up Reserve Gully.

Once in enemy territory, the first challenge would be to reach and then traverse the valley of Aghyl Dere. Two battalions from the 40th Brigade of Kitchener's new army were the covering force assigned to clear the valley for the left assault column to pass through. *A sound principle, but a damned nuisance that they had to wait until the New Zealand covering force got away. Now the 40th Brigade clogged up the only road north and stopped us from forming up to march in a continuous column.*

The 14th Battalion was massing ready to march north, but the tail of the 13th had disappeared into the night.

"McGlinn," John called. "We need to get the next battalion away. They will have to double to catch up with the column. We are falling behind schedule."

"Yes Sir."

Many minutes passed before the next contingent of the 4th Brigade made a start on the journey towards the beach and John immediately sent McGlinn off to start forming up the 15th Battalion.

The way everyone complained about the crowded stink of Reserve Gully, the men might have got themselves a bit better organised to be away. A little moonlight would make it easier, but we'll need the darkness when we attack.

John remained concerned about the condition of his men. The doctors were clear in their assessment. What was being asked of them would test the limits of their endurance. *They can still fire their rifles. When we take the heights, we will have opened a pathway for reinforcements to follow. The Tommies landing at Suvla Bay are fresh and they will bring support to the new firing line. The 1st Brigade have had success at Lone Pine, now we must do the same.*

Topographic maps had been taken from a dead Turkish officer and reproduced to enable the mission, but identifying one's position in complete darkness and reading a map without even the light of a candle was a big ask. This operation went against fundamental principles laid down by British military authorities. *'A thorough reconnaissance'*, said the Field Service Regulations, *'is an essential prelude to a night advance or to a night assault… Every commander who orders a night operation which is not preceded by a complete reconnaissance increases the risk of failure and incurs a heavy responsibility…Reconnaissance from a distance is insufficient.'*

How many men must have died in darkness so that some military strategist could pen those few words? And yet we are completely ignoring the hard-won wisdom.

John had read the Field Service Regulations from cover to cover, but he doubted whether the English Generals Godley or Birdwood were familiar with their contents. When John pointed out that the proposed operation did not comply with the recommended approach, they had dismissed his concerns and said that there simply wasn't enough time to reconnoitre the route, and that if this was done it might alert the Turks to the plan.

They must have been planning this operation for some time in secret. There certainly wasn't time for me to do anything when they gave me the details only days ago.

John's hopes for success on this night mission rested on a sheep farmer from New Zealand. Major Overton of the Canterbury Mounted Rifles had scouted north into the lower reaches of Aghyl Dere in late May. Knowledge gained from Overton's expedition was over two months stale, but it was the only first-hand Anzac experience of the valley. This night, Overton led the left assault column, with ten scouts, a local Greek farmer and an interpreter.

Turks maintained camps and defensive redoubts in this area, but these were believed to be lightly manned. *If the 40th Brigade do their job and clear the path, we might get through. It's hard enough for the men to form up here it's so dark.*

"McGlinn," John called. "Get the 16th Battalion to form up. I know there is barely space before the 15th is away, but we need to get a move on."

That morning, John had addressed the three hundred brigade officers in Reserve Gully and outlined the plan of attack, with details of the objective, timing and contingency plans. He told the officers that they must keep cool under all circumstances to inspire confidence in their men, and then during his speech a volley of shrapnel tore into Reserve Gully. Some men were injured close to John and it took every bit of his fortitude to keep his voice steady to the end, but the situation did give him the perfect opportunity to lead by example.

Now John stood and listened to the men form up and file out in the dark, he felt a different kind of anxiety building within himself, but it was just as real as when the shell burst above him.

By the time the last company marched past No. 5 Supply Depot, on the way out of Reserve Gully, the 4th Brigade was well behind schedule.

"On the double to catch the others," John called and jogged along with the men. They caught up with the next group of men and slowed to a walk, but John ran on beside the advancing column.

At about half a mile out of Reserve Gully, rifle fire crackled in the hills to the right. The sound cut through that of his own heavy breathing. A stray bullet whizzed overhead. His chest felt as if it might burst from the exertion.

Ahead the warship broadside continued to pound the hills and light them up in momentary orange flashes.

A white flare shot into the sky from a Turkish position.

John didn't stop running until he reached No. 2 Outpost. The column of men of the 4th Brigade was still arriving and men stood about in large groups waiting for direction. Some lay on the ground, receiving treatment for wounds. Of some concern to John was the fact that the tail of the covering force battalions of the 40th Brigade were still filing past, taking a parallel course a few yards closer to the sea, scrambling over tussocks and sand-hills.

The sounds of fighting continued inland where the New Zealand Mounted Rifles cleared the way for the right assault column of New Zealand Infantry.

John found his Chief-of-Staff at the agreed meeting place, with other staff officers and the New Zealander guide Major Overton.

"McGlinn," John puffed. "We need to get this column away. What happened here."

"The light of the destroyer dropped too low and touched our column. The men had the good sense to lay down, but bullets fell thickly and caught a few. Our battalions are not all here yet."

"No matter, we are behind schedule. The last of them are on the march from Reserve Gully and will be here before we can get the rest started. Overton be ready to leave at short notice."

"We are ready Sir."

McGlinn relayed the order to junior staff officers and they disappeared into the night to mobilise the four battalions.

It was half an hour after John arrived at No. 2 Outpost when Major Overton led the column out of Anzac territory with his scouts and Greek fisherman. The time was eleven o'clock and the advance of the left assault column was thirty minutes behind schedule.

The men left at a good pace and John was confident they would be able to make up at least some of the lost time. *So long as the 40th Brigade covering force clear the valley of Aghyl Dere for us.*

"McGlinn," John said. "Inform General Cox that the left assault column is on the march and it will soon be time for us to be away."

"Yes Sir."

The column held a steady rate of progress, but still another half an hour passed before the first two battalions were on the march and it was time to take his place in the column with his staff and General Cox in the centre of the brigade.

"I should like to be closer to the front," John said.

"The risk is too great," Frustration in Cox's voice cut through the darkness. "You will stay here with me, as we have already discussed."

"Decisions may be required at the head of the column. Unforeseen circumstances might arise. I cannot lead the men if I am not there."

"They know the plan. You explained it well enough this morning. They can send a runner back if need be."

"We are behind schedule. Runners take time."

"You Australians do struggle with the concept of taking orders. Godley warned me about that. If you were so worried about the schedule, you might have got these men marching sooner."

I am wasting my breath with this man.

John said nothing and marched onwards.

General Godley had placed the left assault column under fifty-five year old General Cox, a newly arrived British veteran from the Indian Army, and so far John was no more impressed with his new commander than he was with General Godley. Cox seemed to come from the same English officer school that taught unquestioning obedience to vague orders, muddling on through and then the making of excuses for failure.

The moon had not yet risen and John could barely make out the form of the man in front, but listened for the crunch of his footsteps so as not to walk into his back.

The pace had dropped to that of a funeral procession and John squinted into the darkness but could see nothing that would explain the delay.

Someone yelled in the distance, then men started diving off the path, into the scrub to the left and right. John dropped for cover himself and listened for sounds of attack but heard nothing more than rifle fire in the foothills to the right that had been chattering away all evening. He wanted to stand and urge the men onwards, but hesitated. *Why did the men in front throw themselves into the bushes?*

He looked back and realised that a tremor of alarm had promulgated back along the column as far as he could see and brought it to a halt.

He stood and looked about. Others rose from hiding.

"Get up, the lot of you!" John yelled. "There is nothing there, we need to keep moving. March on!"

Minutes passed before the column started to move forward again, and the pace was even slower than before.

"I need to go forward," John said to General Cox, "to see what is causing this delay."

"Send one of your staff officers."

"But – very well, Sir." John would have preferred the chance to regain control of the situation himself, but Cox had been adamant from the beginning that John and his staff should stay in the centre of the column. *He's a crotchety old sod, I think the climate in India has affected him.*

The column trudged onwards and John remained none the wiser to the reasons for the delay. Sounds of fighting in the foothills continued. So much for a secret advance. If the enemy doesn't know we're on our way now they must be deaf or stupid.

Ahead, the column of men veered to the right and looked to be turning away from the main trail. One man stood off to the side and looked to be guiding the men at the turn-off. John approached the fellow. It was too dark to recognise him, but he identified himself as one of Major Overton's scouts.

"At least we have made it to the mouth of the Aghyl Dere," John said. "But we are the best part of an hour behind schedule."

"This is not the Aghyl Dere, General."

"What? You were to proceed along the north beach road to the mouth of the Aghyl Dere, then turn inland. The orders were clear."

"The native villager, Sir, the farmer, he knew a short cut. He said his people come this way. This gully leads to a pass that connects with the Aghyl Dere. He said this way is much shorter."

Frustration boiled up from within. *Impulsive changes to plan bring unanticipated problems.*

"This way may well be shorter, but we seem to be moving along awfully slowly."

"Yes Sir, that we do."

John returned to his staff and General Cox in the column that was now at a stand-still.

"We have gone a different way to the plan," John spat. "This is apparently some shortcut known to the Greek native with our guide. I must go forward to see what is causing the delay."

"Send a staff officer", said Cox.

"The last staff officer that I sent never returned. That told us nothing. We cannot afford more delay."

"All the more reason to stay back. If something happens to you then you will not be able to command your men."

"I cannot very well command my men at the moment, Sir."

"Send someone forward. The column has stopped, it should not take them long to reach the front."

"I will go Sir," McGlinn said before John could argue further.

"Very well, see if you can get them moving through to Aghyl Dere, and up the valley at a quicker pace."

"Yes Sir."

The queue of men shuffled forward a few steps and halted again.

John could barely speak from the frustration.

He had told his men to remain calm, imagining circumstances where they might be under enemy fire, not stuck in a line waiting to pass through the wrong gully on the way to attack the enemy.

Many minutes passed and McGlinn did not return.

Somewhere inland a crowd let out a cheer, as if their team just won a grand final. *I hope that was our side.* Distant rifles chattered on.

A few times the men ahead moved another few paces, but otherwise there was no progress being made.

The waiting dragged on until John could bear it no longer.

"I must go forward," he blurted before he organised an argument in his head. "We have no chance of getting close to our objective to attack before dawn if we don't get moving immediately."

After a pause Cox replied "Go then."

John hurried off and shoved past groups of his own men.

"General coming through!" he called several times and they moved over as they could, but the gully narrowed.

John stumbled and caught is breath. *I must be more careful or I will skewer myself.* Each man carried a rifle with a seventeen-inch bayonet blade fixed to the muzzle and darkness prevented anyone from seeing much at all.

In places the prickly undergrowth was so thick that the men were forced to advance in single file, along what appeared to be a freshly cut track. Medical officers were applying field dressings to some who had come under fire.

After what seemed to be a heavy mile, but John knew was less, he pushed over a saddle in the ridge and followed the now stationary line of men down a narrow gully to a junction where it opened out into flatter ground.

At this junction, John found Major Overton in an argument with Colonel Tilney of the 13th Battalion and Captain Eastwood, one of the staff officers that John had sent forward to investigate the slow progress.

"A company of the 13th has gone forward to attack a party of Turks that was firing on us. They have not returned yet. We are considering what is the safest way for the men to proceed."

"What damned nonsense!" John said. "You have a route-plan to follow. Get a move on, quick. We cannot wait for them to return."

"We are still coming under fire from a Turkish Bivouac up the valley."

"Where is the 40th Brigade covering force? They were supposed to clear this area. And where are we anyway?"

"I have not come into the Aghyl Dere this way before." Overton said. "I think we are nearly at the point where the 13th and 14th Battalion are to take a separate course.

"You think? It is half past two, and we are to attack the peak before dawn. We are two hours behind schedule for a coordinated attack, and that relies on our being where you think we are. Why didn't you stick to the plan and enter Aghyl Dere from the end?"

"Our Greek native knew a short cut."

"It wasn't much of a short cut. It slowed us down and the men came under fire. Probably Turks scattered by the New Zealand Mounted Rifles. Any signs of our own covering force?"

"We are not sure, but we believe they are to the west Sir, further down the Aghyl Dere."

"Of course they are! They followed the plan and went the long way around. Now our covering force is behind us and we'll have to fight our own way through. How confident are you of our current location?"

No answer.

A crescent moon hung low over the eastern horizon.

CHAPTER 76

Mustafa

Saturday, 7 August 1915, early hours

Colonel Mustafa Kemal squinted into the pre-dawn black.

His artillery observation emplacement on Sword Slope held a commanding view down the range, but there was little moonlight tonight. It was impossible to make out any details in the distance.

He allowed no flame or other light, that would be far too dangerous, likely to draw enemy fire. Darkness in the trench gave the eyes every chance to adjust. Even so, ears could learn more than eyes for now.

The battle at Bloody Ridge was still raging, but that was not his main concern. The sounds of distant rifle fire in the valleys to the north made him feel sick in the stomach.

No sleep tonight, nor any time soon.

Late on the previous afternoon Mustafa had watched the enemy attack at Bloody Ridge. Their coordination with a naval artillery barrage had been effective. The enemy infantry charge only had to cover a short distance between the frontline trenches and crossed the hundred metres of no-man's-land virtually unmolested. Some of them emerged from new tunnels, blown open with explosive prior to the charge.

Mustafa immediately ordered his howitzers and machine guns to fire on the attackers, but to limited effect.

Pine log cover over the trenches at Bloody Ridge slowed the response of those inside and allowed the enemy to enter in large numbers before anything could be done.

Mustafa had discussed the situation with General Esat and sent a full battalion to reinforce the breached defences, even though Bloody Ridge was outside his zone of responsibility. It was a tough battalion too – Major Zeki's battalion – the First Battalion of the 57th Regiment. *Zeki and his men helped me throw the enemy off this ridge in the first days. I wonder how he's fairing now. Sounds like he's making good use of all those hand bombs he took, the perfect tool to clear the enemy out of our trenches. Rifle fire down there hasn't stopped all night. It must be a hard fight.*

Interesting the enemy is not driving home the attack at Bloody Ridge to full effect.

With more reinforcements they could break through the defensive line and do some real damage. If they fought their way down into the Valley of Black Nomads, they could open up a hole in the middle of our line that would be very difficult to close.

Mustafa drifted back in his memory a hundred days to his decision to execute the nomad trouble-makers in that valley. *It was such a shame for them, a waste. They could have chosen to defend their homeland and die with honour. Instead, their bodies lay there, blackened by the sun, as a reminder to others of the disgrace in desertion.*

The Bloody Ridge attack is a feint.

Mustafa had thought so as darkness fell, and his suspicions were confirmed later in the evening when another weak enemy attack came at Junction Hill. A half-hearted assault, easily fought off.

Distant rifle fire in the gullies to the north had started around midnight. Its continuation gave away the true English objective.

Mustafa recalled the meeting he had held with General Esat two months earlier, at another lookout very close to the observation post where he now stood. He shook his head at the black. Now the enemy was attacking the heights from valleys and ridges to the north, exactly as Mustafa foretold. *I didn't have to be God's holy prophet to see that coming.*

There was no satisfaction in being correct in his predictions about an enemy attack. The heights of Chunuk Bair and Koja Chemen Tepe were always the enemy's objective. Now they were just trying to get there by an alternative route further to the north.

Word had arrived that the light defences in the area had been overcome, and the English were advancing up towards Falcon Ridge.

"Izzettin," Mustafa said. "We need more information about the defence of our high ground. Have we been able to establish communications with Kannengieser's Division up at Chunuk Bair?"

Mustafa had insisted that his full entourage of staff remain with him by the telephone this night. They stood around him in the crowded observation post.

"Not yet Kemal Bey. The engineers are still working on it. I have ordered that they let me know as soon as they make the connection."

"He will need support when the enemy arrives. We will need to determine troop deployment between us."

* * *

Sounds of fighting continued through the night and ignored the beginnings of a grey dawn dissolving the black.

Mustafa peered through binoculars down the ridge. At Bloody Ridge there was just enough light to see an occasional figure emerge from a trench and then disappear again.

A screaming explosive shell disrupted the relative peace on this part of the battleline. It flew into the seaward side of Hill of Valour and sprayed solid earth into the air as if it was mud.

Mustafa looked out to sea and didn't need binoculars to see the muzzle flash when the next gun fired. *The warships have returned.*

Eternal seconds passed as the projectile flew through the air like a deadly bird, flying faster than sound. Then the explosion was delivered, further up Sword Slope from the first, but with the same impact.

Rows of trenches on Sword Slope and Hill of Valour blurred with activity, like a disturbed nest of ants, as men scurried for cover. Even the fresh-faced 18th Regiment knew the meaning of a naval bombardment. Those who didn't learn quickly didn't live long. Machine guns were abandoned and rifles carried away from fire steps all the way down to the enemy front line. Gunners left artillery pieces and bunkered down. No trenches had been hit yet – the first few shots were range-finders.

Another salvo of blasts came in succession.

Thunder ran together and hung in the air like fog.

Crashing war-gongs shook Mustafa to his bones. They were known to bring fear to the surface from any hidden place, no matter how deep it was buried.

"Kemal Bey," Izzettin said. "Perhaps we should move to the rear lines. This bombardment is seeking emplacements like this one."

"I cannot expect men to endure this and hide myself. This is the very time we need to see what is happening." Mustafa forced a grin. "Relax Izzettin Bey, this is only an observation post, the enemy does not even know it is here. They will target our guns and firing trenches. You may yet live to see the end of this day."

"Your safety is my only concern Kemal Bey."

"Of course. We will stay."

Time seemed to stop during the naval artillery bombardment. *Would it never end? How can they afford so many shells?* Fortunately the men could retreat into relative safety in the trenches on the lee side of the hill. The network of trenches had been developed in response to the English warships and their guns.

Naval guns were designed for long range sea-battles and their guns were limited to a low trajectory. Their shells contained high explosive intended to penetrate heavy steel armour. These shells exploded on impact, making them impressive, but ineffective against ground troops hiding behind at hill. Shrapnel burst shells were able to achieve a much more devastating effect against ground troops by exploding in the air and raining deadly metal pellets over a large area, but evidently shrapnel shells were one thing the British navy lacked.

Mustafa sat on the observation step with his entourage of staff crowded around. He desperately wanted to watch what was happening down the ridge, but the risk was unnecessary. He had to wait like everyone else, and rely on the men to do their job when the time came. Such a heavy bombardment usually signalled an imminent attack.

He wondered how Zeki and his battalion were performing down at Bloody Ridge. *Trench warfare is a bloody business.*

A commotion in the trench nearby caused Mustafa to reach for his revolver. He lifted the leather flap on the holster and fingered the timber grip. As always, it was fully loaded.

A small band of men appeared at the entrance to the already crowded observation post.

One man stepped forward, an officer from the 14th Regiment, covered in blood. "Kemal Bey, a strong enemy force has raided the Aghyl Dere sector –"

Naval artillery thundered into the ridge below, making conversation almost impossible.

"Our regiment is mostly destroyed and we have been forced back."

Mustafa surveyed the officer and small band of men. Every one of them was bleeding from wounds. "Take your men to Chunuk Bair. This is where the enemy is heading. We must stop them from claiming the heights. I will send any further reinforcements that I can spare."

The officer's eyes looked to his boots for the briefest moment, then he nodded his head. "Yes Kemal Bey."

He and his men would not likely live to see out the dawning day.

"You and your men have done well this night," Mustafa said. "Your nation will never forget your courage."

"Yes Kemal Bey."

The officer from the 14th Regiment turned to address his men. It was impossible to hear him over the naval bombardment, but the grim determination on the men's faces as they nodded was enough to let Mustafa know that they would give their all.

The bloodied band disappeared into the pre-dawn grey, and the shelling stopped as suddenly as it started.

Mustafa checked his pocket watch. Half past four – the bombardment had lasted about thirty minutes. *Come on my little Mehmets, get back to the firing line. Let's not have another Bloody Ridge today. At least we don't have the pine log covers here to slow us down, and our terraced trenches allow multiple rows to fire on the enemy at once.*

Mustafa reassured himself again that his defence would hold and Bloody Ridge was different.

The dust settled but the acrid cordite smoke hung in the air. The sudden quiet seemed foreign, a peace out of place here. Distant rifle fire from Bloody ridge became audible again for the first time since the shelling started, despite the ringing in his ears. Even the rifle fire off in the distant north could be heard and reminded Mustafa of the bigger problem.

Mustafa checked his pocket watch again – two long minutes since the last naval shell detonated.

No attack.

Finally he saw some movement in the Ottoman frontline trenches. Men scurried to their machine gun posts. Others climbed onto the fire step and raised rifles over the parapet.

Still no attack.

Surely the Australians are not coming now. Their naval bombardment will be wasted. Maybe it was another ruse. The real threat is to the north. That is where the enemy reinforcements have been sent.

The men below will not be thinking like this, and nor should they be. Their sole focus is the enemy trench in front of them. Full of adrenalin after enduring that hell and seeing their brothers killed. Ready to defend their homeland with their lives. Fingers on triggers.

Still no enemy attack.

All smoke had dissipated and silence blanketed the field from the enemy position, past Hill of Valour, up Sword Slope. A high-pitched ringing remained.

Mustafa raised his binoculars and looked across to Bloody Ridge. Still the enemy chose not to flood the area with reinforcements. Maybe they could be contained to a new frontline soon. General Esat had been desperate to regain lost trenches, rushing to reinforce the position. *If a new defensive line can be established there is no great strategic loss. As long as the new enemy position doesn't overlook our other flanks. Our reinforcements will be needed to defend the higher ground.*

A nearby machine gun released a fire-burst. Mustafa turned towards the sound and dropped his field glasses to the end of the neck strap.

Widespread rifle fire erupted from the slope below and the rattle of machine guns blurred together.

He leaned forward to the front of the observation trench. The view to Hill of Valour was unobstructed and close enough to see clearly without the magnification of field glasses.

Australian cavalry held the enemy front line at Hill of Valour, without horses. They had decimated the charge of the 18th Regiment five weeks ago and now they charged back across the same ground. The remains of martyrs lay in vigil as an ongoing reminder of that terrible night.

Hill of Valour compressed any advancement into a narrow bridge of land, an isthmus at the head of the first ridge – a final obstacle to form the junction with the second ridge, like a toll bridge to the heights. The enemy had penetrated here on the first day, but were quickly pushed back and never touched this soil again.

Today they paid the toll in full, but made no serious threat.

The Australian advance withered under fire. Many fell back into their own trench before even reaching the top of their ladders. Some attackers sought cover on their right flank, diving into the upper reaches of the Valley of Fear. Hand bombs followed those ones into the gully and cleared them out.

The attack was over quickly.

The distribution of enemy bodies across the field was evidence of their failure. Dead and wounded were thickest near their own frontline trench. Many lay on the parapet. The scatter thinned out across the narrow strip of no-man's land with very few lying close to the Ottoman frontline trenches.

Men in the Turkish frontline trench stood firm, braced and ready to continue defence of their territory.

Activity in the enemy trenches caught his eye, although it was difficult to determine the details from here.

"See the bayonets," Izzettin said. "The Australians are organising another charge. The troopers are reluctant without their horses. It looks like their officers are beating and prodding them forward with sticks."

"Yes, they will throw more men, but our defences are strong here.

Minutes later another attack came, but it was stopped, even more quickly than the first. Many were shot back into their own trench. Those that cleared the parapet had to negotiate a field covered with their own dead. Enough to slow the most hardened of men. Many added to the pile and none reached the Ottoman frontline trench.

At least this morning the 18th Regiment got its own back at the dismounted Australian cavalry. Any further attacks can be contained here.

Mustafa climbed down from the observation step and turned to his Chief of Staff. "Izzettin, prepare a divisional order for distribution to all regiment commanders and companies, and send a copy to General Esat. Congratulate each regiment by number, for holding firm in defence this past night and inflicting huge enemy losses. I know I can trust in their continuing courage. State that the 9th Division holds Chunuk Bair at our right flank, and plans to attack the enemy advancing on Falcon Ridge tonight. Engineers must establish communications with 9th Division field headquarters at Chunuk Bair – urgently. The 18th Regiment is to reconnoitre valleys on either side of Hill of Valour to be sure no enemy remain after their exceptional defence against this morning's assault. Divisional artillery units are to prepare to fire against enemy positions at Junction Hill and High Ridge. State that I am in the artillery position around Sword Slope."

Major Izzettin nodded while scribbling with pencil on his notebook. "Yes Kemal Bey."

Mustafa stepped back up onto the observation platform and shook his head at the field of dead and wounded Australians. *That was too easy. The English must have a more serious threat for us to deal with in the north.*

CHAPTER 77

Jayjay

Saturday, 7 August 1915, dawn

The flies were on duty early today. They had much work to do.

One crawled across Jayjay's tongue and another bounced against the roof of his mouth.

He drifted again from a semi-conscious daze.

His knee begged for mercy. Slight movement triggered fresh stabs and demanded care.

God please let this be a nightmare, or please let me die.

He inhaled a fly and coughed himself awake, his knee feeling as if it was shaking about on a bed of hot coals. When the convulsions stopped, he spat on the dead Turk lying beside him.

Patches of cool grey between the logs above told Jayjay that he had survived the night. There had been some moments when this seemed unlikely and many when he wished he would not.

Careful not to move his knee, he lifted his left hand in front of his face. The gash across his palm was packed with dirt cemented in congealed blood and felt as if it was being pounded by a meat mallet.

Muffled sounds of rifle fire and yelling hadn't stopped all night, and seemed no further away this morning as they were last night, when Jayjay first found himself to be the only living soul in a trench full of dead.

Keep at them boys. If you let them through, I'm bloody done for. I wonder how Larry and my section are faring. Hopefully better than me.

He dragged himself up to lean against the trench wall. It took a full minute, and much swearing at the reluctant knee. He sat still for a while and the pain subsided to a throbbing ache.

His water bottle was empty, but he removed the lid and held it up to his mouth in case another drop might moisten his tongue. It didn't.

God, I'm thirsty.

Look at this slaughter.

So many dead.

God, how can this happen?

There was plenty of light now to illuminate the display of death. All the actors remained in the same pose as yesterday. The big bearded Turk lay next to him with a gaping hole in the side of his neck. The two men bayoneting each other in the gut held their ground, as if in a competition of endurance, hoping the other might finally concede defeat.

Jayjay sat and counted the dead to pass time.

As far as he could tell they were about half Australians and half Turks, at least from the ones he could identify.

He pulled out his bowie knife and carved another notch in the butt stock of his rifle. Fresh wood stood in contrast to older notches darkened with dirt and dried blood.

"This one's for you Abdul." He rasped, his voice between a croak and a whisper. "You nearly got me, you bastard. I hope you don't mind if I call you Abdul?"

No answer.

"I don't know your real name, so that'll have to do. You're the first man I've killed for over a month. Likely my last, thank God. I've killed a few, but you knew that already. You figured it out from the notches on my rifle. Did you have a family? You're an ugly sod, but you might still have a family somewhere who cares about you, I suppose."

Abdul stared vacantly upwards.

"Was it you who shot my knee?... I think it must have been you… There was no one else alive here, and the bullet came from your direction. You must have hid under the bodies before Larry nearly dropped on top of me."

Jayjay finished carving the notch and returned his bowie knife to its sheath. Maybe no one would ever see it, or know its meaning, but it seemed important to record the final score. He didn't need to count the notches to know that the number was thirty-nine.

"You should have just shot me when you had the chance. I told you to. Then you might have lived instead of me. At least for a little while. But you wouldn't have got out of here alive, not once you were behind our lines, unless you surrendered. You must have known that… Would you have surrendered Abdul?… No I didn't think so…Why didn't you just shoot me? Damn you!"

He counted bodies again and came to a total three lower. He sat and tried to ignore the pain. *Someone will come here eventually, our boys or Turks, but someone will come.*

He counted again and confirmed the original total. There were many more than those he could count, some bodies were lying on others he couldn't see.

Voices caught his attention, close, but around a bend in the trench.

By instinct he reached for his rifle. The rifle he had kept close all night. The rifle that had served him so well since leaving Sydney, but nearly betrayed him in the end.

He eased the safety catch off, but swearing in a familiar drawl let him know he could breathe easy again.

An Australian soldier rounded the corner and paused. "God have mercy, it doesn't end."

Jayjay watched him absorb the scene. *The fellow hasn't seen me. Sitting amongst all these dead bodies, I must be difficult to pick out as alive. He might turn back and leave me here.*

Jayjay lifted a hand and reached towards the soldier. He tried to cry out, but only a hoarse whisper came.

"Stretcher bearer!" the soldier yelled and turned to someone Jayjay couldn't see. "Get those bearers up here!"

Next thing Jayjay knew, he was being rolled onto a stretcher. Movement sent pain shooting up his leg, but when he tried to explain the problem all he could manage was a parched groan.

The bearers were men from the 1st Battalion Regimental Aid Post. Jayjay recognised one who had been with the battalion from the beginning.

The stretcher hovered and took Jayjay feet first away from a place he wanted to escape more than any place he had ever known.

The stretcher ride though the covered Lone Pine trench was bumpy and uncomfortable, but relief pushed fear back in its place. Men continued to fight each other not far away, but he was being evacuated, like so many others he had seen. *As long as they can get me away from the front without getting me shot or blown up, I should be all right.*

A tunnel and new sap joined the captured Turkish trench to the old Anzac front line.

"This is your stop old son." The bearers lowered Jayjay. "The 3rd Field Ambulance boys will take you from here."

Within minutes, another stretcher bearer was standing over him. "Where are you hurt Mate?"

Jayjay pointed to his knee and held out the palm of his left hand. "Water" he managed to croak.

The bearer reached for his water bottle and shook it. "Sorry Mate, I'm all out. They should be able to give you some at the dressing station. I can give you some morphine though."

After the injection, the world dropped away as Jayjay's stretcher rose into the air and started moving forwards. He raised his head a little and looked down Victoria Gully, past his boots and the back of the leading stretcher bearer. The ride was surprisingly smooth. The shoulders of the fellow in front bounced up and down, but he must have been making an effort to avoid transferring the bumps to the stretcher. They travelled around one hundred yards before arriving at the advanced dressing station.

The bearers lowered his stretcher onto the ground in front of the dugout lined with a tin roof and sandbags.

"Good luck sport," one of them offered.

The dugout was big enough for a handful of men to stand inside. The scatter of stretchers out front was the only indication it was a medical station. The bearers sauntered to the stack, picked up an empty blood-stained stretcher and started back up the hill towards Lone Pine.

A fellow moved from the shadow of the dugout and knelt beside Jayjay. He poked at Jayjay's right knee and reflex reaction to the pain caused Jayjay's body to jerk upwards. Movement amplified the pain further.

Jayjay reached up with his hand, but still could not produce more than a weak groan.

"Leg's broke. Bleeding's not too bad. We'll tie it up. Haven't got a tourniquet on have you mate?"

Jayjay shook his head and held up his left hand to show his other wound but the medical officer had turned his back and was fiddling around with his wounded leg. Maybe checking for a tourniquet, but Jayjay felt pressure on his ankle. *You might be a bit gentler about it.*

The medical officer checked Jayjay's identity disk and scribbled something on a white ticket which he pinned it to Jayjay's shirt.

"Take this one down to the beach, head first to stretch the leg out."

What?

Two more stretcher bearers appeared from the shadows. They lifted Jayjay and turned his stretcher about so that when he raised his head he was looking up the hill towards Lone Pine.

The track down Victoria Gully was steep in places and this time Jayjay felt every bump.

They didn't give me any water. I need water.

Gravity pulled Jayjay downhill, but the medical officer had tied Jayjay's right ankle to the stretcher handle. His body started to slip down the slope, but his foot held fast and his wounded knee felt as if it was being pulled apart by the tension.

The journey to the beach was less than a mile, but seemed to go on forever. Nausea swelled in his gut and the world spun about him.

Once he heard a tearing sound come from within his knee, and vomited, then blacked out from the pain. He regained consciousness at the sound of boots crunching on the coarse sand at the beach. Now on level ground, the tension came off his knee and the pain was almost bearable, but his throat was so dry he could barely breathe.

"Water." His voice was weak and went unnoticed.

"Water."

Jayjay's stretcher turned so the soles of his feet aimed at the sea, then he was lowered next to another body lying on the sand.

"Water," he said a bit louder.

One of the bearers unstoppered his water bottle. "Here you go Mate. Go easy, that's all I've got for the morning."

Jayjay nodded, but the water was so sweet he gulped the lot.

"We're going to need that stretcher back."

The stretcher bearer knelt and untied the rope around Jayjay's ankle.

Jayjay rolled himself slowly onto one side, and then, without warning, the stretcher bearer lifted the side of the stretcher and dumped Jayjay face-first into the sand.

The stretcher bearers took the empty stretcher back along the beach, south towards Victoria Gully. Jayjay brushed grit from his face and propped himself onto his elbows to look around.

The cove stretched a few hundred yards in each direction. Men scurried about the beach with greater urgency than usual, and a crowd congregated at the pier directly in front of him. Many of the men loitering near the pier looked to be walking wounded.

A barge approached the pier. *Maybe that will take me to a hospital ship. I wonder how Larry and the others are doing. It'd be nice to say good bye first, but I need to see a doctor.*

To Jayjay's right, a row of wounded lined the back of the beach. Too many men to count easily, maybe a couple of hundred. *A queue of unhealthy passengers, each with a ticket out of here pinned to his uniform.*

Next to him, a fellow lay on his side. His blood-soaked back dotted with four holes showed no signs of life, other than the bright red colour of fresh blood close to the holes.

"Hey," Jayjay said. "Mate? You okay Mate?"

No response.

Jayjay waited a moment before his eyes moved on.

The barge pulled in at the pier. Navy jacktars threw loops of rope to hold the barge in place and walking wounded swarmed on board. They came from all directions, like flies to a tin of jam. The barge was full within a minute, then the jacktars untied the knots and refused to let any more board. One fellow with a bandaged arm jumped on anyway.

A bugle sounded and the barge pulled away from the pier towed by a steam pinnace.

Stretcher bearers approached along the beach with another passenger, and lowered him next to Jayjay. This fellow had blood covering the left side of his face and one ear seemed to be missing, but it was difficult to tell.

"Mate," Jayjay said to one of the bearers. "What's going to happen to us now?"

"That's up to the casualty clearing station, but they're pretty busy today." The bearer looked up at the line of wounded and then gazed towards the pier. "We're just the field ambulance. Our job is to get you here to the beach. Likely you'll be sent out to a hospital ship. Navy looks after sea transport, but there's not much of that available right now. Big landing going on up north. You might be in for a bit of a wait."

The bearers recovered their stretcher and wandered off.

The fellow they left behind stared at Jayjay. His right eye twitched.

"Where you from Mate? Jayjay asked.

No answer. The fellow just stared, one eye twitching.

"Where you from?" Jayjay raised his voice.

A slight shake of the head, and more eye twitches.

"What's your name?"

"Cooper, Sir."

"I'm no Sir, just a shot up Lance Corporal. Listen Cooper, we're going to get out of here. You're going to be okay. Do you understand that Cooper?"

Cooper stared back, eye still twitching. Eventually he gave a single nod and lay back on the sand as if to go to sleep.

Jayjay turned to the bloody back on his other side. Careful not to move his own knee, he reached out and placed his hand on the man's shoulder.

"You okay mate?"

Jayjay half expected him to be dead, and was startled when he made to roll over to face Jayjay.

"How bad does it look?" the fellow asked.

"Looks like you stopped four in your back. Is it shrapnel?" Jayjay asked.

He nodded.

"I'm a gunner and they found our range. Saw it coming and hit the ground, but it was a good shot. Burst right above us. Killed the rest of my crew. Bastards. Where were you?"

"Lone Pine."

The gunner nodded. "The feint."

"Feint?"

"Yeah, a distraction for the main attack on the heights, and the landing up north at Suvla Bay."

"This was no feint mate, we took The Pine, my boys are still fighting to hold it."

The gunner shook his head in a way that reminded Jayjay of his own father when he was younger.

"Lone Pine, Steele's, Quinn's, Pope's – all feints. The main attack is for the higher ground, above The Nek. Trouble is no one's getting through. Light Horse got slaughtered at The Nek this morning, hardly got out of their trenches. Maorilanders couldn't get through on Rhododendron Ridge and the bloody Tommies landing at Suvla are standing around like schoolboys waiting for their teacher."

A sinking feeling gripped Jayjay's gut. The tale had a ring of truth about it. The stretcher bearer had mentioned a big landing to the north.

"How would a gunner know all that then?" Jayjay asked, not wanting to believe what he heard.

"Saw it with me own eyes. I was spotting for our eighteen-pounder at Walker's Ridge. We were supposed to provide some covering fire for an attack that never started. Fired off a few shots to soften the Turks up a bit, but they got us back and they got us good."

Jayjay thought of Larry and the rest. *The whole 1st Brigade. The pride of New South Wales. Four battalions fighting to the death – a feint. A feint for a botched attack in a God-forsaken place on the wrong side of the world. How can this happen?*

Morning sun crept over the escarpment above the beach. A bugle sounded and another barge, full of walking wounded, left the pier. *When are they going to get us onto one of those barges?*

Warmth from the first rays was pleasant for a short while, but soon the heat became harsh and then unbearable.

An occasional orderly wandered along the line with a few bandages, but no water. Anyone who could talk begged for water.

Cramps gripped Jayjay's stomach, then faded.

At around mid-morning the Gallipoli trots defeated his resolve and he unloaded in his trousers. Since he had arrived at the beach the stench of others doing the same hung in the air, but the smell of his own seemed more intense. His ears burned with shame as he was sure that those around him would know it was him.

At least it made the belly ache stop for a while.

Before long the cramps returned.

* * *

Late afternoon sun glared off the water.

Another bugle blast announced the departure of another load of wounded. Still the walking wounded filled the barges. They kept coming from North Beach in a never-ending flow.

The beach at the Cove was full of rows of wounded. These were the more serious cases, carried in by the field ambulance and incapable of moving themselves. A few had been carried to the barges, but at this rate it would take days to clear the beach.

I don't know if I can survive a night in the cold and another day in this heat without water.

"Hey," Jayjay grabbed the gunner's shoulder. "Gunner, we gotta get on one of them barges. Mate."

No response.

Blood on the back facing Jayjay had dried and darkened. Flies crowded around each wound.

Jayjay tugged the shoulder gently and the gunner slumped onto his back. Mouth gaping, lips curled back and eyes staring vacantly at the sky. A storm cloud of flies loomed, as if angry at the disturbance.

"You're not going to be much help then are you? Poor bastard. I didn't even know your name."

Jayjay turned to Cooper.

Cooper was propped on one elbow, watching the one-sided conversation. His right eye twitched.

"Cooper, we gotta get ourselves onto one of those barges, and get to a hospital ship."

Cooper's eyes were as vacant as the dead gunners', but Jayjay persisted.

"They'll give us water and look after us. Look at my eyes Cooper. I need your help. I can't walk myself. My knee is shot, but we can do it together. Look at me. Cooper, do you understand?"

Cooper's eyes flickered and met Jayjay's for an instant. He tilted his head in what might be considered a slight nod.

"It's not far Cooper. I need you to help me up. Together we can get to the pier and get away from this place. Can you do that Cooper?"

Cooper stared into the distance. His face was caked with sand, like coconut shards on a bloody lamington. He looked down at his bloodstained sleeve and Jayjay realised for the first time that Cooper was wounded in his arm as well as his head.

"They shot me," Cooper said.

"I know mate, they shot me too."

"They shot us all," Cooper shook his head slowly. "With bloody machine guns. We had no chance. My mates are all dead. Their blood sprayed all over me. They're still up there. That's where I should be too. I can't just leave them."

"My mates are still up there too. I don't even know if they're alive or dead. Imagine if you were up there, and one of them down here. What would you want him to do? We can get out of here Cooper. We can go home, but we gotta get onto a barge. Will you help me?"

A shell from Beachy Bill screamed over the cove and burst above the beach a hundred yards away. Sudden movement from a few of the casualties lying beneath told of new wounds received by helpless men lying on the sand.

"Do you want to just lie here and wait for a shrapnel shell to finish us off?" Jayjay asked. "We can't do any good here. We'll just end up like this gunner if we stay."

Cooper stared at the small white cloud of smoke that hung in the air where the shell burst.

Jayjay waited long seconds.

He contemplated the idea of dragging himself across the beach to the pier, and begging for help after lying across the start of the pier and blocking the way. *It'll hurt, but I might be able to do it.*

"Okay," Cooper said.

"Okay," Jayjay breathed deep. "Let's take it slow. Can you help me up, I can't use this leg at all."

"What's your name?"

"Jonathan Jones. You can call me Jayjay."

"Okay Jones."

Cooper stood slowly and hauled Jayjay to his feet, then propped him with his good arm. Jayjay lent in, but could only move forward by resting some weight on his bad knee.

Each step sent a stabbing agony up his leg and felt as if it was destroying the knee that carried him forward. But each step was a step towards home.

Crawling couldn't hurt any more than this, but I have to do it. It's good to escape with someone else, even if it's a bloke I only just met who's out of his mind with shell shock.

God, I miss Larry and the others. Please look after them. They're my family here. I was so lonely without them last night, when I needed them the most. If only I could say good-bye. If only I didn't have to leave Ron behind. But I can't do anything for anyone now. It'll take all my strength to get out of here alive. God, please allow me to get home. To get away from this place of killing. To see Mum and Dad. To lie in my own bed without being shot at or shelled.

They reached the pier and a barge approached from the hospital ship. Jayjay hobbled down the centre of the pier with Cooper, to reduce the risk of falling into the water and to make it difficult for the more lightly wounded to shove past.

By the time the barge pulled alongside the pier, he could barely stand, despite leaning all his weight on his good leg.

The jacktars tied the barge off and walking wounded pushed past to get on board, almost knocking Jayjay over.

"Hold your horses mate!" Jayjay raised his voice and sounded angry without having to try. "Give us a hand would ya. We've got seriously wounded here."

Cooper helped Jayjay hobble to the far edge of the barge and the two claimed a small portion of deck space. Cooper sat with his back against the side wall, pulled his knees up tight to his chest and stared towards the top of the Plugge's Plateau looming above the beach.

Jayjay slumped next to Cooper and lay his wounded leg straight. His good leg stayed bent and guarded against impact from other wounded men cramming onto the barge.

His eyes followed Cooper's.

The steep slope dropped into Anzac Cove, barely levelling out at the bottom. Naked earth burned golden brown in the afternoon sun, evidence of human digging scarred its entire surface. Sandbag lined dugouts were lit up to the back corners at this time of day. Green remnants of the prickly scrub that had greeted them at the landing were scant. At the base of the hill, rows upon rows of wounded marked the thin boundary between land and sea. Stretcher bearers delivered a new arrival to the end of the queue, but no one attended to the wounded. A small gap remained where Jayjay and Cooper had spent the day under the scorching sun, next to the gunner who lay on his back, staring lifeless at the sky.

The sea was choppy today. The ride would be bumpy, but Jayjay didn't care. So many times he had thought he would die and be buried at Gallipoli like his brother and all the rest. Even a day ago death seemed a certainty, a day that seemed like a lifetime of torture.

If I never see this bastard of a place again it'll be too soon.

God, please look after Larry and the others.

A bugle sounded.

His conscience accused him of deserting his mates, but he turned his head to face the sun, setting over the water, and forced himself not to look back.

CHAPTER 78

John

Saturday, 7 August 1915, sunset

The sun melted into the distant sea, setting on a scorching day.

Early that morning, after the night march out of Reserve Gully, the men of the 4th Brigade had stopped on the ridge of Damakjelik Bair in readiness to launch a final assault on the summit of Hill 971, but daybreak exposed their positions to enemy machine gunners and would have made the attack suicidal.

At dawn, John had sent out telephone lines to each of his four battalion commanders and asked them to report their position. Each commander confirmed that they were in the agreed position in readiness for the final attack. Colonel Pope's 16th Battalion held the most advanced position and Pope signalled that his right flank reached a spur of Abdel Rahman Bair, the main ridge that led up to Hill 971 from the north. John immediately relayed the reported battalion positions back to higher command, then went forward to assess the situation for himself.

An avid bushwalker back home in Australia, and an experienced cartographer, John took with him a map and compass to confirm the locations and the accuracy of the map. On cresting the Damakjelik Bair, it took John less than a minute to determine that Pope and the others had overestimated their progress, and that they were in fact about half a mile short of where they believed themselves to be.

Being lower on the Damakjelik Bair to this extent meant that an additional spur from that ridge lay between the men and the main ridge of Abdel Rahmen Bair, so instead of crossing a single valley to reach their objective, they would also have to cross the spur and another valley.

John hurried back to the temporary headquarters he had established behind the ridge.

"General Cox," John said to his commander. "I have identified an error in our brigade's position. We are around eight-hundred yards short of the position we believed we had reached."

"And yet, all your battalion commanders reported otherwise."

"Yes they did Sir."

"Is it not possible that you are mistaken?"

"No Sir."

"What of your sheep farmer from New Zealand?"

"Major Overton left our company to take the Gurkhas further up the Aghyl Dere."

"We must push on regardless."

"We cannot Sir," John said. "The enemy has machine guns across the valley. If we follow the ridge as planned, they will have a clear line of fire, and the same if we attempt to cross the valleys. The men are fatigued from marching all night and can barely walk."

"I have ordered the other units in our column to ready for attack. The 4th Brigade will be required to advance at eleven o'clock this morning."

"My battalion commanders have reported to me that they may be able to hold the current line, but that the men are too exhausted even to entrench where they are. Further uphill advance in daylight is impossible."

It was unusual for Cox to stand still, but he did so and stared at John for what seemed to be a long time. John held his commander's gaze.

"Very well," Cox shook his head. "Fortify your line as best you can."

Now, in the fading yellow-orange light of the sinking sun, John stood on a knoll above his headquarters.

From regular telephone conversations with his battalion commanders, John knew that the men had worked through the heat of the day, digging in whilst lying down under sniper fire. Most had emptied their water bottles with no means to refill them.

General Cox approached from the valley, fidgeting with a piece of paper in his hands. He looked as if he was about to say something, but General John Monash decided to get in before his commander.

"We need to establish a supply arrangement," John said. "Bring water, food and ammunition to the new firing line, and move the wounded back towards the beach where they can receive the care they need."

"There is no time for that," Cox snapped. "We are to keep working to gain the summits of Sari Bair."

"The men are exhausted," John said. "We have discussed all this. They were in poor medical condition when we started, and they have been working continuously for a night and a day. We have lost the element of surprise and face strongly defended high ground."

"We have received an order from General Godley." Cox waved the paper about like a flag and then read from it: "The General Officer Commanding wishes you to close the troops… well up the slopes towards the enemy during the preliminary bombardment of the position, so as to be ready to reach the crest as soon as the gun-fire stops tomorrow morning. The assault should be carried out with loud cheering."

"With all due respect, Sir," Monash said. "That is not much of a plan. Godley isn't here to understand our situation. Neither is Birdwood. Did you pass on the information that we are exposed on a ridge half a mile short of where we thought we were?"

"I feel confident that," Cox continued to read the Godley's message, "after today's rest, and starting comparatively fresh, your brigade will make a determined effort to capture the key of the position... Selecting it for this task, I had the original brigade in mind, but we all expect the reconstituted brigade to live up to the traditions of the original."

"I thought not," John said. "Is that all?"

"The attack is to take place at three o'clock tomorrow morning."

"Forget all due respect. That is bloody madness! Our men marched all night and have been digging in, under fire and the hot sun all day. They have no water left and have not had any rest."

"Orders are orders, General."

"We cannot do it."

"We must!"

John drew a deep breath.

This defies all logic. War is a crazy kind of hell.

"If we are even to contemplate this course of action, we will need more men and supplies, water at the very least, and a way to get some more ammunition."

"We can have one Regiment of the Kitchener's New Army, the 6th Kings Own Royal Lancasters. They will bring water and ammunition."

"I cannot rely on a battalion of untried Tommies. The new army at Suvla has not advanced to support us as they were supposed to and I doubt our objective is any longer humanly possible."

"We have no choice. We must follow the order."

"Even if it is damned stupid?"

"Even if you disagree with it, General Monash."

John fought to overcome his own disbelief so he could give rational consideration to his options. *What are our options? We face an uphill battle against a well-armed enemy that is ready for us, without the support that the plan requires. It's like the disastrous May attack on Baby 700 all over again.*

"The Kings Lancasters will have to hold the line with the 13th," John said, "and free up the 14th to join the 15th and 16th Battalions. I will lead our three battalions for the attack, but I must say that I most strongly disagree with this advance. It will cost many lives and is unlikely to achieve the objective. There is no point in going into battle unless you have a reasonable chance of victory."

"I suggest you ready your men and plan for the attack, but you are to command from your headquarters here. Nominate a field commander and we will maintain communications by telephone line that will be run out with the attack."

"I cannot ask my men to attack if I don't have the fortitude to join them, and I cannot command them if I cannot communicate with them. Telephone lines fail at the best of times, and especially during battles."

"You will remain at this line with me. No one is questioning your fortitude. Now I suggest you get on with your preparations."

John stood his ground for several seconds, then turned and walked away.

Anger at Cox and Godley's disregard for his men's lives burned within him, but he fought to push the cold arrogance of the British generals from his mind. He only had a few hours to plan the operation. Having not slept himself for thirty-six hours, he knew he had to allocate his strength deliberately and focus on the task.

John sent messages to each of his four battalion commanders to come to his temporary brigade headquarters for a conference at half past eight that evening. He then rounded up as many of his staff officers as were mobile for a planning reconnaissance during the last of the daylight. His trusted Chief-of-Staff, Colonel McGlinn was unable to join the party due to an injury sustained on the previous night's march when he had impaled himself on a bayonet whilst attempting to hurry to the head of the column to investigate delays.

John checked his pocket watch. *Ninety minutes to take a look from the ridge and form a plan of attack before the conference.*

Minutes later, John gazed from the crest of Damakjelik Bair towards his brigade's most advanced position, being that of Colonel Pope's 16th Battalion.

Abdel Rahman Bair was a key objective of the original night march. This ridge formed the intended passage of the left assault column for the final attack. He looked at his map, and back up at the ridge that led to the summit of Hill 971. There was no denying the truth. *We are not where we thought we were, and we have deviated from the intended path.*

* * *

At half past two the next morning, John stood on the knoll above his headquarters and directed his troops.

The fog of a four-hour sleep lingered in his head, but he knew the men would all be as tired as he was, and they were the ones about to confront the enemy. Many were about to experience the last sunrise of their life.

The 14th, 15th and 16th Battalions had been roused within the past half hour and their men moved with the gait of zombies.

Colonel Pope was designated as field commander of the force of three battalions, as well as his own 16th Battalion and he worked with John to organise the men and communicate the plan of attack.

It was four o'clock when Pope led the 15th Battalion out into the first valley under cover of a warship bombardment of Hill 971, Hill Q and Chunuk Bair, the three highest points of the main ridge.

The men filed out and dropped into the valley without the usual banter. These men had no energy left for such things.

John took his staff officers to an observation post on the ridge where he might see at least some of the activity, and from where he would maintain telephone contact with Pope.

At a quarter past four the bombardment ceased, per the schedule, but the men were nowhere near close to the peak of Hill 971 that General Godley supposed they would be attacking by this time.

In the Anafarta foothills north of the main range, a howitzer launched a shell towards the 4th Brigade advancing in the pale dawn light. *The Turks have seen us.*

The first sounds of rifle fire came in sporadic bursts, then they grew in frequency like the sound of popping corn in a pan of oil that has reached a critical temperature.

Through his field glasses, John could make out a small number of Turks retreating over the first spur. But, before he had time to take any satisfaction in the success of the advance, a machine gun to the right spat fire from a bluff above the next valley. Another machine gun nearby joined in and the Australians dropped to the ground as one. Likely most men were diving for cover as they had learned to do to survive, but some would have taken the hit and would claim this unnamed spur as their final resting place.

Another pair of enemy machine guns opened fire from higher on the main ridge, then a field gun announced its presence on the crest of Hill 971, as if taunting the attackers in defiance.

A warship must have seen the puff of smoke from the field gun and sent in a salvo that silenced the gun, but the machine guns continued to unleash a stream of fire that showed no mercy.

Infantry cannot advance against this kind of resistance. Many will be wounded or die and the rest will be forced to stop in sheltered positions.

"Get me Pope on the telephone," John called to his signalman.

The signalman wound the handle furiously and pressed the handset to his ear. After a minute of trying he shook his head.

"Sorry Sir," the signalman said. "I cannot get through. The line must have been cut. It was probably the artillery shells."

John turned to the officer in charge of the signals unit.

"Get every one of your men out there, trace the line end to end until it can be fixed. Let me know as soon as I can communicate with field command. Hurry, many lives are in your hands!"

"Yes Sir." The officer and his signallers scurried away.

John looked at General Cox who stood fidgeting and wore an anxious look.

"What are you scheming Monash?"

"I am thinking that we may have to pull the men back or we will have nothing left of three good battalions."

"Our orders are to attack Hill 971."

"None of our men is going to get close to that summit today. The enemy has four well-placed machines that command our –.

"Allah! Allah!" The familiar war cry of the enemy drifted across the valley.

John turned to look with his field glasses and saw a mass of Turks surging from the next valley onto the spur that his men occupied.

A fire fight was taking place on the left flank and his men advancing further up the ridge were in danger of being attacked from behind.

Visibility was limited from John's outpost and it was difficult for him to determine what was happening. It appeared that a detachment had split away from the main column to face the attacking Turks.

Machine guns from the next ridge continued to harass the main force as the men pushed up the spur.

Many men fell on that spur, and eventually the remnant drifted back into the valley that they had come from where the spur shielded them from the storm of bullets.

At seven o'clock the signals officer ran back up the hill towards John's outpost with one arm covered in blood. Saying nothing, he went straight to the telephone set and wound the handle with his good hand while the other hung limp by his side.

"General Monash Sir," the signals officer's voice was croaky, but calm. "I have Colonel Pope on the line."

John grabbed the handset.

"Pope," John said. "Monash here. Situation report."

"General," Pope's voice crackled over the telephone system. "Pope here. Our battalions cannot accomplish the set task Sir. We are a long way short of the crest and cannot advance. The enemy has strong defence with several machine guns and are now shelling us as well. Our casualties are heavy and there does not appear to be any advantage in staying here in our current position, Sir."

"I understand the difficulties you are facing and will respond with orders shortly. Stand by Colonel."

"Yes Sir."

John repeated the report to Cox and paused a moment in case his commander wished to come to the right conclusion on his own, but the general only fiddled with his hands.

I will have to make this easier for him.

"General, we have three options here:

"One, we can order the men to entrench at the new position. This would gain us no significant tactical advantage and is likely to end in a bloody massacre.

"Two, we can order an advance. This is clearly impossible with the men available and we would need at least another two battalions for this to be viable." *I doubt that there are any more reinforcements available, and counting on this to be the case. Hopefully he won't call my bluff.*

"Three, we can order a withdrawal, preserve the strength of our force to the extent possible and consolidate our existing position on this ridge."

"Well General Godley –."

"General Godley is not here damn it."

Cox hesitated for a long moment before responding.

"Very well. Order the withdrawal."

"Yes Sir."

John hurried back to the telephone set and picked up the hand-piece.

"Monash here. You there Pope?"

"Yes Sir. Pope here."

"I am ordering a complete withdrawal, back to our firing line held by the 13th. Do you understand that."

"Yes sir, withdraw to the line of the 13th Battalion Sir."

"Yes correct," John said. "But listen, first get our machine gun section to screen that ridge and cover the withdrawal. All four guns, and leave fifty good men to guard the guns. Have you got that?

"Yes Sir, screen the ridge with machine gun section and fifty men."

"The rest should withdraw as soon as the machine guns are in place, and the machine gun section should stay until they can retreat safely, wait until nightfall if necessary."

"Yes Sir, machine gun section to wait until safe withdrawal possible. Got that Sir."

"God be with you Pope."

"Thank you Sir. I'll see you soon Sir."

The connection on the telephone line clicked off and John placed the handset down on the telephone box. The signals officer remained standing nearby with his bloody arm hanging limp by his side.

"The signal got through," John said. "You did well. You better get that arm looked at son."

"Yes Sir, thank you Sir."

CHAPTER 79

Mustafa

Sunday, 8 August 1915, mid-morning

Mustafa could feel his hold on the precious high ground slipping. Anger burned inside him like a forge fire and his fingers crushed the piece of paper into a ball.

Since the day the English and their allies landed over three months ago Mustafa had pushed them back down the hill and held them at bay. Now it might all have been for nothing.

The most infuriating thing was that good brave men were being wasted, thrown at the enemy like weeds into a fire, without thought or an organised plan.

Army command has no awareness or control of the situation.

Esat Pasha knows that the enemy is on Chunuk Bair, close to the summit. He wants me to work with the other field commanders, but how can I when I don't know who is in command. Reinforcements are being sent here from all directions and they have no understanding of what to do when they arrive.

Mustafa unscrewed the ball of paper and read it again, as if the communiqué might tell a different tale the second time:

"An attack on Chunuk Bair has been ordered. To whom shall I pass this order? I am looking for the battalion commanders, I cannot find them. All is confusion and the situation is grave. It is obvious that a person familiar with the terrain should be assigned, but there is no report and no news, I do not know what to do..."

This observation officer is a platoon commander from Army Headquarters' own cavalry company. If he cannot figure out what's happening then God help the rest of us.

The Australians in front of his centre section had been probing around Bomb Ridge and Junction Hill ever since they launched the major assault on Bloody Ridge two days ago. Enemy action had been contained well enough, but it required constant attention to defend this front.

Worrying reports had trickled in since dawn from the right flank. Calls for reinforcements and ammunition from Chunuk Bair. Some companies had run out of hand bombs early in the morning.

Another recent report claimed that the enemy was advancing towards the high point of Koja Chemen Tepe. That area was well outside Mustafa's command sector, but this development would put his right flank further at risk.

"Izzettin Bey, send an order!"

"Yes Kemal Bey?"

"Send reinforcements from 10th and 25th regiments to bolster the defence of Chunuk Bair. They'll need good officers with them to assess the situation and make themselves effective when they arrive. And send another message to General Esat."

"Yes Kemal Bey."

"Tell Esat that the heights will be lost if our defence is not properly organised and lead by an Ottoman officer. Maybe Chunuk Bair is already lost, but we do not know what is happening there. Include the contents of that report from the cavalry observation officer and conclude with this: 'The situation at Chunuk Bair is conspicuously perilous. For the welfare of the country, I implore you to assist in seriously attracting the attention of the Army Commander to this issue.'"

Leadership and ammunition were still in short supply later in the afternoon when Mustafa's Chief of Staff, Major Izzettin answered a telephone call.

He stood a little straighter and nodded his head as he spoke, waving Mustafa over to take the call. "It is Colonel Kazim at Fifth Army Command Headquarters."

Good, it's about time they took this situation seriously.

"Kazim Bey, Mustafa Kemal here."

"Kemal Bey," The voice of the Chief of Staff to Liman von Sanders and the Ottoman Fifth Army was clear enough to betray a note of anxiety. "We have received mixed reports about the current situation at the front line. Von Sanders Pasha has requested your perspective."

Mustafa took a deep breath. "The situation is dire and there is only a moment left to rectify it. If the moment is lost, a disaster is highly probable. The enemy on our central front at the Ariburnu sector is active, but contained. It is to the north where our greatest threat lies and we must take this threat seriously. Large enemy forces have already been landed and are still landing in the Anafarta Hills sector. We must unite the command and organise the dispatch of our brave men effectively, otherwise their lives will continue to be wasted for no benefit."

Mustafa kept the earpiece to his ear, but moved the mouthpiece away. He was breathing heavily as he waited for Kazim to speak.

"Is there a remedy?"

"There is no remedy," Mustafa said. "Other than this – assign all the existing forces under my command."

Another pause.

"Won't that be too many men?"

"No," Mustafa said. "It will be too few."

"Thank you for your view Kemal Bey," Kazim said. "Please keep us informed of any further developments."

The telephone connection went dead.

Mustafa waved away flies and repeated the conversation in his mind. *There will be political difficulty. I know this terrain better than anyone and they know it, but Enver would not approve of my promotion. Damn that man! If we don't organise our defence urgently, we will lose control of the peaks and be overrun.*

Mustafa sent more messages to General Esat during the afternoon, seeking better management of the defensive operation, and clarification about the responses to enemy attacks on peaks. The General didn't help, only sending the usual vague diplomatic responses – that Mustafa should manage his own regiments and determine the extent of their own flank.

A telephone call came in from his aide-de-camp at Chunuk Bair, late in the afternoon. Somehow the support officer had managed to reach the front line and establish a working telephone connection.

"Kemal Bey, our men are dug in and facing off the enemy across the top of Chunuk Bair. The enemy is only 25 to 30 metres away from our front line and no further movement forward is possible. We need more reinforcements, and ammunition and hand bombs."

"I know!" Kemal said. "Tell the men they must hold that position at any cost. Tell the men help is coming."

Into the evening, Mustafa was still trying to obtain more reinforcements and ammunition when another telephone call came from Fifth Army Headquarters. This time it was Field Marshal Liman von Sanders himself.

"You are to take command of the Anafarta Group." The German never wasted words. "Effective immediately. Colonel Fevzi has been relieved of his command. You will coordinate the defence against the enemy attack from Salt Lake to Chunuk Bair. The English are advancing from Salt Lake and must be stopped. You are to launch a counter-attack against these forces at dawn. I suggest you take yourself to the Anafartas Headquarters at Chamlitekke urgently."

"Yes, von Sanders Pasha – thank you. I need more reinforcements at Chunuk Bair also."

"They are on their way."

A click in the earpiece signalled that the conversation was over.

Mustafa pulled his pocket watch from a chest pocket. *A quarter to ten. Dawn is less than seven hours away.*

Mustafa's Chief of Staff, Major Izzettin had been watching and looked to Mustafa as a dog eyeing off a bone in his master's hand.

"I am to take command of the Anafarta Group," Mustafa said. "I need to make arrangements for a handover here, and leave without delay. I am to organise a dawn counter-attack at Salt Lake."

Izzettin looked at the ground and sighed. "Yes, Kemal Bey."

"You are needed here my friend," Mustafa said. "Lieutenant-Colonel Shefik will command the division in my absence, but he will need your help. You know how this division runs better than anyone. We have fought off many enemy attacks these last few days here at the central front – Hill of Valour, Bomb Ridge, Junction Hill. Also, we sent Zeki's battalion to help with the fight at Bloody Ridge. With discipline and vigilance we can hold the central front, but if we are careless now it will have been for nothing. It could be disastrous here like it is further north."

"Yes Kemal Bey."

"Now send for our Chief Physician. And I need to replace my brave aide-de-camp who was martyred at Chunuk Bair today. Select a sharp junior officer that I can take."

"Yes Kemal Bey. Are you ill?"

"Not yet, but I am exhausted and may collapse at any moment. I have not slept for three days and this is the third night. I need the best possible health care so the lives of our soldiers can be used well, otherwise they may regret their heroism."

Major Izzettin departed briefly to send off two runners. By the time he returned, Mustafa was ready to dictate a message to be circulated within the 19th Division. As usual, Izzettin was able to produce a notebook and pencil, as if from nowhere, to record the message:

"I am departing now to undertake command of the Anafarta Hills Group. The 27th Regiment Commander Shefik Bey has been assigned as the Deputy Divisional Commander. I farewell you convinced that with the help of your love and trust in me, I will complete the accomplishment that you brought into being by your ardour and devotion to this duty that I have just undertaken."

* * *

It was half an hour before midnight when Mustafa left 19th Division Headquarters on Flat Hill.

He and his two travelling companions rode horseback. They had around ten kilometres to travel, maybe a little more by the back trails to reduce risk of contact with enemy scouts. *At least it will be dark.* The moon was yet to rise, and had been waning for nearly two weeks so its slender form would bring little light this night.

Mustafa had already mapped a route in his mind. First inland away from the enemy, north of Koja Dere village and then north via the village of Big Anafarta.

Most men would struggle to find their way on such a night, but I cannot afford to lose any time.

Before long, the air in Mustafa's nostrils tasted strangely sweet. He sucked it in and savoured the sensation from the back of his throat and deep into his lungs. Fresh air, not contaminated by the stench of human waste and rotting dead.

Mustafa's memory of the terrain did not let him down. In 1912 and 1913, during the Balkan wars, he held the role of Chief Operations Officer of the Ottoman Army on the Gallipoli Peninsula. A detailed picture of the landscape in his mind served better than any map.

At one-thirty a.m. he led his small entourage into the Anafarta's Group Headquarters. The Group Chief of Staff was expecting them, having talked to Mustafa briefly on the telephone before he left Flat Hill.

After a brief situational update, Mustafa had the outgoing Group commander, Colonel Fevzi, woken to provide the orders outlining the plans for the dawn attack. *The lazy donkey didn't even bother to get out of bed.*

"Huseyin Bey," Mustafa said to his Chief Physician. "I need to sleep, but time is limited. Please stay with me and ensure I can wake."

"Yes Kemal Bey," Huseyin said. "Your body needs rest and will recover best if you can sleep for at least three hours."

"Mustafa checked his pocket watch and shook his head. "We attack at dawn. Wake me in two hours. Do whatever it takes. Beat me if you must."

Without waiting for an answer, Mustafa dropped to the floor and immediately fell into a deep dreamless sleep.

CHAPTER 80

Ellis

Monday, 9 August 1915, Monday

Ellis awoke at dawn to the thunder of Naval guns pounding the Anafarta Hills. He had barely slept.

He huddled behind a stack of crates on the beach near Ghazi Baba at the northern headland of Suvla Bay. He was alive and his water bottle was half full. For that, he was better off than most of the IX Corps of Kitchener's New Army who were spread across the plains and low hills of Suvla.

Hundreds of stragglers lay on the beach and sat in the scrub behind, some walked about in small groups as if they had some good reason to remain back from the fighting front. The blanket of smoke, that yesterday hung over the slopes of the Sari Bair range, had dissipated to reveal silhouette peaks before the sunrise, but from this low position it was impossible to see much of the battlefield across the broken country.

Ellis dragged himself to his feet, urinated on the sand and began the walk around Suvla Bay, across the spit that separated the dry lake from the sea. Beyond the sand spit lay Lala Baba at the southern headland of the bay.

The surface of the spit was composed of soft sand, covered by a coarse grass, into which he sunk, at every step, above his ankles. Rapid movement was impossible. The surface was littered with the debris of battle, abandoned kit, rifles, shreds of uniforms and some graves.

Crossing this ground under shrapnel fire must have been a most unpleasant ordeal.

Across the spit, Ellis climbed Lala Baba, a natural mound that rose barely one hundred feet above the sea, but provided a splendid view across the dry lake and over the terrain in front of the Anafarta Hills. From here the ground could be seen to be immeasurably more difficult than it appeared from the deck of a warship.

In the captured Turkish trenches on the crest of Lala Baba, Ellis re-acquainted himself with Major-General Hammersley, commander of the 11th Division, who had allowed Ellis to use the position as an observation post yesterday.

"Morning Bartlett," the General said gruffly. "We will be continuing our attack on W Hills and Scimitar Hill today. I trust you will enjoy the show."

"I take no pleasure in watching men die, Sir." Ellis wanted the General's ongoing co-operation and refused to allow himself to be antagonised. "I am merely here to observe and report what I see. Will there be a general advance today?"

"The advance is already underway," the general snapped. "Take a look for yourself, and then you can report that."

Hammersley turned his back and walked off with several staff following after him.

Ellis gazed across the battlefield, then raised his field glasses to see what he could make of troop activity. Clusters of movement here and there showed that some were trying to advance, but he could see no evidence of overall co-ordination.

In the distance, beyond the dry lake, two British officers and maybe fifty or sixty men rushed from a position of cover and disappeared into the scrub. Sounds of rifle and machine gun fire followed the attackers and a shrapnel shell burst over their position.

The Turks must have reinforced their numbers overnight, their fire has grown in intensity, and their artillery is better directed – they have moved their guns closer.

One officer and around thirty men emerged from the scrub, the remnant of the platoon Ellis had watched charge into the same patch of bushes moments earlier. They kept running towards the bare yellow slopes that gave Scimitar Hill its name, slopes that formed a natural glacis that favoured the defenders.

Another shrapnel shell burst over the running men and laid them flat on the ground. Some rolled about and some lay still. Two men rose to their knees, then stood and helped a third to his feet. The three men shuffled down the hill, a man on each side supporting one in the middle whose feet dragged across the ground. The three men made five yards, then one of the rescuers collapsed to the ground and lay dead still. The other rescuer paused for a moment and then hurried on, taking sole responsibility for supporting his wounded comrade. Three more steps and both men fell to the ground. The rescuer lay still, but the wounded man lifted himself slowly to his hands and one knee, then he began a lopsided crawl. The fellow dragged himself another ten yards before a bullet left him lying as dead as his two rescuers. On the ground covered by the rest of the platoon, Ellis could see no movement amongst the spread of bodies.

Anguish tightened on his innards like a noose. Ellis lowered his field glasses and looked about the trench he stood in. No one else was watching as he was watching. Likely no one else, other than the Turks, had witnessed the obliteration of a whole platoon of men. He did not know what battalion or brigade the men were from and likely their general had no knowledge of what had become of them.

Not far from the position of cover where the platoon of living infantry had emerged minutes before, then run to their destruction, another like-sized group of men crouched for shelter, as if waiting to see the results of their comrade's efforts, but they could not have seen. Ellis, as usual, had sniffed out a prime vantage position, but the undulating terrain and vegetation obstructed the visibility of those amongst it.

Those men would be lucky to be able to see a dozen yards to the right or left. How can a general advance be organised in such country? Who is even making the attempt? The enemy is consolidating his defensive positions and will soon become immovable.

The sun had only been up for two hours, but the heat was already intense. Behind the front lines, thousands of men lay about, apparently too hot or thirsty even to attempt to deal with the Turkish snipers, who, taking full advantage of the immunity they enjoyed, crept about from scrub to scrub, from tree to tree, and played the devil with the intermixed British battalions.

Ellis watched for the rest of the morning, but little changed. Some groups advanced and many remained inactive. Of the groups that advanced, their numbers thinned as they approached the enemy strongholds, until they were reduced to nothing. The Turks had gravitated to the defensible higher ground and held it with the tenacity of a stubborn foe whilst reinforcing their lines.

Throughout the morning, warships kept up an incessant bombardment of the crest-line of the Anafarta Hills, but the Turks, for the most part, either stayed hidden in their trenches or advanced down the slopes and mingled with the British troops, either way they remained unharmed by the shellfire. For the most part, it seemed to Ellis that the ships' shells were being wasted as they could not even silence the Turkish guns behind W Hills that were doing so much damage. Being on the reverse slopes, these guns could not be touched by direct fire from the warships, but were able to lob their own shells over the hills onto attackers, using the eyes of hidden spotters.

At around midday, explosive shells from the ships started a series of fires, which, wafted by a light wind, swept across the front of Scimitar Hill. Through the smoke, Ellis saw men running back to the trenches for cover, but the wounded could not escape the smoke and flames.

A number of wounded lay hidden in the scrub just beneath the sandy escarpment of Scimitar Hill and they crawled into the open to escape the flames, only to expose themselves to snipers and shrapnel. These men sought safety in vain.

Ellis watched the flames approach another position, closer to where he stood, crawling figures disappeared amidst a dense cloud of black smoke. When the fire passed on, little mounds of scorched khaki marked the places where mismanaged soldiers of the King had returned to mother earth.

The fire showed no favourites and also caught many Turks concealed in the scrub. Some ran like rabbits to return to their own trenches. For some time the combat seemed to pause as the fires burned, and men from each side focused on saving themselves as they could.

Later in the day, when the fires had died down but still spewed forth smoke, Ellis was joined by fellow war correspondent, Henry Nevinson who had walked back from the far side of the dry lake.

"Our infantry," Nevinson said, "are demoralised, weary and absolutely refuse to advance. The muddle is beyond anything I have ever seen. Never since Nicholson's Nek and Lombard's Kopje have I seen British infantry behave so badly."

Nevinson, a veteran reporter from the Boer War, looked exhausted and on the verge of despair. Ellis had seen enough for one day himself, and at his suggestion, the pair of press-men departed Lala Baba headed back along the beach amidst hundreds of stragglers who had drifted away from the front. Men everywhere were desperate for water, clothes burnt black or in shreds, tongues blackened, shrivelled and lolling out of their mouths. Some, when they reached the sea, rushed into it and gulped the salt water. Others waded out to the water barges, but distribution of drinking water was only being issued on shore, by a small ration.

Confusion reigned supreme. No one seemed to know where the headquarters of the different brigades and divisions were to be found. The troops were hunting for water, the staff were hunting for their troops, and the Turkish snipers were hunting for their prey.

On the beach at the northern point of Ghazi Baba, Ellis was surprised to see, standing alone in the distance, the Commander-in-Chief of the Mediterranean Expeditionary Force, General Sir Ian Hamilton. The general's face was pale and worried, his gaze was directed on the columns of smoke rising leisurely from the smouldering fires along the front of Anafarta.

It must be obvious to him now that his final effort to reach the Narrows has failed.

CHAPTER 81

Mustafa

Tuesday, 10 August 1915, small hours

Hooves padded into the earth.

Soft horse sounds resonated in the warm night air, amplified by the black. *It's strange that these animals seem so loud after my ears have been blasted by artillery for months.*

A slither of moon gave the smallest hint of light. *Perfect for travelling by stealth, at least for one who knows the back country as well as I.*

The biggest risk here was a nervous Ottoman patrol or scout. Earlier in the evening he had been forced to change course and travel further inland due to enemy rifle fire from Chunuk Bair. He now approached his forces at the heights from the rear.

English invaders at Salt Lake were kilometres behind now. This morning's dawn counter-attack had achieved as much as Mustafa could have hoped for. His role as commander of the Anafarta Group was barely a day old, and he had successfully achieved his first objective. The enemy landing at Salt Lake was contained, its troops prevented from approaching the heights and linking up with the other enemy forces.

Mustafa smiled into the black with pride in the courageous Ottoman performance. The English landing force was substantial, easily outnumbering his own defensive strength, and yet their advance was more hesitant than aggressive. Towards the end of the day, Mustafa had sent orders to the frontline commanders to dig in. Once entrenched and supported by some well-positioned artillery, being outnumbered was less of a problem for a few days until reinforcements arrived. Attacking cost many more men than a holding position. That much had been proven time and again in this campaign.

Mustafa felt his body relax in the saddle and caught himself drifting from consciousness as his body jerked back upright. *One more day, then maybe I can sleep.*

"Kemal Bey," the young aide-de-camp rode alongside. "I can hear rifle fire from the direction of Chunuk Bair."

Mustafa focused his ears, and could just make out the familiar tap-tap-tap in the distance.

The trail was climbing now, not that it was much of a trail, but a dry creek bed led them up a blind gully towards the pass between Chunuk Bair and Besim Tepe at the heights of the Sari Bair range. *I need to remain alert. Rifle bullets travel as far as their sound. Who knows how far the enemy has advanced this night?*

Mustafa turned to the dark shadow of his aide-de-camp. "You have good ears and eyes. Scout ahead and locate the Eighth Division field headquarters. Inform the commanders that I will arrive shortly and will need a situational report. Then return and escort me to them."

"Yes Kemal Bey!"

The youthful voice urging a horse to gallop faded into the drumbeat of hooves and then that sound too was smothered by the black.

Mustafa turned to his sole remaining travel companion, the Chief Physician Huseyin. "If that horse doesn't break a leg, it should bring him back well within the hour. Listen for any sound of skirmish ahead. I need you to ensure I reach Chunuk Bair safely."

"Of course Kemal Bey."

The taste of the air changed as they approached the heights. The scent of rotting dead and open latrines. Mustafa felt a pang of regret that he had not savoured the clean air more. Rifle fire was becoming louder, but no more intense. *That may be a good sign.*

It seemed that they were almost at the crest when the familiar rhythm of a horse at canter emerged from the black.

"Kemal Bey, this way."

The aide-de-camp turned his horse and led them across the slope.

Field commanders were ready with a situation report, but the circumstances were not as Mustafa hoped. The enemy was entrenching around the seaward side of Chunuk Bair. Promised Ottoman reinforcements from the 9th, 7th and 12 Divisions had not arrived, neither had field artillery. It was unclear when the much-needed support would come.

"We cannot counter-attack without reinforcements." The 8th Division Chief of Staff, captain Galip spoke on behalf of the regimental commanders. He waited for nods of agreement from the officers before continuing.

"The losses will be too great. Our front-line regiments have already taken many casualties and are weakened from battle fatigue. It would be a waste of men, and would leave our defences badly exposed."

Kemal shook his head and pressed fingers into his temples, as if this might help to clear the fog of exhaustion.

In his mind he travelled back to the disastrous slaughter of the Ottoman May offensive, and a more recent attack by the 18th Regiment at Hill of Valour, when he ordered men forward only to be cut to pieces for no gain. Enver was critical of that attack for lacking purpose.

More time, another day or two to allow reinforcements to arrive would strengthen a counter-attack.

Basic principles from military college training were to hold the high ground, and do not let the enemy become established in an advanced position. The enemy had only held the ground for two days. They will also be weakened and awaiting reinforcements. *Chunuk Bair is the key to the peninsula and the straits. We must hold it at any cost. If the enemy captures this peak, Esat's North Group will be surrounded and our whole position will crumble.*

Recent success at Salt Lake drove his thinking in a more aggressive direction. English advance troops in the north had been pushed back and held to a more tolerable front-line position.

If we attack, we must surprise the enemy, under cover of near darkness when the warships cannot see. The Australian charge at Hill of Valour three days ago had shown the disastrous effect of a poorly timed artillery curtain. *We will steal the bone while the dogs sleep.*

"Men." Kemal faced his field commanders in the flickering light of the lantern. "I share your worries about initiating a counter-attack before reinforcements arrive. I agree with your logic. More time will help us, but more time will help the enemy more. Each day they can use to strengthen their defences will cost us dearly. Assemble your regiments, we will advance in silence with bayonets so the enemy is not forewarned. No artillery. No machine guns. No yelling and no rifle fire until we are well into enemy trenches. We attack at dawn."

* * *

Mustafa checked his pocket watch – nearly four-thirty. Darkness was starting to evaporate. Soon day would break and the perfect moment to attack would be missed.

He ran forward.

Rows of infantrymen from the 23rd and 28th Regiments lay on their bellies, facing the enemy. He did not need daylight to sense their eyes following him as he hurried by. It was undignified for an officer to run past his men. *Nothing is dignified about war, there is only success or failure.*

Everything was in place.

Mustafa reached the front line. Here men of the 24th Regiment lay in formation like the others. He dropped to the ground and crawled forward with the scouts. His officer's uniform, the uniform that designated his authority to command the obedience of thousands of men, dragged across the dirt.

He wormed his way towards the enemy – countless armed men. *Every one of them would happily shoot me dead.* Nothing provided protection but a slight rise of bare ground, maybe twenty metres across. He felt naked.

Heartbeats pounded in his ears like distant artillery and energy surged through his body. A strange feeling of calm washed over him. The sound of his leather boots dragging across the ground became more pronounced. Time seemed to slow. *This is what men experience when they are about to die.*

No enemy movement.

The sun, threatening to rise, was pushing the darkness out to sea with each passing second. *This is the moment. The future of our nation will be won or lost on this hill today.*

He turned his head, careful to keep low. To stand here would be to invite immediate death. Rows of invisible assassins lay in wait for his command.

Mustafa raised his riding crop into the air, held it still for a moment and swung it down. The sound of the whip cutting through the air reached his ears and then several things happened at once.

An officer at an observation post on the left flank, known as Saddle Point on the slopes of Besim Tepe, raised the blade of a shovel high into the air – the signal to charge.

Storm clouds of men rose from the ground and rolled towards Mustafa's position, bayonets pumping as they ran. Silent at first, then with a sound like heavy rain approaching across a field.

Rows of brave men, ready to fight to defend our future. How many of them must hate me, sending them to their death. It would only take one to take a moment to kill me on the way past. Any number of them could do it.

The first wave of men parted and surged by him. Mustafa felt the wind from their passing as the sound of many footsteps fell behind.

Another row charged forwards.

Mustafa sat up to reduce the chance of being accidentally run down or run through himself. He could barely see the faces of men charging towards him out of the dawn grey, but he caught the whites of one man's eyes as he ran past, focused straight ahead in grim determination.

Another row surged past, and another like waves passing a small boat on a rough sea. Twenty-two rows – five thousand men running to defend their nation in a stampede of death.

Surprise was achieved.

Still no rifle fire, but the sounds of men being stabbed with bayonets was unmistakable. Friend or foe, any race, there was no difference at the moment of death. Primal groans and cries in a universal language without words.

Mustafa crawled back from no-man's-land and stood facing the carnage he could hear but not see. At that moment he felt a thud and sharp pain in his chest.

I am shot. At least the attack is away. He grabbed at his chest and wondered if he was dying. Looking down, he expected to see a dark stain of blood in the dim light, but there was none. *It hurts, but I am still standing. The pain hasn't made me collapse like so many others I have seen shot.*

His fingers stopped at the watch in his chest pocket. He pulled it out to find it destroyed. He rubbed at his chest and found pain, but no wound.

A wry grin split his face. Relief and surprise effervesced into an involuntary chuckle. His first laugh for months. *Maybe a bullet, maybe shrapnel? Whatever that was, it might have killed me. If there is a God, He must be smiling on me today.*

Mustafa returned the smashed watch to his pocket and crouched low as he moved to an observation post to watch the counter-attack with his regimental commanders.

The first rays of morning sun glistened on rows of bayonets waiting to join the fray behind Chunuk Bair. Mustafa took a long draw of water from his canteen and surveyed Falcon Ridge with the same pride he felt for his men defending Salt Lake to the north. *We must never forget the courage of these martyrs, they are preserving our future although many will not live to see the sunset.*

The first rows of enemy trenches were captured. His troops were forcing the enemy back along the spur and down the gullies.

The battle raged all morning.

Reinforcements followed with ammunition and water to replenish supplies for those at the front line.

It was a slow and bloody business. The close quarter attack and early loss of position by the enemy seemed to catch the warships off guard. Although by mid-morning naval shellfire was preventing advancement down the seaward slopes. By noon Falcon Ridge was clear of enemy forces, except for its lower ridges towards to sea.

Countless dead littered the landscape, as if giant handfuls of men had been scooped up and thrown into the air. Mixed uniforms of the fallen told of heavy losses suffered by both sides.

Much of the frontline fighting was obscured from Mustafa's vantage point, but it was clear from reports, and from what he could see, that the enemy was reinforcing. They were beginning to consolidate a defensive position. Enemy support from the Ariburnu sector was connected and moving freely towards the lower reaches of Falcon Ridge and Sazli Dere. No doubt, that is where all these enemy troops came from to mount the attack three days ago.

At least the enemy is contained, and the high ground is in safe hands again. My little Mehmets have done well this day.

We are approaching the enemy stronghold and they will defend it with vigour. Further attack will waste men with little chance of further success.

Mustafa turned to the 8th Division commander, Colonel Riza. "Issue an order to the regiments on Falcon Ridge. The attack is to stop and men are to dig in and defend their front-line positions. We have pushed the enemy from the heights and our counter-attack is a success. However, further enemy assaults are expected. Vigilance is essential until more reinforcements arrive. Defend our current position with your lives to preserve the good work of the martyrs who gave their lives to defend our nation today."

Colonel Riza scribbled pencil script into his notebook and Mustafa faced back to the lookout and surveyed Falcon Ridge.

Sweat soaked Mustafa's uniform. Flies showed no respect for rank, swarming around him and the others, pestering living and dead alike. He wondered what he should feel at a moment like this. Leading an army to a righteous victory was exhilarating and tragic at the same time. Somehow the extremes cancelled each other out at this moment and he felt – nothing – numb. It might be possible to feel sad for one or a few men, but thousands entered martyrdom this morning. There were no feelings to do justice for suffering and death on this scale.

Mustafa sipped lukewarm water from his canteen and turned northwards, up to the rounded form of Chunuk Bair. The hill had been recovered, but at a very high cost. *I broke the enemy today. They touched the prize, but could not hold it. While I live they will not set foot on this ground again.*

He reached into his chest pocket, withdrew the smashed watch and rubbed a thumb slowly across the bent metal as he spoke to his Chief Physician.

"Huseyin Bey, we must return to the Anafarta front. If the English are still contained there we may be able to sleep this night."

CHAPTER 82

Jayjay

Thursday, 12 August 1915

Heat magnified the stench from Jayjay's clothes, but he barely noticed and didn't care.

This was the beginning of the fourth day since he had been transferred ship-to-ship in Mudros harbour, off the island of Lemnos, onto the black ship.

A nurse from Perth, on the hospital ship at Gallipoli, was the first female he had seen in months. She looked haggard and had little time to converse, but she offered a few brief sentences of explanation and her voice was like honey. Hospital ships were in short supply due to fighting in France, so regular transport ships were taking Gallipoli wounded from Mudros to base general hospitals. She could have been reciting nursery rhymes and Jayjay would have hung on every word.

Hospital ships were painted white and protected from enemy fire by international rules of war under the Geneva Convention. Regular transport ships were known as 'black ships' and knew no such sanctuary. Enemy warships and submarines could not know black ships were being used to carry casualties and medical staff, and so were free to fire upon them at will.

The hospital ship had seemed well equipped, but this black ship was something different. Orderlies were few and far between – well meaning, but exhausted and didn't appear to have any medical training. Jayjay had only seen the nurse once each day, and no doctors since boarding the black ship. Only crowds of wounded, packed like sardines into a tin.

After dark, to reduce the risk of enemy attack, no lights were allowed and smoking was restricted to below decks. Air in the hull was thick, as if every lungful had already been breathed by fifty men, passed through several cigarettes, and picked up the scent of bodily emissions in between times.

Jayjay's knee throbbed and felt as if a bullet was grinding it away from the inside when he moved. He hadn't left his bed since being placed on it four days earlier and a dull ache pulsed through his whole being.

Cooper had taken the lead from some of the other lightly wounded and helped with changing the newspaper under those who couldn't move. There were no bed pans. Not a perfect solution, but a small mercy.

At other times Cooper roamed about in the dark, ignoring orders to stay put. The orderlies' futile attempts to constrain him gave some much needed entertainment.

"Jones," Cooper's voice was a higher pitch than usual. "Jones."

"What is it Cooper?" Jayjay replied.

"We're at Alexandria," Cooper whispered with urgency. "Gonna be unloaded soon. I heard the nurses talking with my good ear."

"About bloody time," Jayjay didn't bother to whisper himself. "I've had enough of this floating tin can. A real hospital would be nice, where they can fix us up a bit. Some fresh air and a few more pretty nurses about the place."

"Hold ya' horses Jones. You'll be wanting flowers on ya' grave next!"

"How about you piss of and see if you can find out when we'll be taken ashore?" Jayjay replied.

Cooper chuckled and darted off. He hadn't returned when an orderly appeared a few minutes later.

"We have arrived at Alexandria." The orderly's sunken eyes were underlined with dark patches. "You will disembark shortly. Please keep any personal belongings with you. Those that are able, please help those that are not and you'll all get off more quickly."

Jayjay checked his small inventory of personal items… two wrist watches, one for each hand, two wallets in his two chest pockets, his own and Ron's with his letters, and a sheathed bowie knife on his belt. Cooper re-appeared and waited by Jayjay as some of the more able-bodied marched themselves out.

"Can you stand Jones?" Cooper looked down as if sizing Jayjay up to carry him.

"I'll try," Jayjay sounded more positive than he felt. "I've gotta get off this damned ship somehow. Might have to wait all day for an orderly to drag me out."

Cooper hauled Jayjay forwards and a crushing ache swelled in his knee. They hobbled together, with the coordination of young boys attempting a three-legged-race for the first time, and moved slowly out the door and along the corridor. Stairs up to the main deck were torture. Cooper showed surprising strength and virtually carried Jayjay much of the way.

A hoist and boom lowered a sick-looking fellow with a bandaged leg from the ship to the dock.

"That crane's for you Jones." Cooper eased Jayjay to the deck and massaged his own wounded arm. Fresh blood soaked through Cooper's head bandage and made him look like he'd done ten rounds in the boxing ring. "I'll see you down there on the dock somewhere."

"Thanks Cooper, I couldn't have got this far without your help."

Cooper gave a slight nod and ambled away towards the gang plank.

Direct sunlight burned exposed skin on Jayjay's legs, arms and face.

Sounds of machinery and men yelling instructions couldn't drown out squawking gulls.

Port smells of fish, spices and rotting garbage took him back to the first time he had arrived at Alexandria and gazed upon the exotic city with Ron and Larry and the other raw recruits. His chest tightened and he fought to push the memory from his mind.

Lowering wounded men to the dock by the hoist was a slow process with a limited number of able-bodied to do the work. An hour later a bed-sized cradle, supported at each corner by frayed rope, lowered Jayjay onto firm ground.

A pair of orderlies man-handled him off the hoist cradle and carried him to a motor ambulance. They loaded him into the back of the vehicle, alongside a semi-conscious fellow with bandages around his chest. There was no sign of Cooper or other walking wounded waiting in the dock area.

The engine spluttered to life and shook the ambulance. Jayjay had never ridden in a motor car before and the sensation reminded him of the engine's constant presence on a steaming ship, felt as much as heard, although these vibrations were much more urgent than pulsations from the ship's steam pistons.

Rumbles from the engine grew louder and the vehicle lurched forward. The ride was rough and Jayjay felt every bump in his knee. *This is a ridiculous form of transport. Only the army would ever use something like this.*

The motor ambulance shook him about for several minutes and crunched to a stop. An orderly poked his head into the back of the ambulance.

"Can you blokes walk?"

"What does it look like? I've been shot in the knee and my friend here is barely conscious."

The orderly disappeared and returned a minute later with a helper. The two of them hauled Jayjay out of the vehicle and onto a train that waited at the station nearby.

"This train will take you to Cairo. They'll look after you at one of the hospitals there."

The two orderlies hurried out and Jayjay lay on the bench in the train for an hour without any other information and no medical staff in sight. Then, without warning, the train started rolling.

A nurse marched along the carriage and Jayjay called for her attention, but she looked to be more interested in counting the patients than administering care and hurried past.

Darkened blood stained the dressing on Jayjay's left hand. A nurse had washed and dressed the wound on the hospital ship, on the first night, but no one had looked at it since. It had not bled for the last two days but his little finger and ring finger couldn't move properly. *Hopefully it's healing. It doesn't feel right.*

Outside the train window, the ancient rural dwellings of the Nile Delta slid past. *Ron was so interested in how they built the mud houses. I can't even picture Emilia's face. What am I going to say to her about her husband?*

Gum trees still slouched in lazy rows, like Australian soldiers refusing to salute an officer.

So much has changed since the last time I made this journey, and yet nothing here has changed. It's a miracle I lived to see this place again. I wonder if Larry will make it back here too one day.

Throbbing pain in Jayjay's knee came and went. The journey was relatively comfortable after the black ship, and even included a warm meal, but the hours passed slowly with none of the excitement of the last time he rode the electric train to Cairo.

The train pulled into the station at Cairo and Jayjay strained to look out the window. People ran in all directions and natives yelled to each other in an unintelligible tongue. Those that could walk disembarked themselves, but Jayjay lay and waited. He lay on the bench for half an hour, then a strong looking fellow, almost as big as Jayjay himself, helped him off the train and into a horse-drawn ambulance next to an unconscious soldier with a bandaged arm. The cart carried the two patients through the streets of Cairo, this ride slower and smoother than the motor ambulance.

Local sounds, and the knowledge that he was back in Cairo, brought back memories of the night he'd given his virginity to a prostitute and been robbed for the privilege. A hint of guilt returned. *Being sent home in disgrace with venereal disease would have been worse than death.*

He felt his chest pocket. *Wallet with Ron's gold sovereign is still there. Ron wasn't robbed because Ron did the right thing. Ron always knew how to do the right thing, except getting himself shot in Shrapnel Valley. Ron copped it for no good reason. He deserved better. He should be going home alive instead of me.*

The horses clopped on along the dusty Cairo road and an opening in the flap at the rear of the ambulance allowed Jayjay to catch glimpses of the passing surrounds. After a short distance, the ambulance stopped at Luna Park.

Why are we stopping here? I'm in no condition to go roller skating. I guess we'll be on our way again soon.

The rear flap flew open and a medical officer stuck his dishevelled head in.

"How many more?" he grumbled.

"Sorry for the inconvenience Mate," Jayjay spat. "But there's a bit of a war going on, in case you hadn't noticed."

The head disappeared but the voice continued to penetrate the canvas walls of the ambulance.

"How can we take any more wounded? The hospital is full. The auxiliary is full..."

The conversation moved away from the ambulance and the voices faded.

Throbbing pain persisted in his knee and the other occupant of the Ambulance cart moaned like an animal about to give birth. *Hopefully they'll find space for us somewhere. I need a doctor to take a good look at this knee, and my hand while he's at it.*

He lay back and waited and the air inside the canvas cocoon of the ambulance grew hotter in the sun.

Several minutes later the flap opened again. This time it moved slowly.

"Hello boys!"

Jayjay's heart quickened at the sound of the cheerful female voice. The nurse's smile was as good as any medicine.

"We weren't expecting more of you," she said. "But you'll be in good Australian hands here. Let's get you out of there and get you cleaned up a bit."

The flap opened all the way. An orderly climbed into the ambulance, hauled Jayjay to the rear of the cart and lowered him gently to a tarpaulin on the ground. The nurse smiled again and cut the remains of Jayjay's clothes away with scissors.

* * *

Next morning Jayjay woke after the best night's sleep he'd had in months.

His knee still throbbed, but it had a clean dressing and bandage. A fresh dressing on his hand showed no evidence of bleeding. *That must be a good sign.* Clean pyjamas felt strange but pleasant on his clean skin. A small basket under his bed held his personal belongings.

Finally things are looking up. With a bit of luck they'll fix the knee, but not too good. I'd rather they send me home with a limp than send me back to bloody Gallipoli. Larry will understand. No sense in all of us getting killed there.

Jayjay propped himself up on elbows and took in his surrounds. Early morning light streamed in through high windows and a skylight that ran the length of a long roof. Internal balconies and bare steel balustrade overlooked a sea of a thousand beds laid out in perfect rows across the floor of the roller-skating rink. Many men lay motionless, some sleeping and some staring up at the arched roof structure high above. Some sat and some wondered about.

Several nurses busied themselves amongst the patients.

I can't see Cooper. I hope he's okay. That bullet to the side of his head knocked his brain about a bit.

A nurse approached Jayay, leant over towards him and examined the notes written on a card at his side. In her early twenties, maybe older, with a tired-looking, but pretty face. Her dark wavy hair was tied back loosely, leaving wisps of hair hanging about both of her ears. Her hips formed perfect curves and her large breasts bulged at the front of her uniform, as if trying to burst out, and pulled at his eyes like magnets.

"Jonathan Jones?"

"Yes Ma'am!"

"I'm going to remove the dressing on your knee so the doctor can take a look."

Her eyes look sad. She must be weary. No wonder considering the number of patients in here.

"Thank you Ma'am," Jayjay sat up and turned his head to see the doctor talking to the patient behind him. *Finally a real doctor.*

The patient looked happy enough. He smiled and nodded, then the doctor left him and approached Jayjay.

"Jonathan Jones?"

"Yes Sir."

"Shot in the right knee is it?"

"Yes Sir."

"How long ago was the injury sustained?"

"We attacked Lone Pine on the sixth of August Sir. That's when I was shot. I don't know what the date is now."

"A week then." The doctor looked across the open hall towards a small room at the end that might once have been the ticket office.

He sat on the edge of Jayjay's bed and examined the wounded leg. He said nothing while he worked and Jayjay didn't interrupt. The Doctor poked in a few places and pulled on the foot, sending shock waves of pain up Jayjay's leg. Jayjay flinched and moaned in reaction, then apologized immediately. The doctor ignored his mumbles, but stood and turned to the nurse who was standing by, waiting to take notes with a pencil.

"We'll have that leg off, above the knee. It can wait a day or two until after we've dealt with the more urgent cases."

The doctor moved on to the next bed without meeting Jayjay's gaze and started examining a light horse trooper with a shoulder wound.

Jayjay sat motionless. He needed to breathe, but could not, as if he had been punched hard in the gut without warning.

The nurse scribbled notes with her pencil.

She doesn't look sad enough.

No one cares.

Someone here should at least care enough to shed a tear.

CHAPTER 83

John

Saturday, 21 August 1915

General John Monash stared at the map entitled 'Kurija Dere' and couldn't shake the feeling he was trapped in a nightmare he had experienced before.

Hill 60. It's a not very imaginative name. I might have suggested we name it Pope's Hill, except that we already have one of those.

The 60 metre contour marked a small neat circle on the map. An almost imperceptible knoll along the gentle slope of the unnamed spur that had been the location of his 4th Brigade's disastrous advance towards Hill 971, barely two weeks earlier. The map in his hands had been printed in preparation for the August offensive by British cartographers at Survey of Egypt, who had plagiarized a map taken from a Turkish officer in May. The Turkish topographical maps showed greater detail and accuracy than the original Anzac landing maps, but showed contours in metres, rather than the usual feet and the ridges and gullies all had difficult Turkish names.

Several days after the failed attack, the English Generals Godley and Birdwood had come to visit the firing line. They congratulated John on his 'excellent trench work' but refused to acknowledge that too much had been asked of the 4th Brigade and the left assault column.

The men who marched out of Reserve Gully with John, two weeks earlier, had started in a depleted medical condition. Since then, John had asked them to hike, fight and work hard without a break and they had been willing to give everything they had. Without their personal kit, men had been sleeping without blankets until two nights ago and bronchitis was rife through the ranks.

When General Cox announced his intention to pluck five-hundred men from the brigade to join the New Zealand Mounted Rifles, and the Connaught Rangers for the attack on Hill 60, the Regimental Medical Officer had trouble identifying enough fit men fit to participate.

"McGlinn," John said. "The orders I gave to the officers yesterday, have they been passed on to every man involved in sufficient detail?"

"Yes, I believe so Sir, I sat in on the 15th Battalion briefing and recorded the following instructions as given to the men." McGlinn opened his notebook and read from it. "Artillery bombardment of Hill 60 will commence at 2:15 and continue until three o'clock this afternoon, at which time it will lift towards Hill 100. Meanwhile, at 2:50, troops on the right flank will target Turkish Trenches on and above Hill 60 with an energetic and sustained covering fire. The enemy front has been divided into sections according to the fields of fire, so no portion of their trenches will be missed. At 2:50 the men involved in the advance are to take position in the minor gullies and at three o'clock, when the bombardment lifts, the first wave of 150 men of the 13th Battalion will advance towards the oak tree on Hill 60. At 3:15 the second wave of 150 men of the 14th Battalion will advance and at 3:30 the third wave with the final 100 men of each of the 13th and 14th will advance with picks and shovels. At 3:45, our new friends from the 10th Hampshire will advance. At this time 50 men from the 13th will move along the gully to clear it of snipers and there will be a quick re-organisation to allow the 15th Battalion to commence digging a communications trench across the gully to connect with the advance party."

"Well," John sighed. "It's a plan of sorts."

"A detailed and complete plan Sir, as I would expect from you."

"A plan that sends men running across the enemy line of fire in broad daylight. We're hoping the artillery buys them enough time to cross two hundred yards of prickly scrub to reach cover on the other side of the gully and attack. Why Godley would not allow us to use the cover of darkness is beyond me. How is your bayonet wound?"

"I'll live Sir."

A disturbance nearby caught John's attention.

General Cox was scrambling up the hill. He reached John's brigade headquarters puffing red-faced and looking more flustered than usual.

He held a piece of paper in one hand and waved it about as if this might demonstrate its significance.

"There is a change of timing," Cox spoke quickly between breaths. "General Godley has generously offered our artillery in support of the British advance on W Hills as well as our attack on Hill –."

"What?" John exploded. "That's our artillery! We need it here. That is the only way our men can advance in the daylight. They'll be cut to pieces!"

"The guns will be turned to Hill 60 at three o'clock," Cox continued. "Your advance is to begin at 3:25."

"You cannot change plans at this late stage." John checked his pocket watch. "It is 1:30 now. The men are preparing to attack in one and a half hours. Orders have been issued. We are about to initiate a complex sequence of events and everyone is working to a pre-arranged timetable."

"You will have to adjust the timing, unless you wish your men to charge at the same moment that the bombardment begins."

John could barely believe what he was hearing and didn't want to believe it.

"If you issue an order," John spat, "followed by a counter order, you create disorder – Napoleon said that for good reason."

He turned and slammed his fist into the makeshift bench that supported his map.

* * *

That afternoon, at half past two, the main bombardment of W Hills began. Shells soared over the Suvla plain and thundered into their target. John watched the display from an outpost on the ridge of Damakjelik Bair, although a haze of dust and shell smoke soon obscured the plain.

Near to John, press correspondent Charles Bean stood with field glasses and a camera, ready to capture his photographic images. *Hopefully he will find something positive that he can write about our achievements. We have been holding this ground with sick men and scant provisions for two weeks. If he has his way, the 1st Brigade feint at Lone Pine will become famous in Australia and the main attack by the 4th Brigade at Hill 60 will never be heard of. Maybe reports of our deeds here would stir more interest at home if we named the place 'The Blood-Soaked Oak of Sacrifice to Superciliousness'.*

John had briefed officers of the 4th Brigade on the change of timing and now he had to rely on them to communicate the information to their men. The men would be watching the shelling while they waited. John had insisted that the whole plan be communicated to them, including the artillery sequence involving W Hills. They would be able to see some of the action to the north and John wanted them to know the relationship it had to their own artillery cover.

Across the valley of Kaiajik Dere, the unnamed spur forked from Damakjelik Bair up at Hill 100, then ran west, parallel to Damakelik Bair for nearly a mile. Turks were well entrenched at Hill 100 and along the unnamed spur down to the knoll now designated as Hill 60. The valley of Kaiajik Dere between the spurs was wide, gentle of slope, and straight as a gun barrel. Anyone attempting to cross it could expect a savage enfilade from defenders uphill.

At three o'clock the artillery bombardment at W Hills, across the Suvla plain, stopped. Several minutes passed before a single shell thudded into the unnamed spur below Hill 60.

John willed the guns on, but they remained quiet.

At 3:15pm, a line of advancing British could be seen on the Suvla Plain in the distance, marked by puffs of Turkish shrapnel in the air above it.

Another shell hit the spur closer to Hill 60, then nothing.

At 3:20 the men below were due to move into the minor gullies in preparation for the charge. Sounds of small arms fire reached John and he knew that some of his men had been seen already.

More artillery was required. Shells had been rationed for the past two weeks, but now they were needed more than ever.

At 3:25 the first wave was due to charge, but there was no sign of movement. *Maybe they are praying for a few more shells at the last moment.*

At 3:30 a machine gun up the valley at Hill 100 opened, and John saw 150 of his fittest men surging across the valley at a full sprint. To travel the distance of two hundred yards, they seemed to take an hour. In the cruel lottery, John estimated that less than one third of them made it to shelter at the far side of the valley, near the base of the solitary oak tree.

John felt as if he might vomit.

We gave them just enough of a shelling to warn them we are coming, but not enough to do any good.

Bean's face was white and his mouth open.

Over one hundred men lay scattered across the valley. Only a few moved. Most likely some were wounded and playing possum, knowing that if they were able lie still until dark, they might have a chance to crawl to safety without being shot. Regardless, the losses were severe. The isolated force across the valley was too small to achieve anything without more men.

At 3:45 the second wave charged. Another hundred and fifty men burst forth and charged by the bodies of their comrades without pausing, but one-by-one they fell themselves. Again, less than one third of their number reached shelter on the far side of the valley.

Further towards the sea, the New Zealand Mounted Rifles made their run across the valley at the same time as the Australian second wave. Some of the New Zealanders fell in the charge, but the Turks had a clearer line of fire at the Australians and it was the Australians who bore the brunt of the fusillade.

Smoke and dust drifted down the valley in a few minutes of hiatus. The tap of small arms fire continued, but the valley floor was devoid of movement other than for a few of the wounded, and those who moved about too much attracted extra bullets for their trouble.

At 4:00 the third wave of Australians made a start, but, being weighed down with picks and shovels they could not move as quickly as they others. As a unit they sought cover barely having entered the valley.

I can't say that I blame them for that.

"Sir," McGlinn called. "A message from General Russell. He says the New Zealand Mounted Rifles are in position and want the Australians to advance."

"Please tell General Russell," John felt Bean's eyes watching him. "That that is exactly what we are trying to do, but in case he hasn't noticed, many of our men are now casualties lying on the valley floor as we are taking the majority of enemy fire up this end of the valley."

Minutes later, the support unit from the 10th Hampshire made their run from the Australian position in the final wave of attack. A well-aimed shell landed in the centre of the cluster of men and threw bodies in the air. When the smoke cleared the 10th Hampshire unit was flattened and a fire burned amongst the bodies. A few dragged themselves up and scurried forward away from the flames. Machine gun and rifle fire from up the valley chased them along until only one man was left. Somehow this one fellow beat the odds and joined the huddle of Australians under the stunted oak on the far side of the valley.

On the valley floor, wounded Australians of the 4th Brigade and Englishmen from the 10th New Hampshire crawled to escape the flames, only to succumb to a renewed storm of Turkish bullets.

John's heart sank further at the sight.

I must do something for those men, the wounded and the ones that made it across, cut off from support. Cox will do nothing. He is incapable is making a decision on his own. Maybe if I approach Godley direct.

"McGlinn," John spoke without taking his eyes from the morbid scene in the valley below. "Who is the fastest runner in our ranks?"

"Private Lewis Sir. Claims he's run a four-minute mile, but had no witnesses. That's obviously an exaggeration on his part, but he is a good runner."

"Get him quick."

"Yes Sir." McGlinn hurried away and John sat to scribble a note to Commander of the New Zealand and Australian Division, General Godley.

John re-read his note and returned his pencil to his pocket. He did not have to wait long until a wiry looking fellow wearing cut-off shorts and a beard came bounding up the ridge."

"Private Lewis?"

"Yes Sir."

"Where is Colonel McGlinn?"

"I think he is still coming Sir, he said you wanted to see me quickly and I shouldn't wait for him, Sir."

"How are things on your part of the front line?"

"We are doing our best Sir."

"I do not doubt that, but that is not what I asked."

"Most of the men are poorly Sir, and we are spread pretty thin."

"Have you seen the plight of the men who attacked across the valley?"

"Yes Sir, we saw it from our trenches."

"We need help here. You can see why. We need reinforcements so we can shorten the section of front line we are defending and to help the survivors in that valley in front of us."

"Yes Sir."

"I want you to take this message to General Godley. It is a request for more men. His headquarters are at No. 3 Outpost, back towards Anzac Cove."

"Is that the Maori-lander country north of Reserve Gully?"

"Yes, that's right."

"The place where we waited about for a while on the night march."

"Yes, just inland from the beach at that point, you should find him. Take my water bottle, it's full."

"Yes Sir, thank you Sir."

"Godspeed Lewis."

"Yes Sir." Lewis pocketed the note, slung the water bottle over his shoulder and jogged away.

John turned towards Hill 60 where smoke from two fires drifted towards the sea. Flames marched towards green bodies and left blackened bodies behind. A crawler found a sudden burst of speed, but the flames enveloped him and then an explosion burst from the place where he was.

Must have been an ammunition pouch or a bomb he was carrying. God help them. Now we must wait.

* * *

One long hour after Private Lewis had departed, he returned to John's outpost through the backline, red-faced and blowing hard.

Lewis approached John, removed the water bottle from his shoulder and handed it back to its owner. The bottle was empty and had a bullet-sized hole in the side.

"Did you find General Godley?"

Lewis nodded, breathing heavily.

"Sorry," Lewis puffed, "Sir."

"Take a moment. Here's some more water."

"Thank… you…Sir..."

"Is General Godley going to send more men?"

Lewis shook his head and pulled a scrap of paper from his pocket.

"He wasn't going to write anything down, but I asked for some paper and a pencil so I would get it right Sir, 'cause what he said didn't make any sense to me."

"What did General Godley say?"

"General Godley said," Lewis read slowly, "Ask General Monash to refrain from using the word survivors as it might provoke alarm and despondency. General Monash ought to talk of an exact number of casualties. Exaggeration can lower morale."

CHAPTER 84

Ellis

Tuesday, 7 September 1915

Ellis Ashmead-Bartlett inhaled warm air through a cigarette and stared at his trusty correspondent's Remington typewriter. Outside, a bitter wind and rain lashed at the canvas of his bell tent. Inside his head, a decision started to crystallise. An opportunity to get the truth out, but the window of opportunity would close very soon.

The risk of being caught was real and the consequences might be severe, but Ellis had never shied away from action in the past, not if a chance presented itself to tell the truth, especially an important truth. The stakes of this game were too high.

For the first time in days, the fog of helpless frustration started to lift from his mind, but it would not clear away in full. The August offensive had been a complete disaster, possibly the greatest reverse ever suffered by the British Army in the field. Every time Ellis thought through the sequence of events, the answer was the same: Sir Ian Hamilton and his General Staff had planned an over-complicated, faulty and almost fantastic scheme of operations. Success was made to depend upon the troops performing impossible feats, in murderous frontal attacks, and, even if there had been no mistakes in execution, the plan could never have succeeded.

The attack on the Sari Bair range was made by the best troops available, seasoned Australians and New Zealanders, reinforced with the 13th Division of the new British Army that had been blooded by several weeks in the trenches at Cape Helles. With such a force, a general might expect to go anywhere and do anything, but the Anzac army was launched against positions, the like of which have never been attacked before under modern conditions of war and expected to climb over unexplored broken ground, at night, under fire, in a prescribed time that would have been difficult to achieve during peacetime in daylight. They were not given even a gambling chance of success. So much effort was required to advance, that positions gained could not be held against Turkish counter attack.

The British landing at Suvla Bay was a fiasco of the highest order. A feasible military operation, depending on two factors – surprise and speed. It was essential to drive away the feeble Turkish forces holding the district and occupy the hills before reserves could be brought from Bulair. Speed required experienced troops, but these men were totally without experience of warfare and unaccustomed to the hot weather. It would have been mere child's play for the Dominion troops to achieve the objectives. Any troops are good enough for feints, like at Lone Pine, or Cape Helles, to draw the enemy away from the real objective. But instead, some of the finest and most seasoned troops were used for feints. Troops who had been tried and never found wanting, and could have been used at Suvla.

Even if we took the Anafarta Hills, the strategic benefit is doubtful. The widest part of the Gallipoli peninsula and the Narrows are still a long way away. We couldn't stop Turkish reserve forces in the north from coming to defend the supply route to their forces in the south.

After four days the offensive ended in overwhelming and decisive defeat. But this was not enough, further cruel and useless frontal assaults on the Anafarta Hills and Hill 60 during the second half of August resulted in thousands more British and Dominion casualties.

A squall of wind reminded Ellis that poor weather had disrupted his plans to visit the Anzac front that day, adding to his frustrations. But an Australian journalist, Keith Murdoch, had been staying in the press camp for the past few nights and was not deterred by the elements. Having only a short time available, he visited the Anzac front despite the heavy rain. Ellis and the Australian had discussed the problems of the campaign at length, ever careful as to who might be listening. Murdoch had some sort of mandate from the Australian Prime Minister and was about to depart for England to make a case against the management of the campaign and the treatment of the Australians. The fellow was an Australian patriot to his shoe-laces and upset at the circumstances in which he found his fellow Colonials, but he was concerned that he lacked the credibility of one who had witnessed the extended operations and he begged Ellis write his own letter that Murdoch would deliver uncensored.

Ellis had signed an agreement to submit all his writing to the censor, but also had a vague feeling that everyone was entitled to write to the Prime Minister without censorship.

The Remington keys called him to tell the truth.

He flicked last of his cigarette through the tent flap into a puddle outside, loaded a sheet of paper and started to type, beginning with tomorrow's date:

September 8th, 1915.

Dear Mr. Asquith,

I hope you will excuse the liberty I am taking in writing to you, but I have the chance of sending this letter through by hand, and

> I consider it absolutely necessary that you should know the true state of affairs out here. Our last great effort to achieve some definite success against the Turks was the most ghastly and costly fiasco in our history since the battle of Bannockburn. Personally, I never thought the schemes decided on by Headquarters ever had the slightest chance of succeeding and all efforts now to make out that it only just failed, owing to the failure of the 9th Corps to seize the Anafarta Hills, bear no relation to the real truth...

Ellis hammered away at the keys until he finished a letter that ran into several pages. He folded the letter and slipped it into an envelope addressed to the British Prime Minister, but did not seal it. That night he would read through it with Keith Murdoch, quietly and secretly. He wanted Murdoch to be clear on the facts, in case anything happened to the letter.

I wish I could deliver the letter myself. Ellis had long been thinking of returning home and had written to the Newspaper Proprietors' Association requesting their permission, but felt that if his employers wished him to remain he could hardly refuse, after all the consideration they had shown him. He hoped to hear back from them soon, but knew there was a good chance he would be asked to stay on and did not want to miss the chance to let the truth be known at home.

* * *

The next day, after a long but discreet night-time discussion, he bid Keith Murdoch farewell. As Ellis watched the ship pull away, he felt relieved for the first time in weeks.

In addition to the letter addressed to the Prime Minister, Murdoch carried letters of introduction from Ellis to others who might be helpful in organising a campaign to save the army on Gallipoli.

Ellis had also arranged for Murdoch to meet Harry Lawson, a representative of the Newspaper Proprietors' Association and one of Ellis's good friends, to urge him to allow Ellis to return home.

In the end, Ellis had promised Murdoch that if he was held up in his mission, or if the authorities refused to listen to his warnings, Ellis would at once resign and join forces with him in London. *I wonder if it will come to that?*

That night the rain and cold wind continued, as if an evil omen. During the storm he received a signal from Sir Ian Hamilton stating that he wished to see Ellis next morning.

Can they have caught my letter already? I wonder if a man can be shot for such a breach of the rules? Ellis lay awake for a long time before he fell asleep that night.

* * *

First thing next morning, Ellis hurried to visit Sir Ian Hamilton.

The Commander-in-Chief wore the look of one who had recently learned of the death of a close friend, but was trying to maintain his composure for an important visitor.

"I have received a cable from the War Office," Hamilton said, "forbidding anyone to take photographs except the official photographer."

Is this what I postponed my trip to Anzac for? He hasn't learned about the letter.

"We have all been taking photographs for the past six months Sir," Ellis replied. "This seems to be a somewhat belated decision. Has the War Office been considering this issue the whole time?"

"Frankly," Hamilton shook his head, ignoring the jibe. "I consider the regulation to be absurd. You might go on using your cameras as far as I am concerned."

Hamilton is going out of his way to be agreeable. And he wants me to know it. He and his General Staff must know that their position is precarious. They are sitting around like condemned criminals.

"General," Ellis probed. "Is there anything you can tell me about the future of the Expedition?"

"There are events in the air," the general pursed his lips until they disappeared into the tight crease of his mouth. "But I do not know if I am right in telling you as much as this. I have no idea what the decision of Cabinet will be."

CHAPTER 85

Jayjay

Friday, 10 September 1915

Pain surged from his knee, or at least from the place where his knee should have been. He ground his teeth against each other and ground the tips of his crutches into the gravel outside the Luna Park skating rink.

Nothing's fair in the whole damned world. Ron copped it for being in the wrong place at the wrong time. If I jumped off the log into the trench at Lone Pine one second earlier, the bullet might have taken me in the heart instead of smashing my knee. I wish it had, then I'd be as dead as Abdul, the big bastard Turk. I'm sure he was the one who shot me.

Jayjay reached into the chest pocket of his pyjamas and fingered the bullet that did the damage. It sat there with a Turkish brass button embossed with a crescent moon and star.

The Turks were decent enough blokes. Seems crazy we spent every day trying to kill each other, every day except the one we worked together to bury the dead. That was a good day.

He leaned on the crutches and shifted his weight. It was too depressing to lie in bed all day, waiting for the leg wound to heal. His left hand relied on the thumb and first two fingers to hold the grip. The little finger and ring finger remained slightly splayed when he tried to make a fist and had no strength. The doctor said tendons were damaged and there was nothing he could do. At least his hand didn't hurt much, not like the knee.

'Phantom pain' the doctor called it. Something to do with the nerves. *Stupid bloody name, the pain's as real now as it ever was.*

He lifted the remnant of his right leg slightly, squeezed the thigh muscles with tired fingers the released, and worked his way along in a routine he had done hundreds of times. He felt the bandage under his pyjamas and massaged to the stump.

There had been no warning on the day of the operation, just a morning bed bath and 'The doctor will be operating on you today.' Then a short wheelchair ride to the ticket office of the roller skating rink hospital.

They called it the 'operating theatre', but it still looked like a ticket office as far as Jayjay could tell, with trays of cutting tools laid out on a pristine white table cloth and a saw hanging on the wall.

The doctor used words like 'septic' and 'gangrene' and reached for the ether. There were no options given. There was no asking whether Lance Corporal Jonathan Jones might mind his leg being cut off before the doctor took a bite of lunch.

The ether worked quickly, and knocked him out cold. When he returned to consciousness the pain was back with renewed intensity.

"Your operation went well." The Nurse from Melbourne smiled, but her eyes glistened with sadness.

"Very funny," Jayjay replied. "I know my leg's still there 'cause it hurts like blazes! Even my foot hurts now."

She saved herself further argument by pulling back the sheet to expose the truth, as if it was some kind of magic trick. The sight nailed Jayjay's tongue to the roof of his mouth. He struggled to breathe and felt the same sensation as when he was first given the news that his leg would be amputated. He said nothing, but stared at the bandaged stump of his leg long after the nurse turned her attention to the next patient.

His question of 'why?' never received a satisfactory answer, but it seemed that amputations due to septic infection and gangrene were common here. Some of the nurses' comments led him to think that the amount of time wounds were left untreated was a contributing factor, but he hadn't been able to get a doctor to say whether his leg could have been saved if it was given proper medical treatment earlier.

Could I have done anything differently? Maybe got off the beach quicker? Maybe demanded more attention on the hospital ship? Maybe not get shot in the first place?

Gravel crunched under the crutch tips.

The entrance to the skating rink was close now and fatigue pushed him along towards a bed where he could lie down. Since the surgery, much energy had drained from his body.

Someone in uniform stood leaning against the entrance watching him, standing strangely, as if one arm was behind his back. Jayjay stopped dead.

"Cooper?"

"Jones." Cooper started down the steps and Jayjay realised that his arm wasn't behind his back. It was missing from the elbow with the shirt sleeve folded up and neatly pinned in place, in a similar way to the leg of his own pyjamas.

"Cooper! Blazes! They took your bloody arm!"

"Yeah, coulda been worse though mate. Coulda' been me bloody leg."

"You're a tough bastard. You were helping me all that time, and your arm was crook. I hardly even realised."

Cooper grinned. "Left the tourniquet on too long. They told me the arm turned poison and it mighta' killed me if they didn't take it off, so I'm probably better off without it eh?"

"Are you right-handed?"

"Not anymore."

"Damn! Does it hurt?"

"Comes and goes." Cooper shrugged.

"Yeah, I know."

"I've learned to bend my left elbow." Cooper made a drinking motion with an imaginary glass in his left hand. "What say we go find ourselves a drink?"

"I'd love to," Jayjay said. "But I'm a cripple in pyjamas, and I'm not carrying any money. I'm not supposed to go far. I haven't even got any clothes. The only ones I had were in a sorry state when I got here and the nurse cut them off me with scissors. There I was for all to see, lying on the road stark naked!"

"Don't worry about that Mate. My shout. How's about you park yourself in the shade of the building over there and I'll go and buy us a bottle o' medicine. What's your preference?"

Jayjay had to stop and think. Other than a few drams of rum on the battlefield, he hadn't taken any alcohol for months.

Beer would be nice, but something stronger might help with the pain.

"Irish whiskey," Jayjay said without conviction.

"Irish!" Cooper laughed. "Johnnie Walker is easy enough to come by, or other scotch, but I'm not so sure about Irish whiskey. I'll see what I can do. No promises mind."

Jayjay hesitated and wanted to say that anything would be fine, but Cooper had disappeared on his mission, so Jayjay turned on his crutches, propelled himself to the shade of the building, then sat on a step and waited.

He sat for twenty minutes and started to wonder whether Cooper would return, then his uniformed frame rounded the corner with a bottle of Jameson Irish Whisky in his one hand.

Cooper sat on the step beside Jayjay and shook his head as if in answer to an unasked question. He pulled the cork with his teeth and spat it on the ground.

"Cheers Jones." Cooper took a swig and held out the bottle.

Jayjay reached across his body with his good hand so as not to risk dropping the bottle. Cooper glanced at Jayjay's left hand resting still, but said nothing.

"Cheers Cooper." Jayjay took sip and passed the bottle back. It warmed the back of his throat and the fumes stung in his nostrils on the way out. He fought the urge to cough, but failed and felt embarrassed, as if he had shown weakness.

"They told me the same thing. My leg was going to kill me if they didn't get rid of it. I thought it might be a bit of a furphy."

"Well, I figure they wouldn't go about cutting off a fella's arm without a good reason."

"But why didn't they treat us sooner? At least get your tourniquet off sooner?"

"I suppose it just took that long to get us back to Egypt, to the hospital." Cooper passed the bottle back.

"They left us lying on the beach, and then on that damn ship. They could have done something."

"I dunno mate. I can't make sense of anything about the war. This ain't no different."

Jayjay nodded in silence. Try as he might, there was much he couldn't make sense of either. He took another gulp. His throat was starting to feel numb and his head light, as if he was drifting away from the reality of his situation.

"You got Irish blood in you Jones?"

"Nah," Jayjay replied. "There were these Irish fellows in the battalion. Got into a bit of strife with them in the Wazza before going to Gallipoli. They introduced me to Irish Whiskey. They're dead now. Seamus, Mick and Poddy. I never really had a chance to pay my respects. Thought I might remember them with a silent prayer and a drop of their favourite."

"Most of my mates are dead – Duck, Macka, Sarge, The Butcher." Cooper stared at the ground. "Unhealthy business bein' a machine gunner – sounds like a great idea – fire hundreds of bullets per minute from a good distance back. Only thing is – enemy doesn't like it – so he spots our possie and sends all hell straight back. Stupid bloody business!"

"The Butcher," Jayjay said. "He must have been a mean bastard."

"Nah, gentle as a lamb. Should never have signed up, only seventeen years old."

"Why'd you call him that then?"

"He was an apprentice butcher in Marrickville. Kept his bayonet so sharp he could shave with it. Never stuck it in the dirt. Never stuck it in another man neither, but if he did, I reckon it would have cut 'em clean in half. Didn't do him no good though. Got blown to hell with the rest of 'em."

Jayjay nodded. "My brother's dead. Didn't last two weeks. Copped it in Shrapnel Gully. Sniper."

"I never had a brother. Got a sister. At least she won't have to fight in no bloody war."

"One of my mates from home is still alive."

"At Gallipoli?"

"Yeah."

"Probably won't live for long then."

"Larry's a tough one. He'll be all right." *Do I really believe that?*

"A lot of tough ones already buried back there mate." Cooper swirled the half-empty bottle in a small circles and stared at the liquid. “I shoulda’ stayed there with ’em and been buried there myself. Shouldn’ta’ gave in to the funk and skived off like a rat.”

He took another drink, then shook his head.

“Funk’s a funny thing,” Cooper continued. “Once saw a bloke shoot his own finger off. He musta’ thought no one was looking. Fixed the bayonet, dunno why he did that. Sat the butt of his bread-winner on the firing step, stuck a finger in the barrel and pulled the trigger with his other hand. Didn’t even cry out, just ran off towards the beach. Left his bread-winner right there on the firing step. I went and wiped off the blood and bits o’ skin off o’ the bayonet. Figured what’s done is done. No use his mate’s thinking he’s deserted ’em.”

Guilt stabbed at Jayjay’s innards. *Why should I leave the place alive when so many can’t? Why did I have to wreck my body to get away? I am a coward.*

There was little reason to live now, with Jayjay’s body the way it was, but he knew deep inside himself, even if he was fit, he would never go back to Gallipoli by choice. Hate for the place burned deep inside him.

The sun climbed in the sky and Jayjay started to sweat in the late morning heat. The two talked some, of mates and war, but mostly sat in silence. The bottle passed between them instead of words.

“I dunno,” Cooper drained the last of the whiskey. “I dunno why I wandered down towards the beach. Maybe I coulda’ done something more. I just left ’em all there. Blown apart and bits o’ their guts lying in the dirt. I just dusted myself off and left ’em lying there. I dunno why I wasn’t killed along with ’em. There was nothing in the way to shield me. Just the way the bullets flew. I can’t figure it any better than that.”

Cooper tossed the empty bottle to the ground and stared at it.

“You feel bad,” Jayjay said, “for leaving your dead mates behind. I feel bad for leaving my mates behind when they were alive. There’s no way out of that damned place, except getting killed, or getting your body wrecked and feeling bad for leaving your mates behind.” Numbness oozed through his veins like sludge and the horizon spun.

“Worst part about it is,” Jayjay continued. “You’re bloody right! Larry and the others are as good as dead. They could be dead already for all I know. They should be here instead of me. Fit and healthy – at least they could get around and have some fun, then go home to their families and have a good life. Instead, the Brass waits for our bodies to be wrecked, then they send us here with no mates. It’s not bloody fair!”

“You got one mate here Jones.”

“Blazes, sorry Cooper. You know what I mean.”

“Yeah, I know.”

CHAPTER 86

Ellis

Tuesday, 28 September 1915

Another visit to the General Staff – like visiting the tombs of the dead. Men living on borrowed time, yet they still insist on censoring my writing to the extreme. Maybe my complaints will fall on deaf ears again today, but I shan't die wondering.

My letter to the Prime Minister must have reached him by now. Three weeks today since I waved Murdoch away and I haven't heard anything about it.

"Ashmead-Bartlett, good morning to you." Colonel Tyrell emerged from his bell tent at General Headquarters. "What trouble are you looking to cook up today?"

"Good morning Sir. I hope to discuss the hefty censorship of my last despatch, and also the state of my most recent work which was submitted three days ago and I believe is still awaiting your attention."

Ellis mostly enjoyed a good working relationship with the Chief of Intelligence, Colonel Tyrell, and knew him from a previous assignment in Constantinople. At the same time, Ellis maintained an ongoing campaign against his blue censor's pencil, urging it to work faster and strike out fewer words.

"Bartlett, you are as persistent as the bloody Turks. I have much more important things to attend to than censoring war correspondents' cables. They are only a secondary matter and a low priority."

"With all due respect Sir," Ellis replied. "We are officially attached to the Army and thus have a right to be properly treated."

"Yes, yes, very well, I shall get to it in good time. But I can't stop now, I must be off to see the Chief of Staff."

"Very well Sir. Thank you Sir."

Ellis sat for a moment and surveyed the camp that constituted General Headquarters. He shook his head. *This is what the might of the British Empire has been reduced to. The command centre of the Mediterranean Expeditionary Force, leading tens of thousands of men with all the modern weapons of war. Sadly it befits the men who live here.* Before him lay a cluster of bell tents and a few simple lean-to structures, centred around a small courtyard of bare earth.

"Bartlett!" Colonel Tyrell returned looking like a man about to kick a stray dog.

"You had better come to see the Chief of Staff yourself."

The Chief Intelligence Officer turned on his heels without further explanation. Ellis followed him into one of the tents and felt his pulse quicken.

General Hamilton's Chief of Staff, General Walter Braithwaite stood with an undisguised sneer that made Tyrell's expression seem like warm sunshine.

"Bartlett, please sit down." Braithwaite waited for Ellis to comply before he continued. "When I had a talk with you in June last, you promised not to criticise the leaders of the Army, the conduct of the campaign, or to break the regulations again."

"I consented to certain things," Ellis replied cautiously. "And as far as I know I have kept my agreement."

"On September 8th you sent off an uncensored letter by Murdoch, who was leaving, addressed to Mr Asquith."

"Yes, I did so and I had a perfect right to address the Prime Minister direct."

"You know you had not, and your letter has got Murdoch into serious trouble."

"How did you find out I had sent this letter?"

"That is not your concern. Suffice it to say that the letter was seized by the military authorities when he landed at Marseilles."

"Did the Prime Minister ever receive it?"

"What?" Braithwaite looked shocked, as if Ellis had just asked him to remove his trousers.

"My letter man, did the Prime Minister ever receive it? He was the intended recipient."

Braithwaite hesitated. "I don't know."

Ellis saw at once that Braithwaite had no conception of the contents of the letter, and if it had been seized off Murdoch in Marseilles, there would have been no time for it to come back, except by cable.

"As you have broken the rules of censorship," Braithwaite continued. "You will no longer be allowed to stay with the Army, and must severe your connection with it and return home."

Braithwaite's sneer grew into a smile of victory, as if he had delivered a knock-out blow.

"May I leave at once?" Ellis jumped to his feet. "I have long been anxious to be relieved of my post, and have in fact applied to the Newspaper Proprietors' Association to be allowed to return."

Braithwaite's eyes narrowed and he said nothing for a long moment before he responded.

"Very well Bartlett, depart as soon as is practical."

"Thank you Sir." Ellis was disappointed his letter had been intercepted, but news of his being sent home left him feeling a sense of relief that he hadn't known in weeks. Without allowing the conversation to continue, he hurried out of the tent fearing the Chief of Staff might change his mind.

"Bartlett!" Colonel Tyrell, the Chief of Intelligence had followed Ellis out. "Bartlett, wait."

"Yes Sir." Ellis turned.

"I shall regret to see you go, despite everything."

"Thank you Sir. I do not have many friends here at G.H.Q. but I am pleased to count you as one of them."

Two junior officers watched the exchange and sniggered like a pair of schoolboys who had just come across a photograph of a woman with bare breasts.

"You lad's better go and pack your things as well," Ellis said to the junior officers. "You'll soon be on your way home. G.H.Q. will not long survive my departure, not once the truth is known at home. I am now absolutely free. I can say what I like, I can write what I like, and I can see whom I like. Good day to you gentlemen."

Ellis turned and left General Headquarters for the last time, without any inkling of an urge to look back over his shoulder. *Never have I known such a collection of unsuitable people to whom to entrust a great campaign, the lives of their countrymen and the safety of the Empire. Their muddles, mismanagement, and ignorance of the strategy and tactics of modern war have brought about the greatest disaster in English history… I must write that down.*

* * *

Five days later, Ellis leaned against the rail on the quarterdeck of the Cressy-class armoured cruiser *Bacchante*. Rays of late afternoon sunshine warmed his shoulder as he gazed across the waters of Mudros Harbour. He remembered the early days of April and the first time his eyes beheld the Dardanelles fleet on this vast expanse of water.

A deep sadness welled up from some place within him, like a spring after heavy rain. *The mightiest fleet ever assembled. So many tragic events have happened since that day, half a year ago.*

Gentle hills on the island of Lemnos slid slowly by and the warship eased out of Mudros Harbour into the Aegean proper, on her way to the British Naval Base of Malta.

Ellis barely noticed the rhythm of tremors from her triple expansion steam engines, or the squawks of the sea gulls chasing her out into open water. The past few days of packing up and saying goodbyes had left him exhausted. In some way, he felt like he had failed.

Thousands of men joined this expedition, from parts of the Empire all over the world. Many of them gave their lives in full trust of their leaders. Not one of those who died had the privilege of seeing what I saw or knowing what I know. It's just as well, or they might well question the cause for which they gave their lives. Now I must go home and expose the truth.

At least I had the chance to let the Navy know the Army was using them as a scapegoat before I left.

The unexpected opportunity to expose General Hamilton's duplicity had presented itself on the Navy flagship *Triad*, whilst saying goodbye to Admiral of the fleet John de Robeck and his Chief of Staff, Commodore Roger Keyes.

Keyes was in a great rage with General Headquarters because of the rumours that had been circulating round for some time, that the Navy was responsible for shelling the Gurkhas off the crest of Sari Bair after they had established themselves on the heights during the August offensive.

Admiral de Robeck had written to General Headquarters, asking for a statement on the subject of these allegations, or else a full denial.

Keyes showed Ellis the reply from General Headquarters, in which Hamilton denied that he had ever used the words complained of, and admitted that it was not the truth that the occupation of Sari Bair had been brought to naught through the fault of the ships.

"Tell me," Commodore Keyes said. "When you visited General Headquarters, did General Hamilton or his staff ever assert that it was only the unhappy intervention of the ships' guns which brought about the disaster?"

"They never ceased to rub it into me," Ellis replied, "that the Navy had shelled the Gurkhas off, and that this cause alone had prevented the retention of Sari Bair."

Ellis pulled a diary from his bag and flicked through the pages until he found what he was looking for. He then showed Keyes a record of an interview with General Hamilton in which the Commander-in-Chief had used exactly these words.

"Further," Ellis said. "This was expressly stated in the official account of these operations issued to the correspondents by the General Staff."

Roger Keyes closed his eyes and pulled a long, slow breath. "Would you be so good to supply all this information to me in a letter?"

"It would be my pleasure Sir," Ellis replied. "I shall type it up right now."

* * *

His Majesty's Ship *Bucchante* zig-zagged down the Mediterranean to dodge enemy submarines on the voyage to Malta, but otherwise the journey to England proved uneventful.

Ellis arrived home on 10 October 1915, exactly one week after departing Mudros harbour. His return to London reminded Ellis of the day HMS *Majestic* was torpedoed, and the moment he burst through the surface of the water gasping for air, clutching at an uninflated life-belt and surrounded by men in various states of panic.

Cabinet and the War Office floundered in confusion as the realisation that the Dardanelles Expedition was a failure had begun to dawn on those in command.

Cabinet was divided. One section favoured the immediate withdrawal of the Expedition. The other anxious to avoid this acknowledgement at any cost, feared the moral effect on our Eastern Empire and the encouragement it would give our enemies.

The military authorities were likewise at loggerheads. The die-hards wished to continue with the Expedition and to send out large reinforcements, still believing that the August offensive had only just failed of success through unfortunate circumstances and that victory was still possible. Their opponents advocated abandonment, and the transference of the Army to some other theatre of war.

Meanwhile, the French clamoured for troops from the Dardanelles to be sent to Salonika for a joint expedition to aid Serbia, now threatened by the cooperation of the Bulgarian and Austro-Hungarian armies.

Another section of military opinion, representing the views of the Western Front, was against any further commitments or adventures in the Near East.

One afternoon, Ellis crossed paths with Winston Churchill who still moped around like a victim of the greatest injustice.

"I remained a member of the Cabinet and of the War Council at their request you know," Winston said.

"The Dardanelles campaign has failed," Ellis replied. "You do understand that."

"It is not too late. If only my wings had not been clipped so. You cannot imagine the frustration. I know everything and can do nothing. The change from the intense executive activities of each day's work at the Admiralty to the narrowly measured duties of a counsellor leaves me gasping. Like a sea-beast fished up from the depths, or a diver too suddenly hoisted, my veins are threatening to burst from the fall in pressure. I have to watch the unhappy casting-away of great opportunities, and the feeble execution of plans which I had launched and in which I heartily believe. At a moment when every fibre of my being is inflamed to action, I am forced to remain a spectator of the tragedy, placed cruelly in a front seat."

"That's all very melodramatic Winston. In my observation, the facts are quite different."

"Maybe I'll take a command on the Western Front. Maybe I'll take up oil-painting."

I cannot waste any more of my time with this fellow. He remains completely delusional.

For anyone else who asked, Ellis was ready to explain that he returned to London with one objective, namely to press for the withdrawal of the Expedition before it was too late, being firmly convinced at the risk of unparalleled disaster in English history if the troops were forced to remain at Anzac and Suvla during the winter months.

In reality, he had to think of money also. His generous war correspondent's salary had been terminated and he had upset the army establishment. He knew they would not allow him to travel to the Western Front. War writing was his profession and his career prospects were not looking good. The declaration of bankruptcy before leaving for the Dardanelles would make it difficult to borrow himself out of a financial hole again.

I will have to visit the Newspaper Proprietors' Association in the next few days. No doubt they will be displeased at my return without their sanction, but they may have some ideas as to how my skills might be used to turn a coin.

If I cannot participate in the rest of the war, or write about what I have seen, I will have to do what I can with what I have. I can sell my cinematograph films if the War Office will allow it and publish all my despatches in a book, censored as they are, people still pay good money for that kind of thing. Maybe I could make a lecture tour and charge admission, tell people about what has really happened until I am made to stop.

Ellis pushed the mundane from his mind to focus on his immediate campaign, the rescue of men from Gallipoli before winter. He formed a plan to contact those he knew and present his case for evacuation of the Gallipoli peninsula. It was a detailed plan as he knew many powerful people in London.

My part in this tragedy is nearly done, but I must do what I can to help cut our losses and relieve the senseless waste of our men. One day, when this business is over, I shall expose the truth more widely and write a full account of the Dardanelles Campaign, uncensored.

CHAPTER 87

Dacre

Friday, 29 October 1915

"Let us," said Archibald coming out into the middle of the room, "let us send this fellow away – I've had enough of him."

"And I!" cried the Bed.

"And I!" said the Floor.

"What is he doing here anyway?" Archibald continued in angrier tones. "When he first arrived I didn't mind, I thought it might be a good thing – that there might be some decent food falling from his table. But is there? Never a crumb! The greed of the brute is disgusting – he gives nothing to me. Have I no dues? Am I not a king in my own right? By right of might, by right of conquest over all my fellows?"

"See the way he treats me," said the Bed. "I am tired of this bony fellow lying on my back hour by hour, day and night, never still, but tossing restlessly from this side to that, until every one of my long-suffering legs and joints cries out in tortured misery. Let us send him away!"

"And is there to be no respect for my age?" groaned the Floor. "Is this endless tramp, tramp, to continue forever – four paces this way, four paces that – until I know to a millionth of an inch the next spot in my aged and broken surface which must bear the crush of his accursed heel! Let us send him away!"

"Fools!" creaked the Door, grating on his broken hinges as the sentry looked in. Worthy of better things was the Door, or had been, tall and commanding in comparison to his surroundings, yet having the sad appearance of genteel poverty. He was certainly down in the world now, and little reason could be seen for his superior manner.

"Fools!" he creaked again, going back to his ajar position.

"Fool yourself!" said Archibald impertinently. "What do you know about it anyway?"

The Door assumed a most majestic look and eyed Archibald witheringly.

"What do I know about it? Have I gained no wisdom in all my years of forest life? Did I learn nothing from the wind whispering to our leaves of the secrets he had found in searching the holes and corners of the earth? Did I learn nothing from the birds chattering among our branches of the sights they had seen?"

"That's all very fine and large," interrupted Archibald. "What's it got to do with the matter in hand, anyway? We're simply saying we've had enough of this confounded man, and we propose sending him away."

"And I say that you are fools," replied the Door. "Do you know who this man is? Do you know that he comes of a race who would capture our city, who would banish our kind rulers afar? And if he and his friends succeeded – what then? Our rest and peace would be gone forever – our very existence at stake! They would scrub and scour you, Floor, beyond endurance. You, Bed, they would destroy and cast away into outer darkness. As for you, Archibald, they would exterminate you and your kind off the face of the earth. I would be tortured with fire. Shreds of paint which I've worn in happiness so many years and learnt to love would be torn from me. Disgusting, evil-smelling new paint would take its place. Cleanliness – that's the awful state we would be brought to! Think of it – think of the horror of endless years passed in the awful discomfort of cleanliness! I tell you, you must guard this man."

"I don't agree at all," growled the Bed. "It's all very well for you – you don't have any of the hard work to do. What about me? Sixteen or eighteen hours a day I have his weight to bear, and I've had enough of it!"

"And what about me?" said the Floor. "Even when he's on you, Bed, I cannot escape his cursed pressure. Send him away!"

But the door would have none of it. "I say NO," he replied, with idiotic pompousness, "and I am the way – the Only Way."

"Excuse me, please," put in a small voice. "I don't wish to intrude myself at all, but you know really – though I say it with the greatest modesty – but really you are not quite the *only* way."

Dacre looked all about, but for a long time could not make out where this small voice had come from. Then, at last he discovered. It was the Window. Way up by the ceiling, he was, and Dacre had been looking about on a level with the others.

A friend of Dacre's was that little window. Dacre was really quite fond of him. He knew the window did his best for Dacre – poor little best, yet Dacre was grateful. But now Dacre could not help smiling pitifully at his claim. Of course, Dacre had thought of trying to escape by him, but all the thought in the world did not suggest it as being a possibility. By putting the table underneath him and standing on it, he might just have been able to reach his lower edge, but how to scramble up noiselessly enough not to attract the attention of the sentry five yards off. Dacre had to smile, much as he liked the Window. But another new voice was speaking.

"I claim to be heard," it was saying. "I claim revenge for my people!"

"We are always pleased to hear Your Bugesty," said the Door, with an overdone politeness of the shabby, down-at-heel failure in life. But his words gave Dacre the clue to the owner of the voice. It was the King of the Bugs.

Now, where are you, my friend the enemy? You think I'm asleep, but in just about two two's you'll know better!

But His Bugesty was not so foolish as Dacre had thought. He had not come out to speak, he was hiding somewhere inside the straw mattress. Yet he could be plainly heard, for his voice was high with indignation.

"I claim revenge," he cried again. "Since the first moment of this man's coming he has waged a never-ending war on my people. When he arrived we had no hatred against him – we were disappointed a little that he was not the usual fat and juicy Turk, but we bore him no malice. We thought he would do for a time. But did he lie down on you, Bed, to let us browse in comfort? No! He declared war at once, with no preliminaries, no warning. Many of my people were innocently waiting to see him, no thought of war or fighting in their hearts – merely the ordinary crowd collected ready to stake out their browsing ground on the newcomer, according to the custom. There they stood, unsuspecting, peaceable citizens" – His Bugesty's voice in a crescendo shriek – "and he fell on them and killed them!"

He calmed himself down somewhat to continue. "The slaughter was terrible, awful, revolting. All who could fled at utmost speed to their holes and hiding-places, but a panic had arisen, and many fell by the way. I caused the roll to be called over my dominions, and wept – yes, even I, a King, wept at the result. Desolation and mourning, not a home but had lost at least two or three of its inmates. The nation clamoured for revenge. Yes, and we should have it! We were confident in our strength. I martialled my forces and waited. A long and weary wait it was – the man would not come. Every now and then he would stop to look at you, Bed, but he ever turned to continue his walking again. Then the moment came – he lay down. 'Attack!' I ordered, and we ran upon him. He fought – oh, yes, he fought hard – but so did we. Blood for blood we drew. The battle raged long and furiously, and then – he withdrew. 'Victory!' I cried. Yes, victory – but at what a cost! Hundreds, thousands of my warriors slain. But, again, they had died in service of their King – what more can a true bug ask? But we were not yet done. At intervals through the night the battle would continue. The man would lie down, we would attack, he would be driven off. We gained great success, but, alas, so did he…. Then the second night. The horror of it! 'Twas not a man we fought, but a fiend in human guise! For" – and again His Bugesty's voice reached a shriek – "he attacked us with Fire! He burned our homes, he burned our wives, our children, even the eggs of our unborn babes he burnt. Words fail me – I cannot describe it! But if that be impossible to describe, how then can I tell of the third night? Indeed it was no man we were fighting, but a very devil. For he fought us with poisoned powder! My bravest warriors, advancing the lead to attack, found themselves amidst a greyish powder from which an evil-smelling gas arose. In a moment they were overpowered by its poisoned fumes, and fell insensible, an unresisting prey to the enemy. Since then all our efforts have been in vain. A ring of impassable powder surrounds the loathsome brute, and we are powerless. Wherefore I come to ask assistance. My armies have been decimated, my civilians slaughtered, my towns and cities burnt to the ground, my lands devastated, and I claim Revenge!"

"'Ere, 'ere," cried Archibald. "I say! You are a talker, old man, aren't you! Let's have some more of it." The others rightly ignored him.

"Your Bugesty," said the Door, "our hearts bleed with sympathy for your wrongs. Such a tale of suffering would move any heart of wood or iron. You are indeed entitled to revenge, and you shall have it."

"Oh, let's send him away," said the Floor, wearily, "that's the simplest thing to do."

But His Bugesty objected strongly. "No, no," he cried, "where is the revenge for my people in that? There is but one revenge which will satisfy us – which could satisfy us. I claim that he must Die!"

Yet again the Door knew better. "No, Your Bugesty," he said. "I have a much better plan than that. You shall have your revenge, but he must not die. There is a revenge sweeter far than that."

"I know of none," replied His Bugesty. "I and my people claim that he must die."

"Listen to me," said the Door. "If you keep this man here in this place in his present state, what do you think will be the result? I will tell you. He will go mad! Mad. Stark, staring mad. A drivelling lunatic! Think of your revenge then, when you send him forth into the world a madman, insane, to be pitied yet shunned by his friends, to be jeered at and jostled by the children in the street. Where could there be a sweeter revenge?"

"That's all nonsense," put in the Bed, "he will never go mad. Only the other day he told the officer that he was quite well and wanted for nothing."

"Fool," said the Door. "Fool, do you see nothing? Are you blind? Did you see the manner in which he said it? No – of course you see nothing. If you were not blind you would have seen him practicing that manner – it is feigned. Do you think he really wants for nothing? He lies. It's all a lie – the way he stands, the tone in which he makes reply, the words he uses. He lies. He wants a myriad of things. He is far from well. I am not blind. I see these things. And I tell you the man will go mad. Sooner or later it must be so, and the time will not be very long now, for he is worrying. His mind is becoming unbalanced. And then think of the revenge!"

Even still His Bugesty was not persuaded. "Your plan would never please my people. It is too risky. There might be a long wait before its realisation, and we would be fearful of failure. And no other revenge could equal that of feasting on his dead body."

"It is very well to talk about his dead body," exclaimed the Bed, "but he seems quite alive now. How are you going to kill him?"

"Archibald must do it," said His Bugesty.

"Go on!" cried Archibald. "Do your own dirty work! What's it got to do with me, anyway?"

"Gladly would I do it if I could," His Bugesty replied, "but, alas, it is no longer possible. I poured all the poison I possessed into him the first two nights, but his constitution was strong then and able to resist it. Now, when he is weak, I have no poison left. But I know you will help us Archibald. It will be easy for you, you are always rich in poison. You are big and strong, and a fighter.

Archibald was far from enthusiastic. Said he, "I fight people my own size, thank you, or smaller for choice. You don't catch me fighting a hulking brute like this! And why should I do it, anyway? I haven't got much of a moan with him – I was only suggesting he should be sent away because I thought I might get more grub." Quite a human sort of rascal he seemed after all.

"But think how easy it will be," His Bugesty insisted. "Listen to my plan. My scouts will watch for a suitable moment when he is sleeping deeply, and then run to tell you. You will only have to jump on the Bed, and long e'er he could have regained consciousness your magnificent teeth will be buried in his throat."

"And what's he going to do then?" Archibald asked sarcastically. "Kiss me, I suppose? No, thanks, I don't care about it."

Whereat His Bugesty waxed eloquent again.

"Archibald," he said, "I appeal to you. Think of my suffering people. Think of the devastated homes, of the murdered women, of the children, aye – of the eggs of the unborn babes. I appeal to you. As a brother King, by our common ties, by our belief in the holiness of cannibalistic rites, as a champion of Right, as a champion of might, as" – and His Bugesty's tone of voice suggested this was the most telling point of all – "as a man of colour! Archibald, I appeal to you!"

Archibald appeared to be moved.

"Oh, well," he said hesitatingly, "I suppose when you put it like that I'll –"

"Archibald!" Dacre cried, rising in the bed for it was near lamp time. "Archibald! Certainly not!"

But the giant rat had fled and Lieutenant-Commander Dacre Stoker, commander of the sunken Australian submarine *AE2*, was alone in his cell again.

This was the seventeenth day of his solitary confinement.

CHAPTER 88

John

Monday, 1 November 1915

John Monash watched the pomp with interest, and waited with four other Generals of the British Empire in a line of dignitaries.

The royal train was not due to leave for another hour, but already the streets leading to the railway station were blocked with people, carriages and motor cars.

The station yard itself was cleared and the whole area lined with city police, in full review order – the patrolmen in white, with red facings, the officers in black and gold, each wearing a red fez. The approaches to the station buildings and platform were lined with the City Fire Brigade, also in white, with shining brass helmets and accoutrements. In the square outside the entrance, Egyptian native troops formed up in a guard of honour, wearing royal blue, white puttees, and white gloves, the officers bedecked with gold, and the commander of the guard mounted on a magnificent white Arab stallion.

The approaches and platforms were covered with purple carpets and rugs. The royal train, consisting of five state cars, rested at the platform. The coaches were lined with white enamel, outlined with gold and light green. The Sultan's carriage had an open observation platform, lined with burnished copper railing.

The summer season at Alexandria had closed yesterday. The Sultan of Egypt and Sudan, along with his court, had left the summer palace early this morning and the entourage was about to leave to take up winter quarters in Cairo.

Winter is coming. Within a month, the weather will become another enemy for us to contend with. We can maintain our stand-off with the Turks, unless the rumours of new German high explosive shells are true, but storms will disrupt supply by sea, rain will play havoc with our earthworks and cold will destroy men's will to fight.

John would soon sail back to Gallipoli and would have to re-focus his mind on the day-to-day operational details of managing a brigade at war. His engineering brain shifted into gear and he thought of how to construct drainage systems on the crowded bare-earth hills and how to create covered areas where men might make fires for warmth.

The past few weeks had left John with much to distract him from the mundane aspects of the battlefield.

After the disastrous week of multiple attacks on Hill 60, John's 4th Brigade was a spent force. Despite reinforcements, the roll call was reduced to a total of 968 men, from an original strength of over 4000. With the New Zealanders, Indians and English, they had managed to gain a toehold astride the tip of the Hill 60 spur, but the peak of the knoll remained in possession of the Turks.

At the end of that terrible week both sides were entrenched and faced off in a stalemate reflective of the whole new front line that now covered a total length of around ten miles, from Old Anzac in the south, across the Suvla Plain in the north and to the sea beyond.

At least, after the trio of British General's Birdwood, Godley and Cox had destroyed my brigade with their inept planning, they put us out to pasture at Bauchop's Hill where the Turks are 300 yards away and life is a bit easier – for those that remain alive.

From Bauchop's Hill, John had continued to argue with his commanders that his men needed a rest. Finally, after an inspection by Birdwood in early September, the 4th Brigade was relieved by the newly-arrived 7th Australian Infantry Brigade, and sent to the Island of Lemnos for a break. Doctors at Lemnos assessed the men and determined that every man needed at least four weeks of rest before returning to active duty, around half the men needed at least eight weeks of rest, and some were declared to be unfit to fight indefinitely.

In the camp on Lemnos, John had found himself in command of multiple brigades and received no respite from army inefficiencies, but after one party of his brigade officers returned from a holiday to Egypt, he managed to escape himself with five other subordinate officers for a two-week excursion to the land of the pyramids.

In Egypt, news of General Hamilton's sacking took John by surprise. At first, he thought it was a false rumour as he liked the Commander-in-Chief and did not want to believe such a thing could have happened, but the truth was confirmed by a number of sources.

On learning of Hamilton's demise, John nursed an unspoken fear for his own reputation, for his part in the disaster.

The August offensive had failed in its objective to secure the heights of Sari Bair, but much new ground had been gained. An English General from the Western Front, Charles Munro, had come as the new Commander-in-Chief of the Mediterranean Expeditionary Force.

After a few days of worry, a telegram from General Birdwood allayed John's concerns with the news that John had been created a Companion of the Order of the Bath, 'for distinguished service in the field.'

My brigade worked itself to the bone and every man fought with great courage. It is right that we should be acknowledged for playing our part, even though the overall operation could not achieve its objective.

The band burst into an anthem to announce the arrival of the Sultan who soon appeared on the train station platform. A small party accompanied him, comprising one aide-de-camp, one bodyguard, the Egyptian Prime Minister, and the Sultan's chamberlain.

The Sultan wore a plain frock coat with a black tie and red fez, and passed between the lines with confidence, shaking hands here and there, and occasionally stopping to chat or joke.

After the foreign consuls, public officials, Arab sheiks and chieftains, the Sultan came to a group of French officers, and then the British officers where John stood.

The chamberlain presented John to the Sultan as one of the last introductions before the boarding of the train.

"Ah, Australien!" The Sultan grinned. "Je vous fais mes compliments, men cher général." *I pay you my compliments, dear general.*

The Sultan stepped onto the train. The guard of honour presented arms and bugles blew. The whole assemblage sprang to attention and came to a salute as the train moved slowly out.

John's last glimpse of the Sultan was of him standing alone in the open compartment with his hand raised in salute.

The sound of bugles died away and the train disappeared around the curve.

Such a simple, dignified and well managed departure that was. I wonder, how will our winter preparations compare?

* * *

A week later, John stepped off a picket boat onto the new pier at North Beach, sheltered in the lee of a breakwater created by the deliberate sinking of a steamer *Milo*. From here he walked to his brigade's position at Bauchop's Hill.

Lieutenant-Colonel McGlinn was acting commander of the 4th Brigade, now re-established on the firing line, having returned from the break on the Island of Lemnos. Reinforcements had the brigade strength up to about 2,000 men.

John inspected the brigade trenches with McGlinn and issued his first brigade order for some time, dated 9 November 1915:

```
1. BRIGADE COMMAND
Brigadier-General J. Monash C.B., V.D., having returned today from
special duty in Egypt, re-assumed command of the Brigade.
```

"It's still pretty quiet along this part of the line Sir," McGlinn said. "Turks are three hundred yards away and don't trouble us too much. We have been considering sending out a midnight patrol to harass a small party of Turks we've heard digging out in front for several nights past."

"Very good," John replied. "How are the preparations for winter coming along?"

* * *

Three days after returning to command of the 4th Brigade, John's jaunt to Egypt had become a distant memory.

"McGlinn," John said, "be sure to paste a copy of the speeches from House of Lords and House of Commons into our Brigade Diary. You know, the ones by Lord Kitchener and Prime Minister Asquith, heaping praise on the Australian troops for their gallantry and resourcefulness."

"Yes Sir." McGlinn extracted a sealed envelope from his pocket. "I think you might want to read this message from General Birdwood Sir,"

Addressed to Brigadier-General Monash, it bore stamps of 'URGENT' and 'SECRET'. John tore open the seal and read the message:

```
Meet Army Corps Commander foot Mule Gully, eleven morning tomorrow,
service dress, belts, leave your A.D.C. and escort at least quarter-
mile from meeting place.
```

For the rest of the afternoon, John wondered what might be afoot. That night he lay in his headquarters with relatively little rifle fire in the background, and speculated in his mind about the upcoming secret meeting. *Perhaps our new Commander-in-Chief, General Munro wishes to hold a conference. Maybe a more distinguished visitor has come from England.*

* * *

Next morning, John allowed himself plenty of time to walk the four miles to Mule Gully, located not far from his former home of Reserve Gully at Old Anzac.

He rendezvoused with the other brigadiers, divisional commanders and General Birdwood. As the party waited, press-correspondent Charles Bean arrived and took a group portrait of the brigadiers, but John didn't like Bean or unnecessary surprises and was in no mood to pose for the camera, so he looked away at the moment the photograph was about to be taken.

Bean seems to know what's about to happen. Sometimes I wonder whether the correspondents are better informed than we field commanders.

At midday a tiny picket boat threaded its way between the throng of lighters, barges, punts, destroyers and submarines that lay off Anzac Cove and North Beach.

John squinted in an attempt to recognise who was on board. Birdwood watched the picket boat with the look of one who knew things, but would not let on. Birdwood left the party and walked alone to the head of North Pier to meet the visitor.

When the boat pulled alongside the pier, John's suspicions were confirmed. Off the boat stepped the great Field-Marshal, British Cabinet Minister and the Secretary of State for War, Earl Kitchener of Khartoum himself.

His tall, ungainly frame dwarfed Birdwood as the two men walked side-by-side and led a small compliment of Kitchener's staff along the pier.

Some amongst the men working on the beach must have recognised the visitor and by the time he reached the beach a small crowd of Australians gathered about Lord Kitchener. Without the lead of an officer, a call came for a cheer, and following the sound that erupted, more men came from all directions and hurried towards the pier.

John looked north-east towards the Turkish position of Snipers Nest. The outcrop perched high on the main ridge commanded a view over North Beach and the gathering crowd created a risk to Kitchener that might have been avoided if such attention was not being drawn to the discrete landing.

Ideally we would disperse the men and get Kitchener to the back of the beach, out of snipers' sights, but Birdwood is in command and I cannot embarrass him by making the suggestion in front of his old commander from the Boer War.

Kitchener has no appreciation of the disregard that Australian soldiers have for senior English ranks. Other than he, no Englishman would receive such a warm reception, save King George himself.

The celebrated visitor shook hands with several men and was shepherded by Birdwood to the cluster of Generals.

"I have brought you a personal message from the King," Kitchener said as he shook John's hand, "He wants me to tell you how much he admires the splendid things you have done here."

"Thank you Sir," John replied.

"You have all done splendidly, better even than I thought you would."

"Come My Lord," Birdwood said. "Let us begin the tour. Up this way if you please. My senior officers will join us."

General Birdwood led Lord Kitchener into Mule Gully, John followed along with the other Generals and Kitchener's small staff. One hundred yards into the gully, the party turned left and climbed the steep track to Walkers Ridge and Russell's Top.

At Russell's Top, Kitchener surveyed the Nek and seaward spurs from a quiet front-line position about sixty yards from the enemy's trench.

"Thank God, Birdie," Kitchener said. "I came to see this for myself. I had no idea of the difficulties you were up against. I think you have all done wonders."

The party then headed south along Russell's Top to Bully Beef Sap at the head of Monash Valley. Here Birdwood pointed out Pope's Hill, Quinn's Post and, further down the Sari Bair range, Lone Pine. From this position it was also possible for Kitchener to see across the plain of Maidos to Kilid Bahr and the hills of Asia.

The Secretary of State for War wore a look of relaxed fascination, like one on holiday in an exotic location, but Birdwood looked ill-at-ease until he had guided Kitchener back to the beach.

Before leaving Gallipoli's shore, Kitchener paused to offer a few more words of encouragement to the men who had gathered in even larger numbers than they had on his arrival.

Lord Kitchener has come a long way from England to have a look at our situation, but given nothing away about why he is here, or what he is thinking. It is difficult to lead the men and prepare for winter when we are not being told the full story.

With a simple salute, Kitchener turned and departed on the picket boat as unobtrusively as he had arrived two hours earlier.

CHAPTER 89

Jayjay

Sunday, 14 November 1915

Gravel crunched under his crutches and single boot as Jayjay shuffled towards the train line. This would be the last time he trod the dirty streets of Cairo.

The kit bag on his shoulder was heavy, but that didn't slow him down so much as the prospect of returning home.

In Cairo, everything was temporary. Despite its ancient history to Old Testament times, it was a place along the journey to somewhere else. Training on the way to Gallipoli was temporary. The Auxiliary Hospital of Number 1 Australian General Hospital was a temporary conversion of a roller skating rink. Recovery in the Helouan Convalescent Hospital was temporary. All as temporary as getting drunk.

Sometimes it seemed that the only reason Egypt was worthy of being part of the British Empire was the canal. *No one wants to stop here too long, just pass through the damned place. Moses and the Israelites didn't want to stay here either.*

The train station was a short walk from camp. Others made their way on the same journey, some in silence and some in subdued conversation. The morning sun still hung low in the desert sky when Jayjay boarded the train with some assistance from a medical general duties private. Jayjay stowed his kit and took a seat next to a window, leaving his crutches leaning against the seat next to him, as if to form a barrier against someone who might want to sit there and start a cheerful conversation.

In his breast pocket was a sheet of paper he had received yesterday. He pulled it out and read the simple explanation of his circumstances again:

> *'Category: C*
> *No immediate need of ministrations.*
> *Unlikely to be fit in three months.*
> *Invalid.*
> *Return to Australia'*

He looked down at his right leg. Uniform trousers neatly folded to the knee, and pinned. *Yeah, pretty bloody unlikely.*

The phantom pain had mostly gone, but a dull ache gave a regular reminder of what once was.

He folded the paper neatly and put it away, back in the pocket with the Turkish button and the bullet that had smashed his knee.

The fading of the pain had given Jayjay capacity to stay sober at times and reflect on the prospect of returning home. He imagined walking down the gang plank on his crutches and one leg, in front of a welcoming Sydney crowd, cheering like the day he departed. He would feel self-conscious, but smile. *Maybe Charlotte will be in the crowd. Maybe her feelings might soften towards me now that her fiancé Alfred McKenzie is out of the picture, or maybe she'll blame me for his death. Maybe I should have sent her a letter as well as the one I sent to Alfred's parents. I wonder if his wallet and pocket watch ever made it home.*

His imaginary homecoming always stopped when he saw his Mum and Dad. They stood motionless in the crowd, starring. A third person was there with them, Ron's wife Emilia. She held a crying baby, but her face was blurred. *Why can't I remember what she looks like?*

Jayjay sat at the dining table at home, next to an empty chair where Ron used to sit. Mum and Dad were there, and Emilia, with her face an unrecognisable haze and a baby on her knee, still crying. No one said anything. They didn't look happy or sad or angry. They just stared, as if waiting for an explanation. The baby turned to face Jayjay and let out a high-pitched scream.

Something bumped into Jayjay's shoulder and woke him. The train guard's whistle was blasting and reminded him for an instant of the trench whistle giving the order to go over the top, as if it was time to charge at death.

"Mind if I sit here Mate? I'm going to have to shove those crutches over a bit."

The crutches were already being pushed up against Jayjay so he just grunted and turned to face the window. The train started to roll out of Cairo and he pretended to go back to sleep, but could not. Cairo faded into sandy desert, flying past in a blur. *What will they say when I arrive home? What will I say? They will ask questions, but I have no answers.*

* * *

The train eased to a stop next to a docked ship.

Despite a hot meal, the five-hour train ride had strained Jayjay's nerves and he was anxious to get off.

He took all of a hundred crutch-aided paces on firm ground at Suez before he was directed up the gang plank to the transport ship. A guard was placed in the dockyard and orders were given that no one was to leave the ship.

Jayjay had no great urge to disobey the order and crutched his way to the upper deck where he propped himself against the balustrade to take in the view. The port town of Suez was grey and dusty, as if it needed a good, heavy rain to wash it clean.

An Australian with his arm in a sling approached the guard on the dock and started yelling something about his kit bag going missing, then a couple of other would-be passengers scurried behind the guard and disappeared. The guard moved to go after the escapees, but the fellow with the bag complaint had positioned himself between the guard and the escape route. A clumsy interaction resulted in the guard lying on the ground entangled with the distracter. The two escapees were nowhere to be seen when the guard scrambled to his feet, and the distracter apologised with exaggerated waving of his good arm, confessing that he now remembered where he had left his kit bag after all.

Jayjay grinned. *Australians can't help themselves. I might have pulled off a stunt like that myself with Larry and Ron. Cooper would have given it a good go if he was here. Maybe he already did it?*

Cooper had left Helouan Convalescent Hospital two weeks before Jayjay. He offered to deliberately miss his train and wait so they could travel together, but he was clearly itching to go home and Jayjay told him to get on his way. If Cooper missed the train there was no certainty that the two would be transported together anyway. His parents lived in the Sydney suburb of Darlinghurst and he seemed happy enough when Jayjay suggested they exchange addresses and plan to meet up again when both were back home.

Others stood about the deck in twos and threes, some sat alone. Most seemed subdued, as if boarding the ship bound for Australia marked the humiliating end of their service. Some had visible impairments like his own, some probably carried the stigma of venereal disease, but every passenger to ride this ship had been declared invalid, of no further use to the King's army. None met his gaze.

No one here knows who I am, or gives a damn whether or not I wake up alive tomorrow morning. I have outlived my usefulness to the Empire and now I'm only a burden. He turned back to the dockyard below where working men scurried about with the purpose of ants.

* * *

Several hours later, surges from the ship's steam engine quickened like the pulse of a waking beast. The last rope was thrown from the dock and hauled onto the ship. The Dockyard glowed under electric lights, as if to announce the importance of good work being done by able-bodied men labouring into the night.

The ship eased away from the dock and Jayjay lent against the balustrade again. The same place where he stood to witness two reluctant passengers escape earlier that day. His kit was stowed, he'd taken a meal and been allocated a place to sleep. Now there was just the journey home.

Just the journey home. God, I'd love to be going home with Ron and Larry and two legs. Why does war have to be like this?

He watched the lights of Suez disappear into the night and stood vigil until his good leg ached.

Moonlight danced on the canal like quicksilver and bore witness to the usual answer to his prayers, the answer of silence. Sandy banks slid by, almost close enough to touch. Defensive emplacements slept under the cool light of his only companion – the three-quarter moon. Now even this old friend seemed to mock him, as if saying 'Who are you? You are nothing.'

Ron was fascinated by this canal. When the rest of us were caught up in the excitement of adventure, Ron had been the one to take interest in foreign surroundings. The challenge of digging a shipping channel across dessert sand, mud construction of huts along the Nile, stonework of the ancient pyramids. Ron had so much more to give. Father to a child he will never meet. Husband to a wife widowed too young. A carpenter who could have helped to build Australia's future.

Instead, I have to go home without him and face the family. I should have done more. I should have done something. They'll think it too, even if they don't say it.

'Why did you come home without your brother?'

'Ron is needed here more than you are after all.'

'You left him behind in a heathen country, pushing up red poppies in a crowded cemetery with nothing but a biscuit box cross to mark his plot.'

Jayjay shifted his weight to free up his left hand and tried to make a fist. The little finger and ring finger ached in the cool night air and refused to close all the way. He reached up to scratch the itch of his beard. Darkness didn't change the fact that it was dusted with grey. *I'll shave it off tomorrow. Twenty years old and I'm a crippled old man.*

Damn this war.

CHAPTER 90

Ishmail

Thursday, 25 November 1915

"Maybe they all went home in the night?"

"If only God would be so kind!"

Ishmail raised his head a little more than was safe and peered over the parapet of Trench 32. He stole a long look into the Valley of Fear. Occasional rifle fire disturbed the crisp morning air, but none appeared to be coming from the enemy.

Osman appeared beside him. "You saw the newspapers, the English are fighting on a new front at Salonika, and are considering withdrawing from here."

"I saw a newspaper." Ishmail jumped down from the knee-high firing step. "It was printed in a language I could not understand."

"But the Mufti gave us the translation. He can read English, or at least he knows someone who can."

"Maybe it's a trick?" Ishmail said. "Maybe they are just pulling back from some of their advanced positions that are difficult to hold? Maybe they are preparing shelters for winter?"

"You could ask them."

"What? Have you lost your brain like Yusuf?"

Osman's eye's narrowed at the mention of the dead friend they had buried together. Ishmail knew immediately that it was a stupid thing to say. He opened his mouth, but found no words.

"You speak French," Osman said. "Write them a note and throw it over in a tin. They will find someone to read it. You can ask them for some cognac!"

Ishmail grinned. With the final retort he knew he was forgiven. "Dear enemy, may I have some of your French poison? I wish to make myself feel sick as conditions in our trench are far too comfortable and pleasant for me!"

"Maybe just wish them a good day, and ask them to respond."

The idea gathered momentum as others from his squad gathered around and urged Ishmail on.

It was not unusual to exchange notes or sometimes food with the enemy. Never when officers or Germans were around, it was forbidden, but when things were quiet, it seemed harmless enough. Care was required. Overconfidence could still result in a bullet to the head, but both sides seemed to respect unwritten local ceasefire rules when exchanges were taking place. Communication was usually in broken French, being the only language of which a few from each side had some understanding.

He surveyed the eight men looking back at him with expectant eyes. Ishmail had been made squad leader and promoted to corporal following the death of the squad's previous leader a month earlier. The choice seemed popular enough within the squad, but maybe it was only because it was better than someone from outside being thrust upon them.

Ishmail found it difficult to be part of the chain of command. The sense of being crushed between millstones came back to him several times each day. Now he wanted to please the men, but it would not look good for him if something went wrong and he was reprimanded in front of them.

"My French is poor, but I will try. Better than walking over to take a look and getting a serve of English lead for breakfast. Ahmet, see if you can find me a piece of paper and pencil."

Ishmail stepped back up onto the earth ledge and reached out to grab an empty tin lying within reach on the parapet. All sorts of rubbish was thrown into no-man's-land by both sides. This tin, with bent lid still attached, hadn't made it as far as most and was yet to be removed during the regular trench tidying duties. He also grabbed a stone about the size of a circle he could make with a thumb and forefinger.

Private Ahmet returned with paper and pencil.

Ishmail closed his eyes and travelled back in time to his first year of architectural studies and evening discussions with another student Phillipe. It was only three years ago, but it seemed like a lifetime. Phillipe's family moved from Paris to Istanbul when he was a child and he provided the perfect opportunity for Ishmail to learn some of the French language. Ishmail was a bit uncomfortable associating with a Christian drinker with loose morals, but to study architecture required an openness to appreciate foreign cultures and designs. French architecture was famous, but the way Phillipe carried on about their gothic cathedrals and the Baroque influence, it was as if the French were the only people in the world who knew anything about architecture.

Ishmail assembled the foreign words in his mind and matched them, as best he could remember, to the strange characters of the Latin alphabet. *I hope this is close enough that they can read it.* He read the words out aloud slowly as he wrote.

"Mes chers Astralyan, comment faites-vous? Nous espérons que vous êtes en bonne santé. Toujours le meilleur. Réponse s'il vous plaît. Soldas Turgo."

"What does it say Ishmail Effendi?" Ahmet asked.

"My dear Australian, how do you do? We hope that you are in good health.

Always the best. Reply if you please. Turkish Soldier."

Ishmail wrapped his note around the stone, placed it in the tin and bent the tin lid closed enough so the stone could not fall out.

"Osman, you have a strong arm. When I say, lob this into the enemy trenches, or beyond."

Ishmail tossed the tin to Osman and climbed onto the firing step again. Still, everything was quiet. He yelled towards the enemy trenches, maybe thirty or forty paces away.

"Australi, Australi! Bonjour! Message!"

He nodded to Osman. "Okay, deliver your message."

Ishmail tracked the arc of the tin as it sailed through the air. It cleared the enemy wire and appeared to bounce into their trench. He watched for a full minute but there was no movement and no response.

Back in the trench he looked at Osman, lifted his chin and made a clicking sound. "Maybe you are right, maybe they snuck away like cowards in the night. Praise to God if it is true."

* * *

Later that night, after evening prayers, the enemy remained dead quiet.

Sergeant Zahid came around midnight with orders of for a surveillance attack at 4:00am.

A thin slither of moon was on the rise.

Ishmail's squad gathered around in the darkness.

"What is this mission, Zahid Efendi?" Ishmail asked. "Is it surveillance or attack?"

"It is Both Corporal. A surveillance team of three squads, including yours, will advance from Trench 32 and occupy enemy trenches. Engineers will follow, reinforce the line and construct a connecting trench to our current position. Extra sandbags and hand bombs are on their way here now to assist. Similar operations will take place along the front line from Hill of Valour to Bloody Ridge."

Sergeant Zahid paused, as if about to deliver important news.

"We have information that the enemy may be retreating! Their front line along this ridge is being held to enable the retreat, but reduced rifle fire and bombing indicates that the place is held lightly, and maybe only some parts are held."

Zahid paused again. It was impossible to see his face in the black. Maybe he expected some reaction, but the enemy withdrawal had been the main topic of discussion all day, so there was no surprise.

"Our Division Headquarters," the sergeant continued, "has determined this to be an important attack point. If we can take the enemy trenches here, we will command the Valley of Fear and be able to see what they are getting up to."

* * *

Four hours later it was time for the surveillance attack.

The crescent moon was high, but gave little light.

Ishmail led his squad up the rickety ladder and over the parapet in silence. Two other squads of nine shadowed them on their left flank. Walking quietly was difficult in the dark as the ground was like a rubbish heap, littered with empty tins and the remains of dead men.

Noises seemed louder just before dawn.

A burst of rifle fire broke the unusual peace some distance down the ridge. Too far away to be of concern. By now the enemy should have heard them and opened fire, but they had not. *That is a good sign.*

Coils of barbed wire were barely visible in front of the enemy position. Ishmail waved Ahmet forward. As previously agreed, he approached the wire and struck a match. The flare of light was horribly bright and Ishmail was relieved to see it replaced by the hissing bomb fuse that then sailed over the wire and into the enemy trench.

There seemed to be sounds of hurried activity, then a muffled blast – then nothing. *Was that my imagination? Maybe there is no one there?*

Ahmet moved to climb over the wire towards a position where he could see into the enemy trench, but it caught on his clothing. He fumbled around to disentangle himself and the wire rattled like a noisy chain.

Sounds of movement from the enemy trench were clearer this time, along with a few foreign words yelled with purpose.

"Drop!" cried Ishmail, and a line of rifle fire burst from the enemy trench. Ahmet's body collapsed into the wire and Ishmail knew that instant he and his squad were all dead men.

The intensity of rifle fire made it clear this was not a lightly held trench. This was a fully manned, well defended enemy position and Ishmail was completely exposed.

His own words from the previous morning returned to haunt him *'maybe it's a trick?'*

Rifle fire stopped. *I am not shot. I don't think I'm shot. Why am I still alive?*

He remembered the crawl back to a friendly trench six months earlier, after his father was killed. Maybe I can do the same again? This time I am not wounded, but I am closer to the enemy. It will soon be light.

He counted to one hundred and raised his head. All was still. Both legs ached. Left calf and right thigh, as if in memory of the last time he crawled away from the enemy with fresh wounds.

Osman was close and looking at him. Ishmail waved a hand and pointed back towards the Turkish trenches. He turned himself around started to crawl as quietly as he could, which was much louder than he would have liked. Others from his surveillance attack group followed his lead and he waved them forwards.

This time he dragged his Mauser.

Maybe I am a coward.

If at least one of us returns safely, maybe the mission will be judged half successful. Not much of an attack, but some good surveillance. We know the enemy remains here in strength.

Somehow all squads returned to their trench unmolested. Only one member of Ishmail's squad, one other than Ahmet, had been left for dead after the initial onslaught, leaving seven of the original nine to return alive. All seven seemed mostly unwounded, except for one. Hadji had a blood-soaked arm, and he was starting to shake all over. In the trench Ishmail called for a medic and looked into the lad's face in the early dawn light.

His eyes were glassy and focused on some non-existent object far away in the distance. His knees buckled and Ishmail caught him to prevent him collapsing to the trench floor. Instead, Ishmail lay the wounded private on the firing step and rubbed his cheeks.

"Hadji!" Ishmail yelled as if the wounded man's hearing was damaged. "Listen Hadji! You are okay. The doctors will look after you. Ahmet has gone to paradise, but this is not your time. Can you hear me, Hadji?

No response.

Two medics arrived with a blood-stained stretcher to take Hadji away. Ishmail watched two good boots on the wounded man's feet bobbing from side to side until they disappeared into the pre-dawn dim.

He stepped onto the firing step and took in the view across no-man's-land. It was the same as yesterday morning, but for the faint outline of a few new bodies down near the Australian trenches. Ahmet led the dead men, still tangled in coils of barbed wire and propped up like a scarecrow keeping watch on the enemy below.

Ishmail looked down at his feet. The boots he had taken from Yusuf's body showed signs of wear, but they held together, for now at least. He wriggled his toes to prove the stitching. *A good thing, the weather is turning cold.*

CHAPTER 91

Larry

Friday, 26 November 1915, late afternoon

Thunder clapped, it sounded strange – this was real thunder.

"Weather's gone crazy," Larry said. "The Brass has gone crazy. The whole damn world's gone crazy. The Joe Bourkes must be sitting in their trenches laughing their lunch up at us."

A pair of stretcher bearers squelched past and one of them lost his footing in the mud. A fellow lay on the stretcher beyond help. Shot in the head. *A common way to go. Let those demons out. No more nightmares for you lad.*

"I'd like to get up there and take a few shots back at Jacko Turk," said Private Timothy Simmonds. "Let him know he can't just pick us off one by one, without getting back as good as he gives."

"Just gotta sit back and soak it all in Simmo," Larry said. "Just like the damned rain."

As a lance corporal and section leader, Larry knew he should be more careful to hold the army line in front of his men, but he was beyond caring.

"Another whole night and day of this. At war with orders not to shoot at the enemy. Pure insanity."

Sergeant Baker had walked away along Leane's trench after delivering the news that the silent stunt was to continue until midnight tomorrow. '*Only fire on the enemy if he attacks or threatens to do so, or offers an exceptionally good target. All normal sniping to cease. There will be no artillery support. Stay hidden from the enemy. Don't light fires.*'

"Must be to trick Jacko into thinking we pissed off," Simmonds said. "Smoke him out, get him to attack."

"The Joe Bourkes might be stupid," Larry said, "but they're not bloody stupid. We're not about to skulk off. They know it, and so do the Germans. Even if we wanted to, it's not as if we could march off across the sea like Moses and the Israelites. I think they might notice all the boats coming to take us. Anyway, no way we would run away from the fight. This madness isn't going to fool anyone."

"Down at the beach," said Albert the Aborigine, "I heard someone say we're gettin' ready for winter. It gettin' harder to land stores with the seas gettin' rough, and thcy might be cutting back the number of men stationed here to hold the line 'til it starts to warm up again."

"What about the poor bastards left here then Darky?" Simmonds asked. "Jacko'd be onto them in a flash. Less men holding the front-line trench, perfect chance for him to attack and take the trench. No way, that's a furphy, sure as a dead man shits himself."

"It's like a nightmare," Albert shook his head. "Stuck here getting shot at, and can't shoot back for a-whole-nother bloody day an' night."

"This is a living nightmare Mate," Larry said without thinking, then bit his tongue. It was the first time he spoke the word out aloud for months. *I won't do that again. I don't think I flinched. If I did then no one noticed.*

Rain grew heavier and the afternoon faded into evening. When time came for first watch and for some to sleep, Larry volunteered for first watch as usual. *Let the others have their dreams.*

* * *

By the end of his watch Larry was almost dozing on his feet. Nothing had happened beyond the usual sporadic rifle fire from the Turks which he had dutifully ignored.

He swapped his post with Timothy Simmonds and took over the sleeping bench cut into the trench wall that Simmonds had vacated. With his Lee-Enfield lying beside him and a damp great coat for a blanket, he curled up and fell asleep in seconds.

It seemed only a moment later when the explosion woke him.

Yelling followed. A mixture of Australian swearing and Turkish gibberish.

Is this another nightmare? Probably not. The nightmares always feel so real that I don't think to question whether I might be dreaming until I wake up. It must be real.

The muffled explosion of a Turkish cricket ball bomb being absorbed by a sandbag was followed by a fusillade of rifle fire.

He grabbed his rifle, flicked off the safety catch, opened his eyes and jumped up onto the firing step.

Clouds smothered any hint of moonlight and light rain deadened the sound of footsteps.

Where are you Joe Bourke?

Muzzle flashes gave enough light for Larry to see that there weren't any Turks within the first few yards of his position. Rifle fire lessened. The enemy raiding party had already turned and retreated.

Off to the left Larry thought he could make out a human form crawling away into the dark, he took aim and fired. The shadow slumped to the ground.

Satisfied that there was no further movement for a few seconds, Larry returned to his resting place in the trench wall and went back to sleep.

* * *

"Only a few hours left of this lunacy," Larry said the following evening. "Then we can get back to the usual madness that we know and love. We let Joe Bourke come a bit too close last night. Nearly got into our trench to greet me personally with a kiss on each cheek and a cricket ball up my arse. That's not the way I like to wake up."

"I just want to make a fire," Simmonds said. "We've hardly got any wood, but at least we could make a little one. It's cold enough to turn my nuts to raisins."

"Got you some waterproof capes lads," Sergeant Baker hollered as he approached up the trench. "There's a pair of india-rubber boots for each man coming as well. They'll help to keep some of the water out."

"Thanks Sarge," Larry said. "These would have been quite handy yesterday, before the rain soaked us to the bone."

"Growling again are we Gillespie? Maybe you and your section would like a to join the Quarter Master's fatigue and carry a few boxes of biscuits up from Watson's Pier?"

Sergeant Baker moved on without waiting for an answer and Larry pulled the cape over his head, careful not to dampen the cigarette that hung from his mouth.

I hope he doesn't come back and make good on that threat. On half rations of hard bloody biscuits, I haven't got the energy. I hate those damned biscuits.

"Don't upset Sergeant Fishface Mate," Albert said. "You'll have us all working as pack-mules."

"Well Darky," Larry sucked warm air through his cigarette and curled his fingers around the glowing tip. *I need to keep it dry. I can't feel any heat in my fingers. If I hold them any closer, I'll burn myself.* "They must have had all this kit yesterday. It's not as if it has been shipped from England since the rain started. Just left us here sitting in the bloody rain to freeze our balls off while they got 'round to sending it to us a day later. Probably had to set up a committee to consider it first."

He finished the cigarette and pulled his evening portion of biscuit from his pocket. He held it out in the darkness in an open palm. *Maybe if it soaks in some rain, it might not break my teeth. I can't feel my fingers in this cold.*

"Corporal," Simmonds said to Larry. "How about you have some rest first tonight. I'll take first watch with Darky."

"Fine, okay Simmo'." Larry didn't want to sleep, but he didn't want to discuss the subject either. He slipped the biscuit back in his pocket and found that all the rest benches in the trench wall were occupied. The best he could do was a high patch of trench floor that was damp, but at least not a puddle. He sat with his back to the wall and rested his head on his knees. *Blazes I'm tired, but it' so damned cold I couldn't sleep.*

I wonder how Jayjay's fairing? And Mum, and Dad, and Gracey… Jayjay might be on a ship bound for Sydney by now, hobbling about on one leg. Lucky bugger. I'd give both my legs to get away from this shithole.

* * *

Larry's Dad lay still beside him on the trench floor. He looked at peace staring at the strip of blue sky above. He might have been resting, but for the gaping hole torn in the side of his head. Scribbly grey-blue mush hung from the opening and lay in the mud beside him. Larry's Mum sat nearby on the trench floor holding handfuls of intestines that spilled from her blood-soaked belly. Her eyes always had that same look, not wide-open in shock or pain, but focused sharp with a knowing sadness.

"Lars, Lars!" Larry's twin sister Grace had called him by that name ever since he could remember. She was the only one who called him that. *Where is she? She must take cover. She doesn't know how things work here.*

A rifle fired in the distance.

"Lars!" Grace's voice was shrill now, almost a scream.

She was in no-man's-land. He didn't know how he knew and it didn't matter. He needed to get up and call her back, go and carry her back if necessary. He made to stand, but his legs wouldn't move. *I need to get up. Why can't I move? Something doesn't feel right.*

Larry cursed his legs and looked down to see bloody stumps at his knees. *What happened to my legs? Maybe a bomb? Maybe an explosive shell? Maybe a machine gun at close range?*

Another rifle shot fired, and another.

"Lars!"

The trench was empty apart from himself and his parents. *It's just us left to hold the whole front line. It's not enough. We're all going to die. Gracey doesn't know she has to stay in the trench. The trench is our home now, until we die here.*

He dragged himself onto the firing step, but could not stand to see over the parapet without legs. *I need a ladder. He turned to look along the trench in the opposite direction, away from his parents. A ladder stood next to him, leaning against the front wall of the trench. That must be how Gracey climbed over the top. She doesn't know any better. It's broad daylight.*

I have to climb the ladder. It's her only hope. How can I climb the ladder without legs? I must try. He grabbed the ladder and pulled himself towards it. The top of the ladder moved against the front wall of the trench and dislodged a lump of earth that fell onto his head. The fallen clod exposed Ron's body buried in the parapet. A lifeless arm swung down and the blackened hand hit Larry in the face.

Larry dragged himself up the ladder. *I have to get to the top. I wish my legs would move quicker. Why can't I move quicker? Strange they don't hurt.*

He reached to top of the ladder and peered over the parapet.

Grace ran towards him. She wore her favourite white Sunday dress, and trod gingerly on bare feet over rocky ground scattered with rusted tins and barbed wire.

"Lars!"

Where are your shoes? Come this way quickly! Larry couldn't speak, but knew he didn't need to. *She's seen me now. She knows she has to get back here. Come on! Hurry!*

Grace reached the parapet and paused.

"Lars, you silly!" she giggled. "How can I climb down the ladder if you're in the way!

A machine gun rattled and a line of three red stains appeared across her chest. Her eye's opened with a mixture of surprise and confusion and she dropped to her knees then collapsed onto Larry.

Her weight knocked him off balance and the twins fell from the ladder into the trench. The sensation of falling backwards was real. So real.

Larry's arms flung out in a reflex action.

At the moment he was about to hit the trench floor he woke up.

* * *

Larry lay on his back in the mud.

Darkness surrounded him, but a grey strip above signalled that dawn was breaking.

Someone crouched over him, laughing.

"It's always fun waking you up Corporal Gillespie," Albert said. You jump like a bloody frog!"

"Piss off Darky." Larry shivered.

"Mate, you gotta get up. Get ya' blood moving else you'll freeze solid. Grab your rifle. We can shoot at Jacko whenever we want now. Gave him a bit of a rude shock I reckon. He got used to the idea of us not firing back for a coupla' days. And get a look at this – it's snowing. Have you seen snow before? I never have. I can't wait 'til morning, everything will be covered in white!"

Larry struggled onto his aching feet and grunted. He hadn't seen snow, but wasn't about to admit to it. *At least I have two legs and I can feel them now, but my toes are numb. I must be awake.*

He moved along the trench to a place where he could see back towards the support lines without exposing himself to enemy fire. Snowflakes drifted from the darkness. The ground dropped away towards the sea and on the ground he could just make out large patches of white.

Maybe this is another dream.

Fuck it's cold.

CHAPTER 92

Ishmail

Sunday, 28 November 1915, mid-afternoon

Ishmail rubbed his icy fingers together and reached towards the small fire.

At this rate we'll all freeze to death in a week.

A biting wind howled along the trench from the northeast, as if direct from the North Pole. Snow had stopped falling hours earlier, but still blew around in the wind like dust. The sun gave light, but its rays lacked the strength to melt the white powder.

He stepped back to make a space for others to reach the fire and slipped on his gloves.

Thank God for the new gloves and socks. Ishmail had received praise worthy of a hero when he distributed the issue of one pair of gloves and one pair of socks to each member of his squad that morning.

Several cases of frost bite had already been sent for medical treatment from other squads in the platoon. One poor fellow was found dead, curled up after sleeping on the trench floor without a greatcoat. Both his boots were wrapped in cloth from emptied sandbags, held in place with knotted string. Stretcher bearers came and took him away as if he was a piece of rubbish,

Why are we here? Who is helped by this suffering? What do our commanders care? They are only interested in looking good to their superiors, strutting about like roosters. They don't care about the men and their hardship. They sleep in bunkers with fires, giving orders and writing reports. The Mufti says 'God has willed it so' and 'true Islam is submission', then he sleeps in warmth like the officers. God when will this end? Let the invaders be preparing to withdraw! Now they have had a taste of winter. Maybe their commanders will have compassion while ours waste men's lives and behave like village boys in a pissing contest.

Ishmail stood on the firing step and gazed across no-man's-land and down into the Valley of Fear.

The devastating effects of rain were covered in a blanket of snow. No evidence could be seen of the torrents that exhumed so many men and took them on a final charge towards enemy trenches. A goal that could not be achieved in life was now reached by some in death as their corpses were washed down the hill.

Ishmail wondered how the flooding affected enemy trenches below in the valleys, and snow and wind. *They must be better equipped than us against the wet and cold. They certainly couldn't be worse off. Each one I've seen had good boots.*

Like many of the men, he had unwrapped his Kabalak headgear and wound the woollen cloth around his head like a turban. The covering gave his ears some protection from the cold, but also dampened his hearing.

Occasional rifle fire could barely be heard over the howling wind. The white blanket laying on the earth also seemed to absorb sound. It covered so much death and destruction, as if there might be a chance for a new beginning. *If the enemy withdraws, maybe I could return to studying architecture and then design fine buildings. I wonder whether we would remain a part of this war if the enemy leaves?*

A distant boom shook his hope.

Then the rattle of an enemy machine gun mocked him.

Another blast confirmed that the peace was temporary and disappointment cut through him like the wind.

Ishmail turned slowly and stepped down from the firing step, pushing aside the thought that he might be put out of his misery by a bullet to the head, rather than have to endure freezing conditions and more fighting.

I must endure. I have nothing left but my life and my men. The men suffer as I do and need someone to look to for direction and hope.

He took a few steps towards the huddle of his squad. A space opened up for him as every man shuffled back a few centimetres without complaint and extended their reach towards the pitiful fire.

* * *

"This is the last of the fire wood Ishmail Efendi," Osman said.

"Enjoy it while you can my brothers. This will be a long night." Ishmail stepped back from the fire.

Stars shone bright and the bitter wind howled as strong as it had all day.

I must complain to Zahid about the lack of firewood being sent forward. We risk our lives for God and country every day and then sit freezing around a tiny fire.

It was impossible to collect fire wood at the front line now. There had been a few attempts during the quiet periods in recent days, but it was a dangerous activity. Now that the enemy was back to their usual aggression levels it would be suicide to wander about in full view. Not that there was much left to pick up any more. Night time wood gathering missions had already cleaned up all but the smallest sticks.

Zahid's deep voice caught Ishmail's attention, carried from the north on the wind. The sergeant's voice was hoarse, but he sounded pleased with himself.

Ishmail might have called his squad to 'stand to', but the burning of last of the fire wood was good enough reason for him to leave them be unless the sergeant had need of them.

Zahid rounded the corner rubbing gloved hands together. He approached Ishmail and spoke to him directly.

"Flags will be delivered tonight," Zahid said. "By first light they must by placed clearly in front of your trench. If you don't do it, you might find hellfire raining on your heads at sunrise! A trainload of artillery reinforcement has arrived. Big bastards! Twenty-four centimetre howitzers – from Germany, now that Bulgaria has joined our alliance and opened the way. We will remind the English whose country this is."

Zahid's teeth reflected the moonlight. His broad grin all the more infectious for the fact that it was so unusual.

Ishmail allowed himself a smile into the darkness. "Thank you Zahid Efendi. We will be ready, and ensure it is done when they arrive."

Zahid disappeared along the trench before Ishmail remembered to ask him about the fire wood. Ishmail turned back towards the fire huddle where several of his squad were looking at him, as if waiting for direction. They had all been through the same disappointment of learning that the enemy remained in force and it showed. They probably heard most of what Zahid said, but regardless, Ishmail relished the chance to relay some desperately-needed good news down the chain of command.

"Looks like there'll be a show for us to watch in the morning Men," Ishmail said. "Some flags will be delivered in the night and we are to position them in front of our part of the trench. They are markers for our artillery. We've had a delivery of big shells."

He paused and looked at the fire, now nothing more than a few embers glowing bright in the wind. *Damn, we need more wood.*

"Keep watch in threes for one hour at a time," Ishmail continued. "You two first with me, then you three. When on watch, talk to each other to keep alert. Otherwise huddle together for warmth and try to sleep if you can. It won't be comfortable but it's better than freezing to death. When the flag's come wake me, and I will set them out with whoever is on watch at the time. I won't wake the others unless I need to."

* * *

Sunrise next morning covered no-man's-land in a welcome glow.

A line of coloured markers stretched from Hill of Valour to Bloody Ridge.

The marker "flags" were actually rigid boards, each supported by a single stake driven into the ground. Ishmail's markers were painted green. Others along the line were red, black or white.

Most of the markers had a least one bullet hole in them and some were riddled like Swiss cheese. One had taken a well-aimed hit to the supporting post and lay flat on the parapet.

Ishmail grinned. *The enemy must have an idea what the markers are for, but there are too many markers for them to destroy them all. Now they will learn what it is like to receive a real artillery bombardment.*

At nine o'clock a rumble came from clear sky and announced that the first howitzer shell was launched – the final stage of its delivery from Germany to the enemy.

The projectile glowed like the sun and made a graceful arc from a place somewhere high, far up the ridge near its peak at Koja Chemen Tepe, over Ishmail's head, then plunged onto Bloody Ridge, behind enemy lines. *A range finder. Better too long than too short.*

Another followed, and the next one landed on the enemy front line, or at least very close to it as far as Ishmail could see. Earth fountained towards the sky and seconds later a distant crump travelled the thousand metres to Ishmail's ears.

Ishmail stopped shivering.

Suddenly the air didn't seem so cold.

Closer to Ishmail's position, an enemy periscope appeared from behind a loophole surrounded with sandbags, around one hundred metres away. A brave soul. Brave or stupid trying to observe during a heavy artillery bombardment. Ishmail had learnt that much from seeing the devastating impact from warship guns. Those who didn't take cover tended not to survive.

Ishmail focused on the periscope, held by an invader from Australia. *So far to come to die. Maybe it's the big fellow with strong hands who helped me bury my father – No, if that fellow is still alive must have learnt by now not to expose himself like that.*

Ishmail's hand reached inside his great coat to the shirt pocket underneath. The silver coin was still where it should be. He fingered it gently, and tried to sense whether he touched the kangaroo and giant bird, or the English king who would conquer the world.

It seemed important to preserve the memory of the day when weapons were put aside and the living worked together to bury the dead. Every other day the living worked against each other with all their might, success measured in death.

A shell landed in front of the periscope, maybe twenty metres from it. Ishmail's trench seemed to shake when the sound wave hit. The periscope disappeared and the enemy observation post was shrouded in smoke and flying earth. Debris rained on no-man's-land, and some small stones fell around Ishmail and his men. The periscope reappeared while dirt and small stones were falling from the sky. *His hands must be shaking now. Stupid goose.*

Ishmail looked up the main ridge, towards the head of Valley of Fear. An Australian machine gun spat, like a child about to receive a beating.

Another blast drew Ishmail's attention back to the enemy observation post nearby, but he could not see the periscope. His eyes tracked left and right from the place where it should have been, in the centre of a shower of dirt. A ragged depression in the ground and a faint cloud of smoke was all that marked the place. No sandbags. No loophole. No periscope.

Serves the goose right.

Cheers and laughter told him others saw it too.

The firing step was lined with men standing tall to witness the artillery attack. Pride swelled in Ishmail's chest as he drew a deep breath and savoured the fresh air. He held his breath for a moment, then released and watched it dissolve into the cold morning. He smiled and nodded slowly.

He didn't like to see his men taking unnecessary risks, but the morale boost from watching the artillery bombardment was important. He decided against ordering them to stand down.

I need to see about some breakfast and fire wood.

Maybe I'll just watch for another minute or two myself.

A howitzer shell sailed over his head towards the enemy.

CHAPTER 93

Jayjay

Saturday, 11 December 1915

Sandstone cliffs glowed orange, reflecting the sunrise. Jayjay felt summer warmth on his back as if welcoming him home, but his breakfast sat in his belly in an indigestible lump.

The transport ship turned slowly to the left, towards Sydney Heads. The change of direction would have been imperceptible, but for changing aspect of the sun and the large arc swept by the tail of aft wash.

At times the voyage from Suez had seemed to drag on too long, but now that he was so close to home, a few more days at sea would be welcome to give the chance to better plan what to say when he faced his family.

The ship rounded South Head and crawled into Port Jackson. Jayjay had long since stopped noticing the rocking motion of the ship at sea, but he missed it as soon as it faded in the harbour. It was as if the ship was sliding across a sheet of ice, with caution to avoid the hazards closing in about her.

Other ships and a ferry blew their whistles as the war transport eased past, and cheers from the decks welcomed her home.

An hour after entering Sydney Heads, a tug dragged her up against Woolloomooloo pier and a gentle lurch announced the end of the journey. There were a few folk at the pier, but nothing like the crowd at the send-off.

Disappointment caught Jayjay off guard. *There should be more people here. Where are all the Sydney-siders who came to see us away? Doesn't anyone care?*

Others stood on deck and watched in silence. *This is worse than arriving at a funeral. At least at the memorial services at Gallipoli, men who cared came and said something, or at least looked each other in the eye with a nod.*

His parents waited at the dock. Mum stood, Dad sat on a bench with his arms folded. They watched the ship, but had not seen him.

His throat tightened and he turned away immediately as if this might stem the unexpected flow of mixed emotions. He bent to pick up his kit bag, threw it over his shoulder and marched on crutches to the other side of the deck. The long way to the gang plank exit would do fine.

He worked his way through the ship and down the ramp off the ship, unable to delay disembarking any longer.

His parents approached slowly.

"Hi Mum, good to see you Dad. How did you know I would be coming in this morning?"

Mum stared at his trousers pinned at the knee and raised both hands to cover her mouth.

Dad moved forward, lifted the bag from Jayjay's shoulder and shook his hand. "Welcome home Son."

"Thanks Dad, that knife you gave me saved my life." Jayjay immediately hoped he didn't have to explain how any time soon.

Mum took a few seconds to regain her composure and gave him a hug. "There's been regular ships coming in with – with boys like you who have been hurt. We didn't know which one you'd be on, but have come to see most of them dock here."

"Jones," the ship's medical officer approached with a notebook and pencil. "Looks like you got family here. You right to get home?"

"Yes Sir."

"Two weeks leave, then report in to Randwick hospital. They're doing some good work with artificial legs made out of wood. You can go there earlier if you need to."

"Yes Sir."

The medical officer scribbled in his book and moved on.

"You still got room for me at home?" Jayjay looked down at his half-leg. "I don't take up quite so much space now."

"Oh Jonathan, don't talk like that. Of course we have your room ready for you. Are you alright to get about on those crutches?"

"Hi Hoppy!" Jayjay hadn't noticed Larry's twin sister Grace, but she must have been watching the family reunion and now stood close by with feet set apart, hands on hips and a defiant smirk on her face. "Race you up the hill?"

Jayjay grinned, relieved at the distraction. "Ah good, Larry asked me to go find you so I could box your ears. You've saved me some trouble."

"You'd have to ask me nicely to stand still then," she stood unmoved. "Else you might be hopping after me all day. Might be good for a laugh."

"I see you've picked up your brother's quick wit and sharp tongue. You'll make some man miserable one day, if you haven't already."

She poked out her tongue with a facial expression that reminded Jayjay of the last time he saw her. She had the same face then, peering through the front window of Larry's house, the morning of signing up.

If only I knew then what I know now. We might not have rushed off to war in such a hurry.

"Well I can't stand around talking to a cripple all day. I've got to hop along. See you hoppy. Bye Mrs Jones, Mr Jones."

Jayjay watched her walk briskly away, and was still trying to think of a suitable retort when she was well out of earshot.

"Pay her no head Jonathan," Mum said. "That young lady certainly speaks her mind. Stirred up her share of trouble in recent months too, but can't say I disagree with everything she says."

Whatever trouble she's decided to stir up, I reckon she'd do a pretty good job of it.

"Let's go home," Jayjay said. "These crutches get uncomfortable when I stand about for too long."

"Of course Jayjay," Dad said. "Can I give you a hand?"

"No, I'll be alright once we get moving."

The tram ride to Rozelle was quiet. More like the homecoming he anticipated. A few heads turned when they saw his leg, but no one said anything. He didn't want to start talking about Ron until they were home and was relieved when Dad asked about the ship's journey. Mum opened her mouth on two occasions, as if about to say something, but held her silence until they were walking home from the tram stop.

"Emilia has been living with us. She's staying in Ron's room with Ronald Junior."

"Righto, great." *That's next to my room. I wonder if the kid cries at night.*

"How's the little fella going?"

"He's going fine Jayjay," Dad said. "Thing is though, Emilia's not so good. She took Ron's passing pretty hard."

"Of course she did!" The hard edge to Mum's voice reminded him of the morning he first raised the idea of signing up. It was as if she was still angry and wanting to continue the same argument from over a year ago.

"Lost her husband for no good reason," she continued. "Threw his life away in a war that's not ours. Now she's left holding a baby with no one else to support her. Her mother died last winter, so now she's just got us. Couldn't afford to keep up the rent and feed the two of them on widow's payments, so we're the last thing between her and the gutter. No sign of King nor country coming to help her now after she's given them everything."

"She doesn't say much," Dad said. "Sometimes she goes several days without a word to anyone but Ronald Junior. Won't even talk to your Mum."

They stopped at the front gate and Jayjay lent on his crutches. He tried not to breathe so heavily, but needed the oxygen.

"I must have got a bit lazy on the ship. I haven't done much walking in the last few weeks."

The scent of jasmine filled his lungs and he knew he was home.

Black ants busied themselves about a tiny mound of sand on a crack in a paving brick outside the front doorstep. Jayjay had stirred up the same ants as a child, sitting on the front door step and poking a stick into the crack. The ants would defend their territory with a fearless courage, unperturbed at the death of their comrades. *I used to wonder what it would be like to be an ant.*

"Come inside Jonathan," Mum said. "I'll make you a cup of tea. Are you hungry?"

"Is Emilia home now?" Jayjay asked. "I have some of Ron's things for her."

"Yes," Dad opened the door for Mum and Jayjay to go through first. "She doesn't leave the house much."

The procession of three marched single file down the narrow corridor to the dining room. It seemed strange that everything was so familiar, as if nothing had changed. The tea towel hanging beside the kitchen sink was the same one that was hanging there on the day he left.

"Hello Emilia," Jayjay said.

Emilia sat at the dining table with a baby at her breast. She adjusted her shawl to cover herself, but didn't appear embarrassed.

First bit of female breast I've seen since Josephine. Don't think like that now. Don't think like that about Ron's wife.

"Hello Jonathan." Her voice was flat.

"This must be Ron Junior."

Emilia looked away. "Ronald. Ron is his father."

The sides of Jayjay's chest ached where the pads pressed when he walked and his good leg was tired from the walking.

"Ah, right, Ronald. It's great to finally see him." Jayjay sat down in a chair at the opposite side of the dining table to Emilia. "How is he?"

"He needs his father." Emilia looked down at Ronald.

"I'm sure he does. I miss him too. I, ah, have some of Ron's things. I thought you might want them."

"Leave them here," Emilia said. "I'll have a look through them later." She stood with the baby still attached and walked out of the room without meeting his eyes.

What just happened? Jayjay felt numb. *It was as if I just told her Ron died, but she received the news months ago.* He sat motionless and repeated the conversation in his head but couldn't think what he might have said differently.

Mum's small hand caressed his shoulder.

"It's not fair that she blames you Jonathan."

"What? Is that it? Damn right it's not fair," Jayjay said in disbelief. "She wasn't there. She isn't me. She doesn't know anything about what it was like. I stayed with Ron from the moment he was shot until we buried him. His last thoughts were of her. The last word he spoke was her name. I thought she might want to know that. I carried him away from where he was shot, most likely in full view of the sniper who fired the bullet. I carried him all the way to the hospital and begged the doctor to do something more. There were so many dying. You can't imagine. I would have carried him all the way home if I could, but he was as good as dead when I reached the hospital. Doctor said so himself. There was nothing he could do and there was nothing I could do! Nothing! I couldn't do anything!"

Jayjay's vision blurred with tears.

"I know it's not fair, but she thinks Ron went away because of you."

"Well that's the most insane thing I've heard for some time, and I've had to listen to some lunatics I can tell you. Since when did Ron ever take advice from his little brother? He was a big boy and he made his own decisions."

Doubt sprouted in his mind and he paused. *Could it be true. Did he come because of me? Why would he do that?*

"Of course you're right Jayjay," Dad said. "Costs in wartime are high. Everyone suffers for the common good. That's just the way it is. Women feel the pain in their own way and sometimes they need to have someone to blame. Emilia can't blame Ron, it'd be too painful for her."

"Oh! Really Stanley?" Mum set a teacup down gently in front of Jayjay. Her hand was shaking and some tea spilled onto the saucer.

"Ah – Thanks Mum for the tea." Jayjay watched her straighten slowly and walk from the room.

"Your mother blames me."

CHAPTER 94

John

Sunday, 12 December 1915

Only a dwarf could have walked along the tunnel without stooping.

General John Monash shuffled forward in the dark, relying on the light of a single candle in the hands of the sergeant in front.

"Nearly there Sir."

"Very good," John replied.

"When we remove the cover Sir," the sergeant said, "there is no loophole, so I suggest stand to the side and take just a quick look, no more than five seconds."

"Do we have any reason to suspect the Turks might know about this one?"

"No Sir. We only broke through last night and the opening is barely big enough to see past the barrel of the machine gun. A clump of prickly scrub out front gives us a bit of camouflage. We don't think they've seen it Sir, but best be careful nonetheless."

At the end of the tunnel, the sergeant extinguished the candle and slowly removed a timber board that once formed the side of a biscuit crate.

"When you're ready Sir."

John took a deep breath and crouched beside the machine gun. In front of the barrel, a small opening revealed the sloping ground of a spur from Cheshire Ridge and overlooked a valley that separated the opposing lines by around three hundred yards. The valley was useless to both sides, impossible to hold under enemy lines of fire, but the tunnels allowed a new perspective on the enemy's position and provided the opportunity to fire upon him from an unexpected angle.

"I see two, no three Turks, carrying something up the back of that ridge."

"We believe that's an enemy supply track Sir."

"Wait until you have a clear shot at ten or more before firing," John said. "A lot of work has gone into this tunnel, we want to be sure to get good value from it. After firing, cover the hole immediately to stop any smoke escaping and get your men out, take the gun with you of course. If the Turks see the muzzle flash, they'll shell the position and the front of the tunnel will be blown to hell, along with everyone in it."

"Yes Sir. We would anticipate that Sir."

John left the sergeant with his machine gun and returned along the tunnel towards the square of daylight at the junction with the firing trench. *He didn't need to be given that warning.*

The machine gun section was affectionately known as the 'suicide squad' amongst the other ranks and maintained a love-hate relationship with the infantry. The troops always wanted a machine gun about to cover their position in defence or attack, but machine guns were known to be a favourite artillery target and a machine gun emplacement was considered dangerous if located too close. Machine gunners lived by a special blend of courage and survival instinct.

On reaching the trench, John straightened his back and gave a stretch, then started on the half mile walk from the left flank of his brigade's territory to his headquarters in the centre.

He wound his way along the gallery of trenches and tunnels with confidence, knowing each interconnected sap well enough to navigate them in the dark.

He exchanged good morning greetings with the men he passed, and indulged himself in a moment of silent self-congratulation on the quality of winter preparations. Now men of his 4th Brigade could access almost any part of their firing line without direct exposure to the enemy. Walking tracks were cut higher than drainage trenches on all major thoroughfares and covered areas allowed for shelter and fires in wet weather. Winter had already delivered a taste of what might be to come, but no other part of the front line was as well prepared for the wet or the cold as his Cheshire Ridge.

Outside brigade headquarters, McGlinn paced about and sucked on a cigarette.

"I do wish you would not go off by yourself like that," McGlinn grumbled.

"Would you have me sit here signing pieces of paper all day?"

"Frankly, yes Sir."

"I'm here now. What have you got for me?"

"The listening patrol returned this morning from the southern sector."

"Any news?"

"A party of around twenty Turks came by their position at two a.m."

"Did the Turks realise they were being observed?"

"No Sir, at least they gave no sign of it."

"Good. The same men are to go out tonight at ten p.m. as a fighting patrol. The usual approach, taking a good supply of bombs, and be ready to ambush the Turks if they pass the same location at two a.m."

"Yes Sir. I will let those lads know they are to rest today."

"Is there any word back from General Headquarters about the extra provisions we have requested? Any variety in food, canned fruits or vegetables, sweets or chocolate?"

"No Sir, they have just sent more Bully Beef and tooth-breakers."

"What about the other items to get the men through the winter – tobacco, playing cards, concertinas, reading material?"

"No Sir, no response from G.H.Q. on any of those things."

In the distance a machine gun unleashed a continuous burst of fire for around ten seconds. With a delivery rate of three-hundred rounds per minute, that was enough to deliver about fifty bullets. If firing into a cluster of men, John knew the best he could about expect was one hit from three bullets. *Maybe ten to fifteen enemy kills.*

Within another ten seconds, an explosive shell blasted into the left flank, in the same area where the sound of machine gun fire had come from. A salvo of shells followed.

I hope the sergeant got his men and machine gun out of that tunnel.

* * *

Next morning John sat on a biscuit box in his brigade headquarters, reviewing the most recent list of provisions sent to the 4th Brigade.

"Sir," McGlinn said as he walked in. "The fighting patrol has returned this morning."

"What news?" John was glad of a distraction from the mundane.

"They ambushed the Turks and everyone scattered as usual, then our boys waited and went back and collected twelve rifles, a few hundred rounds and two wounded prisoners."

"Very good, any casualties of our own?"

"Two Sir, one shot in the arm, looks to be broken, and one shot dead."

"That's a shame, we've gone nearly a week since our last death. Did we bring him back?"

"Yes Sir, his mate carried him all the way."

"What was his name?"

"Private Wilfred Harrison Sir."

"See that Private Harrison is buried with a good service."

"Yes Sir."

"Now, I need to go for a walk to the New Zealand sector to see Godley at Division H.Q. He has called a conference of brigadiers.

* * *

Half an hour later, John sat on a bench at General Godley's headquarters of the New Zealand and Australian Division.

"Gentlemen," Godley spoke with his usual air of self-importance, but quieter than usual. "What I am about to tell you is secret and must be treated as such."

He looked about the dugout, as if an unauthorized listener might be lurking in some dark corner.

"The Allied War Council," Godley continued, "has decided to withdraw from the Gallipoli Peninsula."

It took a moment for the meaning of the words to sink in, then John felt as if the bench he sat on was falling away from underneath him.

This cannot be.

There must be a mistake.

What is the basis?

One does not simply walk away from an engagement such as this. We have tens of thousands of men entrenched, facing off against a hostile enemy.

Sweat prickled John's neck and his heartrate elevated, as if he had just completed a strenuous activity.

Rumours of evacuation had been circulating for some time, but he had paid them no heed.

What of our objective?

We have fought so hard.

I have worked so hard.

How will the men react? They will howl in outrage, and rightly so. So many have given their lives and are buried here. How will the people react at home? We will have to admit defeat. We will be remembered as those who failed, if we are to be remembered at all.

"Planning is already underway. No further stores, mail, reinforcements or munitions will be sent here. You must prepare for this operation, but secrecy is imperative. If the Turks get an inkling of our intention, we could lose half our men. It has been decided that we will put up the bluff to our troops that, owing to severe winter weather, it is intended to form a winter rest camp at Imbros. We will tell the men that they will be taken there by turn in two or three stages. In this way we will remove two-thirds of our army, then the last garrison will make a bolt for the beach in the dead of night."

"How long have you known about this Sir," John asked.

"Apparently, Lord Kitchener recommended the withdrawal soon after his visit and the War Council accepted his recommendation, but British Cabinet only confirmed the decision six days ago. I leaned of this from General Birdwood four days ago, but have only today been given authority to pass this information on to you."

"What is the proposed timetable?" John asked. "This will be a complex operation, and we cannot very well hope to keep it a secret for long. The men are not complete fools."

"The more men we get away before the news is out, the less men are likely to be killed in the process. Spread the word of winter rest camps. The men will want to believe this story as it means they can look forward to a holiday. We shall start the staged withdrawals within the next two days. General Birdwood's Chief-of-Staff, Lieutenant-Colonel White, will be planning the operational details and setting the schedule. The timing of the final bolt is yet to be determined, but we plan to be away by Christmas."

"That's less than two weeks!"

"Yes it is John."

* * *

The walk back to 4th Brigade headquarters gave John a few minutes alone to collect his thoughts.

It will be hard not to tell anyone. I would trust my staff with my life, but I must do it for the men. The longer we can keep the secret, the more men will live. McGlinn could keep the secret and he would be devastated if he found I had lied to him.

I could withdraw the 15th Battalion first, and spread the others thinner across the front line. If possible, I will make sure that I am the last man of the 4th Brigade to leave.

It's such a shame I cannot talk to anyone about it. I must keep a diary each day, and send it on before the final bolt. I wonder what is the chance that I will escape this place alive?

"Good morning Sir." McGlinn gave an inquisitive look on John's return. "Any news from Div. H.Q.?"

"Rest Camps," John said. "We are to send the men to winter rest camps on Imbros – to reduce our numbers here during the harsh weather."

CHAPTER 95

Larry

Sunday, 19 December 1915

Larry retraced his steps and walked back along Artillery Road, from Milo Pier at North Beach. This would be the last time he made the journey from the beach to Leane's Trench.

Like the other members of C party, he considered himself fortunate to have been allowed to be in the final ninety members of the 1st Battalion to evacuate.

The word 'evacuate' had a bitter taste and he had not spoken it aloud since receiving the orders. In the same way, he still refused to say the word 'nightmare'. A small statement of protest against reality, but the best he could manage in the given circumstances.

He would not miss Gallipoli. He hated the place, but he had fought for eight months in the belief that it mattered somehow, for something. Sudden orders to up and leave were hard to swallow. So many good men had died here fighting for a cause. The Turks sided with the Germans, and the Germans had to be stopped. *Maybe something has changed? Something must have changed. One day I will find out and understand so it all makes more sense to me – if I survive this night.*

The plan was that C party would vacate Leane's Trench at around 2:30am. From this time, the firing line would be left unmanned. The plan was then to scarper before the enemy realized what was going on. *Long odds. High stakes.*

The walk from Leane's Trench to Milo Pier had been timed at twenty-eight minutes, and the departure by barge scheduled along with C party members from other Anzac infantry battalions and light horse regiments.

He walked past checkpoint Z, then checkpoint Y and X. At night these were to be marked with coloured lights.

A trail of white rice grains along the centre of the trail designated this as the official departure route. Chunks of icy ground had been cut out from the steeper sections to form steps and reduce the risk of slipping.

Last night's evacuation of half the Anzac force seemed to have gone unnoticed by the Turks. The whole operation appeared to be well organised and this came as a surprise to Larry. Details of the planned sequence and timing had been well communicated to the men. The remaining half of the men would be going tonight. First A party would start to move out in the fading late afternoon light from 5:15pm. Later B party would make their move under cover of darkness from 9:35pm.

Once B party was gone there would be two thousand men holding the Anzac frontline. One day earlier the same line was defended by twenty thousand.

I should've written better letters. If I get away from here alive, by some miracle of God, I'll retrieve those letters and write new ones.

Like many others selected to be in C Party, Larry had written letters home in case he didn't get away alive. Larry sent his two letters with the lanky Private Timothy Simmonds, one letter to Larry's family and one letter to Jayjay.

'Letters' is a generous description of what they were. Less than half a small page each, of pencil scribble. A brief statement that he was well and hoped they were likewise, a description of orders to take part in a dangerous operation was deliberately ambiguous to get past the censor, and best wishes for a merry Christmas. *Yeah, I suppose I could do better than that.*

After the Lone Pine attack, Larry had learned of Jayjay's medical evacuation and the two had managed to exchange brief letters. Neither had ever been strong at writing, but the basic facts were communicated. Larry wrote that he survived Lone Pine to enjoy a seven-week holiday on the island of Lemnos, and learned that Jayjay had his right leg cut off above the knee in Cairo and was waiting to be sent home invalid.

I wonder which would be worse, to be shot dead charging on two legs, or to go home a cripple?

Larry kicked the icy ground and felt suddenly conscious of his action of walking, lifting one leg, then the other.

To his left, a flat area opened out where yesterday troops from the light horse had played a cricket match. The flat area lay within a visible line of sight to Beachy Bill, the Turkish gun emplacement to the south, hence its name, 'Shell Green'. The idea behind the game of cricket was to demonstrate that men were about the place getting on with normal activities. *Funny, I never saw an organised game of cricket there before, so not so normal really.*

Soon after passing Shell Green, Artillery Road turned hard to the left and made its way up the main ridge. Near this area, Sergeant Baker was waiting and looking pleased with himself.

"I've got one final fatigue for you lads," Baker said.

"Come on Serge'," Larry said. "We've only got a few hours left here, then we're going to piss off. We've carried everything out that we're going to take, except our own packs and A party is taking those."

"Growling until the last Gillespie?" Baker had a wicked grin. "Suit yourself. I was going to ask you lads to do smoking duty, even got a pack of Woodbines here for the job. I can always find someone else."

"What's smoking duty?" Albert asked.

"Down this way Darky," Baker said. "Artillery road is visible to Johnny Turk at Gaba Tepe. We want him to think our men have got nothing better to do than loaf about and smoke. Shouldn't be too hard for you lot. Just keep an eye on Beachy Bill as he's likely to start lobbing artillery shells our way."

Larry reached out and took a cigarette from the pack in Baker's hand. "Got a match Sarge?"

* * *

Later that afternoon, up at the front line, Larry stood in a group around a Short Magazine Lee-Enfield rifle that was being wedged in place with several sandbags by a lance corporal from the 7th Battalion.

"We set the two tins up like this," the lance corporal said, "and tie the string like this. Fill this top tin with sea water so it drips out the small hole into the bottom tin. When the bottom tin overbalances and falls, it pulls the trigger like this."

He yanked the string and the rifle fired towards the Turkish trenches.

"Depending on the size of the hole, you have about ten to twenty minutes of delay in firing."

"Thank you Lance Corporal Scurry," Sergeant Baker said. "If you leave that one in place, we'll rig up a few more up like it. You can scurry along now. C party, this is your job. Start with one every twenty yards along the front line. You lot will be relying on them so you set them up and test each one a few times to make sure they all work. Any questions? No? Good."

"Well obviously," Larry said. "I was just about to suggest we do something like this. I mean, I was going to suggest it some time ago, but I was worried I might do myself out of a job."

It grated to be taking advice from another battalion about the final defence of Leane's Trench, but Larry had to admit to himself that the drip rifle was a very clever self-firing arrangement. He knew the rifle he wanted for the first one he would rig up, he had kept it close by since Jayjay left in August. A rifle with thirty-nine neat notches carved in the butt stock, carved with a bowie knife identical to the one he wore at his own hip.

* * *

Men of A party filed past in the orange glow of the setting sun. A few gave nods of acknowledgement to those staying behind, although most kept grim eyes focused straight ahead, as if on their way to the funeral of a loved one.

It's time for our final roll of the dice.

The next phase of waiting began. Sometimes darkness fell quickly, but not tonight. Everything dragged on.

The next four hours felt like four weeks.

Bullets flew in usual quantities from both sides. If anything, the Anzac remnant overcompensated for the reduced numbers and fired more rifle-shots than a full contingent might have.

Time came for B party to move out and there was no indication that the Turks might suspect anything out of the ordinary.

Empty sandbags covered boots to dampen the sound of B party footsteps and the men filed past into the night. B party was smaller than A party. C party was smaller again.

When B Party was gone, ten yards of empty trench lay between Larry and the next man in either direction. *I wouldn't feel this exposed if I ran naked down George Street.*

He pulled the string to fire Jayjay's rifle to prove the mechanism once more, then reloaded it. A few paces along the trench, he climbed up onto the firing step, but kept low and fired over the parapet without looking. *No sense in getting my head shot off at this stage.*

Still crouching, he moved in the other direction and did the same again, then dropped back down to stand on the trench floor.

Five Short Magazine Lee-Enfields leant against the back trench wall within his reach, at much the same angle a private might stand when being addressed by an officer he didn't think highly of. The rifles, each loaded with ten rounds in their respective magazines, stood on duty in place of the men who had cared for them and killed with them. A box of ammunition rested on the firing trench. For the next five hours his job was to shoot as if he was all five men as well as himself.

Time took forever to tick away.

On several occasions, Larry thought he saw movement in the dark shadows, and fired in the direction, but there was none. If the Turks suspected anything they were not acting on it tonight.

After midnight he slipped an empty sandbag over each boot and tied it on with string. He checked each charger clip of five rounds, all accessible in trouser and shirt pockets, eight clips made forty rounds available to reload. *Travel light and get out quick. Don't stop to engage the enemy. Easy said. I haven't lived through all this so I can get shot in the back.*

The last hour before half past two seemed to last as long as a full night. Larry worked through the box of ammunition and kept firing to create the illusion of a fully manned trench. The shooting helped to pass the time. The sounds of rifle fire away in the dark on either side gave some comfort and helped to preserve the remnant of his sanity.

Time came for the first members of C party to move out and Larry picked up the can of sea water he had positioned ready on the firing step. He carefully emptied the can into another can perched above Jayjay's rifle and listened. Drip, drip, drip. *Good, she's working as she should. Soon I'll be away from this shithole, just like you Jayjay old mate. Aim carefully, you always had a good eye. The last shot's for you Jonathan Jones.*

At that moment a heavy fog drifted over the moon and shrouded it with a silver halo. Larry picked up his own Lee-Enfield and moved out with the others. He didn't need to check to know it had a full magazine. *Ten shots to get me out of here. Hopefully I don't have to reload. If I do, we will have been caught out and my luck will have run out.*

Bags muffled the sound. No one spoke a word. Orders were clear, no yelling goodbye to the enemy or leaving notes. The yelling part made sense, alerting the Turks to what was happening would be a disaster, but leaving a note seemed harmless enough.

Larry and a few others from C party had piled a stack of bully beef tins on a biscuit box with a knife and fork, and a pencilled note saying 'Have a good feed Joe Bourke.'

If they get this far to read the note, they'll already know the trench is undefended.

The trail of rice was barely visible in the obscured moonlight, but Larry didn't need it to find his way. Ahead a small white light on a biscuit box marked checkpoint X. An officer sat in silence on another box and marked down a head count in his note book as they passed.

Sounds of rifle fire at the front line were thin, but at least there was something. Drip rifles must have been working as occasional shots could be heard from the direction of the Leane's trench, a trench now empty of men.

The silent stunts were actually quite a good idea. If we pull this off, I'll take back some of the bad things I said about the lunatics at HQ who came up with those orders.

Further along Artillery Road, a green light marked checkpoint Y. Another officer stood beside the light with his notebook and nodded as the men of 1st Battalion C party filed past, muffled footsteps of bagged feet the only announcement of their departure.

Heavy fog continued to obscure the moonlight and sporadic rifle fire in the distance continued.

A red light ahead marked checkpoint Z. Larry passed inside the inner line of defence. A select group of men were stationed along the perimeter of the inner line and would defend it to the last. The rest of C party, including Larry and those he walked with, had orders to continue to Milo Pier and proceed with the evacuation regardless of any Turkish attack once past this point. Of course, if a fire fight erupted, Larry would not run from it and he doubted that many of the others would either, but those were the orders.

They moved like a company of wraiths across the mouth of Shrapnel Gully. The cemetery where Ron and so many others rested lay close by. Sunrise in a few hours would mark the handover of this plot back to the Turks.

Rest in peace lads. I'm glad you don't have to wake up in the morning to realize you've been abandoned. I reckon you might have a bit of a growl at being left behind and I wouldn't blame you one bit for it. Sorry Ron old Mate.

Larry's throat was tight. He fought an urge to punch himself in the leg. *Is it guilt? Or shame? Or both? I'm desperate to get away from this place, but it feels so wrong going like this.*

His boots crunched onto the coarse grit of the beach for the last time. Sounds of distant rifle fire were few and far between now. After several seconds of silence, a rifle shot sounded away to the south.

Maybe that was Jayjay's last round. Ron's dead, Jayjay's gone home with one leg. I guess I'm the lucky one of the three of us that came on this mad adventure. Looks like I'm going to get away alive. Who would have thought it?

At Milo Pier a barge, overloaded with men, pushed slowly away through the water. The steam engine pumped and groaned as if to complain against the burden. Another barge bobbed close, waiting to take its place.

White hospital tents stood pitched behind the beach, outlines barely visible in the dark. The tents remained fully manned with the doctors staying until the last, ready to remain behind and care for the wounded as prisoners of war if the Turks attacked and a party was cut off from the evacuation.

They're good men. True heroes. Insane, but in a good way.

Larry felt a sudden urge to take a souvenir that was a natural part of Gallipoli, rather than a memento of war. *I've seen enough bullets and shell casings.* He crouched down, pushed his fingers into the coarse sand and let them feel their way in the darkness until he found what he was looking for. Then he stood again, brushed the sand off three pebbles and dropped them into a pocket that wasn't full of bullets.

He waited another minute and then it was his time to depart.

Men shuffled along the blanket-lined pier like a mute mob of cleanskin cattle being duffed in the night. He crowded with the others onto the barge and it chugged away into the darkness.

Larry half expected to hear the distant crump of a shell being launched from Beachy Bill, and then for a shrapnel shell to burst over the barge. He stood close to the edge, ready to dive overboard if necessary. But the shell never came.

Each yard the barge pushed through the water made another yard between him and the shore. Men held their silence, as if to speak a word might invite calamity. At one point Larry realized he was holding his breath and forced himself to inhale, but soon the steam engine slowed and the barge eased up against a transport ship. With Lee-Enfields slung over their shoulders, men climbed a rope net and embarked.

On the top deck men lined the balustrade facing the shore they had just left. Larry found a gap and took his station leaning against the rail, rifle still slung over his shoulder, ten rounds in a full magazine. Low clouds drifted apart to allow the moon to shine through and Larry could make out the faintest outline of the hills of Anzac. *So much colonial blood was shed on those hills, thousands of Australians killed for nothing but a name. Now we are sneaking away like cowards in the night. So much for our name.*

He reached into a pocket and felt for the pebbles.

Flash, boom, flash, boom! Two explosions erupted from the top of the ridgeline.

Our mines have been detonated. We must have got away before the Joe Bourkes noticed. I guess we beat the odds.

Larry's fingers tightened around a small stone and he wondered whether he'd left his sanity behind at Gallipoli.

CHAPTER 96

Ishmail

Monday, 20 December 1915, 3:30am

Ishmail stared into the darkness and his heart sank towards his worn-out boots. Two massive blasts faded into the night. *But what do they mean?*

Rumours of enemy evacuation had lost their credibility weeks ago. Disappointment followed earlier periods of quiet when the enemy re-opened savage attacks, seemingly at random. Now it was happening again. In recent days there had been little enemy activity in the trenches in front of Ishmail and the 57th Regiment.

Maybe the Australians are preparing for more cold and wet. No one could forget the snow storm and icy winds that marked the onset of winter three weeks ago.

Ishmail looked up at dull stars fighting to penetrate a heavy blanket of fog. In some dark patches they failed, but the moon shone through, shrouded in a delicate halo. Its crescent took a similar shape to the Ottoman moon on Ishmail's buttons, and the button he had given to the big Australian in exchange for a silver coin. *Maybe the moon is a good omen. Maybe God is smiling on his people tonight.*

Up the ridge, around Hill of Valour, machine gun and rifle fire chased the explosions into the night, but Ishmail could see nothing from his post at Junction Hill. Even distant muzzle flashes were lost in the fog.

"Ishmail!" Sergeant Zahid's lantern approached from the north. "We have reports the Australians have abandoned some forward positions. Send a patrol to investigate and report back when you determine their position."

"Yes, Zahid Efendi. I will lead a patrol of four." Ishmail's response was reflexive, but surprised himself. "Does anyone wish to volunteer to join me?"

"I will come with you Efendi," Osman said.

Two others, Murat and Riza, stepped forward without hesitation.

"Be sure to have full magazines and ammunition pouches, and one canteen of water. Fix bayonets." Ishmail turned to Haydar, his grenadier. How many bombs do you have?"

"Four bombs, Ishmail Efendi."

"Lob two into the enemy trench in front, and give the other two to me, with the matches. Once we have gone, see Sergeant Zahid about more bombs. You three men – stand to, fix bayonets, ready yourselves for possible counter attack. We do not know what we will find. If the enemy has hopped away and you are ordered forward, our password is 'kangaroo'. If he is still here, you will know soon enough, and we will wait for you in paradise.

White teeth reflected the moonlight. Ishmail hoped the nervous grins might release some pre-raid tension.

"There is no God but God," Ishmail said, "and Muhammad is his prophet."

The squad responded as one, "There is no God but God, and Muhammad is his prophet."

Other squads nearby were standing to, under orders to observe the operation and be ready for enemy response. Ishmail watched his men ready themselves and when each had been through his preparations and prayers, he nodded to Haydar the grenadier.

The first bomb cleared the enemy trench and exploded harmlessly on the ground behind. No movement.

Ishmail bit into his lip. "Take your time with this one." Ishmail tried not to sound disappointed.

The next bomb landed on the enemy parapet and rolled on into the trench. The muffled sound of the blast confirmed detonation was down in the trench. Still no movement.

"Beautiful! Very beautiful Haydar." Ishmail turned to Osman and the other two who would follow him. "As God wills."

"As God wills," they replied.

Ishmail climbed the rickety ladder and squatted in front of the parapet to wait for the others. Crouching caused his right thigh to ache where the bullet had been removed from deep in the muscle months earlier, but it was too dangerous to stand exposed and risk creating a silhouette for the enemy to aim at.

Only now did he reflect on his immediate willingness to volunteer to lead this patrol.

It wasn't required of him. It wasn't even expected. He was ordered to send a patrol. The men knew that. It would have been quite reasonable to call for three volunteers and send them on their way, or select three men if no one volunteered. Now the squad might be left without a leader if the party came under attack.

And yet there was no doubt in his mind that he had made the right decision. He knew he must go forward himself. He needed to know if the enemy was gone, and wanted it to be true so badly. If it was not true, he might be killed but he would die a martyr and join the others in paradise. If the enemy was gone and he did not go forward himself, he knew he would never be able to command the respect of his men for having asked them to do something he would not do himself. But if he did go forward and the enemy was gone, then his courage would be remembered. *This time I will die if it is required of me. As God wills.*

A muzzle flash from the enemy trench opposite confirmed that death was a likely outcome. *Strange only one shot, not followed up by a second. They must not have seen us.*

The men crouched and waited.

An artillery shell burst away to the south. *That was probably one of ours. We could be shot at from any direction. Would God consider me to be a martyr if I am accidentally killed by a Muslim brother?*

He signalled for silence and to move forward.

They all walked slowly, hunched low.

Each step ground into the gravel and made too much noise for Ishmail's liking. This mission was about stealth not speed. Unless they came under attack, in which case it would be a sprint home in the darkness, hoping and praying for God's mercy.

They reached the enemy trench and Ishmail signalled for them to wait while he crawled up to the parapet. Inside the enemy trench was blacker than the black that cloaked everything else. He peered up and down. No movement.

He saw a glint of moonlight on a rifle barrel resting on the parapet several paces to the north. Slowly he lifted his Mauser and aimed into the shadow behind the barrel. *He must have heard me by now.* The enemy rifle didn't move.

Suddenly the enemy rifle discharged, harmlessly straight ahead. Ishmail squeezed his own trigger and fired into the black trench, but the enemy rifle remained unmoved. Quickly he worked the action to reload his Mauser. Others beside him fired into the trench also.

"Hold your fire!" Ishmail yelled.

He stepped slowly forward towards the enemy rifle until he was close enough to stand on it. It was unmanned.

The enemy trench appeared to be unmanned, although it snaked along the ridge and was full of treacherous shadows where an assassin might hide.

If anyone is in that trench, now they know we are here.

Ishmail's heartbeats pounded in his ears, so loud it seemed that they might be heard by others and give his position away to the enemy.

Without allowing himself to think further Ishmail slid down into the darkness.

Part way down into the enemy trench, his foot caught on something that moved under his weight and he tumbled to the trench floor. He scrambled to his knees and realised that the trench must be clear of enemy troops, otherwise he would be dead by now.

What is that stink?

A wooden box lay on the ground beside him. It had been up against the front wall of the trench and was the reason for his awkward landing. A puddle formed around the box, and sucked heat from Ishmail's knees.

A latrine!

He stood up quickly and realised that the other three members of his patrol were already in the trench probing bayonet-first to the north and south. He wiped his knees with his left hand, then immediately regretted it and rubbed his hand against the trench wall. The earth was cold and rough. *It feels just like our trench walls.*

He smiled into the night and held back a chuckle. *The Australians have gone, and left their shit as a parting gift.*

He approached the enemy rifle that had fired just before he jumped into the trench.

It had a string attached to the trigger. The string led back to a crude supporting frame and down to a tin half full of water, swinging like the pendulum of a grandfather clock.

He walked further along the trench, following after Osman and rubbing his left hand on the trench wall as he went.

Another rifle was wedged between sandbags at the parapet and a loop of string dangled from it, barely visible in the shadow. He heard the drip of water and paused to inspect the arrangement. One tin was perched above another on steps made of sandbags at the top of the trench wall. It seemed to be a mechanism to fire the unmanned rifle after a period of delay. He dared not touch it in case of another unseen trap that might detonate explosive left in the trench.

The others had progressed some distance along the winding trench and it was clear to Ishmail that at least this part of the enemy frontline had been abandoned. He stared at the tins in the weak moonlight, almost mesmerised. Each drip of water called him to wait a few seconds for the next. The simple delayed firing rifle was ingenious.

Another drip and the bottom tin fell.

The rifle fired before Ishmail could react to stop it. Horror hit him like a slap and he could feel his face flush with guilt. *That bullet might have killed one of my countrymen.* He quickly looked around and on seeing that no one was watching he felt some of the guilt dissipate into the cold night air.

At least I can't be blamed for it. Please God, let that bullet be buried into the earth and not one of our men.

Osman was returning. "Kangaroo." He must have heard the rifle shot, but was taking less care to be quiet now than at first.

"Kangaroos have hopped away." Ishmail grinned into the night.

"Osman, they have gone!" Ishmail wiped his left hand on the trench wall and used his other hand to grab Osman's upper arm.

"At least from this foul trench, but how far?"

"We'll know soon enough."

Murat and Riza approached from the other direction. Murat slid a newly-acquired bayonet into his scabbard, his own Ottoman bayonet was still attached to the barrel of his Mauser.

"Murat, take your souvenir and return to our trenches. Report to Sergeant Zahid that we have found this trench to be unoccupied and are proceeding into the Valley of Fear. Do not try to return to us alone as we might shoot you before we know who you are. Ask Zahid Efendi to send forward reinforcements to occupy this trench immediately."

"Yes, Ishmail Efendi." Murat moved along the firing step to a box latrine similar to the one that Ishmail had overturned, and stepped on it to climb up the front wall of the trench in one nimble action.

My leg wouldn't have allowed me to do that. I feel like an old man.

Walking down into the Valley of Fear was a surreal experience. The ground he trod was so close to his own territory, and yet had remained untouchable since the invasion so many months ago. He passed the place, as close as he could tell, where he had lain in hiding with his father for three days. He smiled with pride at the memory of his father. He focused on the success of killing over fifty invaders between them and then the miraculous escape from behind enemy lines. The arguments and face slap were pushed way to the back of his mind so as not to allow them to darken the memory. *Dad and I might have been the last Ottoman soldiers to tread this ground, and now I am the first one to return.*

The country looked very different now. The scrub that provided cover for both sides during the first days of the invasion was gone, and the hillside was scared from human activity. Natural slopes of the gully and hillsides were covered in a veneer of terraces, sandbags and dugout shelters, all connected by deep cut trenches.

Australian supply trenches resembled Ottoman supply trenches and looked to have been abandoned in a hurry. Kit, clothes and rubbish lay about the place but were difficult to identify in the dark. In a few places the way was blocked with coils of barbed wire, but these were not staked properly and looked to have been thrown in place in great haste.

No traps or self-firing rifles delayed their progress further and the supply trail they were following soon opened out at the mouth of the valley onto a beach.

Stars above, already obscured by the fog, were starting to fade with the first hint of dawn. Lights of enemy ships dotted the sea, and several appeared to be steaming away.

Ishmail, Osman and Riza stood on the shore and stared after them.

Small waves rolled up the beach, as if lazy and yawning, as if this was a normal morning following a normal night. When they dissolved back down into the shingle, they made the most beautiful sound Ishmail could remember. A pure sound of nature that the ocean had been making since God created it. An eternal sound of peace, untainted by the sounds of killing.

After a long silence, Ishmail spoke. "Give me your canteen Riza. Let us drink to celebrate this moment, thanks to God."

The three men passed the canteen around until it was empty.

"Now take this and fill it, with sea water. Take it back the way we came and give it to Sergeant Zahid. Tell him to taste it, and tell him everything we have seen. Tell him troops must be sent forward at once, we must occupy these trenches while they are empty. God only knows what the enemy's plans are. Osman and I will stay here. There may be some enemy still about, but it does not seem so here."

"Yes Efendi." Riza refilled and stoppered the canteen, turned his back to the sea and left a force of two men to defend the shore.

Ishmail and Osman wandered up the beach with crunching footsteps in the growing light of dawn and found an empty packing box with a glass bottle, a packet of cigarettes and a box of matches sitting on it. A note sat beside the cigarettes, written in unintelligible scrawl.

Ishmail was hesitant to touch anything the Australians had left behind, but Osman picked up the bottle. It was about the size of his canteen, but a much more elegant shape – tall and rectangular. The bottle was full of liquid the colour of urine, as might be produced by someone who hadn't drunk any water for a day.

"Maybe this is Cognac for you Efendi? Maybe they heard you had a taste for it?"

"Could be. The bottle of French poison was a different shape from what I remember, but I was in a lot of pain at the time. It looks like donkey piss!"

Osman grinned and picked up the cigarettes, took one out and lit it with the foreign match. Osman sucked deep on the cigarette and it flared up in a bright orange flame. For a moment it looked as if his beard was on fire.

"Treacherous bastards!" Osman slapped himself in the face and splashed water from his canteen to dowse himself.

Once Ishmail could see that Osman was not seriously hurt, he burst out laughing. *The tobacco must be laced with gunpowder.* "Here, pour some enemy piss on your face to put out the fire! Keep those cigarettes, I know a few people I might want to give them to."

Osman was still touching his face gingerly and seemed to realise that the trap was intended to startle but not cause serious harm. He started laughing himself and threw the bottle up the beach.

Ishmail felt a weight lift from him and felt an urge to remove his boots and walk across the beach. The water would be icy, but it would feel like crossing the finish line at the end of a very long running race.

He didn't remove his boots or move towards the sea, but turned to Osman. "They have gone Brother."

He embraced his comrade, and enjoyed the warmth of his hold for a long moment. Smells of gunpowder smoke and singed hair drifted from Osman's beard as it scratched against Ishmail's ear.

"They have gone."

We won.

All the killing achieved something.

Dad's death was not a waste.

Fighting for a just cause is good. If God wants me to keep fighting and defend our Fatherland, then I will do it. I will go where I am needed. Rumours of a move to Irak after this campaign is over might be true.

If I survive the war, then maybe I will become an architect. Maybe I could find a sweetheart, marry and have children to call me Daddy.

If I die then I will die for God, defending my country, defending the right of my people to enjoy a life of peace.

Regardless, I have been part of a great victory here.

As God wills.

CHAPTER 97

Mustafa

Thursday, 20 December 1915, mid-morning

"I had realised that the enemy was about to withdraw."

Colonel Mustafa Kemal dragged his gaze from the cobbled Istanbul street and turned to his friend Salih Bozok.

"And so I had proposed an offensive. But they turned it down. This upset me. I was also very tired, so I came to Istanbul. If the enemy had withdrawn, as successfully as he has done now while I was there, I would have been even more upset."

Mustafa returned to staring out the window of the motor car as it growled along the narrow street. His eyes didn't focus on the wintery scene rolling past.

"Lucky that I'm here."

Details of the enemy's evacuation were limited, but it appeared as if they had simply disappeared in the night like a thief. Of course that was nonsense. *The logistics of moving a force of that number, with their equipment, would be a major operation to take place over many days, if not weeks. How could we not notice? It's embarrassing. The incompetence of others never ceases to amaze me. The enemy would not have escaped unscathed if I was there. I saved Istanbul despite their incompetence. Why can't others see that?*

Much needed rest, since leaving the battlefield ten days earlier, had cleared Mustafa's head and allowed him to time to think.

On being granted medical leave, he had wasted no time in arranging for transport to a hospital in Istanbul. In truth, he was more exhausted and frustrated than sick. *How could I command when I was not allowed to make important decisions? Anyway, it was obvious the enemy could not advance, and would be forced into submission by our strengthened artillery.*

Now there were more serious threats that required his attention than the Chanakkale battle front. The great unknown was whether the Germans or English would win the main conflict in Europe. Both outcomes seemed possible. The Russian threat remained immediate, but if the Germans could crush the Russians and translate success to the western front as well, they would likely leave the remnant of the Ottoman Empire alone for the Turks to restore order. If the greedy English triumphed in Europe, they would be ruthless. *We must be prepared for the worst outcome.*

So much remained uncertain, but one aspect was clear. The Turkish Government was in chaos and the Ottoman Empire was being led by fools. Even calling it an empire now stretched the definition. Other nations in Europe were able to act decisively with their modern systems of government, but the Ottomans remained living in the shadow of a bygone era.

The idea of a caliph as ruler and spiritual leader is antiquated and holds our nation back. An Islamic State is unworkable. The coup leaders have made a mockery of the idea by locking Sultan Abdulhamit under house arrest and installing his weak-minded brother as a puppet sultan. The church and state need to be formally separated so the nation can be run properly without this deceptive farce. A government that can claim to represent God is no longer accountable to its people. A government that is not accountable to its people is destined to become corrupted.

Mustafa had been at Beylerbeyi Palace that morning, where the deposed Sultan Abdulhamit was being held under guard. Before the news arrived, Mustafa was talking in hushed tones, with his childhood friend Salih, of the hypocrisy of the coup leaders. It was a like an infected wound needing treatment before its poison spread. The conversation was interrupted by excited cries announcing the enemy evacuation from the northern front at Channakale.

When it became clear that the messenger knew few details, Mustafa and Salih returned to Mustafa's motor car. Mustafa, in search of more information, told his driver to go directly to the Ministry of War.

Mustafa's breath frosted the motor car window. *I saved this city and no one knows. No one cares. We need strong leaders or our nation will be crushed. Leaders who care about our nation's future. These weak men care only for themselves and do not understand the threats. I must seek recognition and advancement to drag our nation into modern times. Otherwise it might allow itself to be destroyed.*

Mustafa pulled a copy of the December issue of the Ottoman War Magazine from his coat pocket. December was the first issue in which the magazine had mentioned him by name, and it was only a small caption to a terrible photograph, showing Mustafa looking exhausted, standing under a tree. Each previous month's issue talked of the heroic exploits of political leaders from the Committee of Union and Progress and generals at the Chanakkale battlefront. *They did nothing. I saved this city.*

A few weeks earlier, on 30 November, the 57th Regiment was issued with an imperial decree, and its banner was decorated in the presence of Enver, the Minister for War. The regiment was being honoured for valiantly defending the nation. Mustafa crushed the magazine in his fist at the thought. *My 57th Regiment. I led them forwards and committed them to stop the Enemy landing, while the German Field Marshall jumped at shadows fifty kilometres away in the Gulf of Saros. I stopped the enemy on the day he arrived and he never came forward another step because I held him back.*

They didn't even mention my name. I bet Enver made sure of that. He knows full well that I saved this city.

The more Mustafa thought about the circumstances, the less it seemed to matter what was happening at Chanakkale. The enemy was defeated there and Istanbul was safe, at least for now. That chapter was closed. Now Mustafa knew he had to focus on the political enemies within the Turkish government, and think of how a Turkish nation might rise from the ashes of this bloody war.

Mustafa leaned towards Salih's ear. The driver would not likely hear a normal conversation over the roar of the motor, but Mustafa wanted to take no chances any might hear his words that might be considered treasonous.

"The Committee of Union and Progress must be forced to behave like a real government. And we must free our armies from German control, and fools like von Sanders."

Salih grinned and whispered back. "Did you hear that the German Ambassador to the Ottoman Empire died recently?"

"Baron Hans von Wangenheim? Yes, I heard he died of a stroke."

"They say that a certain poison can kill a man with symptoms like a stroke."

"Do you know something more?"

"The German Ambassador was in good health. His unfortunate passing came as a shock to us all." Salih looked forward to the driver who appeared to be focused on the road ahead, then Salih whispered into Mustafa's ear so he could barely hear. "The bastard used us all to further Germany's interests in the war. Poison was too good for him, but he had to be removed cleanly. We need Turks to take control of Turkey's future."

The beginnings of a smile emerged on Mustafa's face.

I need to extend my sick leave and talk to more people. Somehow, I need to gain the recognition I deserve if I am to have any influence over the Turkish future.

Tiredness clawed at him like an old enemy. Months of fatigue took more than a few days of rest to wash away. But his active mind pushed though and started buzzing with ideas. Problems and solutions. So many problems.

There is much to do. Where to start?

The motor car drew to a stop outside the Ministry of War building in the old district of Istanbul.

"Come Salih, my old friend. Let's see what we can learn about this enemy evacuation. Then, we must go for raki. We will drink together and discuss the future of our nation."

CHAPTER 98

Jayjay

Friday, 24 December 1915

Jayjay limped on, through a backstreet of Balmain, Sydney. His stump ached where it sat in the hollow at the top of the wooden leg.

He had hoped to compose his thoughts for a difficult conversation during this walk, but his full concentration was required to avoid falling over. *Maybe I should have brought my crutches, or at least one of them, instead of this walking cane.*

The staff of the army hospital at Randwick had been kind, but all of the wooden legs were too short for someone of Jayjay's height. They took the longest one they had and nailed an extra block on the end. *Hopefully the thing won't fall apart on me.*

"It will seem difficult at first," The doctor said. "But with practice walking will feel more natural."

Not just difficult, it bloody hurts.

Jayjay shuffled along the pavement under the late morning sun, towards the big houses near the water. Beads of sweat formed on his forehead and his shirt stuck to his back.

He had walked this street a thousand times growing up, but it seemed somehow foreign now, almost hostile, as if the place felt he had no right to be there. That he ought not to have returned home alive.

He recognized the house he was seeking, but he had never been inside it before. A large frangipani tree sprawled across the front yard, covered in white and yellow flowers. Paving stones cut a sweeping path across the neatly trimmed lawn towards a wide verandah and double timber doorway.

He paused at the front gate for a moment, still not knowing what he would say, then limped to the front door and knocked.

A sudden urge to retreat was denied by footsteps approaching on the floorboards inside. The door opened slowly.

"Hello Jonathan, I heard you came home. Please come in. I was very sorry to hear about your brother and about your leg. You might like to sit down. Can I offer you a drink?"

Alfred McKenzie senior offered Jayjay his hand with a warm smile.

"Yes, thank you Mr McKenzie." Jayjay shook the hand.

"Was that yes to sitting down, or yes to the drink? How about both? Whiskey? I believe it's close enough to noon."

"Yes sir, thank you." Jayjay followed his host along a wide corridor and into a room with large windows overlooking the Parramatta River.

Mr McKenzie waved towards a deep lounge chair, but Jayjay's attention was drawn to the mantel over the fire place and he hobbled in that direction.

A photograph of Alfred junior held the centre place over the hearth in a what looked to be a shrine to the son. A large oval photograph, almost true to life size and set in an ornate frame hung on the wall, his face as handsome as ever. *I smashed that nose, out of pure spite, but I liked him better when it was crooked. That's when we became mates. I hated him when his nose was straight, but that's how his parents remember him. I won't mention the nose.*

Below the photograph of Alfred, a copy of the *Sydney Morning Herald* from 8 May 1915 rested on the mantel piece, folded open at page 13. Everyone seemed to have kept a copy of this edition with the first account of the landing at Gallipoli by the English war correspondent, Ellis Ashmead-Bartlett.

"AUSTRALASIANS – GLORIOUS ENTRY INTO WAR – HISTORIC CHARGE – BRILLIANT FEAT AT GABA TEPE … MR. ASHMEAD BARTLETT'S STORY …"

Jayjay had read the article previously and didn't want to read it again. It portrayed a more glamorous scene than any he remembered. He had witnessed many wounded men moaning and screaming, but never cheering as the article claimed.

Some bank notes overprinted with Turkish script and spent rifle shells rested on either side of the photograph and two smaller plain frames book-ended the display. One frame held a telegram from the war office, and the other a note that Jayjay recognised, hand written in pencil.

He picked up the frame and read the messy print that he had written himself by moonlight, eight months earlier.

Dear Mrs and Mr McKenzie,
I am very sorry to be writing this letter to you, but I thought you would want to know that your son Alfred is dead.

He was shot by a terkish bullet next to me on the second night after we landed here at galipoly, a place in terky. You might have heard by now that we are fighting here instead of france because terky joined in with the germans.

After landing our platoons got all mixed up and I ended up with Alfred and some others from 2 Btn, even though I am in 1 Btn. We advanced some way and dug in. Alfred fought well and bravely. He was shot in the hart and died quickly so he did not suffer. It was only the toss of a coin that he was shot instead of me. I feel terrible about it and wish he lived on instead.

Yours sincerely,
Private Jonathan Jones
29 April 1915

Jayjay's ears burned with embarrassment. "I see you got my letter."

"Thank you for taking the trouble to write to us Jonathan. It must have been a very difficult time."

"My writing isn't very good, and I only had moonlight to do it. It was a hard night. I thought Ron and Larry were dead too, but they found me next morning." Jayjay shook his head. "You might have also heard that we abandoned Gallipoli and skived off in the night. Alfred, Ron, so many dead – all left behind."

Jayjay knew that everyone in Sydney would have heard the news by now. He didn't believe it himself when he first read the late war news announcement three days ago, way back on page 9 of the *Sydney Morning Herald*. *'Troops at Suvla and Anzac, together with guns and stores, have been transferred to another sphere of operations.'* No further explanation to give it credibility. It seemed ridiculous. *No way we could have got all those men and guns and equipment out without Abdul noticing.* The late news announcement was right next to a transcript of a scathing speech by General M'Cay, branding men who refused to enlist as cowards, not worthy of fathering the next generation of Australians. *It doesn't make sense to be pushing for more reinforcements if we were going to walk away from the fight.*

The morning after hearing the news, Jayjay had risen soon after dawn and gone in search of more details. He bought the early edition of the *Sydney Morning Herald* and stood in the street while he flicked past the sports pages and an advertisement for a summer retreat land release in Cronulla.

The Prime Minister's statement confirmed the fact, and left Jayjay numb.

'I feel that I speak for the people of Australia,' the Prime Minister's statement read, *'when I say that the news that the evacuation of Anzac and Suvla Bay has been carried out with an insignificant loss of life has been received in a spirit of devout gladness chastened with a keen regret that the withdrawal had been found imperative.'*

"The politicians make these decisions," Mr McKenzie said. "The rest of us will likely never know the full truth of the reasons."

"I can't make sense of it. Why did we even go there? We all thought we were fighting for something important. The newspaper called it 'the grandest failure in history.'"

"Can you tell me, was Alfred's body buried?"

Jayjay nodded. "Near the beach at Anzac, and Ron in Shrapnel Gully. I reckon it helped us to keep going, knowing that they were there. We defended that ground like it was part of Australia."

"Was it you who sent his things as well?"

"I took his wallet from his body and gave it to his sergeant. I guess you got that as I can't think how else you might have got that Turkish money. They paid us in those useless notes before we landed. Never got anywhere we could spend them. I dunno what happened to mine. Probably burned them when we were bored."

Mr McKenzie grinned, but his eyes brimmed with sadness. "Yes, we received Alfred's wallet."

"There was a watch too," Jayjay hesitated. "A gold pocket watch, but it might have got lost, or someone might have pilfered it. A lot of that sort of thing went on and it was hard for the sergeants. They had a lot of men to organise, there was a lot of things happening, a lot of men getting killed and wounded. Those first few days were bloody chaos sir, if you want to know the truth of it."

Mr McKenzie nodded slowly and picked up a small box from behind the photograph of Alfred junior.

"I wind this every morning." He withdrew a gold watch and opened the case to reveal the white clock face. "Still keeps good time. Swiss made. No one makes clocks like the Swiss. They just keep on ticking. I knew it would outlast my beating heart and I always planned to give it to Alfred. I suppose I thought that if it did outlast him too, he might be able to leave it to a son of his own."

Alfred senior's voice cracked and he paused a moment before continuing. "We have no other children. Alfred and Charlotte never reached the alter so there will be no grandsons."

"I am sorry for your loss sir, and for Charlotte's." Jayjay was surprised he managed to sound sincere to the end of the statement.

Alfred senior shook his head. "Charlotte's not a widow, even though sometimes she carries on like one. She's young and pretty, she'll find someone else in her own time. Sometimes I wonder if she hasn't already moved on, I've heard she's been getting friendly with another fellow. Mrs McKenzie is the one I worry for. She's still melancholy, and I'm not sure if she'll ever return to her old self. It's a hard thing for a mother to lose her child, no matter his age. It's like a part of her died with him."

Jayjay's throat tightened. He felt embarrassed for all the bad feeling he held towards Alfred over the years, but a deeper feeling of anger welled up from within and smothered the embarrassment. *Charlotte has been as disloyal to Alfred as she was to me. Mr McKenzie doesn't know about my history with Charlotte and I will keep it that way. I wonder who her new fellow is. Actually, I don't care.*

"I am very sorry Sir."

"No Jonathan, I'm glad you were there with him at the end. You oughtn't blame yourself. We are very grateful for all you did."

I'm not sure you'd be so grateful if you knew what I did to his face. "Yes sir, thank you sir."

"I want you to have this."

Alfred senior held out the gold watch and before Jayjay knew what was happening, he was holding it in his own hands.

"I am not sure what to say Sir. It's very valuable. It was Alfred's. Don't you want to keep it here with his things?"

"We have both lost things far more precious that cannot be replaced Jonathan. Hard lessons about what is truly valuable. Keep the watch as a small gesture of my thanks."

"Thank you Sir."

"No, thank you Jonathan. Now, how about that drink?"

Jayjay was much more comfortable to receive the glass than the gold time piece, and welcomed the familiar warmth when the distilled spirit drained down his throat. It was Scotch whisky, and carried a more smoky flavour than the Irish whiskey he had developed a taste for, but not so different that it bothered him.

"To the memory of those who didn't come home." Alfred senior raised his glass.

Jayjay nodded and raised his glass, "To their memory," and then drained it. Mr McKenzie had only taken a sip.

"How is your mother?"

Jayjay was not sure how to answer. "She's sombre too, like you said about Mrs McKenzie. She doesn't smile the same way she did before the war started. I had better be going. It's a bit of a slow walk on one leg. Thanks for the drink."

"Yes, of course. Let me take the glass. Will I see you at church tomorrow?"

"Yes sir, although I don't feel much like celebrating."

"No, I understand. Merry Christmas Jonathan."

"Merry Christmas Sir."

CHAPTER 99

Larry

Sunday, 13 February 1916

He walked alone in the cool of the afternoon, along the Egyptian general's trench. A peaceful place now, since the British Lord Wolseley and his army of 17,000 men had apparently crushed the Egyptian rebellion at this place in 1882.

Larry picked up an old bullet casing from the trench floor. It looked much the same as a modern one.

I never heard of this place, or Lord Wolseley, or his bloody famous victory thirty-something years ago. There are no grave markings for the dead from either side. What memory is left of all the poor bastards who fought and died here for something they thought was important? Thirty more years and Gallipoli will be the same. Abandoned bloody trenches in the middle of bloody nowhere, where thousands of nameless lunatics, miles from home, faced off and killed each other. If we won, Turkey might have become part the British Empire like Egypt, but we lost the fight and skulked off in the night. Why would anyone want to remember that? Turkey has the famous victory this time, and even that will be forgotten by the next generation of Turks. What a waste of men's lives.

He found a quiet place to sit against the trunk of a date palm with the sun peering over his shoulder and pulled Jayjay's letter from his pocket. He had already read it several times, but began to read it once more before setting about his next task that he had put off for way too long.

25.12.1915

Dear Larry,

Merry Christmas! It is a hot Christmas Day at home and I thought I might write you a bit of a letter. From what I read in the paper I guess you are in Egypt now after slipping away, right out from under Adbul's nose. We didn't get many details, but we are being told you all got away without any losses. I don't know what the real truth of it is, but I bet Abdul got the shock of his life when he woke up next morning and found you had all done the get go.

I went and visited Mr McKenzie yesterday, told him I was sorry about Alfred, but didn't tell him about what I did to his nose though! Everyone is a bit sad here, not much of a Christmas this year.

Your mum and dad and sister seem well. They were at church this morning and I said hello. I didn't say much more as I don't know what to say really.

I got a new wooden leg from the army hospital at Randwick, but I'm still getting used to it. It's a bugger to walk with but I can get about with a cane rather than crutches and they told me it will get easier.

I hope you are going well, and getting up to a little bit of mischief at the Wozza, but not too much. Never let an Aussie get outsmarted by a Gyppo! You might even get to France after all if you don't have to stay there and guard the canal.

I don't even know if this will get to you and I am not much of a writer, so I won't write pages, but I hope it does. Try not to get yourself shot or killed.

Your mate,

J.J.

Larry carefully folded the letter, slipped it back into its envelope and returned it to his pocket. From another pocket he pulled more paper and a pencil. This paper was blank.

He rested the paper against his knee and started to write:

13.2.1916

Dear Jay,

Thanks for your letter dated Christmas Day 1915. I received it in record time, a few days back, so it only took less than seven weeks to get here. Probably because the army wasn't involved too much, otherwise it might have taken 6 months or never got here at all.

Here is a place called Tel-el-Kebir. It is in Egypt, so you picked that one like a nose, but let me go back a bit first...

We got orders about the evacuation of Gallipoli only a few days before it was time to get out, but the brass must have been planning it for weeks as they had us doing these silent stunts where we would go for days without firing a shot. Got all the Joe Bourkes used to us being quiet, even though we all thought it was a mad stupid idea at the time. One night, a group of them snuck right up to our trench and damn near blew me up with a cricket ball bomb while I was taking a nap. Anyway, we sent them on their way. We were allowed to shoot them if they got too close.

Crazy thing is that it worked. We cleared out the whole of Anzac in two nights and the Joe Bourkes didn't know about it until after we were gone. I felt pretty bad walking past Ron's grave for the last time I can tell you, and all the others, but I checked on it the day before we left and made sure it was left neat and tidy. I don't imagine you had a last chance to visit it and say goodbye before you left so I did that for both of us. Joe Bourke always fought fair, so hopefully he will respect the graves.

After we were away, mines and ship guns blew the shit out of the place. Didn't want to leave anything worth anything behind I guess. We were taken to Mudros Harbour and got off for three days of rest. Do you remember the first time we were there, I thought we were steaming through the Dardanelles and worried we'd missed the fight. Shows how ignorant and stupid I was. We never even saw the Dardanelles.

Then we were loaded back on a ship bound for Alexandria with nothing but hard biscuits and bully beef for Christmas dinner. Still none of us minded too much as we got off Gallipoli alive and that was more than we expected. At Alexandria they threw us straight on a train and sent us here to Tel-el-Kebir, a place on the train line to the Suez Canal, but it's just few a small gravelly hills in the middle of the dessert (you might like the gravel!). They told us we are to be close by the canal in case it needs to be defended, but I think they just don't want us to cause trouble and go crazy at the Wozza again like a pack of mad rabid dingoes.

So we got here and of course there were no tents, so we bivouacked four nights until the tents arrived in time for new years eve, and everyone was still so tired we mostly slept through. We are just happy to have a bath every day and wear new clothes. Our old clothes were sent straight to the incinerator, bugs and all, but the cunning Gyppos managed to retrieve a heap of them. The joke will be on them when they all get lice!

I have some leave this afternoon and tomorrow and I will go on the train into Cairo tomorrow. I will post this to you by regular Royal Mail so it doesn't have to get past the army censor. I have heard regular mail is not being checked inside the empire.

You would never guess what happened today!

Larry paused and stared across the desolate battleground of Tel-el-Kebir. Some enthusiasts for military history had got all excited when they learned that they would be visiting the place, but as far as Larry was concerned, it was as uninteresting as the rest of the desert, just more depressing.

He tried to imagine Gallipoli abandoned like this after the place had been so crowded and buzzing with activity since the first day. *It's as if the place being attacked and defended is not the important thing at all. It's just a bit of ground like any other, a stage for a contest. It's the fight that needs somewhere to take place. Once it's done, there's a winner and a loser and that means something to some government somewhere. It wasn't really a fight over this shit heap in the middle of nowhere and it wasn't a fight for the ridges of Gallipoli. Just a place for us to come together and try to break each other.*

Larry shook his head slowly and sighed. *I better finish this letter so I can post it tomorrow.* He lowered his gaze and his pencil continued to scratch against the paper.

The orange glow of a desert sunset was starting to fade when he finished writing and rose to return to camp.

CHAPTER 100

Jayjay

Sunday, 26 March 1916

The autumn morning air was mild, but the grip of Jayjay's walking cane was slippery with sweat.

Mum and Dad dawdled in silence on either side. He started to walk faster. He had wanted to leave home early and walk on his own, at his own pace and keeping his own company, but Mum and Dad insisted on walking with him. It would not do for a family to arrive at church separately, that might create the wrong impression.

The stump of his right leg ached in the socket of the squeaky wooden leg. The replacement limb was typical army – functional but not comfortable. At least the walk was nearly over.

Drinking Guinness and Irish whiskey with Cooper the night before hadn't helped. Jayjay could barely remember finding his way home in the black of night with no moon to help. The memory of struggling to the outhouse to vomit and waking this morning with the taste of sick still in his mouth was clearer. A duck's breakfast helped a little, but only a little.

The trio arrived at Saint Thomas' Church of England, Rozelle at a quarter to nine. Dad stopped to talk to Larry's father Jack Gillespie and Mum made a beeline for a brood of women standing in the shade of a gum tree.

Jayjay limped on, into the cool of the church and took his usual pew in the back row. He sat at an angle to fit the length of his rigid leg into the narrow space between his pew and the next.

Mrs McKenzie entered and glanced at Jayjay. She nodded once, slowly. Her smile was both genuine and sad. Alfred McKenzie senior entered close behind his wife and strode directly to where Jayjay sat.

"Good morning to you Jonathan. How's the leg feeling today?" Mr McKenzie's handshake was firm.

"Aches a bit after a walk, but not too bad."

Mr McKenzie looked down at the straight leg and nodded. "You take care of yourself son."

"Yes Sir, thank you."

Mr and Mrs McKenzie made their way down the aisle to their usual place in the front pew.

It had been a difficult thing to face the McKenzies for the first time. Jayjay never mentioned to them that the idea of killing their son to eliminate competition for Charlotte's affections crept into his head on that dark night. Neither did he trouble them with the details of how he intentionally smashed Alfred's nose with his rifle butt on a training exercise in Egypt, leaving the nose with a new shape that would never be the same as the one they knew. Not that it mattered now, the crooked nose was buried with the rest of Alfred Junior's body on the other side of the world.

Jayjay looked up and found his eyes locked with Charlotte's for a brief moment. He couldn't have looked away quicker if he'd been poked in the eye with a stick, but he still felt the poison of her gaze.

Charlotte kept walking and found a pew with her family around halfway to the front, and on the opposite side to the McKenzies. *At least she mostly ignores me now.*

The odd hateful glance still hurt, but the pain was fading with time, like it had in his leg. *Dad was right. Women need someone to blame.*

Jayjay pulled out two folded sheets of paper from his pocket and checked the gold pocket watch that he carried out of the house once each week. *No time to read the letter again now before the church service starts. Later.* He returned the sheets of paper to his pocket without unfolding them and felt eyes on him again. This time it was Grace, Larry's twin sister. She sat apart from her parents. *Why can't I just sit at the back and be ignored in peace?*

The pipe organ announced the beginning of the service with the introduction to a hymn Jayjay hadn't heard since his return. The congregation stood as one, except Jayjay. Jayjay had a sudden vision of The Sphinx above North Beach at Gallipoli, and then of himself lying in the dark, terrified and praying to God to hide him from an unseen enemy.

He stood slowly and flicked through his Hymn Book, but he knew the opening words without having to read them. The rest returned to his mind as if never forgotten…

Rock of Ages, cleft for me,
Let me hide myself in Thee;
Let the water and the blood,
From Thy wounded side which flowed,
Be of sin the double cure,
Save from wrath and make me pure.

Not the labour of my hands
Can fulfill Thy law's demands;
Could my zeal no respite know,
Could my tears forever flow,
All for sin could not atone;
Thou must save, and Thou alone.

Nothing in my hand I bring,
Simply to Thy cross I cling;
Naked, come to Thee for dress;
Helpless, look to Thee for grace;
Foul, I to the fountain fly;
Wash me, Saviour, or I die.

While I draw this fleeting breath,
When my eyes shall close in death,
When I rise to worlds unknown,
And behold Thee on Thy throne,
Rock of Ages, cleft for me,
Let me hide myself in Thee.

Guilt burned within him, but he could not say why. Some words he sang, and some he mouthed without sound. He felt a desperate need to hide and his prayer to the Rock of Ages remained unchanged, although the enemy he sought refuge from had become harder to define than the Turks at Gallipoli.

The rest of the church service washed over Jayjay while he reviewed memories and song words in his mind. Several times he shifted his weight, seeking a way to sit on the wooden pew that did not cause his leg to ache.

When the service was complete, the minister strode to the main entrance and positioned himself in the shade of the doorway. Members of the congregation filed out and received his blessing as they exited.

Jayjay twisted and lifted his foot onto the vacated pew next to him. *Finally a comfortable position.* He sat and watched the congregation drain out, like life blood from a man stabbed in the neck. A building full of human life, quickly transformed into an empty shell.

He stared at the organ. Large pipes lined up in a neat formation like barrels of eighteen pounder artillery guns. *Men can build amazing things. Machines to make music and machines to blow other men into pieces. The wooden housing around the organ looks weak. It needs some steel armour, or a loop hole. Up against an eighteen pounder it'd be silenced pretty quick. Just like the gunner I left dead on the beach, and all his gunner mates. That organ wouldn't last a day at Russell's Top.*

"Good morning to you Jonathan." It was the minister.

"Good morning to you Reverend Davies." Jayjay swung his leg off the pew. "Sometimes the leg gets a bit stiff."

"Call me James please," the minister nodded and offered the cup he held. "Would you like some tea? Milk and one sugar, I hope it's the way you like it."

"Drinking anything while I'm not crouching in a funk hole with someone trying to blow me to kingdom come is the way I like it."

"To everything there is a season. A time of war and a time of peace. You have served your king and country in war and I know you have seen some terrible things Jonathan. Our country remains at war, but now, for you it is time for peace."

This man knows nothing! Maybe drinking this tea here is not the way I like it. How can I end this conversation?

"You don't know what I've seen or what I've done," Jayjay said. "It sounds great to say I served my king and country. It doesn't sound so good to say I broke all of the Ten Commandments while I was at it."

"Jonathan –"

"Every one of them! I cursed God and my parents. I whored and murdered. The first one I killed was barely old enough to shave, unarmed and pleading for mercy. I was scared for my life and didn't know what else to do, so I stabbed him to death – on a Sunday. I coveted his land and stole his life. I called him a heathen, but he was just a boy trying to defend his homeland from attackers. And the one who did this to my leg, at least I think it was him, I stuck a knife in his neck and watched life fade from his eyes. Do you honestly think I can sit here and drink tea and say it's time for peace now? Or ever?"

"There is a time to kill and a time to heal. I think you still have much healing to do."

"That's just words," Jayjay shook his head. "Words are nothing. I know what I've seen and done. I've climbed the pyramids of Egypt where Moses battled with Pharaoh. I sailed by the island of Patmos where Saint John received the Revelation, on my way to war. I've seen Armageddon. I've seen the four horsemen of the Apocalypse and that red one, he's a pure bastard."

Jayjay paused to see if the minister would take offence at his language, but there was no reaction. Instead, James stood and stared, as if watching, for the first time, a cicada coming out of its shell. *That's the first time I've sworn aloud inside a church.*

"The heathen were just men like us," Jayjay continued, "fighting for what they thought was right. The reaper came for us and them the same. His sickle showed us no favour."

"If they were just words of men," the minister replied, "they would be lost to history centuries ago. 'The word of God is quick, and powerful, and sharper than any two-edged sword, piercing even to the dividing asunder of soul and spirit, and of the joints and marrow, and is a discerner of the thoughts and intents of the heart.'"

Jayjay's mind filled with the memory of the moment he drove his bayonet between the ribs of the Turkish boy soldier. He focused on the woodgrain pattern of a floorboard as if this might make the image disappear, but pleading-boy-eyes only became clearer.

"The world has been ever thus," James continued." Saint Paul wrote that Jesus Christ gave himself for us, that he might deliver us from the present evil world. He wrote that in a letter to the churches in Galatia, not far from your battleground, nearly two thousand years ago."

"I can't be delivered from the evil world if I'm the worst part of it."

"They that are whole need not a physician; but they that are sick. Jesus came not to call the righteous, but sinners to repentance."

"Why would God want to have anything more to do with me?"

"Jonathan, you are closer to knowing God's true love than half the congregation here today. You stood at the precipice and gazed into the abyss. You almost fell in yourself. You know all men need to be ready to meet their maker when He calls their name. You have a broken spirit and a heavy heart, but only when you know you need God's mercy can you truly receive it. 'Blessed are the poor in spirit, for theirs is the kingdom of heaven.'"

Jayjay remembered the rage he felt after Ron's death, and his blood lust when the Turks charged. He had wanted to kill as many as he could. He hated God for allowing it all and shook his head.

"No man can be right with God by works of the law," James continued as if reading Jayjay's thoughts. "Not you, not I, not anyone. Do not frustrate the grace of God, for if righteousness come by the law, then Christ is dead in vain."

Jayjay stared at the floor. *I shouldn't have quoted scripture to a minister without expecting more to be thrown back at me.*

James stood and rested his hand on Jayjay's shoulder. The warmth was comforting despite the heat. Without speaking further he walked out and left Jayjay alone in the church.

Jayjay sat a while longer, then pulled two folded sheets of paper from his pocket. Sunlight streamed in through the tall windows, separated into its spectrum of colours by the stained glass. *Maybe if I re-read Larry's letter, I can forget that the conversation happened.*

He found the paragraph he was up to part way through the letter and continued to read.

I have some leave this afternoon and tomorrow and I will go on the train into Cairo tomorrow. I will post this to you by regular Royal Mail so it doesn't have to get past the army censor. I have heard regular mail is not being checked inside the empire.

You would never guess what happened today! They split our old 1st Battalion in two, can you believe it? We've had shiploads of reinforcements and some of the lads who have been having a holiday in hospital came back to join us. A lot of the old hands were pretty upset about the change as you can imagine, but the brass wanted to spread us across the two battalions and I didn't mind too much. Now I'm part of the 53rd Battalion, same black and green colours on our patches, but beside each other instead of one over the other. I figure now I am more than half way to ending up in the 100th Battalion like we talked about when we went for our holiday to Mudros last summer, remember that? At least I could keep the old section together, Simmo, Darky and Sunny from your time, and four more. All good blokes.

A few weeks before we evacuated Gallipoli we had some heavy rain and even some snow. It was terrible just like you imagined, and so cold, like sitting in a giant pot of Gallipoli soup left outside for three nights in the middle of winter. It was the only time I have seen snow. Have you seen snow? I don't think you have.

There are rumours we might be going to France, but you know what the rumours are like, a hundred furphies for each grain of truth. Still, maybe I'll get there after all, meet my own Josephine, a real French girl!

Have you caught up with Charlotte, or shouldn't I ask? You mentioned the McKenzies in your letter, but not her.

I hope you get better at walking with your cane like an old man!

Say hello to everyone at home and if you see my sister Gracey, give her a hug from me.

Your mate, Larry

"Did Reverend Davies give you fire and brimstone Hoppy?" Jayjay's head jerked towards Grace's voice. That girl always seemed to have her hands on her pert hips. The long sandy hair and impish face was quite attractive in an angry kind of way.

"No, not really. He just told me a whole lot of things that are true, but I didn't want to hear them right now." Jayjay folded the paper slowly and returned it to his chest pocket.

"What are you reading? Is it a love letter from your girlfriend?"

"You're half right, it's a letter from a friend."

"Not a girl?"

"No, it's from your brother."

Grace's eyes narrowed. The cheeky smirk disappeared and she stepped forward. "When did it come?"

"Two days ago."

"Can I read it?"

"No."

"Why not?"

"He wrote it to me."

"Let me read it."

"There's things that are personal. Mate talk."

"Blazes Jon, he's my twin and I haven't seen him for over a year. He wrote me too, but –." Grace leaned forward, braced herself against the pew and hung her head. A tear dropped and spattered on the pew next to Jayjay's leg.

Grace's face no longer looked like that of a defiant child. Her pain tormented him worse than the minister's words.

She stood silent.

He waited.

Another tear fell.

"Here," Jayjay pulled the letter slowly from his pocket. "Read it, but you have to promise to give it right back. I only just got it and I want to read it again and keep it. I was meaning to let you know he says hello."

Grace nodded, took the letter and read it quicker than Jayjay thought would have been possible.

"Who's Josephine?" She wiped her eyes.

"What?"

"Who's Josephine?"

"I don't know, maybe he hopes to meet a girl called Josephine if he goes to France. We go for months at a time without seeing any girls. You can't imagine –."

"No, I understand that, but the way he says it, it's like there was another one. Did you have a girl called Josephine?"

"Is this the bloody Spanish Inquisition? You wanted to read Larry's letter and you read it, now give it back."

"So, you did then?"

"Give it back, you promised!" *Why did I let her read it?*

"Was she a prostitute?"

"Larry didn't say that!"

"I don't care if she was."

Jayjay hesitated and looked down at the droplets from her tears. For a long moment he pondered what, if anything, he might say next.

"I did a lot of stupid things, a lot of things that I'm not proud of. Plenty worse than that."

"I don't care that you know about me either."

"Know what?"

“That I fancied you. I’m sure he must have told you.”

“No, he didn’t.”

“He didn’t ask you to say hello to me, he asked you to give me a hug. When were you going to do that?”

“I wasn’t sure that you’d want me to.”

“Did you think to ask?”

“Well, would you?”

“Not anymore,” she said quietly, then handed back the letter, turned and walked away.

CHAPTER 101

Dacre

Friday, 7 April 1916

He imagined himself on the open water, cruising along the surface in a submarine, batteries charged and ready to dive at his command. Never did Dacre feel more at home, nor more free, than when he was as sea.

But now, his feet ached and his belly growled with hunger. He pushed himself on, over the rocky ground. He could not let the other two men down. His two companions were Cochrane, commander of British submarine *E7* and Price, an officer from British submarine *E15. They must be struggling as much as I am.*

On evacuation of the Gallipoli Peninsula, the British and allied forces had taken away with them any hope of rescue for the prisoners-of-war at Afyonkarahisar. Hope was something each man owned for himself and Dacre refused to allow his hope to be taken away by someone else, but the day the commandant announced the Turkish victory, it was as though the collective spirit of the men was crushed.

When discussing the possibility of escape, most had openly declared it impossible and some were of the view that it was irresponsible to try, as those left behind could expect to be made to suffer for the crimes of the escapees.

Dacre disagreed and felt he had a duty to make the attempt. *Nothing is impossible until it has been given a good go and proven to be so.*

One could not achieve anything as a submarine commander without a can-do attitude. There are always risks and reasons why a scheme might fail.

After his stint in solitary confinement in a Constantinople prison, where his only conversation was with Archibald the rat, Dacre had been sent back to the prisoner of war camp at Afyonkarahisar in central Turkey. Conditions were harsh, but while the Gallipoli campaign continued, hope that the Turks might capitulate and release their prisoners outweighed the risks of attempting escape.

However, soon after hearing the news of the Gallipoli evacuation, Dacre decided to attempt escape. Officers had been separated from the rest of the men, and the other officers from his beloved submarine *AE2* were not in a physical or mental state to make the attempt. Instead, Dacre schemed with the two men of submarines *E7* and *E15* that the three would make a run for it together.

Lieutenant Clarence Palmer seemed of sound mind. He might have been a handy companion if we invited him along. His control of the Turkish language would have been helpful. But the way he described his interrogation by the Turks, and his claim that he fed them misinformation about the troop landings. It was hard to know whether he could be trusted. Anyway, just the three of us are here now.

The plan was simple: make for the coast, steal a boat and sail it to a Greek Island. By Dacre's estimate the distance was one hundred and thirty miles, as the crow flies, to the nearest point on the coast.

They had scrambled out a window with what supplies they could carry and walked due south, mostly by night to reduce the risk of discovery, and rested by day when the cold was not so severe.

This was the fifteenth day since their escape.

The food was nearly gone, enough remained for one more lean day, and Dacre's boots barely held together. His legs protested at each step, but he forced them on, one step at a time, careful not to stumble up the rocky slope.

He crested the hill and the view that awaited him stopped him like a wall. His mouth moved but no words came, then he started to smile.

Below him the hill sloped down into a valley, but beyond the next range lay the great blue spread of the Mediterranean Sea. Bright under the spring sun, the colour of the water was more beautiful than that of any jewel. Tiny fishing boats with white sails dotted the surface near a river mouth. *How happy must those fellows be? Sailing and fishing and free.*

Turks the lot of them.

Not an Englishman in sight. The English have forgotten us. The Admiral was happy for my men and I to take the risks. The prize was worth it.

'If you succeed,' the Admiral said, 'there is no calculating the result it will cause, and it may well be that you will have done more to finish the war than any other act accomplished.'

He dominated the whole Mediterranean with a fleet of warships – from here to Egypt over that blue horizon. Where is he now?

'Try again tomorrow.' The Admiral said. 'If you succeed in getting through, there is nothing we will not do for you.'

But he has forgotten about us. Everyone has forgotten about us. They just up and left with no thought for those they left behind.

He promised me much but delivered nothing, the English submarine commanders got their Victoria Crosses, but at this moment I would be happy with a small sailing boat and a crust of stale bread.

Dacre sat on the hillside and forced negative thoughts from his mind. His two travelling companions were close behind.

"Well, look at that!" Price exclaimed. "The Mediterranean! Can't be more than ten miles.

"We might reach it this very night," Cochrane said. "The hills are growing lower towards the coast."

Three weary submariners sat and stared at the sea for a long while.

After nearly a year of captivity, Dacre could feel it replenish his soul and strengthen his body.

He looked about the valley below, bathed in early afternoon sunshine. The country was wild and deserted.

"When we're ready lads," Dacre broke the spell. "I suggest we push down into that valley. There doesn't look to be anybody around these parts.

With greater enthusiasm than any of the trio had shown for the past few days, they began the scramble down. After an easy start, the ground dropped away in a precipitous slide of loose shale. The descent became dangerous, but there was no way around without climbing back up an unacceptable distance, so they struggled down throughout the afternoon.

Exhausted and bleeding, the three reached the bottom of the valley and stopped by a stream where they agreed they must rest for the night.

The night was cold, the ground hard and stony.

Next morning, after broken sleep, Dacre felt unrested and without the return of the strength he hoped for. The one remaining range of hills seemed like an impassable barrier.

Price and Cochrane stared up at the range ahead as if sharing Dacre's thoughts.

"Maybe we could find a way around," Price mused. "Rather than climb over?"

They reached unanimous agreement on this plan, but after another day and night of trying to find a way though or around, the men remained in the clutches of the valley. Their boots were in ribbons, food finished and strength ebbing.

Dacre felt panic clawing at him from his stomach. The need for food would soon drive them into acts of desperation.

Onwards along the valley floor they continued.

Cochrane clutched at his belly, then groaned and took a squat where he was.

"You two keep going," Cochrane said. "I'll catch up."

Dacre and Price slowed the pace, and paused a hundred yards ahead.

"We need to find food," Price said.

Dacre nodded.

In the distance, a square shape caught his eye.

"There's a hut." Dacre was not sure if it was good or bad.

"There might be food."

"There might be trouble."

"No worse than starving to death out here in the middle of God-only-knows-where."

Cochrane caught up, looking pale.

"There's a hut," Dacre said again.

"What are we going to do?" Cochrane had the look of a man who didn't trust himself to make an important decision.

"We had better stop in to see if we can find or beg some food." Dacre looked at Price who nodded without hesitation. "If we come across someone who speaks French, let's tell them we are German surveyors. A simple villager will not know the difference between Europeans."

Closer to the hut, a goat perched on a rock and watched them pass, then sauntered towards a herd of around twenty scrawny goats that all watched the approach of the oncoming strangers.

"Guten Tag?" Dacre called into the doorway of the hut. "Bonjour Monsieur? Hello?"

"Bu kim? Qu'est-ce?"

At least some of that was French. So we are Germans who speak some broken French. That will do.

A short man appeared in the doorway. His weather-beaten face peered out from under a tangled mop of grey hair. Though not young, the goatherd stood upright and looked like a man who could hold his own if he needed to. *Best if this does not come to violence.*

Dacre continued in broken French with the story of the three being German surveyors looking to buy food.

They actually had no money, since having been held up, threatened with death and robbed several days earlier, but that was another problem yet to be overcome.

However, at the mention of being German, the goatherd's eyes narrowed and he spat on the ground in the doorway to his own hut which struck Dacre as quite a silly thing to do, but also gave clear signal that the old man hated Germans.

Price continued to argue in shabby French, but the negotiation was going nowhere.

If he hates Germans, he might sympathize with the honest truth. He might turn us in, but what other choice do we have?

Dacre raised his hand and put a new plan of desperation to his comrades in English. Both nodded.

"We are not Germans," Dacre spoke slowly in French. "We hate the Germans as much as you do. We are escaped British officers. We are dying of starvation and if you do not give us food, we are likely to die at your door."

"Ingiliz!" The goatherd grinned in the first sign warmth he had shown them, and revealed a mouthful of crooked yellow teeth with a notable gap towards one side.

The goatherd disappeared inside and returned moments later with a loaf of bread and jug of white liquid that looked like milk. He motioned for the three escapees to sit down on the ground against the side of his hut, then handed the bread to Price and the jug to Dacre.

"Merci! Merci!" The three responded in unison and obeyed without hesitation.

Dacre tasted the liquid, straight from the jug. Rather than plain milk, it tasted like a mixture of runny yoghurt and sour milk. After the initial surprise, he decided that it was quite delicious. Price tore the bread into three pieces and handed them around. Dacre passed the jug on to Cochrane.

After the three escapees had eaten what Dacre considered the best meal they had had for a week, Dacre felt strength and hope returning to his body again. The goatherd motioned for them to follow and led them further down the valley. He fired a few clipped words at the goats and they followed him immediately. A few hundred yards on, another hut lay nestled in a hollow. The goatherd motioned for the three men to go inside, and when they did so the old man darted off. Dacre stuck his head out the doorway and saw him disappear over a rise.

"Maybe he has gone to turn us in?" Cochrane said, his face back to its usual colour.

"He seemed kindly enough," Dacre said, but he could hear the uncertainty in his own voice, "at least, once he realised we aren't Germans."

"Why would he have given us all that good food and drink if he only meant to hand us over?"

"We could run."

"We wouldn't get far with no shoes."

"Night is nearly upon us. We all need to rest."

In the end they agreed to wait in the shelter where the old goatherd had left them, rather than exert more energy that they didn't have.

Later, as darkness was falling, footsteps outside approached and the three escapees all scrambled to their feet. There was more than one person coming towards the door.

The goatherd strode in, holding a hunting knife with a blood-stained six-inch blade in his bony hand.

Dacre felt the release of adrenalin and his heart quickened.

He knew he didn't have the strength to put up much of a fight. He stood frozen as a statue, neither did the other two move. *So here it ends, butchered by a village goatherd.*

Another man stood behind and blocked the doorway, much taller and broader, with some form of bundle draped over his shoulders. A third stood outside.

The old goatherd muttered something that Dacre didn't understand and pointed towards a small table, the only item of furniture in the single room hut. The tall man came inside. It was now clear that he carried a dead goat which he lifted over his head and dumped onto the table without ceremony.

The old goatherd leant over the table and started to skin the beast. At the same time, he explained in heavily-accented French that he and his two sons had killed a goat which he was going to skin and butcher. From this animal, he would give the escapees some meat and a skin to make shoes. The three men would be welcome to sleep in the hut this night, but must be on their way next morning.

Dacre could barely believe the good news, but drank in relief that welled up like water from a spring.

"Merci! Merci!"

* * *

Next morning, Dacre was roused by Price. There was no sign of the goatherd or his two sons.

Cochrane snored.

By the door was a pile of goatskin, and wrapped inside were several chunks of meat. Beside the pile was a jug of white liquid.

"Wake up Cochrane! It's sour milk for breakfast, then we must be away."

The three escapees rose and gathered their belongings, including the new provisions, and left the hut without delay.

Outside they peered about like nervous rodents in the early morning sunshine, but there was no one to be seen.

"The kindly old goatherd suggested that we follow the valley this way." Dacre said. "But I should like to hide a bit in case he has a loose tongue."

"How about down there?" Price pointed down a steeper side valley. "It's more heavily wooded. A mile or so down that way and we could stop to make a fire, cook some meat and dry out the goatskin to make some coverings for our feet."

The plan was agreed and the party of three moved out with a renewed spring in their steps.

About an hour later they found a hiding place deep in the valley, surrounded by thick bushes. Dacre sat on a log and examined his bleeding feet. *Any form of crude shoe will be better than nothing.*

Price and Cochrane threw themselves on the ground and no one moved for the first few minutes, then Dacre stood and gathered together a few sticks.

The others joined him in silence and soon they had a small fire burning. Cochrane lay the goatskin out over a forked green branch beside the fire and each of them took a chunk of meat to roast on a stick. The remaining meat was placed around the edge of the fire where it cooked more slowly in preparation to be packed for the final stage of their journey. This would be the last fire before reaching the coast. They had agreed that none of them wanted to further risk drawing unwanted attention.

Dacre leant back against the log. Warmth from the fire soothed his feet and the aroma of charring meat tantalized his nostrils.

I could almost eat it now, but it might make me sick. Better cook it a few more minutes.

Crash! – something charged through the bushes behind him.

Dacre, Price and Cochrane turned as one towards the noise and found themselves looking down the barrels of several rifles held by uniformed gendarmes with intense looks on their faces, as if they might pull the triggers at any moment.

Confused shouts followed from all directions, but the message was clear enough. Dacre raised his hands and his chunk of partially cooked goat fell to the dirt.

One of the gendarmes stepped forwards with his rifle aimed square at Dacre's chest.

With a weary fascination, Dacre watched the twitchings of his trigger finger as another gendarme grabbed Dacre from behind and cuffed his hands together.

Highly excitable people should not be entrusted with firearms. It is very dangerous.

Price and Cochrane were handcuffed to each other, wrist to wrist.

As the three submariners were led away, Dacre spied the goatherd's tall son standing and watching from the bushes at the edge of the clearing.

* * *

Two weeks later, Dacre paced in his cell like a caged animal.

Four steps.

About face.

Four steps.

About face.

His cell was located in the same Constantinople prison where he served his last stint of solitary confinement. Last time, the reason for his transfer and isolation had been explained by the commandant as a necessary diplomatic reprisal for harsh treatment of Turkish prisoners in Egypt – an "entirely impersonal matter".

At least this cell has a little window to the outside world. My sanity might last a bit longer for that window.

The effects of starvation were gradually wearing off as he had been given more food this time than on his last visit.

The bugs, if anything, had grown stronger in numbers and remained most active at night, turning sleep into unbearable torture. Dacre found that he was able to sleep during the daylight hours, and so paced his room during the night without lying down in the dark.

If they ever send me back to camp with the other prisoners of war, they will keep me under close watch. I don't know if I have another escape attempt left in me. We were so close to reaching the sea! One day this war must end. Then I will be free to go home, if I can stay alive that long. One day. God, how long until that day?

He stared at the wall where he made a daily mark. He could not see anything there in the darkness, but he knew the number of marks he had made. *This night is precisely one year since I took the Australian submarine* AE2 *into the Dardanelles. We accomplished our mission for whatever good it did. It has been a long year.*

He recited to himself a poem-prayer that he had been working on since being shown into his new accommodation. *I must ask for a pencil and paper so I can write it down. They might give me that much…*

Standing at my window, gazing at the stars,
Winking at me sagely, through the iron bars;
Thinking of the Hand that's guiding them thro' space.
Praying to Him silently, asking Him for Grace.
God of Love and Pity, God of Mercy, too,
Give me grace in this place that my faith in You,
Which alone can help these trials to be borne,
May grow ever stronger, like the light at dawn
Peeping first so shyly in the eastern sky,
Gradually grows and grows, till bye and bye
All the world is bathed in beams of strongest light;
Gone the powers of darkness, past the dreaded night.
Man's mad machinations cannot check its flow,
Only Thou, the Ruler, causing it to grow.
God of Love and Pity, give me the grace that I
May by Faith be lightened like that eastern sky.
In my prison cell there are not two or three
Gathered here together to ask these things of Thee.
Only one is praying from his heart to You,
God of Love and Pity, God of Mercy too. …
Standing by my window, gazing at the stars,
Winking now more faintly through the iron bars,
Somehow things seem better, sorrow's soothed away,
Dawn is surely coming, it will soon be – Day.

CHAPTER 102

John

Tuesday, 25 April 1916

As I anticipated, Australia has chosen, yet again, to let her forces be exploited to find jobs for unemployed senior British officers. Cox is a Kitchener man, and Birdwood's old colleague from India, it is no surprise that Birdwood has entrusted Cox with my division.

John pushed aside the sting of being passed over. For today, at least, he determined not to dwell on the injustice. Today was too important for such things. Today was the first anniversary of the landing at Gallipoli. Today was Anzac Day.

Following the split and re-organisation of brigades in February, John's new-look 4th Brigade was restored to a strength of five thousand men. But of these men under John's command, all of whom stood in formation on the desert sand before him, such a small number wore both the blue ribbon and red ribbon on their breast at today's ceremony.

"Today we remember the sacrifice made by our fellow Australian soldiers," Chaplain Lieutenant-Colonel Wray continued his address to the brigade through a megaphone. The Chaplain wore a blue ribbon and a red ribbon. "Especially sacrifice of the fallen, for it is they who have paid the highest price. These men have laid down their lives for those of us that remain, for their families and for our families.

"Jesus Christ said 'This is my commandment, That ye love one another, as I have loved you. Greater love hath no man than this, that a man lay down his life for his friends,' and that is indeed what our fallen brothers have done, as Jesus himself did for those of us who will place our trust on him.

"It is right and proper, at this time, to remember God's word to Israel through his servant Moses, not far from this place where we stand together today: 'Then beware lest thou forget the LORD, which brought thee forth out of the land of Egypt, from the house of bondage.'

"The sun grows hot, despite the early hour. Thank you for your respect and patience. Let me conclude with Rudyard Kipling's poem, 'The Recessional':

"God of our fathers, known of old,
        Lord of our far-flung battle line,
Beneath whose awful hand we hold
        Dominion over palm and pine –
Lord God of Hosts, be with us yet,
Lest we forget – lest we forget!

"The tumult and the shouting dies;
        The Captains and the Kings depart:
Still stands Thine ancient sacrifice,
        An humble and a contrite heart.
Lord God of Hosts, be with us yet,
Lest we forget – lest we forget!

"Far-called our navies melt away;
        On dune and headland sinks the fire:
Lo, all our pomp of yesterday
        Is one with Nineveh and Tyre!
Judge of the Nations, spare us yet,
Lest we forget – lest we forget!

"If, drunk with sight of power, we loose
        Wild tongues that have not Thee in awe,
Such boastings as the Gentiles use,
        Or lesser breeds without the Law –
Lord God of Hosts, be with us yet,
Lest we forget – lest we forget!

"For heathen heart that puts her trust
        In reeking tube and iron shard,
All valiant dust that builds on dust,
        And guarding calls not Thee to guard,
For frantic boast and foolish word –
Thy Mercy on Thy People, Lord!"

As soon as Chaplain Wray concluded reciting the poem, the massed bands of the 4th Brigade began to play Handel's Dead March in Saul and all the men stood to attention as one.

For around five minutes the music played, building through the crescendos and diminuendos of the funeral piece. The men looked straight ahead, as did

John who was glad during that time not to have to look another man in the eye.

At the conclusion of the Dead March, the men stood like an army of statues. Silence hung heavy for a few seconds, then the tone of a single bugle sounded. At this signal, other buglers joined in up and down the lines, together they played The Last Post.

* * *

Later that day, after the heat of desert sun had brought an end to the games of cricket, John watched the 4th Division sports and swimming carnival on the Suez Canal at Serapeum, around fifty miles north of Suez. He stood on the deck of a steam launch that had been nominated as the flagship for the event.

General Cox's newly formed 4th Division consisted of three Brigades, including the two brigades formed from John's original 4th, being the new 4th and 12th Brigades, and also the new 13th Brigade built from half of the original 3rd Brigade.

The canal was full of swimmers, participating in races and bobbing about to keep cool. For a mile along the canal, both of the sloping banks of sand were covered in naked humanity.

At one time, virtually all fifteen thousand men were in the water, then the flag ship tooted warning that the course must be cleared and men scampered from the water before the bows of an advancing cargo steamer. Many stayed in the water and some seemed to be so close to the ship that there was a risk they might be sucked into the screw, but no one was harmed and the frolic continued once the steamer passed.

We have a lot of men here to defend this strip of water.

As far as John was concerned, any threat to the canal was more imagined than real. Occasional demonstrations by the Turks seemed to be directed at tying down the large garrison of British troops along the waterway, rather than the mounting of a serious attack.

A smaller force would be adequate here. We are needed in France. That is where the real fight must be taken to the Germans, and how I would love to get away from this dreadful desert.

The 1st Division had already departed for France and the prospects for John to follow with his brigade in the coming months were looking positive. More fighting would cost more lives, but that was the reality of war.

John bowed his head in a moment of reflection. On his breast he wore a blue ribbon and a red ribbon. At that morning's church parade, the blue ribbon was worn by all who had served at Gallipoli, and the red ribbon by those who took part in the original landing.

I am pleased to have given the men a holiday on this day, especially those who endured such hardship at Gallipoli. The living must get on with living, but it is right to remember the sacrifices and mistakes that have been made. If I survive this war, I will do all I can to ensure that Australians at home understand, and remember, and enjoy many happy returns of this famous day – Our Day.

CHAPTER 103

Jayjay

Tuesday, 8 August 1916

Jayjay poured himself a generous glass of Jameson Irish Whiskey.

The winter morning sun was weak and Jayjay's breath visible without cigarette smoke. Despite the cold, he chose to sit outside as he usually did when alone.

Mum and Dad didn't approve of strong drink in their home, but Dad was working at the ironmongery store and Mum was at the markets. Emilia had finally taken Ronald Junior out for a walk and left Jayjay at home alone with some peace and quiet. A chair on the balcony facing the small back yard was his favourite place to sit and forget everything. The winter sky was clear and the first sip warmed his throat. The first sip was always the best, almost sweet before the true sour taste came through.

He unfolded the three-day-old *Sydney Morning Herald* to re-read it and flicked past the advertising that filled the first few pages. Much of the space in the first pages was filled with house and land promotion, but real estate in Sydney was too expensive for Jayjay to contemplate, with some houses in good suburbs asking in excess of £1000.

The headline on page eight read "CURRENT LITERATURE", normally one that Jayjay would not bother with, but the caption "GALLIPOLI" caught his eye. He read on about an account by an Australian Mr S. de Loghe, 'The Straits Impregnable', telling of his experiences as a gunner during the campaign. Jayjay's mind went back to the day he lay on the sand at the back of the beach at Anzac Cove with a wounded gunner who didn't live to see out the day. *He never did tell me his name.*

On page ten, he read 'CASUALTIES. – 37 MORE SOLDIERS KILLED. – 190th LIST.'

When will this end? He scanned through the list of those from New South Wales and confirmed again that it contained no one he knew.

On page twelve, an article headed 'CONSCRIPTION' anticipated a possible split in the Political Labour organisation over the issue. The acting Prime Minister had authorised the military to seize the trades union pamphlets against conscription. *Larry's sister Grace will tell anyone who'll listen that conscription's a stupid bloody idea. His encoded letter must have got through to her.*

On page 13, a small article was circled in pencil:

'LONE PINE. – ANNIVERSARY TO-MORROW. The article announced a special parade of returned servicemen, starting at the corner of Bathurst and Pitt Streets at 10:15am.

Jayjay massaged his leg, still aching from the special parade march to St. Mary's Cathedral and then back to St. Andrew's Cathedral. *Over a thousand of us. All invalids. No wonder everyone was drunk by mid-afternoon.*

On the same page, an article of ten lines in length, headed 'GALLIPOLI INQUIRY' quoted British Lord Cromer giving his assurance that "there would be no white-washing." *I wonder what they'll find? It was all a bit of a mistake. Sorry about that chaps.*

A familiar finger of guilt poked at his innards.

If I'm not careful, I'll start talking like Mum. I ought to be more loyal. The war needs to be fought and sacrifices have to be made. The commanders might have made some errors, but they need to be allowed to push towards victory, rather than being distracted by an enquiry into the past.

Banging at the front door disturbed the quiet. *Is that someone knocking? They're making a bit of a fuss about it.*

He stared at his glass for a second. *Damn!* He promised himself he would return smartly and placed the glass on the balcony next to the bottle.

Knocking continued.

"Hold your horses, I'm coming. I've only got one bloody leg you know."

He limped through the house on his artificial leg and wrenched the door open. Larry's twin sister Grace stood in the doorway with hands hanging by her side and tears streaming down her cheeks.

He knew immediately what it meant. The moment he saw her he lost the ability to breathe. He opened his mouth, but only air came out.

"Can I come in Jon?" Grace whispered.

Jayjay nodded, and ushered her through to the dining room. Pain gripped his chest.

"Tell me."

Grace shook her head and covered her mouth with both hands.

"The Somme offensive?" Jayjay asked.

Grace gulped a mouthful of air and looked like she was trying to hold it in with all of her fingers. She nodded slowly, hands unmoved.

"Pozieres. Killed in action at Pozieres. That's all they told us, we don't even know how he died. Only that the King, Queen and Commonwealth Government convey deep regret and sympathy. What a lot of rot. They couldn't care less about

Lars. They didn't even know him."

"I could have a good guess how he died. 'Killed in action' is better than 'died of wounds'. Hopefully he didn't suffer for too long. You want a drink? Tea, or something stronger? Whiskey?"

She shook her head.

"I'm going to have one." Jayjay limped out the back door and found his glass where he left it. He swigged half the glass and turned to see Grace watching him, hands on hips. She marched forwards and picked up the bottle. *She must have changed her mind about the drink.*

"You want a glass?"

She didn't answer, but took the bottle into the outhouse for a moment, came back out and threw the empty bottle into the garden before Jayjay could react.

"Did you just tip it down the dunny? It was nearly full. Why?"

Her bloodshot eyes opened wide and she took a swing at Jayjay's face.

Reflex responded before Jayjay realised what was happening. He stopped her right hook by grabbing her forearm with his left hand and reached with his other hand for a knife at his right hip. For an instant he was in a log covered trench at Lone Pine, fighting for his life.

Beats from his racing heart pounded his ears like artillery. There was no other sound. Their eyes locked and time seemed to slow.

There was no knife and she was not the enemy. *I should have let her hit me. Does she realise what I might have done to her?* He let go of her arm and she stared back, eyes brimming with defiance.

"I'm sorry Grace," Jayjay stepped back. "I didn't mean to hurt you."

"You didn't hurt me, you just grabbed my arm like a drunk. It's the first time you've touched me. You didn't even give me a hug – again."

"I thought you said you didn't want a hug." *And why did you waste all that good whiskey?*

"Bloody Hell Jon, how can you be so stupid?"

Well, that needs a bit more explanation before I can respond.

"That language doesn't suit a young lady. What would you know about bloody hell?"

"You're talking nonsense!"

"Me? You're talking like a crazy woman. What do you think bloody hell even is? Imagine living in a grave you dug yourself, surrounded by your own shit, getting shot at, mates getting shot and blown to bits all around you. Death is everywhere. You can hardly sleep because you know there's a thousand men trying to kill you and if you rest you might never wake up. Nowhere is safe. Nowhere."

"I want to know. Tell me what it was like."

Jayjay shook his head. "I knew this day would come. Larry knew it too.

Neither of us thought we would ever leave Gallipoli alive. By the grace of God we both did. There was no other way for him. At war they push you and push you and push you. You can't stop until you are dead or broken. He didn't want to come home broken. That's the truth, he told me himself." *I said it too, but I didn't mean it. No need to mention that.*

"Lars wouldn't have wanted to die."

"Everyone dies. It's just a question of when."

Grace bit her lower lip and it looked as though it might bleed. "He was so young."

"Sometimes it's so hard and painful and horrible that today seems like a better time to go than tomorrow. If not at Gallipoli, then in France. If not the Somme offensive, then the next bloody battle. Larry was tough and cunning, but you can only run at machine guns under raining shrapnel so many times before your luck runs out."

Jayjay's leg started to ache. "I need to sit down."

Two chairs occupied the balcony, Grace remained standing. Jayjay reached down for his glass and drained the remaining whiskey in a single gulp.

"Emilia told me that you get drunk often. Does it help you forget?"

"Only for a little while – unfortunately."

"Do you want to forget my brother?"

"Of course not! I want to forget what this war did to him, and to the others, and to me, and what it made us do."

"When are you going to stop?"

"Stop what?"

"Stop feeling sorry for yourself and start thinking about other people."

"Think about who? I can't do anything for my mates anymore. I'm a useless invalid. That's why they sent me home. They pinned a ticket to my chest that said as much."

"What about your Mum, your Dad, Emilia, little Ronald Junior. What about me?"

"Maybe you'd all be better off without me."

"So many are dead and dying, but you have come back. You're a war hero and it's time you bloody-well started behaving like one. Stop and think about everyone around you that you're hurting."

"I'm no bloody hero, don't call me that!"

"We need you to be a hero Jon, can't you see?"

"How can I be something I'm not?"

Grace's hands were clenched in tight fists and starting to shake. *If she takes another swing, I'll let her hit me this time.*

A tear ran down her nose and fell to the balcony floor. It left a small dark patch on the timber. Jayjay stared at the perfect circle. Another appeared near it.

"Larry once wrote that I should give you a hug, you're right. I always felt bad that I never did it, but you said you didn't want me to anymore, so I didn't, but if you would like a hug now then I'd be happy to give you one, but if not, then that's fine too – he was a good mate and I wouldn't want to let him down."

Jayjay stared at the timber floor and felt tears welling in his own eyes. His throat tightened and he could barely breathe. He knew he wouldn't be able to talk for a moment. *I'm drowning in an ocean of Gallipoli soup.*

Grace took a step closer and a dark circle appeared on the deck below Jayjay from his own tear.

I don't want to cry in front of her. It'll just make her think I'm a coward and make her more upset.

She sat across his lap, wrapped her arms around him and nuzzled her face into his neck. For many minutes her sobs and his were the only conversation.

He held her tight and warmth from her body seeped into his. After some time, the flow of tears eased and he drew in deep, slow breaths of good air.

Those heroes that shed their blood and lost their lives ... You are now lying in the soil of a friendly country. Therefore rest in peace. There is no difference between the Johnnies and the Mehmets to us where they lie side by side here in this country of ours ... You, the mothers who sent their sons from far away countries wipe away your tears; your sons are now lying in our bosom and are in peace. After having lost their lives on this land they have become our sons as well.

– Mustafa Kemal Ataturk, 1934[6]

---

6 As President of the newly established Republic of Turkey. These words are set in a monument above Anzac Cove.

ACKNOWLEDGEMENTS

I acknowledge with gratitude, the assistance and support that I have received in writing this work.

My good friend and fellow author Julian Musgrove walked with me on the hard road of writing a first book. We bounced ideas off each other and told each other to keep going. I needed to be told this more than once.

Members of my family – my wife, children, parents and aunt – had patience while I prioritised the time commitment of writing, and invested the time to review early copies. Thanks to Melis Knight, Corey Knight, Lara Knight, Bryce Knight, Joel Knight, Elissa Knight, Michael Knight, Janet Knight and Hiliary Carne.

My mother Janet Knight, great uncle Max Day and great uncle Allan Day told me about my great grandfather George William Day who served as an Anzac medical orderly and later as an officer in France.

My mother-in-law Verda Cimilli told me about her father who served in the Ottoman forces defending the Gallipoli peninsula against the Anzac invasion.

The staff at the Australian War Memorial in Canberra and the NSW Mitchell State Library in Sydney helped me to find obscure reference material. This helped me to fill this dramatised work with maximum factual content and minimal joining of the dots.

Other reviewers who gave me helpful feedback and encouragement to publish include Rebekah Lee, Zubin Meher-Homji, Son Vu, Frank Steele, Mark de Lacey, Elizabeth Webb, Cameron Ballantine-Jones, Bruce Ballantine-Jones, Andrew Barry and Michael Smithers.

Local tour guide Ercan Yavuz spent days walking tirelessly over the battlefields of the Gallipoli peninsula with me. His knowledge of the area is exceptional.

A list of books and other sources consulted is included in the bibliography and referenced in the end notes which are accessible online at: www.gallipolisoup.com.

BIBLIOGRAPHY

Adam-Smith, Patsy, *The Anzacs*, Penguin Books, 2002

Adam-Smith, Patsy, *Prisoners of War – From Gallipoli to Korea*, Ken Fin, 1998

Anzacs (the Men of Anzac), *The Anzac Book*, Cassell and Company, 1916

Ashmead-Bartlett, Ellis, *Despatches from the Dardanelles*, George Newnes, 1915

Ashmead-Bartlett, Ellis, *Personal Diary*, (Unpublished, NSW State Library online copy), 1916

Ashmead-Bartlett, Ellis, *Port Arthur: The Siege and Capitulation*, William Blackwood and Sons, 1906

Ashmead-Bartlett, Ellis, *The Uncensored Dardanelles*, Hutchinson & Co, 1928

Ashmead-Bartlett, Ellis, *With the Turks in Thrace*, George H Doran Company, 1913

Austin, Ron, *The Fighting Fourth – A History of Sydney's 4th Battalion 1914–1919*, Slouch Hat Publications, 2007

Australian Department of Defence, *Musketry Small Book for the Australian Imperial Force*, Angus and Robertson, 1916

Australian War Memorial, *1st Infantry Battalian War Diary*, 1914–1915

Barrett, James, et al., *The Australian Army Medical Corps in Egypt in 1914–15*, H. K. Lewis & Co, 1918

Barwick, Archie, *In Great Spirits – The WWI diary of Archie Barwick*, Harper Collins 2013 (A First Infantry Battalion soldier's diary, 1914–1919, edited by the NSW State Library)

Bean, Charles, *Anzac to Amiens*, Australian War Memorial 1983 edition (First published 1946)

Bean, Charles, *Gallipoli Mission*, Australian War Memorial, 1952

Bean, Charles, *Official History of Australia in the War of 1914–18, volume I, The story of Anzac from the Outbreak of War to the end of the First Phase of the Gallipoli Campaign, May 4 1915*, Angus and Robertson, 4th ed. 1935

Bean, Charles, *Official History of Australia in the War of 1914–18, volume II, The story of Anzac from 4 May,1915 to the Evacuation of the Gallipoli Peninsula*, Angus and Robertson, 4th ed. 1936

Bean, Charles, *Official History of Australia in the War of 1914–18, volume III, The A.I.F in France: 1916*, Angus and Robertson, 12th ed. 1941

Bean, Charles, et al *Official History of Australia in the War of 1914–18, volume XII, Photographic Record of the War*, Angus and Robertson, 12th ed. 1939

Birdwood, William, *Khaki and Gown*, Ward, Lock & Co, 1941

Blair, Dale, *Dinkum Diggers – An Australian Battalion at War*, Melbourne University Press, 2001

Brenchley, Fred and Elizabeth, *Mythmaker, Ellis Ashmead-Bartlett – The Englishman Who Sparked Australia's Gallipoli Legend*, John Wiley & Sons, 2005

Brenchley, Fred and Elizabeth, *Stoker's Submarine*, Harper Collins, 2001

Broadbent, Harvey, *Gallipoli, The Fatal Shore*, Penguin 2005

Broadbent, Harvey, *Defending Gallipoli*, Melbourne University Press, 2015

Broadbent, Harvey, *Gallipoli, The Turkish Defence*, The Miegunyah Press, 2015

Broadbent, Harvey, *The Boys Who Came Home*, ABC Books, 2001

Brodie, Charles, *Forlorn Hope 1915 – The Submarine Passage of the Dardanelles*, Frederick Books, 1956

Butler, Arthur, *Official History of the Australian Army Medical Services, 1914–1918; Volume I – Gallipoli, Palestine and New Guinea,* Australian War Memorial, 2nd edition, 1938

Butler, Arthur, *Official History of the Australian Army Medical Services, 1914–1918, Volume 1, Part 1: The Gallipoli Campaign*, Australian War Memorial, 2nd edition, 1938.

Butler, Arthur, *Official History of the Australian Army Medical Services, 1914–1918; Volume III – Special Problems and Services,* Australian War Memorial, 1st edition, 1943.

Cameron, Simon, *Lonesome Pine – The Bloody Ridge*, Big Sky Publishing, 2013

Cameron, David, *The August Offensive at Anzac, 1915*, Australian Army History Unit, 2011

Cameron, David, *The Battle for Lone Pine*, Penguin Viking, 2012

Carlton, Mike, *First Victory 1914 – HMAS Sydney's Hunt for the German Raider Emden*, William Heinemann, 2013

Carlyon, Les, *Gallipoli*, Pan Macmillan Australia, 2001

Churchill, Winston, *Savrola*, Hodder and Stroughton, 1915

Churchill, Winston, *Painting as a Pastime* (essay), 1932, Charles Scribner's Sons

Cutlack, Frederic, *Official History of Australia in the War of 1914–1918, Vol VIII, Australian Flying Corps*, Angus and Robertson, 12th Edition, 1942

Curran, Tom, *Who was Responsible for the Dardanelles Fiasco?*, Article in Australian Journal of Politics and History: vol 57, no. 1, 2011, pp 17–33.

Dawood, N, English Translation of *The Koran*, Penguin Classics, 2014

Dolan, Hugh, *36 Days, The Untold Story Behind the Gallipoli Landings*, Pan Macmillan Australia, 2010

Dolan, Hugh, *Gallipoli Air War – The Unknown Story of the Fight for the Skys over Gallipoli*, Pan Macmillan Australia, 2013

Doyle, Peter, et al., *Trench Talk – Words of the First World War*, The History Press, 2012

Ekins, et al, *Gallipoli, A Ridge Too Far*, Exisle Publishing, 2013

Erickson, Edward, *Gallipoli, The Ottoman Campaign*, Pen and Sword, 2010

Fasih, Mehmed, *Bloody Ridge (Lone Pine) Diary of Lt. Mehmed Fasih 5th Imperial Ottoman Army Gallipoli 1915*, Denizler Kitabevi, English translation 2001

Fewster, Kevin; Başarın, Vecihi; Başarın, Hatice Hürmüz, *Gallipoli, The Turkish Story*, Allen and Unwin, 2003

Fewster, Kevin, *Bean's Gallipoli – The Diaries of Australia's Official War Correspondent*, edited by Kevin Fewster, Allen and Unwin, 2009

Fewster, Kevin, *Ellis Ashmead Bartlett and the Making of the Anzac Legend*, Article in Journal of Australian Studies, volume 6, 1982 – Issue 10, pp. 17–30

Gammage, Bill, *The Broken Years*, Penguin Books, 1990 Illustrated Edition (originally published 1974)

Hamilton, John, *Gallipoli Sniper – The Life of Billy Sing*, Pan Macmillan Australia, 2008

Hamilton, Ian, *Gallipoli Diary*, Edward Arnold, 1920

Hankey, Maurice, *The Supreme Command 1914–1918*, George Allen and Unwin, 1961

Herbert, Aubrey, *Mons, Anzac and Kut*, Edward Arnold, 1919

Idriess, Ion, *The Desert Column*, Angus & Robertson,1932

James, Robert Rhodes, *Gallipoli*, Papermac, 1989 (originally published 1965)

Jenkins, Roy, *Churchill*, Pan MacMillan Australia, 2001

Jose, Arthur, *Official History of Australia in the War of 1914–18, vol IX, The Royal Australian Navy*, Angus and Robertson, Seventh Edition 1939

Keyes, Roger, *The Naval Memoirs of Admiral of the Fleet Sir Roger Keyes – The Narrow Seas to the Dardanelles 1910–1915*, Thornton Butterworth,1934

King, Jonathan, *Gallipoli Diaries*, Kangaroo Press, 2003

Kipling, Rudyard, *A Diversity of Creatures*, Macmillan and Co., 1917

Kipling, Rudyard, *Rewards and Fairies*, Macmillan and Co., 1910

Kyle, Roy, *An Anzac's Story – Roy Kyle A.I.F.* (Introduced by Bryce Courtenay), Penguin Viking, 2003

Laffin, John, *Damn the Dardanelles – The Story of Gallipoli*, Doubleday, 1980

Loch, Sydney, *To Hell and Back – The Banned Account of Gallipoli*, Harper Collins, 2007 (originally published as *The Straits Impregnable*, under pseudonym Sydney De Loghe 1916)

Mango, Andrew, *Atatürk*, John Murray Publishers, 1999

Masefield, John, *Gallipoli*, New Holland Publishers, 2014 (first published 1916)

Monash, John, *War Letters of John Monash*, Angus and Robertson, 1935

Moorehead, Alan, *Gallipoli*, Perennial Classics, 2002 (First published 1956, Harper & Brothers)

Morgenthau, Henry, *Secrets of the Bosphorus*, Hutchinson & Co, 1918

Murdock, Keith, *The Gallipoli Letter* (Introduction by Michael McKernon), Allen & Unwin, 2010

Oral, Haluk, *Gallipoli 1915 - Through Turkish Eyes*, Bahçeşehir University Press, 2012

Örnek, Tolga and Toker, Feza, *Gallipoli – The Front Line Experience* (2nd Edition), Currency Press, 2006

Paget, Gregory, *The November 1914 Straits Agreement and the Dardanelles-Gallipoli Campaign* Article in The Australian Journal of Politics and History, Vol 33, 1987

Pederson, Peter, *Monash as a Military Commander*, Melbourne University Press, 1985

Perry, Roland, *The Australian Light Horse*, Hachette Australia, 2009

Perry, Roland, *Monash – The Outsider Who Won a War*, Random House Australia, 2007

Plowman, Peter, *Voyage to Gallipoli*, Rosenberg Publishing, 2013

Rees, Peter, *The Other Anzacs – Nurses at War, 1914–1918*, Allen & Unwin, 2008

Reid, Richard, *Gallipoli 1915*, ABC Books, 2002

Roberts, Chris, *The Landing at ANZAC*, Australian Army History Unit, 2013

Robertson, John, *Anzac and Empire*, Hamlyn Australia, 1990 (reprinted 2010)

Scott, Ernest, *Official History of Australia in the War of 1914–1918, Vol XI, Australia During the War*, Angus and Robertson, Fifth Edition, 1939

Smithers, Alan, *Sir John Monash – A Biography of Australia' Most Distinguished Soldier of the First World War*, Angus and Robertson, 1973

Stacey B.V, Kindon F.J, Chedgey, H.V, *The History of the First Battalion A.I.F. 1914–1919*, (Publisher unknown, NSW State Library online copy), Sydney 1931

Stoker, Henry "Dacre", *Straws in the Wind*, Herbert Jenkins Publishers, 1925

Stoker, Bram, *Dracula*, Archibald Constable and Company, 1897

Taylor, F.W and Cusack, T.A. *Nulli Secundus – A History of the Second Battalion, A.I.F. 1914–1919*, New Century Press, 1942

Travers, Tim, *Gallipoli 1915*, Tempus Publishing, 2002

Tyquin, Michael, *Gallipoli – An Australian Medical Perspective*, Australian Army History Unit, 2012

Uyar, Mesut, *The Ottoman Defence Against the ANZAC Landing – 25 April 1915*, Australian Army History Unit, 2015

Various, *The Bible, King James Version*, King James I of the United Kingdoms of England, Ireland and Scottland, 1611

Various, *The Anglican Hymn Book* (Second Edition), Novello Ewer and Co, 1871

Wheat, John, *Diary of a Torpedoman on the Submarine AE2* (Unpublished, NSW State Library online copy), 1915

Wren, Eric, *Randwick to Hargicourt – History of the 3rd Battalion, A.I.F.*, Ronald G. McDonald, 1935

Australian Imperial Force War Diaries

AIF War diaries are accessible via Australian War Memorial website: *http://www.awm.gov.au/collection/awm4/*

1st Infantry Battalion War Diary, 1914–1915

1st Infantry Brigade War Diary, 1914–1915

4th Infantry Brigade War Diary, 1914–1915

ANZAC 1st Division War Diary, 1915

ANZAC Headquarter Intelligence War Diary 1915

Australian War Memorial Maps

Anzac reference maps from the Australian War Memorial digital collection include:

G7432G1S65V_2b, Anzac Monash landing map 1:40,000, with contours in feet, including notes from aerial reconnaissance to 18 April 1915, shows grid numbering referenced in Anzac landing orders

G7432G1S65VI_11a, Karija Dere 1:20,000, with contours in metres, including details from maps taken from a Turkish officer and used for the August 1915 Anzac offensive

G7432G1S65II_7, Anzac sector topographical map with place names

G7432G1S65II_8, Anzac sector topographical map with place names and trench locations

G7432G1S65II_10, Anzac sector maps

G7432G1S65V_1a, Anzac Monash landing map 1:40,000, with contours in feet

G7432G1S65XV_6, Anzac trench diagrams

G7432G1S65XXVI_25, Anzac sector map with Turkish division positions in May 1915

Documentary DVDs

Gallipoli 1915 – Frontal Assault on Turkey, Cromwell Productions 2002

Gallipoli From Above – The Controversial Truth About the Gallipoli Landing – The Untold Story, Wain Fimeri and Hugh Dolan, 2008

Gallipoli Submarine, Australian Broadcasting Corporation, 2008

Gallipoli, The Frontline Experience, (to accompany the book of the same title), Ekip Films and Tolga Örnek

Monash – The Forgotten Anzac, Australian Broadcasting Corporation, 2014

The War That Changed Us, Australian Broadcasting Corporation, 2014

NON NOBIS

NOT unto us, O Lord, to tell
Thy purpose in the blast,
When these, that towered beyond us, fell
And we were overpast.

We cannot guess how goodness springs
From the black tempest's breath,
Nor scan the birth of gentle things
In those red bursts of death.

We only know – from good and great
Nothing save good can flow;
That where the cedar crashed so straight
No crooked tree can grow;

That from their *ruin a taller pride –*
Not for these eyes to see –
May clothe one day the valleyside . . . .
Non nobis, Domine

– Charles Edwin Woodrow Bean, 1916[7]

7 *The Anzac Book*, written and illustrated in Gallipoli by the Men of Anzac, 1916, page. 11.

LET'S REMEMBER